Preface

Family law is a dynamic subject, constantly changing, and a challenge to everyone involved with it. We have taken on the challenge in preparing this book. Our main aim has been to prepare a book which provides the legal background and a springboard for students to use to practise the skills learned during their course. We hope it will also be of use to trainees and newly qualified solicitors who are using these skills for the first time in the real world.

Throughout the book, for uniformity, we have generally referred to the client as 'he'. In reality, it is usually the woman who initiates proceedings on the breakdown of the relationship.

In the book the terms 'husband and wife' or 'spouses' should be taken to include civil partners unless the text states otherwise. Similarly 'matrimonial home' includes a civil partnership home.

We would like to acknowledge with thanks the contribution made to this book in the past by Jo Theobald. Our thanks also go to our colleagues at The University of Law who have helped us with this book, and to our long-suffering families and friends who have endured its rebirth.

Unless otherwise mentioned, the law is stated as at 1 September 2021.

NANCY DUFFIELD
JACQUELINE KEMPTON
CHRISTA SABINE
The University of Law

Contents

PREFACE   v

TABLE OF CASES   xi

TABLE OF STATUTES   xxi

TABLE OF STATUTORY INSTRUMENTS AND CODES OF PRACTICE   xxv

TABLE OF ABBREVIATIONS   xxvii

Chapter 1		INTRODUCTION: THE FAMILY PRACTICE	1
	1.1	The family client	1
	1.2	The family practitioner	3
	1.3	Support for family clients	6
	1.4	Litigants in person	6
	1.5	The court system	7
	1.6	Human Rights Act 1998	8
	1.7	Family law in the future	8
	1.8	Conclusion	9
		Summary	9
Chapter 2		FUNDING AND PROCESS OPTIONS	11
	2.1	Introduction	11
	2.2	Legal aid	11
	2.3	Human rights	16
	2.4	Other methods of funding	17
	2.5	Dispute resolution	20
		Summary	24
Chapter 3		DIVORCE LAW AND PROCEDURE	25
	3.1	Introduction	25
	3.2	One-year rule	26
	3.3	Jurisdiction of the English courts to hear suits for divorce	26
	3.4	The ground for divorce	29
	3.5	Children	36
	3.6	Nullity	36
	3.7	Judicial separation	37
	3.8	Presumption of death and dissolution of marriage	38
	3.9	Divorce procedure	38
	3.10	Defended divorces	46
	3.11	Costs	47
	3.12	The Divorce, Dissolution and Separation Act 2020	47
		Summary and checklist	49
Chapter 4		FINANCIAL ORDERS: THE LAW	51
	4.1	Introduction	51
	4.2	The powers of the court	52
	4.3	Income orders	52
	4.4	Capital orders	54
	4.5	Deciding what orders to make	56
	4.6	The clean break	68
	4.7	Pensions on divorce	70
	4.8	Financial cases in the future	73
	4.9	Financial provision during marriage	73
		Summary	74

Chapter 5	TAX ON MARRIAGE BREAKDOWN	77
	5.1 Introduction	77
	5.2 Tax on marriage breakdown	77
	Summary	81
Chapter 6	WELFARE AND LOCAL AUTHORITY HOUSING	83
	6.1 Introduction	83
	6.2 Child benefit	84
	6.3 Universal credit	84
	6.4 The benefit cap	87
	6.5 Other help	87
	6.6 Welfare benefits and marriage breakdown	87
	6.7 Local authority housing	88
	Summary	90
Chapter 7	CALCULATING CHILD MAINTENANCE	91
	7.1 Introduction	91
	7.2 When does the CSA 1991 apply?	92
	7.3 The jurisdiction of the court	93
	7.4 Maintenance agreements and consent orders	94
	7.5 The formula	97
	7.6 Special cases	99
	7.7 Variations	100
	7.8 Default and interim maintenance decisions (CSA 1991, s 12)	102
	7.9 Voluntary payments	102
	7.10 Review	102
	7.11 Reform	102
	Summary	103
Chapter 8	MAINTENANCE FOR A SPOUSE	105
	8.1 Introduction	105
	8.2 High income families	106
	8.3 Middle income families	106
	8.4 Low income families	108
	Summary	109
Chapter 9	DEALING WITH THE CAPITAL ASSETS	111
	9.1 Introduction	111
	9.2 Selling the home	112
	9.3 Retaining the home	113
	9.4 The interests of third parties	116
	9.5 The rented home	118
	9.6 Protecting the capital assets	118
	9.7 Lump sums	121
	9.8 Pensions	123
	9.9 Bankruptcy	125
	Summary	126
Chapter 10	PROCEDURE FOR OBTAINING A FINANCIAL ORDER	127
	10.1 Introduction	127
	10.2 Public funding	128
	10.3 Overview of the procedure	128
	10.4 Procedure pre-application	129
	10.5 The application	130
	10.6 Filing and service	131
	10.7 Obtaining the evidence	132
	10.8 Court hearings	134
	10.9 Interim orders	138
	10.10 Fast-track procedure	138

	10.11	Costs	139
	10.12	Negotiations	140
	10.13	Consent orders	141
	10.14	Drafting financial orders	141
	10.15	Summary of court procedure	157
	10.16	Procedure following agreement by collaborative law process or by arbitration	160
	10.17	The Financial Remedies Working Group	160
Chapter 11		ENFORCEMENT, APPEALS, SETTING ASIDE AND VARIATION	163
	11.1	Introduction	163
	11.2	Enforcement of financial orders in the Family Court	164
	11.3	Collection and enforcement by the Child Maintenance Service	167
	11.4	Property adjustment orders	168
	11.5	Appeals	168
	11.6	Setting aside	169
	11.7	Variation	171
		Summary	175
Chapter 12		PRE-MARITAL AGREEMENTS AND SEPARATION AGREEMENTS	177
	12.1	Introduction	177
	12.2	Pre-marital agreements	177
	12.3	Postnuptial and separation agreements	179
	12.4	Reform	182
		Summary	182
Chapter 13		CHILDREN	183
	13.1	Introduction	183
	13.2	Parental responsibility	184
	13.3	Section 8 orders	189
	13.4	Welfare principle	204
	13.5	Checklist of factors to be taken into account in applying welfare principle	206
	13.6	The 'no order' presumption	209
	13.7	Avoiding delay	209
	13.8	Procedure for s 8 orders	210
	13.9	Protection of children	220
	13.10	Financial provision and property orders for children	224
		Summary	227
Chapter 14		CHILDREN: PUBLIC LAW	229
	14.1	Introduction	229
	14.2	Local authority support for children and families (CA 1989, Pt III)	231
	14.3	Preventing neglect or abuse	234
	14.4	Care and supervision orders (CA 1989, Pt IV)	236
	14.5	Contact (s 34)	241
	14.6	Discharge of care orders (s 39)	243
	14.7	Effect of a supervision order	243
	14.8	Care or supervision order	244
	14.9	Interim orders (s 38)	244
	14.10	Emergency protection and assessment (CA 1989, Pt V)	246
	14.11	Procedure for care and supervision orders	249
	14.12	Human rights implications	256
	14.13	Compensation for local authority failings	258
		Summary and checklists	259
Chapter 15		DOMESTIC ABUSE	261
	15.1	Introduction	261
	15.2	Protection under Pt IV of the Family Law Act 1996	263
	15.3	Human rights implications	277
	15.4	Protection from Harassment Act 1997	277

	15.5	Coercive and controlling behaviour	278
	15.6	Forced Marriage (Civil Protection) Act 2007	278
	Summary		279
Chapter 16	THE COHABITING FAMILY		281
	16.1	Introduction	281
	16.2	Setting up home together	282
	16.3	Breaking up	285
	16.4	Children	290
	16.5	Bankruptcy	292
	16.6	Death	292
	Summary		294

APPENDICES   **295**

Appendix 1 – Legislation			297
	(A)	Matrimonial Causes Act 1973	297
	(B)	Inheritance (Provision for Family and Dependants) Act 1975	315
	(C)	Domestic Proceedings and Magistrates' Courts Act 1978	318
	(D)	Child Abduction Act 1984	320
	(E)	Children Act 1989	322
	(F)	Child Support Act 1991	380
	(G)	Family Law Act 1996	390
	(H)	Trusts of Land and Appointment of Trustees Act 1996	407
	(I)	Family Procedure Rules 2010 (SI 2010/2955)	408
Appendix 2 – Code of Practice for Resolution Members			435
Appendix 3 – Court Forms			437
	(A)	Divorce application	437
	(B)	Form A (Application for a financial order)	453
	(C)	Form E (Statement for a financial order)	469
	(D)	Form D81 (Statement of information for a consent order)	497
	(E)	Parental responsibility agreement (1)	503
	(F)	Parental responsibility agreement (2)	505
	(G)	Form C1 (Children Act application)	507
	(H)	Form C100 (Application for a s 8 order)	517
	(I)	Form C1A (Allegations of harm and domestic violence)	541
	(J)	Form C110A (Application for a care or supervision order)	553
	(K)	Form FL401 (Family Law Act application)	575

INDEX	595

Table of Cases

A

A (A Child) (Intractable Contact Dispute: Human Rights Violations), Re [2013] EWCA Civ 1104 — 200
A (Contact: Separate Representation), Re [2001] 1 FLR 715, CA — 207
A (Minors) (Parental Responsibility), Re [1993] Fam Law 464 — 186
A (Section 8 Order: Grandparent Application), Re [1995] 2 FLR 153 — 196
A and S v Lancashire County Council [2012] EWHC 1689 — 256
A and S v Lancashire County Council [2012] EWHC 1689 (Fam) — 258
A Local Authority v YZ and Others [2006] 2 FLR 41 — 203
A v A [2012] All ER (D) 108 (Dec) — 140
A v A [2018] EWHC 340 (Fam) — 175
A v N (Committal: Refusal of Contact) [1997] 1 FLR 533 — 199
A v T (Ancillary Relief: Cultural Factors) [2004] 1 FLR 977 — 57
A, Re [2009] EWCA Civ 1141 — 200
AB v CB [2014] EWHC 2998 (Fam) — 60
AB v CD (Jurisdiction Global Maintenance Orders) [2018] 2 FLR 150 — 96
AC v DC [2012] EWHC 2420 (Fam) — 121
AC v SC [2015] EWFC B76 — 137
AD (A Minor) (Child's Wishes), Re [1993] 1 FCR 573 — 211
AH v PH (Scandinavian Marriage Settlement) [2013] EWHC 3873 (Fam) — 136, 178
Airey v Ireland (1979) 2 EHRR 305 — 17
Alireza v Radwan and Others [2017] EWCA Civ 1545 — 61
Allington v Allington [1985] FLR 586 — 207
Amin v Amin [2017] EWCA Civ 1114 — 163
An application by Denise Brewster for Judicial Review, Re [2017] UKSC 8 — 293
An application by Siobhan McLaughlin for Judicial Review (Child Poverty Action Group and another intervening), Re [2018] UKSC 48 — 293
Arbili v Arbili [2015] EWCA Civ 542 — 133

B

B (A Child) (care order: proportionality: criterion for review), Re [2013] UKSC 33 — 239
B (a child) (residence order), Re [2009] UKSC 5 — 190
B (A child) (Unnecessary private law applications), Re [2020] 9 WLUK 317 — 20
B (Contact Application: Costs), Re [1995] Fam Law 650 — 199
B (No 2) (A Child) (Welfare: Child Arrangements Order) (Inherent Jurisdiction), Re [2017] EWHC 488 (Fam) — 188
B and C (Change of Names: Parental Responsibility: Evidence), Re [2017] EWHC 3250 (Fam) — 192
B v A and Others (Parental Responsibility) [2006] EWHC 2 (Fam) — 186, 189
B v B (A Minor) (Residence Order) [1992] 2 FLR 327 — 209
B v B (Financial Orders: Proportionality) [2013] EWHC 1232 (Fam) — 59
B v B (Occupation Order) [1999] 1 FLR 715 — 265
B v B [2008] 2 FLR 1627 — 59
B v S (Financial Remedy: Marital Property Regime) [2012] EWHC 265 (Fam) — 178
Balfour v Balfour [1919] 2 KB 571 — 284
Bank v Dobson and Dobson [1986] 1 FLR 171 — 287
Barder v Barder [1988] AC 20 — 170
Barnes v Barnes [1972] 3 All ER 872 — 59
BD v FD (Maintenance Pending Suit) [2014] EWHC 4443 (Fam) — 53
Behzadi v Behzadi [2008] EWCA Civ 1070 — 138
Bernard v Josephs [1982] Ch 391, [1983] 4 FLR 178 — 289
Birch v Birch [1992] 1 FLR 564 — 32
Birch v Birch [2017] UKSC 53 — 174
B-J (Power of Arrest), Re [2000] 2 FLR 443 — 264
Bokor-Ingram v Bokor-Ingram [2009] EWCA 412 — 133
Brack v Brack [2018] EWCA Civ 1306 — 178
Bradley v Bradley [1973] 1 WLR 1291 — 32
Brickell v Brickell [1973] 3 All ER 508 — 35
Briers v Briers [2017] EWCA Civ 15 — 131, 179

Browne (formerly Pritchard) v Pritchard [1975] 1 WLR 1366   112
B-S (Adoption: Application of s 47(5)), Re [2013] EWCA Civ 1146   239
Burns v Burns [1984] Ch 317   287
Burris v Azadani [1995] 4 All ER 802   277
Burrow v Burrow [1999] 1 FLR 508   72

C

C (A Child) (Suspension of Contact), Re [2011] 2 FLR 912   195
C (A Minor) (Interim Care Order: Residential Assessment), Re [1996] 4 All ER 871   246
C (Care Order or Supervision Order), Re [2001] 2 FLR 466   244
C (Change of Surname), Re [1998] 1 FLR 549   189
C (Internal Relocation), Re [2015] EWCA Civ 1305   194
C (Minors) (Parental Rights), Re [1992] 1 FLR 1   186
C (Welfare of child: Immunisation), Re [2003] EWCA Civ 1148   189
C and B (Care Order: Future Harm), Re [2001] 1 FLR 611   244
C and V (Contact and Parental Responsibility), Re [1998] 1 FLR 392   186
C v C (Minors: Custody) [1988] 2 FLR 291   207
C v C (Variation of Post-Nuptial Settlement: Company Shares) [2003] 2 FLR 493   123
CA v DR (Schedule 1 Children Act 1989: Pension Claim) [2021] EWFC 21   226
CB v KB [2020] 1 FLR 795   94
CH v WH [2017] EWHC 2379 (Fam)   142
Chalmers v Johns [1999] 1 FLR 392   265
Charman v Charman (No 4) [2007] EWCA Civ 503   58, 73
child X and another, Re; A mother v A father [2021] All ER (D) 92 (Apr)   188, 192
Citro, Re [1991] 1 FLR 71   125
CL v East Riding Yorkshire Council and Others [2006] EWCA Civ 49   237
Cooke v Head [1972] 1 WLR 518   287
Coombes v Smith [1986] 1 WLR 808   288
Cornick v Cornick [1994] 2 FLR 530   170
Coventry City Council v C, B, CA and CH [2012] EWHC 2190 (Fam)   232
Cowan v Cowan [2001] 2 FLR 192   64
CR v SR (Financial Remedies: Permission to Appeal) [2013] EWHC 1155 (Fam)   168
Crossley v Crossley [2007] EWCA Civ 1491   178
Crozier v Crozier [1994] 1 FLR 126   171
CS v SBH and Others [2019] EWHC 634 (Fam)   211
CT (A Minor) (Wardship: Representation), Re [1993] 2 FLR 278   211
Curley v Parkes [2004] EWCA Civ 1515   286
Curling v Law Society [1985] 1 All ER 705   15
Curran v Collins [2015] EWCA Civ 404   287

D

D (A Minor) (Child: Removal from Jurisdiction), Re [1992] 1 FLR 637   201
D (Care Proceedings: Preliminary Hearing), Re [2009] EWCA Civ 472   238
D (Children) (Shared Residence Orders), Re [2001] 1 FLR 495   191
D (Minors) (Conciliation: Disclosure of Information), Re [1993] Fam 231   428
D v D and B Ltd [2007] EWHC 278 (Fam)   122
D v East Berkshire Community Health NHS Trust, K and Another v Dewsbury Healthcare NHS Trust and
    Another, K and Another v Oldham NHS Trust and Another [2005] UKHL 23   258
Dawson v Wearmouth [1999] 1 FLR 1167   192, 257
DB v DLJ (Challenge to Arbitration Award) [2016] EWHC 324 (Fam)   24, 171
Delaney v Delaney [1990] 2 FLR 457   62
DFX (A Protected Party) v Coventry City Council [2021] EWHC 1382 (QB)   258
Director of Legal Aid Casework v IS [2016] EWCA Civ 464   17
Dixon v Marchant [2008] 1 FLR 665   170, 172
Dolan v Corby [2011] EWCA Civ 1664   265
Donohoe v Ingram (Trustee in Bankruptcy of Kirkup) [2006] EWHC 292   125
Dorney-Kingdom v Dorney-Kingdom [2000] 2 FLR 855   102
Dutfield v Gilbert H Stephens & Sons [1988] Fam Law 473   5
Duxbury v Duxbury [1987] 1 FLR 7   123
DW (A Minor), Re [1984] Fam Law 17   206

E

E (Residence: Imposition of Conditions), Re [1997] 2 FLR 638   194

E v E (Financial Provision) [1990] 2 FLR 233 — 65
E v E (Premature Remarriage) [2008] 1 FLR 220 — 130
E v L [2021] EWFC 60 — 64
E, Re [2016] EWCA Civ 473 — 216
Edgar v Edgar [1980] 3 All ER 887 — 181
Evans v Evans [1989] 1 FLR 351 — 65
Evans v Evans [1990] 1 FLR 319 — 135
Evans v Evans [2013] EWHC 506 (Fam) — 62, 139
Ever's Trust, Re [1980] 1 WLR 1327 — 289
Eves v Eves [1975] 1 WLR 1338 — 287

F

F (A Child) (International Relocation Cases), Re [2015] EWCA Civ 882 — 193
F (A Minor) (Blood Tests), Re [1993] 1 FLR 598 — 185
F (Child: Surname), Re [1993] 2 FLR 837 — 192
F (children) (internal relocation), Re [2010] EWCA Civ 1348 — 194
F (Contact: Child in Care), Re [1995] 1 FLR 510 — 242
F v F (Clean Break: Balance of Fairness) [2003] 1 FLR 847 — 122
F v G (Child: Financial Provision) [2005] 1 FLR 261 — 226
F v Kent County Council and Others [1993] 1 FLR 432 — 242
Flavell v Flavell [1997] 1 FLR 353, [1997] Fam Law 237 — 173
Fleming v Fleming [2003] EWCA Civ 1841 — 172
FRB v DCA (No 3) [2020] EWHC 3696 (Fam) — 18

G

G (a child), Re [2013] EWCA Civ 965 — 239
G (A Minor) (Parental Responsibility Order), Re [1994] 1 FLR 504 — 186
G (Children), In re [2006] UKHL 43 — 207
G (Costs: Child Case), Re [1999] 2 FLR 250 — 218
G (Domestic Violence: Direct Contact), Re [2000] 2 FLR 865 — 242
G (Interim Care Order: Residential Assessment), Re [2005] UKHL 68 — 246
G (Minors) (Ex parte Interim Residence Order), Re [1993] 1 FLR 910 — 214
G (Minors) (Interim Care Order), Re [1993] 2 FLR 839 — 245
G (Residence: Same Sex Partners), Re [2005] EWCA Civ 462 — 191
G v G (Financial Provision: Separation Agreement) [2000] 2 FLR 18 — 57
G, Re [2006] UKHL 43 — 208
Gillick v West Norfolk and Wisbech Area Health Authority [1986] AC 112 — 184
Gojkovic v Gojkovic [1990] 1 FLR 140 — 63
Grant v Edwards [1986] Ch 638 — 287
Greasley v Cooke [1980] 3 All ER 710 — 289
Grey v Grey [2009] EWCA Civ 1424 — 135, 174
Grubb v Grubb [2009] EWCA Civ 976 — 265
GS v L (Financial remedies: Pre-acquired assets: Need) [2011] EWHC 1759 (Fam) — 61
GS v L (No 2) [2011] EWHC 2116 (Fam) — 140

H

H (A Child) (Interim Care Order), Re [2002] EWCA Civ 1932 — 245
H (A Minor) (Custody: Interim Care and Control), Re [1991] 2 FLR 109 — 207
H (A Minor), Re (1990) The Times, 20 June — 208
H (Contact: Domestic Violence), Re [1998] 2 FLR 42 — 196
H (Minors) (Local Authority: Parental Rights) (No 3), Re [1991] 2 WLR 763 — 185
H (Parental Responsibility), Re [1998] 1 FLR 855 — 189
H (Prohibited Steps Order), Re [1995] 1 FLR 638 — 202
H (Residence Order: Child's Application For Leave), Re [2000] 1 FLR 781 — 212
H and R (Child Sexual Abuse: Standard of Proof), Re [1996] 1 FLR 80 — 237
H v H (Financial Relief: Attempted Murder as Conduct) [2005] EWHC 2911 (Fam) — 65
H v H [2016] EWFC B81 — 179
H v M (Property: Beneficial Interest) [1992] 1 FLR 229 — 286
H v O (Contempt of Court: Sentencing) [2004] EWCA Civ 1691 — 277
H v W (Cap on Wife's Share of Bonus Payments) [2013] EWHC 4105 (Fam) — 106
Haghighat (A Bankrupt), Re [2009] EWHC 90 (Ch) — 125
Hale v Tanner [2000] 2 FLR 879 — 276
Hamilton Jones v David & Snape (A Firm) [2003] EWHC 3147 (Ch) — 222

Hammersmith and Fulham LBC v Monk [1992] 1 AC 478   118
Hammerton v Hammerton [2007] EWCA Civ 248   276
Hanlon v Law Society [1980] 2 All ER 199   15
Hart v Hart [2017] EWCA Civ 1306   61
Hart v Hart [2018] EWCA Civ 1053   163
Harvey v Harvey [1982] 3 FLR 141   114, 115, 116
Hayley v Hayley [2020] EWCA Civ 1369   23
Hewett v First Plus Financial Group PLC [2010] EWCA Civ 312   117
Hill v Haines [2007] EWCA Civ 1284   125
H-N and others (Children) (Domestic Abuse: Finding of Fact Hearings) (Rev 2) [2021] EWCA Civ 448   197
Hopes v Hopes [1948] 2 All ER 920   33
Hope-Smith v Hope-Smith [1989] 2 FLR 56   112
Hoppe v Germany [2003] 1 FLR 384   205
Hvorostovsky v Hvorostovsky [2009] EWCA Civ 791   174
HW v WW [2021] EWFC 34   129

I

I (Children: Child Assessment Order), Re [2020] EWCA Civ 281   249
Imerman v Imerman [2010] EWCA Civ 908   133
Ipecki v McConnell [2019] EWFC 19   96

J

J (Child's Religious Upbringing and Circumcision), Re [2000] 1 FLR 571   189
J (Children) (non-accidental injury: past possible perpetrator in new family), Re [2013] UKSC 9   238
J (Costs of Fact Finding Hearing), Re [2009] EWCA Civ 1350   218
J (Specific Issue Order: Leave to Apply), Re [1995] 1 FLR 669   234
J and Another v C and Others [1969] 1 All ER 788   205
J v B (Ultra-Orthodox Judaism: Transgender) [2017] EWFC 4   195
J v J (A Minor: Property Transfer) [1993] 2 FLR 56   226, 289
J v J (Financial Remedies: Disproportionate Costs) [2014] EWHC 3654 (Fam)   139, 161
J v J [2014] EWHC 3654 (Fam)   17
Jackson v Secretary of State for Work and Pensions [2020] EWHC 183 (Admin)   293
JD and A v United Kingdom [2020] HLR 5   85
JL v SL (No 2) (Appeal: Non-Matrimonial Property) [2015] EWHC 360 (Fam)   61
JL v SL (No 3) [2015] EWHC 555 (Fam)   123
Johansen v Norway (1996) 23 EHRR 33   257
Johnston v Ireland (1987) 9 EHRR 203   26
Jones v Kernott [2011] UKSC 53   285, 286, 287
Joy v Joy-Morancho & Others (No 3) [2015] EWHC 2507 (Fam)   140
Joy-Morancho v Joy [2017] EWHC 2086 (Fam)   173, 174
JS (Disposal of Body), Re [2016] EWHC 2859 (Fam)   202
Judd v Brown [1998] 2 FLR 360   125
Julian v Julian (1973) 116 SJ 763   35

K

K (A Child) (Contact: Ouster Injunction), Re [2011] EWCA Civ 1075   196
K (A Child) (Shared Residence Order), Re [2008] EWCA Civ 526   191
K (Care Proceedings: Notification of Father without Parental Responsibility), Re [1999] 2 FLR 408   251
K (Contact: Mother's Anxiety), Re [1999] Fam Law 527   197
K (Supervision Orders), Re [1999] 2 FLR 303   234
K and H (Children), Re [2015] EWCA Civ 543   19
K v K (Ancillary Relief: Prenuptial Agreement) [2003] 1 FLR 120   66
K v K (children) (removal from jurisdiction) [2011] EWCA Civ 793   193
K v K (Conduct) [1990] 2 FLR 225   65
K v K (Minors: Property Transfer) [1992] 2 FLR 220   226
K v L [2010] EWCA Civ 125   65
K, Re [1999] 3 FCR 673   193
KD (A Minor) (Access: Principles) [1998] 2 FLR 139   257
Kehoe v United Kingdom [2008] All ER (D) 198   168
Kent County Council v M and K [2016] EWFC 28   233
KG v LG [2015] EWFC 64   133
Kimber v Brookman Solicitors [2004] 2 FLR 221   133
Kingdon v Kingdon [2010] EWCA Civ 1251   169

Kokosinski v Kokosinski [1980] Fam 72   63
Krystman v Krystman [1973] 3 All ER 247   63
KSO v MJO and JMO (PSO intervening) [2008] EWHC 3031 (Fam)   139

L

L (A child), Re [2019] EWHC 867 (Fam)   200
L (Care: Threshold Criteria), Re [2007] EWHC 3527 (Fam)   237
L (Children), Re [2012] EWCA Civ 2012   265
L (Contact: Domestic Violence), Re [2000] 2 FLR 334   197, 198, 242
L (Police Investigation: Privilege), Re [1996] 1 FLR 731   255
L and H (Residential Assessment), Re [2007] EWCA Civ 213   246
Lancashire County Council v B [2000] 1 FLR 583   238
Langley v Liverpool City Council [2005] EWCA Civ 1173   248
Lawrence v Gallagher [2012] EWHC 394   51
Le Foe v Le Foe and Woolwich plc; Woolwich plc v Le Foe and Le Foe [2001] 2 FLR 970   287
Livesey (formerly Jenkins) v Jenkins [1985] AC 424, [1985] FLR 813   60, 133, 142, 169
Lloyds Bank plc v Rosset [1990] 2 WLR 867, [1990] 1 All ER 1111   286, 287
LM v DM (Costs Ruling) [2021] EWFC 28   20
Lomas v Parle [2003] EWCA Civ 1804   277
Lord Lilford v Glynn [1979] 1 WLR 78   67
L-W (children) (contact order: committal), Re [2010] EWCA Civ 1253   201

M

M (A Minor) (Care Order: Threshold Conditions), Re [1994] 2 FLR 577   237
M (Care: Contact: Grandmother's Application for Leave), Re [1995] 2 FLR 86   242
M (Children), Re [2017] EWCA Civ 2164   195
M (Contact: Violent Parent), Re [1999] 2 FLR 321   196
M (Intractable Contact Dispute: Interim Care Order), Re [2003] EWHC 1024 (Fam), [2003] 2 FLR 636 200
M (Minors) (Sexual Abuse: Evidence), Re [1993] 1 FLR 822   251
M (Section 91(14) Order), Re [1999] 2 FLR 553   242
M v D (Family Law Act 1996: Meaning of Associated Person) [2021] EWHC 1351 (Fam)   263
M v M (Parental Responsibility) [1999] 2 FLR 737   186
M v M (Third Party Subpoena: Financial Conduct) [2006] 2 FLR 1253   135
M v M (Transfer of Custody: Appeal) [1987] 1 WLR 404   206
M v M [2009] EWHC 1941 (Fam)   140
M v M and Others (Costs) [2013] EWHC 3372 (Fam)   140
MacLeod v MacLeod [2008] UKPC 64   179, 181
Maharaj v Chand [1986] AC 898   289
MAP v RAP [2013] EWHC 4784 (Fam)   171
Martin v Martin [1978] Fam 12   114
Martin-Dye v Martin-Dye [2006] EWCA Civ 681   124
Maskell v Maskell [2001] EWCA Civ 858, [2001] 1 FLR 1138   124
Matthews v Matthews [2013] EWCA Civ 1874   69
McCartney v Mills McCartney [2008] EWHC 401 (Fam)   106
McFarlane v McFarlane [2009] EWHC 891 (Fam)   106, 172, 174
McMichael v UK (1995) 20 EHRR 205   189, 291
Merritt v Merritt [1970] 1 WLR 1121   284
Mesher v Mesher and Hall [1980] 1 All ER 126   114
MF v SF (Financial Remedies: Litigation Conduct) [2015] EWHC 1273 (Fam)   139
MG v JF (Child Maintenance: Costs Allowance) [2015] EWHC 564 (Fam)   218, 226
Michael v Michael [1986] 2 FLR 389   55, 60
Migliaccio v Migliaccio [2016] EWHC 1055   166
Miller v Miller; McFarlane v McFarlane [2006] UKHL 24   58, 106, 173, 178
Miller-Smith v Miller-Smith (No 2) [2010] 2 FLR 351   45
Mills v Mills [2018] UKSC 38   173
Minkin v Lesley Landsberg (Practising as Barnet Family Law) [2015] EWCA Civ 1152   3
Moher v Moher [2019] EWCA Civ 1482   66
Morgan and Others v Legal Aid Board [2000] 3 All ER 974   15
Mossop v Mossop [1988] 2 All ER 20   285
Mountney v Treharne [2002] EWCA Civ 1174   125
Mubarak v Mubarak [2001] 1 FLR 698   166
Myerson v Myerson (No 2) [2009] EWCA Civ 282   171
Myerson v Myerson [2008] EWCA Civ 1376   137

N

N (Adoption: Jurisdiction), Re [2015] EWCA Civ 112   232
N v F (Financial orders: pre-acquired wealth) [2011] EWHC 586 (Fam)   61
N v N (Consent Order: Variation) [1993] 2 FLR 868   174
N v N (Financial Provision: Sale of Company) [2001] 2 FLR 69   122
Nasim v Nasim [2015] EWHC 2620 (Fam)   170
ND v GD [2021] EWFC 53   61
Negus v Bahouse and Another [2007] EWHC 2628 (Ch)   293
NG v SG [2011] EWHC 3270 (Fam)   132
Norris v Norris [2002] EWHC 2996 (Fam), [2003] 1 FLR 142   124
Nottinghamshire County Council v P [1993] 1 FLR 115   236
Nunn (Bankruptcy: Divorce: Pension Rights), Re [2004] 1 FLR 1123   125
Nwogbe v Nwogbe [2000] 2 FLR 744   269
NXS v Camden London Borough Council [2009] EWHC 1786 (QB)   258

O

O (A Minor) (Care Order: Education: Procedure), Re [1992] 2 FLR 7   236
O (A Minor) (Contact: Imposition of Conditions), Re [1995] 2 FLR 124   196
O'Neill v O'Neill [1975] 1 WLR 1118   31
OG v AG [2020] EWFC 52   65, 140
Owens v Owens [2018] UKSC 41   29, 32, 47

P

P (A Minor) (Adoption), Re [1990] 1 FLR 96   208
P (A Minor) (Education: Child's Views), Re [1992] 1 FLR 316   206
P (Child Financial Provision), Re [2003] EWCA Civ 837   226
P (Parental Responsibility), Re [1998] 2 FLR 96   186
P (Section 91(14) Guidelines) (Residence and Religious Heritage), Re [1999] 2 FLR 573   218
P (Terminating Parental Responsibility), Re [1995] 1 FLR 1048   188
P, C and S v United Kingdom [2002] 2 FLR 631   257
Parkes v Legal Aid Board [1997] 1 FLR 77   15
Pascoe v Turner [1979] 1 WLR 431   288
Payne v Payne [2001] EWCA Civ 166, [2001] 1 FLR 1052   193, 205
P-B (Children) (Contact: Committal), Re [2009] EWCA Civ 143   242
Pearce v Pearce [2003] 2 FLR 1144   172
Pettit v Pettit [1970] AC 777   282
PF v CF [2016] EWHC 3117 (Fam)   266
Phillips v Peace [2004] EWHC 3180 (Fam)   225
Piglowska v Piglowski [1999] 2 FLR 763   112
Poole BC v GN [2019] UKSC 25   258
Practice Direction (Ancillary Relief: Costs), 20 February 2006   140
Practice Direction (Applications: Liberty to Apply) [1980] 1 All ER 1008   173
Practice Direction (Minor: Preventing Removal Abroad) [1986] 1 WLR 475, [1986] 1 All ER 983   222
Prest v Petrodel Resources Ltd and Others [2013] UKSC 34   54

Q

Q (A Child), Re [2015] EWCA Civ 991   195
Q v Q [2014] EWFC 31   19

R

R (A Minor) (Blood Transfusion), Re [1993] 2 FLR 757   202
R (A Minor) (Residence: Religion), Re [1993] 2 FLR 163   208
R (CD) v Isle of Anglesey County Council [2005] 1 FLR 59   234
R (on the application of DA and others) v Secretary of State for Work and Pensions [2019] UKSC 21   87
R (on the application of Kehoe) v Secretary of State for Work and Pensions [2005] UKHL 48   168
R (on the application of Pantellerisco) v Secretary of State for Work and Pensions [2020] EWHC 1944 (Admin)   86
R (on the application of SC) v Secretary of State for Work and Pensions [2021] UKSC 26   85
R (on the application of SG) v Secretary of State for Work and Pensions [2015] UKSC 16   87
R (on the application of Steinfeld and Keidan) v Secretary of State for International Development [2018] UKSC 32   281
R (Parental Responsibility), Re [2011] EWHC 1535 (Fam)   187
R (Residence Order: Finance), Re [1995] 2 FLR 612   206
R v Cornwall County Council, ex p LH [2000] 1 FLR 234   235

R v Kayani; R v Solliman [2011] EWCA Crim 2871   222
R v London Borough of Barnet, ex p B [1994] 1 FLR 592   231, 234
R v London Borough of Brent, ex p S [1994] 1 FLR 203   234
R v R (Financial Remedies) [2012] EWHC 2390 (Fam)   123, 140
R v R (Lump Sum Repayments) [2004] 1 FLR 928   122
Radmacher v Granatino [2009] EWCA Civ 649   178
Radmacher v Granatino [2010] UKSC 42   57, 177
Rattan v Kuwad [2021] EWCA Civ 1   53
RC v JC [2020] EWHC 466 (Fam)   58
RM v TM [2020] EWFC 41   139
Roberts v Roberts [1986] 2 FLR 152   55
Robinson v Murray [2005] EWCA Civ 935   277
Robson v Robson [2010] EWCA Civ 1771   58, 61
Roocroft v Ball [2016] EWCA Civ 1009   169
Rothschild v de Souza [2020] EWCA Civ 1215   66
Royal Bank of Scotland v Etridge (No 2) [2001] 4 All ER 449   117
Rubin v Rubin [2014] EWHC 611 (Fam)   18

S

S (a child) (care proceedings: challenge to findings of fact), Re [2014] EWCA Civ 25   255
S (A Minor) (Independent Representation), Re [1993] 3 All ER 36   211
S (Adoption Order or Special Guardianship Order), Re [2007] EWCA Civ 54   203
S (Care Proceedings: Split Hearing), Re [1996] 2 FLR 773   255
S (Child: Financial Provision), Re [2004] EWCA Civ 1685   225, 226
S (Children) and W (A Child), Re [2007] EWCA Civ 232   240
S (Children), Re [2015] UKSC 20   218, 256
S (Contact: Children's Views), Re [2002] EWHC 540 (Fam), [2002] 1 FLR 1156   206
S (Minors: Access), Re [1990] 2 FLR 166   208
S (Minors) (Care Order: Implementation of Care Plan), Re; W (Minors) (Care Order: Adequacy of Care
    Plan), Re [2002] UKHL 10, [2002] 1 FLR 815   241
S (parental alienation: cult), Re [2020] EWCA Civ 568   200
S (Removal from Jurisdiction), Re [1999] 1 FLR 850   194
S v H [2020] EWFC B16   126
S v P (Settlement by Collaborative Law Process) [2008] 2 FLR 2040   160
S v S (Child Abduction: Child's Views) [1992] 2 FLR 492   206
S v S (Financial Provision: Departing from Equality) [2001] 2 FLR 246   63
S v S [2014] EWHC 7 (Fam)   160
SA v PA (Pre-Marital Agreement: Compensation) [2014] EWHC 392 (Fam)   58
Samuels v Birmingham City Council [2019] UKSC 28   88
Santos v Santos [1975] 2 All ER 246   34
S-B (children) (non-accidental injury), Re [2009] UKSC 17   238
Sears Tooth (A Firm) v Payne Hicks Beach (A Firm) and Others [1997] 2 FLR 116   18
Secretary of State for Work and Pensions v Johnson [2020] EWCA Civ 778   85
Sharland v Sharland [2015] UKSC 60   170
Sims v Dacorum BC & Secretary of State for Communities & Local Government [2014] UKSC 63 118
SJ v RA [2014] EWHC 4054 (Fam)   139
Slater v Slater and Another [1982] 3 FLR 364   60
Smallwood v UK (1999) 2 EHRLR 221   291
South Glamorgan County Council v W and B [1993] 1 FLR 574   244, 248
Southwell v Blackburn [2014] EWCA Civ 1347   288
SS v NS (Spousal Maintenance) [2014] EWHC 4183 (Fam)   105, 172
Stack v Dowden [2007] UKHL 17   285
Sutton v Mischon De Reya and Gower & Co [2003] EWHC 3166 (Ch), [2004] 1 FLR 837   283

T

T (A Child) (Non-molestation Orders), Re [2017] EWCA Civ 1889   264
T (A Child) (Order for Costs), Re [2005] EWCA Civ 311   218
T (A Minor) (Care or Supervision Order), Re [1994] 1 FLR 103   240, 244
T (A Minor) (Parental Responsibility: Contact), Re [1993] 2 FLR 450   195
T (Accommodation by Local Authority), Re [1995] 1 FLR 159   234
T (Care Proceedings: Costs), Re [2012] UKSC 36   218, 256
T (Judicial Review: Local Authority Decisions Concerning Child in Need), Re [2003] EWHC 2515 (Admin) 234
T v T (Financial Relief: Pensions) [1998] 1 FLR 1072   72

T v T (Interception of Documents) [1994] 2 FLR 1083   66
Talbot v Talbot (1971) 115 SJ 870   35
Tanner v Tanner [1975] 3 All ER 776   288
Taylor v Warners (1988) 85(25) LSG 26   282
Thakkar v Thakkar [2016] EWHC 2488 (Fam)   46
Thiry v Thiry [2014] EWHC 4046 (Fam)   133
Thompson v Thompson [1986] Fam 38   173
Thursfield v Thursfield [2013] EWCA Civ 840   133
TL v ML and Others [2006] 1 FLR 465   53
Treharne & Sand v Forrester [2004] 1 FLR 1173   125
Trowbridge v Trowbridge [2003] 2 FLR 231   121
Truex v Kitchin [2007] 2 FLR 1203   13
TW v TM (Minors) (Child Maintenance: Jurisdiction and Departure from Formula) [2015] EWHC 3054 (Fam) 93

U

UL v BK (Freezing Orders: Safeguards: Standard Examples) [2013] EWHC 1735 (Fam)   120, 133

V

V v V (Contact: Implacable Hostility) [2004] 2 FLR 851   200
V v V [2011] EWHC 3230 (Fam)   178
Vaughan v Vaughan [2007] EWCA Civ 1085   124
VB v JP [2008] 1 FLR 742   173
Veluppillai v Veluppillai [2015] EWHC 3095 (Fam)   66
Versteegh v Versteegh [2018] EWCA Civ 1050   178
Villiers v Villiers [2021] EWFC 23   73
Vince v Wyatt [2015] UKSC 14   130

W

W (A Minor) (Consent to Medical Treatment), Re [1993] 1 FLR 1   207
W (A Minor) (Residence Order), Re [1992] 2 FLR 332   201, 208
W (Children), Re [2010] UKSC 12   207, 216
W (Section 34(2) Orders), Re [2000] 1 FLR 502   243
W and B, Re; W (Care Plan), Re [2001] EWCA Civ 757, [2001] 2 FLR 582   240, 245
W v A (Child: Surname) [1981] 1 All ER 100   191
W v H (Divorce financial remedies) [2020] EWFC B10   124
W v W [2009] 1 FLR 92   173
W, A, B (Change of Name), Re [1999] 3 FCR 337   192
W, Re [1997] 1 FLR 793   196
Waggott v Waggott [2019] EWCA Civ 727   59
Walkden v Walkden [2009] EWCA Civ 627   171
Walker v Hall [1984] FLR 126   282
Waterman v Waterman [1989] 1 FLR 380   70
Westbury v Sampson [2001] EWCA Civ 407, [2002] 1 FLR 166   172
White v White [1998] 2 FLR 310; [2000] 2 FLR 981   57, 123, 135
Whitehouse-Piper v Stokes [2008] EWCA Civ 1049   130
Williams v Lindley [2005] EWCA Civ 103   170
WL v HL [2021] 2 FCR 394   20
WL v HL [2021] EWFC B10   128
Work v Gray [2017] EWCA Civ 270   64
WS v HS (Sale of Matrimonial Home) [2018] EWFC 11   56

X

X (Emergency Protection Orders), Re [2006] EWHC 510 (Fam)   247
X (Parental Responsibility Agreement: Children in Care), Re [2000] 1 FLR 517   241
X & Y (Bundles) [2008] EWHC 2058 (Fam)   137
X Council v B (Emergency Protection Orders) [2004] EWHC 2015 (Fam)   246
X v Y [2021] EWFC 72   19
XW v XH [2019] EWCA Civ 2262   65

Y

Yates v Yates [2012] EWCA Civ 532   172
Yemshaw v London Borough of Hounslow [2011] UKSC 3   88

YM v NM [2020] EWFC 13   120
Young v Young [2013] EWHC 3637 (Fam)   126
YXA v Wolverhampton City Council [2021] EWHC 1444 (QB)   258

Z

Z (Schedule 1: Legal costs funding order; Interim financial provision), Re [2020] EWFC 80   19
Z v Z (Divorce: Jurisdiction) [2010] 1 FLR 694   27
Z v Z (No 2) [2011] EWHC 2878 (Fam)   178
Zamet and Others v Hyman and Another [1961] 3 All ER 933   284

Table of Statutes

Access to Justice Act 1999 155
Administration of Justice Act 1960
  s 12(1) 7
Adoption and Children Act 2002 241
  s 46 188
Anti-social Behaviour, Crime and Policing Act 2014 279
  s 121 279
Arbitration Act 1996 169
  Part I (ss 1–84) 23
Attachment of Earnings Act 1971 164, 269

Child Abduction Act 1984 192, 221, 222, 223, 227, 320–1
  s 1 221
  s 2 221
Child Abduction and Custody Act 1985 223
Child Maintenance and Other Payments Act 2008 91, 92,
  94, 95, 167
Child Support Act 1991 2, 51, 67, 68, 69, 91, 92, 93, 95, 96,
  97, 100, 103, 109, 113, 114, 143, 150, 167, 168, 180, 224,
  225, 226, 284, 291, 380–9
  s 3(1)–(2) 92
  s 3(3) 93
  s 4 95
  s 4(10) 95, 96
  s 8 93, 94, 164
  s 8(1) 93
  s 8(3) 53, 93, 94, 95
  s 8(3A) 93, 96
  s 8(4) 93
  s 8(5) 95
  s 8(6)–(9) 94
  s 9(2)–(4) 95
  s 11 92
  s 12 102
  s 26 93
  s 28A 100
  s 28G 100
  s 28J 102
  s 28J(4) 102
  s 30(2) 167
  ss 32A–32L 167
  s 44(2A) 93, 97
  s 55(1) 92
  Sch 1
    para 6 99
    para 7 99
  Sch 4B 100
Child Support Act 1995 91
Child Support, Pensions and Social Security Act 2000 91
Children Act 1989 97, 180, 183, 184, 186, 192, 222, 224,
  225, 226, 227, 229, 254, 284, 291, 294, 322–79
  s 1 193, 198, 239, 243, 244
  s 1(1) 204, 247, 249, 257
  s 1(2) 207, 209
  s 1(2A) 183, 195, 205
  s 1(2B) 205
  s 1(3) 204, 206, 227, 247, 249

Children Act 1989 – *continued*
  s 1(3)(g) 239
  s 1(4)(a) 205
  s 1(5) 204, 209, 247, 249
  s 1(6) 205
  s 1(6)(a) 205
  s 1(6)(b) 206
  s 1(7) 205, 206
  s 2(2)(a) 290
  s 2(5) 188
  s 2(7) 189
  s 2(9) 189
  s 3(1) 184
  s 3(5) 189
  s 4 241
  s 4(1)(a) 184
  s 4(1)(b) 185
  s 4(1)(c) 185, 206
  s 4(2A) 206
  s 4A 187, 189
  s 4A(1)(b) 187
  s 4ZA 188
  s 4ZA(1)(c) 206
  s 4ZA(5) 206
  s 5 187
  s 5(1)(a) 187
  s 7 215, 217, 251
  s 8 183, 189, 190, 201, 202, 203, 204, 209, 210, 213, 218,
    219, 221, 223, 224, 226, 227, 236, 242, 243, 245, 254,
    260, 290
  s 9(2) 233
  s 9(5) 201
  s 9(6) 219
  s 10 211
  s 10(5)(b)–(c) 203
  s 10(8) 212
  s 10(9) 242
  s 11(1) 207
  s 11(5)–(6) 219
  s 11(7) 194
  ss 11A–11B 198
  ss 11C–11H 198
  ss 11I–11P 200
  s 12(1) 187
  s 12(1A) 187
  s 12(2) 190
  s 12(2A) 191, 211
  s 13(1) 191, 192, 221
  s 14 221
  s 14A 203, 260
  s 14A(7) 204
  ss 14B–14F 203
  s 15 225, 288, 289, 292
  s 16 202, 239
  s 16A 203, 214
  Part III (ss 17–30A) 231–4
  s 17 232, 233

Children Act 1989 – *continued*
   s 17(10) 231
   s 20 89, 232, 233, 234
   s 20(11) 232
   ss 22–24 243
   s 24B 243
   ss 25A–25C 256
   s 26 234, 241
   Part IV (ss 31–42) 236–41, 251
   s 31 204, 236, 245, 256
   s 31(3A) 240
   s 31(10) 236
   s 31A 240
   s 33(3) 188
   s 34 241, 242–3, 250, 260, 290
   s 34(1) 242, 243
   s 34(11) 240
   s 37 200, 204, 235, 245, 251
   s 37(1) 209
   s 38 235, 244, 254
   s 38(6) 245, 246
   s 38(7B) 245
   s 38A(2) 246
   s 39 243, 250
   s 41(3) 253
   Part V (ss 43–52) 246–9
   s 43 249
   s 43(3) 249
   s 44 246, 247
   s 44A(2) 247
   s 46 248
   s 47 235, 258
   s 47(6) 235
   s 91(10) 190, 219
   s 91(11) 219
   s 91(14) 218, 242
   s 91A 218
   s 97(2) 7
   Sch 1 18–19, 131, 160, 218, 225, 226, 266, 267, 288, 289,
     292
     para 4(1) 225
   Sch 2
     para 9 232
Children and Adoption Act 2006 200
Children and Families Act 2014 36, 183, 190, 191, 198, 205,
   230
   s 10 21, 184, 210
   s 10(1) 128, 129
   s 13 215, 254, 255
   s 13(7) 255
Children (Leaving Care) Act 2000 243
Civil Evidence Act 1968
   s 11 30
   s 12 30
Civil Partnership Act 2004 25, 29, 51, 281, 282, 292
   s 66 145
   Sch 5
     Part 9 73
Civil Partnerships, Marriages and Deaths (Registration etc)
   Act 2019 26, 281–2
Crime and Courts Act 2013 7
Criminal Justice Act 1967
   s 9 273, 274

Criminal Justice and Court Services Act 2000 184

Data Protection Act 1998 133
Debtors Act 1869 165, 269
Divorce, Dissolution and Separation Act 2020 26, 47–8
Divorce (Religious Marriages) Act 2002 46
Domestic Abuse Act 2021 197, 261–2
   s 67 218
Domestic Proceedings and Magistrates' Courts Act 1978 73,
   74, 75, 177, 210, 224, 225, 226, 318–19
   s 1 74
   s 2 26, 74
   s 3 74
   s 6 74
   s 25(1) 74
Domicile and Matrimonial Proceedings Act 1973
   s 5 26
   Sch 1 29

Equality Act 2010 196

Family Law Act 1986 29, 221
   s 33 221
   s 34 199, 221
Family Law Act 1996 2, 46, 47, 118, 126, 154, 210, 235, 262,
   264, 270, 277, 279, 289, 290, 294, 390–406
   Part IV (ss 30–63) 16, 26, 263–77, 288
   s 30 119, 126, 264, 268
   s 30(3) 119, 267
   s 30(4)–(6) 267
   s 33 264–6, 267, 268, 269, 270
   s 33(5) 119
   s 33(6) 265
   s 33(7) 265
   s 35 264, 266, 267, 268, 269, 270
   s 35(6) 266
   s 36 264, 266, 267, 268, 269, 270
   s 36(6) 267
   s 36(13) 267
   s 37 264, 268, 270
   s 38 264, 268, 270
   s 40 269
   s 42 263
   s 42(5) 264
   s 42(7) 264
   s 42A 272, 275
   s 43 263
   s 45 271
   s 46 271, 272
   s 47 276
   s 62 263
   Part IVA (ss 63A–63S) 278
   s 63A 278
   s 63CA 279
   Sch 7 118, 290
Family Law Reform Act 1969
   s 20(1) 185
Family Law (Scotland) Act 2006 282
Finance Act 1985
   s 83(1) 286
Finance Act 2003
   Sch 3
     Part 3 81

Financial Services and Markets Act 2000 72
Forced Marriage (Civil Protection) Act 2007 278–9
Fraud Act 2006 133

Homelessness Act 2002 88
Housing Act 1985 89
  s 79 290
Housing Act 1988
  Part VII 290
Housing Act 1996 88, 289
Human Fertilisation and Embryology Act 2008 188, 291
Human Rights Act 1998 8, 16, 17, 67, 166, 189, 205, 242,
  256, 257, 258, 291

Inheritance (Provision for Family and Dependants) Act 1975
  67, 146, 292, 294, 315–17
  s 2 70, 149, 153, 156
  s 3 292
  s 15 70
Inheritance Tax Act 1984
  ss 10–11 80
  s 18 80

Law of Property Act 1925
  s 30 289
  s 53(1)(b) 282, 287
Law of Property (Miscellaneous Provisions) Act 1989
  s 2 179
Law Reform (Succession) Act 1995 292
Legal Aid, Sentencing and Punishment of Offenders Act
  2012 11, 12, 14, 18
  s 10 17
  s 25 15
Legitimacy Act 1976
  s 1 37
Life Assurance Act 1774
  s 1 283

Maintenance Enforcement Act 1991 164
Marriage (Same Sex Couples) Act 2013 25
Married Women's Property Act 1882
  s 17 56, 145, 285
Matrimonial Causes Act 1973 25, 29, 34, 47, 51, 56, 67, 70,
  71, 91, 97, 109, 118, 120, 126, 180, 210, 224, 226, 281,
  297–314
  s 1(1) 29
  s 1(2) 29, 37, 39
  s 1(2)(a) 29
  s 1(2)(b) 31, 32, 47
  s 1(2)(c) 32
  s 1(2)(d) 33, 150
  s 1(2)(e) 35
  s 1(4) 29
  s 1(6) 30
  s 2 37, 44
  s 2(1) 31
  s 2(2) 31
  s 2(3) 32
  s 2(5) 33, 34
  s 2(6) 33
  s 3 26, 47
  s 4(1) 38
  s 4(2) 30

Matrimonial Causes Act 1973 – *continued*
  s 5 35
  s 5(1) 35, 49
  s 5(2) 35
  s 5(3) 35
  s 9(2) 46
  s 10 34, 47
  s 10(1) 34
  s 10(2) 34, 35, 36, 45, 49
  s 10(3) 34, 45
  s 10(4) 34, 35, 45
  s 10A 45, 46
  s 11 36
  s 13(1) 36
  s 13(4) 37
  s 17(2) 37
  s 22 52, 53, 142
  s 22ZA 18
  s 22ZA(10) 18
  s 22ZB 18
  s 23 16, 52, 56, 74, 142
  s 23(1)(a) 53, 68, 69, 148, 153, 156
  s 23(1)(b) 54, 68, 69, 148, 153, 156
  s 23(1)(c) 55, 68
  s 23(1)(d) 53
  s 23(1)(e) 54
  s 23(1)(f) 55
  s 23A 266
  s 24 16, 52, 55, 56, 68, 118, 126, 142, 266
  s 24A 52, 55, 56, 68, 112, 126, 142, 165, 172, 173, 175
  s 24A(2) 112
  s 24B 16, 52, 56, 72, 142
  s 24B(3)–(4) 73
  s 24C 142
  s 24D 142
  s 25 51, 56, 57, 58, 62, 63, 65, 67, 72–5, 106, 109, 111,
    112, 113, 122, 123, 126, 133, 137, 169, 173, 174, 177,
    180, 181, 226, 282, 286
  s 25(1) 56, 57, 63, 67, 71, 75, 93
  s 25(2) 57, 65, 75
  s 25(2)(a) 57, 61, 64, 68, 71
  s 25(2)(b) 57, 62, 68
  s 25(2)(c) 57, 63, 68
  s 25(2)(d) 57, 63
  s 25(2)(e) 57, 68
  s 25(2)(f) 57, 64
  s 25(2)(g) 57, 65, 66
  s 25(2)(h) 57, 66
  s 25(3) 57, 67, 75, 93
  s 25(3)(a)–(d) 67
  s 25(3)(e) 68
  s 25(4) 57, 67, 68, 75, 93
  s 25(4)(a)–(c) 68
  s 25A 68, 75, 122, 145
  s 25A(1) 68, 69
  s 25A(2) 54, 69
  s 25A(3) 69
  s 25B 57, 71
  s 25B(4) 172
  s 25C 71, 172
  s 25D 71
  s 27 26, 73, 75, 225, 226
  s 28 54

Matrimonial Causes Act 1973 – *continued*
  s 28(1A) 70, 153, 171–2
  s 28(3) 52, 130
  s 29 54
  s 29(3) 54, 74
  s 31 70, 73
  s 31(2) 171
  s 31(2A) 172
  s 31(7) 173, 174
  s 31(7A) 16
  s 31(7B) 16
  s 34 181
  s 34(2) 181
  s 35 181, 182
  s 35(2) 182
  s 36 181, 182
  s 37 118, 120, 121, 126, 129, 167
  s 37(2)(a) 120
  s 37(2)(b) 121
  s 37(2)(c) 121
  s 40A 155
  s 40B 155
  s 41 36
Matrimonial and Family Proceedings Act 1984 68
  s 31 168
  s 31K(1) 168

Pensions Act 1995
  s 166 71
Pensions Act 2008 56
Pensions Act 2014
  s 30 293
Presumption of Death Act 2013
  s 1 38
Protection from Harassment Act 1997 262, 277–8,
  279
  s 2 278
  s 2A 278
  s 3 277
  s 3(6) 278
  s 3(9) 278
  s 4 278
  s 4A 278
  s 5 278
  s 5A 278
  s 7 277

Rent Act 1977 118, 290

Senior Courts Act 1981
  s 39 168

Serious Crime Act 2015
  s 76 278
Social Security Contributions and Benefits (Northern
  Ireland) Act 1992 293
Stamp Act 1891
  s 57 286

Taxation of Chargeable Gains Act 1992
  s 21 79
  s 225 79
  s 225B 78, 79
  s 251 79
Terrorism Act 2000 249
Trusts of Land and Appointment of Trustees Act 1996 289,
  407
  s 13 56
  s 14 56, 284, 285, 289, 290
  s 15 289

Welfare Reform and Pensions Act 1999 72
  ss 11–12 126

Bills
Divorce (Financial Provision) Bill 106, 182
Nuptial Agreements Bill (draft) 182

International legislation
Brussels IIa 223
European Charter of Fundamental Rights
  Art 47 218
European Convention on Human Rights 8
  Art 3 8, 258
  Art 5 8
  Art 6 8, 16–17, 166, 168, 194, 210, 218, 233, 241, 245,
    247, 258, 276, 277, 291
  Art 6(1) 211
  Art 8 8, 118, 125, 135, 194, 195, 200, 205, 218, 233, 239,
    241, 245, 247, 248, 256, 257, 258, 277, 291, 293
  Art 8(2) 257
  Art 9 196
  Art 12 26
  Art 14 8, 196, 291, 293
  First Protocol
    Art 1 118
  Seventh Protocol
    Art 5 67
European Convention on Recognition and Enforcement of
  Custody Decisions 223
Hague Convention on International Child Abduction 1980
  223
IFLA Rules 23

Table of Statutory Instruments and Codes of Practice

Access to Justice Act 1999 (Destination of Appeals) (Family Proceedings) Order 2014 (SI 2014/602) 168

Child Maintenance (Written Agreements) Order 1993 (SI 1993/620) 95
Child Support Maintenance Calculation Regulations 2012 (SI 2012/2677) 98, 100
  reg 68 101
  reg 69 101
  reg 70 101
  reg 71 102
Civil Legal Aid (Merits Criteria) Regulations 2013 (SI 2013/104) 12
Civil Legal Aid (Procedure) Regulations 2012 (SI 2012/3098) 12, 13
  Sch 1 12
Civil Legal Aid (Statutory Charge) Regulations 2013 (SI 2013/503) 15
Civil Partnership (Jurisdiction and Recognition of Judgments) Regulations 2005 (SI 2005/3334) 27
Civil Procedure Rules 1998 (SI 1998/3132) 134, 167
  r 44.3 140
  r 44.13 146
  r 47.17 156
  r 71 164
Community Legal Service (Financial) Regulations 2000 (SI 2000/516) 146, 155

Family Court (Composition and Distribution of Business) Rules 2014 (SI 2014/840) 7, 213, 251, 272
Family Procedure (Amendment) Rules 2018 (SI 2018/440) 127
Family Procedure (Amendment No 2) Rules 2021 (SI 2021/875) 273, 274
Family Procedure Rules 2010 (SI 2010/2955) 20, 25, 134, 160, 167, 253, 408–34
  Part 1
    r 1.1(1) 128
  Part 3 20, 128
    r 3 129
    r 3.1 129
    r 3.4 128
    r 3.8 129
  PD 3A 128, 129, 210
    para 13(2) 129
  Part 4 47
    r 4.4(1) 130
  PD 5A 44
  Part 6 43, 48
    r 6.5(3) 42
    r 6.9 42
    r 6.14 43
    r 6.15 41
    r 6.16 42
    r 6.19(2) 42
    r 6.20 43

Family Procedure Rules 2010 – *continued*
  PD 6A
    para 6.2 42
  PD 6B 43
  PD 6C 43
  Part 7 48
    r 7.6 41
    r 7.8 41
    r 7.12(1) 43, 46
    r 7.12(8) 44, 46
    r 7.12(12) 34
    r 7.13 40
    r 7.20 44, 45
    r 7.32 45
    r 7.32(2) 45
    r 7.33 46
  PD 7A 30, 45
    para 2.1 31
  Part 9 128
    Ch 5 174
    r 9.7 138
    r 9.9A 155, 171
    r 9.12(1) 132
    r 9.13(3) 132
    r 9.14(5) 134
    r 9.17(3) 136
    r 9.27 139
    r 9.28 137
    r 9.31 132
    r 9.33 132
    r 9.40 132
  PD 9A 128, 134, 141
    para 6.3 136
  Part 12 210, 249, 250, 253
  PD 12A 249, 250, 253, 255
  PD 12B 210, 212
  PD 12C 213
  PD 12J 197, 198, 214
  PD 12.3 213
  Part 16 252
    r 16.6 211
  PD 16A 213, 252
  Part 17
    r 17.2 216
  Part 18
    r 18.11 271
  PD 18A
    para 5.1 120
  Part 21
    r 21.2 135
    r 21.2(3) 135
  Part 25 135, 215, 255
    r 25.7 135
  PD 25A–25F 215
  Part 27
    r 27.11 7

Family Procedure Rules 2010 – *continued*
  PD 27A 137, 217, 255
  Part 28
    r 28.3 139, 140, 161

    r 28.3(6) 66
  PD 28A 140
    para 4.4 20
  Part 30 168
  Part 33
    r 33.3(2) 164
  Pre-application protocol for applications for a financial
    remedy 129
    para 7 133
Family Proceedings (Amendment) Rules 2003 (SI 2003/184)
  166
Family Proceedings Rules 1991 (SI 1991/1247)
  rr 7.4–7.6 166

Insolvency (Amendment) Rules 2005 (SI 2005/527) 126

Jurisdiction and Judgments (Family) (Amendments etc) (EU
  Exit) Regulations 2019 (SI 2019/5190) 26

Legal Aid, Sentencing and Punishment of Offenders Act
  2012 (Amendment of Schedule 1) Order 2013
  (SI 2013/748) 12
Local Government Pension Scheme (Benefits, Membership
  and Contributions) Regulations (Northern Ireland) 2009
  (NISR 2009/32) 293

Marriage (Same Sex Couples) (Jurisdiction and Recognition
  of Judgments) Regulations 2014 (SI 2014/543) 27

Parental Responsibility Agreement Regulations 1991
  (SI 1991/1478) 185

Stamp Duty (Exempt Instruments) Regulations 1987
  (SI 1987/516) 286

EU secondary legislation
Regulation 2201/2003 (Brussels IIa) 223

Codes and guidance
SRA Code of Conduct for Solicitors
  para 1.2 6
  para 2.5 223
  para 6.2 3
  para 6.3 3
  para 6.5 3
Family Mediation Council's Mediators Code of Conduct
  21
Inland Revenue SP 27 April 1990 286
Law Society's Family Law Protocol
  Part II, para 2.4 284
  Part III, para 4.10 222
President's Guidance on Allocation and Gatekeeping 213,
  251
President's Guidance on Family Court - Duration of Ex Parte
  (Without Notice) Orders 264, 271, 273
President's Guidance on Radicalisation Cases 237
President's Guidance on Standard Financial and
  Enforcement Orders 142
Public Law Outline 2010 230, 249, 250, 251, 253, 255
Resolution Code of Practice 4–5, 435
Resolution Guidelines (Section F: Assessing Understanding)
  211

Table of Abbreviations

CA 1989	Children Act 1989
CAA 1984	Child Abduction Act 1984
CACA 1985	Child Abduction and Custody Act 1985
Cafcass	Children and Family Court Advisory and Support Service
CETV	Cash Equivalent Transfer Value
CGT	capital gains tax
C-MEC	Child Maintenance and Enforcement Commission
CMH	Case Management Hearing
CMOPA 2008	Child Maintenance and Other Payments Act 2008
CMS	Child Maintenance Service
CPA 2004	Civil Partnership Act 2004
CPR 1998	Civil Procedure Rules 1998
CSA 1991	Child Support Act 1991
CSMCR 2012	Child Support Maintenance Calculation Regulations 2012
CS(MCSC) Regs 2000	Child Support (Maintenance Calculations and Special Cases) Regulations 2000
CSPSSA 2000	Child Support, Pensions and Social Security Act 2000
DAA 2021	Domestic Abuse Act 2021
DRA	Dispute Resolution Appointment
DPMCA 1978	Domestic Proceedings and Magistrates' Courts Act 1978
DWP	Department for Work and Pensions
ECHR	European Convention on Human Rights
EPO	emergency protection order
FDR	Financial Dispute Resolution
FHDRA	First Hearing Dispute Resolution Appointment
FLA 1996	Family Law Act 1996
FPR 2010	Family Procedure Rules 2010
HMRC	HM Revenue and Customs
HRA 1998	Human Rights Act 1998
IRH	Issues Resolution Hearing
I(PFD)A 1975	Inheritance (Provision for Family and Dependants) Act 1975
IRO	Independent Reviewing Officer
LASPO 2012	Legal Aid, Sentencing and Punishment of Offenders Act 2012
LHA	local housing allowance
MCA 1973	Matrimonial Causes Act 1973
MIAM	Mediation Information and Assessment Meeting
MWPA 1882	Married Women's Property Act 1882
PHA 1997	Protection from Harassment Act 1997
PLO	Public Law Outline
PPO	periodical payments order
SRA	Solicitors Regulation Authority
TLATA 1996	Trusts of Land and Appointment of Trustees Act 1996

CHAPTER 1

INTRODUCTION: THE FAMILY PRACTICE

1.1	The family client	1
1.2	The family practitioner	3
1.3	Support for family clients	6
1.4	Litigants in person	6
1.5	The court system	7
1.6	Human Rights Act 1998	8
1.7	Family law in the future	8
1.8	Conclusion	9
Summary		9

LEARNING OUTCOMES

After reading this chapter you will be able to:

- appreciate the varied issues facing a family client
- understand the nature of family law cases.

1.1 THE FAMILY CLIENT

There is a wide range of reasons why a client would wish to discuss family problems with a solicitor. The most common reason is that a relationship has permanently broken down. Some clients, however, may seek advice because they are encountering temporary difficulties and have no wish to terminate the relationship formally. Yet others may have some domestic problem that they need to resolve, but they are undecided and unclear as to the future of the relationship.

Whether or not a client has made a firm decision about the relationship, he will usually be reasonably clear about his more immediate problems which prompted him to seek legal advice. The three most common problem areas concern money and property (see **Chapters 4 to 11**), children (see **Chapters 13** and **14**) and protection from domestic abuse (see **Chapter 15**). How these problems are to be dealt with depends in the first place on whether the couple are married (or in a civil partnership) or living together. The problems and concerns of cohabiting couples are virtually indistinguishable from those of married couples or civil partners; the legal remedies, however, are by no means the same and are more limited for cohabiting couples. A large part of this book is devoted to married couples as these will form the majority of the clients for most family solicitors. However, the cohabiting family is considered in detail in **Chapter 16**, and comparisons between the positions of cohabiting couples, civil partners and spouses are made throughout this book.

In the case of married couples, there is a broad range of solutions to the key problems. The skill of the family lawyer is to match the appropriate solution to the needs of the individual client. Which measures are to be taken will depend on whether the client has made the decision to end the marriage, or whether a more temporary solution is favoured. The marriage may be terminated formally by divorce (or nullity), or the couple may separate formally by judicial separation (these options are considered in **Chapter 3**). Alternatively, the client may not wish to make any final decision about the relationship itself but merely wish to seek advice on a particular problem: for example, a wife may be anxious about her position in the matrimonial home, or a father may be being denied contact with his children.

It is worthwhile pausing to consider some of the likely issues and concerns facing a family client. Whilst there is no such thing as a 'typical' family client (and it would be a mistake to assume that there was), there are certain concerns which are common to many families.

EXAMPLE

Beverley is a mother with two young children. She has been married to Colin for the last 10 years, but is seeking a divorce because Colin has recently begun to be violent towards her and on one occasion to her son. Beverley does not work and has no savings. She has fled the family home and her main worry is to be able to return to the home in safety.

One of the first issues for the solicitor to consider is how the client will pay for the legal advice. This will also be high on the client's list of concerns. The question of costs, including legal aid, is considered in context throughout this book and in **Chapter 2**. A private client should be advised about the costs policy of the firm and will usually be asked to make a payment on account. As with most contentious work, it is difficult to give an accurate prediction of costs in the initial interview as so much depends on the attitude of the other party, and indeed of the client himself. In this example, Beverley may be eligible for legal aid.

Beverley's primary need is to seek protection from the violence and to be able to return home. It will be necessary, therefore, to take instructions to prepare for proceedings for a non-molestation and occupation order under the Family Law Act 1996 (FLA 1996) (see **Chapter 15**). As Beverley wishes to obtain a divorce, the solicitor will also need to obtain the information and prepare the documentation required to institute divorce proceedings (see **Chapter 3**). Since the order under FLA 1996 will provide only a temporary solution to Beverley and the children's housing needs, the solicitor must also discuss the future arrangements in relation to the former matrimonial home (see **Chapter 9**). Although it will be some time before this can be dealt with, the solicitor needs to think ahead and decide on the best method of resolving financial issues. The solicitor should also be aware of the need to protect their client's interest in the matrimonial home. They will, therefore, need to establish how the property is held between the parties and make any necessary registrations against the title. In addition, Beverley should be advised to make (or alter) a will. Further, there may be a problem regarding the mortgage, as Colin may stop paying the mortgage if he is ordered to leave the home (although, if an occupation order is made, provision can be included instructing Colin to continue to pay the mortgage). It will probably be necessary, therefore, to advise Beverley regarding maintenance, and possibly to write to the lender to explain any short-term difficulties there may be in relation to the mortgage. The procedure for obtaining financial orders is considered in **Chapter 10**, and their enforcement and variation is considered in **Chapter 11**.

As it will be some time before any application for maintenance for Beverley can be considered in detail, she should be advised of her entitlements to welfare benefits (see **Chapter 6**) and for maintenance for the children under the Child Support Act 1991 (see **Chapter 7**).

The other important consideration is, of course, the children (see **Chapters 13** and **14**). At an early stage, it is likely to be necessary to raise the question of the arrangements for the children. As with the other issues, this may be agreed upon between the parties (after, say, negotiation), but in Beverley's case, in view of her husband's violence towards her son, she may well object to him having contact with the children, and this could involve further proceedings.

The topics covered in this book deal with all of the problems faced by Beverley in the example above. Of necessity, the book takes each issue in turn, but it is important to appreciate from the beginning that all the issues are strongly interrelated and that several disputes and difficulties can occur concurrently.

The past few years have seen a change in the manner in which family clients seek legal advice. Historically, it was usual for a client to instruct a solicitor to initiate and conduct whatever proceedings and/or negotiations were necessary to deal with each and every aspect of the client's case: divorce, children, finances etc. No doubt those clients who are eligible to have their legal fees paid by legal aid and those clients who are wealthy enough to have legal fees well within their means will continue to instruct solicitors in this way. However, there is an increasing number of family clients who fall between these two extremes and who are simply unable to afford to have a solicitor acting from the beginning of their case until the end. As a consequence, many family clients are having to be much more selective in the use they make of their solicitor. It is now common for a solicitor to be instructed to deal only with particular elements of the case (for example, the drafting of a complex document) or to act for the client for an isolated event (for example, a court hearing).

Whether the solicitor is instructed to deal with the client's entire case or is confined to dealing with individual aspects of it, they will need to be aware of the wider picture. Family cases are by their nature multi-faceted. A family solicitor must raise the various issues at an appropriate stage and encourage their client to confront the future and make reasoned and informed decisions.

1.2 THE FAMILY PRACTITIONER

1.2.1 Professional conduct

Family solicitors owe the same duties towards their clients as those of any other solicitor. The solicitor may not act for both parties, no matter how amicable their separation, as there is an inherent client conflict (see SRA Code of Conduct for Solicitors, para 6.2). Confidentiality towards clients' affairs must also be observed, for example a client's address cannot be disclosed without his consent. There are, however, particular professional conduct issues which may arise in the context of a family law case. The solicitor may, for example, have previously acted for the husband and wife jointly in a property or business matter during the marriage. On the breakdown of the marriage the husband may ask the solicitor to act for him in the divorce. The solicitor will need to consider whether they have relevant confidential information about the wife which will require the solicitor to decline to act for the husband (see SRA Code of Conduct for Solicitors, paras 6.3 and 6.5).

A solicitor acting in a children case may be given information by their client which the client does not wish to be disclosed, and yet which causes the solicitor to believe that the mental or physical safety of a child is at risk. The solicitor will need to consider whether it is an exceptional situation, which would justify the solicitor breaching client confidentiality under the SRA Code of Conduct for Solicitors, para 6.3.

The shift towards solicitors being instructed only in relation to selected aspects of the client's case (ie acting on a 'limited retainer') gives rise to its own professional conduct issues. It is, for example, essential for the solicitor to clearly define the limits of his retainer at the outset so that there is no uncertainty as to the services the solicitor has agreed to provide (see the Law Society practice note, 'Unbundling civil legal services'). An example of a client suing a solicitor for negligence in such circumstances is provided in *Minkin v Lesley Landsberg (Practising as Barnet Family Law)* [2015] EWCA Civ 1152. In that case the solicitor was instructed to redraft a consent order to reflect the financial agreement reached directly between husband and wife. Once the order had been redrafted and approved by the court, the wife decided that its terms were unfavourable to her and brought an action claiming that her solicitor had been negligent in failing to warn her of the potential unfairness of the agreement. The claim failed. The Court found that the solicitor was acting under a defined and limited retainer to redraft the order, and that this did not extend to advising on the merits of the agreement. The Court stressed the importance of clarity and said that, as a matter of good practice, any limitations placed on a retainer should be confirmed by the solicitor to the client in writing.

1.2.2 Adviser – not decision-maker

There are certain special considerations to be borne in mind when dealing with a family matter. Family clients are likely to be more vulnerable than other clients. They may have only recently (or are even yet to) come to terms with the breakdown of their relationship and the consequent break-up of their home and family. They will invariably face many problems, be presented with a bewildering array of options, and be called upon to make many important decisions. It is hardly surprising, therefore, that such clients may be tempted to pass the responsibility to make these decisions on to their solicitor. However, it is important that the family solicitor is able to distinguish between advising the client of his choices and influencing the client's decisions, or even assuming certain choices on the client's behalf. However much a client's marriage appears to the solicitor to be irredeemably lost, the solicitor must be careful to advise the client fully of all the options and not to push the client prematurely down the route to divorce. If the solicitor is in any doubt as to what the client really wants to do about his relationship, the solicitor should pause to allow the client time to make a free and firm decision. Many clients will find the initial interview an emotional and stressful experience and, bearing in mind that many important and complex matters will have been discussed in the interview, it is sensible to confirm advice given and to set out the options in a letter following the interview. This enables the client to absorb the advice and reflect upon it before embarking upon a particular course of action.

1.2.3 Objectives

A further important consideration for the family solicitor is to keep sight of the client's overall long-term objectives. If a relationship has finally broken down, it is fair to assume that a family client's ultimate objective is to be able to unravel the legal ties of that relationship and to begin life afresh with the minimum of pain and bitterness. This will apply particularly where children are involved. There will be times when a client may be so involved in the detail of a particular dispute that he loses sight of this wider aim. It is here that the good family practitioner can make a positive contribution; by maintaining a sufficiently detached viewpoint the professional may enable a client to refocus on his goal and to regard matters in the round.

In pursuing these long-term objectives the good family solicitor has a very positive role to play. The approach taken by the solicitor can significantly influence a client's response. If a solicitor takes an aggressive stance, advising in terms of 'winning' and 'losing' and 'fighting' and 'giving in', then this is likely to serve to stir up bitterness and lead a client to set his face against compromise. Conversely, the solicitor who attempts to defuse tensions, concentrating on important issues rather than petty matters, and who talks in terms of arriving at fair solutions and compromise is likely to find that his client is more willing to follow this lead. It is important to address the advantages of a negotiated settlement whilst at the same time assuring the client that, where appropriate, a firm stance will be taken to protect his interests. The people most likely to come through the trauma of a divorce or separation successfully are those who have been involved in reaching agreement about important issues. A party is also much more likely to abide by such an agreement than by an arrangement imposed by the court. Most important of all is the benefit of reducing the impact of the disputes on any children who are at risk of being caught in the cross-fire. The Resolution Code of Practice (set out in **Appendix 2**) advocates a constructive and non-confrontational approach in family matters. Resolution has a membership of over 6,500 family law solicitors and other legal justice professionals. Its Code of Practice is endorsed by The Law Society and supported by many senior members of the judiciary (see, for example, *Dutfield v Gilbert H Stephens & Sons* [1988] Fam Law 473).

In order to achieve these objectives, the family practitioner must acquire negotiating skills (see **Skills for Lawyers**); they must know when and how to employ methods of dispute resolution (see **2.5**) to achieve a settlement. Having successfully reached a settlement, the family solicitor must use their drafting skills to draw up a clear and enforceable agreement (see **Skills for Lawyers**). This document may take the form of a consent order (see **Chapter 9**), or a separation agreement (see **Chapter 11**).

If a settlement cannot be achieved, the matter must be determined in court. Often in family cases the solicitor will have rights of audience. This will call for the use of advocacy skills (see **Skills for Lawyers**).

1.2.4 Interviewing skills

The success of the solicitor–client relationship in family cases is to a large extent dependent upon the impression created in the first interview. The practitioner may be in the privileged position of being the first person with whom the client has discussed his relationship difficulties. The client will be sensitive to the atmosphere in that interview, and it is of crucial importance that the solicitor attempts to create the right environment and to adopt an appropriate tone for the interview.

Preparation for the interview is vital. Thought should be given to the length of the interview and its venue, as well as to the information which should be obtained from, and given to, the client. In family matters the interview could also be complicated by the fact that the client may bring his children with him, or have chosen to bring a friend for support. This field of interviewing is a hugely important subject in itself which cannot be considered in detail here, but reference should be made to the section on interviewing in **Skills for Lawyers**.

1.2.5 Awareness and balance

When a relationship is in crisis, each party may experience a wide range of feelings. These will inevitably vary between individuals, but may variously include disappointment, anger and blame, hurt, sadness, self-doubt, loss, guilt, uncertainty and anxiety. For some time, there may be a sense of relief that an unhappy situation is being addressed. Sometimes, there may be worry and concern for the other partner. It is not uncommon for people in this crisis situation to move inconsistently from one feeling to another. There is no standard reaction to relationship breakdown, and family solicitors need to be aware of the sensitivity of the situation in which they are intervening.

Most clients need, and are entitled to have, solicitors who will advise and support them in these difficult times. Their solicitors may have to act as their champions, protecting their rights and position. However, while maintaining awareness of these legitimate expectations, the family solicitor also needs to be aware that supporting the client can sometimes mean helping him to understand and come to terms with unpalatable consequences, or seeking compromises which the client may prefer not to make. Parents may be able to keep their children's best interests in mind, but in that situation those interests may sometimes blur with the client's own preferences, antagonisms or strength of feeling; and here again the solicitor may have a role in helping the client to be aware of the children's needs and interests as well as the client's.

The family solicitor accordingly has to maintain a balance between the supportive, partisan role and the need to confront the client's perceptions where appropriate. As previously stated, an objective view, sympathetically but not patronisingly expressed, may be necessary to help the client make necessary shifts. The solicitor must also appreciate the extent to which his actions and approach can have an effect, whether helping or damaging, on the client and on the relationship between the parties and their children. Communications with the other side can always be courteous and sensitive, even where tough positions are being stated. Opportunities for dialogue can be established early on and maintained even when confrontation is indicated. This is all consistent with having a sympathetic and effective relationship with the client.

1.3   SUPPORT FOR FAMILY CLIENTS

Family clients often need emotional support through the process of family breakdown. Whilst the family solicitor provides support in the form of guiding the client through the process, it is important to be able to recognise the boundaries of the solicitor's role and the limitations of their skills. There is a range of support services available to complement the work of the family practitioner. The family solicitor should be aware of the local agencies and services which are more suitable and capable of meeting the client's emotional needs and recommend them, as appropriate.

The client may, for example, benefit from counselling. Counselling takes different forms and may have different aims. It may involve working with an individual, the couple, members of the family or the whole family together. It may be relatively short-term or may involve longer-term marital or family therapy; and there are different theoretical perspectives.

One of the aims of counselling may be to try to save the relationship where it is under stress, or to establish a reconciliation where it has already broken down. Another may be to explore whether there is any basis for continuing with the relationship and, if so, what has to happen to make this possible. Not uncommonly, a couple may disagree about the future of the relationship, one wishing to end it and the other to continue with it. Counselling may assist the couple to come to their own conclusion, whether this proves to be preserving the relationship or bringing it to an end. Counselling may therefore help a couple to accept the ending of their relationship, if that is appropriate.

1.4   LITIGANTS IN PERSON

In recent years there has been a significant rise in the number of individuals who conduct their family case without the involvement of a solicitor – 'litigants in person'. To a large extent the increase is the result of the removal of legal aid from most types of private family cases (see **Chapter 2**). It has therefore become increasingly common for the family solicitor to have to correspond, negotiate and/or conduct litigation with a lay person rather than another legally qualified professional.

When faced with a case involving a litigant in person, there may be a tendency on the part of the solicitor to automatically view this as a 'problem'. However, just as there is no 'typical' family client, there is no 'typical' litigant in person. At one end of the spectrum, the litigant in person may be legally sophisticated and able to conduct the case in a dispassionate and conciliatory manner; at the other end, however, the litigant in person may have little understanding of the legal process and/or may find it impossible to put their personal feelings aside. Whether or not the case can truly be considered a 'problem', dealing with a litigant in person certainly requires the family solicitor to exercise both care and caution.

The family solicitor should be mindful of potential professional conduct issues when dealing with a litigant in person. Obviously the solicitor must not abuse their position: the SRA Code of Conduct for Solicitors, para 1.2 states that a solicitor must not take unfair advantage of others. Conversely, the family solicitor must be wary of being overly helpful to the litigant in person, the danger being that the solicitor may overstep the mark and stray into giving legal advice to the litigant in person.

Helpful guidance can be found in Resolution's 'Guide to Good Practice on Working with Litigants in Person' and the joint Law Society, CiLEX and Bar Council publication, 'Litigants in Person: Guidelines for Lawyers'.

1.5 THE COURT SYSTEM

The family practitioner must not only be able to identify the client's needs and determine the correct approach to meet these, but must also decide when and how to seek appropriate remedies through the courts. Proceedings will usually be brought in the Family Court or, in limited cases, the High Court. The Court of Appeal and the Supreme Court have jurisdiction to hear appeals in family cases.

1.5.1 The Family Court

After calls for reform stretching back decades, in April 2014 the Crime and Courts Act 2013 finally introduced the Family Court. The Family Court replaced the previous three-tier structure of High Court, county court and family proceedings court, each with their own individual jurisdiction, procedures, administration and buildings. The Family Court provides a single, unified and coherent venue for the conduct of family cases.

For the purpose of setting up the Family Court, England and Wales has been divided into geographical areas, each with one central designated family centre (three in London) presided over by the designated family judge. The designated family centre is the location for the court's administration and the place where cases will be heard. Some areas have additional hearing centres where cases can be heard. The former Principal Registry of the Family Division located at First Avenue House is the designated family centre for central London and has been renamed the Central Family Court. Within the Family Court there are also specialist courts, such as the Financial Remedies Courts (see **10.5.3**).

All family cases must be commenced in the Family Court. The only exceptions are cases invoking the inherent jurisdiction (eg wardship) and certain international cases which are reserved to the Family Division of the High Court.

Various levels of judiciary, from lay magistrates to High Court judges, sit as judges of the Family Court. On the issue of proceedings, a case is allocated to a judge of the appropriate level in accordance with the Family Court (Composition and Distribution of Business) Rules 2014 (SI 2014/840).

1.5.2 Transparency in family cases

Family court hearings normally take place in private, ie members of the public have no right to attend. This is a reflection of the personal and sensitive nature of their content. However, in recent years there has been a move towards more openness in family cases driven by a desire to promote a greater understanding of the family court system amongst the general public and by a determination that 'justice be seen to be done'.

One result of the move for greater transparency is that r 27.11 of the FPR 2010 allows 'duly accredited representatives' of the media to attend family court hearings. The provisions cover most types of family hearings, with the exception of those specifically conducted for the purpose of conciliation or negotiation. The court has the power to exclude the media if this is necessary to protect the interests of a child or the safety of a witness or to ensure the proper conduct of the proceedings. There is currently a pilot project underway which extends r 27.11 to allow 'duly authorised lawyers attending for journalistic, research or public legal educational purposes' (known collectively as 'legal bloggers') to attend hearings.

The ability to attend family hearings does not, however, give the media access to the documents in the case nor grant an unfettered right to report on or publish details of the proceedings. Indeed s 12(1) of the Administration of Justice Act 1960 and s 97(2) of the CA 1989 impose automatic reporting restrictions on cases involving children. Reporting restrictions can be lifted by application to the court.

The President of the Family Division has been conducting a review of transparency in the Family Courts. His findings are due to published in late 2021.

1.6   HUMAN RIGHTS ACT 1998

The Human Rights Act 1998 (HRA 1998) incorporates the European Convention for the Protection of Human Rights and Fundamental Freedoms (ECHR or 'the Convention') into the law of England and Wales. It provides a scheme whereby domestic legislation must be read and given effect so as to be compatible with the rights and freedoms guaranteed by the Convention as far as is possible. If a Convention right is infringed then an application for judicial review, or proceedings against the appropriate public body for failure to act compatibly with the Convention, may be appropriate. The most relevant of the Convention rights for the purposes of family law is Article 8 (right to respect for family and private life), which provides:

1. Everyone has the right to respect for his private and family life, his home and his correspondence.

2. There shall be no interference by a public authority with the exercise of this right except such as is in accordance with the law and is necessary in a democratic society in the interests of national security, public safety or the economic well-being of the country, for the prevention of disorder or crime, for the protection of health or morals, or for the protection of the rights and freedoms of others.

Public law relating to children (see **Chapter 14**) is an obvious example of an area of UK law where this Article will need to be taken into account.

Other Convention rights which could give rise to litigation and, potentially, changes in UK law are Article 3 (prohibiting inhuman or degrading treatment); Article 5 (the right to liberty and security of person); Article 6 (right to a fair hearing); and Article 14 (prohibiting discrimination on any ground, including sex, birth or other status). The significance of these Articles will be considered in more detail in the relevant chapters of this book.

1.7   FAMILY LAW IN THE FUTURE

Family law has gone through a series of radical changes in the past few years. Some of those changes, such as the introduction of the single Family Court, have been almost universally welcomed, whilst others, such as the removal of legal aid for most family cases (see **Chapter 2**), have proved highly controversial. The process of reform is ongoing. For example, the Law Commission is currently consulting on aspects of family law to include in its latest Programme of Law Reform.

The family courts are making use of information technology. The e-filing of some documents is compulsory in some cases, and courts are moving over to the use of e-files in the court office and e-bundles in the courtroom. Online procedures and paperless platforms are already a feature of family law. Whilst the aim of digitisation of the entire court system has not yet been fully achieved, progress has undoubtedly been rapid.

In the office, family solicitors, in common with their colleagues in other legal areas, are identifying how new technology can streamline and enhance the service they provide for their clients. Case management systems are now relatively commonplace, and automated document assembly systems are increasingly being employed in family law practices. Some firms are also using 'onboarding' or engagement software to assist with data collection and process selection.

These rapid changes are taking place against a political backdrop. For some years now, the determination has been to enable and encourage individuals to make arrangements for themselves following family breakdown. This certainly does not mean that family solicitors no longer have a place. The inevitable consequence is, however, that today, in addition to coming to terms with new law and procedure, the family solicitor must constantly evaluate and adapt their practice of family law.

At the time of writing, the family justice system is slowly and cautiously emerging from an unprecedented period of upheaval as long-term policies and objectives were overtaken by the need to tackle the immediate impact of a global pandemic. 'Lockdown' led to an increase in private children law disputes and an upsurge in the incidence of domestic abuse, whilst simultaneously making access to the family justice system extremely problematic at a practical level. Solicitors have been forced to hastily find new ways of engaging with their clients, and the courts have had to rapidly adapt procedures and grapple with remote and hybrid hearings. The future is, even now, uncertain, but these new ways of working that circumstances have forced upon the profession are likely to remain a feature of family law going forward. These are challenging times indeed for family law practitioners.

1.8 CONCLUSION

The problems facing a family client are as diverse as families themselves. The challenge facing the family practitioner is to steer a client through those problems on to a new life. This requires the practitioner to fit the appropriate solution from a diverse range of remedies to meet the specific needs of each individual client. To succeed in this, the family solicitor must acquire a firm grasp of a broad range of law and develop a variety of legal skills. A healthy measure of common sense and a sense of humour are also invaluable. Thus equipped, the family practitioner can look forward to a highly interesting and rewarding career.

SUMMARY

(1)   The family client will usually want advice on money and property, children and protection from violence.

(2)   The family practitioner will need to consider professional conduct, the need to advise but not take decisions for a client, and the need to keep in mind long-term objectives.

(3)   Outside agencies can also help a client, for example counselling services.

(4)   Most family cases are dealt with in the Family Court.

CHAPTER 2

FUNDING AND PROCESS OPTIONS

2.1	Introduction	11
2.2	Legal aid	11
2.3	Human rights	16
2.4	Other methods of funding	17
2.5	Dispute resolution	20
Summary		24

> **LEARNING OUTCOMES**
>
> After reading this chapter you will be able to:
>
> - outline the application of legal aid in family cases
> - describe the various methods of funding legal fees
> - explain the process options available to resolve family cases.

2.1 INTRODUCTION

The question of how to pay for legal advice will be a concern for all clients from the outset of their case. Even where the client is of modest means, public funding or, as it is more commonly known, legal aid will only be available in limited circumstances. Some clients will simply pay for their solicitor to conduct the entire case calculated on the basis of an hourly charging rate, although for the reasons considered below (see **2.4**) this is becoming less common, with the result that the family solicitor must be prepared to consider more creative funding options.

At the first interview, the client will also wish to know how best to resolve his case. Litigation is but one option and, in view of its cost and adversarial nature, is often the least attractive. The family solicitor will need to consider, advise on and engage in the range of process options available.

This chapter provides an outline of the system of legal aid in relation to family work. It also considers other funding options available to the client. The chapter concludes with an overview of the various methods of resolving family cases, other than litigation.

2.2 LEGAL AID

For over 50 years, those of modest means who could demonstrate that their case had merit were entitled to have their legal fees paid through the legal aid scheme. This is no longer the case. Following the implementation of the Legal Aid, Sentencing and Punishment of Offenders Act 2012 (LASPO 2012), since April 2013 legal aid has not been available for most family cases. This was a fundamental shift in the provision of legal services, which has had a profound effect on the work of all family solicitors.

The changes implemented by LASPO 2012 were highly controversial at the time. The controversy has never abated and there have been a number of 'reviews' in the intervening years. Most recently, in July 2021, the House of Commons Justice Committee completed its report on the legal aid scheme. The Committee said that 'there is a strong case for fundamental changes to the civil legal aid scheme'. The Committee called for urgent reform both to protect the fairness of the justice system and to ensure that the most vulnerable in society continued to have access to justice. It is yet to be seen whether any such reforms will be forthcoming.

In the limited circumstances where legal aid is available, in essence the scheme enables a client to obtain free or low-cost legal services, usually subject to meeting a means and a merits test. Eligibility and procedures are governed mainly by the Civil Legal Aid (Merits Criteria) Regulations 2013 (SI 2013/104) and the Civil Legal Aid (Procedures) Regulations 2012 (SI 2012/3098).

The scheme is administered by the Legal Aid Agency, an executive agency of the Ministry of Justice. Solicitors (as well as law centres and some charities) conduct legal aid work under a contract with the Legal Aid Agency. To obtain a contract, a firm must meet various quality assurance requirements. Usually, the contract enables the provider to deliver legal services face to face.

2.2.1 The scope of legal aid

The basic position is that legal aid is not available for family cases unless the case is of a type specified under LASPO 2012 as being within the scope of the legal aid scheme.

Some types of family case are within the scope of the scheme, namely:

(a)   public law children proceedings (see **Chapter 14**);

(b)   cases involving the obtaining of protective injunctions, eg non-molestation orders, occupation orders, forced marriage protection orders (see **Chapter 15**);

(c)   cases where a child under 18 is an applicant, respondent, or joined as a party to the proceedings (legal aid is available to the child);

(d)   cases involving securing an order to prevent the unlawful removal of a child from the UK, or to secure the return of a child unlawfully removed from or within the UK (see **13.9**).

Other family cases (eg private children cases, financial applications and divorce) are outside the scope of the scheme *unless* the client can demonstrate that she has been a victim of or is at risk of domestic violence, or, in children cases, that the case is for the purpose of protecting a child who would otherwise be at risk of abuse.

The term 'domestic violence' is defined in the Legal Aid, Sentencing and Punishment of Offenders Act 2012 (Amendment of Schedule 1) Order 2013 (SI 2013/748) as 'any incident, or pattern of incidents, of controlling, coercive or threatening behaviour, violence or abuse (whether psychological, physical, sexual, financial or emotional) between individuals who are associated with each other'. This is a wide definition. However, in order to bring the case within the scope of the scheme, the client must be able to provide evidence of the violence. Only certain forms of evidence are acceptable for this purpose. They are listed in Sch 1 to the Civil Legal Aid (Procedure) Regulations 2012 and include evidence of an arrest for a domestic violence offence, a protective injunction having been made in the past, or a report from a health professional that an examination showed injuries/condition consistent with those of a victim of domestic violence. (Similar prescribed evidence is required to demonstrate that a child is at risk of abuse.)

It can be seen that the scope of legal aid is now severely restricted. Even where a case falls within the scope of the scheme, clients must still go on to establish their entitlement to legal aid based on the merits of their individual case and their financial means.

Where a solicitor is instructed by a client and takes the view that the client may be eligible for legal aid, she must advise the client accordingly, even though the solicitor or her firm do not themselves undertake legal aid work. This advice must be given promptly, before the client incurs significant costs on a privately paying basis. In the case of *Truex v Kitchin* [2007] 2 FLR 1203, a solicitor who did not give this advice was required to repay virtually the whole of the amount which the client had already paid towards the solicitor's fees.

2.2.2 Types of funding

For those cases within the scope of legal aid, the Civil Legal Aid (Procedure) Regulations 2012 set down various types of funding, based broadly on how litigious the case becomes. The types of funding that are most relevant to the family practitioner are Legal Help, Family Help (Lower), Family Help (Higher) and Legal Representation. Not all types of funding will be relevant in every case. The types of funding operate slightly differently in public law cases such as care proceedings (see **14.11.4**).

For most family cases, the type of funding corresponds with a level of standard fixed fee which the solicitor will receive for the work undertaken on the client's behalf. The amount of the fixed fee depends on the type of case (financial cases receiving a higher fee than children cases, for example) and the geographical location of the firm (higher fees being paid in London). If appropriate, the solicitor can claim one fixed fee for, say, the children case and a second fee for the financial case. Similarly, if the case progresses through all four types of funding then four separate fixed fees may be claimed.

2.2.2.1 Legal Help

This enables people who are eligibile financially and on merit to obtain initial advice from a solicitor on any question of English law or procedure, for example in relation to domestic abuse. It will usually extend to only very limited steps following on from that advice, such as writing a letter. However, when advising a petitioner in a divorce, Legal Help covers all the steps taken by the solicitor throughout the divorce process itself.

To be financially eligible a client must come within the financial limits for both capital and income. If the client is in receipt of certain welfare benefits, he will automatically qualify on income grounds. The capital limit is presently £8,000. If the client is eligible, he will not have to pay a contribution, although the statutory charge (see **2.2.4**) may be relevant.

The case itself must also merit Legal Help. Legal Help will be provided only where there is sufficient benefit to the client, having regard to the circumstances of the case, including the personal circumstances of the client, to justify work being carried out. Legal Help will not be provided, therefore, if the claim is clearly hopeless, vexatious or would be an abuse of the process, or if the client is seeking advice on non-legal matters.

It is for the solicitor to ensure both that the client is financially eligible and that Legal Help is justified on merit.

2.2.2.2 Family Help (Lower)

This covers work done by the solicitor up to, but not including, the issue of proceedings (except proceedings to obtain a consent order in financial proceedings). The solicitor will be able to advise the client, draft documentation, write correspondence, negotiate and/or support the client through mediation. However, Family Help (Lower) is available only where the help required is more than simply taking instructions and providing follow-up written/ telephone advice, the solicitor is involved in substantive negotiations with a third party and the case is a significant family dispute (ie the case must be one which, if unresolved, would result in family proceedings). Family Help (Lower) is not available for divorce, or those cases where the issues relate to child maintenance and the Child Maintenance Service has jurisdiction, or where the client requires only general advice about the dispute and method of dispute resolution, such as mediation.

Family Help (Lower) may be provided only where the client comes within the capital and income limits and where the benefits to be gained from the help justify the likely costs, such that a reasonable private paying client would be prepared to proceed having regard to the chances of success and all the circumstances of the case, and the provision of Family Help (Lower) would help to avoid contested proceedings.

2.2.2.3   Family Help (Higher)

In essence, Family Help (Higher) will be justified only where it is necessary to litigate or proceedings are already underway and all reasonable alternatives to litigation have been exhausted. Family Help (Higher) is available for financial and children cases, but not for domestic abuse cases. In financial cases, Family Help (Higher) covers all work from the issue of proceedings up to and including the Financial Dispute Resolution hearing. In children cases, all work undertaken from the issue of proceedings is covered save in relation to or at the final hearing.

The client's capital and income must come within the current financial limits. A contribution may be payable from capital or income depending on resources. It is essential that the solicitor explains to the client the effect of the statutory charge (see **2.2.4**).

Family Help (Higher) may be provided only where the benefits to be gained for the client justify the likely cost, such that a reasonable private paying client would be prepared to proceed in all the circumstances.

Family Help (Higher) may be refused if alternative funding is available to the client. This might occur where the client could raise the money to pay his legal fees by selling assets or taking out a loan.

2.2.2.4   Legal Representation

This covers preparation for and representation at the final hearing.

Eligibility for Legal Representation, the application process and the criteria by which it is granted are the same as for Family Help (Higher) (see **2.2.2.3**), and additionally there must be a demonstrable need for Legal Representation in view of the circumstances of the case.

2.2.2.5   Help with family mediation

This type of funding was introduced by LASPO 2012. It covers legal advice given to support a client participating in family mediation.

2.2.3   Effect of legal aid

2.2.3.1   Duty to notify the court and other parties

Immediately upon receipt of the certificate or, if proceedings have not yet commenced, when they do, the solicitor must file the original legal aid certificate at court and must inform all other parties of the fact that the client is publicly funded by serving upon them a notice of issue of certificate.

2.2.3.2   Relationship between solicitor and client

The solicitor will continue to owe the normal solicitor–client duties to a client in receipt of legal aid. In addition, the solicitor will owe duties to the Legal Aid Agency. If the client acts unreasonably (eg refuses a reasonable offer of settlement) or has given inaccurate, misleading or incomplete information, the solicitor must report this to the Legal Aid Agency. This duty to the Agency overrides the solicitor's usual duty of confidentiality to their client.

2.2.4   The statutory charge

Legal aid does not necessarily amount to free legal representation for the client. In broad terms, if the client benefits financially from the case, any property that he receives can be taken by the Legal Aid Agency and applied in payment of his solicitor's fees. This is the so-called statutory charge. The underlying principle is to put the funded client as far as possible in the same position as the privately paying client.

The statutory charge is potentially relevant to all types of public funding, and consequently the solicitor is obliged to explain the effect of the statutory charge to the client. Given its obvious financial implications, it is vital that client fully understands the charge, and he should be reminded of it throughout the proceedings. The client should also be advised periodically as to the approximate costs accumulated.

2.2.4.1   The operation of the charge

The Legal Aid Agency will be responsible for paying the assisted party's legal fees. The Agency will attempt to recoup these fees where possible. In order to do so, it first claims any money paid pursuant to an order for costs made in favour of the assisted party. Secondly, if a shortfall remains, it will retain any contribution paid by the assisted party under the terms of the offer of legal aid. Thirdly, if there is still a deficit, the statutory charge will apply (LASPO 2012, s 25). The effect of this is that any property (including money) 'recovered or preserved in the proceedings' may be applied to make up the shortfall.

It was said in the case of *Hanlon v Law Society* [1980] 2 All ER 199:

> [P]roperty has been recovered or preserved if it has been in issue in the proceedings: recovered by the claimant if it has been the subject of a successful claim, preserved by the respondent if the claim fails ...

So, property is 'recovered' if the funded client successfully obtains that property – ie, he makes a net gain. Property is 'preserved' if the funded client successfully defends a claim – ie, he retains property which he regarded as his own. The Legal Aid Agency will determine from the statements of case, correspondence and order what the issues of the case were.

To facilitate collection of the charge, the assisted party's solicitor is required to pass any money payable to the assisted party under an agreement or court order to the Legal Aid Agency. In addition, the solicitor must notify the Legal Aid Agency of any property recovered or preserved by their client. If a party receives a lump sum well in excess of the anticipated statutory charge, the solicitor may apply to the Legal Aid Agency for authority to release some of the money to the client, provided sufficient sums are retained to cover the firm's costs. In all cases, once the solicitor's costs have been finally determined and the statutory charge has been satisfied, any balance is sent to the assisted party.

The statutory charge may even apply where the ownership of the property has not been in dispute but proceedings were brought to determine what should happen to the property, ie whether it is to be sold, transferred or retained (see *Curling v Law Society* [1985] 1 All ER 705 and, similarly, *Parkes v Legal Aid Board* [1997] 1 FLR 77).

The costs are not limited to property obtained as a result of contested proceedings. Whilst a settlement will reduce the overall costs of the case, the Civil Legal Aid (Statutory Charge) Regulations 2013 (SI 2013/503) ensure that a settlement will not avoid the effect of the statutory charge unless the settlement occurs at an early stage. Where there has been a compromise, the property itself does not need to have been in issue for the statutory charge to apply, provided that it has been recovered or preserved in substitution for property which was in issue. For example, if the parties were arguing over the matrimonial home and a compromise was reached which instead transferred a holiday home (which had not been in issue) from the husband's sole name to the wife, the statutory charge can apply to the holiday home (see *Morgan and Others v Legal Aid Board* [2000] 3 All ER 974).

2.2.4.2 Exemptions

Some cases are not subject to the statutory charge. Those cases which conclude using Legal Help are exempt from the operation of the charge. Those cases which conclude using only Family Help (Lower) are also exempt provided only the standard fixed fee is claimed. Otherwise, the statutory charge applies to all costs, including those incurred under Legal Help and Family Help (Lower), and applies to the costs incurred in all proceedings, meaning the entire cause or matter and not just the financial proceedings.

Some types of property will be exempt from the charge, irrespective of the level of funding that led to their being recovered or preserved. The following are not subject to the statutory charge:

(a)   periodical payments;

(b)   payments on or after the making of an occupation order under Pt IV of the FLA 1996;

(c)   lump sums or property adjustment orders made after divorce in substitution for spousal maintenance under s 31(7A) or (7B) of the Matrimonial Causes Act 1973 (MCA 1973); and

(d)   pension attachments or pension sharing orders (other than lump sum pension attachments) under ss 23, 24 and 24B of the MCA 1973.

2.2.4.3 Postponing the charge

The Lord Chancellor has the power to waive the statutory charge in limited circumstances. More commonly, the Legal Aid Agency will agree to postpone enforcement of the charge where it is charged on either:

(a)   property which is expressly stated (in the order or agreement) to be used as a home by the assisted person or his dependants; or

(b)   a lump sum which is agreed or ordered with the express purpose of it being used to purchase a home (the purchase to be made within one year).

In both cases, before agreeing to postponement, the Legal Aid Agency will need to be satisfied that the property represents adequate security for the charge.

Postponement will not be allowed if, for example, the client could pay the statutory charge immediately by increasing the mortgage on the property. Even where the Legal Aid Agency has initially exercised its discretion to allow the statutory charge to be postponed, that postponement will be kept under review and repayment sought immediately in the event of an improvement in the client's financial circumstances.

The charge will be protected by registration against the title of the property and simple interest will accrue. This may influence a client's decision to pay or postpone the charge. In most cases, the charge and interest will be enforced when the home is sold. However, it is possible for the charge to be transferred to a substitute property, provided, first, that the consent of the Legal Aid Agency is obtained before the charged property is sold and, secondly, that the substitute property represents adequate security.

Where an assisted party recovers both a lump sum and property, the Legal Aid Agency will look to take its charge from the money first, attaching the charge to property only as a last resort.

2.3 HUMAN RIGHTS

The Legal Aid Agency is a public body, and therefore it cannot act in a way that is incompatible with Convention rights under the HRA 1998.

Article 6 of the ECHR provides that 'everyone is entitled to a fair and public hearing within a reasonable time by an independent and impartial tribunal established by law'. Article 6 thus focuses on effective access to the courts. In *Airey v Ireland* (1979) 2 EHRR 305, a wife wanted to bring proceedings for judicial separation. She could not afford legal representation and her application was complex but she was refused public funding. The European Court of Human Rights held that Article 6 might sometimes compel the State to provide legal assistance if such assistance was indispensable for effective access to court. The Court said that complexity of procedure, complicated points of law, the need to call expert witnesses or the emotional involvement of the parties might all result in a requirement that legal assistance be provided. In *Airey*, for access to be effective, the wife required legal representation which, in her case, meant granting legal aid.

Subsequently, the European Commission on Human Rights has attempted to confine the application of the *Airey* principles. It recognised that, due to limited resources, States might legitimately restrict the grant of public funding, provided the decision whether or not to grant such funding was not taken arbitrarily. However, under HRA 1998, the Legal Aid Agency may potentially be liable to challenge if it fails to grant public funding in circumstances that result in a litigant being unable to have effective access to the court.

Partially in an attempt to avoid any possible challenge under the HRA 1998, a blanket exception to the general non-availability of legal aid in family cases was created under s 10 of LASPO 2012. Legal aid therefore remains available in those exceptional cases where without legal aid there would be a breach, or risk of a breach, of the applicant's human rights (exceptional case funding). To qualify, the case must be outside the ordinary scope of legal aid; exceptional case funding is not available where the case is within the ordinary scope, but legal aid had been denied because the applicant does not satisfy the means or merits tests. At the time LASPO 2012 was passing through Parliament, it was envisaged that s 10 would operate as a safety net, ensuring that legal aid would continue to be available when required in the interests of justice and that a significant number of cases would qualify as 'exceptional'. However, despite the softening of the initial guidance issued by the Lord Chancellor on the operation of s 10, the number of successful applications in family cases remains low. The treatment of s 10 applications remains controversial – see, for example, the attempt at judicial review, albeit ultimately unsuccessful, in *Director of Legal Aid Casework v IS* [2016] EWCA Civ 464.

2.4 OTHER METHODS OF FUNDING

Traditionally, a family client, unless he qualified for legal aid, simply paid his solicitor privately on the basis of an hourly charging rate. This remains an option and will continue to apply to those clients who have sufficient means. Whilst it might be said that legal fees are a matter between the solicitor and their client, the level of fees in family cases has attracted some judicial criticism. For example, in *J v J* [2014] EWHC 3654 (Fam), Mostyn J made a number of caustic remarks about the costs incurred in the case (which equated to a third of the total family assets) and called for the introduction of compulsory fixed fees in family cases, or for the court to be able to put a cap on costs at the outset of the case.

The curtailing of legal aid means that it has become increasingly common for the family solicitor to encounter clients who are not eligible for assistance and yet who do not have sufficient resources to pay fees on a privately paying basis. A solicitor cannot enter a conditional fee agreement with a client in relation to family proceedings. In appropriate cases there are other possible ways in which this problem can be resolved.

In discussing funding options with the client, the solicitor must not stray into engaging in a regulated activity under the Financial Services and Markets Act 2000 (see **Legal Foundations**). There is something of a fine line between providing 'financial information' and giving 'financial advice', and the family solicitor must take care not to step over it.

2.4.1   Deferred payment of legal fees

A firm may be prepared to carry out work but defer payment of its fees until the end of the case. Given the uncertainty of litigation, this is a risky option for the firm, and consequently the circumstances in which a solicitor will be prepared to act on this basis will be rare. However, it may be appropriate, for example, in a case where there is substantial capital but little or no income and/or liquid assets.

Where a firm does defer payment, it will almost certainly wish to take steps to ensure that it will in fact be paid at the end of the case. This could take the form of an authority from the client that the eventual lump sum or proceeds of sale are paid direct to the firm for the purpose of deducting fees before passing on the balance to the client. A more formal arrangement would be a so-called *Sears Tooth* agreement from the case of *Sears Tooth (A Firm) v Payne Hicks Beach (A Firm) and Others* [1997] 2 FLR 116, where its validity was discussed. In this case, Sears Tooth acted for a wife in financial proceedings. She agreed to assign any award for financial relief (other than for maintenance) or costs to them as far as was necessary to pay their fees. The court stated that this device was a valid contract to assign a future chose in action and was not contrary to public policy.

2.4.2   Court orders

In some circumstances, the court can order one party to contribute towards the other party's ongoing legal fees. These orders must be distinguished from the costs orders that the court can be invited to make at the end of the case (see **Chapter 10**).

The statutory provision that is likely to be invoked most frequently is s 22ZA of the MCA 1973, which enables the court to make a legal services order requiring one party to pay an amount for the purposes of enabling the other party to obtain legal services (an order for payment in respect of legal services). Section 22ZA was introduced by LASPO 2012 in part in order to 'compensate' for the restrictions on the availability of legal aid which the same statute imposed. Section 22ZA only applies to divorce/civil partnership and financial applications connected with divorce/civil partnership. Whilst the most obvious use of such orders is the funding of ongoing litigation, s 22ZA(10) makes it clear that 'legal services' in this context includes all types of dispute resolution (see **2.5**).

The court will only make an order if satisfied that the recipient would not reasonably be able to obtain legal services without the order. In particular, the court must be satisfied that it would not be reasonable for the applicant to obtain a loan or enter into a *Sears Tooth* agreement. Section 22ZB sets out the matters that the court should take into account in deciding whether to make an order; these include whether the other party is legally represented, and the steps taken by the applicant to avoid litigation (eg proposing mediation).

In *Rubin v Rubin* [2014] EWHC 611 (Fam), Mostyn J refused to make an order under s 22ZA, but he did provide some helpful guidance. He made it clear that the purpose of an order under s 22ZA was to enable the applicant to obtain legal services in respect of ongoing and future proceedings. Orders cannot therefore be made in respect of historic legal costs, unless it can be shown that the effect of non-payment of those costs would be to prevent the applicant from obtaining legal services in the future. Mostyn J indicated that in determining whether the applicant could obtain other funding, the court would not normally consider it reasonable to expect the applicant to sell or charge his home or to deplete modest savings, or to take on a loan with a very high rate of interest. That approach was followed in *FRB v DCA (No 3)* [2020] EWHC 3696 (Fam) where the judge took the view that it would not be appropriate to expect the wife to charge what little capital she had, when the husband was very wealthy and had been found by the judge to have been deceitful.

In private children cases, similar provision for a contribution towards costs (a 'legal costs funding order') can be made, albeit via the more circuitous route of an order under Sch 1 to the Children Act 1989. The guidance provided in *Rubin v Rubin* is equally applicable to such orders. In *Re Z (Schedule 1: Legal costs funding order; Interim financial provision)* [2020] EWFC 80, the judge refused the mother's application in respect of the unpaid costs of her previous solicitors on the basis that those costs remaining outstanding would have no impact on her ability to obtain legal services to continue with the case. In contrast, the court was prepared to make a legal costs funding order to cover a proportion of the historic (and future) costs incurred by her current solicitors as it was not fair or reasonable to expect the firm to act without payment. In an interesting development, when the case later came back before the same judge as *X v Y* [2021] EWFC 72, Cobb J, whilst affirming his earlier comments about solicitors not being expected to work without payment, said that he was '... dismayed to discover that the solicitors in this case have billed the mother sums significantly in excess of the amount which I awarded to cover the costs'. The judge declined to make an order to cover the funding of the 'excess' costs in full, adding, '... I set a budget within which I expected the mother's solicitors to work ... I am not prepared for my legal funding orders, and the rationale which lies behind them, simply to be disregarded.'

In *Q v Q* [2014] EWFC 31, the President of the Family Division raised the intriguing prospect of costs in some family cases being borne by the Lord Chancellor via Her Majesty's Courts and Tribunal Service. However, this ingenuity was thwarted in *Re K and H (Children)* [2015] EWCA Civ 543, where the Court of Appeal held that the court does not have the power to order the Lord Chancellor to provide funding for legal representation. However, the Court of Appeal did go on to suggest that the Ministry of Justice should consider introducing such a power (as exists in criminal cases).

2.4.2.1 Loans

In some instances the only practical solution may be for the client to borrow money in order to pay his legal fees. This could involve the client taking out an ordinary loan with a mainstream bank or borrowing money from a friend or on a credit card. However, it is now more common for clients to borrow from a specialist family litigation funding provider.

Family litigation funding is a burgeoning market with various providers offering a range of products and services. The basis on which loans are given will vary in terms of interest rate, how interest is calculated, how repayment is made, whether security is required and so on. Whilst the true cost of such loans must be understood and factored into the litigation, they will be appropriate for some clients.

2.4.3 Litigation insurance

Whilst litigation insurance has been available in many areas of law for some considerable time, this has not been the case in family law. Historically, insurers have been unwilling to provide cover for legal fees in family cases, which are so multi-faceted, emotional and potentially very expensive. However, recently, litigation insurance has been making some inroads into family cases.

2.4.4 Creative funding options

The changing face of family law means that solicitors have to be more creative in the way in which they approach costs. Fixed fees, which in the past were often reserved for the initial client interview, are now being increasingly offered for the entire case or for conducting certain stages of the case. The curtailing of legal aid means that many more people are having to primarily conduct their own cases, instructing solicitors only to deal with certain elements of the case (known as 'unbundling'). As a result, most solicitors offer a menu of fees for different aspects of a case. Some firms are prepared to act on a 'pay as you go' basis whereby a litigant in person will pay for face-to-face time with a solicitor as and when they need it to help them to progress the case. It is clear that solicitors must be ready to adapt and respond to the client's needs.

2.5 DISPUTE RESOLUTION

Dispute resolution exists across a range of legal disciplines. It is the generic term used to describe any process aimed at resolving disputes without going to court. Even in the context of family law, dispute resolution is nothing new. For years, responsible family solicitors have recognised that litigation is not the best way to resolve family disputes and have sought more constructive and consensual methods of dealing with cases. However, recent years have seen a significant increase in dispute resolution, both in terms of the number of family cases being resolved through its use and the range of processes available. The demand for dispute resolution has received an additional boost due to the difficulty in accessing the courts during the pandemic.

The importance of resolving family cases other than through the courts was emphasised rather forcefully by HHJ Wildblood QC in *Re B (A child) (Unnecessary private law applications)* [2020] 9 WLUK 317:

> ... the message in this judgment to parties and lawyers is this, as far as I'm concerned. Do not bring your private law litigation to the Family Court here unless it is genuinely necessary for you to do so. You should settle your differences (and those of your clients) away from court, except where that is not possible. If you do bring unnecessary cases to this court, you will be criticised, and sanctions may be imposed upon you. There are other ways to settle disagreements ...

The Family Procedure Rules (FPR) 2010 (SI 2010/2955) place emphasis on dispute resolution in family cases. Part 3 of the FPR 2010 focuses on the courts' powers to encourage and facilitate the use of dispute resolution. The court is obliged to consider at every stage of family proceedings whether dispute resolution is appropriate, and it may adjourn the case for the purpose of obtaining information about dispute resolution and, with agreement, for it to take place. Judges are becoming increasingly prepared to use their powers under Part 3. In *WL v HL* [2021] 2 FCR 394 the judge was concerned that the costs already incurred were disproportionate to the issues involved and so adjourned the case three times to enable the parties to explore resolving the matter out of court, adding directions requiring the parties to keep him informed of the attempts made to settle the progress made.

In some cases, it may be that an unreasonable refusal to engage in negotiations has costs implications. In *LM v DM (Costs Ruling)* [2021] EWFC 28, the judge reduced the costs order that he would have made in the applicant's favour by half because she had been '... determined to fight the application come what may'. In relation to making costs orders in financial remedy proceedings, para 4.4 of PD 28A of the FPR 2010 says that a refusal to negotiate will usually result in the court considering an order for costs (see also **4.5.1.8** and **10.11.2**). Such orders are becoming increasingly common.

A variety of process options fall within the term dispute resolution. In family law, the best known are mediation and, perhaps, collaborative law (see further below), but the number of options continues to grow. Although each option is a distinct process, it would be wrong to view them in isolation. It may be that each element of the client's case is best resolved using a different process or that the case moves naturally from one process to another. It is also important that the family solicitor considers the viability of each of these options at the beginning and throughout the case.

Many family law solicitors are trained in one or more dispute resolution processes. Therefore, for example, the work of an individual solicitor may, with appropriate training, include conducting mainstream litigation for some clients, negotiating settlements for others, practising collaborative law and acting as a mediator. However, every solicitor must be aware of the various dispute resolution processes available and be able to inform their clients about them even though the solicitor does not offer a particular process as part of their own practice.

2.5.1   Solicitor negotiations

Historically, negotiation through solicitors has not been viewed as a dispute resolution process as such. However, negotiation is an essential part of the role of a family solicitor and a common means of achieving a consensual resolution of family cases.

Negotiation can take place through correspondence, with, say, a series of offers and counter-offers being put forward with the aim of ultimately reaching a settlement. Negotiation can also take the form of a 'round table meeting'. Despite the name, the parties are not necessarily gathered together around the same table. More commonly, the parties are gathered in the same building, with the solicitors negotiating face to face and taking time out to take instructions from their client as the negotiations progress.

2.5.2   Mediation

In family mediation, a couple (or family members) engage the assistance of a mediator (or sometimes two co-mediators), who has no authority to make any decisions for them but who uses certain skills to help them to resolve their issues by negotiated agreement without adjudication. Mediation does not aim to save the relationship but to help parties deal, by agreement, with the consequences of its breakdown.

The mediator will usually meet the parties together and will try to help them to clarify and resolve their issues on a basis which they find mutually acceptable. Depending on the issues, this may involve obtaining all relevant facts, including, where appropriate, financial data, exploring alternative settlement options and their acceptability and viability, and generally helping the couple to communicate and make decisions. The mediator may give information but will not advise the couple what terms they should agree, this being a matter for them. The mediator may help the couple to examine different solutions but will not try to press the one which the mediator may prefer.

Typically, the mediator will meet with the parties together in the same room in a series of 90-minute mediation sessions over a period of weeks or months. The process is characterised by openness and transparency between the parties and the mediator. The 'gaps' in between the sessions allow the parties to reflect and, if necessary, consult their solicitor. However, mediation is a flexible process. For example, the couple may be 'in separate spaces' with the mediator 'shuffling' in between, or the mediation conducted online; and there has been a recent increase in 'child-inclusive mediation' (where a specially trained mediator speaks with the children involved in the case) which enables the children to have a voice in the process. The mediator can, with the parties' consent, invite solicitors or other professionals (such as financial advisers) to attend mediation sessions. This flexibility makes mediation suitable for resolving a huge variety of family issues.

There are various facilitation, communication and management skills which mediators should have, and which generally necessitate special training. Family mediators are regulated by five organisations, all of which are members of the Family Mediation Council. Mediators work to a Code of Conduct which regulates the ethical and practical approach which they adopt. Many solicitors have undergone training to become accredited mediators. Family mediators are also drawn from other ranks, including social workers, probation officers, children and family reporters, psychotherapists, counsellors and mental health professionals.

A solicitor cannot act as a mediator for their own client and would need to refer to an outside organisation or individual mediator. The solicitor should take the earliest opportunity to assess the suitability of mediation as a means of attempting to resolve the client's case. If relevant, information should be given to the client about the availability of mediation and the nature of the process.

Under s 10 of the Children and Families Act 2014, anyone wishing to start court proceedings in most types of family cases (not including the divorce itself) must first attend a Mediation

Information and Assessment Meeting (see **10.4.1**). The purpose of the meeting is for a mediator to provide information about the process of mediation and to assess whether the particular case is a suitable one in which to attempt mediation. There is no compulsion to proceed with mediation following the meeting.

In a bid to encourage the use of mediation to resolve cases during the pandemic, in March 2021 the government launched the mediation voucher scheme. The voucher entitled the recipient to a contribution of £500 towards the costs of mediation in cases concerning children. The vouchers were originally limited in number, and although that number was increased in August 2021, it is uncertain whether the scheme will be continued.

2.5.3 Hybrid mediation

Hybrid mediation is so called because it combines elements of conventional family mediation (see **2.5.2**) and elements of the mediation model used in civil/commercial cases. In conventional family mediation, the solicitor effectively refers the client on to the mediator and then steps into the background (although the solicitor retains an ongoing advisory role). However, in hybrid mediation, the solicitor retains a much more active role in the process.

The aim of hybrid mediation is to enable the parties to reach an agreement. The mediator is 'in charge' of the process and their role is to facilitate negotiations. The mediator will discuss and agree the terms of reference and conduct of the mediation with the parties' solicitors in advance of the actual meetings. The process is flexible. The parties may have joint or separate meetings with the mediator with or without their solicitor present. The mediation may take place over the course of a single day, or the meetings may be spread over several days. Unlike conventional mediation, the mediator is able to have separate private discussions with each party.

The role of the solicitor in hybrid mediation is essentially to support and advise the client. If an agreement is reached, the solicitors may also draft the terms of the agreement.

2.5.4 Collaborative law

Collaborative law is based on a model of dispute resolution used in Canada and has been used in England and Wales for some 20 years. Family solicitors who employ this method of dispute resolution are trained as collaborative lawyers. The process operates as a series of meetings aimed at enabling the parties to resolve the issues resulting from the breakdown of a relationship. The process requires the parties and their solicitors to sign up to a participation agreement promising to try to reach an amicable consensus on all issues without recourse to court proceedings. If it transpires that a settlement cannot be reached, then usually the parties cannot continue to instruct their collaborative lawyers and must instruct other solicitors to represent them in subsequent court proceedings. Therefore, both the parties and their solicitors have an interest in making the process work.

Collaborative law views the breakdown of a relationship in the round and enables the parties to explore the issues and find solutions outside the constraints of court proceedings. Mainstream legal issues, such as the financial consequences of the ending of the relationship, are explored and, if possible, agreed upon. But collaborative law also recognises that the concerns which a client has when a relationship ends may not be of a 'legal' nature, and yet those concerns must be addressed if the parties are to be able to make sensible decisions about the future. Collaborative law also allows these issues to be looked at through the involvement of other collaborative professionals, such as family consultants and financial planners, as necessary.

There is some anecdotal evidence to suggest that the take-up of collaborative law has declined. Nevertheless, it remains a viable method of dispute resolution advocated by a significant number of family solicitors.

2.5.5 Early neutral evaluation

Early neutral evaluation is a relatively recent development. However, it is becoming increasingly common in both children cases and in financial cases. It can be used to resolve a particular issue or the case as a whole.

In early neutral evaluation, the parties jointly appoint an evaluator (there are barristers, solicitors, retired judges and others who are willing to act as evaluators). The parties, usually through their solicitor/barrister, present their respective positions to the evaluator. The evaluator then gives their opinion on the likely outcome were the case to go to court. The parties can then negotiate in the light of the evaluator's opinion.

The evaluator's opinion is not binding and so the parties are free to accept or reject it as they wish. Even if the case is not settled on the terms of the evaluator's opinion, it may help to narrow the issues between the parties.

A form of early neutral evaluation which has gained in popularity recently is private financial dispute resolution, or a private FDR. This is intended to effectively replicate an FDR appointment. An FDR appointment is a court hearing which takes place in the early stages of litigation at which a judge facilitates discussions between the parties with a view to settlement (see **10.8.3**).

2.5.6 Arbitration

In arbitration, the parties agree to put the matter before an independent third party who will consider the dispute and make a decision for them. The family arbitration scheme was launched by the Institute of Family Law Arbitrators (IFLA) in 2012. Initially the scheme covered only financial and property issues, but in 2016 it was extended to cover most types of private children disputes. The scheme operates under Part I of the Arbitration Act 1996 and the IFLA's own Arbitration Rules. The arbitrator's decision is known as an 'award' in financial cases and a 'determination' in children cases.

In agreeing to arbitration, the parties sign up to the rules of the arbitration scheme and agree to be bound by the arbitrator's award/determination. The parties may nominate their own arbitrator or ask the IFLA to choose an arbitrator for them. In the arbitration, the parties will usually be represented by a solicitor or barrister, but, as with court proceedings, they are free to represent themselves.

Arbitration can be used to resolve a case in its entirety, or to decide one discrete issue, for example, where the parties have been able to agree all other points for themselves. Arbitration gives the parties greater control and flexibility; they can, for example, stipulate whether the arbitrator's decision is to be made by way of a 'hearing', over the telephone or based on paperwork alone. The parties have 'access' to the arbitrator who will be able to offer guidance, for example, on the process generally or specific points such as how to instruct an expert. Confidentiality is also assured, which may be very important for certain clients.

The arbitrator's award is binding on the parties in the sense that the scheme envisages that a court order will subsequently be obtained which mirrors the arbitration award. The procedure for doing so is set out in *Arbitration in the Family Court: Practice Guidance*, issued by the President of the Family Division. In the vast majority of cases, the court will simply make the order reflecting the award. However, it is not possible to oust the court's jurisdiction. The court may therefore decline to make the order based on good and substantial grounds, in much the same way as a higher court may overturn the decision of a lower court on appeal. In *Hayley v Hayley* [2020] EWCA Civ 1369, Lady Justice King confirmed the test to be applied: the court will only substitute its own order '... if the judge decides that the arbitrator's award was wrong; not seriously, or obviously wrong, or so wrong that it leaps off the page, but just wrong'. The court also retains the power to interfere with an arbitration award where there has been fraud, mistake or a supervening event (*DB v DLJ (Challenge to Arbitration Award)* [2016] EWHC 324 (Fam)).

Many family solicitors are also qualified arbitrators.

2.5.7 The Certainty Project

Arbitration has increasingly been used in conjunction with mediation, so that the parties agree as much as they can through mediation and then move on to arbitration to determine the outstanding issues. This approach has been given a degree of formality through this recent initiative.

Essentially, this process requires the parties to sign up to arbitration. The arbitrator will immediately give directions on the next steps, such as information to be provided by each party or the instruction of an expert, and then adjourn the arbitration to enable the parties to attend mediation. The parties will then attend a limited number of mediation sessions (usually no more than four). The mediation may be conventional or hybrid. If a complete agreement is reached in mediation then that is the end of the process, save embodying the agreement in a court order where appropriate. If all or some issues remain unresolved at the end of the mediation sessions, they proceed to arbitration, where the arbitrator will make a binding decision as above (**2.5.6**).

SUMMARY

(1)   In limited cases where a client is of modest means, legal aid may be available to enable that client to pay for legal advice and representation.

(2)   There are various types of funding that may need to be provided by the family law solicitor:

    (a)   Legal Help;

    (b)   Family Help (Lower);

    (c)   Family Help (Higher);

    (d)   Legal Representation.

(3)   Legal aid is not 'free' and will need to be repaid from any property 'recovered or preserved' (with some exceptions) – the statutory charge.

(4)   Where legal aid is not available, other methods of paying for legal fees could be considered:

    (a)   deferred payment of legal fees;

    (b)   court orders;

    (c)   loans;

    (d)   litigation insurance.

(5)   There is a range of process options available for resolving family law disputes, including:

    (a)   negotiation;

    (b)   mediation;

    (c)   hybrid mediation;

    (d)   collaborative law.

    (e)   early neutral evaluation;

    (f)   arbitration;

    (g)   the Certainty Project;

CHAPTER 3

Divorce Law and Procedure

3.1	Introduction	25
3.2	One-year rule	26
3.3	Jurisdiction of the English courts to hear suits for divorce	26
3.4	The ground for divorce	29
3.5	Children	36
3.6	Nullity	36
3.7	Judicial separation	37
3.8	Presumption of death and dissolution of marriage	38
3.9	Divorce procedure	38
3.10	Defended divorces	46
3.11	Costs	47
3.12	The Divorce, Dissolution and Separation Act 2020	47
Summary and checklist		49

LEARNING OUTCOMES

After reading this chapter you will be able to:

- identify those situations in which the court has jurisdiction to deal with divorce cases
- apply the ground and facts for obtaining a divorce to a given set of facts
- outline the procedure for obtaining a divorce.

3.1 INTRODUCTION

3.1.1 Terminology

The language used in the FPR 2010 was intended to modernise legal terminology in family cases. However, funding issues with the court computer system meant that, initially, this modernisation could not be carried through to court documentation. The result is that there are inconsistencies between the Rules and the documentation. This chapter will in the main retain traditional terminology of 'petition' and 'petitioner', not least because this remains consistent with the current underlying legislation (although see **3.12** for future changes).

3.1.2 General

According to the Office for National Statistics, some 107,000 opposite sex couples divorced in England and Wales in 2019. By comparison, relatively few proceedings for judicial separation and nullity are brought. This chapter therefore deals in detail with the law relating to divorce, and contains an outline of the law relating to judicial separation and nullity. Although the terms 'husband' and 'wife' will be used for ease of reference, since the implementation of the Marriage (Same Sex Couples) Act 2013, with very limited exceptions, the same procedures are, with very limited exceptions, available to same sex married couples under the MCA 1973. There were 822 same sex divorces in 2019.

The same procedures are also available to civil partners under the Civil Partnership Act 2004 (CPA 2004), although termed 'dissolution', 'separation' and 'nullity'. Although initially restricted to same sex couples, the Civil Partnerships, Marriages and Deaths (Registration etc) Act 2019 extended civil partnerships to opposite sex couples.

The chapter also deals with the procedure for divorce. Since less than 1% of all divorces are defended, only the undefended procedure is dealt with in detail. A checklist summarising the undefended divorce procedure is given at **3.12.2**.

The content of this chapter is current at the time of writing. However, the Divorce, Dissolution and Separation Act 2020 is set to come into force on 6 April 2022. The Act will effect fundamental changes to divorce law, and procedures will be altered as a consequence (see **3.1.2**).

3.1.3 Human rights

Article 12 of the ECHR gives 'men and women of marriageable age the right to marry and found a family according to the national laws governing the exercise of that right'. Marriage is the only relationship that is given special treatment under the Convention. The protections of Article 12 are limited to unions between members of the opposite sex and Article 12 has no application to same sex relationships.

By way of contrast, there is no similar right to divorce, whether this is to re-marry or for any other reason (*Johnston v Ireland* (1987) 9 EHRR 203).

3.2 ONE-YEAR RULE

A petition for divorce cannot be presented to the court before the end of a period of one year from the date of the marriage (MCA 1973, s 3). The reason for this restriction is to discourage over-hasty decisions to end such short marriages.

The rule cannot be waived in any circumstances. However, provided that grounds for divorce can be satisfied, a petition may be presented after one year based on matters that occurred during this time; for example, the respondent's adultery or other behaviour during the first year of marriage can form the basis of a petition as soon as the year has expired. A solicitor should also bear in mind the alternative solutions that exist to protect a client with matrimonial problems, even during the first year. A decree of nullity or judicial separation is not affected by the one-year rule (see **3.6** and **3.7**). Maintenance can be applied for under either s 27 of the MCA 1973 or s 2 of the Domestic Proceedings and Magistrates' Courts Act 1978 (DPMCA 1978). A spouse could be protected from violence by using Pt IV of the FLA 1996 (see **Chapter 15**).

3.3 JURISDICTION OF THE ENGLISH COURTS TO HEAR SUITS FOR DIVORCE

3.3.1 General

The English courts do not have the right to deal with a person's matrimonial affairs merely because that person is a British citizen or is present in this country. Following the UK's departure from the European Union, jurisdiction is now determined solely by domestic legislation. The position is governed by s 5 of the Domicile and Matrimonial Proceedings Act 1973 (as amended by the Jurisdiction and Judgments (Family) (Amendments etc) (EU Exit) Regulations 2019 (SI 2019/5190)). The English courts have jurisdiction to hear a divorce suit only where:

(a) both parties are habitually resident in England and Wales; or

(b) both parties were last habitually resident in England and Wales, and one of them still resides there; or

(c) the respondent is habitually resident in England and Wales; or

(d) the petitioner is habitually resident in England and Wales and has resided there for at least a year immediately before the application was made; or

(e)   the petitioner is domiciled and habitually resident in England and Wales and has resided there for at least six months immediately before the application was made; or

(f)   both parties are domiciled in England and Wales; or

(g)   either of the parties is domiciled in England and Wales.

The same jurisdictional bases for hearing a same sex divorce appear in the Marriage (Same Sex Couples) (Jurisdiction and Recognition of Judgments) Regulations 2014 (SI 2014/543) and for a civil partnership dissolution in the Civil Partnership (Jurisdiction and Recognition of Judgments) Regulations 2005 (SI 2005/3334). Rather strangely, both Regulations appear to make the sole domicile basis ((g) above) dependent on none of the other bases in (a) to (f) being applicable (as was the case for all divorces/dissolutions pre-Brexit); however, this may simply be a legislative oversight. The Regulations make an additional provision that the courts of England and Wales will also have jurisdiction if the courts of no other country have jurisdiction under the Regulations, and either one party is domiciled in England and Wales or the marriage/civil partnership took place in England and Wales and it would be in the interests of justice for the court to assume jurisdiction. This is aimed at the possibility of a couple moving to a country where the legal system does not recognise their marriage/civil partnership and consequently does not provide any means for them to end the relationship. In that scenario, rather than leaving the couple without a remedy, the courts of England and Wales can step in and assume jurisdiction.

The various bases of jurisdiction are not ranked in any order of precedence. More than one basis may apply on the individual facts of the case, but only one needs to be satisfied. In practice the easiest approach is for the family solicitor to work down the list and to rely upon the first basis that is applicable to the client's case.

> **EXAMPLE**
>
> Sophie, who is French, marries Tim, who is English. The couple make their married home in England for 10 years. The marriage breaks down and Sophie returns home to France; Tim remains in England. Six months later Tim decides to seek a divorce through the English courts. On the facts, Tim has been habitually resident and domiciled in England throughout. Sophie has been habitually resident and in England during the marriage, but she is now both habitually resident and domiciled in France. The English courts have jurisdiction to deal with Tim's divorce on the basis of (b), (d), (e) or (g) above. Tim needs to satisfy only one basis, and in practice the simplest approach is rely on the first, ie (b).

3.3.2   Habitual residence

Habitual residence is a term which can be found in a variety of statutory provisions, and its meaning differs according to the context in which it is used. The essence of habitual residence lies in establishing the 'centre of interests' of a person's life. This is a question of fact to be decided in the individual circumstances of each case. To establish a person's place of habitual residence therefore requires a careful consideration of the facts of the case. In *Z v Z (Divorce: Jurisdiction)* [2010] 1 FLR 694 Ryder J offered some guidance and said:

> A centre of interests may be established quickly or slowly, depending on the circumstances. Habitual residence in one country may not be lost despite a lengthy period in another ... There is no requirement that the centre of interests has to be permanent; it need only be habitual. But it must have a stable character.

3.3.3   Domicile

Domicile is a more universal concept. However, no simple definition of 'domicile' is possible and, if issues arise in this respect, reference should be made to textbooks on private international law.

Broadly, a person is said to be domiciled in a territory having a single legal system if he has his permanent home there. Everyone has a domicile and can only have one operative domicile at any one time. However, a person's domicile may alter as his circumstances change throughout his life. A person may acquire, and lose, any of three types of domicile. Each is described in outline below.

3.3.3.1 Domicile of origin

A person acquires domicile of origin at birth. In the case of a child whose parents are married, it is the father's domicile. In the case of a child whose parents are not married, it is the mother's domicile. It is therefore irrelevant where the child was born.

A domicile of origin is never lost, and even though it may not be operative for any period during which the person acquires a domicile of choice, it will revive if the domicile of choice is lost until another domicile of choice is acquired.

EXAMPLE

Maria's domicile of origin is Italy. She marries an Englishman, Nigel, and moves to London, intending that England will be her permanent home. Maria acquires a domicile of choice of England. The marriage breaks down and Maria permanently leaves England to take up temporary residence in Paris whilst she contemplates her future. Maria has lost her English domicile of choice. Her Italian domicile of origin is therefore revived until such time as she acquires a new domicile of choice.

3.3.3.2 Domicile of choice

Every person aged 16 or over may acquire a domicile of choice. This requires, first, residence in a country other than the domicile of origin and, secondly, an intention to remain there permanently or indefinitely. This intention may be shown by becoming a citizen of that country, by the purchase of a home or by the length of time spent in that country. No single factor will be decisive.

3.3.3.3 Domicile of dependence

A child can acquire an independent domicile only at 16 years of age, or on marriage under that age. If he is under 16 years old and unmarried, his domicile will follow his father's domicile if his parents are married, or his mother's if his parents are not married. If married parents separate, the child will acquire the domicile of the parent with whom he lives.

EXAMPLE

Assume that Maria and Nigel, in the example at **3.3.3.1**, had a daughter, Olivia, who lives with Maria after the marriage breaks down. At birth Olivia acquired her domicile of dependence from Nigel, ie England. After the separation, Olivia's domicile follows that of her mother as a domicile of dependence. Olivia therefore has an Italian domicile of dependence.

3.3.4 Choice of forum

In many cases, it will be clear that the divorce will take place in England and Wales. In other cases, for example where one of the couple has been habitually resident in England for the past year but the other has not, it may be possible to choose whether to start proceedings in England and Wales or elsewhere. Such a choice will be governed by a number of factors, such as convenience and the law of the other jurisdiction(s) involved.

Pre-Brexit, where the other jurisdiction concerned was within the EU (apart from Denmark), the position was clear cut in that the State first seized of the matter had exclusive jurisdiction.

The position post-Brexit is less specific. Now the courts of England and Wales adopt the same approach as previously applied to countries outside the EU, namely that jurisdiction issues are determined by looking at which is the most appropriate court to deal with the divorce, taking account of such matters as convenience and family connections (Domicile and Matrimonial Proceedings Act 1973, Sch 1).

Where choice of forum is an issue, the solicitor must contact a lawyer in the other jurisdiction as soon as possible for advice on the legal position should a divorce be started there. Speed will normally be of the essence, since foreign courts will vary in their approach and it may be that proceedings will continue in the jurisdiction where they were first started, any which commence later in an alternative jurisdiction being stayed.

3.3.5 Recognition of foreign decrees by the English courts

A relevant factor when dealing with foreign marriages is to check that the English courts recognise a foreign decree, for example, of divorce. If the English courts recognise the foreign decree then the parties are free to remarry in England and Wales, and no English divorce is necessary or, indeed, possible. However, in these circumstances, the English courts can make financial orders. If, on the other hand, the foreign decree is not recognised, the parties are still married and they will have to petition for a divorce through the English courts, in which case financial orders can be made in the normal way. The law is set out in the FLA 1986 and reference should be made to this, and to relevant textbooks, should an international aspect arise.

3.4 THE GROUND FOR DIVORCE

3.4.1 General

There is only one ground on which a petition for divorce may be presented to the court by either party to the marriage; that is, that the marriage has broken down irretrievably (MCA 1973, s 1(1)) (see **3.4.2** to **3.4.6** below). However, the court cannot hold that the marriage has broken down unless the petitioner satisfies the court of one or more of the five facts specified in s 1(2) of the MCA 1973. There is no need for there to be a causal relationship between the fact and the breakdown. Therefore, it is no defence to a divorce suit that, for example, the respondent committed adultery after having left the petitioner because the marriage had broken down; the fact does not have to precede and cause the breakdown, but can follow and merely evidence it. As Lady Hale said in *Owens v Owens* [2018] UKSC 41, 'The marriage has to have broken down irretrievably. One of the "five facts" … has to be proved. But the Act does not require that there be a causal connection between them.'

If the court is satisfied that a fact is proved, it must grant the decree nisi unless it is satisfied that the marriage has not broken down (MCA 1973, s 1(4)). This could occur if the parties began living together again before the divorce was granted.

The equivalent process to end a civil partnership is dissolution. The statutory provisions are to be found in the CPA 2004, although they effectively mirror those of the MCA 1973.

3.4.2 Fact A: adultery and intolerability

> (a)   That the respondent has committed adultery *and* the petitioner finds it intolerable to live with the respondent. (MCA 1973, s 1(2)(a), emphasis added)

There are two elements to this fact, which must both be proved to the court:

(a)   adultery; and

(b)   intolerability.

It should be noted that this fact is not available as the basis for a petition to dissolve a civil partnership.

3.4.2.1 Adultery

Section 1(6) of the MCA 1973 provides that only conduct between the respondent and a person of the opposite sex can constitute adultery.

Case law defines adultery as voluntary sexual intercourse between two persons of the opposite sex, one or both of whom is or are married, but not to each other.

Adultery may be proved or inferred from the following:

(a)   A confession of adultery by the respondent. This is the method often used in undefended divorces. Proof can either be by way of a separate confession statement signed by the respondent, or by the respondent answering 'yes' to a question in the Acknowledgement of Service form which is served on the respondent with the petition. If this method is to be used, the Acknowledgement must be returned to court signed by the respondent personally.

(b)   Birth of a child to the wife on proof that the husband was not the father.

(c)   Circumstantial evidence showing both guilty purpose and the opportunity to gratify it, for example, an enquiry agent's report which shows that the respondent and a member of the opposite sex are cohabiting.

(d)   A finding of paternity against the respondent in Children Act proceedings (Civil Evidence Act 1968, s 12).

(e)   Conviction of the respondent in a criminal court of an offence entailing sexual intercourse, for example, rape (Civil Evidence Act 1968, s 11). Although by definition the act of sexual intercourse is not voluntary on the part of the victim, a conviction for rape will be sufficient to satisfy the definition of adultery as against the perpetrator.

(f)   A finding of adultery against the respondent in an earlier case (Civil Evidence Act 1968, s 12). If the petitioner had already been granted a decree of judicial separation on the grounds of adultery, the court can treat the judicial separation decree as sufficient proof of the adultery (MCA 1973, s 4(2)).

3.4.2.2 Intolerability

Intolerability must be proved as well as the adultery, but this element rarely causes any problem. In the first place, the petitioner does not have to show that it was in consequence of the adultery that he found it intolerable to live with the respondent. He could say, for example, that he found it intolerable to live with her because of her treatment of the children, or because of some behaviour of the respondent other than the adultery. Secondly, the test of intolerability is subjective. The petitioner has merely to convince the court that he finds it intolerable to live with the respondent.

The intolerability can be proved by an assertion of intolerability in a statement sent to the court as part of the divorce proceedings. In practice, in undefended cases, courts do not even require the petitioner to state the reason why he finds it intolerable to live with the respondent.

3.4.2.3 The co-respondent

The person with whom the respondent committed adultery can be made a party to the divorce proceedings and is called the co-respondent. However, even if the co-respondent is made a party, it is not necessary to obtain an admission of adultery from the co-respondent if the respondent admits the adultery, because the fact requires only evidence that the respondent has committed adultery.

For many years the rules have given a petitioner the option not to name the co-respondent in the petition, in which case it is not necessary to make the co-respondent a party to the divorce. It has become established good practice to refrain from naming a co-respondent so as to reduce animosity between the parties. The FPR 2010 Practice Direction 7A goes a little further in saying, at para 2.1, that the co-respondent *should not* be named unless the petitioner believes that the respondent is likely to object to the divorce. Consequently, naming a co-respondent should be reserved for those cases in which there is a genuine risk of the proceedings being defended.

3.4.2.4 Effect of cohabitation

Adultery

The petitioner is not entitled to rely on adultery committed by the respondent if the parties cohabit for a period, or periods together, exceeding six months after the petitioner has discovered the adultery (MCA 1973, s 2(1)).

The purpose behind this provision is to allow the parties a reasonable length of time in which to achieve a reconciliation without prejudicing their ground for divorce.

The time begins to run when the petitioner discovers the adultery. It is not relevant how long ago the adultery was actually committed. The six months can be made up of a number of periods of cohabitation, they need not constitute a continuous period. If the respondent has committed adultery on several occasions, time will not begin to run until after the petitioner learns of the last act of adultery.

Intolerability

Where the parties have lived together for a period or periods not exceeding six months in total after the petitioner knew of the adultery, the court must disregard the cohabitation when considering whether the petitioner finds it intolerable to live with the respondent (MCA 1973, s 2(2)).

This is another attempt to encourage the parties to attempt reconciliation. Without it, any cohabitation after discovery of the adultery could be used by the respondent as evidence that the petitioner did not in fact find it intolerable to live with the respondent.

> **EXAMPLE**
>
> Abigail and Brian marry in 2005. In 2007 Brian has an affair, which ends after one month. In December 2021 a friend tells Abigail about Brian's affair. Initially the couple stay together and try to make the marriage work. However, in February 2022, Abigail decides that she cannot forgive Brian for the affair and she chooses to start divorce proceedings. The lengthy cohabitation since the affair took place is irrelevant. Time begins to run only when Abigail knew of the affair, ie December 2021. As fewer than six months have elapsed since that date, Abigail's petition can proceed based on the adultery in 2007.

3.4.3 Fact B: behaviour

> (b) That the respondent has behaved in such a way that the petitioner cannot reasonably be expected to live with the respondent. (MCA 1973, s 1(2)(b))

3.4.3.1 The respondent's behaviour

The phrase 'cannot reasonably be expected to live with the respondent' lays down an objective test. The court must make a value judgement about the respondent's behaviour and its effect on the petitioner. In contrast to the test for intolerability (see **3.4.2.2**), the petitioner's word alone is not enough. However, the court must have regard to the history of the marriage as well as to the personalities of the individual spouses. In the case of *O'Neill v O'Neill* [1975] 1 WLR 1118, the respondent, after retiring, bought a flat for himself, his wife and teenage daughter. He then personally began extensive renovation, involving mixing cement in the living room and leaving the toilet without a door for eight months, embarrassing his wife and daughter. After two years of the upheaval the wife left, and was entitled to a decree using this fact.

In the case of *Birch v Birch* [1992] 1 FLR 564, the wife's main complaint against the husband was that he was dogmatic and dictatorial, with nationalistic, male chauvinistic characteristics which she had resented for many years. The court granted the divorce and acknowledged that the wife's sensitive nature made it unreasonable for her to go on living with him.

It is a question of fact in each case whether the behaviour is such as to entitle the petitioner to a decree; it does not have to be grave and weighty behaviour. There is also no need to prove that the respondent had any intention to inflict misery on the petitioner. Nevertheless, it seems that there must be something of substance. In *Owens v Owens* [2018] UKSC 41, the Supreme Court expressed some misgivings on the facts, but refused to interfere with the trial judge's decision to refuse the wife a divorce based on allegations which he described as being 'at best flimsy'. Lord Wilson, in the Supreme Court, summarised the court's approach to establishing whether the requirements of s 1(2)(b) MCA 1973 are satisfied as follows:

> The inquiry has three stages: first (a), by reference to the allegations of behaviour in the petition, to determine what the respondent did or did not do; second (b), to assess the effect which the behaviour had upon this particular petitioner in the light of the latter's personality and disposition and of all the circumstances in which it occurred; and third (c), to make an evaluation whether, as a result of the respondent's behaviour and in the light of its effect on the petitioner, an expectation that the petitioner should continue to live with the respondent would be unreasonable.

In practice, again, each case depends on its facts, but typically, in an undefended divorce the court will look for three to six examples of behaviour. A further guide to follow in drafting a behaviour petition is 'first, worst and last'. This will ensure that the length of time that the behaviour has been suffered will be established, the major incidents included and when the latest example occurred.

The type of conduct that can be included will always depend on the particular circumstances of the case, but relevant matters include physical violence, verbal abuse (which could include insults, threats, nagging), demanding sexual intercourse too often or not agreeing to intercourse at all, intimate relationships with people of the same or opposite sex (even if they fall short of sexual acts), cruelty, and failure to provide money or food as well as failure to provide affection or attention. However, the mere fact that the petitioner has become bored with the marriage, or that the parties are simply incompatible, will not be sufficient.

3.4.3.2 Effect of cohabitation on behaviour

The fact that the petitioner and respondent have lived with each other for a period or periods not exceeding six months in total after the last incident of behaviour relied on must be disregarded in deciding whether the petitioner can reasonably be expected to live with the respondent (MCA 1973, s 2(3)). This is to encourage the parties to consider reconciliation as cohabitation will not immediately prevent a divorce.

If the parties have lived together for longer than six months, this will not be an absolute bar to a petition being granted. However, the court will take the length of the cohabitation into account in determining whether the petitioner can reasonably be expected to live with the respondent. The longer the cohabitation, the less likely it will be that the court will grant the petition. It would always be open to the petitioner to show a good reason why the cohabitation continued. In *Bradley v Bradley* [1973] 1 WLR 1291, the wife had continued to cohabit, but proved to the court that she had no choice but to do so as she had seven children, nowhere else to go and was frightened that unless she went on sleeping with the husband and looking after the house he would seriously injure her.

3.4.4 Fact C: desertion

> (c) That the respondent has deserted the petitioner for a continuous period of at least two years immediately preceding the presentation of the petition. (MCA 1973, s 1(2)(c))

3.4.4.1   What constitutes desertion?

The elements needed to constitute the fact of desertion are as follows:

(a)   There must be a separation. In calculating the period of separation, the date of separation itself will not be included. In most cases the parties are living apart, but people who are living under the same roof can be separated in law if the common home and the common life have ceased altogether. The petitioner must establish that there are, in fact, two separate households under the same roof (see *Hopes v Hopes* [1948] 2 All ER 920). The court will examine the extent to which the parties share domestic life; whether they cook for each other, eat together and sleep together will all be relevant considerations.

(b)   There must be an intention to desert, ie to bring the matrimonial union permanently to an end.

(c)   The petitioner must not consent or agree to the separation.

(d)   The respondent must not have a just cause for leaving. This could apply if the respondent were away on business, or if his leaving was because of the wife's adultery.

(e)   The desertion must be continuous. Normally, several periods of separation cannot be added together to form the two-year period.

(f)   The desertion must immediately precede the presentation of the petition, ie the date when it is filed.

In practice, desertion is rarely cited in a petition because it is so technical and because other facts can usually be cited where the parties are living separately.

3.4.4.2   Effect of cohabitation on desertion

In considering whether a period of desertion has been continuous, no account is to be taken of a period or periods not exceeding six months in total during which the parties cohabited (MCA 1973, s 2(5)). However, any period of cohabitation cannot be counted as part of the period of desertion.

> **EXAMPLE**
>
> Lisa deserted Martin on 31 January 2020. They make an attempt at reconciliation and live together for two months in 2021. The cohabitation will not prevent Martin from petitioning on the basis of desertion, but he cannot file the petition until a period of two years and two months has expired since Lisa first deserted. Martin will therefore be able to start divorce proceedings on 1 April 2022.

3.4.5   Fact D: two years' separation and consent

(d)   That the parties to the marriage have lived apart for a continuous period of at least two years immediately preceding the presentation of the petition ... *and the respondent consents to a decree being granted.* (MCA 1973, s 1(2)(d), emphasis added)

The elements that are necessary for this fact are, first, separation and, secondly, the respondent's consent to the decree.

3.4.5.1   Separation

Two years' separation is necessary. The spouses are treated as living apart unless they are living with each other in the same household (MCA 1973, s 2(6)). The test is similar to the test of separation in desertion cases (see **3.4.4.1**); accordingly, people can be living apart even though living under the same roof if they are living completely separate lives. The actual date of separation will not be included when calculating the period of separation.

A physical separation does not of itself constitute living apart. There must also be a mental element, ie one of the spouses must regard the marriage as a mere shell, never intending to live with the other spouse again (*Santos v Santos* [1975] 2 All ER 246). This intention does not necessarily have to be communicated to the other spouse and the petitioner could, in theory, rely on the respondent's intention. However, in practice, it is almost always the petitioner's intention that is relied on, and the standard-form divorce documents are drafted on this basis.

3.4.5.2 Consent

The respondent must consent to the divorce. This consent can be given any time after the service of the petition. Consent must be given in writing (FPR 2010, r 7.12(12). In practice, in an undefended divorce, this is given in the Acknowledgement of Service form returned by the respondent to the court following service of the petition on him. All a respondent has to do is answer 'yes' to one of the standard questions and sign the form personally.

The respondent may give notice to the court that he does not consent, or that he withdraws consent already given. No reason for this is needed (FPR 2010, r 7.12(12)).

Any attempt to withdraw consent once decree nisi has been obtained is likely to be ineffective. However, even after the decree nisi, the court has discretion to rescind the decree nisi on the respondent's application if satisfied that the petitioner misled the respondent (whether intentionally or unintentionally) about any matter which he took into account in deciding to give his consent (MCA 1973, s 10(1)). This could apply in a situation where the respondent was misled about a financial or property matter, but could also apply where the respondent was misled about the petitioner's intention to remarry. However, in many cases the court will use its discretion to grant the decree absolute even though the respondent has been misled by the petitioner, so long as this does not have serious consequences.

3.4.5.3 Effect of cohabitation on separation

Section 2(5) of the MCA 1973 applies to the continuity of separation in the same way as it does to desertion (see **3.4.4.2**). Therefore, in deciding whether the living apart has been continuous, a period not exceeding, or periods together not exceeding, six months will be ignored. However, they must be added to the total period of separation so that the time that the parties have actually lived apart is at least two years.

3.4.5.4 Financial position of the respondent (MCA 1973, s 10(2))

If the only fact found is Fact D (or Fact E, see **3.4.6**) the respondent may apply to the court for a consideration of his financial position following the divorce (MCA 1973, s 10(2)).

If such an application is made, the court must consider all the circumstances, and will not make the decree absolute unless satisfied that:

(a)   the petitioner should not be required to make any financial provision for the respondent; or

(b)   the financial provision made is fair and reasonable, or the best that can be made in the circumstances (MCA 1973, s 10(3)).

The court may proceed without observing the above requirements if it is satisfied that the circumstances make it desirable that the decree should be made absolute without delay *and* that the court has obtained a satisfactory undertaking from the petitioner that he will make such financial provision for the respondent as the court may approve (MCA 1973, s 10(4)).

In practice, s 10 is rarely used, and is often treated as something of a negotiating mechanism. The court has no power under this section actually to make financial orders, so it will generally insist that a court order is obtained in financial proceedings under MCA 1973 before the decree absolute is granted.

If the court exercised its discretion under s 10(4) to enable the decree absolute to be granted without satisfactory provision being made (it might do so, eg, if the petitioner's new partner was about to have his child and he urgently wanted to marry her), it would still insist on detailed provisions being included in any undertaking given by the petitioner.

3.4.6 Fact E: five years' separation

> (e)   That the parties to the marriage have lived apart for a continuous period of at least five years immediately preceding the petition. (MCA 1973, s 1(2)(e))

After five years' separation, there is no need for the petitioner to obtain the respondent's consent to the divorce and either party can petition. Living apart has the same meaning as in Fact D (see **3.4.5.1**).

There is no defence to a Fact E petition except to deny the separation, or to prove grave hardship under s 5 of the MCA 1973 (see **3.4.6.1**).

The decree may also be delayed by the respondent asking for his financial position to be considered under s 10(2) of the MCA 1973 (see **3.4.5.4**).

3.4.6.1 Grave hardship

It is a defence to proceedings for divorce, where the only fact found is Fact E, that the dissolution of the marriage would result in grave financial or other hardship to the respondent *and* in all the circumstances it would be wrong to dissolve the marriage (MCA 1973, s 5(1)).

In deciding whether s 5 applies, the court must take account of all the circumstances, including the parties' conduct, the interests of the parties, and the interests of any children or other persons concerned (MCA 1973, s 5(2)).

In *Talbot v Talbot* (1971) 115 SJ 870, the husband left his wife for another woman and ceased maintaining his wife and children. He obtained a divorce under Fact E. The court held that the s 5 defence did not apply as his wife's hardship arose from the breakdown of the marriage and not from the prospective divorce. Accordingly, granting the decree would not add to it. The court may also grant the decree even though grave hardship does result, provided it is satisfied that it is not wrong to grant it. In *Brickell v Brickell* [1973] 3 All ER 508, the Court of Appeal looked at the surrounding circumstances, including the conduct of the parties, and concluded that the husband was entitled to a decree, even though the wife would suffer grave financial hardship, because the wife had behaved so badly during the marriage.

The grave hardship most commonly pleaded is financial; this will include the loss of the chance of acquiring any benefit the respondent might acquire if the marriage were not dissolved (MCA 1973, s 5(3)). If, for example, the husband was contributing to an occupational pension scheme, his wife could be faced with grave financial hardship if he obtained a divorce, because she would then cease to be entitled to a widow's pension under his pension scheme (*Julian v Julian* (1973) 116 SJ 763). However, the defence would not succeed if the petitioner could show that the hardship was not grave because, for example, the wife was entitled to her own occupational pension, or the husband could compensate her for the loss with, say, a deferred annuity, or by 'earmarking' the pension or 'splitting' it (see **4.7**). In practice, this defence is usually used by the respondent to persuade the petitioner to make satisfactory financial provision.

Grave hardship may take other forms and may necessitate examination of hardship caused by religious censure or social ostracism. In practice, it is very difficult to establish that such other hardships are grave enough to warrant refusing a decree.

3.4.6.2 Distinction between MCA 1973, s 5 and s 10(2) of the MCA 1973

Section 5 is a complete defence; therefore, if the defence succeeds, the couple remain married. Section 10(2) merely delays the decree absolute. Section 5 requires the respondent to establish 'grave' financial or other hardship, whereas under s 10(2) the respondent must merely show that the provision is not fair and reasonable. It is easier to establish that s 10(2) applies, but its effect is less drastic.

3.4.6.3 Effect of cohabitation on separation

The effect of cohabitation on Fact E is the same as on Fact D (see **3.4.5.3**).

3.5 CHILDREN

Although children are not parties to the divorce, they are often deeply affected by the breakdown of the marriage. For this reason, until April 2014, s 41 of the MCA 1973 required the court in every divorce to consider the welfare of the children and to sanction any agreed arrangements for them, and even gave the court the power to delay finalising the divorce whilst the arrangements for the children were considered further. However, s 41 was repealed by the Children and Families Act 2014. The result has been to remove any consideration of the children from the divorce process itself. Consequently, parents are left to pursue appropriate remedies separately in the event of there being a dispute.

3.6 NULLITY

This section gives an outline of the decree of nullity, which can, in certain circumstances, be sought as an alternative to a decree of divorce. In comparison with divorce, relatively few decrees of nullity are sought.

3.6.1 General

A decree of nullity may declare that a marriage is either void from the outset, in which case it is treated as never having existed at all, or voidable, in which case it will be treated as being valid and subsisting until the decree is obtained.

3.6.2 Void marriages

A marriage will be void in situations that include the following:

(a)   where the parties are too closely related to each other; or

(b)   either party was under 16 years of age at the time of the ceremony; or

(c)   either party was already lawfully married (MCA 1973, s 11).

If a marriage is void, it never existed. Therefore, a decree is not needed to end it. However, since a decree is needed if financial orders are required, a decree is usually obtained.

3.6.3 Voidable marriages

A marriage will be voidable in situations which include the following:

(a)   non-consummation, either due to incapacity of one party or wilful refusal (non-consummation does not give rise to a voidable civil partnership or same sex marriage); or

(b)   lack of consent, for example, due to duress; or

(c)   one party was suffering from a mental disorder such as to make them unfit for marriage; or

(d)   an interim gender recognition certificate was issued to the respondent after the marriage.

A voidable marriage exists until such time as a decree of nullity is obtained. A bar to obtaining a decree can exist if the respondent satisfies the court, first, that the petitioner, knowing that the marriage could be ended, behaved in such a way as to lead the respondent reasonably to believe that he would not seek to end it and, secondly, that it would be unjust to the respondent to grant the decree (MCA 1973, s 13(1)).

Generally, the petitioner must apply for the decree within three years of the date of the marriage. This does not apply to non-consummation cases, nor to cases based on an interim gender recognition certificate; and, in any event, the court also has a discretion to extend the time limit (MCA 1973, s 13(4)).

3.6.4 Consequences of a decree of nullity

3.6.4.1 Ancillary orders

The parties to a suit for nullity are entitled to apply for all those orders in relation to children, property and finance as are available on divorce.

3.6.4.2 Children

Children born to parents who subsequently obtain a decree of nullity are automatically legitimate if the parents' marriage is voidable, because the marriage existed up to the time of the decree. If the marriage is void, the children will be legitimate if, at the time of conception (or the celebration of the marriage if this is later), both or either of the parents reasonably believed the marriage was valid and the father was domiciled in England and Wales at the time of the birth, or, if he died before the birth, was so domiciled immediately before his death (Legitimacy Act 1976, s 1).

3.6.4.3 Wills

A voidable marriage revokes a previous will, whereas a void marriage, as it never existed, does not have this effect.

When a decree of nullity is granted, whether in respect of a void or voidable marriage, it will have the same effect on a will as a decree of divorce. This means that the former spouse is to be treated as having died on the date of the decree.

Neither party will be able to claim in the event of the other's intestacy.

3.6.5 Divorce or nullity?

In some cases, there may be grounds for both divorce and nullity. It is then for the client to choose which to pursue. Influencing factors may be the fact that nullity can be obtained in the first year of marriage, or there may be religious reasons for wanting to have the marriage declared non-existent rather than dissolved, making nullity the preferred option.

3.7 JUDICIAL SEPARATION

An alternative to a decree of divorce is a decree of judicial separation (or separation order for civil partners). It does not dissolve the marriage but can be used, for example, if religious beliefs forbid divorce.

3.7.1 Grounds for judicial separation

The grounds on which a decree of judicial separation may be obtained are the same as the facts that need to be proved to obtain a divorce (MCA 1973, s 1(2)) (see **3.4.2** to **3.4.6**). This means that s 2 of the MCA 1973 will apply regarding periods of reconciliation and cohabitation. However, the parties do not need to show irretrievable breakdown (MCA 1973, s 17(2)). The same procedure available in undefended divorces applies to undefended petitions for judicial separation although, in contrast to divorce, there is only one stage to the decree.

3.7.2 Effect of decree of judicial separation

When a decree of judicial separation has been obtained the parties are still married, as the decree does not dissolve the marriage but only releases the parties from the duty to live together.

3.7.3   Reasons for seeking judicial separation

Reasons for seeking judicial separation include the following:

(a)   Judicial separation may be sought at any time after the marriage, so this could assist a spouse who separates within the first year who cannot start divorce proceedings.

(b)   Broadly, the same financial and other ancillary orders can be obtained on judicial separation as on divorce.

(c)   Some clients have religious or moral objections to divorce and so this decree offers an alternative.

(d)   The fact used in the judicial separation proceedings can subsequently be used as proof of a fact in later divorce proceedings (MCA 1973, s 4(1)).

Note that judicial separation does not affect existing wills and advice should be given to clients recommending that they review their wills in the light of their separation. If, subsequently, a spouse dies intestate, his or her property will devolve as if the other spouse was already dead, so the surviving spouse will not benefit.

3.8   PRESUMPTION OF DEATH AND DISSOLUTION OF MARRIAGE

There will occasionally be cases where the respondent leaves the marital home and later simply disappears without trace. In such circumstances, the petitioner can apply to the court under s 1 of the Presumption of Death Act 2013 for a declaration that the respondent is presumed to be dead. The court will make a declaration under s 1 if it is satisfied that the respondent has died, or has not been known to be alive for a period of at least the last seven years. The effect of such a declaration is to end the marriage.

3.9   DIVORCE PROCEDURE

The process for obtaining a divorce is going through a transitional period at present with the gradual introduction of online divorce. The current position is that where the petitioner is represented, the solicitor must complete the petition online via *MyHMCTS* and, if the divorce is undefended, follow the online process for the entire divorce; otherwise, the online divorce process is optional. Civil partnership dissolution and judicial separation proceedings currently still follow the paper process.

There is no separate online procedure as such. It merely allows for the completion and online submission of digital versions (with some adaptations) of the various paper forms. The steps required in an online divorce are the same as those in a paper divorce, with some minor modifications to cater for the online environment.

This chapter focuses on the paper divorce process, noting any particular points of relevance for the online process.

3.9.1   The first interview

The first interview is of crucial importance. It is the first meeting with the client and gives the opportunity for the solicitor to obtain information needed from the client as well as to give advice and plan what is to be done (for general advice on interviewing, see **1.2.4**).

When a client seeks advice on his marriage, it is important to discover the client's intentions. The solicitor must not assume that the client wants a divorce. Instead the solicitor must establish whether the client regards the marriage as at an end, or whether he is still hopeful of a reconciliation.

Assuming that the client wants to obtain a divorce, the following areas will need to be covered in the interview. Appropriate use of a checklist or instruction sheet may help to obtain the information. For example:

(a)   general advice on divorce and alternatives, for example, grounds, timing, mediation;

(b)   information sufficient to complete the divorce petition and the supporting documents;

(c)   advice on costs;

(d)   financial matters, for example, property and maintenance principles and orders that could be made;

(e)   children, for example, advice on general principles and orders available;

(f)   welfare benefits;

(g)   legal aid: statutory charge. If the client is eligible for legal aid for ancillary matters, advice must be given on the effect that the statutory charge will have on any order obtained (for a more detailed explanation, see **2.2.4**);

(h)   injunction law and procedure. If the client has problems with domestic abuse, appropriate advice should be given (see **Chapter 15**).

A file note of the interview should be made as soon as possible after the interview. A letter should be written to the client reminding him of what happened at the interview and what advice was given, as well as reminding the client of any action he has asked for. Advice given on costs, including legal aid, should be repeated.

3.9.2   The petition

3.9.2.1   The prescribed form

A divorce is commenced by filing a petition in a standard form. The current standard form divorce petition was drafted with the litigant in person in mind. The form is intended to be straightforward and easy for a lay person to complete; consequently, terminology has been simplified and the legal requirements covered in a series of tick boxes and short questions.

The standard form petition is drafted (see **Appendix 3(A)**) to enable certain required information to be inserted. This is as follows:

(a)   A statement that the petitioner seeks a divorce on the ground that the marriage has irretrievably broken down.

(b)   The petitioner's name and address and their solicitor's details (if any). There are provisions enabling the petitioner's address to be concealed if this is necessary for the protection of the petitioner, for example where there is a fear of violence from the respondent.

(c)   The respondent's name and address and their solicitor's details (if any) (online, the solicitor's details will be added automatically if they are registered with *MyHMCTS*). If there is a co-respondent in a Fact A petition, the co-respondent must be served with the petition, and his or her name and address must be added.

(d)   The date of the marriage and the parties' names as they appear on the marriage certificate.

(e)   The ground on which it is alleged that the court has jurisdiction.

(f)   The Fact under s 1(2) of the MCA 1973 relied upon, together with, in the case of petitions based on adultery, behaviour or desertion, brief details of the incidents relied on, but not the evidence by which these will be proved. The wording used to describe the incidents relied upon is a drafting matter for the solicitor. However, an example for a petition based on adultery is as follows: 'In or about November 2019 in Barchester, Wessex, the Respondent committed adultery with a person whom the Petitioner does not wish to name.'

(g)   Information about any other court proceedings in England and Wales or elsewhere relating to the marriage, property or children.

(h)   A statement as to whether the petitioner wishes to apply for a financial order. It is important that the petitioner answers in the affirmative if a financial order might be needed as this will be considered to be the 'application'. Orders for periodical payments can be backdated to the date of application, which will be the date of the petition. If the petitioner remarries, they will be prevented from making a claim for a lump sum or property adjustment order. If they had applied in the petition, ie before remarriage, a hearing could take place after remarriage. There is also provision on the standard form to indicate an intention to seek financial orders for any children of the family. In most cases, the Child Maintenance Service (CMS), rather than the court, will have jurisdiction to deal with periodical payments. However, other forms of financial order, for example a lump sum order, could be applied for.

(i)   The standard form concludes with a prayer for the following:

   (i)   dissolution of the marriage;

   (ii)   a claim for costs, if required. When the petition is drafted, it is not certain whether the proceedings will be defended or not. It is possible to claim costs in the petition but abandon that claim if the divorce proceeds undefended. Where the petitioner is paying privately, costs may be claimed in relation to fault-based divorces. The costs being sought in the prayer will only cover costs incurred in dissolving the marriage. Costs for ancillary matters, for example financial orders, can be sought separately during the financial proceedings;

   (iii) a claim for a financial order, if required.

The petition is verified by a statement of truth signed by the petitioner or by the solicitor acting for him or her. The online petition does not permit a physical signature.

In practice, it is common for the parties' solicitors to agree the contents of the petition in advance, with the intention of reducing animosity and ensuring from the outset that the divorce will proceed undefended.

3.9.2.2   Amendments

If an error or omission is discovered in a petition – for example, the prayer does not include an application for financial relief, or the petitioner's domicile is stated incorrectly – it will have to be amended. The petition can be amended without permission of the court, unless an answer has been filed in which case permission is required. After the application for decree nisi, permission of the court will generally be needed for amendments (FPR 2010, r 7.13).

Permission may be given without notice if the respondent agrees to the amendment. If the respondent does not agree, an on notice application to the district judge will have to be made. Whenever a petition is amended after service, the amended petition will have to be served on the respondent (and co-respondent, if any).

In practice, very minor amendments – for example, an incorrect date of birth of a child, or incorrect occupation of a party – can be corrected by referring to the error in the petitioner's statement in support of petition (see **3.9.8**). The district judge can then give permission for the petition to stand as corrected without the need for re-service.

In an online divorce, the court may ask for an amended petition to be submitted, for example if there is an obvious mistake or the original is incomplete.

3.9.3   The supporting documents

The following additional documents must be prepared and filed with the petition.

3.9.3.1   Marriage certificate

If the client cannot produce the original marriage certificate, a certified copy may be obtained on payment of a small fee either from the Superintendent Registrar of Marriages for the district where the marriage took place, or from the General Register Office. The online process enables a copy of the marriage certificate to be uploaded. If the marriage certificate is in a foreign language, an authenticated translation must also be obtained and filed with the divorce documents.

3.9.3.2 Statement of reconciliation

Where a solicitor is acting for a client, there is an obligation to file a statement of reconciliation, which states whether or not the solicitor has discussed with the petitioner the possibility of a reconciliation and has given him details of agencies that are qualified to help effect a reconciliation (FPR 2010, r 7.6). In the online process, the 'statement' is a tick box at the start of the application.

There is no duty on a solicitor to discuss reconciliation in every case in which they act, although it will usually be good practice to do so. If they decide not to discuss this matter, they will inform the court of this in the statement.

3.9.3.3 Service copies of the petition

It is necessary to file the original petition plus one copy for each party who is to be served. One copy will be sufficient unless a co-respondent is involved in a Fact A petition, in which case two service copies will be needed.

3.9.3.4 Fee or application for remission from fees

A fee is payable on filing the petition. The client will be entitled to full or part remission from paying the fee if his income and his capital fall below certain thresholds. However, a form applying for remission must be completed and filed at court, and supported by financial documentation evidencing the client's means.

3.9.4 Filing

The filing of papers at court is done by post, in person or, in the case of online process, via the online platform.

For some time, there has been a centralised administrative scheme for divorce cases via a number of divorce centres across England and Wales. With the increase in numbers of online divorces, the divorce centres are currently being phased out. It is anticipated that only the centre at Bury St Edmunds will remain in order to deal with paper divorces.

3.9.5 Service of the petition

The petition and other appropriate documents must be served on the respondent and any co-respondent (FPR 2010, r 7.8).

3.9.5.1 Usual method of service

The court will usually serve the petition by sending it by first-class post to the address given in the petition.

The court attaches the following to each service copy of the petition:

(a) A Notice of Proceedings. This is a general explanation to the respondent of the divorce procedure with detailed instructions on completing and returning the Acknowledgement of Service.

(b) An Acknowledgement of Service. This is an important procedural document which could furnish proof of service of the petition or of the fact relied on as well as other useful information, for example, whether the respondent intends to defend (see **3.9.7**).

If the respondent then completes and returns the Acknowledgement of Service to the court, this is proof of service (FPR 2010, r 6.15). When the court receives the Acknowledgement from the respondent, it will send a copy to the petitioner's solicitors.

In an online divorce where the petition gives details of the respondent's solicitor and that solicitor is registered with MyHMCTS, the solicitor will additionally receive notice of proceedings by email. The solicitor will be able to complete and submit the Acknowledgement of Service online.

3.9.5.2   Alternative methods of service

If postal service by the court is unsuccessful or inappropriate, alternative methods of service are available, and proof of service will depend on which method is used.

Personal service

(a)   *Service through the petitioner.* Service is carried out through the petitioner. A process server will be instructed, or the petitioner's solicitors will themselves serve the documents. The Rules prohibit the petitioner himself from serving the documents on the respondent (FPR 2010, r 6.5(3)). Proof of service in these cases will be by certificate of service by whoever served the documents.

(b)   *By court bailiff.* The petitioner may request bailiff service by lodging the appropriate form (FPR 2010, r 6.9). A fee is payable unless the petitioner has filed a remission form. A request for bailiff service must be accompanied by evidence that postal service has already failed or an explanation as to why postal service is not appropriate. A description of the respondent, normally a photograph, must also be lodged in order to enable the bailiff to identify the respondent. The bailiff will then serve the documents personally and file a certificate of service. If the Acknowledgement of Service is then returned by the respondent, this will be proof of service; if not, the bailiff's certificate will be used. A request for bailiff service will rarely be granted where the petitioner is legally represented, as it is unlikely that the petitioner will be able to demonstrate the need to serve by bailiff rather than by process server.

Deemed service

If the respondent does not return the Acknowledgement of Service to the court, the petitioner can apply for deemed service if he can satisfy the court that the respondent has in fact received the petition (FPR 2010, r 6.16).

An application without notice should be made, supported by evidence showing why the petitioner is of the view that the respondent has received the petition. This can be done by using evidence from a third party, or, for example, even from the petitioner himself, that the respondent read the petition and then threw it away, or an open letter from solicitors instructed by the respondent to act for him referring to the petition.

Service by alternative means

Service by alternative method or at an alternative place will be relevant when all the petitioner's efforts to serve by post and personal service have failed and there is insufficient evidence to apply for deemed service.

An application should be supported by evidence setting out the attempts made to serve personally/by post and the basis on which alternative means are thought likely to be successful (FPR 2010, Practice Direction 6A, para 6.2).

If the order is granted, it will specify the alternative method to be used. This could be by advertisement if there is a reasonable likelihood that it will come to the respondent's notice, for example by placing it in a newspaper which he is known to read regularly. Another method that could be specified is service on another person, for example a relative whom he visits regularly, or a person with whom he lives or works.

An application for service by alternative means may also be used retrospectively. If the respondent has in fact already received the papers by some alternative means, an application may be made for this to be accepted as good service (FPR 2010, r 6.19(2)).

Dispensing with service

Dispensing with service is used only as a last resort where all other methods have failed and the district judge is of the opinion that it is impracticable to serve the petition (FPR 2010, r 6.20). It is treated by the court very seriously as, by granting the order, the respondent can find that he is divorced without knowing that a divorce petition had been filed and having had no opportunity to defend. An application without notice should be made to the court setting out the grounds for the application (ie why there is a problem and what has been done to trace the respondent). The judge can require the petitioner to attend to give evidence. Service will be dispensed with only where the petitioner can show that every effort has been made to trace the respondent.

3.9.5.3   Other problems with service

Finding the respondent

If the petitioner does not know the whereabouts of the respondent, enquiries must be made so that postal or personal service can be used. If particular difficulty is encountered, reference should be made to FPR 2010 Practice Direction 6C. This enables the court to request a search for the respondent's address in the records of the Department of Work and Pensions or the Passport Service. If the respondent is in the Armed Services, the relevant service department can be asked for the respondent's address.

Serving on the co-respondent

The petition must also be served on any co-respondent. The same methods of service are available as for the respondent.

Service of the petition must also be proved, and this will normally be done by the co-respondent returning the completed Acknowledgement of Service to the court. If this is not done, another method of proving service will have to be used, for example, a certificate of service following bailiff service or personal service. Otherwise an order for deemed service, service by alternative means or, as a last resort, an order dispensing with service will have to be obtained.

Service outside England and Wales

The divorce petition may be served outside England and Wales. Special rules apply and reference should be made to FPR 2010, Pt 6 and Practice Direction 6B.

Service on children and protected parties

The court cannot serve the petition if the respondent is a minor (under 18 years of age) or a protected party (eg someone who lacks capacity). Special rules apply and reference should be made to r 6.14 of the FPR 2010.

3.9.6   Return of the Acknowledgement of Service

The respondent is required to complete and return the Acknowledgement of Service to the court within seven days of service of the petition (FPR 2010, r 7.12(1)). In an online divorce, time runs from service of the paper petition even though the respondent's solicitor may have received notice of proceedings by email.

The respondent is given guidance as to how to complete this form in the Notice of Proceedings. He may also have instructed his own solicitors. When the court sends a copy of the Acknowledgement of Service to the petitioner, the replies to the straightforward questions it contains may reveal the following information:

(a)   Proof of service (see **3.9.5**).

(b)   Whether the respondent intends to defend the petition. Since the reply is not binding on the respondent, he can later change his mind.

(c)   Whether the respondent has admitted adultery or consented to the decree. If the petition is based on Fact A, the respondent can admit the adultery and, provided he has signed the form personally, this will be sufficient proof of his adultery. If the petition is based on Fact D and the respondent has given his consent in this form, this will be proof of his consent, provided he has signed the form personally.

3.9.7 Application for decree nisi

Provided the respondent has not given notice of intention to defend and a period of seven days after service of the petition has expired, the next step is for the petitioner's solicitors to file an application for decree nisi, together with a statement containing proof of the fact relied on and other essential matters via the online platform. If the respondent has given a notice of intention to defend, the petitioner must wait 28 days from service of the petition to file an application for decree nisi.

3.9.8 Petitioner's statement in support of the petition

The petitioner's statement in support of the petition is filed with the application for decree nisi. The Rules provide standard forms to suit each Fact (see FPR 2010, Practice Direction 5A). The statement is in question and answer form. The main matters which are dealt with are as follows:

(a)   The petitioner must confirm that the contents of his petition are true and that no amendments or alterations are required.

(b)   If the parties have cohabited since the date of the incidents relied on, the affidavit requires the petitioner to give details of the periods of cohabitation to ensure that the fact is not barred by s 2 of the MCA 1973.

(c)   The Acknowledgement of Service will need to be attached if the petitioner is relying on it as proof of service, or if it has been signed by the respondent to admit adultery (Fact A), or to consent to the divorce (Fact D).

3.9.9 Directions for hearing

On receipt of the application for decree nisi the court will check the following:

(a)   that the petition has been served. The court will check that proof of service is evident from the documents lodged. If the petitioner is relying on return of the Acknowledgement of Service and it is a case where this has been signed personally by the respondent, the court will check that the petitioner's affidavit identifies the respondent's signature;

(b)   that the case is undefended. The case will be undefended if:

    (i)   the respondent has told the court that he does not intend to defend (usually in the Acknowledgement of Service), or

    (ii)   no notice of intention has been given and seven days have elapsed since service of the petition, or

    (iii)   the respondent has filed a notice of intention to defend but the time limit for filing the answer has expired. Rule 7.12(8) of the FPR 2010 provides that this time limit is 28 days from the date of service of the petition;

(c)   if the petition relies on Fact D, that the respondent's consent has been given. Consent may be given either in the Acknowledgement of Service, or in a separate document.

If all the above matters are satisfied, the court will consider the evidence of the petitioner on the court file and in particular the petition, the Acknowledgement of Service, the petitioner's statement in support of petition and any exhibits. If the court is satisfied that the petitioner is entitled to a decree nisi, it will do the following:

(a)   direct that the application for the decree nisi be listed for the making of the decree nisi on the next available date (FPR 2010, r 7.20);

(b)   if there is a prayer for costs in the petition, make a direction for costs if it considers that the petitioner is entitled to them, or if not so satisfied, make no direction as to costs.

The court will then send a notice of the date on which the decree nisi will be granted, together with any direction as to costs, to both parties (via the online platform if relevant). If either party objects to the direction as to costs, he must give notice not less than 14 days before the decree nisi hearing of his wish to make representations at the hearing (FPR 2010, r 7.20).

If the court is not satisfied that the petitioner has proved his case, it may:

(a)   ask for further evidence. This could clarify, for example, an uncertainty revealed in the petition relating to domicile or habitual residence, or an ambiguity in the petitioner's statement in support of petition relating to any period during which the petitioner cohabited with the respondent;

(b)   list the case for a case management hearing.

If there is a problem that cannot be resolved by supplying further information, eg a question of whether there was sufficient behaviour to amount to grounds for a Fact B divorce or a complex jurisdictional issue, the court will set a procedure and timetable as to how to progress the case. This could lead to a hearing to resolve the problem. If the problem is resolved and the ground for divorce is proved, the decree nisi will be made at the hearing. If not, the petition will be dismissed.

3.9.10   Decree nisi

The decree nisi (or conditional order for civil partners) will be ordered on the appointed day by the judge in open court. However, unless there is any dispute as to costs, neither party need attend. Indeed, under the centralised scheme, any party wishing to attend the pronouncement of the decree nisi must first notify the court, setting out the reason for their attendance. A copy of the decree nisi is sent to the parties. This decree does not dissolve the marriage. Even when the online process is extended beyond the initial application, the decree nisi will continue to be pronounced in open court.

3.9.11   Decree absolute

The final step in the undefended divorce procedure is to obtain the decree absolute (or dissolution order for civil partners), which will end the marriage.

3.9.11.1   Petitioner's notice

Once six weeks have elapsed since the grant of the decree nisi, the petitioner can give notice that he wishes the decree nisi to be made absolute (via the online platform if relevant) (FPR 2010, r 7.32). In extremely rare cases, the court does have the power to reduce this six-week period (FPR 2010 Practice Direction 7A). However, when urgency is anticipated it is better to speed up the earlier part of the divorce proceedings rather than relying on this power.

The court will grant the decree absolute, provided that the matters set out in r 7.32(2) of the FPR 2010 are satisfied, for example:

(a)   that there is no appeal relating to the decree nisi;

(b)   that the provisions enabling the respondent's financial position to be considered under s 10(2)–(4) of the MCA 1973 do not apply or have been complied with;

(c)   that any order under s 10A of the MCA 1973 has been complied with (see **3.9.11.3**).

In the case of *Miller-Smith v Miller-Smith (No 2)* [2010] 2 FLR 351 the court decided that, in addition to the statutory grounds for delaying the decree absolute to be found in the MCA 1973, the court also has a discretionary power under its inherent jurisdiction to stay or delay the decree absolute. However, the court emphasised that this is a power to be exercised in 'special and exceptional' circumstances.

The decree absolute certificate is sent to the petitioner and the respondent. The marriage is now dissolved.

It is important not to seek to obtain the decree absolute automatically after the six-week period as there could be good reasons to delay. For example, it might be important to preserve the petitioner's right of occupation under the FLA 1996 (see **9.6.2.1**), or to preserve pension rights until a pension sharing order becomes effective, or even at this late stage the petitioner might be considering a reconciliation.

If the petitioner delays obtaining the decree absolute for more than 12 months after the decree nisi, the notice must be accompanied by a written explanation for the delay. This is to ensure that there has not been an attempted reconciliation which may have prejudiced the grounds.

3.9.11.2   Respondent's application

The petitioner may choose not to obtain the decree absolute for the reasons mentioned above, or perhaps where the petitioner knows that the respondent is anxious to remarry and wishes to use the delay as a negotiating weapon in the financial proceedings. In this situation, the respondent can apply for the decree absolute once a period of some four and a half months has elapsed from the date of the decree nisi (ie three months after the earliest date (ie six weeks after decree nisi) on which the petitioner could have obtained the decree absolute) (MCA 1973, s 9(2)). The petitioner must be served with notice of the application. The court will then consider the respondent's application and any objections that the petitioner has made. The court can then decide to make the decree absolute, require further investigations or, if necessary, rescind the decree nisi (FPR 2010, r 7.33).

Broadly speaking, the court will make the decree absolute unless there are special circumstances which demand that the court exercises its discretion to delay. In *Thakkar v Thakkar* [2016] EWHC 2488 (Fam), the court found such special circumstances in the form of the complex offshore assets involved in the case which made it uncertain whether the making of the decree absolute at that stage would prejudice the petitioner's financial claims.

3.9.11.3   Religious marriages

Historically, some family clients have found themselves in the difficult position of being divorced in law and yet their marriage remains intact according to their own religious rules and customs, usually because the other party refuses to co-operate in ending the marriage according to religious practices. The Divorce (Religious Marriages) Act 2002 inserted provisions into the MCA 1973 designed to overcome this problem. Section 10A applies where the parties have been married according to particular religious usages and must co-operate if the marriage is to be dissolved according to those usages. The court may, on application by either party, order that the decree nisi is not to be made absolute until such time as the parties produce a declaration to the court confirming that they have taken such steps as are necessary to dissolve the marriage according to the appropriate religious usages.

3.10   DEFENDED DIVORCES

As defended divorces are so rare, the detail of defended procedure is outside the scope of this book and reference should be made to specialist textbooks.

If the respondent intends to defend, he will normally return the Acknowledgement of Service stating that he intends to defend the petition. He must give this notice within seven days from service of the petition (FPR 2010, r 7.12(1)).

If he does not file this notice, he can still file an answer. If he does give notice, he is under no obligation to file an answer if he changes his mind. The answer is the defence to the petition and must be filed within 28 days of service of the petition (FPR 2010, r 7.12(8)).

Where a divorce becomes defended, the court will fix a case management hearing for the purpose of deciding how to progress the case. The court will set a procedure and a timetable using its general case management powers in Pt 4 of the FPR 2010, ultimately leading to a hearing in open court.

3.11 COSTS

On an application for costs, the decision is always in the discretion of the court, but the general principle is that an order for costs will be made in favour of the successful party. Often such applications are not made, or are expressed as to be pursued only if the divorce is defended. This is particularly common where the divorce is not fault-based and it is thought that to pursue costs would introduce animosity into the proceedings, or where the petitioner is a litigant in person and it may be uneconomic to pursue costs of only a small amount.

3.12 THE DIVORCE, DISSOLUTION AND SEPARATION ACT 2020

Many have argued for some time that divorce law based on a statute enacted in 1973 is hopelessly out of step with modern family life. At various times over the years there have been numerous calls for, and even attempts at, reform. The FLA 1996, for example, as originally envisaged, would have brought a radically different divorce regime into being. However, these changes were eventually abandoned, and those parts of the Act that would have introduced them were never implemented.

Renewed impetus towards reform came with the case of *Owens v Owens* [2018] UKSC 41, in which the husband successfully defended the wife's petition on the basis that it did not meet the requirements of s 1(2)(b) of the MCA 1973, despite the trial judge's finding that the marriage had indeed broken down. Mrs Owens took her case as far as the Supreme Court, but the conclusion reached was that a correct application of the MCA 1973 was to refuse her a divorce. During the progress of the case, several of the judges involved took the opportunity to express their views on the current state of the law. In the Supreme Court, Lord Wilson concluded his judgment with the following sentence:

> Parliament may wish to consider whether to replace a law which denies to Mrs Owens any present entitlement to a divorce in the above circumstances.

As it transpires, Parliament did 'consider' this, and the result was the Divorce, Dissolution and Separation Act 2020 (DDSA 2020). The DDSA 2020 is set to come into force on 6 April 2022. The DDSA 2020 will introduce the most radical changes to divorce law in half a century. The DDSA 2020 also provides for equivalent changes to dissolution of civil partnerships and judicial separation.

The DDSA 2020 is not a free-standing piece of legislation; instead, it makes a few specific amendments to the MCA 1973. Various elements of the MCA 1973 are retained, for example, the one-year rule in s 3, consideration of the respondent's financial circumstances in s 10 (albeit in amended form) and the two-stage divorce process. The DDSA 2020 amends, at last (see **3.1.1**), the terminology of the MCA 1973 (and other legislation). For example, a 'petition' becomes an 'application for a divorce order', 'decree nisi' becomes a 'conditional order' and 'decree absolute' becomes a 'final order'.

Under the DDSA 2020, irretrievable breakdown of the marriage remains as the sole ground for divorce. The key change introduced by the DDSA 2020, of course, is that there is no longer any need to evidence irretrievable breakdown by establishing one of the five Facts. Instead, irretrievable breakdown is established by the applicant making a statement to that effect. The statement itself is conclusive evidence. Therefore, it will not be possible for a divorce to be 'defended' by arguing that the marriage has not broken down irretrievably. A divorce may only be 'disputed', for example where the court's jurisdiction is contested.

Under the DDSA 2020, joint applications for divorce will be permitted for the first time. Part of the rationale behind the campaign for no fault divorce was that the ending of a marriage should not be seen as an adversarial process, initiated by one party and imposed on the other. The availability of a joint application is intended to encourage the couple to come to a mutual decision about their future and to enable that mutual decision to be reflected in the manner in which the process is presented to the court.

The DDSA 2020 sets a timetable for divorce. A minimum of 20 weeks must elapse from the presentation of the initial application before the court can be asked to make the conditional order. There is then a further six-week delay before the final order can be obtained (as now, it will be possible to shorten the time period in appropriate cases). In other words, it will take a minimum of six months to obtain a divorce. Interestingly, whilst the DDSA 2020 allows the Lord Chancellor to adjust the time limits by secondary legislation, the overall timeframe cannot be reduced to below six months. Under the current law, of course, a good many divorces are concluded in half that time. Essentially, the six-month timeframe was introduced to address concerns voiced when the legislation was going through Parliament that no fault divorce would equate to 'quickie' divorce.

At the time of writing, the court forms are not available and the amendments to the FPR 2010 (principally to Rules 6 and 7) which will introduce the new divorce procedure are only in draft form. Some key features of the draft Rules appear below (although obviously there may be changes in the final version):

- The procedure will be primarily an online process.
- An 'undefended' case will be termed a 'standard' case.
- Once an application has been made, it will not be possible for the respondent to make their own application without the court's permission (to avoid cross-applications and a race to final order).
- The default position is that service of the papers will be carried out by the court. The applicant can elect to serve, but must effect service within 28 days.
- Service can be effected by email, but this must be coupled with postal notice that email service has taken place (the wording of the Rules suggest that this will be the court's preferred method of service).
- The respondent will have 14 days to acknowledge service.
- In a joint application, both parties will be served with notice of proceedings and must acknowledge within 14 days (this is intended to prevent fraud).
- A joint application can proceed as a sole application at the conditional order stage.
- A joint application can proceed as a sole application at the final order stage, but the applicant will have to give the respondent 14 days' notice of their intention to apply for the final order.
- The conditional order will be made at a court hearing.
- The costs rules remain unchanged (the government says that it may consult on changes once the new procedure is up and running).

SUMMARY AND CHECKLIST

(1)   No divorce proceedings can begin until one year after the marriage. Decrees of nullity and judicial separation can be sought at any time after the marriage.

(2)   The English courts will have jurisdiction to hear a divorce only if one of the grounds relating to the parties' habitual residence or domicile is satisfied.

(3)   The only ground for divorce is that the marriage has broken down irretrievably.

(4)   One or more of 'the five facts' must be proved:

Fact A: Adultery and Intolerability (not applicable to civil partners)

Fact B: Behaviour

Fact C: Desertion

Fact D: Two Years' Separation and Consent

Fact E: Five Years' Separation.

(5)   Section 10(2) of the MCA 1973 enables a respondent in a Fact D or Fact E divorce to ask the court to consider his financial position after the divorce.

(6)   Section 5(1) of the MCA 1973 is a defence to a Fact E divorce. The respondent must prove that the divorce would result in grave financial or other hardship and it would be wrong to dissolve the marriage.

(7)   A decree of nullity can declare that a marriage either never existed at all (a void marriage), or that it did exist but, due to certain circumstances, it has been ended (a voidable marriage).

(8)   A decree of judicial separation can be obtained by proving one of the five facts.

Undefended divorce: procedure checklist	
Petitioner	Respondent

(1) Files at divorce centre:
   (a) Marriage certificate;
   (b) Petition + copy(ies);
   (c) Statement of reconciliation (only if solicitor on court record);
   (d) Fee or application for exemption.
(2) Receives notification of case number allocated.	

	(3) Receives from divorce centre:
	   (a) Copy petition;
	   (b) Notice of Proceedings;
	   (c) Acknowledgement of Service.
	(4) Returns completed Acknowledgement of Service.

(5) Receives photocopy of completed Acknowledgement of Service.
(6) Files:
   (a) Application for decree nisi;
   (b) Statement in support of petition.	

	(7) Both parties receive a notice of the date fixed for pronouncement of decree nisi. (8) Decree nisi pronounced. (9) Both parties would be notified of any directions, eg further information or appointment at court. (10) Both parties receive copy of decree nisi.
(11) Petitioner files notice for decree nisi to be made absolute (after 6 weeks from grant of decree nisi) and the fee (if appropriate).	
	(12) Both parties receive copy decree absolute.

CHAPTER 4

FINANCIAL ORDERS: THE LAW

4.1	Introduction	51
4.2	The powers of the court	52
4.3	Income orders	52
4.4	Capital orders	54
4.5	Deciding what orders to make	56
4.6	The clean break	68
4.7	Pensions on divorce	70
4.8	Financial cases in the future	73
4.9	Financial provision during marriage	73
Summary		74

LEARNING OUTCOMES

After reading this chapter you will be able to:

- explain the court's powers to make financial orders
- understand how the court decides on the appropriate financial orders to make
- outline the application of the factors in s 25 of the Matrimonial Causes Act 1973.

4.1 INTRODUCTION

This chapter deals with the law relating to financial provision on marriage breakdown. It covers the range of financial orders available to spouses under the MCA 1973 and to civil partners under the CPA 2004, and the principles applied by the court when making those orders. Although the law applicable to married couples and that applicable to civil partners derive from different statutes, the provisions are to all intents and purposes identical, and the court will apply them in the same way. This was confirmed in the first reported case concerning civil partnerships, *Lawrence v Gallagher* [2012] EWHC 394. In that case, Thorpe LJ described the fact that the case arose from the dissolution of a civil partnership rather than a divorce as being 'of little moment'.

This chapter also deals with the wide range of orders available for children under the MCA 1973. However, in the majority of cases, maintenance for children is governed by the Child Support Act 1991 (CSA 1991) to the exclusion of the MCA 1973. The CSA 1991 will be considered in **Chapter 7**. However, as financial provision between spouses is closely linked with provision for any children, it is important to appreciate the impact of the CSA 1991 on orders made by the court under the MCA 1973.

A significant minority of maintenance applications for children will continue to be dealt with by the court, and the court also retains sole jurisdiction to make lump sum and property adjustment orders in favour of children.

4.2 THE POWERS OF THE COURT

4.2.1 Orders available

The powers of the court to make financial orders are found in ss 22 to 24B of the MCA 1973 (see **Appendix 1(A)**). The orders fall into two main categories: income orders and capital orders. The *income orders* are:

(a)   maintenance pending suit;

(b)   periodical payments;

(c)   secured periodical payments.

The *capital orders* are more diverse and include:

(a)   lump sum orders;

(b)   property adjustment orders (for property to be transferred or held on trust);

(c)   orders for sale;

(d)   pension sharing orders;

(e)   pension sharing compensation orders.

4.2.2 When available

Spouses may apply for any of these orders, or indeed all of them, on or after the filing of the divorce petition. However, with the exception of maintenance pending suit (MPS), the application cannot be heard until decree nisi, and no order will take effect until decree absolute (or, in the case of a pension sharing order, 28 days after the making of the order if later than decree absolute). By contrast, most applications for provision for children may be made and heard at any time, and such orders take immediate effect.

Availability of financial orders

Petition	Decree nisi	Decree absolute
Application for financial provision can be made	Order for financial provision for spouse can be made	Order for financial provision can come into effect ⟶
		(Periodical payments can be back-dated to the date of the application)
Order for MPS for spouse can be made and take effect	⟶	MPS ends
Order for financial provision for child(ren) can be made and take effect		⟶

In most cases, the arrangements for financial provision for a spouse are finalised after the divorce itself has gone through. However, parties should take care to apply for financial provision before remarrying, because after they have remarried they are no longer entitled to apply (see MCA 1973, s 28(3) in **Appendix 1(A)** and **10.5.2**).

4.3 INCOME ORDERS

4.3.1 Maintenance pending suit

As the name suggests, MPS is an order for regular payments designed to provide for a spouse in the short term until the divorce is determined (the equivalent for civil partners is maintenance pending the outcome of dissolution proceedings). As stated above, an order for periodical payments for a spouse cannot take effect until decree absolute, and yet the client may be in urgent need of money before then. In such cases an application for MPS under s 22 of the MCA 1973 may be appropriate. The application for MPS may be made, heard and take effect at any time after the petition has been filed.

An order for MPS will terminate on the grant of decree absolute. At that time, an order for full periodical payments may take effect. In practice, however, the court will often not hear a financial application until some time after decree absolute is granted. If the client is in need of money in the meantime, an application for an interim periodical payments order could be made.

Case law would indicate that the courts do not consider it necessary to approach applications for MPS and/or interim periodical payments with quite the same level of forensic detail as is applied to a final order. Instead the court's task is to make a broad assessment to ensure that the applicant is in receipt of a reasonable sum to meet their immediate needs, with needs, resources and the marital standard of living being key factors in determining 'reasonableness' (see, for example, *TL v ML and Others* [2006] 1 FLR 465). In *BD v FD (Maintenance Pending Suit)* [2014] EWHC 4443 (Fam), Moylan J ordered the husband to pay MPS of £202,000 (the amount that he was already paying voluntarily) on the basis that it was within the 'bracket of reasonableness', adding:

> In coming to this conclusion, I do not consider that I should either err on the side of generosity or parsimony; I should simply determine what sum it is reasonable for the wife to receive to enable her to meet her interim income needs from the resources available to her.

Further guidance was given in *Rattan v Kuwad* [2021] EWCA Civ 1. The Court of Appeal said that the correct approach was to be pragmatic and that the court was only required to undertake sufficient analysis to be satisfied, on the facts of the particular case, that the ultimate award was 'reasonable'. In terms of the items of expenditure covered by MPS, the Court added that the fact that some items of the applicant's expenditure were not incurred every month did not mean that they should be excluded for the purposes of determining what maintenance was reasonable; further, that school fees could form part of the applicant's immediate needs and so be included in the maintenance award.

In practice, MPS applications are rarely pursued. The primary reason for this is simply that the cost of bringing such an application will usually be disproportionate to the short-term benefit to be gained. In *BD v FD* (above), where the legal costs incurred were in the region of £80,000, Moylan J advised restraint, saying that

> interim hearings should be pursued only where, on a broad assessment, the court's intervention is manifestly required. Otherwise, parties will be encouraged to engage in what can often be an expensive exercise when the proper forum for the determination of the proceedings is the final hearing.

Despite its drawbacks, MPS may be worth pursuing, particularly if a party with ample means leaves another with onerous responsibilities and no ability to meet them. It should also be noted that some family litigation funding providers now offer maintenance loans to meet living expenses pending the final hearing which, in the right case, may be a suitable alternative to an application for MPS.

Maintenance pending suit is not available for a child; neither is it necessary, because periodical payments may be obtained for a child of the family (if appropriate) as soon as the petition is filed, or alternatively an application may be made to the CMS for a child maintenance calculation.

4.3.2   Periodical payments

Periodical payments usually take the form of weekly or monthly sums. Periodical payments may be paid to a spouse (MCA 1973, s 23(1)(a)), or, in exceptional cases, to a child of the family (see CSA 1991, s 8(3), discussed at **7.4**) or to the spouse caring for the child on that child's behalf (MCA 1973, s 23(1)(d)). Periodical payments may be ordered for children even if the divorce petition is dismissed, either at the time of dismissal or within a reasonable period after the dismissal.

All periodical payments to a party terminate on the death or remarriage of the recipient. Unsecured periodical payments terminate on the death of the paying spouse (MCA 1973, s 28). A periodical payments order (PPO) is unaffected by the remarriage of the payer, save that remarriage could prompt an application to discharge (or reduce) the order if the payer would then be supporting his new spouse.

The court may limit the term of the PPO to years or months if it considers that a party should be able to become independent after a period of adjustment, for example, to allow a wife to retrain and obtain employment. The court is under a duty to consider whether such a limitation on maintenance is feasible (see MCA 1973, s 25A(2) and **4.6.2.1**).

In the few cases where the court has jurisdiction to make a PPO in favour of a child, it will terminate on the child's 17th birthday unless it is in the child's interest for it to continue until he is 18 (see MCA 1973, s 29, in **Appendix 1(A)**). The usual reason for such an extension is that the child will be continuing with full-time education.

The maintenance may continue beyond a child's 18th birthday only if the circumstances in s 29(3) apply, ie:

(a)   the child is (or intends to be) in further education, academic or vocational; or

(b)   there are special circumstances, for example, the child has a mental disability.

4.3.3   Secured periodical payments (MCA 1973, s 23(1)(b) and (e))

A party may be ordered to secure periodical payments which are payable to the other party or a child of the family. This is a device to ensure that the recipient will continue to receive the periodical payments even if the payer's income fluctuates, or if problems of enforcement are anticipated. Secured PPOs work by charging an asset with a sum fixed by the court from which the periodical payments can be met. Typically, that asset will be income producing, for example, shares or rented property. The income yielded by the charged asset will be paid to the recipient up to the amount specified in the PPO. Alternatively, a non-income-producing asset, such as a valuable painting, could be secured. If the periodical payments were not made from other sources, the asset would be liable to be sold and the proceeds used to pay the sum secured.

Secured PPOs terminate in the same circumstances as unsecured PPOs, save for one exception: unlike ordinary PPOs, secured PPOs do not terminate on the death of the payer. However, his death would be taken into account on any application by his estate to vary or discharge the order.

4.4   CAPITAL ORDERS

The purpose of capital orders is to settle once and for all any disputes in respect of the couple's capital. For most couples the matrimonial home represents the main, if not the only, family capital. This is considered in detail in **Chapter 9**. Some couples will, of course, have considerable assets in addition to the home, including savings, securities, etc which may be the subject of a lump sum order, a property adjustment order, an order for sale or, in the case of pensions, a pension sharing order or pension sharing compensation order.

The high-profile case of *Prest v Petrodel Resources Ltd and Others* [2013] UKSC 34 serves as a reminder that the court only has power under the MCA 1973 to make capital orders in respect of assets in which one or both parties actually has a legal or beneficial interest. In *Petrodel* the Supreme Court made it clear that whilst the existence of a number of properties owned by the husband's company was a fact which the court should take into account, there was no power under the MCA 1973 to make orders in respect of those assets if they were found to be genuinely in the ownership of a third party; the court could only make orders in respect of assets where it could be shown that one or both parties had an interest. On the particular facts of *Petrodel*, the Supreme Court was able to conclude that the company held the properties on trust for the husband and the existence of the husband's beneficial interest enabled the court to make an order transferring the properties to the wife.

4.4.1 Lump sum orders

Under s 23(1)(c) and (f) of the MCA 1973, the court can order a party to pay to the other, or to a child of the family, a cash lump sum. There are two main reasons for making such an order:

(a) to adjust the final division of the parties' assets. The order is frequently used in conjunction with an order dealing with the matrimonial home;

(b) to recompense the applicant for expenses incurred prior to the application as a result of inadequate support from the respondent for the applicant or a child of the family.

A spouse is entitled to apply for one lump sum order only (although see **11.8.1**, which deals with the court's power to make a second lump sum or property adjustment order on an application for variation or discharge of a periodical payments or a secured periodical payments order). The lump sum order may specify payment by several instalments. In common with the other capital orders, a lump sum order cannot be varied. However, there is jurisdiction to deal with an application to vary, suspend and even to discharge instalments of a lump sum. Where the court orders payment of the lump sum to be by instalments or to be deferred, for example to allow the payer time to raise the money, it may order interest to be paid at a specified rate. There is also power to secure payment of the instalments in the same way as for periodical payments.

It is sometimes the case that although there may be no funds immediately available for the payment of a lump sum, it is anticipated that money will be forthcoming. Examples include an expected dissolution of a partnership, or maturity of an insurance policy releasing capital. In such a case, the court may adjourn an application, although it will do so only where there is a real likelihood of a change of circumstances within a relatively short period. The court has said that an application should not be adjourned for longer than about five years (see *Roberts v Roberts* [1986] 2 FLR 152). It has also refused applications for adjournment based on a party's hopes of inheritance on the grounds that it was too uncertain whether and when the inheritance would occur (see *Michael v Michael* [1986] 2 FLR 389 and **4.5.1.2**).

Lump sum orders are also available for children. Whilst they are not common, they may be appropriate in high income families or if a child has a special need, for example he is disabled or has special educational needs. Unlike for spouses, more than one lump sum order can be made for a child, so several orders could be made over a period of time. The Child Maintenance Service has no jurisdiction to make capital awards for children.

4.4.2 Property adjustment orders

Under s 24 of the MCA 1973, the court has wide powers to redistribute family property between the parties and the children of the family. It may do so by ordering that property be transferred, for example, from one party to the other, or held on trust. Such orders are intended to be final. Consequently, no application may be made (not even for a child) for further property adjustment, neither is it possible to vary these orders (but, again, see **11.8.1** on the court's powers to make a property adjustment order on a variation of a periodical payments order).

4.4.3 Orders for sale

The court has power under s 24A of the MCA 1973 to order a sale of any property in which either party is beneficially entitled. The court can make this order only once it has also made one of the following orders:

(a)   a secured PPO;

(b)   a lump sum order;

(c)   a property adjustment order.

The order for sale may be made at the same time as the above orders or later. The order cannot take effect until decree absolute. Consequently, if an earlier order for sale is needed, this cannot be made under s 24A and will have to be sought, if possible, under other legislative provisions, such as s 17 of the MWPA 1882 and ss 13 and 14 of the TLATA 1996. (See *WS v HS (Sale of Matrimonial Home)* [2018] EWFC 11.)

The court has power to order that the sale shall not take place until a specified event has taken place or period has expired. For example, it may order that the property in question is not to be sold until essential works on it have been completed. Alternatively, the court may defer the sale to enable a party wishing to avoid the sale and remain in the property (or keep the car/ shares, etc) to raise a lump sum to 'buy out' the other party's interest.

Orders for sale may also be used as a method of enforcement by ordering the sale of an asset if the owner has defaulted on a lump sum order (see **Chapter 11**).

The order for sale may contain consequential and supplementary provisions, directing, for example, how the sale price is to be fixed, or who should have the conduct of the sale.

If a party owns property jointly with another person, for example where a husband and his new partner are co-owners of a flat, the court must give the third party, here the partner, the opportunity to make representations on the matter before it decides whether to order the sale of the property. Alternatively, it may be, say, that the partner is living in a property but has no interest in it. In such a case, the s 24A order may include a consequential direction that she is to be given first refusal on the property before it is placed on the open market.

Although ss 24 and 24A apply to all types of property, for most families the matrimonial home is the most significant asset and, therefore, the issue on which feelings often run high. There are various ways of resolving disputes over the home and these are considered in detail in **Chapter 9**.

4.4.4   Pension sharing orders and pension sharing compensation orders

The court can make pension sharing orders under s 24B of the MCA 1973. The benefits that have accrued to one party under a pension scheme can be a valuable asset and yet they are not realisable until the pension scheme member reaches retirement. A pension sharing order enables the court to divide the pension rights between the parties at the time of the divorce. Pension sharing orders are considered further at **4.7.3**.

The Pensions Act 2008 inserted further provisions into the MCA 1973, which enable the court to make pension compensation sharing orders. These orders enable the court to divide compensation payments made by the Pension Protection Fund. The Fund was set up by the Government to compensate members of pension schemes which have failed.

4.5   DECIDING WHAT ORDERS TO MAKE

The court has a great deal of discretion and flexibility when deciding on the appropriate division of matrimonial assets on divorce.

When the court is considering provision, whether for the parties to the marriage or for a child of the family, it must begin by considering the statutory criteria laid down in s 25 of the MCA 1973 (in **Appendix 1(A)**).

Section 25(1) states:

> It shall be the duty of the court in deciding whether to exercise its powers under sections 23, 24 or 24A above and, if so, in what manner, to have regard to all the circumstances of the case, first consideration

being given to the welfare while a minor of any child of the family who has not attained the age of eighteen.

The section goes on to list factors applicable to provision for spouses (s 25(2)), children of the family (s 25(3)) and further factors for children of the family who are not natural children of both parties (s 25(4)). Those factors are examined below.

Section 25 does not represent an exhaustive list of factors. Indeed, s 25(1) makes it plain that the court must take into account 'all the circumstances of the case'. Thus, the interests of third parties, for example a party's new partner and children, will also be taken into account. A separation agreement or prenuptial agreement previously entered into by the parties (see *G v G (Financial Provision: Separation Agreement)* [2000] 2 FLR 18 and *Radmacher v Granatino* [2010] UKSC 42) would also be considered as part of 'all the circumstances'.

Any significant feature of the case not covered elsewhere can be considered. For example, the case of *A v T (Ancillary Relief: Cultural Factors)* [2004] 1 FLR 977 was unusual on its facts. An Iranian national living in England married an Iranian woman under a marriage contract entered into in Iran. The marriage ended after seven weeks and divorce proceedings were brought in England. In deciding the financial application the court found the cultural background of the parties to be a dominant factor, justifying the court taking into account (and indeed largely following) the way in which the courts of Iran would have dealt with such a case.

4.5.1   Provision for a spouse

Section 25(2) of the MCA 1973 lists the following eight factors to be considered by the court when dealing with financial orders for a spouse:

(a)   the income, earning capacity, property and other financial resources which each of the parties to the marriage has or is likely to have in the foreseeable future [but see s 25B and **4.7.2.1**], including in the case of earning capacity any increase in that capacity which it would be in the opinion of the court reasonable to expect a party to the marriage to take steps to acquire;

(b)   the financial needs, obligations and responsibilities which each of the parties to the marriage has or is likely to have in the foreseeable future;

(c)   the standard of living enjoyed by the family before the breakdown of the marriage;

(d)   the age of each party to the marriage and the duration of the marriage;

(e)   any physical or mental disability of either of the parties to the marriage;

(f)   the contributions which each of the parties has made or is likely in the foreseeable future to make to the welfare of the family, including any contribution by looking after the home or caring for the family;

(g)   the conduct of each of the parties, if that conduct is such that it would in the opinion of the court be inequitable to disregard it;

(h)   in the case of proceedings for divorce or nullity of marriage any benefit which, by reason of the dissolution or annulment of the marriage, that party will lose the chance of acquiring.

4.5.1.1   The courts' approach

A process of re-evaluating the approach taken by the courts when exercising their powers under s 25 began in the landmark case of *White v White* [2000] 2 FLR 981. Until that point, in very broad terms, the courts' approach had been that on marriage breakdown the entitlement of the financially weaker party (usually the wife) was to have her reasonable needs or requirements met, and nothing further. That approach was abandoned in *White*, where the House of Lords said that the courts should not focus exclusively on one factor in this way. Lord Nichols of Birkenhead stated, 'the objective must be to achieve a fair outcome'. All the s 25 factors are ranked equally at the outset and just gain or lose importance in each case, according to the relevant facts of that particular case and what seems to be fair between the parties.

Although emphasising 'fairness', the House of Lords rejected the idea of a presumption, or starting point, of equal division, preferring to leave it to the judge in each particular case to go through the exercise of weighing up all the s 25 factors. Significantly, though, Lord Nichols did go on to say:

> Before reaching a firm conclusion and making an order along these lines, a judge would always be well advised to check his tentative views against the yardstick of equality of division. As a general rule, equality should be departed from only if, and to the extent that, there is a good reason for doing so.

Mrs White was eventually awarded approximately 40% of the total net assets. The 'good reason' to depart from equality in her case was that Mr White's father had loaned the couple some money when they started out, without which they would not have been able to buy the first farm.

The House of Lords expanded on the courts' approach in *Miller v Miller; McFarlane v McFarlane* [2006] UKHL 24. The House of Lords said that the general principles to be applied when making financial awards were 'needs, compensation and sharing'. It was recognised that in many cases, of necessity, achieving fairness did not go beyond the stage of dividing the assets so as to try to meet the parties' housing and financial needs, and that often those assets were insufficient to provide adequately for the needs of two homes. However, in appropriate cases, fairness demanded that the court should exercise its discretion so as to compensate one party and redress the financial disadvantage suffered by one party arising from the way in which the couple had conducted their marriage. The House of Lords went on to state that there was additionally an 'equal sharing' principle deriving from the basic concept of equality which underlies modern marriages. Echoing his words in *White*, Lord Nichols said that 'when their partnership ends each is entitled to receive an equal share of the assets of the partnership unless there is a good reason to the contrary'.

Subsequent cases have wrestled with these principles of 'needs, compensation and sharing'. There has been much comment and debate on the order in which they should be addressed, the balance to be struck between them and how they should be applied to particular assets. In *Robson v Robson* [2010] EWCA Civ 1771, the Court of Appeal took the opportunity to issue a timely reminder that the focus must be on s 25, where Parliament had set out the factors to be considered. The Court went on to say that the objective is to achieve a just result and that 'needs, compensation and sharing' would inform and usually guide that search for fairness.

In broad terms, the baseline is that needs must be met; the principles of sharing and compensation then dictate the extent to which the award will go beyond this. Awards based on compensation are unusual. In *SA v PA (Pre-Marital Agreement: Compensation)* [2014] EWHC 392 (Fam), Mostyn J said that compensation could only be successfully argued in 'very rare and exceptional cases'. A case in which compensation was successfully argued is *RC v JC* [2020] EWHC 466 (Fam). The court said that but for the compensation element, the assets would have been divided equally between the parties. The court accepted the wife's argument that as a result of the marriage she had sacrificed her career as a solicitor and awarded her an extra £400,000 in compensation. However, in making the order, Moor J was at pains to emphasise that the facts of the case were highly unusual:

> ... litigants should think long and hard before launching a claim for relationship generated disadvantage and they should not take this judgment as any sort of 'green light' to do so unless the circumstances are truly exceptional.

Cases are usually dealt with on either a 'needs' or a 'sharing basis'. In *Charman v Charman (No 4)* [2007] EWCA Civ 503, Sir Mark Potter said:

> It is clear that, when the result suggested by the needs principle is an award of property greater than the result suggested by the sharing principle, the former result should in principle prevail ... It is also clear that, when the result suggested by the needs principle is an award of property less than the result suggested by the sharing principle, the latter result should in principle prevail ...

Although the House of Lords in *White v White* was at pains to avoid a presumption of equal division, over time an equal sharing principle has established itself. However, it is not always easy to apply. Perhaps a summary of the up-to-date approach to 'equality' can be found in the words of Coleridge J in B *v* B *(Financial Orders: Proportionality)* [2013] EWHC 1232 (Fam):

> The principle that the marital acquest (ie the wealth generated by the parties' joint efforts during the marriage) should, on divorce, be split equally between them is now both uncontroversial and normally the starting point for the determination of financial remedy proceedings, at least in so far as they involve the distribution of capital assets. However, the actual process of achieving that equal split can, in all but straightforward cases, be fraught with complex argument ...

White and *Miller* and *McFarlane* were 'big money' cases where resources exceeded the parties' needs. Whilst the principles expressed in these cases are of universal application, the reality in many cases will be that most of the resources are required to meet the parties' basic needs (eg, to house the children and the spouse primarily caring for them), and this will provide good reason to depart from equality. In the case of B *v* B [2008] 2 FLR 1627 the court said that fairness is not necessarily the same as equality. Fairness will always depend on the individual facts of the case.

4.5.1.2   Resources

Although the statute does not list the factors in any specific order of importance, it is clear that, generally, the determining factor will be the parties' resources, income and capital. This is as much the case for PPOs as for lump sums and property adjustment orders. Whilst it is convenient to consider the various orders for financial provision separately, in reality the orders interrelate. For example, a husband with a high income may be able to transfer the home to his wife because he is able to raise a mortgage to purchase a new home for himself, but this would be a sensible solution only if the wife has enough income to finance the costs of running her home.

Earning capacity

The court will take into account the parties' income from all sources. Earnings are the starting point. Fringe benefits, such as a company car, free petrol, paid telephone bills, etc will also be taken into account.

As well as looking at actual earnings, the court will also consider potential earnings. When assessing a party's earning capacity, the court will take a realistic approach. If a wife has qualifications which are in demand and has recent work experience, the court will bear in mind her ability to earn a living, taking into account her commitments to the children. Before deciding on a party's earning capacity, the court will carefully consider the person's skills, age and time out of work, the possibility and cost of retraining and the job market. If the court is of the view that a party is perversely refusing to work in order to frustrate a financial application against him, it could make an order by attributing a notional earning capacity to him.

Earning capacity may be significant in determining the duration of periodical payments or a party's occupation of the matrimonial home. If the court considers that a party could reasonably be expected to take steps to increase his earning capacity by, say, undertaking further training, this could prompt the court to limit the period for which maintenance is payable (see **4.6**). It might also result in a reduction of a party's share on sale of the home if a return to work or significant promotion is anticipated with reasonable certainty.

Although future earning capacity is a factor to be taken into account, in *Waggott v Waggott* [2019] EWCA Civ 727 the Court made it clear that earning capacity is not in the nature of an asset to be shared between the parties.

Welfare benefits

As a general rule, means tested welfare benefits will not be regarded as a resource since the supporting spouse cannot free himself of his responsibilities to maintain his family by casting that burden onto the taxpayer (*Barnes v Barnes* [1972] 3 All ER 872). However, there will frequently be cases where there are insufficient resources to maintain two households. In such cases, it would be an affront to common sense to ignore the availability of state benefits. If both parties are claiming benefits, it would be rare for the court to make any order because, as a general principle, the court would not make an order reducing the payer's income below subsistence level.

New partner

Income from other members of the household, such as 'board' paid by a working child or lodger, will be taken into account as a resource. More problematic is the extent to which the means of a party's new partner are taken into account. The court cannot redistribute a third party's income or assets, and therefore it cannot, for example, order a new wife to pay maintenance to the former wife. However, if a second wife was earning and contributing to the household expenses, it would be wrong if the court was unable to take that fact into account. The practice which has emerged, therefore, is that the court will assess the extent to which contributions made by the new partner reduce the party's outgoings, thereby increasing the money available for maintenance payments (see *Slater v Slater and Another* [1982] 3 FLR 364). The paying spouse would still be expected to share the living costs with his new partner, and, therefore, even if that partner was very wealthy and meeting all the expenses, this would not result in the payer being liable to pay his entire income to his first family. If the applicant has a new partner, the same principles apply: to the extent that he is supporting the applicant, her needs will be reduced. Clearly, the court will have regard to the stability of that relationship and may decide to preserve the party's option to apply to vary an order should the relationship break down. If the recipient remarries, she will lose her entitlement to maintenance altogether.

The existence of a new partner can also influence capital provision. In *AB v CB* [2014] EWHC 2998 (Fam), the judge said that he could not ignore the fact that the wife was in a 'strong' nine-month relationship (which she had failed to disclose in the proceedings) even though the wife's evidence was that she did not intend to cohabit. The relationship was reflected in the capital order made in the wife's favour, as the judge said that if the wife had been single and he could see that continuing then he would have doubts as to whether the capital amount would be sufficient to meet the wife's needs.

If a party is not in a new partnership, the court will not speculate on that party's prospects of improving his or her financial circumstances by finding a partner. Nevertheless, if a party does have a firm intention to remarry or cohabit at the time an order for provision is being sought (including an order by consent), this will amount to a material fact which should be disclosed to the other party and to the court. This information may affect the outcome of proceedings or negotiations, for example as periodical payments terminate on remarriage they may be more appropriate than a lump sum or property adjustment order if a party is soon to be amply supported and housed by a new spouse. If remarriage plans are not disclosed then any order made is liable to be set aside (see *Livesey (formerly Jenkins) v Jenkins* [1985] AC 424 and **11.7**).

Future prospects

The court will give a wide interpretation to 'property' and 'financial resources'. The court is not limited to considering assets acquired jointly or during the marriage, or even existing assets. As with income, the court may take into account a party's future prospects, for example, a terminal gratuity, or an interest under a settlement or inheritance (but generally only if the donor has already died). If it is uncertain whether or when a party might acquire the anticipated property, or how much that property will be worth, it might be appropriate for the court to adjourn the application. In such a case, no final decision will be made, leaving the parties to wait and see whether (and to what extent) the anticipated property materialises during the period of the adjournment. In the case of *Michael v Michael* [1986] 2 FLR 389, Nourse LJ said it would be wrong to take into account the possibility of a wife's inheritance from her mother who was in her sixties and suffered from high blood pressure, saying the world was full of women in their eighties who had high blood pressure in their sixties. Although in *Alireza v Radwan and Others* [2017] EWCA Civ 1545, the fact that the inheritance was subject to forced heirship rules (which operate in some jurisdictions and dictate that certain family members must benefit from an estate) created sufficient certainty for the court to take the inheritance into account as an asset that one party was likely to have in the foreseeable future.

Non-matrimonial assets

In recent years, a considerable body of case law has developed on the issue of the proper treatment to be given to assets which can be categorised as 'non-matrimonial'. Such assets might include those which were inherited or owned by one party before the marriage, or which have been acquired by one party after separation. What has emerged from these cases is a reiteration that s 25(2)(a) is not confined to assets accumulated during the marriage, and the courts have the power to deal with the parties' resources whenever and however acquired. Consequently, if one party asserts that there are non-matrimonial assets deserving of different treatment, it is for him to prove it.

Initially, these cases revealed a divergence of opinion amongst the judiciary as to how non-matrimonial assets should be taken into account. Some judges took a scientific approach, attributing a value to the non-matrimonial assets and then excluding them from the resources available for division (see, eg, *N v F (Financial orders: pre-acquired wealth)* [2011] EWHC 586 (Fam)). Other judges preferred a less clinical approach, treating the nature and source of the assets as an unmatched contribution by one party or as one of the circumstances of the case to be taken into account when determining the requirements of fairness and which may provide a justification to depart from equality (see, eg, *Robson v Robson* [2010] EWCA Civ 1771). However, more recently, in *Hart v Hart* [2017] EWCA Civ 1306 the Court of Appeal discouraged both a too forensic approach to establishing the existence of non-matrimonial assets and a too formulaic approach in deciding upon their treatment.

The approach which seems to have emerged from these cases is that the court will first consider whether there is any property which can be categorised as non-matrimonial. If there is a clear distinction to be made between matrimonial and non-matrimonial property then the court will usually apply it so as to effectively leave the non-matrimonial property out of the equation when dividing the assets. As Mostyn J observed in *JL v SL (No 2) (Appeal: Non-Matrimonial Property)* [2015] EWHC 360 (Fam):

> Given that a claim to share non-matrimonial property (as opposed to having a sum awarded from it to meet needs) would have no moral or principled foundation, it is hard to envisage a case where such an award would be made. If you like, such a case would be as rare as a white leopard.

Ultimately, however, the court will make an overall assessment so as to achieve fairness and, as Moylan LJ said in *Hart v Hart*, '… fairness has a broad horizon'. As part of that overall assessment, the court may conclude that whilst there are non-matrimonial assets, they should not be treated any differently from the other assets in the case. This may be because the non-matrimonial assets have become so intermingled with the parties' other assets that it is not possible to distinguish them. Similarly, at the end of a long marriage, the fact that some assets were acquired before the marriage began may have lost its significance with the passage of time.

As indicated in the quote from *JL v SL* above, a much more common reason for the court refusing to afford non-matrimonial assets different treatment is that they are required in order to meet the parties' needs. In *GS v L (Financial remedies: Pre-acquired assets: Need)* [2011] EWHC 1759 (Fam), King J refused to entertain the husband's attempt to ring-fence approximately £1.5m of the total £4m assets on the grounds that he had owned prior them to the marriage. The judge said that it was simply unnecessary to consider the 'vexed question' of whether those assets were non-matrimonial assets or not because they were required in order to meet the needs of the parties and the children. Similarly, in *ND v GD* [2021] EWFC 53, the bulk of the assets were non-matrimonial, having been inherited by the husband five years before the separation. Nevertheless, the court was prepared to make an order 'invading' the non-matrimonial assets in order to meet the particular needs of the wife who had been diagnosed with Young Onset Alzheimer's.

Whilst it is clear from the recent cases that the existence of non-matrimonial assets is capable of having a significant bearing on the outcome, whether this will in fact be so depends on the facts of the individual case and the operation of the other s 25 factors. It is worth remembering that s 25 itself draws no distinction between matrimonial and non-matrimonial assets. As Moylan LJ put it *Hart v Hart*, 'It is, perhaps, worth reflecting that the concept of property being either matrimonial or non-matrimonial property is a legal construct. Moreover, it is a construct which is not always capable of clear identification.'

Lost assets

In some cases, the resources the parties have when they come before the court would have been much greater were it not for the fact that one party has lost money or frittered assets away, for example as a result of gambling debts. In such cases, the courts may sometimes be prepared to 'add back' the value of the lost assets so that the other party does not suffer any reduction in his entitlement. In the case of *Evans v Evans* [2013] EWHC 506 (Fam), the court said that for assets to be added back, there must be evidence that one party had wantonly dissipated assets, and a notional reattribution must be necessary in order to enable the court to achieve a fair outcome. (See also **4.5.1.8.**)

4.5.1.3 Needs

Section 25(2)(b) of the MCA 1973 directs the court to consider the parties' needs, obligations and responsibilities: for most couples the primary task will be to assess each party's essential needs. The most basic of these needs is the provision of accommodation for both parties and any children. Also important will be the expenses connected with the accommodation, and the costs of food and clothing.

These costs will vary from case to case, depending on the size of the home, the number of people living in it and the general cost of living in the particular locality. In addition to considering these basic needs, the court must also consider the parties' existing obligations, for example, hire-purchase, bank loans, school fees, insurance premiums, etc. The courts have tended to construe s 25(2)(b) as confining them to have regard only to such requirements as are reasonable – as Ward J stated in *Delaney v Delaney* [1990] 2 FLR 457:

> In all life, for those who are divorced as well as for those who are not divorced, indulging one's whims or even one's reasonable desires must be held in check by the constraints imposed by limited resources and compelling obligations.

However, there will usually be little to gain in increasing the legal costs burden by challenging a party's existing outgoings unless he is being excessively extravagant. If a party is already committed to make certain payments, the courts will be reluctant to disregard the impact of those liabilities on that party's disposable income.

One of the most controversial obligations is that of the respondent who has 'indulged' himself by forming a new relationship (and possibly by having further children). It was noted (at **4.5.1.2**) that the resources of a party's new partner would be borne in mind when assessing that party's disposable income. It is, therefore, only reasonable that if the new partner is financially dependent upon the party, this fact will be taken into account. The court will consider the extent to which the financially dominant party can meet the needs of the other party and the children of the family, bearing in mind his additional responsibilities towards his new partner (and family). The result may be that a substantially reduced order is made, in some cases leaving the applicant to look to the State to meet her needs. The point was made graphically in the case of *Delaney* (above):

> Whilst this court deprecates any notion that a former husband and extant father may slough off the tight skin of familial responsibility and may slither into and lose himself in the greener grass on the other side, nonetheless this court has proclaimed and will proclaim that it looks to the realities of the real world in which we live, and that among the realities of life is that there is a life after divorce. The respondent husband is entitled to order his life in such a way as will hold in reasonable balance the responsibilities to his existing family which he carries into his new life, as well as his proper aspirations for that new future.

In S v S (*Financial Provision: Departing from Equality*) [2001] 2 FLR 246, the good reason for the (in this case, small) departure from equality was that the husband needed more to meet his responsibilities towards his new family. Similarly, if a respondent has obligations to wives and children of former marriages, these will also be taken into account when considering the application of any subsequent spouse.

In April 2018 the Family Justice Council published the second edition of its Guidance on Financial Needs on Divorce. The Guidance does not seek to redefine 'needs', nor fetter judicial discretion, but it does provide a helpful overview of relevant case law. The Guidance acknowledges that 'needs' is a broad concept in family cases.

Where the parties are well off, the court will look beyond their basic needs, and the other s 25 factors are likely to play a more significant role in determining the outcome.

4.5.1.4   Standard of living

In applying s 25(2)(c), the court will not attempt the impossible by seeking to preserve both parties' standard of living at the level prior to the breakdown of the marriage. On separation, there will be the increased costs of running two households, usually without any increase in either party's income. Instead, the court will endeavour to ensure that the inevitable reduction in the parties' standard of living is borne by them evenly.

Where a couple have lived frugally and enjoyed only a modest standard of living, perhaps preferring to invest their resources in their business or to save for their retirement, the court will look at the wider picture. An applicant would not be penalised for having lived carefully during the marriage by an order for humble provision. On the contrary, the order should reflect the contributions made by the thrifty housekeeper towards the family's prosperity.

4.5.1.5   Ages of the parties and the duration of the marriage

Taken in isolation, the importance of s 25(2)(d) is not immediately obvious. However, taken in conjunction with the other factors, its significance is more apparent: a young spouse ending a short marriage is likely to have an earning and borrowing capacity, and therefore a package of orders to enable a couple to achieve financial independence (known as a clean break: see **4.6**) may be appropriate. On the other hand, an older spouse leaving a long marriage may have little or no earning capacity, but is likely to have made a greater contribution to the marriage, and there are usually more family assets to distribute.

In terms of the duration of the marriage, it is the cohabitation during the marriage which is relevant in s 25(2)(d): the Court of Appeal in *Krystman v Krystman* [1973] 3 All ER 247 refused to order financial provision where the couple lived together for only two weeks of their 26-year marriage. As for cohabitation prior to marriage, the court is not required to take this into account under s 25(2)(d); however, it may be taken into account when the court considers 'all the circumstances of the case' under s 25(1) (*Kokosinski v Kokosinski* [1980] Fam 72). In the case of *Gojkovic v Gojkovic* [1990] 1 FLR 140, the wife received a substantial award based on her contributions to the family fortune made largely during their pre-marital cohabitation.

One issue which has occupied the courts in a number of cases over the years is the impact of a 'short' marriage on the award. In *Miller and McFarlane* (see **4.5.1.1**), the House of Lords said that the general approach in short marriages was to consider whether and to what extent there was a good reason to depart from equality. Lord Nichols referred to the 'instinctive feeling' that parties would generally have less call upon each other following the breakdown of a short marriage. Nevertheless, the House of Lords was at pains to emphasise that each case would turn upon its own facts. On the facts of *Miller*, the high standard of living that the parties had enjoyed and the fact that Mr Miller's wealth had increased dramatically during the marriage justified Mrs Miller receiving £5 million after less than three years of marriage.

The relevance of a short marriage was considered again in *E v L* [2021] EWFC 60. In this case, the couple were married in June 2017 and a decree nisi was pronounced in October 2020. During that time, there were two periods of separation totalling six months; the couple finally separated in late 2019 although the exact date was disputed. The total assets were £9.2 million. The husband argued that because the marriage was childless and short, the wife was only entitled to a sum which was sufficient to meet her conservatively assessed needs. Mostyn J dismissed the first point, saying that the fact that the marriage was childless was irrelevant and '... should be banished from any consideration of whether there should be a departure from the application of the equal sharing principle'. Secondly, Mostyn J said that the shortness of a marriage was not (save in the most exceptional of cases) a reason to depart from equality. Accordingly, the wealth generated from the start of the relationship to the date of trial was to be divided equally, with the result that the wife was awarded a little over £1.5 million.

4.5.1.6 Disability

If a party suffers from a physical or mental disability, this may affect that party's resources as he may have a reduced (or no) earning capacity. It will also affect the sufferer's needs if, for example, expensive care, treatment or equipment is required. The court will also bear in mind the effect of any future deterioration in the party's condition. It has been held that damages awarded to compensate a party for personal injury are rightly to be regarded as a resource for that party under s 25(2)(a), notwithstanding that they were assessed to compensate that party for his loss, pain and suffering.

4.5.1.7 Contributions to the family

The court is required by s 25(2)(f) to consider the parties' past and anticipated future contributions to the welfare of the family, both materially and otherwise. Where a spouse has contributed in non-financial terms to the marriage, it is not necessary for them to show the extensive contributions in kind of the sort required to establish a proprietary interest under a constructive trust (see **Chapter 16**). The court is not deciding the ownership of the family assets, but rather how each party's assets should be shared.

It has been recognised for some time that a spouse who cares for the home and the family contributes as much to the family as the spouse who goes out to work. Indeed in *Miller and McFarlane* (see **4.5.1.1**) Lord Nichols described as 'a principle of universal application' the fact that in assessing the parties' contributions there should be no bias in favour of the money-earner and against the home-maker. The court will bear in mind the impact of that role on the carer's career. It will also take into account the continuing contributions that the parent will make as the children grow up.

In *Cowan v Cowan* [2001] 2 FLR 192, the Court of Appeal recognised that one party may have made a special contribution in some way. In the case of Mr Cowan, this was demonstrated by his 'entrepreneurial flair, inventiveness and hard work'. The Court found that fairness permitted, and sometimes required, a departure from equality in order to reflect that special contribution. However, subsequent cases have demonstrated that the circumstances in which one party will be able to successfully argue that they have made a special contribution which must be reflected in the court's final award are restricted to the truly exceptional. In *Work v Gray* [2017] EWCA Civ 270, the Court said:

The contribution has to derive from something the contributor has done. Accordingly, if the contribution does not derive from the exceptional and individual quality of the contributor, it could not be a special contribution.

In *XW v XH* [2019] EWCA Civ 2262, the Court re-emphasised the need for exceptional circumstances and added that the approach should be to consider whether there was such a disparity in the parties' respective contributions that it would be inequitable to disregard it.

Conversely, the court may also take into account any negative contribution made by a party: in the case of *E v E (Financial Provision)* [1990] 2 FLR 233, Mrs E, while having an adulterous affair, was said to have spent thousands of pounds on clothes and to have withdrawn from family life. The judge found that 'the wife's contribution to the welfare of the family was negative' and added, 'I do not find it necessary to consider conduct as a separate item. Such conduct as has been shown can properly be dealt with by considering the contribution the wife has made to the welfare of the family'. Whilst, then, it would be exceptional for adultery to be taken into account under s 25(2)(g) (see **4.5.1.8**), if affairs have resulted in a party failing to contribute to the family, this may be taken into account.

4.5.1.8 Conduct

Under s 25(2)(g), the court is required to have regard to conduct that it would be inequitable to disregard. However, either party to the divorce may apply for financial provision: it is not a case of the 'guilty respondent' maintaining the 'innocent petitioner'. Whether, and to what extent, one party will be required to support the other will depend on all the factors appearing in s 25, of which conduct is but one.

Conduct in the context of s 25(2)(g) may take the form of personal misconduct by one party towards the other during the marriage and/or post separation. Such misconduct will usually only influence the overall award by the court where it has a financial impact. Examples of cases where conduct was an issue include:

(a) *K v K (Conduct)* [1990] 2 FLR 225: the husband had a serious drink problem, which contributed to his refusal to obtain employment and his neglect of the house, which ultimately forced its sale. Although the husband succeeded in obtaining a lump sum, his application for periodical payments was dismissed.

(b) *H v H (Financial Relief: Attempted Murder as Conduct)* [2005] EWHC 2911 (Fam): the husband subjected the wife to a vicious knife attack and was subsequently convicted of attempted murder. As a result of the attack, the wife could no longer continue with her career as a police officer. The court considered it fair in all the circumstances that the wife should receive the greater share of the matrimonial assets, including the entire sale proceeds from the former matrimonial home. The husband's conduct had had the effect of placing the wife's needs as a much higher priority than the husband's in the court's consideration of s 25 of the MCA 1973, because the situation in which the wife found herself was clearly the husband's fault.

(c) *Evans v Evans* [1989] 1 FLR 351: the court discharged a maintenance order made in favour of the wife after she was convicted (and imprisoned) for inciting others to murder the husband.

There have been cases in which conduct which did not have a bearing on finances was taken into account. For example, in *K v L* [2010] EWCA Civ 125, the husband was awarded a negligible sum despite the wife's wealth of £4.3 million and a 24-year marriage. The husband had been convicted of the sexual abuse of two of the wife's grandchildren. The Court decided that such conduct was the ultimately decisive factor which overrode all the other s 25(2) factors. However, such cases are rare. As Mr Justice Mostyn said in *OG v AG* [2020] EWFC 52:

... times have changed. The financial remedy court is no longer a court of morals. Conduct should be taken into account not only where it is inequitable to disregard but only where its impact is financially measurable. It is unprincipled for the court to stick a finger in the air and arbitrarily to fine a party for what it regards as immoral conduct.

The conduct complained of may be that one party has deliberately dissipated assets which otherwise would have been available for the court to distribute. In such a case, the court may adopt the approach of notionally 'adding back' the dissipated assets and basing its award on the increased pot.

Another possibility is that a party's misconduct may relate to the proceedings themselves. This may take the form of a failure to make full and frank disclosure of means. In such a case, the court will draw inferences in order to form a view of the individual's wealth and make its order accordingly. The court does not need to put a precise value on the undisclosed assets but must be satisfied that there is sufficient wealth to meet the order (*Moher v Moher* [2019] EWCA Civ 1482).

Litigation misconduct, such as failing to produce required documentation or unreasonably refusing to negotiate (see **2.5** and **10.11.2**), will not usually affect the quantification of order the court makes but may be penalised in costs under r 28.3(6) of the FPR 2010. For example, in *T v T (Interception of Documents)* [1994] 2 FLR 1083, the wife intercepted the husband's mail and broke into his office in an attempt to ascertain his true financial position. The court's approach was that, whilst this misconduct would not be brought into the reckoning of the substantive award, it was relevant in respect of costs.

However, it is not the case that litigation misconduct will never affect the financial award. In *Rothschild v de Souza* [2020] EWCA Civ 1215, the Court of Appeal confirmed that litigation misconduct, whether in relation to the financial proceedings or other litigation, could be taken into account under s 25(2)(g), pointing out that the depletion of matrimonial assets could not always be remedied by a costs order. In this case, the litigation was described as being on a 'massive scale', and the judge at first instance referred to an 'unnecessary haemorrhage of money' in costs due to the manner in which the husband had conducted both the financial case and other litigation. The result was that the court awarded the wife £1.73 million which was necessary to meet her needs and those of the children; the husband would be left with £24,000 (after repaying a loan to his mother). Moylan LJ said that 'a party cannot "fritter away assets" on litigation and then claim as great a share of what is left as he would have been entitled to had he not acted in a manner within the scope of s25(2)(g)'.

An example of extreme litigation conduct, and the court's reaction to it, is provided by *Veluppillai v Veluppillai* [2015] EWHC 3095 (Fam). By the time of the final hearing there had already been over 30 separate hearings, including four appeals, even though the parties' total assets amounted to only £1.3m. The husband's conduct, which the judge described as 'truly abysmal', included failing to disclose assets, assaulting and threatening to kill the wife and her counsel, and sending threatening and abusive e-mails to the judge and his clerk. The judge not only ordered the husband to pay the wife's costs, he also directed that his judgment be published without anonymisation, in order to expose the husband's conduct, and that the husband's e-mails be passed to the Police Commissioner to see if criminal charges could be brought against the husband.

Whilst the majority of cases on s 25(2)(g) deal with misconduct by one party, it should be noted that the wording of the sub-section is not restricted to 'wrongdoing'. In *K v K (Ancillary Relief: Prenuptial Agreement)* [2003] 1 FLR 120 the court found that the fact that the parties had previously entered into a prenuptial agreement was conduct it would be inequitable to disregard.

4.5.1.9 Potential financial loss

When dealing with applications ancillary to divorce or nullity (but not judicial separation), s 25(2)(h) requires the court to consider any potential benefits a party might lose as a result of the termination of the marriage. The loss of certain types of pension rights is an example. As a widow or widower, the applicant may be entitled to the deceased spouse's pension: that right would be lost on the termination of the marriage. This can be a serious problem to, say, a financially dependent middle-aged wife of a long marriage. In such cases there may be an argument for giving that spouse a greater share of the other matrimonial assets to mitigate the problem, and perhaps also for preserving the wife's claim under the Inheritance (Provision for Family and Dependants) Act 1975 (I(PFD)A 1975).

Other contingent benefits which a party might lose include a share in life policies which are yet to mature. The lost opportunity to share in the other party's prospective inheritance will be taken into account only if it is sufficiently certain in time and amount (see **4.4.1**).

4.5.1.10 Human rights

Some legislative provisions, including s 25 of the MCA 1973, cannot be interpreted in accordance with the ECHR. Article 5 of the Seventh Protocol states that 'spouses shall enjoy equality of rights and responsibilities of a private law character between them, and in their relations with their children, as to marriage, and in the event of dissolution'. Yet, under s 25, the starting point in a financial application is not necessarily equality between the spouses. Because of the difficulty in interpretation of s 25 and other provisions, Article 5 was specifically excluded from being incorporated into the HRA 1998.

4.5.2 Provision for children

The interests of the children of the family are borne in mind when any financial order is made under the MCA 1973. Section 25(1) requires the court 'to give first consideration to the welfare while a minor of any child of the family' when making any financial order on divorce. Therefore, when considering its powers to provide for the parties, any order made will reflect not only the needs of those parties but also the needs of the children.

The court has wide powers to make capital orders in favour of the children of the family. However, it is not usual for the court to make capital orders in favour of children: in *Lord Lilford v Glynn* [1979] 1 WLR 78, Orr LJ stated that

> a father, even the richest father, ought not to be regarded as under financial obligations or responsibilities to provide funds for the purpose of such settlements that are envisaged in this case on children who are under no disability and whose maintenance and education are secure.

In contrast, provision will be required for children's maintenance. It has already been noted (at **4.1**) that applications for children's maintenance will usually be dealt with under the CSA 1991, either by agreement or by application to the CMS rather than to the court. This is considered in detail in **Chapter 7**. However, the court will continue to have limited jurisdiction to deal with maintenance orders for certain children, and in such cases the factors in s 25 must be taken into account.

When considering what orders should be made for children, the court is guided by s 25(3) in all cases. Section 25(4) lists further factors to be taken into account where the payer is not the natural parent of the child.

4.5.2.1 Children of the family

Section 25(3) directs the court to consider the following factors when making orders for children of the family:

(a)   the financial needs of the child;

(b)   the income, earning capacity (if any), property and other financial resources of the child;

(c)   any physical or mental disability of the child;

(d)   the manner in which he was being and in which the parties to the marriage expected him to be educated or trained;

(e)   the considerations mentioned in relation to the parties to the marriage in section 25(2)(a), (b), (c) and (e).

The factors are generally self-explanatory, but one or two points are worth noting. Clearly, the needs of the child will increase with age: the section does not refer to the child's future needs as these are best dealt with by further applications for increased maintenance as and when required.

Most young children do not have any income or earning capacity. However, maintenance may be sought for children who are receiving wages, grants or scholarships whilst in education or training, and such sums would be taken into account. In wealthier families, children may have trust income to be borne in mind.

The court will wish to ensure that adequate provision is made for children with a disability. It might, in particular, consider making secure PPOs to provide for a stable income. It might also be appropriate to make lump sum orders to meet capital expenditure on, for example, special equipment adapted for the child's handicap. The disability may also affect the duration of the order, as special circumstances could lead to the provision continuing well into adulthood.

Section 25(3)(e) requires the court to look at the parties' resources, needs, standard of living and any disability. This is because the parties' ability to provide for their children is directly related to and dependent upon their own circumstances.

4.5.2.2   Step-children

Section 25(4) requires the following additional factors to be considered where the child in question, although a child of the family, is not the natural child of the party against whom an order is being sought:

(a)   whether that party assumed any responsibility for the child's maintenance, and, if so, to the extent to which, and the basis upon which, that party assumed such responsibility and to the length of time for which that party discharged such responsibility;

(b)   whether in assuming and discharging such responsibility that party did so knowing that the child was not his or her own;

(c)   the liability of any other person to maintain the child.

The section recognises that a child may be a child of more than one family and, as a consequence, several people may be liable to maintain that child. For example, a husband may have treated his wife's child from a previous relationship as his own: in such a case both the husband and the father could be looked to for support. Clearly, the factors in s 25(4) will be highly relevant in determining the extent of this support. If the child's father is meeting the child's maintenance requirement under the CSA 1991 (see **Chapter 7**), this may relieve the step-father from paying maintenance.

4.6   THE CLEAN BREAK

4.6.1   The principle

The object of the clean break is to settle once and for all the parties' financial responsibility towards each other and to end their financial interdependence, to enable them to leave their past behind them and begin anew. The advantages of such an approach have long been recognised, but with the enactment of the Matrimonial and Family Proceedings Act 1984, which introduced s 25A into the MCA 1973, the concept of the clean break was given statutory backing. The court has a duty to consider whether a clean break should be achieved.

Section 25A(1) states:

Where on or after the grant of a decree of divorce or nullity of marriage the court decides to exercise its powers under sections 23(1)(a), (b) or (c), 24 or 24A above in favour of a party to the marriage, it shall be the duty of the court to consider whether it would be appropriate so to exercise those powers that the financial obligations of each party towards the other will be terminated as soon after the grant of the decree as the court considers just and reasonable.

The wording of the section only imposes a duty to consider the appropriateness of a clean break, it does not oblige the court to make a clean break wherever possible. Nevertheless, s 25A(1) has been described as a 'statutory steer' towards a clean break. In practice the judiciary view a clean break as the preferred outcome. In *Matthews v Matthews* [2013] EWCA Civ 1874, Tomlinson LJ said:

> We are here considering an exercise of discretion, but it is an exercise of discretion in which Parliament has indicated that there should be a clear presumption in favour of making a clean break, in the sense that it is something which the court is mandated to consider ... as an initial consideration.

But the clean break is not to be imposed at all cost. In reality the court must weigh all the statutory factors in deciding whether a clean break is appropriate on the facts of the particular case; as Lord Nichols said in *Miller and McFarlane* (see **4.5.1.1**):

> [I]f the claimant is owed compensation and capital assets are not available, it is difficult to see why the social desirability of a clean break should be sufficient reason for depriving the claimant of that compensation.

It will never be appropriate to have a clean break between a parent and child, as a party can never sever his responsibility towards a child of the family. It is possible, however, to have a clean break between the parties even where there are children involved. In cases where the court has jurisdiction to make orders for children, it might award less than it would otherwise do because the parent with whom the children are residing has agreed a clean break settlement. For example, the father might be using a significant amount of his income to pay for a loan which was raised in order to make a generous lump sum payment for the mother who is caring for the children. The father would clearly have less income available to support the children directly, but they will be benefiting indirectly from the lump sum payment. However, should the mother subsequently apply for a maintenance calculation under the CSA 1991, the father might then find himself being required to pay substantially more maintenance than he had bargained for. This is because when calculating the liability to pay maintenance under the 1991 Act, no account is taken of any clean break made on divorce.

4.6.2 The practice

4.6.2.1 Income orders

So far as periodical payments are concerned, the most extreme form of clean break is an order dismissing the application coupled with a bar against the making of any further applications. Section 25A(3) empowers the court to make such an order:

> Where on or after the grant of a decree of divorce or nullity of marriage an application is made by a party to the marriage for a periodical payments order in his or her favour, then, if the court considers that no continuing obligation should be imposed on either party to make or secure periodical payments in favour of the other, the court may dismiss the application with a direction that the applicant shall not be entitled to make any further application in relation to the marriage for an order under section 23(1)(a) or (b) above.

Less extreme than this immediate clean break is an order for 'term maintenance'. Such an order allows a party to receive maintenance for a limited period only in order to tide him over while he adapts to becoming financially self-sufficient. The clean break will be deferred to a future date. The term of the maintenance will vary from case to case: it may be for six months to enable the party to find a job, or for two or three years to allow for retraining. If there are children, it may be for a longer period until they are less dependent on the applicant.

The benefits of term maintenance have been given statutory support by s 25A(2), which states:

> Where the court decides in such a case to make a periodical payments or secured periodical payments order in favour of a party to the marriage, the court shall in particular consider whether it would be appropriate to require those payments to be made or secured only for such term as would in the opinion of the court be sufficient to enable the party in whose favour the order is made to adjust without undue hardship to the termination of his or her financial dependence on the other party.

If events do not work out according to plan and the applicant fails to achieve the anticipated financial independence, in most cases the applicant will be able to apply under s 31 of the MCA 1973 to extend the maintenance for a further period. It is essential that any such application is made before the expiry of the term as the order itself ceases at that point. In deciding whether to grant such a request, however, the court would enquire into the reason for the applicant's failure to become self-sufficient. If, for example, the availability of work decreases and the court is satisfied that the applicant has made genuine efforts to seek employment, it is likely to deal with the application sympathetically.

The court is empowered under s 28(1A) to direct that the applicant will not be entitled to make any application to extend the term regardless of any change of circumstances. Whilst this has the advantage for the payer of certainty, in that he will eventually be rid of the obligation to maintain his ex-spouse, the inflexibility can lead to hardship to the recipient (see *Waterman v Waterman* [1989] 1 FLR 380). If the children are very young, the court is unlikely to consider non-extendable term maintenance to be appropriate.

4.6.2.2   Capital orders

A clean break is commonly achieved by means of a lump sum payment in return for a dismissal of all other claims. One party may prefer to pay a relatively substantial lump sum rather than have the burden of even modest maintenance hanging over him for an indefinite period. This is possible, though, only if there are sufficient capital assets available. A party may need to borrow in order to raise the necessary capital.

Particular problems arise if the main asset involved is a business. Selling the business to realise capital may be 'killing the goose that lays the golden egg'.

Lump sums are discussed further at **9.7**. It may be that there is no clean break initially between the parties, but that one occurs later on; see **11.8.1**, which deals with the court's power to impose a clean break at a later stage, by making lump sum adjustment orders, on an application for variation or discharge of an existing periodical payment or secured periodical payments order.

There are only two ways of dealing with the matrimonial home to achieve an immediate clean break: by immediate sale, or by a transfer into one party's sole name. These and other orders for the matrimonial home are considered in detail in **Chapter 9**.

As part of a clean break package a provision is often included under s 15 of the I(PFD)A 1975. This enables the court to direct that neither party may apply under s 2 of the 1975 Act for financial provision out of the other's estate.

4.7   PENSIONS ON DIVORCE

A pension is often a person's most valuable asset, or it will be when it comes to being paid, so it is not surprising that dividing it should be a major consideration in settling the financial aspects of divorce, particularly for older couples. Since its original enactment, the MCA 1973 has been the subject of significant amendments which have radically altered the treatment of pensions on divorce. As a result of these amendments, there are three possible ways of dealing with pension rights on divorce. These are:

(a)   the traditional approach of adjusting the other matrimonial assets to take account of pension rights ('off-setting');

(b)   an order which allows for all or part of any pension or lump sum arising at retirement to be 'earmarked' for the other spouse ('pension attachment');

(c)   splitting the pension so that the pension benefits are physically subdivided at the time of the divorce; the parties will then have two entirely separate pensions which they can contribute to in the future in the normal way ('pension sharing').

4.7.1   The traditional approach – 'off-setting'

As originally enacted, the MCA 1973 was limited both in terms of taking pension rights into account and the orders that could be made regarding those rights. Section 25(2)(a) says that when the courts consider the 'financial resources' of the parties this can include those which will be available 'in the foreseeable future'. However, this phrase is not defined. Historically this often meant that at best, pension rights were afforded a passing acknowledgement as one of 'all the circumstances of the case' in s 25(1), or at worst completely ignored despite their potential value.

Added to this, the courts, in the past, did not have any powers to make orders specifically dealing with the parties' pension arrangements. Historically, the best that the courts could do in making appropriate settlements on divorce was to allocate to one spouse (normally the wife) a proportion of the matrimonial assets equivalent to the approximate value of the pension benefits lost. This meant that a trade-off was being made between the pension rights and other matrimonial assets. However, this is not always an entirely appropriate solution: there are problems of valuation, and there is the fact that the trade-off must be made immediately at the time of the divorce, yet the pension benefits themselves will be in the future and are contingent on certain events (eg retirement, death) and possibly may never materialise. Despite subsequent amendments to the MCA 1973, off-setting is still available to the courts, and may remain the appropriate approach on the individual facts of the case.

4.7.2   'Pension attachments'

The obvious limitations to off-setting prompted the Government of the day to introduce reforms. The first step was taken in s 166 of the Pensions Act 1995, which inserted three new sections into the MCA 1973, namely ss 25B, 25C and 25D (see **Appendix 1(A)**). These sections allow the court to make pension attachment orders so that certain payments under a pension are to be paid not to the member of the pension scheme but to his former spouse. The amendments addressed the issue of the court being able to take pension rights into account.

Section 25B provides that, in relation to benefits under a pension scheme, the words 'in the foreseeable future' in s 25(2)(a) shall not apply. This means that the court can take into account any future pension benefits.

In terms of the orders that the court can make, s 25B gives the court the power, when making a financial provision order, to direct the trustees or managers of a pension scheme to pay some (or even all) of the pension to the spouse without the pension rights. If the pension is not yet payable (ie the member-spouse has not yet retired) the court may make a deferred order. Such orders are effectively deferred periodical payment orders.

Most pension schemes include a lump sum benefit payable on retirement, or on the death of the member before retirement. Section 25C gives the court the power to make a lump sum order which directs the trustees or managers of the pension scheme to pay the whole or part of that lump sum, when it becomes due, to the other spouse.

Although these amendments gave the courts more possibilities for redressing the harsh effects of loss of pension rights on divorce, there were still problems.

Pension attachments will usually be deferred until the member-spouse retires or dies. This means that the other spouse has no control over the money until that time and, for example, the member-spouse could decide to retire early or late. Also, such orders are contrary to the clean break principle. As a result of these problems, few pension attachments have been made in practice. They are likely to be rarer in the future now that changes to the pension rules introduced in April 2015 enable some pension holders over 55 to withdraw their pension in cash (see **9.8**).

There have only been a few reported cases involving pension attachments (eg T v T (*Financial Relief: Pensions*) [1998] 1 FLR 1072, and *Burrow v Burrow* [1999] 1 FLR 508). In both these cases, the courts confirmed that the court, in determining whether to make a pension attachment and the amount, if any, should exercise its discretion under the established s 25 criteria.

4.7.3 'Pension sharing'

The final step in reform came with the Welfare Reform and Pensions Act 1999, which inserted s 24B into the MCA 1973, creating a new type of financial order – a pension sharing order (now further extended by the addition of a pension sharing compensation order). This additional power enables the courts to split pension rights at the time of divorce. This is done by directing a transfer payment equal in value to a proportion of the member-spouse's pension rights to be made to a pension arrangement which could then provide retirement benefits for the other spouse. In this way, both parties would have immediate control over their own pension provisions. Pension sharing orders can be made on divorce (or nullity) but not on judicial separation.

A pension sharing order may be made against an occupational pension scheme or personal pension scheme. Pension sharing also applies to most public service pensions and the State Earnings Related Pension Schemes (SERPS), but not to the basic State retirement pension.

The effect of a pension sharing order, is that the transferor loses the percentage required to be transferred which reduces the value of his fund – 'the pension debit'. The transferee acquires the right to be credited with that amount – 'the pension credit'. The transferee thus gains an amount which will fund a quite separate pension of her own, which is not in any way contingent on the transferor taking his own pension. The order cannot take effect until decree absolute.

Depending on the type of pension scheme involved, the transferee may have a choice as to whether to become a member of the transferor's pension scheme, but in her own right (known as an 'internal transfer'), or to transfer to a different pension scheme (an 'external transfer').

Pension rights will be valued using the method already in use for valuing the rights of 'early leavers' from occupational pension schemes, or of members of personal pension schemes who wish to transfer their accrued rights to another pension scheme. This is known as the Cash Equivalent Transfer Value.

Any solicitor advising a client about pension sharing must be careful not to infringe the provisions of the Financial Services and Markets Act 2000. For advice on, for example, whether to opt for an internal or external transfer, the client needs to be referred to an independent financial adviser.

4.7.3.1 Pension sharing and the other options

There is no obligation on the court to make a pension sharing order, and 'offsetting' or pension attachment orders remain alternatives. The court must, as always in financial matters, consider each case on its facts by applying the principles and factors set out in s 25 of the MCA 1973 (see **4.5**).

One restriction on the options available to the court is that it is not possible to make both a pension sharing order and a pension attachment in relation to the same pension arrangement. Therefore, the court could not, for example, make a pension attachment in relation to the lump sum death benefit and share the member's other rights. Also, a pension sharing order may not be made in relation to a pension arrangement which is already subject to such an order in respect of that marriage (MCA 1973, s 24B(3) and (4)). However, the fact that a pension is already subject to a sharing order made in respect of a previous marriage would not prevent a further order being made as a result of a second divorce.

The very nature of pensions makes them difficult for the court to deal with on divorce. A pension is a complex investment which represents both a capital asset and future source of income. The court's approach will vary according to the facts of the case. For example, in a case being dealt with on a sharing basis (see **4.5.1**), the court is more likely to focus on dividing the capital value of the pension, whereas in a needs based case, utilising the pension to provide an income may be more appropriate.

4.8 FINANCIAL CASES IN THE FUTURE

Calls for a review of the law on financial relief have been growing louder in recent years. The legislation remains in substantially the same form as when originally enacted over 30 years ago. Financial relief has always been an area dominated by judicial discretion. Yet the flurry of litigation which followed *White* and, later, *Miller and McFarlane* has arguably only served to add to the law's uncertainty. In *Charman v Charman* [2007] EWCA Civ 503 the President of the Family Division commented: 'Arguably ... [the MCA] is ... in need of modernisation in the light of social and other changes as well as in the light of experience.'

4.9 FINANCIAL PROVISION DURING MARRIAGE

It may be that a spouse is in need of financial provision during a marriage and yet is not ready to make a decision regarding divorce or judicial separation. In such circumstances, a spouse may bring proceedings under s 27 of the MCA 1973 in a divorce county court (under CPA 2004, Sch 5, Pt 9 for civil partners), or under the Domestic Proceedings and Magistrates' Courts Act 1978 (DPMCA 1978) in the family proceedings court (see **Appendix 1(C)**).

4.9.1 Matrimonial Causes Act 1973, s 27

Section 27 of the MCA 1973 allows either party to a marriage to apply for financial provision on the ground that the respondent has failed to provide reasonable maintenance for the applicant, or has failed to provide or make a proper contribution towards the reasonable maintenance of any child of the family. The court can make orders for periodical payments (including secured provision) and lump sums. In contrast to the DPMCA 1978, there is no ceiling on the amount of any lump sum, although as with the 1978 Act there is no power to make property adjustment orders. In determining whether to make provision, the court will have regard to all the circumstances of the case, including many of the factors set out in s 25 (see **4.5.1**).

The duration of periodical payments orders made under s 27 is precisely the same as for ordinary periodical payments made on divorce (see **4.3.2**). The court also has power to make interim orders, and orders for periodical payments may be varied under s 31 of the MCA 1973 in the usual way (see **11.8**).

The need for applications under s 27 is diminished by the fact that where a married couple are separated and have natural children, the appropriate application for maintenance for the children will be to the CMS rather than under s 27 of the MCA 1973. Applications under s 27 of the MCA 1973 have never been common. However, a recent example is *Villiers v Villiers* [2021] EWFC 23. The wife's application fell at the first hurdle as she was unable to satisfy the judge that the husband had in fact failed to provide reasonable maintenance. The judge did, however, comment that reasonable maintenance was to be judged 'by reference, first, to the respondent's ability to pay and, second, to the marital standard of living', and that what the applicant might obtain on a financial claim in divorce was irrelevant.

4.9.2   Domestic Proceedings and Magistrates' Courts Act 1978

The DPMCA 1978 enables a party to a marriage to seek limited financial provision during the subsistence of the marriage. The court may make orders for periodical payments for a spouse as well as for a child of the family, and it may make lump sum orders. There are two main types of application under the DPMCA 1978: contested applications under s 2; and applications by consent under s 6.

4.9.2.1   Contested applications

In order to bring an application under s 2 of the DPMCA 1978, the applicant must establish one of the grounds in s 1, ie that the respondent has not sufficiently provided for the applicant or a child of the family, or the respondent's behaviour has been unreasonable, or the respondent has deserted the applicant. The court will have regard to the factors listed in s 3, which are broadly similar to s 25 of the MCA 1973.

Any lump sum order made on a contested application is limited to £1,000, although, unlike s 23 of the MCA 1973, there is no bar against making further applications.

4.9.2.2   Agreed applications

If the parties agree financial provision, either may apply for an order under s 6 of the DPMCA 1978 to endorse their agreement.

The court is also able to approve agreements to pay a lump sum of any amount.

4.9.2.3   Duration of periodical payments

Whether the order is made pursuant to s 2 or s 6, it may be backdated to the date of application. The order will cease on the death of either party, or on the remarriage of the recipient. It is unaffected by the termination of the marriage, although it will usually be discharged and replaced by any order made under s 23 of the MCA 1973 by the divorce county court. Periodical payments to a spouse for himself or for the benefit of a child will cease if the parties resume cohabitation for a continuous period of more than six months (DPMCA 1978, s 25(1)). Payments ordered to be payable direct to a child will be unaffected by cohabitation. The child's maintenance will terminate in the same circumstances as under s 29(3) of the MCA 1973 (see **4.3.2**).

SUMMARY

(1)   On divorce, the Family Court can make one or more of the following financial orders in favour of a spouse:

    (a)   maintenance pending suit;

    (b)   periodical payments;

    (c)   secured periodical payments;

    (d)   lump sum order;

    (e)   property adjustment order;

    (f)   order for sale;

    (g)   pension sharing order;

    (h)   pension sharing compensation order.

(2)   The court can also make any of these orders (except for maintenance pending suit and pension sharing orders) in favour of a child. However, in most cases, periodical payments for a child are now dealt with by the CMS, and it is unusual to obtain the other types of order, such as a lump sum order, for a child.

---

(3)   Whenever the court considers making a financial order on divorce, it must consider:

     (a)   the general principle in s 25(1), ie all the circumstances of the case, with first consideration given to the welfare of any child of the family under 18 years; and

     (b)   the factors in s 25(2):

         (i)   income, earning capacity and other resources;

         (ii)   needs and responsibilities;

         (iii)   standard of living;

         (iv)   age of the parties and duration of the marriage;

         (v)   disability;

         (vi)   contributions to the family;

         (vii)   conduct;

         (viii)   potential financial loss.

The House of Lords in *White* and *Miller and McFarlane* has reaffirmed that no one s 25 factor is more important than the others. The objective for the court is to achieve fairness.

There are other factors for the court to refer to when considering making financial orders for a child or step-child (s 25(3) and (4)).

(4)   Under s 25A, the court always has a duty to consider whether a clean break should be achieved.

(5)   It is important to be aware of the significance of pensions on divorce and the ways in which the court can try to adjust the financial position of the parties on retirement.

(6)   A spouse who is not divorcing can still apply to the court for financial provision, either:

     (a)   under s 27 of the MCA 1973, for periodical payments and/or a lump sum order; or

     (b)   under the DPMCA 1978, for periodical payments and/or a maximum £1,000 lump sum order.

CHAPTER 5

TAX ON MARRIAGE BREAKDOWN

5.1	Introduction	77
5.2	Tax on marriage breakdown	77
Summary		81

LEARNING OUTCOMES

After reading this chapter you will be able to:

- understand the relevance of the main taxes on marriage breakdown
- recognise those situations which give rise to tax implications on divorce.

5.1 INTRODUCTION

This chapter deals with the effect of marriage breakdown on the tax position of the couple.

5.2 TAX ON MARRIAGE BREAKDOWN

Where the assets owned by the divorcing couple are numerous and complicated, it may be wise to enlist the help of an accountant when considering tax planning. Nonetheless, the solicitor should be aware of the major tax effects of marriage breakdown and some basic tax planning points. For a reminder of the basic principles of income tax, capital gains tax and inheritance tax, see *Legal Foundations*.

5.2.1 Income tax

Changes to the income tax regime that came into effect in April 2000 effectively removed the scope for tax planning. There is:

(a) no tax relief on maintenance payments, whether for a spouse or a child (maintenance is tax free in the hands of the recipient);

(b) no married couple's or single parent allowance;

(c) no tax relief on mortgage interest payments.

Consequently, how maintenance payments are arranged is not influenced by fiscal considerations.

There are four ways in which maintenance may be paid:

(a) purely voluntary payment;

(b) under a written agreement;

(c) by court order (whether made by consent or after a contested hearing);

(d) in compliance with a maintenance calculation by the CMS.

Voluntary payments are normally only a short-term arrangement. As between a written agreement and a court order, it is a question of balancing the potential advantages of speed, lower costs and flexibility of an agreement against the better provisions for disclosure and enforcement with a court order (see **12.3.3** and **12.3.4** for a more detailed comparison).

It should be noted that from April 2015, a married couple, neither one of whom is a higher rate taxpayer, have been able to engage in some limited tax planning, in that one spouse is able to transfer a small amount (currently £1,260) of his or her unused personal allowance to the other in order to achieve an overall tax saving. The ability to make this transfer will cease at the end of the tax year of separation.

5.2.2 Capital gains tax

Capital gains tax (CGT) is charged on the chargeable gains made by a person on the disposal of chargeable assets. In effect, tax is charged on the increase (gain) in the value of the asset during the taxpayer's period of ownership. On marriage breakdown, capital assets commonly have to be sold or divided between the spouses, and this may give rise to a chargeable gain. The impact of CGT cannot be ignored as it may alter the effect of any negotiated settlement or court order.

Ordinarily transfers of assets between spouses are deemed to have occurred at a consideration that gives rise to neither a gain nor a loss. However, the benefit of this rule is lost at the end of the tax year of separation. Even when the rule applies, there may still be some tax implications for the recipient spouse who is deemed to have acquired the asset at the same value as the transferring spouse. As a result, when the recipient eventually disposes of the asset, he or she will, in effect, be taxed on the transferor's gain as well as his or her own.

> **EXAMPLE**
>
> In 2009 Said bought a holiday cottage for £200,000. As part of their divorce settlement in 2016, Said transfers the cottage to his wife, Farhat. At the time of the transfer, the cottage is worth £250,000, but as it takes place within the tax year of separation, it is deemed to create neither a gain nor a loss and so no CGT is payable. In 2022 Farhat sells the cottage for £275,000. Even though the cottage has only increased in value by £25,000 during her ownership, Farhat is deemed to have acquired the cottage at the same value as Said. As a result, Farhat will be taxed on a gain of £75,000 (£275,000 – £200,000).

5.2.2.1 Capital gains tax and the home

The home is often the largest capital asset and any transfer of it, or of a share in it, could potentially give rise to CGT. However, liability may be avoided due to two important exemptions:

(a)   The private residence exemption: to qualify for full exemption, an individual must have occupied the home as his only or main residence throughout the period of his ownership. If he has occupied during part only of his ownership then the relief will be proportionately reduced, except that he is deemed to have occupied during the last nine months of ownership whether or not this is in fact so. (Further details of this exemption can be found in **Property Law and Practice**.)

(b)   Taxation of Chargeable Gains Act 1992, s 225B: this will apply where:

(i)   a husband and wife separate or divorce and one of them moves out of the home whilst the other continues to live there;

(ii)   under the subsequent financial settlement the non-occupying spouse transfers the home or an interest in it to the occupying spouse; and

(iii) the non-occupying spouse has not elected to treat another property as his only or main residence.

If these conditions are fulfilled, the non-occupying spouse will be treated as having continued to occupy so that his gain will be exempt.

How do these exemptions work in practice?

Sale of the home to a third party

If the sale is within nine months of the separation, any gain is exempt, being covered by the private residence exemption. If the sale is later, the proportion of the non-occupying spouse's gain not covered by the exemption may be taxable. The annual exemption, if available, can be applied to reduce the gain. (The spouse who has continued to occupy will, of course, be covered by the private residence exemption.)

Transfer of the home between spouses

This will be necessary where the court orders an outright transfer, or deferred trust of land or deferred charge where this requires a transfer, ie disposal of some interest in the home. The transferor's gain may be exempted under the following rules:

(a) where the transfer takes place in the tax year of separation, the rule relating to inter-spouse disposals; or

(b) where the transfer takes place within nine months of separation, the deemed occupation rule; or

(c) Taxation of Chargeable Gains Act 1992, s 225B, if later.

Where none of the above applies, probably because the transferor has made an election in respect of another home and the separation exceeds three years, the gain will be taxable in the same way as above. A proportion of the gain will thus be exempt due to the private residence exemption. The annual exemption, may help to reduce the remainder.

Future sale of home subject to a deferred trust of land or deferred charge

When the deferred trust of land or deferred charge is set up, one spouse may be required to transfer some, or all, of their interest in the home to the other. The CGT consequences of this have been dealt with above. However, when the house eventually comes to be sold, possibly many years into the future, a further CGT liability may arise.

The occupying spouse's gain will be exempt under the private residence exemption. The position of the non-occupying spouse will depend on whether the home was subject to a deferred trust of land, or a deferred charge:

(a) *Deferred trust of land.* As the court order created a settlement, it would appear that the non-occupying spouse will avoid CGT liability completely because of rules exempting gains on property occupied by a beneficiary entitled to do so under a settlement (Taxation of Chargeable Gains Act 1992, s 225).

(b) *Deferred charge.* Where the charge is expressed as a proportion of the proceeds, for example, one-third, the value of that share may have increased by the time the property is sold. In this situation, the non-occupier is likely to be liable to CGT, the redemption monies being a capital sum derived from an asset, ie the charge (Taxation of Chargeable Gains Act 1992, s 21). The annual exemption, may help to reduce the bill. However, if the deferred charge is for a fixed sum (rather than a proportion of the proceeds), there is no charge to CGT when the debt is paid (Taxation of Chargeable Gains Act 1992, s 251).

5.2.2.2 Other assets

Disposals giving rise to liability to CGT are most likely to arise, for example, on sale of an asset (say a valuable painting) to raise a lump sum, or on the transfer of property (say shares) between the parties.

> **EXAMPLE**
>
> Jim and Kate bought a painting jointly seven years ago for £10,000. They separated two years ago. The financial order is made today, when the painting is worth £16,000. Under the order Jim must transfer his share in the painting to Kate. Jim has made a gain of £3,000 (£16,000 – £10,000 = £6,000, Jim's gain is half of this).

The gain on many disposals of matrimonial property may, however, be eliminated or reduced by an exemption or relief. The following should be considered:

(a)   wasting assets, for example, the family car or electrical items;

(b)   tangible moveable property disposed of for a consideration of less than £6,000;

(c)   the annual exemption;

(d)   the rule relating to inter-spouse transfers.

But these exemptions and reliefs will not eliminate CGT in every case. Consequently, the family solicitor must always have the impact of CGT in mind, and ensure that settlements and orders are framed in a legitimate tax-efficient manner where possible. There may, for example, be merit in arranging a financial settlement so as to enable assets to be transferred between spouses before the tax year of separation expires. Similarly, the family solicitor may need to structure a financial settlement so as to stagger the disposal of assets across two tax years, so that the transferor can take advantage of two annual exemptions.

5.2.3   Inheritance tax

Inheritance tax (IHT) is charged on the value transferred by a chargeable transfer. Transfers of assets or money between spouses on marriage breakdown have the potential to give rise to a charge to IHT as lifetime transfers. However, in reality there is rarely any liability to IHT on marriage breakdown. This is due to a number of exemptions and reliefs.

5.2.3.1   The spouse exemption (Inheritance Tax Act 1984, s 18)

The spouse exemption exempts transfers between the parties before decree absolute, even if separated. However, this exemption will rarely apply since lump sum and property adjustment orders are not effective until decree absolute (see **4.4.1** and **4.4.2**).

5.2.3.2   Dispositions for family maintenance (Inheritance Tax Act 1984, s 11)

This relief provides that a disposition is not a transfer of value if made by one spouse for the maintenance of the other spouse or of a child of either spouse, and applies both before and after divorce. The term 'maintenance' is not defined in the Act but clearly covers periodical payments. There is, however, doubt as to whether it is wide enough to cover capital provision, such as lump sum or property adjustment orders. However, capital orders should be covered by the following relief.

5.2.3.3   Dispositions without donative intent (Inheritance Tax Act 1984, s 10)

This provides that a disposition is not a transfer of value if it was not intended to confer a gratuitous benefit and that either:

(a)   it was made in a transaction at arm's length between unconnected persons; or

(b)   it was such as might be expected to be made in such a transaction.

To avoid any doubt about the application of this exemption to transfers on marriage breakdown, the Senior Registrar of the Family Division, with the agreement of the then Revenue, issued the following statement:

> Transfers of money or property pursuant to an order of the court in consequence of a decree of divorce or nullity will, in general, be regarded as exempt from [IHT] as transactions at arm's length which are not intended to confer any gratuitous benefit. ((1975) 119 SJ 596)

Care must be taken if the disposition concerned is a payment into or creation of a trust. Although at the time of the disposition there will be no IHT consequences by virtue of s 10, there may be anniversary charges during the lifetime of the trust and exit charges to be paid when the trust comes to an end.

5.2.4 Stamp duty land tax

Where property is transferred under a separation agreement or court order on divorce, the instrument effecting the conveyance is exempt from stamp duty land tax (Finance Act 2003, Sch 3, para 3).

SUMMARY

(1)   The payment of maintenance, whether to a spouse or child, does not give rise to any income tax consequences.

(2)   CGT may have to be paid when the matrimonial assets are divided on divorce.

(3)   Where the asset is the home and it is transferred from one spouse to the other, CGT will not usually be payable. However, if the home is sold to a third party, some CGT may have to be paid by the non-occupying spouse.

CHAPTER 6

WELFARE AND LOCAL AUTHORITY HOUSING

6.1	Introduction	83
6.2	Child benefit	84
6.3	Universal credit	84
6.4	The benefit cap	87
6.5	Other help	87
6.6	Welfare benefits and marriage breakdown	87
6.7	Local authority housing	88
Summary		90

> **LEARNING OUTCOMES**
>
> After reading this chapter you will be able to:
>
> - describe what welfare benefits may be available on divorce
> - explain how maintenance, lump sum orders and property adjustment orders made on divorce may affect any welfare benefits payable
> - describe what housing duties local authorities owe to those who are homeless.

6.1 INTRODUCTION

When a married couple or civil partners separate and the main earner leaves the home, the other spouse may be left with little or no money. Although this may be only a temporary situation, and it is possible to apply for maintenance (see **4.3** and **4.9**), it may be preferable for that spouse to apply for welfare benefits (for reasons explained at **4.3.1**). In addition, since it is more expensive to run two households than one, many people, particularly if they are lone parents, find themselves reliant on welfare benefits on a more permanent basis after marriage breakdown.

In terms of eligibility for welfare benefits, cohabiting couples (ie those who are 'living together as a married couple' or 'living together as civil partners') are treated in the same way as married couples and so, for example, their income will be aggregated.

The matrimonial solicitor thus needs to have a working knowledge of the main benefits available and how they may be affected by any financial settlement the couple later reach.

The following is an outline of the most important current benefits for the family client. Further detail on these and other benefits can be found in specialist publications, such as *Welfare Benefits and Tax Credits Handbook* (Child Poverty Action Group, 2021–22). Online benefits calculators, such as <https://benefits-calculator-2.turn2us.org.uk/>, can be useful in helping work out likely amounts of benefit.

Major reforms are being carried out to the system of welfare benefits, with most benefits such as income support; working tax credit; child tax credit and housing benefit being replaced by one benefit, universal credit. Initially, universal credit was piloted in a number of areas, with national implementation for new claimants taking place from October 2013 to December

2018. Now, all new claimants, save for those receiving the Severe Disability Premium, will claim universal credit. Claimants with a change of circumstances, such as a new partner joining the household or a former partner leaving, must also move onto universal credit. Other claimants in receipt of the benefits that universal credit replaces will be gradually transferred onto universal credit. The government plan is for all transfers to be completed by 2024.

6.2 CHILD BENEFIT

Child benefit is a weekly sum payable in respect of each child or qualifying young person to the person responsible for maintaining that child or qualifying young person. A 'child' is defined as being someone aged under 16. A 'qualifying young person' is defined as being someone who is under 20 and still in full-time secondary education or training. A higher amount of benefit is paid for the eldest child.

Child benefit is paid irrespective of the claimant's income and is non-taxable. However, an income tax charge will apply to a taxpayer whose income exceeds £50,000 pa who receives child benefit or whose partner receives child benefit. Where both partners have an income which exceeds £50,000, the charge will apply to the partner with the highest income. Where the taxpayer liable to the charge is not the person who receives child benefit, he will only be liable for the charge when living with the claimant and not after separation.

Taxpayers whose income is between £50,000 and £60,000 will be charged 1% of the amount of child benefit they receive for every £100 of income above £50,000. Taxpayers whose income is above £60,000 will be charged equivalent to the full amount of child benefit.

EXAMPLE

Mo and Jess are married with two children. Mo earns £56,000 pa and Jess works part time, earning £17,000 pa. Jess receives £1,752 pa child benefit. Mo will have to pay extra income tax as follows:

1% x £1,752 = £17.52

Mo earns £6,000 above the £50,000 threshold, ie 60 x £100.

Mo will pay 60 x £17.52, ie £1,051.20 extra income tax.

If Mo and Jess separate, Mo will no longer pay the extra income tax. Jess will continue to receive the full amount of child benefit throughout.

Child benefit claimants may elect not to receive child benefit to which they are entitled if they or their partner do not wish to pay the tax charge.

6.3 UNIVERSAL CREDIT

Universal credit is a means-tested benefit for people of working age. Where the claimant is part of a couple (whether married, civil partners or cohabiting) a joint claim must be made. Most claims must be made online.

6.3.1 Eligibility

For a claimant to be eligible to claim universal credit, he must:

(a)   be 18 or over. Some exceptions will apply so that, for example, those aged 16 or 17 will be able to claim if they have dependent children;

(b)   be under state pension age;

(c)   be in Great Britain, have a right to reside and be habitually resident in the UK;

(d)   not be in education. Some exceptions apply, so that students will be eligible to claim if they have dependent children;

(e)   have accepted a claimant commitment; and

(f)   not have capital which exceeds £16,000. Some capital will not count, eg the home.

6.3.2   Amount

Universal credit is paid monthly in arrears. The amount consists of:

(a)   a standard allowance, which will differ depending on, for example, whether the claimant is a single person or part of a couple and whether the claimant is over 25;

(b)   a child element where a claimant is responsible for a child and that child normally lives with him. The child element will be paid at a higher rate for the eldest child. From April 2017 new claimants can only claim the child element for a maximum of two children unless the children were all born before 6 April 2017; the claimant has a multiple birth or there are other 'exceptional circumstances', such as where the child was born as a result of a 'non-consensual conception'. The two child limit was challenged but ruled lawful by the Supreme Court in R (*on the application of SC*) *v Secretary of State for Work and Pensions* [2021] UKSC 26;

(c)   a housing costs element where the claimant is renting. Claimants who rent from a private landlord will receive the local housing allowance (LHA) for the relevant size of property that the family is assessed as needing. The LHA is generally the amount of the lowest third of local market rents.

For local authority or housing association tenants, the amount will generally be 100% of the rent payable (subject to any reductions mentioned below). The amount paid will be reduced if the tenant lives in a property which is too big for them (the 'spare room subsidy' or 'bedroom tax'). Housing benefit is reduced by 14% if there is one bedroom more than needed in the house and by 25% if there are two or more extra bedrooms. The amount will also be reduced if one or more non-dependants share the property. In *JD and A v United Kingdom* [2020] HLR 5, the European Court of Human Rights decided that the spare room subsidy/bedroom tax unlawfully discriminates against victims of domestic violence living in 'Sanctuary Scheme' homes. These are properties which have been modified to enable victims to live safely in their own homes through, for example, provision of a 'panic room'. The government is 'carefully considering' the Court's decision.

Where the claimant is an owner-occupier, he may be able to claim help with mortgage interest by way of a Support with Mortgage Interest Loan. This can cover mortgages of up to £200, 000 and is paid at a standard rate. The amount will be reduced if there are non-dependants living at the property. The loan will need to be repaid when the property is sold or transferred. The claimant must have been claiming universal credit for nine months before such a loan will be payable. However, if either the claimant or his partner is working, he will not be eligible for any help with mortgage payments;

(d)   a childcare costs element of up to 85% of the cost of childcare, up to a maximum of £646.35 per month for one child and £1,108.04 per month for two or more children.

6.3.3   Income

Any income the claimant may have will reduce the amount of universal credit payable. The claimant's income will include:

(a)   any earnings of the claimant net of tax, national insurance contributions and pension contributions. There is a work allowance for those with children or a disability, which sets out an amount that such claimants can keep before wages will affect the amount of benefit. The amount of this depends on whether the claimant gets help with his housing costs or not and is higher if not in receipt of assistance with housing costs. Universal credit will taper at the rate of 63%, ie a claimant can keep 37p for every extra £1 of net earnings (or earnings above any allowance where relevant). In *Secretary of State for Work and Pensions v Johnson* [2020] EWCA Civ 778, the Court held that the system of calculating earned income was irrational in circumstances where people had their wages paid later in months where payment was due on a weekend or Bank Holiday. This sometimes led to two monthly salary payments falling within one of the monthly assessment periods for universal credit, meaning that universal credit would be substantially reduced for the claimant for that month. Following *Johnson*, the court reached a similar result in R (*on the application of Pantellerisco*) *v Secretary of State for Work and Pensions* [2020] EWHC 1944 (Admin) where the claimant was paid four-weekly rather than monthly;

(b)   any maintenance payments paid to the claimant for his own benefit. Such payments will reduce universal credit pound for pound. Any child maintenance, for example under a child maintenance calculation, will not be included as income;

(c)   income from capital. If the claimant has capital of more than £16,000, he will be ineligible for universal credit (see **6.3.1**). Any interest actually earned on capital of less than that amount will be ignored. However, capital of over £6,000 will be deemed to produce income at the rate of £1 per week (£4.33 per month) for every £250 of capital over the £6,000 limit. So, for example, capital of £8,000 will be deemed to produce income of £34.80 per month (£8,000 – £6,000 = £2,000/250 x 4.33 = £34.64). Any such income will reduce universal credit pound for pound.

Any child benefit will not count as income.

6.3.4   Claimant commitment

The claimant commitment will generally refer to work-related requirements. The claimant will be in one of the following groups:

(a)   No work-related requirements. This group includes families where there is a child under one and applies to the carer or main carer of the child.

(b)   Work-focused interview only requirement. This group includes families where there is a child aged one and applies to the carer or main carer of the child. Members of this group must attend periodic interviews to discuss plans for returning to work.

(c)   Work preparation requirement. This group includes families where there is a child aged two and applies to the carer or main carer of the child. Members of this group must take reasonable steps to prepare for work, such as participating in training or undertaking a work placement.

(d)   Anyone else must be looking for and available for work, although where the claimant is the main carer of a child under 13, the hours available for work can be restricted to school hours.

Claimants who do not comply with their claimant commitment may be sanctioned, that is, have their universal credit reduced for a certain period.

6.3.5   Passport benefits

Depending on the claimant's circumstances, universal credit may be a 'passport' to certain other benefits, ie the claimant will automatically be entitled to these other benefits as well. These passport benefits include:

(a)   free school meals;

(b)   exemption from NHS charges for prescriptions, dental treatment and eye-tests, and vouchers to help with the cost of glasses;

(c)   Healthy Start food vouchers and Healthy Start vitamins for expectant and nursing mothers and pre-school children. Healthy Start food vouchers can be exchanged for cows' milk, cows' milk formula, fruit or vegetables.

6.4 THE BENEFIT CAP

There is a maximum amount of benefit that each household can receive based on the average earnings of working households in Great Britain. The amount of the benefit cap is £20,000 pa for couples and lone parents (or £23,000 within Greater London). Those in receipt of carer's allowance or guardian's allowance are exempt from the cap, as are those claiming universal credit due to a disability. Also exempt are those who receive universal credit and they and their partner together earn more than the amount they would get on the national minimum wage for 16 hours work per week. There is a 'grace period' in certain situations where a claimant's job has ended for up to 39 weeks when the benefit cap will not apply. The benefit cap was challenged but ruled lawful by the Supreme Court in R *(on the application of SG) v Secretary of State for Work and Pensions* [2015] UKSC 16 and R *(on the application of DA and others) v Secretary of State for Work and Pensions* [2019] UKSC 21.

6.5 OTHER HELP

6.5.1 Council tax support

Each local authority has its own council tax support scheme to provide help for people on low incomes with their council tax bill.

6.5.2 Discretionary housing payments

Discretionary housing payments can be paid by the local authority to anyone entitled to the housing costs element of universal credit who appears to require additional financial assistance to meet their housing costs. This may be, for example, due to the benefit cap or the 'spare room subsidy/bedroom tax'. They are paid by the local authority from a cash-limited fund.

6.5.3 Local welfare assistance schemes

Loans, grants or other forms of assistance (for example, food vouchers for a food bank) may be provided by the local authority. Each local authority runs its own scheme.

6.5.4 Budgeting advance

Budgeting advances are available to those who have been on universal credit for at least 26 weeks to meet large, one-off expenses, for example a replacement cooker or furniture. Claimants will be expected to use any savings they have in excess of £1,000 before a loan will be made. The loans are interest-free and repaid by deductions from benefit, the amount of the deduction depending on the claimant's individual circumstances.

6.5.5 Flexible Support Fund

This is a discretionary fund, allocated by Jobcentre Plus advisers to help with extra costs associated with finding a job, such as travel expenses to attend an interview or clothing/uniforms to start work. Payments made do not need to be repaid.

6.5.6 Further assistance

Sure Start maternity grants; funeral grants; cold weather payments and/or winter fuel payments may also be available depending on the claimant's circumstances.

6.6 WELFARE BENEFITS AND MARRIAGE BREAKDOWN

6.6.1 Maintenance and universal credit

Any maintenance paid to the claimant for herself will count as income and will reduce universal credit paid pound for pound. Thus, where the maintenance is not sufficient to take the claimant above the universal credit level, she will receive her income partly from maintenance payments and partly from universal credit. However, any child maintenance will be disregarded in full.

6.6.2 Lump sum payments

Where a lump sum payment brings the claimant's capital above the relevant capital limits, entitlement to the appropriate benefit will be eliminated.

Where a lump sum payment brings the claimant's capital to over £6,000 but under the relevant capital limits, the capital will be deemed to produce income (see **6.3.3**).

6.6.3 Property adjustment

The value of the claimant's home is generally ignored in assessing benefits.

6.7 LOCAL AUTHORITY HOUSING

The family solicitor must be able to give immediate advice to a client who finds herself in a situation where she is, or might be, without a roof over her head. The two most common situations where this might occur are where the client has been subjected to domestic abuse (see **Chapter 15**), or when she cannot stay in the former matrimonial home for financial reasons (eg because there are large mortgage arrears and the home must be sold).

Local authorities are under certain duties to provide help (including, in some cases, accommodation) to people who are homeless or threatened with homelessness. These duties are set out in the Housing Act 1996, as amended by the Homelessness Act 2002. The duty owed will depend upon whether the person applying is homeless or threatened with homelessness, whether that homelessness is intentional and whether the applicant has a priority need.

6.7.1 Homelessness

A person is homeless if:

(a)   there is no reasonable accommodation which he and his family are entitled to occupy; or

(b)   he has such accommodation but he cannot secure entry.

A person may also be entitled to local authority help if he is 'threatened' with homelessness, which means that he is likely to become homeless in the next 28 days.

6.7.2 Intentional homelessness

A person is intentionally homeless if he deliberately does or fails to do anything in consequence of which he ceases to occupy accommodation that was available for occupation by him and his family, and which it would have been reasonable for him to continue to occupy. The Supreme Court stated in *Samuels v Birmingham City Council* [2019] UKSC 28 that an applicant was not intentionally homeless where they could not pay their rent because their housing benefit was insufficient to cover it. The applicant could not be expected to subsidise the rent using other benefits. The Court made it clear that this would continue to be the case under universal credit.

It is not reasonable for a person to continue to occupy accommodation if it is probable that this will lead to domestic violence or other violence against her or other members of her household. In *Yemshaw v London Borough of Hounslow* [2011] UKSC 3, the Supreme Court held that 'domestic violence' in the Housing Act 1996 includes physical violence, threatening or intimidating behaviour and any other form of abuse which, directly or indirectly, may give rise to the risk of harm.

6.7.3 Priority need

The following have a priority need:

(a)   a pregnant woman or member of her household;

(b)   a person who has dependent children living with them or might reasonably be expected to live with them;

(c)   a person who is vulnerable as a result of old age, mental illness or handicap or physical disability or other special reason, or with whom such a person lives or might reasonably be expected to live;

(d)   a person who is homeless or threatened with homelessness as the result of an emergency such as flood, fire, or other disaster;

(e)   a person who is homeless as a result of that person being a victim of domestic abuse;

(f)   a person aged 16 or 17, who has not been in care and no duty to accommodate is owed to them under s 20 of the CA 1989;

(g)   a person aged under 21 who was in care whilst aged 16–18, but has now left care;

(h)   a person who is 'vulnerable' as a result of having been in care, having served in the armed forces, or having been in prison, custody or detention; or

(i)   a person who has ceased to occupy accommodation as a result of violence or threats of violence.

6.7.4 Local authority duties

The local authority has the following duties:

(a)   to rehouse a homeless person with a priority need who did not become homeless intentionally;

(b)   to provide temporary housing for a homeless person with a priority need who did become homeless intentionally. This accommodation must be provided for such period as the authority considers will give the homeless person a reasonable opportunity of finding his own accommodation. The authority is under a further duty to give advice and assistance to help him find such accommodation;

(c)   to advise and assist a homeless person without a priority need to help him find his own accommodation. In addition, if satisfied that he did not become homeless intentionally, the authority *may* secure that accommodation is available for his occupation.

6.7.5 Local connection provisions

Generally, the local authority to which the applicant applies will be the one under the duty mentioned at **6.7.4**. However, that local authority may not be under such a duty if the applicant has no local connection with its area. This is so that local authorities in, for example, seaside areas do not become overwhelmed with applications. In this case, the local authority can refer the applicant to a local authority with which he does have a local connection (provided that the applicant is not at risk of domestic abuse in that authority's area).

The applicant will have a local connection with the area in which he is normally resident, or where he is employed, or where he has family associations.

6.7.6 Local authority tenancies

A local authority tenancy is classed as a secure tenancy under the Housing Act 1985. This means that a council tenant has a great deal of security of tenure. In particular, he cannot be evicted without an order for possession from the court, and such an order is available only on specified grounds, for example, non-payment of rent. This security depends partly on the tenant (or one of them where the property is on a joint tenancy) remaining in occupation.

On divorce, the court can order the tenant spouse to transfer the tenancy to the other spouse, and when this is done security of tenure is not lost (see further **9.5**).

SUMMARY

(1)   On marriage breakdown one or both of the parties may need to claim welfare benefits. The following may be available:

    (a)   child benefit;

    (b)   universal credit;

    (c)   loans or grants.

(2)   Local authorities have duties towards homeless people. Where a person is homeless unintentionally and has a priority need (eg if she has a child with her), the local authority must generally rehouse her.

CHAPTER 7

CALCULATING CHILD MAINTENANCE

7.1	Introduction	91
7.2	When does the CSA 1991 apply?	92
7.3	The jurisdiction of the court	93
7.4	Maintenance agreements and consent orders	94
7.5	The formula	97
7.6	Special cases	99
7.7	Variations	100
7.8	Default and interim maintenance decisions (CSA 1991, s 12)	102
7.9	Voluntary payments	102
7.10	Review	102
7.11	Reform	102
Summary		103

LEARNING OUTCOMES

After reading this chapter you will be able to:

- describe the role of the Child Maintenance Service
- explain when child maintenance can be agreed between the parties and how any agreement can be embodied in a court order
- set out when the court will be able to order child maintenance
- calculate child maintenance using the gross income formula.

7.1 INTRODUCTION

This chapter covers the Child Support Act 1991 (CSA 1991), which deals with maintenance for most children. In response to some of the criticisms raised against the Child Support Agency ('the Agency'), the CSA 1991 was amended by the Child Support Act 1995, the Child Support, Pensions and Social Security Act 2000 (CSPSSA 2000) and the Child Maintenance and Other Payments Act 2008 (CMOPA 2008). Throughout this book, any reference to the CSA 1991 includes the 1995, 2000 and 2008 Acts.

Chapter 4 dealt with the statutory criteria used by the court when considering applications for child maintenance under the MCA 1973 on marriage breakdown. These factors are of a general nature and do not assist the court in arriving at specific figures for maintenance. Accordingly, the orders for children's maintenance could vary enormously from one court to another.

However, the approach under the CSA 1991 is entirely different. This legislation introduced a precise method of assessing maintenance using a formula. The CSA 1991, as it was originally enacted, used a detailed and complex formula. This led to long delays in assessing liability and enforcement. The Act was amended by the CSPSSA 2000, which replaced the detailed formula with a calculation based on a simple percentage of the non-resident parent's net income. Further amendments to the formula were made under the CMOPA 2008. Under these amendments, calculations are based on the gross income of the non-resident parent. This formula is considered in detail at **7.5**.

The original idea behind the CSA 1991 was that the Child Support Agency ('the Agency') would deal almost exclusively with child maintenance. However, the Agency was beset with problems from the beginning, and the CMOPA 2008 established the Child Maintenance and Enforcement Commission (C-MEC) which assumed responsibility for the Agency. The Commission itself was abolished in July 2012 and its responsibilities transferred to the Department of Work and Pensions (DWP). The current scheme is administered by the Child Maintenance Service (CMS).

The prevailing emphasis for child maintenance is now private maintenance arrangements, with resort to the CMS only when these would not be appropriate. To help accomplish these objectives, C-MEC set up an information and support service for parents called Child Maintenance Options, which the DWP and CMS are continuing. This service aims to help parents understand the options available for child maintenance and choose the one which is most suitable for them. The Child Maintenance Options website hosts a web app, 'Sorting out Separation', which includes a diagnostic tool to help separated couples work out what support they need and signpost them to the relevant expert organisations that can help them. Any parent wishing to apply to the CMS must first phone Child Maintenance Options to discuss the choices available to them.

Parents may be further encouraged to avoid CMS by the introduction of a £20 application fee (there is an exemption from this fee for an applicant who is a victim of domestic violence or abuse). Indeed, since the introduction of the fee in July 2014, there has been a substantial drop in applications of over 30%. In addition, if the parties opt to use CMS's 'Collect & Pay' service, where CMS will calculate, collect from the paying parent and pay the receiving parent child maintenance, they will be subject to charges. The paying parent must pay an additional 20% on top of the maintenance calculation, and the receiving parent will lose 4% of the maintenance in charges (see further **11.3**). These new fees were controversial and so the DWP was required to review their impact within 30 months of introduction. In December 2016 the DWP produced its report. The report concluded that the charges did not have an excessive impact on parents' decisions about whether to use the CMS or not, but they were a key way to encourage parents to collaborate. On this basis, the DWP has stated that it has no plans to change the charging structure.

7.2   WHEN DOES THE CSA 1991 APPLY?

Section 11 of the CSA 1991 provides:

> For the purposes of this Act, each parent of a qualifying child is responsible for maintaining him.

This calls for a number of definitions to be considered.

Section 55(1) defines 'a child' as an unmarried person under 16, or under 20 receiving full-time education which is not advanced education.

Section 3(1) defines the 'qualifying child' as such if:

(a)   one of his parents is in relation to him a non-resident parent; or

(b)   both of his parents are, in relation to him, non-resident parents.

As the name suggests, a non-resident parent is one who is not living in the same household as the child (s 3(2)). The term 'parent' takes its usual meaning of being a person who is in law the mother or father of the child, ie the natural parent or adoptive parent of the child. Where the child has been born through artificial insemination, the non-biological parent will also be treated as a 'parent' under the CSA 1991 if he or she is a spouse or civil partner. If the non-biological parent is not married or a civil partner, he or she can choose to become a 'parent' with the mother's consent. Clearly, the definition includes unmarried as well as married parents, and it is immaterial whether or not the non-resident parent knows that the child is his. The definition does not extend to a step-parent. In cases of disputes over parentage, the CMS may make a maintenance calculation in certain cases, for example, where the alleged father was married to the mother throughout the period of conception to birth, where the alleged father has been registered as the father of the child or where the alleged father has refused to take a scientific paternity test (CSA 1991, s 26). In other cases the CMS may not make a maintenance calculation until the court has determined parentage.

The CSA 1991 also refers to the person with care. Section 3(3) defines this person as one with whom the child lives and who usually provides the child's day-to-day care (this may not necessarily be the child's parent). If the child spends time with both parents, then the person with care will be the person who provides care to the greatest extent. The CMS will presume that the person with care is the person who claims child benefit, but this is only a presumption and can be rebutted by evidence. It will generally be the person with care who will apply for the maintenance calculation, although the non-resident parent may choose to apply for a calculation against himself.

The CMS has jurisdiction to make a maintenance calculation only if the qualifying child, the person with care and the non-resident parent are all habitually resident in the UK. This is subject to exceptions under s 44(2A) of the CSA 1991, relating to certain non-resident parents who are not habitually resident in the UK. These include civil servants and members of the armed forces working abroad, and employees of UK companies who are working abroad but whose employer calculates and arranges payment within the UK.

7.3 THE JURISDICTION OF THE COURT

By virtue of s 8 of the CSA 1991, the DWP, rather than the court, has almost exclusive jurisdiction to deal with child maintenance.

Section 8(3) states:

> Except as provided in subsection (3A), in any case where subsection (1) applies, no court shall exercise any power which it would otherwise have to make, vary or revise any maintenance order in relation to the child and non-resident parent concerned.

The cases covered by s 8(1) are those where the CMS would have jurisdiction to make a maintenance calculation with respect to a qualifying child and his non-resident parent. In other words, if an application could be dealt with by the CMS, it must be pursued there. However, the court retains jurisdiction to deal with those cases in which the CMS has no jurisdiction. The court, therefore, continues to deal with maintenance for step-children who are children of the family, and for those natural children who are too old to be qualifying children, for example, those aged 20 or over who are in education or training. If either the child, or the non-resident parent or the person with care is not habitually resident in the UK, the CMS will have no jurisdiction, but the court would have jurisdiction. The court also retains jurisdiction to make capital orders on behalf of children, ie a lump sum or property adjustment order. The court has power to vary or revoke existing maintenance orders in all cases (CSA 1991, s 8(3A) and (4)).

In the limited cases where the court retains jurisdiction, it will have the widest discretion to determine the amount of a child's periodical payments. It will consider the factors listed in s 25(3) and (4) of the MCA 1973, giving first consideration to the child's welfare as directed in s 25(1) (discussed in **Chapter 4**). In practice, the court will almost invariably take as its starting point for a child maintenance order the figure produced by a maintenance calculation under the CSA 1991 (*TW v TM (Minors) (Child Maintenance: Jurisdiction and Departure from Formula)* [2015] EWHC 3054 (Fam)). The solicitor should therefore calculate what a parent would be ordered to pay for a child were an application to the CMS possible. Indeed, in proceedings for a financial order the parties must generally include the figure a maintenance calculation would produce in Form E (see **10.7.2** and **Appendix 3(C)**). If the child is a step-child, regard must be had to the liability of the child's natural parents to maintain the child. Consequently, the step-parent may be ordered to pay an amount significantly less than a natural parent would be required to pay under the CSA 1991 formula, particularly if the parent with care could claim against the natural parent through the CMS.

In cases where a maintenance calculation has been (or is about to be) made, this must be taken into account in proceedings by the carer for maintenance for herself, as it will have a direct bearing on both parties' means (see **8.3**).

As well as dealing with those cases which cannot be dealt with by the CMS, the court retains jurisdiction to make maintenance orders for children in the three circumstances specified in s 8. These are discussed in **7.3.1** to **7.3.3** below.

7.3.1 Supplementary maintenance

Under s 8(6), the court will have jurisdiction if it is of the view that maintenance should be paid in addition to that assessed by the CMS. This will apply to wealthy families only, as it is a prerequisite that the CMS has already made a calculation up to the maximum level and therefore that the non-resident parent has a gross income of over £3,000 per week (see **7.5.1**). The judge in *CB v KB* [2020] 1 FLR 795 suggested that, where a parent is applying for supplementary maintenance, the starting point should be the amount produced by the formula applied by the CMS on earnings of up to £650,000 pa. On earnings above that, the starting point would be the amount produced by applying the CMS formula to £650,000 pa.

There are not very many applications under this subsection as the courts will rarely be persuaded that further sums should be paid. The circumstances when a child might require further assistance, for example, because he needs school fees or because of a disability, are in any event separately provided for in s 8(7) and (8).

7.3.2 Educational expenses

Section 8(7) provides that the court may continue to exercise its jurisdiction if the child is in education and provision is required to meet some or all of the expenses connected with it.

Typically, applications under this section will be made to cover the cost of school fees which are not fully met from the maintenance calculation. They may also be made to cover the payment of school uniforms, sports equipment, books, etc.

7.3.3 Children with a disability

If a child has a disability, this is not taken into account by the CMS when making the maintenance calculation. Such children, however, will frequently have additional expenses to meet their needs. Section 8(8) enables the court to make an order to supplement the maintenance calculation to meet expenses attributable to that disability.

Section 8(9) defines a child as disabled if he is blind, deaf or dumb, or is substantially and permanently handicapped by illness, injury, mental disorder or congenital deformity, or such other disability as may be prescribed.

7.4 MAINTENANCE AGREEMENTS AND CONSENT ORDERS

Section 8(3) restricts the jurisdiction of the court to determine maintenance for children. However, it is still open to parents to arrange maintenance for children without going to the CMS. The principle underlying the CMOPA 2008 is that it is preferable for parents to come to an agreement between themselves over child maintenance, only involving the state where this is not possible or the non-resident parent is trying to evade his or her responsibilities.

7.4.1 Family-based arrangements

To assist parents to make voluntary maintenance arrangements, which it refers to as 'family-based arrangements', the Child Maintenance Options website has a proforma which can be downloaded (www.cmoptions.org). However, this proforma clearly states that it is only a 'statement of commitment' rather than a legally binding document, so that such family-based arrangements are likely to be unenforceable. Thus, for the sake of certainty, the following options may be preferable.

7.4.2 Maintenance agreements

Maintenance agreements are frequently used by those who are unable or do not wish to obtain a court order, and who have agreed their own arrangements and wish to put their agreements in writing. A maintenance agreement is not a court order but is enforceable in the same way as any other binding contract (see **12.3.4.1**).

Following the CSA 1991, parents may still make maintenance agreements, and s 9(2) specifically preserves this right. However, just as in the past such agreements could not oust the jurisdiction of the court to determine maintenance, neither can the jurisdiction of the CMS be ousted. Section 9(3) and (4) rules out any attempts to prohibit applications to the CMS. As a result, any carer who enters into a separation agreement (even one which expressly purports to restrict the parties' rights to make any further claims) will, nevertheless, be able to apply to the CMS for a maintenance calculation.

7.4.3 Consent orders

Some couples may want to do more than just put their agreement in writing; they may want their agreement embodied in a court order. If so, they can apply for a consent order.

In spite of the clear wording of s 8(3), which prohibits the court from making (varying or reviving) maintenance orders where the DWP would have jurisdiction, s 8(5) preserves the power of the court to make an order if:

(a) a written agreement (whether or not enforceable) provides for the making or securing by a non-resident parent of the child of periodical payments to or for the benefit of the child; and

(b) the maintenance order which the court makes is, in all material respects, in the same terms as that agreement.

This provision was implemented by the Child Maintenance (Written Agreements) Order 1993 (SI 1993/620). Therefore, a maintenance agreement may be converted into a court order in the same terms. All that is required is for there to be a written agreement (this can be evidenced in a separate agreement, or incorporated in the recitals to the consent order). As a result of s 8(5), parents may continue to side-step the CMS and embody a clean break agreement in a consent order.

Where a consent order was made before 3 March 2003, no application can be made to the CMS under s 4 whilst that order is in force. If a consent order is made after 3 March 2003, no application can be made to the CMS under s 4 for one year (CSA 1991, s 4(10)). Thus consent orders made after 3 March 2003 will be binding as to child maintenance for only one year, after which the parent with care can apply for a maintenance calculation. Failure to advise a client of this is one of the most common grounds for complaints and negligence claims against family solicitors. The Family Law Committee of The Law Society recommended in its 2003 report, 'Financial Provision on Divorce: Clarity and Fairness – Proposals for Reform', that this provision be scrapped and that couples should still be able to agree consent orders in relation to child maintenance which will bind until the child(ren)'s majority. Unfortunately, the CMOPA 2008 has not introduced this reform. Thus family law practitioners are having to use various devices to try to mitigate the effect of s 4(10) of the CSA 1991.

One way is to enter a contract ancillary to the consent order whereby the parties agree to pay (or repay) any difference between the agreed maintenance order and a maintenance calculation subsequently made by the CMS. Another is to agree to an annual child periodical payments order (or 'Christmas order'). Such an order lasts for a day short of a year and is then replaced by an order in identical terms the following day. However, there is some criticism of such Christmas orders as contrary to public policy (see, for example, Nicholas Mostyn QC in *Child's Pay*, a computer package by Class Publishing). Another device used is a '*Segal* order', which is a global order combining maintenance to both spouse and child. The amount to be paid is reduced by the amount of any subsequent maintenance calculation by the CMS. Such orders are possible only if there is a substantial element within them for the financial support of the parent with care. The court's jurisdiction to make such '*Segal* orders' was confirmed in the case of *AB v CD (Jurisdiction Global Maintenance Orders)* [2018] 2 FLR 150. In *Ipecki v McConnell* [2019] EWFC 19 the court made a lump sum order on the basis that the parent with care would not make an application for a child support assessment under the CSA 1991. This was backed up by an indemnity, so that, if such an application were made, the non-resident parent would have a right to recoup any money paid out under the child support assessment. It is arguable that this device is also contrary to public policy (see, for example, Alex Woolley and James Webb 'Child Maintenance in *Ipecki v McConnell*: court ordered indemnity against a statutory right?' [2019] Fam Law 861).

Irrespective of s 4(10) of the CSA 1991, if the order or agreement is revoked, an application may be made to the CMS immediately. The decision whether or not to revoke an existing order rests with the court. It may not be prepared to revoke its original order, which would in effect block an early application to the CMS. In the case of *B v M (Child Support: Revocation of Order)* [1994] Fam Law 370, an order was made for the maintenance of three children in 1986. The mother wanted to apply under CSA 1991 for an assessment in respect of the two younger children, and applied for the original maintenance order to be revoked to enable her to do so. The father successfully appealed against the district judge's revocation. The court stated that the proper course would be to vary the original order, and that it was inappropriate to exercise its discretion to revoke the order purely because the mother wished to apply to the Agency. However, the court made it clear that each case must be considered on its merits.

Where a court order has been made, the court will retain its power to vary the order (CSA 1991, s 8(3A)).

7.4.4 Child maintenance flowchart

In practical terms, parents with care will have three choices when it comes to obtaining child maintenance: entering an agreement with the non-resident parent (which should be in writing for clarity and certainty); applying to the court; and applying to the CMS. The following flowchart may help to clarify when each of these options is appropriate.

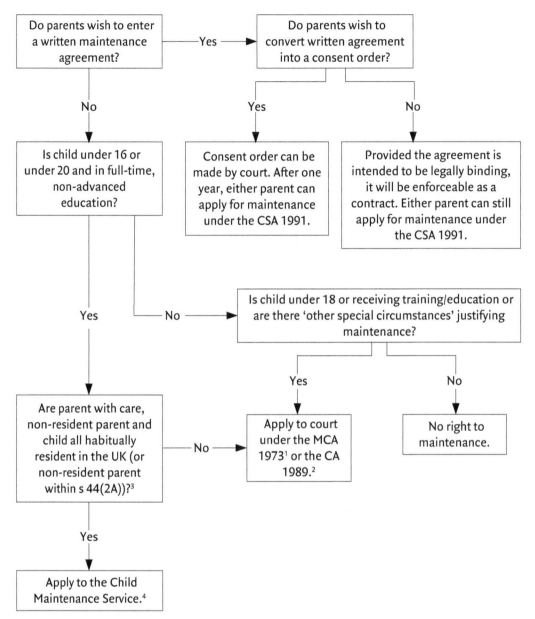

1 For MCA, see **4.3.2** and **Appendix 1(A)**.
2 For CA, see **13.10.4** and **Appendix 1(E)**.
3 See **7.2**.
4 Court may order additional maintenance if child is disabled, to cover educational expenses or where the family is very wealthy – see **7.3.1–7.3.3**.

7.5 THE FORMULA

When an application is made to the CMS, a formula is applied in order to calculate the maintenance payable in respect of a child by the non-resident parent. This is based on the non-resident parent's gross income and the number of children for whom that parent is responsible. Gross income is income before income tax and national insurance contributions are taken off; pension contributions will be deducted. When calculating gross income, the latest available information from HMRC will be used unless there are no HMRC records for the last six years or income has risen or fallen by 25% or more since the last HMRC record. In these circumstances current income will be used. The maintenance calculation is at one of four rates: the basic rate, the reduced rate, the flat rate or the nil rate.

7.5.1 The basic rate

This will be the usual rate. It provides that the non-resident parent should pay a proportion of his gross income as follows:

Number of children	Proportion of gross income up to £800 per week	Proportion of gross income between £800 and £3,000 per week
One	12%	9%
Two	16%	12%
Three or more	19%	15%

As can be seen, where a non-resident parent earns £800 or more per week, the top slice will be subject to a lower percentage.

> **EXAMPLE**
>
> Paul has separated from his partner and their three children. He earns £1,500 per week. The maintenance assessment Paul must pay will be:
>
> £800 x 19% = £152
>
> £700 x 15% = £105
>
> Total   = £257

Gross weekly income of over £3,000 (£156,000pa) will be ignored.

If the non-resident parent has other children living with him, for whom either he or any partner he is living with receives child benefit, his gross income is reduced by the following amount before the basic rate is applied:

Number of other children	Proportion gross income is reduced
One	11%
Two	14%
Three or more	16%

> **EXAMPLE**
>
> George is living with Linda and her two children, Doug (9) and Chloe (4). His ex-wife lives with their only child, Patricia (7). George has gross income of £500 per week. The maintenance payable for Patricia will be:
>
> £500 x 14% = £70
>
> £500 - £70 = £430
>
> £430 x 12% = £51.60

7.5.2 The reduced rate

This will apply where the non-resident parent's gross weekly income is more than £100 but less than £200. The amount payable increases in proportion to the amount by which the non-resident parent's income exceeds £100. The exact method of calculation is contained in the Child Support Maintenance Calculation Regulations 2012 (SI 2012/2677).

7.5.3 The flat rate

This will apply if the non-resident parent's gross weekly income is £100 or less, he is in receipt of certain benefits, pensions or allowances (including income support, jobseeker's allowance, universal credit and incapacity benefit), or his partner is in receipt of income support or income-based jobseeker's allowance. The flat rate is currently £7 per week.

7.5.4 The nil rate

This applies where the non-resident parent has gross income of below £7 or comes within a prescribed category (including people receiving an allowance in respect of work-based training for young people and prisoners).

7.6 SPECIAL CASES

7.6.1 Apportionment

The position where a non-resident parent has more than one qualifying child and those children are looked after by more than one person with care is covered by para 6 of Sch 1 to the CSA 1991. In such a case, the maintenance calculation is divided by the number of qualifying children and then shared between the parents with care in proportion to the number of qualifying children in each family.

> **EXAMPLE**
>
> Jon has four qualifying children, one being cared for by Lisa and three by Anita. His gross income is £800. The maintenance calculation is therefore 19% × £800 = £152. Lisa will receive £38 maintenance (one-quarter) and Anita the remaining £114 (three-quarters).

7.6.2 Existing court order

Where there is an existing court order in respect of one or more of the non-resident parent's qualifying children, the maintenance calculation will be similarly apportioned, although the actual amount paid to any children in respect of whom there is a court order will be the amount under that order.

> **EXAMPLE**
>
> Red has four children. His eldest, from a previous marriage, is now living with her mother, Maria, in Spain. He pays maintenance of £75 for her under a court order. Emily, from whom he has recently separated, applies for a maintenance calculation for his other three children. Red has gross income of £1,000. The maintenance calculation is therefore (19% x £800) = £152 + (15% x £200) = £30 = £182. Emily will receive £136.50 (three-quarters). Red will continue to pay £75 under the court order to Maria.

7.6.3 Shared care

Where both parents share care, the maintenance calculation will be reduced. The amount of this reduction will depend on the number of qualifying children and the amount of time they spend in the care of each parent (CSA 1991, Sch 1, para 7).

Shared care – basic and reduced rates

The amount of reduction for one child is as follows:

No of nights per year	Fraction to subtract
52–103	one-seventh
104–155	two-sevenths

No of nights per year	Fraction to subtract
156–174	three-sevenths
175 or more	one-half

Where the parent with care is looking after more than one qualifying child of the same non-resident parent, the reduction will be the sum of the relevant fractions divided by the number of children. Put simply, this means that where the children stay the same number of nights each with the non-resident parent then, generally, the maintenance calculation will be reduced by one-seventh for each night of the week that they stay.

> **EXAMPLE**
>
> Nick and Maria have three children. They all stay with Nick on Friday and Saturday night each week. The initial maintenance calculation is £210. This will be reduced by $\frac{2}{7}$ (ie $\frac{2}{7}$ + $\frac{2}{7}$ + $\frac{2}{7}$ ÷ 3). $\frac{2}{7}$ × £210 = £60. So the final maintenance calculation will be £210 – £60 = £150.

However, note that there is a further reduction of a flat rate of £7 per child where that child is looked after by the non-resident parent for 175 nights or more. Care must also be taken in the calculation where the children stay for a different number of nights with the non-resident parent.

> **EXAMPLE**
>
> Duncan and Nicola have two children, Jack and Georgia. Jack stays with Duncan for 180 nights a year, Georgia for 156. Duncan's maintenance calculation will be reduced by $\frac{13}{28}$ ([$\frac{7}{14}$ + $\frac{6}{14}$] ÷ 2), and then by a further £7.

Finally, in cases where care is shared exactly equally between the parents, neither parent will be a 'non-resident parent' and there will be no liability for child support maintenance under the CSA 1991. In such circumstances, jurisdiction for child maintenance is likely to return to the court.

Shared care – flat rate

Where:

(a)   child support maintenance would be payable at the flat rate because the non-resident parent is in receipt of prescribed benefits, pensions or allowances, or his partner is in receipt of prescribed benefits; and

(b)   the non-resident parent cares for one or more qualifying children for at least 52 nights a year,

then the maintenance calculation will be nil.

7.7   VARIATIONS

The application of a rigid formula may inevitably lead to harsh results in certain cases. For this reason, the CSA 1991 (as amended) allows for applications for variation. Any such application can be made either before a final maintenance calculation has been made (CSA 1991, s 28A) or after (CSA 1991, s 28G). However, variations will be allowed only in certain tightly defined circumstances as set out in Sch 4B to the CSA 1991 and the Child Support Maintenance Calculation Regulations 2012 (SI 2012/2677) (CSMCR 2012). In addition, the CMS must be of the opinion that, in all the circumstances of the case, it would be just and equitable to agree to a variation.

7.7.1 Special expenses

These are:

(a)   costs incurred by the non-resident parent maintaining contact with a qualifying child;

(b)   costs attributable to a long-term illness or disability of another relevant child;

(c)   certain debts incurred before the parent became a non-resident parent (generally only if these debts were incurred for the benefit of both parents or the child);

(d)   the maintenance element of boarding school fees for the child in relation to whom the application for a maintenance calculation is made; and

(e)   mortgage payments on the home the non-resident parent and parent with care shared, provided the non-resident parent no longer has an interest in the property and the parent with care and child still live there.

These expenses must be of at least a 'threshold' amount to be taken into account (unless the expense relates to ground (b) when there is no threshold). The threshold amount is £10 a week for each expense (they cannot be aggregated to achieve the threshold). If the CMS considers any of these special expenses to be unreasonably high or to have been unreasonably incurred, it may substitute such lower amount as it considers reasonable, including nil (CSMCR 2012, reg 68).

Generally speaking, if allowable, these expenses will be deducted from the gross weekly income of the non-resident parent before making the maintenance calculation.

7.7.2 Additional cases

Non-resident parents may apply for a downwards variation of any maintenance calculation on the basis of special expenses as set out above. There are in addition rules which may result in an increase to the maintenance calculation. These are:

(a)   The non-resident parent has unearned income of £2,500 or more per annum. The amount of such income will be determined by reference to the non-resident parent's latest tax return and will include such things as income from rental properties, investments and dividend income. The non-resident parent will be treated as having an additional weekly income equal to the amount of unearned income divided by 365 and multiplied by 7 (CSMCR 2012, reg 69).

(b)   The non-resident parent has assets, such as cash, virtual currency (provided this is capable of being exchanged for money), shares or land with a net value exceeding £31,250. Some assets, such as the non-resident parent's home, business assets and assets which have been purchased from the gross weekly income which has already been taken into account for the purposes of the maintenance calculation, are excluded. The value of these assets is calculated by applying the statutory rate of interest (currently 8% pa) and dividing it by 52. This amount is then added to the non-resident parent's gross income. For example, if the non-resident parent owned shares worth £80,000, these would be taken to produce income of (£80,000 x 8%) ÷ 52 = £123.08 per week.

(c)   The maintenance assessment is at the nil rate due to the non-resident parent coming within a prescribed category, or at the flat rate due to the non-resident parent being in receipt of a prescribed benefit, pension or allowance, but the CMS is satisfied that the non-resident parent is in receipt of gross income over £100 which would otherwise be taken into account. This would cover, for example, the income of a non-resident parent who was a child. The whole of this income will be taken into account as gross income (CSMCR 2012, reg 70).

(d)   The CMS is satisfied that the non-resident parent has unreasonably reduced the amount of his income that would otherwise be taken into account as gross income or unearned income, eg where a non-resident parent reduces the amount of his gross income by making excessive payments into a pension scheme. The whole amount of the reduction will be taken into account as income (CSMCR 2012, reg 71).

7.8 DEFAULT AND INTERIM MAINTENANCE DECISIONS (CSA 1991, S 12)

In certain circumstances, it will not be possible to make a final maintenance calculation straightaway. If this is because there is insufficient information to complete the calculation, the CMS may make a default maintenance decision. If it is because an application for variation is outstanding, the CMS may make an interim maintenance decision.

7.8.1 Default maintenance decision

Where there is insufficient information to make a final maintenance calculation, maintenance can be calculated at the default rate. This is £39 per week if there is one qualifying child, £51 per week if there are two qualifying children and £64 per week if there are three or more qualifying children. When the relevant information is provided, a new maintenance calculation will be made. If non-provision of information by the non-resident parent led to the making of the default maintenance decision, his maintenance liability for the period that the default rate was in place will be recalculated only if the full rate is higher than the default rate. The Government hopes that this will provide an incentive for non-resident parents to provide information quickly. It will also avoid the situation where overpayments need to be recovered from the parent with care.

7.8.2 Interim maintenance decision

Where there is an application for a variation outstanding, maintenance may be calculated as normal, ignoring the variation application. If the variation application is successful, this interim rate will be replaced with the new level of maintenance calculated taking into account the variation. The maintenance calculation at this new level will have retrospective effect.

7.9 VOLUNTARY PAYMENTS

A non-resident parent may wish to ensure that he is given credit for any payments of child support maintenance that he makes whilst a maintenance calculation is being made. Section 28J of the CSA 1991 provides that voluntary payments can be set off against any child support maintenance liability under a maintenance calculation, but, by s 28J(4), such a voluntary payment must be made to the CMS unless agreed otherwise.

Another possible device was discussed in *Dorney-Kingdom v Dorney-Kingdom* [2000] 2 FLR 855. The court stated that a provision in an order for spouse maintenance which incorporated some of the costs of caring for the children and which was reduced once the CMS had assessed child support was legitimate provided it included a substantial amount of spousal support. Such orders ('*Segal* orders') are useful since the financial order proceedings are often heard before the child maintenance has been calculated, and such an order will ensure that the parent with care has sufficient money to support the children in the interim.

7.10 REVIEW

Under the new scheme, the CMS will carry out an annual review to ensure that the correct amount of maintenance continues to be paid.

7.11 REFORM

A consultation by the Department for Work and Pensions on proposals designed to modernise and improve the CMS closed in August 2021. Many of the proposals are on points of detail but they also include allowing unearned income to be included in CMS calculations.

SUMMARY

(1) Where parents do not enter an agreement, the CMS will deal with maintenance for a child where the child is:

    (a)   under 16;

    (b)   under 20 and in full-time, non-advanced education.

(2) The courts will deal with maintenance for a child in the following circumstances:

    (a)   where the child is a step-child;

    (b)   where the child is aged 16–19 and in advanced education or is aged over 19;

    (c)   where either parent or the child is not habitually resident in the UK;

    (d)   to provide top-up maintenance;

    (e)   to cover education expenses;

    (f)   to cover disability expenses; or

    (g)   by making a consent order.

(3) A simple formula is applied to calculate maintenance for a child under CSA 1991, based on a two-tiered percentage of the non-resident parent's gross income.

(4) Variations from the simple formula are possible in certain tightly defined cases.

CHAPTER 8

MAINTENANCE FOR A SPOUSE

8.1	Introduction	105
8.2	High income families	106
8.3	Middle income families	106
8.4	Low income families	108
Summary		109

LEARNING OUTCOMES

After reading this chapter you will be able to:

- explain what principles the court will apply when deciding on the amount of maintenance for a spouse in a high income case
- describe how the court will evaluate the amount of maintenance to be paid to a spouse in a middle income case
- set out how to test whether a particular figure suggested as maintenance for a spouse would be appropriate on the facts
- explain the factors which should be taken into account when considering the amount (if any) of spousal maintenance which would be appropriate in a low income case.

8.1 INTRODUCTION

The amount of maintenance to be paid by one spouse to the other will depend on numerous variables, and a case-by-case approach will be taken by the solicitor and the court. Figures cited in reported decisions are of little assistance as there are rarely two cases with identical facts. However, one variable will always be significant and that is the presence or otherwise of dependent children. If there are children to provide for, this will have a significant impact on each party's needs and resources. The maintenance being paid and received for children must be taken into account when calculating maintenance for a spouse. In many instances, there will be insufficient resources remaining for maintenance to be paid to a spouse after paying maintenance for children. It is especially so in low income families. In middle and higher income families, spouses may wish to pursue claims for their own provision in addition to maintenance for their children.

In *SS v NS (Spousal Maintenance)* [2014] EWHC 4183 (Fam), the court gave guidance on maintenance payments including:

(1) That maintenance should be paid when decisions made by the couple during the marriage meant that the recipient needed such maintenance.

(2) However, if needs were not generated by the marriage itself, any maintenance award should be aimed at alleviating significant hardship only.

(3) In addition, the court must consider in every case whether term maintenance would be appropriate. Term maintenance would be appropriate unless the recipient could not adjust to financial independence without undue hardship. A degree of (not undue) hardship in making the transition to independence is acceptable.

(4) Where the choice between an extendable term and a joint lives order is finely balanced, the 'statutory steer should militate in favour of the former'.

(5)   If the choice between an extendable and non-extendable term is finely balanced, the decision should normally be in favour of the economically weaker party, ie to allow the term to be extended.

Note that where a significant proportion of the payer's income is made up of a bonus, the court may provide for part of the recipient's maintenance to be paid from the bonus. Any maintenance paid from the bonus would be calculated as a percentage of the bonus but subject to a cap to avoid unintentional unfairness should an unanticipated substantial bonus be paid – see *H v W (Cap on Wife's Share of Bonus Payments)* [2013] EWHC 4105 (Fam). In addition, where possible, essential needs of the recipient should be met from non-bonus income, with discretionary items met from the bonus (*SS v NS (Spousal Maintenance)*).

In its report on 'Matrimonial Property, Needs and Agreements', the Law Commission acknowledged that no formula for spousal maintenance 'can take account of all aspects of each unique case' but stated that guidelines would be useful, especially for litigants in person. As a result, the Ministry of Justice 'is working to develop an online tool supported by formulae to assist separating couples and help provide confidence in making private financial arrangements on divorce'. The Divorce (Financial Provision) Bill has been introduced by Baroness Shackleton into the House of Lords and has received a first reading. This Bill proposes that there should generally be a five-year limit on maintenance orders, save in cases of 'serious financial hardship', but stops short of proposing a formula.

8.2   HIGH INCOME FAMILIES

In high income families, the courts will be less concerned about meeting an applicant's basic needs than ensuring a fair apportionment of the family's wealth. In doing so, they will bear in mind the standard of living enjoyed prior to the breakdown of the marriage, as well as all the other relevant factors in the s 25 of the MCA 1973 (see **4.5.1**). Commonly, where significant capital is available, it will not be appropriate for there to be any maintenance payable between spouses. In such cases, a clean break will be favoured instead (see **4.6**).

A clean break will not always be appropriate in wealthy families as there may be insufficient liquid capital. Assets may be tied up in land or in a business. It will frequently be counter-productive to realise such assets, as their loss could have a disproportionately adverse effect on the income generated by the assets as a whole. In such cases, it would be more sensible and profitable for the assets to be retained and for a maintenance order to be made instead.

In certain cases there may be insufficient capital for an immediate clean break but a very large amount of income (perhaps, for example, a young person 'up and coming' in the City). In *Miller v Miller; McFarlane v McFarlane* [2006] UKHL 24, the House of Lords upheld an award of £250,000 per annum to Mrs McFarlane and extended its duration for her lifetime. The size of the award was partly to compensate her for the couple's joint decision that she should give up her successful career to care for the children. The House of Lords made it clear that it was in fact unlikely to be appropriate for maintenance to continue at this level indefinitely. However, their Lordships took the view that the onus should be on the husband to seek a variation once Mrs McFarlane had revived her earning capacity and he had reduced his outgoings, by which time a clean break might be possible. Subsequently, Mrs McFarlane successfully applied for an increase in her periodical payments to enable a clean break to occur on or before the husband's retirement (see *McFarlane v McFarlane* [2009] EWHC 891). However, in the majority of cases, the compensation principle will not apply. In these cases, the court is likely to use the applicant's needs (generously interpreted) as a guiding principle (see eg *McCartney v Mills McCartney* [2008] EWHC 401 (Fam)).

8.3   MIDDLE INCOME FAMILIES

The approach taken by the courts to the large group of people who are neither wealthy nor on or near subsistence level has varied over the years. The current guiding principle would appear to be needs, which may be generously interpreted where funds allow. In cases where there are minor children and a figure for maintenance for the children has been agreed or a maintenance calculation has been or is to be made by the CMS, the court is likely to calculate whether the non-resident parent can afford to make any additional periodical payment to the parent with care of the children.

In order to decide what figure (if any) is appropriate for spouse maintenance, or to decide on whether a figure proposed by the other party is reasonable, the solicitor must make a calculation.

It is important to consider the reality behind a particular figure to ensure that the payer can afford to make any payment proposed and that the recipient can manage to live off her income (which will of course include the proposed maintenance). It is important to compare the size of their respective households and the extent of their liabilities. If maintenance is also being paid for children, this must also be borne in mind, as it represents an additional obligation for the paying parent and an additional resource for the receiving parent.

The solicitor should calculate the parties' net income, taking into account any income tax, national insurance and pension contributions. The figure for any child support maintenance must be added to the recipient's income and correspondingly deducted as an expense from the payer's income. A budget will need to be drawn up for each household, which should be compared against the available income. Clearly, there is scope for argument about what represents a reasonable budget, and the solicitor will need to look at the figures carefully. However, care must be taken not to waste costs in a disproportionate manner.

EXAMPLE

This simple example uses *notional figures* to establish whether maintenance should be paid to a wife in addition to child support. In reality, a budget is likely to include a number of other expenses, for example, holidays, etc.

Fergus and Rose have two children, aged 8 and 10. Fergus earns £35,000 annually (gross) and Rose earns £7,000 annually (gross). After applying the formula under the CSA 1991, the parties have agreed that Fergus will pay £100 per week child support maintenance. Rose has remained in the family home with the children and Fergus is in rented accommodation.

Stage 1: Calculate each spouse's net income:

	Fergus	Rose
	£	£
Earnings	675.00	135.00
Less tax	105.00	14.00
National Insurance	55.00	12.00
Pension	30.00	5.00
	485.00	104.00
Child benefit	–	30.00
Child tax credit		10.00
	485.00	144.00

Stage 2: Take child maintenance of £100.00 into account:

	Fergus		Rose
	£		£
Net income	485.00	Net income	144.00
less	100.00	plus	100.00
	385.00		244.00

Stage 3: Deduct each spouse's budgeted expenses:				
	Fergus			Rose
	£	£	£	£
Net income		385.00		244.00
Less expenses:				
Gas and electricity	10.00		15.00	
Council tax	25.00		30.00	
Mortgage	–		135.00	
Rent	115.00		–	
Car insurance, tax and petrol	35.00		–	
TV licence	3.00		3.00	
Bus fares	–		10.00	
Childcare	–		20.00	
Clothing	40.00		20.00	
Food, etc	50.00		75.00	
Total		278.00		308.00
Balance available		107.00		– 64.00

Thus it would appear that Fergus would need to pay maintenance of over half his available income to enable the books to balance. Even so, clearly money is very tight, as there are no allowances for entertainment or holidays in the figures. However, it can be seen that Fergus claims he needs £40 per week for clothes, whereas Rose is claiming she needs only £20 for herself and the two children. Thus it would be sensible to query Fergus's budgeted figure for clothes.

It is likely that for any family, a number of such budget calculations will need to be made before an appropriate settlement is reached. An online tool which can help with this is the divorce and separation budget calculator on the Money Advice Service's website.

8.4 LOW INCOME FAMILIES

If there are clearly insufficient resources for both parties to be independent of welfare benefits, the court and practitioners take a pragmatic approach. Although generally a spouse cannot cast his or her responsibility to maintain the other and their children onto the state, common sense dictates that in low income cases the availability of welfare benefits must be taken into account. The calculation of maintenance in such cases will often be a relatively straightforward process, as it will be a matter of identifying how much the recipient needs to live on and how much the payer can spare. The court will never order a party to pay a sum which would place him below a notional subsistence level. This means the payer would be allowed to keep sufficient money to pay his housing costs, as well as the sum he would be entitled to were he to claim universal credit. The reason for this is plain: there would be little incentive for such a person to earn a living or to pay the maintenance if he would be worse off than if he were unemployed.

The court is even reluctant to make an order that would reduce the payer to this subsistence level. It is more common for the payer to be able to retain a percentage (say 15%) of his net earnings above his subsistence level.

If the recipient is receiving universal credit and will continue to do so when maintenance is paid, she will not be any better off as a result. This is because any maintenance she receives forms part of her income when calculating her benefit entitlement and reduces her entitlement pound for pound.

EXAMPLE

Lucy is 45, unemployed and has no dependent children. She receives £45 universal credit. Her husband Bill is ordered to pay her £10 per week maintenance. Thereafter, she will receive only £35 universal credit, but when this is added to her maintenance her income remains at £45 per week.

In such circumstances, clients may be unenthusiastic about claiming maintenance. However, if the client has any prospects of finding employment, even modest maintenance when combined with wages may, in time, assist her to become independent of state benefits altogether.

Careful calculation must be made in the case of low income families to ensure that the recipient is not worse off with maintenance than without it. This can arise if the maintenance raises the recipient's income to, or only slightly above, her universal credit payment. This is since she may lose other benefits such as free prescriptions and school meals for her children, and as a result would be worse off. It may be appropriate to accept a reduced sum of maintenance to ensure that the recipient is still eligible for universal credit, thereby enabling her to continue to qualify for these other benefits.

Where both parties are in receipt of universal credit, it will not usually be appropriate to apply for maintenance for a spouse. The position is different, however, with children's maintenance. Even parents on universal credit may be expected to pay maintenance for their children under the CSA 1991 (see **Chapter 7**). In low income families in particular, if maintenance is payable for children, it is likely that the non-resident parent will have insufficient resources to pay maintenance for the parent with care as well. If, after paying the child maintenance, the payer's income is close to his subsistence level, no spouse maintenance will be paid.

SUMMARY

(1)   In practice, it is not possible to isolate issues of maintenance from other issues, such as where the children are going to live and what is going to happen to the matrimonial home and other property.

(2)   Maintenance for a spouse is dealt with by the courts under the MCA 1973. The court will consider what the child maintenance calculation under the CSA 1991 will be for any relevant children and then decide whether any payment in addition for the spouse can be afforded and is appropriate, bearing in mind the s 25 factors. The court will consider the effect of any proposed order on both household's budgets.

(3)   In higher income cases the courts will use a guideline of needs (generously interpreted) when calculating the amount of maintenance to be paid. If significant capital is available, maintenance is likely to be capitalised to effect a clean break.

CHAPTER 9

DEALING WITH THE CAPITAL ASSETS

9.1	Introduction	111
9.2	Selling the home	112
9.3	Retaining the home	113
9.4	The interests of third parties	116
9.5	The rented home	118
9.6	Protecting the capital assets	118
9.7	Lump sums	121
9.8	Pensions	123
9.9	Bankruptcy	125
Summary		126

LEARNING OUTCOMES

After reading this chapter you will be able to:

- describe the various types of property adjustment order which may be made
- explain which of these orders may be appropriate on a given set of facts
- explain the legal position of co-owners and lenders in financial order proceedings
- protect the matrimonial assets so that they are available for distribution on divorce
- demonstrate how the amount of a lump sum payment will be assessed
- explain how pensions will be valued and divided
- describe what effect the bankruptcy of one spouse will have on financial orders on divorce.

9.1 INTRODUCTION

The matrimonial home is generally the most important property owned by the family. As well as providing a home for the parties and their children, it is an important capital asset. The court must decide whether it is appropriate to retain the property so that it will continue to provide a home, or whether to sell it and thereby realise the capital. The home also represents a liability, as it must be maintained and in most cases it will be subject to a mortgage. In deciding what should be done with the home, the court is required to have regard to the factors in s 25 of the MCA 1973, considered in **Chapter 4**. These factors assist the court in deciding which type of order to make and what size each party's respective share in the home should be. Although the court will take into account the financial contributions made by the parties to the purchase of the home, it is not fettered by proprietary interests, and such contributions will frequently be outweighed by other factors. The court has a wide discretion to determine how the property should be held and in what shares. It will take into account the parties' past and future non-financial contributions, as well as the other factors referred to in s 25, in an attempt to reach a fair outcome. The House of Lords has made it clear that there is no presumption that both spouses invariably have a right to be able to buy a new home from the assets available to the family. Instead, the court will exercise its discretion in each and every case, in the light of the relevant s 25 factors as applied to that case (*Piglowska v Piglowski* [1999] 2 FLR 763).

Although this chapter is confined to considering the matrimonial home, lump sum orders and pensions, it is important to bear in mind that the court will not look at the capital assets in isolation. It will decide upon a package of complementary orders dealing with income and capital. Any agreement will require careful drafting. In **Chapter 10**, consideration is given to drafting the various orders examined in this chapter.

The following property adjustment orders may be made and are considered below:

(a)   Immediate sale.

(b)   Outright transfer.

(c)   Deferred trust of land.

(d)   Deferred charge.

9.2   SELLING THE HOME

There is a variety of reasons why the court might exercise its powers under s 24A of the MCA 1973 to order the immediate sale of the matrimonial home and the division of the proceeds between the parties. Typically, an immediate sale of the house will be appropriate where the court is effecting an immediate clean break. Each party will be able to use his or her share of the equity towards purchasing separate homes. They will first redeem the existing mortgage from the proceeds of sale, which benefits the parties by releasing them from a significant debt which bound them together. For the sake of clarity, any order for sale should deal with the liabilities to be met out of the proceeds of sale, such as the existing mortgage, estate agent's commission and solicitor's conveyancing fees. When calculating the value of the equity, the costs of purchase and removal should also be borne in mind. For a publicly funded client the statutory charge will also be paid out of the proceeds of sale. However, it may be possible for the payment of the charge to be postponed by registering it against the assisted party's new home (see **2.2.4**).

When making an order that the home be sold (whether immediately or on the triggering of a deferred trust of land or deferred charge – see **9.3.2** and **9.3.3** below), it is generally preferable to specify that the parties should receive a set percentage of the proceeds of sale rather than a set sum (*Browne (formerly Pritchard) v Pritchard* [1975] 1 WLR 1366 and *Hope-Smith v Hope-Smith* [1989] 2 FLR 56). This is fairer, since both parties will be equally at risk in a fluctuating property market.

Section 24A(2) (see **Appendix 1(A)**) provides that the order may contain such consequential or supplementary provisions as the court thinks fit. This therefore gives the court the widest discretion to make directions about the sale, for example, which party's solicitors should have the conduct of the sale, how the price is to be determined and what payments should be made out of the proceeds, etc.

There will not usually be sufficient equity for both parties to be able to purchase alternative homes outright. However, if the couple are both earning, they may be able to do so with the aid of a new mortgage. If one party has only low earnings (or low earning capacity), that party may receive a greater proportion of the equity to enable him to reaccommodate himself. A party may be willing to forgo some of his share of the equity in order to achieve a clean break. This may be regarded as the lesser of two evils if the only other viable alternative is for the other party to remain in the property for many years. If the parties are relatively young and without children, the house is likely to be sold even if the equity is very small, as there is a strong presumption in favour of a clean break in these circumstances. If there are minor children, the court must give first consideration to their welfare when determining what should happen to the matrimonial home, and will thus wish to be satisfied that they will be suitably accommodated. The court will also have regard to the disruption which a move might cause to the children and to the adverse effect this could have on their stability and security. If a move to a cheaper area would involve a change in the children's schooling, the court may be hesitant to order this. However, children frequently adapt well to change and if the home (or the school) has been unhappy, a move might benefit them. If the house is larger than needed and has a substantial equity, it may well be unduly harsh on the non-resident parent to deny him the opportunity to realise some of his capital. In such a case, the court may order sale and perhaps give a weighted share of the equity to the parent caring for the children, as she will require a larger property than the non-resident parent and will frequently have a smaller income.

An immediate sale may be ordered out of necessity if there are insufficient resources to retain and maintain the house. If the couple's finances were already stretched before the marriage breakdown, then plainly it would not be possible for one party to remain in the home and for the other party to accommodate himself as well. It may be that both parties will have to rent properties. Typically, the couple may have purchased the property relatively recently with the aid of a large mortgage, and consequently there may be little or (in times of falling house values) no equity.

If one party wishes to sell the home while the other wishes to remain in it, the former could transfer his interest in the home to the latter in return for a lump sum. Whether or not such a 'buy out' can be achieved depends upon whether the spouse who wishes to stay has the means to make the lump sum payment. He may have savings, or sufficient income to raise the sum by borrowing. Provided the equity is sufficient, the sum may be raised by increasing the mortgage. The spouse who wishes to sell may agree to a smaller lump sum rather than have the delay and inconvenience of sale on the open market.

9.3 RETAINING THE HOME

The matrimonial home may be retained for the occupation of one party and the children of the family. This occupation may be permanent in the case of an outright transfer, or in the medium to long term in the case of a deferred trust of land or deferred charge.

9.3.1 Outright transfer

Outright transfer is another method of achieving a clean break between the parties as it determines immediately and finally the ownership of the home. The court is unlikely to order an immediate outright transfer unless the transferee spouse has the means to pay the outgoings on the house, including the mortgage. It will also wish to ensure that the transferor spouse has suitable alternative accommodation. He need not necessarily own this accommodation: he may, for example, be provided with accommodation through his employment, or he may be living in his new partner's home.

If the transferor is giving up a significant amount of capital, the court will seek to compensate him for this loss. An order for the transfer of a property may be coupled with a lump sum payment from the transferee to the transferor (see the example of Shah at **10.13.13**). The extent to which the transferor spouse will be compensated depends on the value of the equity and on s 25 of the MCA 1973 factors in general. If the equity is small, the transferor may not receive anything in return. In a sluggish market, a party may be glad to be relieved of responsibility for the property.

Another means of compensating a transferor is by releasing him from paying maintenance to the transferee. However, a spouse cannot generally be compensated by being released from his obligations to pay maintenance for his children. This is because, in many cases, the transferor will be bound to pay maintenance for the children under the CSA 1991. When assessing the amount payable, the CMS will not generally take into account any disposals of capital made by the non-resident parent on divorce. Similarly, any agreement by the transferee to forgo any claim under the CSA 1991 will be unenforceable (see **7.4.2**). In the less common cases, where the court, rather than the CMS, has jurisdiction to make periodical payment orders for children, it will take into account all the circumstances of the case, including a sacrifice by the transferor of his interest in the matrimonial home. As a result, the court may take the view that the transferor should pay only modest maintenance for the children.

Faced with the prospect of forgoing capital in the matrimonial home and paying substantial income in the form of CSA 1991 maintenance, outright transfers of the matrimonial home are used infrequently. If the transferee spouse is unable to pay a lump sum to the transferor by way of compensation, the transferor may prefer to preserve his interest in the matrimonial home by means of a deferred charge or trust of land.

9.3.2 Deferred trust of land

The deferred trust of land is a compromise solution to the problem of the matrimonial home. Where the court is of the view that an immediate sale is inappropriate and an outright transfer too harsh on the transferring spouse, it can order the house to be held in the parties' joint names on trust of land. It will specify which spouse is to occupy the home pending sale. The sale of the property is postponed until the first of a number of specified triggering events occurs. The order will also settle how the net proceeds of sale are to be shared between the parties. The main advantage of the trust of land is that it allows a party and the children to remain in the home after the divorce, and it enables the non-occupying spouse to retain an interest in the home which may be realised at a later date.

There are several variations on the trust of land; the differences lie in the events which trigger sale. The main variations are known as the '*Mesher*' order (see *Mesher v Mesher and Hall* [1980] 1 All ER 126), the '*Martin*' order (see *Martin v Martin* [1978] Fam 12) and the '*Harvey*' order (see *Harvey v Harvey* [1982] 3 FLR 141), named after the cases in which they were considered.

9.3.2.1 *Mesher* order

Triggering events

Typically, the events which will trigger the sale in a *Mesher* order will be the first of the following to occur:

(a)   the occupying spouse dies, remarries or voluntarily leaves the property; or

(b)   the youngest child reaches a specified age (usually 17 or 18 years), or ceases full-time education (if this happens earlier/later).

For an example of a *Mesher* order, see Levy at **10.13.13**.

The advantage of this order is that it provides a secure home for the children of the family and offers medium-term security to the occupying spouse. In addition, each party will know fairly clearly when the sale will take place and can plan accordingly. The non-occupying spouse can be confident that the day will come when he will realise his capital and be released from making any contributions towards the outgoings on the former matrimonial home.

The court's attitude towards the sale of the home on the occupying spouse's remarriage varies. Given that the court's primary consideration is the welfare of the minor children, there is some force to the argument that the children's home should not be jeopardised by the remarriage of their parent. Their step-parent may have little or no resources of his own. On the other hand, the non-occupying spouse will feel aggrieved to watch another person living in his property with his ex-spouse and children. Consequently, most judges are prepared to order that the sale is triggered by the occupying spouse's remarriage. A more controversial trigger for sale is cohabitation by the occupying spouse with a new partner. Such orders require careful drafting, as cohabitation is by no means as clearly definable as marriage. Further, a cohabitee would be under no obligation to maintain his partner or her family. It is also arguable that such a trigger would be unduly restrictive on the occupying spouse's personal freedom. Given these problems, and the fact that sale on cohabitation may put minor children at risk, such a clause in unlikely to be imposed by the court.

If the occupying spouse gives up occupation of the home, this would trigger sale. The order may, however, provide for the occupying spouse to move to an alternative property without having to settle the non-occupying party's share. Care must be taken when drafting such a clause; the non-occupying spouse will wish to ensure that the substitute property will adequately protect his interest by being marketable and of sound construction, etc. The substitute property may also be cheaper or more expensive than the original property, which requires further consideration.

Reference to the youngest child may be drafted so that the sale is triggered on the child reaching the specified age whether or not he or she remains in education. Alternatively, it may be worded so that the sale is postponed while the child is in full-time secondary (or even higher) education on the basis that the adult child will still require a home.

Use

As we have seen, the *Mesher* order is a compromise solution; it does not resolve all the difficulties with the matrimonial home. Its main shortcoming is that it is only a medium-term solution. The widespread use of *Mesher* orders has been criticised for simply postponing the 'evil day' so as to avoid facing the harsh reality of the present (*Harvey v Harvey* [1982] 3 FLR 141). Sooner or later the occupying spouse will have to leave the home and then start from scratch to find new accommodation. A wife may have to take that step at a vulnerable time in her life when she has a diminishing earning capacity. The court cannot predict with any accuracy how much time the occupying spouse will need to reaccommodate herself, or what the housing and job market will be many years ahead. The court has no discretion to postpone the sale beyond the triggering events and it may not interfere with the apportionment once it has been settled in the original order. On the other hand, the very fact that the sale is postponed will enable the wife to look to the future and make efforts to become financially independent. Her position may be eased to a certain extent by giving her a greater share of the net proceeds of sale on the assumption that the non-resident parent will have been able to establish himself and secure accommodation in the years which have elapsed since divorce.

9.3.2.2 Martin order

The *Martin* order operates in a similar way to the *Mesher* order, save that the triggers for sale make no reference to the children of the family. The result is that the house need be sold only if the occupying spouse so chooses by leaving or remarrying, or, ultimately, when she dies. Thus, she has the right to remain in the home for life. The *Martin* order will be most appropriate where one spouse is in a significantly weaker financial position than the other. For example, a middle-aged wife may not have worked for many years having cared for the home and family, whereas the husband may be living with a new partner and have reasonable earnings. In such a case, the capital realised by the sale would be a bonus to the husband, whereas the wife would have to apply her money towards a new property. The court is likely to order that the house should be retained to be used as a home for the wife for life. However, it would not make such an order if the matrimonial home were manifestly surplus to her needs. In such a case, an order for sale and division of the proceeds would be more appropriate.

The obvious advantage of this variation on the trust of land is that it avoids the 'evil day' encountered with the *Mesher* order. Provided the occupying spouse remains in the home and unmarried, she will not be faced with the prospect of a forced sale. The disadvantages of this type of order are equally apparent: the non-occupying spouse has an indefinite wait to realise his capital. Indeed, he may predecease his wife, in which case only his estate would benefit. As the occupying spouse has a secure home for life with this type of order, she will not have the same need for capital when the house is sold. The non-occupying spouse may therefore acquire a greater share of the equity than is usually the case with a *Mesher* order. This may go some way to compensate him for the indefinite wait to realise his capital. The court would be unlikely to make a *Martin* order if the occupying spouse could not afford to pay the outgoings on the property, as this would be unduly harsh on the non-occupying spouse. If, exceptionally, the non-occupying spouse is required to pay maintenance to the occupying spouse, he could expect that fact to be reflected by an order giving him an even larger share of the equity upon sale.

9.3.2.3 *Harvey* order

In *Harvey v Harvey* [1982] 3 FLR 141, the court sought to mitigate the hardship which a *Martin* order causes to the non-occupying spouse. A *Harvey* order has triggers similar to the *Martin* order, but in addition it provides for the payment of an 'occupation rent' by the occupying spouse. The obligation to pay the 'rent' is itself triggered by the children growing up or the mortgage being paid off, whichever first occurs. Although the order attempts to do justice between the parties, it is not without its difficulties and is not commonly made. Consideration would have to be given as to how the 'rent' is to be assessed and paid. The rent is taxable in the hands of the recipient spouse.

9.3.3 Deferred charge

A deferred charge is a further method of retaining a home for a spouse and the children. Although similar to the trust of land, the property remains (or is transferred) into the sole name of the occupying spouse. The non-occupying spouse's interest in the home is represented by a charge over the property. This charge cannot be enforced until one of the triggering events discussed in **9.3.2.1** and **9.3.2.2** occurs (*Mesher* or *Martin* triggers). If the occupying spouse cannot pay the charge, at this point the property must be sold. The charge will usually be expressed as a proportion of the net proceeds of sale, thereby allowing the charge holder to benefit from any increase in the value of the property (as in the Brown example at **10.13.13**). Less commonly, the charge may be expressed as a fixed sum, but this has the obvious disadvantage of its value being eroded by the effects of inflation. The charge will be registered against the title and will take priority over any subsequent liabilities incurred by the owner.

In practical terms, there is very little difference between the deferred charge and the trust of land, although the former is less advantageous from a CGT point of view (see **5.2.2**). If the property is already in the parties' joint names, a trust of land will be the preferred method as it avoids interfering with the legal estate. On the other hand, if the property is already in the name of the occupying spouse, the deferred charge may be the preferred method.

9.4 THE INTERESTS OF THIRD PARTIES

9.4.1 Co-owners

If a party owns property with a third party the court may make an order only with respect to the spouse's share of the asset. It cannot interfere with the third party's interest. A third party who is not a legal owner but claims to be beneficially entitled to a property may intervene in proceedings for sale and make representations. So, for example, a parent of one of the parties who has been living in the matrimonial home, having contributed towards the deposit or mortgage, may apply to have the extent of his beneficial interest determined by the court. If the court decided that the property should be sold in such a case, it would probably direct that the parent should be offered the right of first refusal.

9.4.2 Lenders

9.4.2.1 Undue influence

Where both husband and wife are parties to a mortgage, they will both be bound by the mortgage. This is true unless one of them can argue that the mortgage should not be enforced against them because their consent to the mortgage was obtained by undue influence. For example, a wife may argue that the mortgage should be set aside as against the husband because she was induced to enter into the mortgage as a result of his undue influence. In *Royal Bank of Scotland v Etridge (No 2)* [2001] 4 All ER 449, the House of Lords reviewed the law on undue influence, and it is now the leading case in this area. The wife may either prove actual undue influence (ie overt act(s) of the husband actually putting unfair pressure on her or making misrepresentations), or raise a 'rebuttable evidential presumption' of undue influence.

This 'rebuttable evidential presumption' arises where the wife shows that her relationship with her husband is one of trust and confidence in such matters and that the transaction 'calls for explanation' (ie if it is explicable only on the basis of undue influence). This may rarely be the case since such transactions will generally be likely to benefit the family as a whole, although there will be cases where the remortgage is to finance the husband's debts, for example *Hewett v First Plus Financial Group PLC* [2010] EWCA Civ 312.

If there is such undue influence, the wife can have the mortgage set aside as against the lender (ie the lender will not be able to enforce the mortgage against her) only if the lender had actual or constructive notice of the risk of this. The lender will now be 'put on inquiry' (ie fixed with constructive notice) whenever the relationship between debtor and guarantor is non-commercial (eg spouses). However, this will not apply where the money is being advanced jointly, as opposed to the wife acting as guarantor, unless the lender is aware that the loan is being made for the husband's purposes.

Where the lender has notice, either actual or constructive, it must take reasonable steps to satisfy itself that the transaction was properly entered into. In order to do this, the lender must comply with the requirements now laid down in *Royal Bank of Scotland v Etridge* regarding explanations and warnings. The lender may either do this itself, or send the necessary information to the wife's solicitor and obtain confirmation from the solicitor that the transaction and its practical implications have been fully explained. If the lender fails to comply with the requirements it may not be able to enforce the mortgage against the wife, who will be entitled to take her share of the house free from the mortgage. As these requirements are quite stringent, it is likely that, in future, most lenders will rely on the wife's solicitor, rather than attempting to comply with them themselves.

As a result of the House of Lords decision in *Royal Bank of Scotland v Etridge*, in future it will be more difficult for wives to argue undue influence; lenders are less likely to be 'put on inquiry' where the money is advanced jointly. Even where they are, the insistence on confirmation from solicitors is likely to mean that most transactions have been properly entered into and are therefore enforceable.

9.4.2.2 Property adjustment orders on divorce

Leaving aside the cases of possible undue influence and returning to more usual circumstances, what is the position of a lender when a court is considering making a property adjustment order with respect to a matrimonial home on divorce?

If a property is ordered to be sold immediately, there will be no problem with the lender: on completion the mortgage (including any arrears which may have built up) must be paid. It may be necessary to obtain the lender's agreement to postpone any possession proceedings to allow a private sale if substantial arrears have built up. The lender may agree to extend the mortgage term, or perhaps to accept only interest payments in the short term. Mortgage interest at a standard only rate may be paid through income support, jobseeker's allowance or universal credit (and full mortgage interest will not be immediately included in a claim, see **6.3.2**).

If the property is to continue in the parties' joint names under a trust of land, this should not cause any difficulties with the lender. The parties may agree between themselves how the mortgage is to be paid. The occupying spouse may undertake to indemnify the non-occupying spouse for his liability under the mortgage. However, as joint owners and joint borrowers, the lenders have the right to look to both spouses to make the repayments. The lender's rights are unaffected by the terms of the trust. However, if the court alters the legal estate by transferring the property into a party's sole name, the lender is entitled to object. Invariably, the lender will be asked to release the transferor spouse from his liability under the mortgage and thereby relinquish the right to pursue the transferor for payment of the debt. Before agreeing to do so, the lender will need to be satisfied that the transferee spouse will be able to meet the payments. If the lender is not confident that this will be the case, it may refuse to release the transferor. This condition may defeat the object of the transaction, ie of achieving a clean break. Full disclosure of the transferee's resources should be made to the lender in advance of any hearing or agreement to avoid such an objection.

9.5   THE RENTED HOME

If the former matrimonial home is a rented property, the court will have to consider whether the tenancy can and should be transferred into the sole name of one party. Section 24 of the MCA 1973 allows the court to transfer 'property': most tenancies will be regarded as 'property' for this purpose. If the tenancy contains a prohibition against assignment, the court cannot order the transfer under this provision unless the landlord consents. As with lenders, the landlord should be contacted at an early stage in the proceedings.

Statutory tenancies that arose under the Rent Act 1977 on the termination of a protected tenancy do not amount to 'property' for the purposes of s 24 of the MCA 1973, and cannot therefore be transferred under this section. However, under Sch 7 to the FLA 1996, a statutory tenancy can be vested in the name of one spouse. Strictly speaking this is not a transfer of the tenancy and so may be ordered notwithstanding a prohibition in the tenancy against assignment. However, the landlord would be entitled to make representations before the court, and if his objections were reasonable they would be unlikely to be overridden. Protected, assured and secured tenancies may be transferred under s 24 of the MCA 1973. Protected, assured and secured tenancies may also be transferred under FLA 1996. There will, therefore, be a choice (in most cases) of whether to deal with the tenancy under the MCA 1973, or under the FLA 1996. Any public funding for financial orders will normally specify that orders may be made only under the MCA 1973, and as proceedings will already have been brought under that Act, it will normally be convenient to use this jurisdiction.

Where the tenancy is in joint names, either tenant may serve a notice to quit on the landlord, and this will be effective even if done without the knowledge or consent of the other joint tenant (*Hammersmith and Fulham LBC v Monk* [1992] 1 AC 478). The Supreme Court has confirmed that this rule is not incompatible with the other joint tenant's rights under ECHR, Protocol 1, Article 1 (peaceful enjoyment of property) or Article 8 (right to respect for private and family life) – *Sims v Dacorum BC & Secretary of State for Communities & Local Government* [2014] UKSC 63. Joint tenants should be advised of this and, if they have reason to believe that their spouse may serve notice to quit, it may be appropriate to apply for an injunction under s 37 of the MCA 1973 to prevent this (see **9.6.2.3** below).

9.6   PROTECTING THE CAPITAL ASSETS

The matrimonial home is almost invariably the most important (and valuable) family asset. It is also true to say that the issue of what to do with the home is among the most contentious on marriage breakdown. It is a subject on which emotions frequently run high. One fear which a party may have is that the other party will seek to avoid his responsibilities by disposing of the property. Such a suspicion may be well founded. There is a variety of measures available to prevent a party from disposing of (or charging) the matrimonial home, or any other property, and to reverse any attempt by a party to do so.

Whether or not any action need be taken will depend upon how the property is held.

9.6.1 Property in joint names

If the parties hold the property in joint names, neither party can deal with it unilaterally. Any sale or mortgage will require the consent and signature of both parties; therefore, no steps need be taken to guard against this other than advising the client not to sign anything without legal advice (see also **9.4.2** and the possible problem of undue influence).

However, consideration should be given to the question of the parties' beneficial interests in the property. If the parties hold the property jointly in law and equity then their interests will automatically pass to the survivor on death. Given the breakdown of the relationship, the parties are likely to want their shares in the property to form part of their own estates. If this is the case, the joint tenancy must be severed to allow the parties to become beneficial tenants in common. This may be achieved by giving written notice of severance to the other party. The severance should be recorded on the title of the property, by a restriction on the proprietorship register (if the property is registered) or by a memorandum of severance on the conveyance to the parties (if the title is unregistered).

Even if this step is taken, if a party dies intestate prior to decree absolute, the spouse is liable to inherit by default through the rules on intestacy. Clearly, the client should be advised to make a will, or any existing will may need to be reviewed.

9.6.2 Property in a party's sole name

9.6.2.1 Matrimonial home rights: FLA 1996, s 30

If a spouse is not a legal owner of the property, she may feel in a vulnerable position. In such a case, the spouse should be advised of her matrimonial home rights with respect to the matrimonial home by virtue of s 30 of the FLA 1996 (see **Appendix 1(G)**). These rights protect a non-owning spouse (husband, wife or civil partner) against eviction from the matrimonial home without the leave of the court. A spouse will be non-owning for these purposes even if she owns an equitable interest. The rights exist in respect of only one property at a time and it must have been the matrimonial home at some stage.

The rights under s 30 of the FLA 1996 terminate on the death of the owning spouse or on the grant of a decree absolute or dissolution order, although the court has power under s 33(5) of the FLA 1996 to direct that the rights should continue beyond these events.

The matrimonial home rights should be registered so that they bind any subsequent buyers and lenders. As always, the rights will not take priority over any pre-existing interests, such as a prior mortgage.

In order to ascertain where the registration should be made, it may be necessary to carry out an Index Map Search at Land Registry. This will indicate whether or not the property is registered and, if it is, its title number. If it is registered, an agreed notice should be placed on the register (despite the fact that this is an 'agreed notice', it does not need the owning spouse's consent to be registered). If the title is unregistered, a Class F land charge should be registered against the name of the owning spouse. If a spouse fails to register the rights, she will be unable to assert her rights against any third party.

In practice, Land Registry automatically notifies the registered proprietor that an entry relating to the matrimonial home has been made. It will also hold any application made for a period of one week to give the applicant the opportunity to consider fully the effect of her application.

A non-owning spouse may also have concerns about the payment of the original mortgage. Whether or not a spouse has registered her rights, s 30(3) of the FLA 1996 obliges a lender to accept payments from a non-owning spouse (a similar principle applies to payments of rent by a non-tenant spouse). If possession proceedings are brought, the non-owning spouse must be notified (if she has registered her rights) and she may apply to be made a party to the proceedings. If the court is persuaded that the non-owning spouse is able to pay the mortgage and the arrears within a reasonable time, it will usually refuse an order for possession.

A non-owning spouse may also feel vulnerable if the owning spouse faces bankruptcy, because bankruptcy vests the owning spouse's property in his trustee in bankruptcy. Once registered, the matrimonial home rights are binding on the trustee and on the creditors. However, the trustee may apply to the court to terminate the rights. If the application to terminate is made more than a year after the bankruptcy, the court is bound to grant it unless the circumstances are exceptional. The client should be advised of this and warned that having no alternative accommodation for herself and her children will not amount to exceptional circumstances.

9.6.2.2 Pending land action

The limitations of the matrimonial home rights may leave a spouse with inadequate protection. For this reason the registration of a pending land action should be considered. This can be done once proceedings have commenced in relation to property. A request for a property adjustment order in the prayer of the petition or Form A suffices. The registration is not confined to the matrimonial home and it is effective beyond the termination of the marriage. If the property in question is registered land, a unilateral notice should be lodged in the proprietorship register. If the land is unregistered, registration is by way of a pending action against the name of the owning spouse. This prevents any new dealing with the property taking place without first being brought to the attention of the non-owning spouse.

9.6.2.3 Injunctions: MCA 1973, s 37

Preventing disposals

It is possible to seek an injunction from the court under s 37(2)(a) of the MCA 1973 (see **Appendix 1(A)**) to prevent a party from disposing of property. This can be done in relation to any type of property, but if the property is land in England or Wales, it is usually easier to protect it by registering a matrimonial home right or pending land action (as explained at **9.6.2.1** and **9.6.2.2**).

If a client wishes to make use of s 37, he must first have made an application for financial relief under the MCA 1973 (eg for a lump sum or property adjustment order). An injunction may then be granted where the court is satisfied that the other party is about to make a disposition of property with the intention of defeating the claim for financial relief, or with the intention of frustrating or impeding its enforcement. The court has power to make whatever order it thinks fit to restrain the party from making the disposition. The applicant must have placed evidence before the court that the disposition is likely and the application is not simply being taken as a precautionary measure (YM *v* NM [2020] EWFC 13). There is a (rebuttable) presumption that the respondent to the injunction application intends to make the disposition in order to jeopardise the applicant's claim, if it would have that consequence.

> **EXAMPLE**
>
> Mrs Edwards learns that her husband is about to transfer the funds in his savings account to his girlfriend's account. Mrs Edwards can apply for an injunction to freeze the savings account. A copy of the injunction should be served on the bank.

In suitable cases, it may be appropriate to apply for an injunction under s 37 of the MCA 1973 without notice being given to the respondent. The Family Procedure Rules 2010, PD 18A, para 5.1 allows without notice applications (inter alia) 'where there is exceptional urgency'. In UL *v* BK (*Freezing Orders: Safeguards: Standard Examples*) [2013] EWHC 1735 (Fam), Mostyn J stated:

Short informal notice must be given to the respondent unless it is essential that he is not made aware of the application. No notice at all would only be justified where there is powerful evidence that the giving of any notice would likely lead the respondent to take steps to defeat the purpose of the injunction.

Setting aside

If the spouse does not learn of the disposition until after it has taken place, all is not lost. Section 37(2)(b) empowers the court to grant an injunction setting aside a reviewable disposition made with the intention of defeating a claim for financial orders, if financial provision or different financial provision would be made to the applicant as a result. The case of *AC v DC* [2012] EWHC 2420 (Fam) makes it clear that a s 37 order operates retrospectively, avoiding transactions ab initio.

A disposition will be reviewable unless it was made for valuable consideration to a bona fide purchaser without notice of the respondent's intention. A transaction at an undervalue, provided it was not purely nominal, would constitute 'valuable consideration' (*Trowbridge v Trowbridge* [2003] 2 FLR 231). If the disposition took place less than three years before the application, the malevolent intention will be presumed.

> **EXAMPLE**
>
> Mr Philips gave his valuable yacht to his brother 18 months ago. Regardless of whether the brother was aware of Mr Philips' purpose, the disposition may be set aside as it was not made for valuable consideration.

Avoiding enforcement

If a reviewable disposition is made after financial proceedings have been determined, with the object of avoiding enforcement of an order for financial relief, it may be set aside under s 37(2)(c) of the MCA 1973.

> **EXAMPLE**
>
> Mr Clark is ordered to pay a lump sum of £10,000 to his wife. In order to frustrate this, he transfers his entire investments to his mother. Mrs Clark can seek an injunction to reverse this disposition and enforce the lump sum by means of an order for sale against the investments.

Dispositions

A disposition includes any disposal of property except one contained in a will.

Other options

The procedure above under the MCA 1973, s 37 is by far that most commonly used. However, it may instead be possible to obtain an injunction in the High Court using the court's inherent jurisdiction, or to obtain a *Mareva* injunction. Neither of these options will be considered in any further detail here.

9.7 LUMP SUMS

9.7.1 Lump sums generally

The power of the court to make lump sum orders is discussed at **4.4.1**. Lump sums have also been examined throughout this chapter in the context of a division of the net sale proceeds of the matrimonial home. The assessment of the amount of a lump sum remains to be considered here.

Generally, no lump sum would be awarded where the family assets are modest, otherwise than in relation to a division of the net proceeds of the matrimonial home. However, if following the breakdown of the marriage the applicant spouse has incurred debts due to the failure of the respondent to maintain her, the court may remedy the problem by ordering a lump sum. Careful thought should be given to the impact of any lump sum on the recipient's eligibility for welfare benefits (see **Chapter 6**).

The impact of the statutory charge could also seriously erode the net value of any lump sum awarded (see **2.2.4**).

9.7.2 Lump sums in 'big money' cases

If the family assets are substantial, the court will usually consider making a lump sum order in addition to making an order regarding the matrimonial home. The reason for this can be traced to s 25A of the MCA 1973, which requires the court to facilitate a clean break wherever appropriate. If the family assets are substantial, there will be ample opportunity to achieve a clean break by making a lump sum order and dismissing any claim for spousal periodical payments.

In determining how much the lump sum should be, the court will have regard to the s 25 factors and the cases of *White* and *Miller v Miller; McFarlane v McFarlane* (examined in detail in **Chapter 4**). Any contributions made by a spouse towards the family prosperity or to the welfare of the family generally will be particularly influential.

As a result of the case of *White* and the 'yardstick of equality', lump sum awards in 'big money' cases will generally be substantial. A difficulty that may arise is one of liquidity, as one spouse may not have sufficient available resources to pay the other such significant sums of money. This may mean that a clean break may be more difficult to achieve in certain cases. It is particularly problematic if the main asset is a business (or various businesses). In the past, the courts tended to be very reluctant to break up such a business in order to give the other spouse their due. However, the case of *N v N (Financial Provision: Sale of Company)* [2001] 2 FLR 69 suggests that this attitude has changed. As Coleridge J graphically explained:

> There is no doubt that had this case been heard before the *White* decision last year the court would have strained to prevent a disruption of the husband's business and professional activities except to the minimum extent necessary to meet the wife's needs.
>
> However, I think that it must now be taken that those old taboos against selling the goose that lays the golden egg have largely been laid to rest; some would say not before time. Nowadays the goose may well have to go to market for sale, but if it is necessary to sell her it is essential that her condition be such that her egg laying abilities are damaged as little as possible in the process. Otherwise there is a danger that the full value of the goose will not be achieved and the underlying basis of any order will turn out to be flawed.

So, whilst the business may have to be sold, it is important to consider how and when and to give the husband every opportunity to raise funds to buy out the wife's share if at all possible as an alternative.

However, as was emphasised in *D v D and B Ltd* [2007] EWHC 278 (Fam), despite the desirability of achieving a clean break, there will be some cases, especially those involving private companies, where the commercial reality was that a fairer result would be achieved by not selling the business. Thus it will not always be practical or desirable to value and sell the business and then divide the proceeds. The courts have used a variety of different devices where it is either not practical or not desirable to sell the business. For example, in *F v F (Clean Break: Balance of Fairness)* [2003] 1 FLR 847, the court ordered substantial periodical payments to the wife instead of imposing a clean break. In *R v R (Lump Sum Repayments)* [2004] 1 FLR 928, the court made a 'frankly unusual order for a lump sum payment'. This order provided that the husband would pay an initial lump sum instalment of £30,000, followed by 240 further monthly instalments of the amount needed to repay the wife's mortgage liability under a mortgage of £225,000. The judge explained that the reason that these payments were to be made by lump sum rather than periodical payments was that 'it will endure beyond remarriage, ie will in that regard equate to conventional capital provision, and will bind the husband's estate in the unlikely event of his death within the 20-year period'. The lump sum order was secured by giving the wife a first charge over the husband's shares in the company. In R v R *(Financial Remedies)* [2012] EWHC 2390 (Fam), the court ordered the husband to pay a series of lump sum orders together with ongoing periodical payments which would mean that the wife continued to benefit from the profits of the company. Should the husband argue that he was unable to raise the lump sums, shares in the company would be awarded to the wife equivalent to the value of any outstanding lump sums. In C v C *(Variation of Post-Nuptial Settlement: Company Shares)* [2003] 2 FLR 493, the court varied a post-nuptial settlement to give the wife a shareholding in the company.

In cases where a lump sum is used to capitalise maintenance, the courts have in the past based awards on actual assessments of the capital sum required to produce a given income for the remainder of the wife's life (see *Duxbury v Duxbury* [1987] 1 FLR 7). Computer programs have been devised by accountants and lawyers that can calculate the lump sum which, if invested, will produce enough to meet the recipient's requirements for the rest of her life. The calculations are based on certain assumptions, such as to life expectancy and rates of inflation, etc. This complicated method is designed to produce an index-linked net income where both the capital and income are used with the result that the fund would be exhausted, in the main, on the recipient's death. This method cannot, however, protect a spouse against unforeseen future adversity: it may be appropriate to increase the lump sum to provide additional resources to cushion a spouse against such unfortunate eventualities. Whichever method of assessment is used, such calculations can only ever be a guide to the court. The court will keep sight of its wide discretion and its obligation to consider all relevant factors in s 25. In various recent cases, the court has stressed that '*Duxbury* is a tool and not a rule' (as observed by Thorpe LJ in *White v White* [1998] 2 FLR 310 in the Court of Appeal).

Indeed, it has been recognised for some time that *Duxbury* calculations result in the paradox that the longer the marriage, and hence the older the wife, the less the capital sum required for a *Duxbury*-type fund. The case of *White* brought about the demise of the reliance on 'reasonable requirements' and emphasised the importance of considering all the relevant s 25 factors, including contributions. Since, after a long marriage, a spouse will almost certainly have made substantial contributions, whether financial or not, to the welfare of the family, this will have to be reflected in the award made.

Nevertheless, *Duxbury* continues to be used widely. As Mostyn J opined in JL v SL *(No 3)* [2015] EWHC 555 (Fam),

> the Duxbury tables are used in countless cases. Their underlying methodology and assumptions are widely accepted as the usual starting point, and where there is no countervailing evidence, the usual finishing point. In that sense they do represent an 'industry standard'.

9.8 PENSIONS

In many cases the pensions of either or both of the spouses will be a most valuable asset, and in some cases, the most valuable. Previously, pensions were not generally realisable as a capital sum. However, where the pension is a defined contribution pension (eg a personal or stakeholder pension), under rules introduced in April 2015, the policy holder may withdraw some or all of their pension fund as cash once they reach 55. Twenty-five per cent of the sum can be taken tax free with the remaining 75% being treated as income and taxed accordingly. Those in a defined benefit scheme (eg a final salary scheme) will also be able to take advantage of these new rules but only if they first transfer to a defined contribution scheme. Thus, where the pension holder is 55 or over, the pension fund will be realisable, although there may be substantial tax to pay for doing this. The case of JL v SL *(No 3)* [2015] EWHC 555 (Fam) suggests that the courts are now likely to treat the 25% tax-free sum as capital available to be distributed.

There are three possible ways of dealing with pension rights on divorce: off-setting; pension attachment; and pension sharing (see **4.7**). In many cases, the parent with care will give up their pension claim, instead taking the whole equity in the family home so that they can remain there with the children. In other circumstances, off-setting may be the only sensible option, for example where the pension is small in value and the costs of sharing would be disproportionate. One potential problem to be resolved in deciding which option to choose is how to value the pension rights.

The problem of valuation is particularly acute when off-setting is being considered, since it is almost impossible to decide what amount of non-pension assets represents the equivalent of the pension value. For this reason, it may be preferable to opt for pension attachment or pension sharing. Nonetheless, a study on *Pensions on Divorce* (Woodward with Sefton, 2014) showed that off-setting is by far the most common way of dealing with pensions. However, solicitors should ensure that they consider whether other options would be preferable to avoid a negligence claim. In addition, the reduced lifetime pension allowance (the total amount of pension savings attracting tax relief that a person can have) means that pension sharing may be less attractive in some circumstances. In *W v H (Divorce financial remedies)* [2020] EWFC B10, the court emphasised that off-setting may be unfair, firstly due to difficulties in valuation and, secondly, if offsetting would mean that one party would not have sufficient capital to rehouse themselves.

9.8.1   Valuation of the pension

The starting point is the Cash Equivalent Transfer Value ('CETV'), but it would often be inappropriate simply to include this sum as if it were extra capital. This problem was raised in two cases: *Maskell v Maskell* [2001] EWCA Civ 858, [2001] 1 FLR 1138 and *Norris v Norris* [2002] EWHC 2996 (Fam), [2003] 1 FLR 142. In *Maskell*, the Court of Appeal took the view that the pension should be valued at the amount of capital which could be taken on retirement, the rest providing an income stream. This amounted to only 25% of the CETV. However, in different circumstances in *Norris*, the court held that it would not be unfair to include the full CETV as part of the assets.

Equally, it is common for the CETV to undervalue the true value of the pension. The case of *Martin-Dye v Martin-Dye* [2006] EWCA Civ 681 may provide a solution. In this case the Court of Appeal took the view that the best way to achieve fairness was to exclude the pensions from the capital assets altogether and instead make a pension-sharing order in the same percentages as the capital had been divided. Thus, as the capital assets had been divided 57:43 in favour of the wife, there should also be an order sharing the pensions 57:43 in favour of the wife. This case involved a pension in payment, but could equally apply when the respondent has not retired. However, it would not necessarily be fair in all cases. Cases will inevitably turn on their own facts, and in a case where pension rights are substantial, expert advice should be sought as to their valuation.

In *W v H* (above), the court considered whether the pre-marital portion of the pension should be excluded from the calculation. The court held that this may be possible in a sharing case. However, it would potentially be unfair and is unlikely to be justified in a needs case.

9.8.2   A practical approach

In *Vaughan v Vaughan* [2007] EWCA Civ 1085, Wilson LJ suggested that when setting out the parties' capital assets, first the capital other than the pensions should be totalled. Then the CETV of the pensions should be set out underneath, leading to a grand total. It is then possible to apply the 'yardstick of equality' to the resultant figures. The court in *W v H* (above) also looked at the question of whether the court, in promoting equality, should aim for capital equality or equality of income. It stated that much would depend on the facts of the individual case. However, in cases where the pension represents a large proportion of the assets, the parties are older and/or the pension is a defined benefit scheme, then equality of income is likely to be preferred. When the pension is small, the parties are younger and the pension is a defined contribution scheme, equality of capital may be the fair approach.

Further detail and guidance on how to approach pensions on divorce and when expert advice should be sought can be found in the final report of the Pensions Advisory Group which was published in July 2019.

9.9 BANKRUPTCY

9.9.1 Bankruptcy and the matrimonial home

When a spouse becomes bankrupt, his property will vest in the trustee in bankruptcy. The making of a bankruptcy order will sever any joint tenancy. Where the matrimonial home is in the sole name of the bankrupt spouse, the non-owning spouse's matrimonial home rights bind the trustee and creditors (see **9.6.2.1**). However, the trustee in bankruptcy can apply to the court for the sale of the matrimonial home to satisfy the creditors, whether the home is in the sole name of the bankrupt or in the joint names of the bankrupt and spouse. In deciding whether to order a sale the court must take into account the following factors:

(a)   the interests of the bankrupt's creditors;

(b)   the conduct of the spouse or former spouse, so far as contributing to the bankruptcy;

(c)   the needs and financial resources of the spouse or former spouse;

(d)   the needs of the children; and

(e)   all the circumstances of the case other than the needs of the bankrupt.

However, if the trustee applies more than one year after the bankruptcy, the court must assume that the interests of the creditors outweigh all other considerations unless the circumstances are exceptional. There is no definition of what amounts to 'exceptional' circumstances and cases coming within this are likely to be rare. Two examples are *Judd v Brown* [1998] 2 FLR 360, where the wife was suffering from cancer and needed to undergo a course of chemotherapy, and *Re Haghighat (A Bankrupt)* [2009] EWHC 90 (Ch), where there was a seriously disabled adult child who needed constant care. However, the fact that the wife and children will be rendered homeless is unlikely to be regarded as exceptional circumstances (*Re Citro* [1991] 1 FLR 71). In *Donohoe v Ingram (Trustee in Bankruptcy of Kirkup)* [2006] EWHC 292, the court held that such an interpretation of 'exceptional circumstances' did not breach Article 8 of the ECHR. Thus, generally, the non-bankrupt spouse and any children will have a one-year 'breathing space' in which to find themselves alternative accommodation.

9.9.2 Bankruptcy and financial orders

9.9.2.1 Financial orders against a bankrupt spouse

If the court has made a property adjustment order in favour of the spouse of a bankrupt, it would seem that the trustee will take subject to that spouse's interest, provided that the property adjustment order has become effective (ie, decree absolute has been pronounced) at the date of presentation of the bankruptcy petition (*Mountney v Treharne* [2002] EWCA Civ 1174). The only exceptions to this would be if there was evidence of fraud (eg collusion between the spouses designed adversely to affect the creditors) or some other vitiating factor, such as a failure to make full and frank disclosure (*Hill v Haines* [2007] EWCA Civ 1284). If the property adjustment order has not been made and become effective by the date of the presentation of the bankruptcy petition, any property adjustment order made will be void (*Treharne & Sand v Forrester* [2004] 1 FLR 1173).

In *Re Nunn (Bankruptcy: Divorce: Pension Rights)* [2004] 1 FLR 1123, the court held that a pension attachment order made in 1994 was not enforceable against the trustee in bankruptcy as the order did not give the wife an equitable interest in the proceeds of the pension lump sum. However, since May 2000 pension rights under an approved pension scheme are excluded from the bankruptcy estate, and they may be excluded where the scheme is unapproved (see Welfare Reform and Pensions Act 1999, ss 11 and 12).

Under the Insolvency (Amendment) Rules 2005 (SI 2005/527), where the bankruptcy order was made on or after 1 April 2005, lump sum orders and costs orders made in family proceedings are provable in bankruptcy. Thus, where a lump sum order has been made and the payer then becomes bankrupt, the recipient spouse will be in the same position as the bankrupt's other creditors. Arrears of periodical payments and child support maintenance arrears are not provable.

The case of *Young v Young* [2013] EWHC 3637 (Fam) makes it clear that the court can still make a lump sum order against an undischarged bankrupt. In this case the court made a substantial lump sum order in favour of the wife, and made the point that the lump sum would continue to exist until it was paid off and would not be automatically written off if and when the husband obtained a discharge from bankruptcy.

9.9.2.2 Financial orders in favour of a bankrupt spouse

The court will not usually make a capital order in favour of a bankrupt spouse, since such an order would vest in the trustee in bankruptcy and would not meet the applicant's need for housing and an income. However, in S v H [2020] EWFC B16, the court ordered the respondent wife to pay off the husband's debts on the basis that the debts were of a reasonable amount, had been incurred following separation and were due to the fact that the husband had received no financial support from the wife. The wife was also ordered to buy a property for the husband on trust, to revert to her on his death.

SUMMARY

(1) Under ss 24 and 24A of the MCA 1973, the court may make the following orders with respect to the matrimonial home:

    (a) immediate sale (and division of the proceeds, if any);

    (b) outright transfer to one spouse;

    (c) home retained under a deferred trust of land (eg a *Mesher* order) or subject to a deferred charge.

When deciding what order to make, the court will consider the factors in s 25 of the MCA 1973. It must also take into account the interests of any third party, such as a lender.

(2) If the matrimonial home is rented, the court has powers under the MCA 1973 and FLA 1996 to order the transfer of the tenancy to one spouse.

(3) Several measures are available (eg an injunction under MCA 1973, s 37) to protect against one party disposing of property in order to thwart the other party's financial claim. In particular, a non-owning spouse's matrimonial home rights, under s 30 of the FLA 1996, should be registered to prevent the owning spouse selling the matrimonial home.

(4) Lump sums are most commonly ordered either in the context of a division of the net sale proceeds of the home (or other property), or as a form of capitalised maintenance, particularly in cases of substantial assets.

(5) Where one spouse becomes bankrupt, the non-bankrupt spouse and any children will generally have one year in which to find alternative accommodation.

CHAPTER 10

PROCEDURE FOR OBTAINING A FINANCIAL ORDER

10.1	Introduction	127
10.2	Public funding	128
10.3	Overview of the procedure	128
10.4	Procedure pre-application	129
10.5	The application	130
10.6	Filing and service	131
10.7	Obtaining the evidence	132
10.8	Court hearings	134
10.9	Interim orders	138
10.10	Fast-track procedure	138
10.11	Costs	139
10.12	Negotiations	140
10.13	Consent orders	141
10.14	Drafting financial orders	141
10.15	Summary of court procedure	157
10.16	Procedure following agreement by collaborative law process or by arbitration	160
10.17	The Financial Remedies Working Group	160

LEARNING OUTCOMES

After reading this chapter you will be able to:

- explain the procedure to be followed to obtain a financial order
- describe how the court will deal with the issue of the costs of obtaining the financial order
- explain the importance of negotiating throughout the procedure and what safeguards should be considered when negotiating
- draft a consent order.

10.1 INTRODUCTION

This chapter deals first with how to obtain a court order in divorce proceedings providing for the distribution of the matrimonial assets. The order may follow a court hearing or an agreement between the parties. Throughout this chapter, the spouse who is applying for the order is called the applicant and the other spouse is called the respondent (regardless of who was the petitioner or respondent in the divorce itself).

The Family Procedure (Amendment) Rules 2018 have set up two distinct procedures – the 'standard procedure' and the 'fast-track procedure'. This chapter will initially consider the 'standard procedure', which, as its name suggests, is the procedure that will be used most frequently. It will then deal briefly with the fast-track procedure.

The drafting of an order to record any agreement between the parties or order of the court will then be considered.

10.2 PUBLIC FUNDING

Where the client is eligible (eg because she has been a victim of domestic violence), initial advice and negotiations can be carried out using Legal Help and Family Help (Lower). Once proceedings are about to be issued, the solicitor will need to apply for Family Help (Higher).

10.3 OVERVIEW OF THE PROCEDURE

The rules relating to financial procedure are set out in Pt 9 of the FPR 2010 (see **Appendix 1(I)**) which came into force on 6 April 2011. There is an accompanying Practice Direction (PD) 9A, which has a pre-application protocol annexed to it. Also relevant are Pt 3 of the FPR 2010 (non-court dispute resolution) and PD 3A, which accompanies it. These give effect to the Children and Families Act 2014, s 10(1), which requires a potential applicant for a financial order to attend a mediation information and assessment meeting before commencing proceedings (see further **10.4** below).

The FPR 2010 contain an overriding objective 'of enabling the court to deal with cases justly, having regard to any welfare issues involved' (FPR 2010, r 1.1(1)). Dealing with a case justly includes dealing with it expeditiously and proportionately. To this end, similar to the CPR, the court is given a duty to manage cases actively and a number of general case-management powers.

Note that under the FPR 2010, r 3.4, if the court considers that non-court dispute resolution is appropriate at any stage in the proceedings, it may direct that the proceedings be adjourned to enable the parties to obtain information and advice about, and consider using, non-court dispute resolution and, where the parties agree, to enable non-court dispute resolution to take place. An example of the court's use of this power is *WL v HL* [2021] EWFC B10. In this case, the judge adjourned the proceedings to enable the parties to obtain information and advice about, and consider using, non-court dispute resolution and, if the parties agreed, to enable that non-court dispute resolution to take place. Further directions were given requiring fortnightly updates informing the judge by joint letter of their engagement in such a process and dates of offers made and responded to (though not the contents of those offers). The parties did engage in mediation and reached agreement. In his judgment, the judge noted that this judicial encouragement had assisted the parties in reaching settlement. The order took the matter out of the court arena and the inevitable focus on the next court hearing. It allowed the parties to maintain a direct dialogue rather it being conducted in writing via their solicitors (with the potential for polarisation and the inevitable increase in costs). It also allowed them to discuss with a third party and eventually agree a solution that worked for them (rather than having one imposed). The judge also noted that it was important that this was in the context of knowing that he, as the judge, was maintaining an overview of the progress of their negotiations. Although the courts are now heavily encouraging the use of non-court dispute resolution, r 3.4 cannot be used to compel its use, only encourage it.

Once proceedings for a financial order have commenced, the procedure falls into three phases, each of which ends with a court hearing:

Phase 1:   Filing of the application until the end of the First Appointment.

Phase 2:   End of the First Appointment until the end of the Financial Dispute Resolution (FDR) hearing.

Phase 3:   End of FDR until the Final Hearing.

In many cases, only the first two phases will be needed to achieve a final consent order.

Parties can agree to vary the court procedure to attempt non-court dispute resolution, provided that the court sanctions such a variation. One method being encouraged by the courts is the private FDR which takes the place of the in-court FDR (see also **2.5.5**). When parties agree to a private FDR, they will pay a financial remedy specialist (who may be a solicitor, barrister or retired judge) to carry out the FDR. The FDR can then take place at a time and location which is convenient for the parties. This has the advantage that the FDR can take place over as long a time period as needed to reach a settlement. In *HW v WW* [2021] EWFC 34, Mostyn J stated that 'Private FDRs are to be strongly encouraged – they have a higher success rate than in-court FDRs and take pressure off the court system'.

10.4 PROCEDURE PRE-APPLICATION

10.4.1 Mediation information and assessment meeting

Under the Children and Families Act 2014, s 10(1), before making an application to court in relevant family proceedings, all applicants will be required (unless an exemption applies) to attend an information meeting about family mediation and other forms of non-court dispute resolution (a 'mediation information and assessment meeting' or 'MIAM'). Relevant family proceedings for this purpose are all proceedings for a financial remedy (apart from under s 37 of the MCA 1973) and private law proceedings relating to children. This requirement does not apply when the proceedings are for a consent order (FPR 2010, PD 3A, para 13(2)). Exemptions to the requirement include where the mediator is satisfied that the case is not suitable for mediation; where there is an allegation of domestic abuse against a party; where the application is urgent; and where the applicant (or his legal representative) has contacted three mediators within 15 miles of the applicant's home and none is able to conduct a MIAM within 15 working days of the date of contact (see FPR 2010, r 3.8; and **Appendix 1(I)**).

Thus, unless the applicant comes within an exemption, before making any application to court he (or his solicitor) should contact a family mediator to arrange for the applicant to attend a MIAM. The mediator should be provided with contact details for the respondent so that he can contact the respondent to discuss her willingness and availability to attend a MIAM.

The applicant should then attend the MIAM arranged by the mediator. If the parties are willing to attend the MIAM together the meeting may be conducted jointly, but where necessary, separate meetings may be held.

If the applicant then makes an application to court in respect of the dispute, he should complete the relevant part of the application form (Form A – see **10.5.1**) confirming attendance at a MIAM or giving the reasons for not attending. Note that the FPR 2010, r 3 and PD 3A do not require a client to undertake mediation, only to obtain information and advice.

The court will expect all applicants to have complied with this requirement before commencing proceedings, and will also expect respondents to have attended a MIAM if invited to do so. In considering the conduct of any relevant family proceedings, the court will take into account any failure to comply and may refer the parties to a meeting with a mediator before the proceedings continue further (FPR 2010, r 3.1).

10.4.2 Pre-application protocol for applications for a financial remedy

This protocol states that pre-application disclosure should be encouraged only where both parties agree to it and disclosure is not likely to be an issue. Where pre-application disclosure and negotiation are appropriate, they must be carried out in accordance with the overriding objective and be proportionate. Solicitors should bear in mind the advantage of a court timetable and a court-managed process. Thus, making an application to court should not be regarded as a hostile step or as a last resort, but rather as a way of starting the court timetable, controlling disclosure and endeavouring to avoid the costly final hearing and the preparation for it. In addition, solicitors should consider at an early stage and keep under review whether it would be appropriate to suggest mediation, collaborative law or arbitration to the clients as an alternative to solicitor negotiation or court-based litigation.

10.5 THE APPLICATION

10.5.1 Making the application for a financial order

The method of application will depend upon whether the applicant is the petitioner or the respondent in the divorce.

The petitioner-applicant makes the formal application in the summary (prayer) to the petition.

The petitioner-applicant must follow up the formal application in the petition by filing a notice of intention to proceed in Form A (see **Appendix 3(B)**). A respondent-applicant merely has to file Form A.

It is good practice to apply for a financial order (see **Chapter 4**). This not only prevents the client falling into the remarriage trap (see **10.5.2**), but also allows for a change in circumstances or for a clean break to be effected (see **4.6**).

10.5.2 Potential danger areas

Generally, the application should be made at an early stage. There are several reasons for this:

(a)   The remarriage trap: this is caused by s 28(3) of the MCA 1973, which states: 'If after the grant of a decree ... either party remarries ... that party shall not be entitled to apply ... for a financial provision order in his or her favour, or for a property adjustment order'. Thus the court cannot make an order in such circumstances, even by consent; see E v E (*Premature Remarriage*) [2008] 1 FLR 220).

> **EXAMPLE**
>
> Henry has petitioned for divorce. His wife Eileen is very pleased since she wishes to marry her new partner. The decree absolute is granted and Eileen remarries. Only at this stage does she consult her solicitor about obtaining a lump sum order. It is too late – she has fallen into the remarriage trap.

A potential solution to this problem was found in the case of *Whitehouse-Piper v Stokes* [2008] EWCA Civ 1049. Here, the husband had remarried and thus could not apply for a financial order himself. However, his wife applied for a property adjustment order against herself which would transfer the former matrimonial home to her husband with a balancing lump sum for herself. The court made the property adjustment order in favour of the husband but declined to make the lump sum order for the wife. The Court of Appeal made it clear that a party is entitled to make a claim against him or herself.

Note that, in the above example, if Eileen had applied for a lump sum order at any time before remarrying, that application could be heard after her remarriage, as s 28(3) of the MCA 1973 prevents only the *making* of an application after remarriage (*Whitehouse-Piper v Stokes*).

(b)   A lengthy delay in making or proceeding with the application may result in a less advantageous order being made if, for example, the delay has prejudiced the respondent. However, even a very lengthy delay will not lead to a claim being struck out under the FPR 2010, r 4.4(1). In *Vince v Wyatt* [2015] UKSC 14, the wife applied for financial orders 18 years after the divorce. The Supreme Court held that an application could only be struck out under FPR 2010, r 4.4(1) if:

(i)   there were 'no reasonable grounds' for the application which meant that the application was not legally recognisable; or

(ii)   the statement of case amounted to an abuse of process. This application was not such an abuse.

Thus Ms Wyatt's case was not struck out. The Supreme Court commented that there was no limitation period for seeking financial remedy orders on divorce. However, the consequence of such a lengthy delay was that it was likely to 'reduce or even eliminate' any financial provision. In *Briers v Briers* [2017] EWCA Civ 15 the Court reduced the wife's share of the assets from equality to 30% on the basis of a five-year delay.

(c) The court has power to backdate a periodical payments order to the date of the application (provided it believes the respondent has the means to pay). Therefore, the earlier the application, the further it can be backdated.

It is particularly important to remember to apply where the applicant is the respondent in the divorce, as the solicitor must file Form A without the benefit of any reminders. In contrast, the petitioner's solicitor is reminded by the petition itself.

Although the application should be made as soon as possible, the court has no power to make the order before decree nisi (and if it purports to do so, any order it makes is void). Also, most orders will not take effect until decree absolute (see **4.2**).

10.5.3 Financial Remedies Courts

Following calls from a number of people, including the former President of the Family Division, Sir James Munby, a pilot Financial Remedies Court began operation in the West Midlands in spring 2018. These courts have now been rolled out across the whole of the country and have become an established and permanent part of the Family Court. Decisions in these courts are made by specialist family judges with the aim of producing consistency. Such courts also have a greater ability to signpost parties to other resources for alternative dispute resolution, such as mediation or arbitration. The Financial Remedies Courts deal with all financial remedy applications (for example, those arising under the Children Act 1989, Sch 1 as well as divorce). They will also deal with enforcement of financial remedy orders.

A Good Practice Protocol has been produced for use in Financial Remedies Courts. This includes, for example, use of an Accelerated First Appointment procedure. Under this procedure, by agreeing directions, the parties and their legal representatives can avoid the need to physically attend the First Appointment. The procedure requires the parties to email the court at least 14 days before the date fixed for the First Appointment: the body of each party's Form E, the First Appointment documentation (for details on both of these see **10.7.2**) and a draft consent order in standard form containing agreed directions. The parties must also agree a date for the FDR with each other and the court. The application will then be considered by a district judge, and the court will either approve or not approve the order and email its decision at least 7 days prior to the date fixed for the First Appointment hearing. The district judge may telephone the parties to seek clarification. Should the court not approve the draft consent order then the First Appointment will go ahead in the normal way.

10.5.4 The Financial Remedies Unit

The Financial Remedies Unit ('FRU') is a specialist court within the Central Family Court. It handles complex financial cases. Where a case is complex, for example where there are complex asset structures or substantial arguments about which assets are 'non-matrimonial assets', Form A can be issued in the FRU at the Central Family Court provided that a Certificate of Financial Complexity is completed and filed at the same time. A judge of the FRU will then decide whether the matter is sufficiently complex to be dealt with by the FRU or should be transferred. Any family court may transfer cases to the FRU where by reason of complexity or for other good reason they would be better dealt with by the FRU.

10.6 FILING AND SERVICE

10.6.1 Filing

The applicant needs to file at the local Financial Remedies Court:

(a)   Form A in duplicate;

(b)   legal aid certificate and notice of issue (if relevant);

(c)   application fee;

(d)   notice of acting where the client received Legal Help in the divorce and now has Family Help/Legal Representation. This is because the client will have been acting in person in the divorce. Now a solicitor is acting, they will need to ensure that their firm appears on the court file.

Upon filing the Form A, the court will at once (on Form C) fix the date for the First Appointment between 12 and 16 weeks ahead. The timing of this First Appointment cannot be altered without permission from the court. Within this period, much, if not most, of the important financial information-gathering and appraisal of the case will take place.

A pilot scheme allowing applications for consent orders to be filed online was commenced in August 2018. This scheme has now been made compulsory. A similar pilot scheme in relation to contested orders commenced in May 2019 and is running until the end of March 2022.

10.6.2 Service

The court must serve on the respondent a copy of Forms A and C within four days of filing (FPR 2010, r 9.12(1)).

The applicant must serve on the respondent:

(a)   notice of issue of legal aid (if relevant);

(b)   copy of notice of acting (Legal Help divorce case only).

The Form A must also be served on any lender or person responsible for a pension arrangement mentioned in the application (FPR 2010, rr 9.13(3), 9.31, 9.33 and 9.40). Although the applicant is required to confirm to the court prior to the First Appointment (see **10.8.1**) that this step has been taken, if it is overlooked and the lender or person responsible for a pension arrangement is not served with a copy of the application, the hearing may have to be adjourned while the mistake is rectified, with a consequent costs penalty.

Once served, the mortgagee can apply for a copy of the financial statement within 14 days and the pension provider can apply for a copy of section 2.13 of the financial statement within 21 days. Either may then file a statement in answer if they wish.

10.6.3 Pensions

Unless the party with pension rights has a valuation less than 12 months old at the date of the first appointment, he must, within seven days of receiving notification of the date of the first appointment, request one from the pension arrangement. The pension arrangement must provide a valuation within six weeks. When the party with pension rights receives the valuation, he must send it to the applicant within seven days of receipt. Where the Pension Protection Fund has become involved with the pension scheme, the party with pension rights must also send to the applicant a copy of any notification received from the Pension Protection Fund.

10.7 OBTAINING THE EVIDENCE

10.7.1 Duty of disclosure

Each party is under a duty of full and frank disclosure. This duty is underlined in the pre-application protocol for applications for financial relief. This duty of disclosure is ongoing and includes the duty to disclose any material changes after initial disclosure has been given. Should the parties not give full disclosure, this may result in the court drawing adverse inferences and making an increased order (if the party is the respondent – see *NG v SG* [2011] EWHC 3270 (Fam)); a reduced order (if the party is the applicant); a penalty in costs (see, eg,

Thiry v Thiry [2014] EWHC 4046 (Fam)); the forfeiture of legal professional privilege protection (see *Kimber v Brookman Solicitors* [2004] 2 FLR 221); the final order being set aside at a later date (see, eg, *Livesey (formerly Jenkins) v Jenkins* [1985] AC 424 and **11.7**); a party being imprisoned for contempt of court (*Thursfield v Thursfield* [2013] EWCA Civ 840); or even criminal sanctions under the Fraud Act 2006 (see para 7 of the protocol). The bulk of the information needed should be contained in each party's Form E (see **10.7.2**).

The case of *Bokor-Ingram v Bokor-Ingram* [2009] EWCA 412 makes clear that the duty of disclosure not only applies to current resources but extends to facts relevant to resources that parties may have in the foreseeable future. In that case the husband omitted to disclose job negotiations with new employers which had reached a very advanced stage. The consent order reached was set aside.

The duty also applies to cases settled following negotiation, including those where the parties have decided not to use the formal Form E procedure (*KG v LG* [2015] EWFC 64). The duty is owed to the court, so that it is not possible for the parties to agree to release either or both of them from this duty (*Gohil v Gohil* [2015] UKSC 61).

In many cases, the applicant may believe that the respondent is concealing, or will conceal, assets to avoid his financial responsibilities. In such a situation in the past, the so-called Hildebrand rules have enabled the applicant to take and copy documents belonging to the respondent, provided that no force is used, the originals are returned and the existence of copies is disclosed. However, the case of *Imerman v Imerman* [2010] EWCA Civ 908 makes it clear that there is no legal basis for the Hildebrand rules and that such 'self help disclosure' was an actionable breach of confidence. It may also amount to a criminal offence, such as theft or burglary or under, for example, the Data Protection Act 1998. In such a situation the correct approach is for the applicant to apply for an injunction preserving assets, a freezing (*Mareva*) order, a disclosure order (under the *Norwich Phamacal* principle) or even a search (*Anton Pillar*) order.

In a situation where the applicant supplies such documents to her solicitor, the solicitor must not read them and must return them (together with any copies) to the respondent's solicitor. In turn, the respondent's solicitor should read them and disclose those that are relevant. Should disclosure not be made then the applicant spouse is entitled to rely on her recollection of their contents and this evidence will be admissible (*Arbili v Arbili* [2015] EWCA Civ 542). Should the respondent not have a solicitor then the applicant's solicitor should ask the court for directions (*UL v BK (Freezing Orders: Safeguards: Standard Examples)* [2013] EWHC 1735 (Fam)).

10.7.2   The evidence

Both parties must complete and swear a financial statement (Form E) (see **Appendix 3(C)**). This form is quite lengthy and gives details of: the parties and any children; means (including pension); capital and income needs; standard of living; contributions made to the family; conduct (in exceptional cases only); and any other relevant circumstances. Thus, all the essential information required by s 25 of the MCA 1973 should be included in Form E. Each party should also set out any order sought in Form E.

Certain essential documents must be filed and served with Form E:

(a)   last three payslips and last P60 or, if self-employed or in partnership, a copy of the latest tax assessment;

(b)   bank/building society statements for the last 12 months for all accounts;

(c)   any property valuation obtained during the last six months;

(d)   most recent mortgage statement(s);

(e)   the last two years' accounts for any business, and any documentation relating to a valuation of the business;

(f)   valuation of any pension;

(g)   surrender value quotations for any life insurance policies; and

(h)   the latest statement or dividend counterfoil for any investments.

Any necessary explanatory documents must also be annexed.

Various computer packages have been developed to help the solicitor complete Form E, for example *Quantum* (Class Legal). Both Form Es should be filed and simultaneously exchanged at least 35 days before the First Appointment. What if one party's solicitor is ready to exchange Form E but the other side is refusing to? In such a situation, the solicitor who is ready to exchange should send a copy of Form E to the court (but not to the other side) to prove compliance with the FPR 2010. Additionally, the solicitor could apply for a without notice order that the defaulting party should comply, although it is probably better to wait until the First Appointment to ask for such an order.

Both parties should then draft the following documents:

(a)   A concise statement of the issues. This will require the parties to focus on the real issues in the application.

(b)   A chronology.

(c)   A questionnaire of further information and documents requested from the other party. This must be drafted with reference to the issues raised in the statement of issues. In many cases it may be that Form E and the attachments leave no matters outstanding and, in these cases, the parties will file a statement that no further information and documents are required.

(d)   A notice stating whether that party will be in a position at the First Appointment to proceed on that occasion to an FDR appointment. This will be the case where both parties feel that they have all the disclosure they need, and it allows a form of 'fast tracking' in these cases.

These four documents must be filed and served by both parties at least 14 days before the First Appointment (FPR 2010, r 9.14(5)).

As well as the documents required by r 9.14(5), Practice Direction 9A states that the parties should, if possible, exchange and file with the court:

(a)   a summary of the case agreed between the parties;

(b)   a schedule of assets agreed between the parties; and

(c)   details of any directions they seek, including, where appropriate, the name of any expert they wish to be appointed.

In addition, at least one day before the First Appointment, the solicitors for both parties must file and serve a written estimate of the costs incurred so far and those estimated to be incurred by the FDR in Form H. Note that this is something separate from the statement of costs required by the CPR 1998 (see **10.11.2**). Thus, if the solicitor wishes to claim the costs of the First Appointment, they must complete and serve a statement of costs at least 24 hours before the hearing.

10.8 COURT HEARINGS

10.8.1 The First Appointment

The court will fix a date for this when the applicant files Form A (see **10.6.1**). The short timetable is to allow the court to monitor the application and its progress from an early stage, with a view to limiting the issues and saving costs. Both parties and all legal representatives must attend. At this appointment, the district judge will give directions and decide how the application should proceed from then on. Also, unless there are considerable assets involved or the assets require further investigation, the district judge will treat the First Appointment as an FDR appointment.

The directions will deal with:

(a)   the extent to which the questionnaires need to be answered;

(b)   documents to be produced;

(c)   valuations or other expert evidence (joint independent experts should be instructed wherever possible). Part 25 of the FPR 2010 deals with experts, and under r 25.7, the court can direct evidence to be given by a single joint expert;

(d)   the production of other evidence, such as schedules of assets or, in some cases, affidavits.

The normal procedure for incorporating use of a private FDR is that the order made at the First Appointment will record the agreement to have a private FDR in a recital. The order will then provide for a short directions hearing to take place after the private FDR. This hearing can be vacated if the private FDR is successful and a consent order agreed. If it is unsuccessful then directions for the Final Hearing can be given.

Particular considerations that may arise at the First Appointment stage include the following:

(a)   *Valuation of the home.* Directions will usually require that the parties agree a valuation, and if they are unable to agree, that they appoint a joint expert valuer. If they cannot agree on a valuer then the court will appoint one.

(b)   *Valuation of the family business.* There may be a family business which the client wants to be valued. The court will not generally order a sale of the family business, nor make an order which would mean in effect that the owner was forced to sell to comply with the order or where such an order would prejudice third party investors (see **9.7**). The court will also be anxious to ensure that the family assets are not needlessly wasted on expensive valuations of the business (*Evans v Evans* [1990] 1 FLR 319). Therefore, usually, an approximate valuation is all that is needed. However, since *White v White* [2000] 2 FLR 981, a more exact valuation may be required in big money cases. Again, the court is likely to restrict the use of experts by giving a direction for joint appointment or, in default, only allowing one per party.

(c)   *New partners.* One party may claim that the other party has a new partner who is working, and who therefore is able to contribute to the outgoings, thus freeing more cash for the former family or reducing the new family's needs. Say, for example, that the wife had a new partner. The husband might want to know what that partner's assets were. Rule 21.2 of the FPR 2010 allows a party to apply to court for an order that a non-party disclose relevant documents. However, case law states that the court will not order disclosure unless the non-party is to attend the final hearing as a witness. Thus it would appear that the correct procedure in such a situation is to apply for a subpoena for the new party to attend the final hearing. In deciding whether to grant such a subpoena, the court will take into account that any requirement for a third party to disclose financial information is potentially a breach of that party's right to respect for his private life under Article 8 of the ECHR. Thus ordering disclosure must be necessary and proportionate (*M v M (Third Party Subpoena: Financial Conduct)* [2006] 2 FLR 1253; FPR 2010, r 21.2(3)).

   Alternatively, a practical answer to any potential difficulties was set out in *Grey v Grey* [2009] EWCA Civ 1424. The judge can require the party to proceedings to produce evidence of the new partner's means and, in default, the court could draw adverse inferences.

(d)   *Pensions.* Where a pension sharing or pension attachment order is sought, the court is likely to direct the completion of all or part of a Pension Inquiry Form (Form P) within a set time limit before the FDR. When a pension compensation sharing order or a pension compensation attachment order is sought, the court is likely to direct the completion of all or part of a Pension Protection Fund Inquiry Form (Form PPF1 or PPF2) within a set time before the FDR.

(e)   *'Millionaire's defence'*. In some cases the respondent may seek to claim that he need not give detailed disclosure on the basis that he is so wealthy that he can meet any reasonable order that the court may make. This is known as the 'millionaire's defence'. The court in *AH v PH (Scandinavian Marriage Settlement)* [2013] EWHC 3873 (Fam) stated that, provided the respondent gives a broad outline of his overall wealth, this defence is appropriate in cases where the sharing principle would not apply. Thus, for example, where the assets were mainly non-matrimonial, this defence may be utilised as it would be proportionate and cost effective.

The district judge will then give a date for an FDR appointment unless the First Appointment has been treated as a FDR appointment and has been effective, or there are exceptional reasons which make a referral to a FDR appointment inappropriate. In these exceptional cases (which are likely to be those which are very complicated), the district judge must give one of the following directions:

(a)   that a further directions appointment be fixed;

(b)   that an appointment be fixed for an interim order;

(c)   that the case be fixed for a final hearing; or

(d)   that the case be adjourned for mediation or negotiation.

Both parties' representatives will produce their written costs estimates. The district judge must consider whether they should make a costs order at this stage, having regard to the general rule on costs and the extent to which the parties have adhered to the rules (see **10.10.2**). Thus if, for example, one party fails to provide the relevant documentation with Form E, and this wastes the opportunity of having an FDR, he is likely to have a costs order made against him.

10.8.2   From First Appointment to FDR

Both parties should comply with all directions made at the First Appointment before the FDR. Neither party can insist on any further disclosure without leave of the court.

The applicant must inform the court of all offers or proposals and responses made to him at least seven days before the FDR (FPR 2010, r 9.17(3)). This should give the lawyers sufficient time to consider any proposals and ensure that their clients are not surprised by them at the hearing. The court will expect the parties to make offers and proposals, to give them proper consideration and not to attempt to exclude their consideration at the FDR (PD 9A, para 6.3).

At least one day before the FDR, both parties must produce a second written costs estimate in Form H setting out the costs incurred so far and estimating the costs to be incurred up to the final hearing.

10.8.3   The FDR appointment

The aim of the FDR is to produce a settlement. Both parties and all legal representatives must attend. The FDR will be conducted by a district judge who will then have nothing more to do with the case (including any applications relating to enforcement or variation). The district judge will attempt to help the parties towards settlement by exploring common ground. Any offer made so far can be referred to at the FDR, even 'without prejudice' offers. All discussions at the FDR will be completely privileged. Documents referring to prior offers must be returned to the party who filed them at their request and not kept on the court file.

Where a settlement is reached at the FDR, the district judge may make a consent order reflecting the agreement. The district judge may also adjourn the FDR to allow one or both parties time to consider their position. Where no agreement is reached, the judge must make further directions, including, where appropriate, setting a hearing date. These are likely to include directions that the parties must produce statements of issues, schedules of assets and chronologies for use at the final hearing. In addition, a direction that the parties should file s 25 statements setting out their case with reference to the s 25 factors is likely to be made. These statements will generally stand as the parties' evidence in chief.

Where heads of agreement reached at the FDR need to be converted into a court order, the FDR judge can be consulted about the necessary wording. However, if the agreement leaves some peripheral issues outstanding, to be later agreed by the parties or, if they cannot agree, the court, any subsequent dispute about these terms must be dealt with by a different judge (*Myerson v Myerson* [2008] EWCA Civ 1376). Where some matters are agreed at the FDR, that agreement will usually be binding. The final hearing should deal only with those matters that the parties have not agreed and the court should not re-open agreed matters at this stage (*AC v SC* [2015] EWFC B76).

10.8.4   From FDR to hearing

Any directions made at the FDR should be complied with. Either party can apply for further directions, and the court may direct a further FDR.

Where no further FDR is directed, each party must file and serve open proposals for settlement within 21 days or by such date as the court directs. Where there has not been an FDR, such proposals must be filed and served not less than 42 days before the date of the final hearing (FPR 2010, r 27A).

Before the final hearing, both parties must draft a statement of proposed orders, file this at court and serve it on the other party. The applicant must do this at least 14 days before the hearing, and the respondent within seven days of being served with the applicant's proposals (FPR 2010, r 9.28). These statements are open and no privilege will attach to them. However, these rules have no effect on without prejudice offers and such offers may continue to be made at any time.

At least 14 days before the final hearing both parties must file and serve on the other party a statement of costs in Form H1. This requires full details of all costs incurred to date in the proceedings and an estimate of those to be incurred (including the estimated costs of implementation of the order).

The applicant's solicitor should ensure that the relevant bundle of documents is prepared and lodged with the court at least two working days before the hearing, in accordance with FPR 2010, PD 27A. The bundle must be limited to one file containing no more than 350 pages unless a specific direction to exceed this limit has been obtained from the court. Failure to comply with this Practice Direction may result in costs orders, the case being moved to the end of the list or being adjourned altogether, or the naming and shaming of offenders – *X & Y (Bundles)* [2008] EWHC 2058 (Fam). Where the applicant is a litigant in person, responsibility for preparing the documents shifts to the respondent's solicitor.

10.8.5   The Final Hearing

The hearing is usually before a district judge, in chambers and in private.

In theory, the hearing should follow the same course as ordinary civil proceedings. However, such hearings are often much more informal. Having read the papers, the district judge may open by letting the parties know what they have in mind and inviting the parties to discuss and negotiate around this for a while.

If this does not succeed, or if the district judge wishes the proceedings to follow a more formal course, then the applicant's solicitor (or counsel) will open. They will outline the case and then call their evidence. The evidence will often consist only of that of the applicant, but other witnesses, for example a new partner or valuer, may be called. Generally, a party's witness statement will be his evidence in chief. He may amplify his witness statement or give evidence of new matters which have arisen since the statement was served only with permission from the court. The witnesses will then be cross-examined by the respondent's solicitor. They will then present their own client's case. Once all the evidence has been given, the district judge will make the order (or may reserve their judgment until a later date). A careful note should be taken of exactly what is said in case it should be necessary to appeal.

In the case of *Behzadi v Behzadi* [2008] EWCA Civ 1070, the Court of Appeal stated that the court should produce a balance sheet of the parties' assets and the effect of the order, and distribute this to the parties to enable them to see how the sharing principle has been applied in their case.

It is possible that the district judge will not feel able to make a final order at this time, for example, because it appears that the respondent is about to obtain (or lose) a job, or because the respondent has not turned up to the hearing. In such a situation, the district judge could make an interim order on such terms as they consider just.

Copies of any order made are sent to both parties by the court. In addition, where a pension sharing, pension attachment, pension compensation sharing or pension compensation attachment order is made, within seven days of the making of the order or of the decree absolute (whichever is the later) the court must send, or direct one of the parties to send, a copy of the decree nisi, a copy of the decree absolute and a copy of the relevant pension order and annex to the pension sharing arrangement or Pension Protection Fund Board, as appropriate.

10.9 INTERIM ORDERS

Despite the fact that one of the aims of the procedure is to save time, it may still be many months before a final order is made. Thus, FPR 2010, r 9.7 allows a party to apply at any stage of the proceedings for an order for maintenance pending suit (see **4.3.1**), interim periodical payments or an interim variation order. The application will be made by application notice. The notice must state what order is being sought and why the order is required. It should be verified by a statement of truth. Where the application is made before filing a financial statement, up-to-date information about the applicant's financial circumstances must be given. On filing the application notice, the court will give a hearing date which must be at least 14 days later. The applicant must then immediately serve the respondent with a copy of the application notice (and accompanying documents where relevant). Where the respondent has not already filed Form E, he must file and serve a short sworn statement setting out his means at least seven days before the hearing.

10.10 FAST-TRACK PROCEDURE

The fast-track procedure should be used where the application is:

(a)   for a periodical payments order only, or

(b)   for variation of a periodical payments order. However where the application is seeking to substitute the periodical payments order with a lump sum order, property adjustment order, pension sharing order or pension compensation sharing order, it should be made using the standard procedure.

Application is made using Form A1. Either the applicant or the respondent can request the court to direct that the standard procedure should apply. The applicant must do so in the application, the respondent within seven days of being served with the application. In either case, reasons for the request must be given. The court will then decide before the first hearing which procedure should apply and will notify the parties.

The fast-track procedure is similar to the standard procedure but with a number of the time limits reduced and the possibility for earlier resolution of the claim. Thus, when the application is filed, the court will fix a first hearing date not less than six weeks or more than 10 weeks later. As with the standard procedure, this date cannot be cancelled without the court's permission. The parties must then simultaneously exchange Forms E within 21 days of issue of the application.

The applicant must produce to the court all offers and proposals and responses to them at the first hearing. The court may then decide the application at the first hearing or give directions, including directing that the application be referred to an FDR appointment. Alternatively, the court can use the first hearing, or part of it, as an FDR appointment. After any FDR, the application will continue as on the standard procedure.

10.11 COSTS

10.11.1 Costs generally

The importance of costs in financial proceedings cannot be over-emphasised. It is essential that the question of costs is kept in sight and in proportion to the overall assets in dispute. In the case of *Evans v Evans* [2013] EWHC 506 (Fam) the costs amounted to £2.7 million; in *KSO v MJO and JMO (PSO intervening)* [2008] EWHC 3031 (Fam) the costs amounted to over 70% of the total matrimonial assets, leaving insufficient funds to both house the children and pay their school fees; and in *RM v TM* [2020] EWFC 41 the parties ended up with approximately £5,000 each of liquid assets, having incurred nearly £600,000 in costs in what the judge described as 'self-defeating litigation'. In the long-running litigation between the Russian oligarch Farkhad Akhmedov and his ex-wife Tatiana Akhmedova, Tatiana paid the company that funded her litigation nearly £75 million (out of an award of £150 million).

The impact of costs on the family finances is so significant that, under r 9.27 of the FPR 2010, each party must, not less than one day before every hearing or court appointment, file and serve a written estimate of costs in Form H. In addition, at least 14 days before the Final Hearing, both parties must file and serve a written statement of costs in Form H1 (see **10.8.4**). The parties must bring copies of their Forms H or H1 to the hearing, and any order made will include a recital setting out the amount of the costs estimates and any failure to comply with the requirement to file such estimates.

Despite the provisions of the FPR 2010, disproportionate costs continue to be a problem. In *J v J (Financial Remedies: Disproportionate Costs)* [2014] EWHC 3654 (Fam), Mostyn J suggested that there could be fixed fees for each stage of the financial remedy proceedings and the imposition of a cap on costs by the court (variable if circumstances significantly changed). He stated that he intended to bring this to the attention of the President of the Family Division with a view to the matter being raised urgently by the President with the Family Procedure Rules Committee.

10.11.2 The costs rules

The costs rules are set out in r 28.3 of the FPR 2010 (see **Appendix 1(I)**). The general rule is that the court will not make a costs order in financial order proceedings, unless such an order is justified by the litigation conduct of one of the parties. Costs will normally be treated as a liability of the relevant party and be taken into account when making the substantive order. Thus in *MF v SF (Financial Remedies: Litigation Conduct)* [2015] EWHC 1273 (Fam), the court departed from equality due to the litigation conduct of the wife in unreasonably pursuing her allegations relating to her husband's alleged dishonesty and incurring grossly disproportionate costs. Where one party has expended significantly more on costs, the court may adjust the award made to equalise the costs position (eg in *J v J (Financial Remedies: Disproportionate Costs)*). In *SJ v RA* [2014] EWHC 4054 (Fam), the court stated that the respondent may be ordered to pay the high interest costs on the applicant's loan if he has forced her to borrow when he could have funded her legal costs.

In deciding whether to make a costs order on the basis of a party's litigation conduct, the court must take into account the following factors:

(a)   any failure to comply with the rules, any court order or any practice direction which the court considers relevant. Thus, for example, where a party does not make any proposals for settlement before the FDR and in consequence the FDR is adjourned, he is likely to be ordered to pay the costs of the wasted hearing. In *A v A* [2012] All ER (D) 108 (Dec) the court made a costs order against a husband who had filed a deficient Form E and failed to attend the hearing;

(b)   any open offer to settle made by a party;

(c)   whether it was reasonable for a party to raise, pursue or contest a particular allegation or issue. Thus, for example, the wife was ordered to make a contribution towards the husband's costs where she had made a wholly misconceived application to transfer the husband's shares to her weeks before the final hearing and this had vastly increased the costs (*M v M* [2009] EWHC 1941 (Fam));

(d)   the manner in which a party has pursued or responded to the application or a particular allegation or issue. The husband was ordered to pay a proportion of the wife's costs in *GS v L (No 2)* [2011] EWHC 2116 (Fam) where he had erroneously insisted that the case should be determined in Spain or by Spanish law (for example, engaging four Spanish lawyers, one of whom flew from Spain for the hearing). This had meant that the proceedings had been transferred to the High Court and become far lengthier than they should have done;

(e)   any other aspect of a party's conduct in relation to the proceedings which the court considers relevant. This is a general sweeping-up factor, which could cover, for example, where one party instructed a sole expert after a joint expert report had been prepared;

(f)   the financial effect on the parties of any costs order. Thus the court will bear in mind that any costs order will be paid from the pot of assets available to the parties and may not make a costs order on this basis – see, for example, *R v R (Financial Orders: Contributions)* [2012] EWHC 2390 (Fam).

The Practice Direction on Costs (PD 28A) states that the court will take 'a broad view of conduct' and 'will generally conclude that to refuse openly to negotiate reasonably and responsibly will amount to conduct in respect of which the court will consider making an order for costs'. In *OG v AG* [2020] EWFC 52, the husband was ordered to pay the costs, which exceeded £1 million, due to his litigation misconduct. However, the wife failed to negotiate reasonably and so the costs order in her favour was reduced by £50,000. Mostyn J stated, 'It is important that I enunciate this principle loud and clear: if, once the financial landscape is clear, you do not openly negotiate reasonably, then you will likely suffer a penalty in costs. This applies whether the case is big or small, or whether it is being decided by reference to needs or sharing.'

A party who intends to seek a costs order at a hearing must give advance notice of that fact in open correspondence or in his skeleton arguments (*Practice Direction (Ancillary Relief: Costs)*, 20 February 2006). If a summary assessment of costs is likely, the claiming party must also file a statement of costs in CPR Form N260, as Form H1 is insufficiently detailed for such an assessment. In cases where the litigation misconduct is sufficiently bad, indemnity costs may be awarded (*M v M and Others (Costs)* [2013] EWHC 3372 (Fam) and *Joy v Joy-Morancho & Others (No 3)* [2015] EWHC 2507 (Fam)).

Note that the costs rules in r 28.3 of the FPR 2010 do not apply to proceedings for maintenance pending suit or for an interim order. In these cases CPR r 44.3 will apply, giving the court discretion as to whether or not to order costs.

10.12 NEGOTIATIONS

One of the key features of the financial order procedure is the promotion and facilitation of settlements. Most cases do, in fact, settle by agreement, often during informal discussions following the FDR. However, negotiations are an on-going process and may well commence at a very early stage. This is generally to be encouraged as it will probably be quicker and will cost the parties less, so leaving more of the assets available to be divided between them. Further, it may help to lessen any ill-feeling caused by the breakdown of the marriage and, therefore, aid the parties' future relations, in particular with the children. In addition, the respondent is more likely to comply with an order to which he has agreed, thus avoiding the need for enforcement proceedings.

However, the client must beware of settling at any price. Any agreement represents a compromise, but the solicitor must ensure that negotiations are carried out with full knowledge of all material facts. Both parties are under a duty of full and frank disclosure (see **10.7.1**). Do not be afraid to ask the other party for the same level of disclosure as he would give if the matter was to proceed to a hearing.

In addition, the solicitor should be aware of the type of order which the court might be expected to make, thus ensuring that he does not allow his client to accept too little or offer too much. Take care to check that the client is not willing to accept a very low offer simply because he is in an emotionally vulnerable state following the breakdown of the marriage.

If a settlement is reached, heads of agreement should be drawn up and signed by the parties and their legal representatives to evidence the necessary consensus.

10.13 CONSENT ORDERS

Once the parties have reached agreement, the applicant's solicitor should draw up a draft consent order and send it to the respondent's solicitor. To enable the court to investigate the parties' means, a statement of information must also be completed (Form D81 – see **Appendix 3(D)**). This statement sets out information such as an estimate of the approximate value of the capital resources and net income of each party and of any minor child of the family; what arrangements are intended for the accommodation of the parties and any minor child of the family; and whether either party has remarried, or has any present intention to remarry or to cohabit with another person.

Both applicant and respondent may complete the relevant information on one statement of information, or each may each complete his own. A party must sign a statement of truth on any statement of information he completes. Each party must also certify that he has read the contents set out by the other party.

The applicant must then file the statement(s) of information together with two copies of the draft order sought, one of which must be endorsed by the respondent to signify his agreement. Practice Direction 9A states that this rule is complied with if the endorsed statement is signed by solicitors on the record as acting for the respondent, with the important proviso that, if the consent order includes undertakings, it must be signed by the party giving the undertaking as well as by that party's solicitor. The applicant must also file Form A if agreement was reached at such an early stage that this has not yet been done.

The district judge will then peruse the filed documents and, if satisfied, can make an order in the agreed terms. If they are not satisfied, they can return the forms to ask for clarification or order the parties to attend a hearing.

If agreement is reached at a hearing, the district judge can dispense with the need for filing a statement of information.

The consent order is then drafted immediately by both parties' solicitors, and approved and made by the district judge.

10.14 DRAFTING FINANCIAL ORDERS

It is very important for a family solicitor to be able to draft orders which give effect to any financial agreement between husband and wife (or order of the court) in the way intended. It is equally important for the solicitor to be able to spot any errors in a draft order that is sent to them for approval. At **10.14.13**, there are three specimen orders: Shah, Levy and Brown. These should be read carefully, as they will be referred to throughout **10.14** to illustrate a variety of drafting points. In November 2017 Standard Financial and Enforcement Orders were introduced with Practice Guidance from the President of the Family Division. The guidance states that, although use of the Standard Orders is not mandatory, it is strongly to be encouraged. Thus the specimen orders have been drafted in accordance with the Standard Orders.

10.14.1 Form of order

The order should be set out in three parts as follows:

(a)   Title of suit.

(b)   Preamble. This can deal with matters the court has no power to order. In the past, on the basis of *Livesey v Jenkins* [1985] AC 424, this was thought to include payments for the mortgage and for outgoings on the house (unless this was contained in a deferred trust of land – see **10.4.5.3**). However, in *CH v WH* [2017] EWHC 2379 (Fam), Mostyn J was of the view that any family court could order one spouse to make payments on behalf of the other and this would include payments of the mortgage. The family court also has power to order one spouse to indemnify the other in relation to mortgage payments. The standard form of financial order approved by the Financial Remedies Working Group (of which Mostyn J was a member) has been drafted on this basis. The judgment in *CH v WH* was approved by the President of the Family Division. On this basis, and despite the fact that the authors doubt the rationale of *CH v WH*, the specimen orders at **10.14.13** have been drafted in accordance with that judgment and the Standard Financial and Enforcement Orders.

The Preamble:

(i)   states whether the order is made by consent (as in Shah and Levy) or (in a contested case) after hearing representations from the parties (and their solicitors/counsel) (see Brown);

(ii)   may indicate the basis on which the order is made, for example on the basis that the applicant pays the mortgage instalments out of her maintenance payments (see Levy);

(iii)   recites any undertakings given by either party, for example to take out a life insurance policy.

(c)   Operative part of order. This is prefaced by the words 'It is ordered'. It must be couched in clear and unambiguous terms so that each party can see, for example, what he or she is required to do, by when and/or until when. It must also reflect what the court's powers under ss 22–24D of the MCA 1973 actually are. Even by consent, the court cannot order a party to do something which it has no power to do (eg order the husband to pay the premiums on a life insurance policy).

Note that third parties cannot be ordered to do anything, for example, a building society cannot be ordered to grant or transfer a mortgage.

10.14.2 Undertakings

The court may accept undertakings to do things which it cannot itself expressly order. The terms of an undertaking will be set out in the preamble to the order. Common examples would include provisions for one party:

(a)   to take out a life insurance policy for the benefit of the other;

(b)   to pay for medical insurance cover;

(c)   to guarantee a mortgage;

(d)   to purchase property.

Failure to comply with an undertaking to do or abstain from doing any act other than the payment of money may be punished by imprisonment for contempt of court. The undertaking must be endorsed with a notice setting out the consequences of disobedience. The person giving the undertaking must also sign a statement that he understands the terms of the undertaking being given and the consequences of failing to comply with it.

An undertaking for the payment of money can be enforced like an order, for example by attachment of earnings or third party debt order (see **11.2.2**). It will also be contempt of court to fail to comply with such an undertaking. An undertaking for the payment of money must be endorsed with a notice setting out the consequences of disobedience. The person giving the undertaking must also sign a statement that he understands the terms of the undertaking being given and the consequences of failing to comply with it.

See, for example, the specimen orders in Shah and Brown at **10.14.13** below.

10.14.3 Periodical payments

The order must indicate in relation to the payments:

(a)   by whom they are payable;

(b)   to whom they are payable;

(c)   period by reference to when calculated, eg £2,000 per annum;

(d)   period by reference to which payable, eg monthly in advance;

(e)   from what date or event payments are to commence; and

(f)   until what date or event they are to continue (remember the age limits for children (see **4.3.2**)).

EXAMPLE

The Respondent shall pay periodical payments to the Applicant. Payments shall be at the rate of £5,000 per annum payable monthly in advance. Payments shall commence on 1 April 2021. They will end on the first to occur of:

(a)   the death of the Respondent or the Applicant; or

(b)   the Applicant's remarriage; or

(c)   further order of the court.

Spouse and child provision (if any) should appear in separate clauses. In cases where maintenance for a child is not covered by the CSA 1991, child provision should clearly indicate whether the payer is to:

(a)   pay direct to the child; or

(b)   pay to a third party (usually the other parent) for the child's benefit.

Where (as is usual) the order provides for payment to continue until the child reaches 17 (or 18) or ceases full-time education, the words 'whichever is the later' should be added.

Note that, where the CMS makes a calculation, this will not appear in the operative part of the order.

10.14.4 Lump sums

Remember that an order may provide that payment be deferred until a later date or an event and/or be by instalments (see **4.4.1**). The order must indicate in respect of each sum:

(a)   by whom it is payable;

(b)   to whom it is payable;

(c)   by what date or contingency it is to be paid;

For example, 'on or before the 30th day of June 2021'.

10.14.5 Property adjustment orders (not requiring an immediate sale)

Remember that although such orders usually affect only the home, any property may be covered, such as furnishings, stocks and shares, other land, cars (see Shah). The following points primarily relate to land, including the home.

10.14.5.1 Preliminary considerations

The order must make sense from a conveyancing and property law point of view. The solicitor will need to ascertain the following:

(a)   Where is the legal estate now? Is it in joint names, or his or hers alone?

(b)   Where is the legal estate going? Is it to stay in joint names, or to be put into joint names for the purposes of a deferred trust of land? Or is it to be transferred into the sole name of one? This will be so for an outright transfer (with or without a lump sum in return), or a deferred charge.

(c)   What are the equities now, and what are they going to be? This is relevant in two main cases:

    (i)   where the house is in one spouse's sole name but the other spouse may have an equitable interest from contributions to purchase or improvement. If the owning spouse is to keep the home outright, perhaps paying the other a lump sum, the non-owner should agree she has no interest in the property in the preamble;

    (ii)   a *Mesher-* or *Martin*-type order creating a deferred trust of land, where the new equities will be set out in the order.

10.14.5.2 Outright transfers (with or without lump sums in return)

The legal estate and/or equitable interests must be ordered to be transferred to one party as appropriate (see, eg, Shah, clause 2) and a date or event for compliance must be inserted. This date/event must be after the decree absolute (see **4.2**).

10.14.5.3 Deferred trusts of land

The legal estate must be vested in trustees (usually but not necessarily the parties) and ordered to be transferred if need be, with a date for compliance if that is so. The terms of the trust must be set out, including:

(a)   a statement of who has the right to occupy until sale;

(b)   the determining (or 'triggering') event(s) for sale to take place, for example, the occupying spouse's remarriage;

(c)   the proportions of the sale proceeds to which the parties will be entitled on sale.

Other provisions may be included, for example, detailed provisions to enable the original property to be sold and another bought on the same trusts if the occupier wishes to move, or as to who should have responsibility for repairs (see, eg, Levy, clause 1).

10.14.5.4 Deferred charge

If necessary, the legal estate must be ordered to be transferred into the sole name of the intended occupier with a date for compliance. She will then be ordered to execute a legal charge (within a specified time) to secure payment to the non-occupier of a sum representing a proportion of the value of the property as defined in the order, or a fixed sum (as agreed). (See Brown in **10.14.13**.)

The order will require the charge deed to specify the events which will make the statutory power of sale arise and become exercisable, and may provide for matters such as removal and repairs to be covered by covenants to be set out in the deed.

10.14.5.5   Transfer of tenancies

The court also has power to order the transfer of most types of tenancy (see **9.5**). The wording of an order to effect this is relatively straightforward, for example, 'The Respondent do transfer his tenancy in Flat 2, The Broadway, Guildshire, to the Applicant within one month of decree absolute'. Remember that the landlord should be contacted at an early stage so that his consent can be obtained.

10.14.5.6   Further points

The orders do not operate to vest or transfer legal estates, nor to create legal charges. Conveyancing documents will be required to do this.

10.14.6   Orders for sale

In some cases, property may need to be sold in order to realise and divide the cash value. Remember that orders for sale cannot be made on their own, and the court must also have made an order for secured periodical payments, a lump sum order or a property adjustment order (see **4.4.3**). Where the home is in the sole name of one party this will most commonly be achieved by ordering the property owner to pay a lump sum to the other party equivalent to the desired share. The owner may raise the sum either by borrowing against the property, or by selling it, at his option. The non-owner is unaffected either way so long as the cash is paid.

Where property is in joint names, the court has power under s 17 of the the Married Women's Property Act 1882 (MWPA 1882) to order simply that the trust of land be executed and the proceeds divided. On divorce, the court may exercise its powers under s 17 of the MWPA 1882 without a separate formal application. A similar power exists in relation to civil partnerships under s 66 of the CPA 2004. This means that, where the property is in joint names, no lump sum, etc order needs to be made.

10.14.7   Pensions

The order must state that there is to be a provision by way of pension attachment, pension sharing, pension compensation sharing order or pension compensation attachment order in accordance with an annex in Form P1 (pension sharing), Form P2 (pension attachment), Form PPF1 (pension compensation sharing order) or Form PPF2 (pension compensation attachment order).

10.14.8   Dismissals

Just as an application for a particular type of order may be granted by the making of an order, for example for the payment of a lump sum, so an application may be dismissed. Any application by either party which is not granted by the making of an order should be dismissed to prevent that party from reactivating his or her claim in the future. The dismissal may be of an individual application, or the order may provide for the dismissal of all outstanding applications (see, eg, Levy, clause 5).

However, an application can be dismissed only if it has been made. If the husband is the respondent in the divorce, he may not have made any applications. Some courts will require that he files Form A so that his applications can be dismissed. However, no fee will be required if Form A is marked 'for dismissal purposes only'.

10.14.9   Clean break orders

Remember that such orders involve either an immediate dismissal of all maintenance claims, or an order that maintenance should be paid for a finite term only (see **4.6.2**).

Where an application for periodical payments for a spouse is dismissed to effect a clean break, the order should go on (under MCA 1973, s 25A) to direct that she 'shall not be entitled to make a further application in relation to the marriage' for a secured or unsecured periodical payments order (as in Shah, clause 6).

Where the order is for term maintenance, to effect a clean break it should direct that the applicant 'shall not be entitled to apply for an order to extend this deadline' (see Levy, clause 3).

The order should normally state that neither party, on the death of the other, shall be entitled to apply for an order under the I(PFD)A 1975 (see Shah, clause 6).

10.14.10 'Liberty to apply'

The words 'Liberty to apply' are conventionally included in an order. They simply envisage that the parties may need to come back to the court to resolve any difficulties over the interpretation of the order in the light of circumstances which may occur on putting it into effect, for example if, when the house is sold, there is a dispute over which/how many estate agents to use. They do not in any way affect the court's power to vary an order and the restrictions on that power (see **11.7**).

10.14.11 Costs

The costs of each ancillary matter is a separate matter distinct from the main suit and any other application. When considering the costs of the financial order proceedings, remember that the general rule is that the court will not make a costs order unless it is appropriate to do so because of the litigation conduct of one of the parties. On an earlier hearing, there may already have been a summary assessment of costs. Alternatively, if the order was silent as to costs, no party is entitled to costs in relation to that order (CPR 1998, r 44.13).

Where the court orders one party to pay the costs of the other party, it may either make a summary assessment, or order a detailed assessment of the costs (for further details, see **Civil Litigation**).

Where the general rule applies, the order will say that there be 'no order as to costs'. Where it is an application for a consent order (see **10.13**), the parties should agree a figure for costs to be inserted in the order, or agree there should be no order as to costs, as otherwise it will be necessary for attendance at the hearing.

If the receiving party is legally aided:

(a)   there must be a detailed assessment of costs, if not agreed (see, eg, Brown, clause 8); and

(b)   where property or cash 'recovered or preserved' is intended to provide a house, a statement to that effect must be included in the body of the order to enable the Legal Services Commission to exercise its discretion to postpone the enforcement of the statutory charge. The Lord Chancellor has prescribed the following clause:

> And it is certified for the purpose of the Community Legal Service (Financial) Regulations 2000 [that the lump sum of £X has been ordered to be paid to enable the applicant/respondent to purchase a home for himself/herself (or his/her dependants)] [that the property (address) has been preserved for/ recovered by the applicant/respondent for use as a home for himself/herself (or his/her dependants)].

See Brown, clause 1.

Lastly, remember to deal with the costs of implementing the order, for example conveyancing costs.

10.14.12 Side-letters

In some cases, it may be useful to record in a side-letter the background to the order and the result that it is trying to achieve. This can aid the court if at a later date one of the parties seeks to vary the order (see **11.7.3**).

10.14.13 Specimen orders

There follow three specimen orders: Shah, Levy and Brown. These should be read carefully as they are referred to throughout **10.14** to illustrate a variety of drafting points.

SHAH *v* SHAH

[Order for transfer of property with lump sum back or sale in default.]

There follows an outline of the facts of the case which resulted in the order below (note that these facts are *not* part of the order):

Mr and Mrs Shah are both working and self-supporting. There are no children. The matrimonial home is owned in joint names and is subject to a mortgage to the Halnat Building Society. It was agreed at the FDR that Mrs Shah (respondent) will transfer to Mr Shah her half share in the property in return for £15,000, being approximately half the net equity. Mr Shah will finance this by a second mortgage. Should it not be possible for him to raise the money within three months of decree absolute the house will be sold and the proceeds divided as to £15,000 to Mrs Shah and the balance to Mr Shah. Each party is to pay their own costs.

	Case No
	In the Family Court
	sitting at

The Matrimonial Causes Act 1973

The marriage of Raj Shah and Gita Shah

ORDER MADE BY DISTRICT JUDGE JONES ON … July 2021 BY CONSENT

> **WARNING: IF YOU DO NOT COMPLY WITH THIS ORDER, YOU MAY BE HELD TO BE IN CONTEMPT OF COURT AND YOU MAY BE SENT TO PRISON, BE FINED, OR HAVE YOUR ASSETS SEIZED.**

The applicant is Raj Shah

The respondent is Gita Shah

The 'family home' shall mean 93 Brook Court, Hullpool 1HP 2ER registered at HM Land Registry with title number HPO1234.

The 'mortgage' shall mean the mortgage secured on the family home in favour of the Halnat Building Society.

The 'payment date' shall mean the date which is 3 months after the date of decree absolute in this matter.

1.   It is recorded that the applicant has filed with the court and served on the respondent a costs estimate in Form H, stating that: (a) the applicant has incurred costs of £xx up to today's hearing and (b) the applicant expected to incur further costs of £xx after today's hearing up to and including the final hearing if settlement had not been reached.

2.   It is recorded that the respondent has filed with the court and served on the applicant a costs estimate in Form H, stating that: (a) the respondent has incurred costs of £xx up to today's hearing and (b) the respondent expected to incur further costs of £xx after today's hearing up to and including the final hearing if settlement had not been reached.

3.   The parties agree that the terms set out in this order are accepted in full and final satisfaction of:

    (a)   All claims for income;

    (b)   All claims for capital, that is payments of lump sums, transfers of property and variations of settlements;

    (c)   All claims in respect of each other's pensions;

(d)   All claims in respect of the contents of the family home and personal belongings including but not limited to furniture, art work, jewellery and motor vehicles;

(e)   All claims in respect of legal costs including those of the divorce proceedings;

(f)   All claims against each other's estate on death;

(g)   All other claims of any nature which one may have against the other as a result of their marriage howsoever arising either in England and Wales or in any other jurisdiction.

BY CONSENT IT IS ORDERED THAT:

1.   The applicant shall pay to the respondent a lump sum of £15,000 by the payment date.

2.   On payment of the lump sum ordered in paragraph 1 the respondent shall transfer to the applicant:

(a)   all her legal estate and beneficial interest in the family home subject to the mortgage; and

(b)   all fixtures and chattels now in the family home which belong to her alone and her interest in any such items which are jointly owned.

3.   The applicant shall use his best endeavours to procure the release of the respondent from any liability under the mortgage on or before completion of the transfer provided for by paragraph 2.

4.   Upon transfer in accordance with paragraph 2 the applicant shall discharge as and when each payment becomes due, be solely responsible for and in any event indemnify the respondent against:

(a)   all interest and capital payments due in respect of the mortgage;

(b)   all sums due in respect of service charge, council tax, utilities (including but not limited to gas, electricity, water and telephone accounts), and buildings and contents insurance premiums in respect of the family home.

5.   If the lump sum is not paid by the payment date then the family home shall be sold on the open market and the following consequential provisions shall apply:

(a)   the home shall be sold for such price as may be agreed by the parties or in default of agreement determined by the court;

(b)   both parties shall have the conduct of the sale;

(c)   the applicant's solicitors shall have the conduct of the conveyancing work relating to the sale;

(d)   the home shall be offered for sale by such estate agents as may be agreed by the parties or in default of such agreement nominated by the court.

(e)   The proceeds of sale of the home shall be applied as follows:

(i)   to discharge the mortgage

(ii)   in payment of the applicant's solicitors' conveyancing costs and disbursements in connection with the sale;

(iii)   in payment of the charges of the estate agents;

(iv)   in payment to the respondent of the lump sum of £15,000 referred to in Clause 1 of this order;

(v)   in payment of the balance to the applicant.

6.   Except as provided for in this order, the applicant's and the respondent's claims for periodical payments orders, secured periodical payments orders, lump sum orders, property adjustment orders, pension sharing orders and pension attachment orders shall be dismissed, and neither the applicant nor the respondent shall be entitled to make any further application in relation to the marriage for an order under the Matrimonial Causes Act 1973 section 23(1)(a) or (b) and neither the applicant nor the respondent shall be

entitled to apply on the other's death for an order under the Inheritance (Provision for Family and Dependants) Act 1975, section 2.

7.   The parties shall have liberty to apply to the court concerning the implementation and timing of the terms of this order only.

8.   There shall be no order as to costs.

Dated the   day of   2021.

Signed ....   Signed ....
Applicant   Respondent

We request that the court make an order as set out above to which our clients respectively consent.

Signed ....   Signed ....
Solicitors for the Applicant   Solicitors for the Respondent

LEVY v LEVY

[*Mesher* order: periodical payments to wife (linked to payment of mortgage) and step-child; dismissal of prayer for lump sum and respondent's application.]

Background information (note that this is *not* part of the order): Michelle Levy has recently obtained a decree absolute against Michael Levy under s 1(2)(d) of the MCA 1973. The parties have agreed that the three children of the family, Anthony (7) (who is Mrs Levy's child by her first husband who is now dead), Robert (5) and Peter (3), will remain with Mrs Levy. Mr Levy will pay maintenance for all three children (for his natural children by written agreement based on a calculation made using the formula under the Child Support Act 1991). The parties are in their mid-thirties. Mr Levy is a partner in a firm of surveyors. Mrs Levy has not been in paid employment since the birth of their first child. The former matrimonial home is in joint names and subject to a mortgage. Mr Levy has agreed that Mrs Levy and the children will remain in the home while the children are being educated. Mr Levy now lives in a flat. During mediation Mr and Mrs Levy agreed to the terms of the following order. Mr Levy has agreed to pay Mrs Levy's costs, the sum has already been agreed.

Case No

In the Family Court

sitting at

The Matrimonial Causes Act 1973

The marriage of Michelle Ann Levy and Michael James Levy

ORDER MADE BY DISTRICT JUDGE SMITH ON ... October 2021 BY CONSENT

> **WARNING: IF YOU DO NOT COMPLY WITH THIS ORDER, YOU MAY BE HELD TO BE IN CONTEMPT OF COURT AND YOU MAY BE SENT TO PRISON, BE FINED, OR HAVE YOUR ASSETS SEIZED.**

The applicant is Michelle Ann Levy

The respondent is Michael James Levy

The 'children of the family' are:

a)   Anthony Levy born on 2/06/13

b)   Robert Levy born on 17/3/16 and

c)   Peter Levy born on 29/11/17

The 'family home' shall mean Twintrees, Hill Road, Highbridge, HB4 9LX registered at HM Land Registry with title number HB9876

The 'mortgage' shall mean the mortgage secured on the family home in favour of Barcloyds Bank

1.   The parties attended mediation with Harriet Johnson. They have now invited the court to make this order in agreed terms, reflecting the agreement reached at mediation.

2.   The parties agree that the terms set out in this order are accepted in full and final satisfaction of:

(a)   All claims for income;

(b)   All claims for capital, that is payments of lump sums, transfers of property and variations of settlements;

(c)   All claims in respect of each other's pensions

(d) All claims in respect of the contents of the family home and personal belongings including but not limited to furniture, art work, jewellery and motor vehicles;

(e) All claims in respect of legal costs including those of the divorce proceedings;

(f) All other claims of any nature which one may have against the other as a result of their marriage howsoever arising either in England and Wales or in any other jurisdiction

3. The applicant and the respondent agree that the contents of the family home and their personal belongings shall be divided in accordance with schedules attached to this order.

This order is on the basis that the applicant will use the periodical payments made to her by clause 3 of this order to discharge the mortgage on the family home

BY CONSENT IT IS ORDERED:

1. With effect from the making of this order the family home shall be held by the applicant and respondent upon a trust of land for themselves as beneficial tenants in common as to 75% to the applicant and as to 25% to the respondent upon the following terms and conditions:

(a) The applicant shall be entitled to occupy the family home rent free to the exclusion of the respondent until the determining event

(b) The family home shall not be sold without the prior written consent of both parties or further order until the first to happen of the following events ('the determining event'), namely:

(i) the applicant remarries;

(ii) the applicant dies;

(iii) all the surviving children of the family reach the age of 18 or finish full-time undergraduate education if later save that, if prior to this all the surviving children of the family have ceased to live permanently with the applicant, the determining event shall arise upon such cessation;

(iv) the applicant's failure to occupy the property for a period of 4 months in any 12 month period;

(v) the applicant's failure to occupy the property as her primary residence; or

(vi) further order of the court,

provided that in any event the property shall not be sold without the permission of the court while any child of the family in occupation of the property is still a minor or of full age but receiving full time education or training.

(c) The applicant shall with effect from the date of this order be solely responsible for all payments of capital and interest on the mortgage

(d) The applicant shall be responsible for all routine maintenance and decorative repairs to the family home

(e) The cost of insuring the family home and of any structural repairs shall be shared equally between the applicant and the respondent provided that no works of structural repair shall be carried out to the family home save by agreement between the parties or by further order of the court

(f) If the applicant wishes to spend money on the property to improve its amenities then the parties shall enter into a deed recording their interests in the net proceeds of the sale of the property. The applicant shall acquire such further share in the net proceeds of the property as may be agreed between the parties or in default of agreement as shall be determined by the court as reflecting the likely increase in the sale price (when the family home is eventually sold) referable to her outlay. The applicant shall be responsible for the costs of preparing and executing the deed of trust

(g)   In the event of the applicant wishing to move to another home with the agreement of the respondent (such agreement not to be unreasonably withheld) during the subsistence of this trust:

  (i)   the trustees shall, if requested by the applicant, sell the family home and re-invest the proceeds in the purchase of such other freehold or leasehold property ('the new home') as she shall direct for her occupation

  (ii)   the applicant shall pay the costs of and incidental to such sale and purchase

  (iii)   the new home shall be held on the same trusts terms and conditions as the family home and the trustees shall have full power as if they were beneficial owners to execute such mortgage deed as may be necessary to enable the purchase to be completed

  (iv)   if the purchase price excluding stamp duty land tax, Land Registry fees and conveyancing costs of the new home shall be less than the net proceeds of the family home the difference shall be divided as to 75% to the applicant and 25% to the respondent and if the purchase price excluding stamp duty, Land Registry fees and conveyancing costs of the property purchased shall be more than the net proceeds of sale of the property the difference shall be met by the applicant. The parties shall then enter into a written deed recording their interests in the net proceeds of sale of the property purchased as proportionate to their contributions towards the purchase price or such other arrangement as may be agreed between them. The applicant shall be responsible for the costs of preparing and executing the deed of trust

(h)   If the applicant shall remain in occupation of the property for more than 6 months after the determining event, she shall pay to the respondent from that date such sum by way of occupation rent as may be agreed or in default of agreement determined by the court

(i)   On or before the determining event the applicant shall have the right to purchase the respondent's interest in the family home at an open market valuation to be agreed, or in default of agreement, to be determined by a valuer nominated by the court

(j)   If either the applicant or the respondent shall die during the currency of the trust, the power of appointing a substitute trustee shall be exercised by his or her personal representatives.

2.   That upon sale (except in accordance with clause 1(g), the proceeds shall be applied in redeeming the mortgage, and paying the costs of the sale. The balance remaining shall be divided in the proportion of 75% to the applicant and 25% to the respondent.

3.   The respondent shall pay periodical payments to the applicant.

Payments shall be at the rate of £X per annum payable monthly in advance.

Payments shall commence on   .

They will end on the first to occur of:

(a)   the death of either the applicant or the respondent; or

(b)   the applicant's remarriage; or

(c)   (subject to clause 1(g)) the applicant voluntarily vacating the family home for a period in excess of 3 months in any 12 month period; or

(d)   all the children of the family reaching the age of 18 or finishing full-time undergraduate education if later; or

(e)   further order of the court

after which the applicant's claims for periodical payments shall be dismissed, and it is directed that:

    (i)   upon the expiry of this term, the applicant shall not be entitled to make any further application in relation to the marriage for an order under the Matrimonial Causes Act 1973 section 23(1)(a) or (b) for periodical payments or secured periodical payments;

    (ii)   pursuant to the Matrimonial Causes Act 1973 section 28(1A), the applicant may not apply for an order to extend this term;

    (iii)   upon the expiry of the term, the applicant shall not be entitled on the respondent's later death to apply for an order under the Inheritance (Provision for Family and Dependants) Act 1975, section 2.

For the avoidance of doubt, the applicant may not apply for an order to extend this term. Further, paragraph (iii) above shall not apply in the event of the respondent's death prior to the expiration of this term.

4.   The respondent shall make periodical payments to the applicant for the benefit of the children of the family. Payments shall be at the rate of £X per annum per child.

    (a)   Payments shall be made monthly in advance on the 1st of each month

    (b)   They shall commence on 1st November 2021

    (c)   They shall end on

        (i)   each child respectively attaining the age of 18 years or ceasing their full-time secondary education whichever shall be the later; or

        (ii)   a further order.

The court may (prior to the expiry of the term or subsequently) order a longer period of payment.

5.   Except as provided for in this order, the applicant's and the respondent's claims for periodical payments orders, secured periodical payments orders, lump sum orders, property adjustment orders, pension sharing orders and pension attachment orders shall be dismissed, and the respondent shall not be entitled to make any further application in relation to the marriage for an order under the Matrimonial Causes Act 1973 section 23(1)(a) or (b) and he shall not be entitled on the applicant's death to apply for an order under the Inheritance (Provision for Family and Dependants) Act 1975, section 2.

6.   The parties shall have liberty to apply to the court concerning the implementation and timing of the terms of this order only.

7.   The respondent shall pay the applicant's costs of this application in the sum of £   .

Dated the   day of   2021.

Signed ....   Signed ....

Applicant   Respondent

We request that the court make an order as set out above to which our clients respectively consent.

Signed ....   Signed ....

Solicitors for the Applicant   Solicitors for the Respondent

BROWN *v* BROWN

[Deferred charge on *Martin* contingencies; order for nominal maintenance.]

Background information (note that this is *not* part of the order): Eileen and Arthur Brown are in their fifties and were married for 35 years. Mr Brown is an office manager and Mrs Brown is a typist. The children of the family are married and self-supporting. Mrs Brown has obtained a decree absolute based on Mr Brown's adultery with a woman with whom he now lives permanently. Mrs Brown continues to live at the former matrimonial home, a small three bedroomed terraced house which is in Mr Brown's sole name. The mortgage was paid off two years ago, and Mrs Brown can afford to pay the outgoings from her earnings. Mrs Brown has arthritis and has been advised that she will probably have to stop work in about three years' time. Mr Brown wants the house sold and has offered Mrs Brown one-third of the net proceeds. Mrs Brown, who has registered an agreed notice under the Family Law Act 1996, has rejected the offer, saying this will be insufficient to rehouse her. She wishes to remain in the house. Following a heated argument about finances, Mr Brown became violent towards Mrs Brown, who subsequently sought, and obtained, a non-molestation order. Mrs Brown then obtained legal aid and applied to the court in relation to her application for financial orders. The district judge makes the following order.

Case No

In the Family Court sitting at

The Matrimonial Causes Act 1973

The marriage of Eileen Audrey Brown and Arthur George Brown

After hearing Polly Newby for the Applicant and hearing Justin Powell for the respondent

ORDER MADE BY DISTRICT JUDGE WATSON ON ... November 2021 SITTING IN PRIVATE

> **WARNING: IF YOU DO NOT COMPLY WITH THIS ORDER, YOU MAY BE HELD TO BE IN CONTEMPT OF COURT AND YOU MAY BE SENT TO PRISON, BE FINED, OR HAVE YOUR ASSETS SEIZED.**

The applicant is Eileen Audrey Brown

The respondent is Arthur George Brown

The 'family home' shall mean 34, Lower Lane, Loke LK5 7AA registered at HM Land Registry with title number LK7543

1. It is recorded that the applicant has filed with the court and served on the respondent costs particulars in Form H1, stating that the applicant has incurred costs of £xx and expects to incur further costs of £xx in respect of these proceedings.

2. It is recorded that the respondent has filed with the court and served on the applicant costs particulars in Form H1, stating that the respondent has incurred costs of £xx and expects to incur further costs of £xx in respect of these proceedings.

Upon the basis that the family home be used as a home for the applicant

AND UPON the respondent UNDERTAKING not to change employment and not to retire until the pension sharing provision in clause 5 of this order is implemented

> **You, Arthur Brown, may be held to be in contempt of court and imprisoned or fined, or your assets may be seized, if you break the promises that you have given to the court.**

> I understand the undertakings that I have given, and that if I break any of my promises to the court I may be sent to prison for contempt of court.
>
> ....Respondent

IT IS ORDERED:

1. That the respondent shall on or before the   day of   transfer all his legal and beneficial interest in the family home into the name of the applicant AND it is certified for the purpose of the Community Legal Services (Financial) Regulations 2000 and the Access to Justice Act 1999 so as to provide security for the postponement of the statutory charge, and subject to the agreement of the Legal Aid Agency that the family home has been preserved for the applicant for use as a home for herself.

2. As from the date of the said transfer the family home shall be charged by way of legal charge as security for the payment to the respondent of a lump sum equal to 50% of the net proceeds of sale, such charge to be in the form annexed to this Order ('the Charge').

    (a) But this charge shall not become enforceable/exercisable without the permission of the court or the consent of the parties until:

        (i)   the death of the applicant;

        (ii)   the applicant's remarriage or cohabitation with another person as man and wife for a continuous period of more than 6 months;

        (iii) the applicant's failure to occupy the property for a period of 4 months in any 12 month period;

        (iv)   the applicant's failure to occupy the property as her primary residence; or

        (v)   any sale of the family home by the applicant

        whichever shall first occur or further order of the court

    (b) And so long as the applicant remains entitled to occupy the property under the terms set out above, the respondent shall not seek to exercise his power of leasing under the charge.

3. The applicant shall discharge as and when each payment becomes due, be solely responsible for and in any event indemnify the respondent against all sums due in respect of service charge, council tax, utilities (including but not limited to gas, electricity, water and telephone accounts), and buildings and contents insurance premiums in respect of the family home.

4. The respondent shall pay periodical payments to the applicant.

    Payments shall be at the rate of 5 pence per annum payable in advance.

    Payments shall commence on the   day of   2021.

    They will end on the first to occur of:

    (a) the death of either the respondent or the applicant; or

    (b) the applicant's remarriage; or

    (c) further order of the court.

5. There shall be provision by way of a pension sharing order in favour of the applicant in respect of the respondent's rights under his pension arrangement with [   ] in accordance with the annex to this order it being agreed between the parties that in the event of the respondent predeceasing the applicant after this order has taken effect but before implementation the applicant shall have the respondent's personal representative's consent to apply to vary or to set aside the terms of this order under FPR 2010, r 9.9A or to appeal out of time against the order under the Matrimonial Causes Act 1973, s 40A or s 40B (as shall in the circumstances be appropriate).

6.   Except as provided for in this order, the applicant's and the respondent's claims for periodical payments orders, secured periodical payments orders, lump sum orders, property adjustment orders, pension sharing orders and pension attachment orders shall be dismissed, and the respondent shall not be entitled to make any further application in relation to the marriage for an order under the Matrimonial Causes Act 1973 section 23(1)(a) or (b) and he shall not be entitled on the applicant's death to apply for an order under the Inheritance (Provision for Family and Dependants) Act 1975, section 2.

7.   The parties shall have liberty to apply to the court concerning the implementation and timing of the terms of this order only.

8.   There shall be no order as to costs save for the detailed assessment of the applicant's publicly funded costs in accordance with the Civil Procedure Rules 1998 Part 47.17

Dated the   day of   2021.

    Signed:

        District Judge

10.15 SUMMARY OF COURT PROCEDURE

Financial order procedure can effectively be illustrated by way of checklists. Two such checklists follow. One shows the contested procedure and the other the procedure to be followed where the parties have reached agreement.

10.15.1 Application to the court for a financial order

	Applicant (A)	Court	Respondent (R)
(1)	Files at court: — Form A — court fee — legal aid certificate (where appropriate) — notice of issue of legal aid (where appropriate) — notice of acting (Legal Help divorce cases only)		
		(2) Fixes First Appointment (FA) 12–16 weeks ahead (Form C) (3) Serves on Respondent within 4 days copy Forms A and C	
(4)	Serves on Respondent — notice of legal aid (where appropriate) — copy notice of acting (Legal Help divorce cases only) Serves on lender and person responsible for any pension arrangement copy Form A		(4) Requests information from pension arrangement. Serves information on Applicant within 7 days of receipt.
(5)	Completes, files and exchanges Form E at least 35 days before FA		(5) Completes, files and exchanges Form E at least 35 days before FA

	Applicant (A)		Court		Respondent (R)
(6)	Drafts, files and serves: (a) statement of issues; (b) chronology; (c) questionnaire and documents requested; (d) notice whether ready to proceed to FDR at least 14 days before FA			(6)	Drafts, files and serves: (a) statement of issues; (b) chronology; (c) questionnaire and documents requested; (d) notice whether ready to proceed to FDR at least 14 days before FA
(7)	Files and serves costs estimate at least one day before FA in Form H			(7)	Files and serves costs estimate at least one day before FA in Form H
(8)	Attends FA with client			(8)	Attends FA with client
		(9)	Makes directions; fixes FDR (unless FA treated as FDR/ exceptional circumstances)		
(10)	Complies with directions			(10)	Complies with directions
(11)	Gives notice to court of all offers and responses 7 days before FDR				
(12)	Files and serves costs estimate at least one day before FDR			(12)	Files and serves costs estimate at least one day before FDR
(13)	Attends FDR with client			(13)	Attends FDR with client
		(14)	May: (a) make consent order; (b) give directions; (c) fix final hearing; (d) adjourn for non-court dispute resolution		
(15)	Drafts, files and serves open proposals within 21 days after FDR			(15)	Drafts, files and serves open proposals within 21 days after FDR

Applicant (A)	Court	Respondent (R)
(16) Drafts, files and serves on R statements of proposed orders 14 days before hearing		
		(17) Drafts, files and serves on A statement of open proposals 7 days after receipt of A's proposals
(18) Files and serves costs statement (H1) at least 14 days before hearing		(18) Files and serves costs statement (H1) at least 14 days before hearing
(19) Attends hearing with client		(19) Attends hearing with client
	(20) Makes order	

10.15.2 Consent orders

There are two possible procedures. Which is appropriate depends on how far (if at all) the application has progressed on a contested basis when the parties reach agreement. Whichever is used, Form A must be filed before an order can be made. This will either have taken place before the steps described below, or (if not) can be incorporated into para 3 (see note (ii) below).

10.15.2.1 Normal consent procedure (no court attendance)

Applicant (A)	Court	Respondent (R)
(1) Completes Statement of Information Prepares draft order and submits it to R for approval/amendment		
		(2) Completes Statement of Information. Endorses consent on draft order. Returns both documents to A
(3) Files at court: (a) Draft order, endorsed with R's (and A's) consent, plus (b) 2 copies; (c) Statement of Information signed by both parties		

Applicant (A)	Court	Respondent (R)
	(4) If satisfied, makes order. Sends copy to A and R. If not satisfied, may require parties to attend	

Notes

(i)   Where appropriate, public funding certificate, notice of issue of certificate and notice of acting should be filed and/or served.

(ii)   If A has not yet filed Form A, the draft order can conveniently be incorporated into that application which will be endorsed with R's consent.

10.15.2.2   Where attendance at court

The normal contested procedure will be followed up to the date of the hearing.

Once agreement has been reached, provided the district judge has the prescribed information as to parties' resources etc, an order may be made despite the lack of a draft order and written statement of information.

10.16   PROCEDURE FOLLOWING AGREEMENT BY COLLABORATIVE LAW PROCESS OR BY ARBITRATION

In S v P (*Settlement by Collaborative Law Process*) [2008] 2 FLR 2040, the court approved a short-cut procedure where a settlement has been reached through the collaborative law process. Application for approval of the agreement can be dealt with in the urgent without notice applications list before the applications judge of the day on short notice. This avoids the need to lodge the order at the court and wait for the court to peruse and approve it. Coleridge J stated that a full day's notice must be given and that this could be done by telephone. Every aspect of the documentation must be agreed, the hearing must be expected to last for not more than 10 minutes and the documentation must be lodged with the judge the night before the hearing.

In S v S [2014] EWHC 7 (Fam), the court approved this short-cut procedure where the parties had submitted to binding arbitration under the Institute of Family Law Arbitrators Scheme. In such cases the parties would need to lodge with the court both the agreed submission to arbitration (Form ARB1) and the arbitrator's award.

10.17   THE FINANCIAL REMEDIES WORKING GROUP

The Financial Remedies Working Group was established by the President of the Family Division in June 2014. One of its remits is to formulate a more efficient method of progressing financial remedy cases through the courts. The group published its final report on 15 December 2014. Its recommendations included the following:

(1)   There should be one unified procedure for all financial remedy applications (eg 'first' applications on divorce; variation applications and applications under the Children Act 1989, Sch 1).

(2)   An amendment to the FPR 2010, clarifying that Forms A 'for dismissal purposes only' are not a necessary requirement for approval of a consent order provided one of the parties has made an application.

(3)   The Accelerated First Appointment procedure should be adopted nationwide and incorporated in an FPR Practice Direction.

(4)   The FDR should generally take place on the first occasion that the parties attend court even if this is against the wishes of one or both parties.

(5)   Financial orders should be separated completely from divorce proceedings (this has now been done).

(6)   The FPR 2010, r 28.3, enabling the court to make orders for costs where there is litigation misconduct, should be applied more generally. The Financial Remedies Working Group noted Mostyn J's suggestion of fixed-price costing and judicial costs capping in J v J *(Financial Remedies: Disproportionate Costs)* [2014] EWHC 3654 (Fam). However, it also noted that these are complex and difficult issues for practitioners, and it would not be appropriate to take the issues further until professional bodies such as Resolution, The Law Society and the FLBA had been given the opportunity to engage in a discussion on the subject.

(7)   The formal adoption under the FPR 2010 of standard orders for directions; final orders and enforcement orders.

CHAPTER 11

ENFORCEMENT, APPEALS, SETTING ASIDE AND VARIATION

11.1	Introduction	163
11.2	Enforcement of financial orders in the Family Court	164
11.3	Collection and enforcement by the Child Maintenance Service	167
11.4	Property adjustment orders	168
11.5	Appeals	168
11.6	Setting aside	169
11.7	Variation	171
Summary		175

LEARNING OUTCOMES

After reading this chapter you will be able to:

- explain what enforcement methods are available in the Family Court and which may be appropriate on the facts
- describe the enforcement methods that can be utilised by the Child Maintenance Service
- explain the circumstances in which an appeal may be possible
- describe in what circumstances the court may set aside a financial order
- demonstrate when a financial order may be varied and assess whether the court is likely to do so on the facts of a particular case.

11.1 INTRODUCTION

Frequently, the respondent to an order for financial relief will fail to comply with some, or all, of the provisions of that order. It is essential, therefore, that the solicitor should be aware not only of the methods of enforcement that are available, but also which of those methods is most appropriate in the circumstances. The potential need for enforcement should also be considered before any order is made or agreed to. It may be possible to build in potential enforcement methods within that order. Thus in *Amin v Amin* [2017] EWCA Civ 1114, the wife was able to 'enforce' the order against the husband's pension. The judge had ordered that the balance of her award should come from a share in the husband's pension. When the husband did not pay the lump sum ordered, the wife's share in his pension was increased to make up the deficit.

Although not a 'method of enforcement', it should also be remembered that disobeying a court order is contempt of court. In the recent case of *Hart v Hart* [2018] EWCA Civ 1053, the Court of Appeal upheld a sentence of 14 months' imprisonment for the husband's deliberate and sustained breaches of the court's orders in financial remedy proceedings.

A client may wish to appeal against an order he thinks is unfair. In certain situations an order may even be set aside. If the circumstances have changed since the order was made, the client may wish to have that order varied. This chapter deals with what action the solicitor can take on these occasions.

11.2 ENFORCEMENT OF FINANCIAL ORDERS IN THE FAMILY COURT

Financial orders in the Family Court comprise all orders apart from property adjustment orders (which are considered at **11.4**), but most commonly will be spouse PPOs or lump sum orders. Enforcement of child maintenance calculations will be effected by the Child Maintenance Service (CMS) (see **11.3**), but where a child maintenance order has been made by the court, enforcement will generally be through the court in the usual way. However, the CMS can collect and enforce 'top-up' child maintenance orders made by the court under s 8 of the CSA 1991.

Payments of money orders made by the Family Court are generally made direct between the parties. This can sometimes lead to problems since not only may the parties have to remain in direct contact (which could result in continued acrimony), but, as there is no independent record of payments, proof of payment (or non-payment) may be difficult. These problems can be mitigated by use of the Maintenance Enforcement Act 1991. This Act provides that, when granting or varying a periodical payments order, or at any time after doing so, the High Court or Family Court can order:

(a)   payment by standing order;

(b)   the payer to open a bank account;

(c)   attachment of the payer's earnings (see **11.2.2**).

11.2.1 Preliminary steps

When the order is first obtained the solicitor should tell their client to contact them immediately if the respondent defaults. This is particularly important in the case of periodical payments, because permission will be required to enforce arrears that are more than 12 months old. The court may refuse permission, remit the arrears and give the respondent a fresh start.

The method of enforcement used will depend upon the decision as to which method would be most effective. This in turn will usually depend upon the assets the respondent owns. The applicant will already have this information where the respondent has defaulted shortly after the order was made. However, in other cases, the applicant can apply to the court for an order to obtain information under CPR, r 71. If the court agrees to the application, the respondent will be ordered to attend court and asked to bring relevant documents with him. He will then be thoroughly examined by a court officer (or exceptionally by a judge) as to his means. Failure to attend is contempt of court.

Under r 33.3(2) of the FPR 2010, when applying for enforcement an applicant may either specify the method of enforcement, or apply for an order for such method of enforcement as the court may consider appropriate. Should the applicant chose the latter option then an order for the respondent to attend court will be made, and he will be questioned as to his assets so that the court can decide on the appropriate method of enforcement. The order to attend should be served on the respondent personally, and he should be offered travelling money to attend the hearing. If these steps are taken and the respondent subsequently fails to attend the hearing then the judge may make a committal order.

11.2.2 Methods of enforcement

11.2.2.1 Attachment of earnings

Under an attachment of earnings order (made under the Attachment of Earnings Act 1971) the respondent's employer will deduct a specified sum from his earnings. This sum will represent the amount of the maintenance order plus, possibly, a proportion of the arrears. The order must also specify a minimum amount, known as the 'protected earnings rate', below which the respondent's wages cannot fall. This rate is generally the amount that the respondent would be entitled to if he was reliant on welfare benefits. The employer will forward the money deducted from the respondent's wages to the court.

An attachment of earnings order is probably the best method of enforcement for a periodical payments order. It can be applied for either when the order is first made, or later when the respondent defaults. Fear of embarrassment with his employer may prompt the debtor to pay. However, the drawback of this method of enforcement is that the respondent must be in employment. It cannot be used if the respondent is self-employed or unemployed, and can be administratively difficult if the respondent frequently changes jobs.

11.2.2.2 Warrant of control

A warrant of control enables the High Court enforcement officer (or County Court bailiff where the sum to be enforced is under £5,000) to seize and sell assets belonging to the respondent sufficient to meet the outstanding amount. The solicitor applies to the court for a warrant; no hearing is needed. This method is most useful for unpaid lump sums, but could also be used for substantial arrears of maintenance.

11.2.2.3 Third party debt order

A third party debt order enables the applicant to receive payment direct from a third party who owes the respondent money, for example a bank or building society. Any account must be in the sole name of the respondent rather than in joint names with another. The third party must be within the jurisdiction (so a third party debt order cannot be used, for example, against an offshore account). Third party debt order proceedings involve two stages. At first, an interim third party debt order (obtained without notice) will freeze the account. At the subsequent 'on notice' hearing the court can make a final third party debt order, which will require the bank or building society to pay the applicant the amount outstanding. This method is most useful for unpaid lump sums.

11.2.2.4 MCA 1973, s 24A

Under s 24A of the MCA 1973, the court can make an order for sale to enforce, for example, a lump sum or secured periodical payments order (see **4.4.3**). The s 24A order for sale can be made at the same time as the original order as a type of precaution. Thus, for example, an order could provide that the respondent is to pay the applicant a lump sum of £30,000 (representing her share in the home) and that, if that sum is not paid within three months of decree absolute, the home is to be sold and the £30,000 paid to the applicant out of the proceeds of sale. Alternatively, the order for sale can be made later, if the respondent defaults.

11.2.2.5 Charging order

The applicant can apply to charge land (and/or certain securities) that the respondent owns, or in which he has an interest, with the amount outstanding. However, the procedure involved is protracted. The applicant needs to apply for an interim charging order, which can be made final at the subsequent hearing. This will give the applicant security for the debt, but a further hearing is needed to obtain an order for sale. At that further hearing, the court will have total discretion as to whether to order sale, and it may decide not to, for example if the charging order is over the respondent's home and the amount owed is relatively small. It is usually far better to use s 24A (see **11.2.2.4**).

11.2.2.6 Judgment summons

Under the Debtors Act 1869, the court has power to commit to prison a respondent who has not paid a periodical payments order or a lump sum order. This can be done provided:

(a) the respondent has defaulted; and

(b) the respondent has the means to pay but is neglecting or refusing to do so.

Until recently, the judgment summons procedure provided that the respondent must attend before the judge and be examined as to his means. However, in *Mubarak v Mubarak* [2001] 1 FLR 698, the Court of Appeal held that this procedure was in breach of the ECHR, Article 6 in particular, since it breached the respondent's right not to incriminate himself. As a result of *Mubarak*, it is now necessary for the applicant to produce evidence to show beyond reasonable doubt that the respondent has the means to pay. This may be very difficult for the applicant to do. The Family Proceedings (Amendment) Rules 2003 (SI 2003/184) subsequently amended the relevant procedure (under FPR 1991, rr 7.4–7.6) to make it compliant with the HRA 1998. The judgment summons procedure was already rarely used, partly because public funding is not available in the Family Court. A consequence of *Mubarak v Mubarak* and the amendments to the procedure mean that it is likely to be used even more rarely in the future and only as a last resort. However, it can still prove a useful method of enforcement, as in *Migliaccio v Migliaccio* [2016] EWHC 1055. In this case, a sentence of 14 days' imprisonment was imposed and then suspended provided that the husband paid the arrears owing plus costs within 28 days.

11.2.3 Reform

The Law Commission published its report 'Enforcement of Family Financial Orders' on 15 December 2016. The report highlights four key problems with the current law:

(a)   the complexity of the rules;

(b)   a lack of information about the debtor, making it difficult to identify the most effective enforcement option;

(c)   the fact that some of the debtor's assets could not be enforced against (eg joint bank accounts);

(d)   there are insufficient means to coerce debtors who will not pay into complying with court orders.

The Commission made a large number of wide-ranging recommendations to solve these problems, including the following:

(1)   Recommending that judges consider whether enforcement terms should be included whenever they make a financial order. Judges should also consider noting on the court file a summary of their main findings in relation to the debtor's assets that may be relevant to enforcement proceedings.

(2)   The appointment of an enforcement liaison judge for each designated family judge area.

(3)   Clearer rules, including a new Enforcement Practice Direction.

(4)   Information given on enforcement at the time the financial order is made – perhaps by way of a summary on the back of the order.

(5)   A new Enforcement Financial Statement. If the debtor fails to adequately complete this or provide supporting documents then the court could coerce them (perhaps by holding them in contempt). However, the Law Commission was of the view that it may be more effective for the court to instead obtain the relevant evidence from third parties such as HMRC, the DWP, a bank or building society or a pension provider.

(6)   Power for the court to make pension sharing or attachment orders by way of enforcement of financial orders which did not originally relate to a pension.

(7)   Power for a court to make a third party debt order over a joint bank account. There would be a presumption that any such account was owned in equal shares. Third party debt orders should also be able to operate on a periodic basis (eg each month). This would be particularly helpful in enforcing orders against a self-employed debtor.

(8)   The introduction of orders disqualifying debtors from driving or prohibiting them from travelling outside the UK where the court is satisfied that the debtor has the ability to pay. Such orders would last for a maximum of 12 months and would be discharged upon full payment of the amount owing.

In July 2018 the Government agreed to take forward those recommendations of the Law Commission that do not require primary legislation to put into effect. The Family Procedure Rules Committee plans to begin this process by amending the FPR 2010 to:

(a)   transpose some of the provisions of the Civil Procedure Rules to the FPR 2010 so that the key rules for enforcement in family law are in one place;

(b)   remove any ambiguities or gaps in the rules and promote uniform practice across courts.

11.3   COLLECTION AND ENFORCEMENT BY THE CHILD MAINTENANCE SERVICE

Where child maintenance is calculated by the CMS, the parents can opt for payment to be either through a system known as 'Direct Pay', or by 'Collect & Pay'. Under Direct Pay, the CMS will calculate the amount that the paying parent should pay and provides guidance on setting up regular payments. These are most likely to be made by standing order. Under Collect & Pay, the CMS will calculate child maintenance, collect payments from the paying parent and pay them to the receiving parent. The CMS will levy charges for this service: the paying parent will have to pay an additional 20% on top of the child maintenance calculation; the receiving parent will have 4% of the maintenance payment deducted before it is paid to her. If the parent with care wishes to use Collect & Pay but the non-resident parent does not, the CMS will usually decide on the basis of how the non-resident parent has dealt with the application process (or their history of child support) whether they are 'unlikely to pay'. If the CMS decides that the non-resident parent is unlikely to pay then payment will be by Collect & Pay despite the non-resident parent's objections. Where payment is by Collect & Pay, this is likely to be by direct debit or deduction from earnings request. This works in the same way as an attachment of earnings order but there is no court involvement (see **11.2.2.1**). Although the majority of payments are made using Direct Pay, statistics produced by the CMS show that in March 2021, 35% of payments were being made via Collect & Pay.

Whichever method is used, should the non-resident parent not pay child maintenance, the CMS can serve a deduction from earnings order on the non-resident parent's employer by way of enforcement (CSA 1991, s 30(2)). The CMOPA 2008 has amended the CSA 1991 so that now, where the non-resident parent is self employed, the CMS can make an order requiring the non-resident parent's bank or building society to make regular deductions from his account and pay the money to the CMS (CSA 1991, ss 32A–32D). Alternatively, the CMS can make a lump sum deduction order, which is a two-part process similar to a third party debt order (CSA 1991, ss 32E–32K). Regulations which came into force in December 2018 allow for regular deduction orders and lump sum orders to be made from joint accounts and partnership accounts where the non-resident parent is an account holder. Under those Regulations, lump sum deduction orders can also be made from the non-resident parent's sole trader accounts. Charges for enforcement, to be paid by the paying parent, were introduced in 2014.

Where one or more payments remain unpaid and the above methods of enforcement are inappropriate or have proved ineffective, the CMS can apply for a variety of other methods of enforcement including, as a last resort, committal for up to six weeks or disqualification from driving or holding or obtaining a UK passport for up to two years.

Anti-avoidance provisions have been introduced and are contained in s 32L of the CSA 1991. These provisions are very similar to s 37 of the MCA 1973 (see **9.6.2.3**) and allow the court to prevent a non-resident parent from disposing of property. The non-resident parent must have failed to pay child support maintenance and must be disposing of the property with the intention of avoiding payment of child support maintenance. However, if the disposition would have the effect of frustrating the enforcement of the unpaid child support maintenance, the intention will be presumed. Alternatively, where the property has already been disposed of, the court can set aside the disposition, unless it was made for valuable consideration to a person who was acting in good faith and without notice of an intention to avoid payment of child support maintenance.

Despite the wide array of enforcement methods at its disposal, the *Missing Maintenance* report by Gingerbread shows that the total child maintenance debt is almost £4 billion. In 2014/15 the CMS collected just 53% of maintenance charged via its collection service. However, it is not possible for parents with care to take enforcement proceedings themselves.

In R (*on the application of Kehoe*) v *Secretary of State for Work and Pensions* [2005] UKHL 48, Mrs Kehoe sought a declaration that her inability personally to enforce arrears of child maintenance under a maintenance calculation by the Agency breached her rights of access to the court under Article 6 of the ECHR. The House of Lords held that Mrs Kehoe had no right under the CSA 1991 that she could exercise against Mr Kehoe entitling her to play any part in the assessment or enforcement process. Thus her 'civil rights' had not been engaged for the purposes of Article 6 and her claim failed. Mrs Kehoe then appealed to the European Court of Human Rights. Her appeal failed, the Court stating that her ability to apply for a court order via judicial review directing the CSA to take appropriate enforcement action meant that there was no breach of Article 6 (*Kehoe v United Kingdom* [2008] All ER (D) 198).

11.4 PROPERTY ADJUSTMENT ORDERS

If the respondent fails to execute the documents required to effect a property adjustment order then the court has power to order the document to be executed by another person, usually the district judge, on his behalf (Senior Courts Act 1981, s 39 and Matrimonial and Family Proceedings Act 1984, s 31). Should there be a problem with drafting the documents, the court can refer the matter to conveyancing counsel. In such a case, the court can direct that the granting of any decree be deferred until the documents have been executed.

11.5 APPEALS

11.5.1 Financial orders

The Matrimonial and Family Proceedings Act 1984, s 31K(1) and the Access to Justice Act 1999 (Destination of Appeals) (Family Proceedings) Order 2014 (SI 2014/602) provide that appeals from decisions made by a district judge (other than a Senior District Judge of the Family Division or a district judge of the Principal Registry of the Family Division) lie to a circuit judge or a High Court judge sitting in the Family Court. Appeals from a district judge of the Principal Registry of the Family Division ('Central Family Court') or a Senior District Judge of the Family Division lie to a judge of High Court judge level sitting in the Family Court.

Under Pt 30 of the FPR 2010, permission to appeal must first be obtained. Permission may be sought from the lower court at the hearing at which the decision to be appealed was made, or to the appeal court in an appeal notice. The appeal notice must be filed at the appeal court within 21 days unless the lower court specifies a different period. Permission to appeal will be given only where the court considers that the appeal would have a real prospect of success, or where there is some other compelling reason why the appeal should be heard. A 'real prospect of success' means that the applicant must show a realistic, rather than fanciful, prospect of success (*CR v SR (Financial Remedies: Permission to Appeal)* [2013] EWHC 1155 (Fam)).

Generally an appeal will be limited to a review of the decision of the district judge, unless the appeal court considers that in the circumstances it would be in the interests of justice to hold a rehearing. An appeal will only be allowed where the earlier court has erred in law; the decision is outside the range of reasonable disagreement and is plainly wrong; or there was a serious procedural or other irregularity that makes the decision unjust.

Further appeal to the Court of Appeal will be available only where the Court of Appeal considers that the appeal would raise an important point of principle or practice, or there is some other compelling reason for it to be heard.

11.5.2 Maintenance calculation

Where the non-resident parent or the person with care is unhappy with the amount awarded, he can ask for a review of the maintenance calculation within one month of the date of the decision. If still dissatisfied, he can usually appeal to the First-tier Tribunal (Social Security and Child Support) (SSCS), again within one month of the decision. A decision of that tribunal can be appealed on a point of law to the Upper Tribunal. There is a further right of appeal on a point of law to the Court of Appeal.

Where a person is dissatisfied with the actions (or inactions) of the CMS, he can make use of the internal review procedure. If still dissatisfied, he can apply to the Independent Case Examiner within six months of the final decision of the internal review. Compensation may be available for any maladministration.

11.5.3 Welfare benefits

Generally, most decisions relating to welfare benefits will be reviewed internally on request. An appeal on fact or law can then be made to the SSCS, provided that the appeal is lodged within one month from the decision. Further appeal on a point of law then lies to the Upper Tribunal.

11.5.4 Arbitral awards

Under the Arbitration Act 1996, an arbitral award can be challenged on the basis that the arbitrator had no jurisdiction to make the order, or that there was a serious irregularity, for example a failure to deal with all the issues. An appeal on a point of law may be made with the consent of the other party or leave of the court.

11.6 SETTING ASIDE

One of the parties may attempt to have the order set aside. Generally, the court is reluctant to set aside orders for reasons of certainty – divorcing couples should be able to organise their future lives without fear of their divorce settlement being reopened. An application to set aside therefore can be made only on narrow grounds, the scope of which are not totally clear. These grounds include:

(a) *Non-disclosure of material evidence.* In the case of *Livesey (formerly Jenkins) v Jenkins* [1985] AC 424 (see **10.7.1**) the House of Lords stated that each party owed to the other a duty of full and frank disclosure. Where this duty is breached the order may be set aside. It must be emphasised, however, that not every non-disclosure will justify setting an order aside. The non-disclosure must have resulted in the court granting an order substantially different from that which it would have granted had the true facts been known or the court will not agree to set the original order aside. If the non-disclosure is deliberate, then it is presumed to be 'material' and the original consent order will be set aside unless the party who has failed to disclose can prove, on the balance of probabilities, that the order would have been substantially the same even if full disclosure had been made. If, on the other hand, the non-disclosure is inadvertent or innocent, the burden is on the party seeking to set aside the order to prove that the non-disclosure was 'material' (*Roocroft v Ball* [2016] EWCA Civ 1009).

The court in *Kingdon v Kingdon* [2010] EWCA Civ 1251 made it clear that in cases of non-disclosure it would not always be necessary to set aside the whole order and conduct the entire s 25 exercise again. The final order should reflect the order the court would have made had there been no material non-disclosure. It may be possible, as in this case, to achieve this simply by adding further provision to the order already made rather than starting from scratch.

(b)   *Fraud*. For example, if one party deliberately misrepresents the size of his assets. In this situation, the order will be set aside unless the perpetrator of the fraud proves that the court would not have made a significantly different order had it known the true position (*Sharland v Sharland* [2015] UKSC 60).

(c)   *Mistake*, that is, where the relevant facts exist when the order is made but are unknown to the parties or the court. In *DB v DLJ* [2016] EWHC 324 (Fam), the court stated that in such cases the following conditions would need to be fulfilled before the order would be set aside:

   (i)   The claimant must show that the true facts would have led the court to have made a materially different order from the one it in fact made.

   (ii)   The absence of the true facts must not have been the fault of the claimant.

   (iii) The claimant must show, on the balance of probabilities, that he could not with due diligence have established the true facts at the time the order was made.

   (iv)   The application to set aside should be made reasonably promptly in the circumstances of the case.

   (v)   The claimant must show that he cannot obtain alternative mainstream relief which has the effect of broadly remedying the injustice caused by the absence of the true facts.

   (vi)   The application, if granted, should not prejudice third parties who have, in good faith and for valuable consideration, acquired interests in property which is the subject matter of the relevant order.

(d)   *Events occurring after the order is made*. The House of Lords in *Barder v Barder* [1988] AC 20 laid down four conditions which must be fulfilled before the order will be set aside:

   (i)   the subsequent events must have invalidated the basis upon which the order was made; and

   (ii)   these events must have occurred within a relatively short time of the original order; and

   (iii) the application to set aside must be made promptly; and

   (iv)   the granting of the application must not prejudice the rights of a bona fide purchaser for value of any property in question.

The facts of *Barder v Barder* provide a useful example of the extreme circumstances which are necessary for the court to set aside an order on this ground. As part of a consent order, Mr Barder agreed to transfer the home to his ex-wife within 28 days so that she could live in it with their children. Before he had done so, Mrs Barder killed both children and committed suicide. Under her will, all her property would go to her mother. The House of Lords agreed to set the order aside. In *Williams v Lindley* [2005] EWCA Civ 103, the Court of Appeal set aside a consent order where the wife became engaged to (and subsequently married) a wealthy man within one month of the making of the order. This event invalidated the basis of the original order, which had been to provide the wife and children with a home. In *Nasim v Nasim* [2015] EWHC 2620 (Fam), the original order was for an unequal split of the proceeds of sale of the matrimonial home, giving 70% to the wife. This was on the basis that the children would spend significantly more time with her than with the husband, and she would therefore need a suitable home. Six weeks later an incident occurred that resulted in the children going to live with their father for 100% of the time. Giving permission to appeal out of time, Holman J stated that the criteria in *Barder* were satisfied. In other cases, where the basis of the original order is not invalidated, remarriage will not lead to the order being set aside (*Dixon v Marchant* [2008] 1 FLR 665).

What if the order involves assets that change dramatically in value a short time after the order is made? In the case of *Cornick v Cornick* [1994] 2 FLR 530, Hale J (as she then was) set out three possible causes of the change in value of the assets:

(i) An asset that was taken into account and correctly valued at the date of the hearing changes value within a relatively short time owing to natural processes of price fluctuation. This would not justify setting aside the order as it would amount to varying a capital order, which the court has no power to do (see **11.7.2**).

(ii) A wrong value was put upon that asset at the hearing, which had it been known about at the time would have led to a different order. Provided that it is not the fault of the person alleging the mistake, it is open to the court to give leave for the matter to be reopened. (This is a 'mistake' case – see (c) above.)

(iii) Something unforeseen and unforeseeable has happened since the date of the hearing that has altered the value of the assets so dramatically as to bring about a substantial change in the balance of assets brought about by the order. Then, provided that the other three conditions are fulfilled, the *Barder* principles may apply. However, Hale J went on to state that the circumstances in which this can happen are very few and far between.

In the case of *Myerson v Myerson (No 2)* [2009] EWCA Civ 282, the parties had reached an agreement at an FDR that the wife was to receive 43% of the assets and the husband 57%. The husband's share consisted of shares in his business, the value of which over the following year fell dramatically such that his share now represented, at best, only 14% of the assets. The Court of Appeal held that this case fell within the first of Hale J's categories and that 'the natural processes of price fluctuation, whether in houses, shares or any other property, and however dramatic, do not satisfy the *Barder* test'. Similarly, where a shareholding dramatically increased in value, the Court of Appeal held that this fell within the first of Hale J's categories (*Walkden v Walkden* [2009] EWCA Civ 627).

A subsequent maintenance calculation by the CMS will not be sufficient grounds for setting aside a clean break order (see *Crozier v Crozier* [1994] 1 FLR 126).

(e) *Lack of capacity*, for example, due to mental health issues (*MAP v RAP* [2013] EWHC 4784 (Fam)).

An application to set aside should generally be made within the proceedings to the same level of judge who made the original order (FPR 2010, r 9.9A).

In *DB v DLJ* [2016] EWHC 324 (Fam), Mostyn J held that where evidence emerges following an arbitral award that would, if the award had been a court order, entitle the court to set it aside on the basis of mistake or supervening event, then the court is entitled to refuse to incorporate the arbitral award in its order and instead make a different order.

11.7 VARIATION

11.7.1 Types of county court order that can be varied

It is possible to apply to the court to vary an order not only where that order was made after a contested hearing, but also where the order was made by consent. However, it will not be possible to vary an order that effected a clean break.

Orders that can be varied are set out in s 31(2) of the MCA 1973 (see **Appendix 1(A)**), and include orders for:

(a) maintenance pending suit and interim maintenance;

(b) periodical payments and secured periodical payments. Periodical payments orders are the type of order most commonly varied. Applications are made either by the recipient to increase the amount being paid, or by the payer to reduce or extinguish the payments. Several points should be noted:

(i) Where the court makes an order for fixed-term maintenance, the term can usually be extended, provided that the application for an extension is made before the original order has expired (although the actual hearing may take place after expiry). However, this can be prevented by the court including a direction in the original order that no application for an extension may be made (see MCA 1973, s 28(1A) and **4.6**). Where there is no s 28(1A) 'bar', it would seem that the guidance in *Fleming v Fleming* [2003] EWCA Civ 1841 should still be followed (*Yates v Yates* [2012] EWCA Civ 532). This states that term orders should only be extended in exceptional circumstances. However, this is far from clear. In *SS v NS (Spousal Maintenance)* [2014] EWHC 4183 (Fam), Mostyn J, relying on Charles J's dicta in *McFarlane v McFarlane* [2009] EWHC 891 (Fam), stated, 'There is no criterion of exceptionality on an application to extend a term order. On such an application an examination should to be made of whether the implicit premise of the original order of the ability of the payee to achieve independence had been impossible to achieve and, if so, why.'

(ii)   The court may impose a 'deferred clean break'. To achieve this, the court has power when discharging a periodical payments order or varying it to last for a further limited time only, also to make a lump sum order, or one or more property adjustment orders, or one or more pension-sharing orders. It may also include a direction that no application for an extension of a limited-term periodical payments order can be made. Whether a deferred clean break is appropriate will depend on much the same factors as those taken into account when deciding whether a clean break is appropriate (see **4.6**). In particular, the payer should consider whether the recipient is likely to remarry in the near future, since the court is unlikely to set aside the order if he does (*Dixon v Marchant* [2008] 1 FLR 665). If legally aided, the recipient should be reminded that a lump sum payment will attract immediate enforcement of the statutory charge, unless the money is to be used to purchase a home and the order includes the necessary clause to enable the Legal Services Commission to postpone the charge (see **2.2.4.3**). In *Pearce v Pearce* [2003] 2 FLR 1144, the Court of Appeal made it clear that when making such a deferred clean break the court was only entitled to capitalise the remaining periodical payments and could not reopen capital claims and further redistribute the capital assets. The court also stated that, in deciding what substitute order to make, a pension sharing order should be the first choice if it were available. This is because no capital would have to be raised or paid by the payer, and the recipient would continue to get regular income.

(iii)   When varying a periodical payments order the court has power to remit any arrears due under the order (MCA 1973, s 31(2A)). This power could be used, for example, where the payer had become unemployed and arrears had built up before he had a chance to apply for a downward variation;

(c)   payment of a lump sum by instalments. Generally, this power will only enable the court to vary the number and amount of the instalments, so that the amount payable overall will remain the same. However, the Court of Appeal stated in *Westbury v Sampson* [2001] EWCA Civ 407, [2002] 1 FLR 166 that the power to vary included varying the overall sum. Nevertheless, the court made clear that, in order to achieve finality, this would be done only in exceptional cases where the anticipated circumstances had changed significantly, making it unjust to hold the payer to the original quantum agreed;

(d)   payment of a lump sum ordered in relation to pensions under s 25B(4) or s 25C of the MCA 1973;

(e)   the sale of property under s 24A of the MCA 1973. This could be used, for example, where the order for sale was made as a way of enforcing a lump sum order. If the payer could find some other means to pay, he could then apply to have the order for sale discharged.

11.7.2 Types of county court order that cannot be varied

Orders for capital provision usually cannot be varied. This is to avoid uncertainty and so that the parties can make plans for the future on the basis that the distribution of capital is permanent.

(a) Lump sum orders cannot be varied unless they are payable by instalments, or ordered in relation to a pension (see **11.7.1**).

(b) Transfer of property and settlement of property orders cannot be varied. So, for example, if the court orders a deferred trust of land on *Mesher* contingencies, the occupier will not be able successfully to apply to court at a later date to have the sale further postponed. However, it may sometimes be possible to obtain a sale at a date earlier than that set out in the original order by applying for an order for sale under s 24A of the MCA 1973. The court can make an order for sale either at the same time as making the original order, or at a later date (see **4.4.3**). It is totally in the court's discretion whether to make such an order, but it may do so if, for example, it is the spouse in occupation who is seeking the sale against the wishes of the non-occupying spouse. On the other hand, an application by the non-occupying spouse is likely to be rejected if the home is still needed for the children (see, eg, *Thompson v Thompson* [1986] Fam 38).

(c) Pension sharing orders cannot generally be varied. The only exception to this is when the variation takes place before the order comes into effect and before the decree absolute. Once the decree has been made absolute, or if the order is in effect, it cannot be varied.

Many orders contain a clause that gives the parties 'liberty to apply'. This does not allow the parties to return to court to vary the order. Instead, it gives the parties the opportunity to return to court if they experience trouble implementing the order, for example, due to conveyancing difficulties or misunderstanding of minor terms where property is settled (see *Practice Direction (Applications: Liberty to Apply)* [1980] 1 All ER 1008). In *W v W* [2009] 1 FLR 92 the court differentiated a 'working out' of an order under a liberty to apply clause and a variation by considering the end result. Under a 'liberty to apply' clause, the court could select a different method of achieving the stated objective provided that the end result was, as far as practicable, the same as the original order. If the end result was more favourable to one of the parties, then this was a variation and not permitted.

11.7.3 Factors to be considered on a variation

The factors to be considered on a variation are set out in s 31(7) of the MCA 1973 (see **Appendix 1(A)**), which requires the court to have regard to all circumstances of the case, giving first consideration to the welfare of any child of the family who is not yet 18. This subsection also states that 'all the circumstances of the case' includes any change in the matters which the court was required to consider when making the original order, ie any change in the s 25 factors. However, case law makes clear (see, eg, *Flavell v Flavell* [1997] Fam Law 237) that the court is not restricted to considering changes in the matters that were taken into account when making the original order, but can consider the case afresh. Nonetheless, where an order has been made by consent, it will not usually be varied unless there has been a change in circumstances (*Joy-Morancho v Joy* [2017] EWHC 2086 (Fam)).

The principles set out in *Miller and McFarlane* (see **4.5.1.1**) apply equally on a variation application (*VB v JP* [2008] 1 FLR 742). Needs are likely to be the dominant factor. However, where those needs have been created by the recipient's own financial mismanagement or extravagance, the payer is unlikely to be expected to meet them (*Mills v Mills* [2018] UKSC 38). Conversely, needs are not a limiting factor, so that the principles of compensation and sharing can lead to an increase in maintenance where the payer's income has increased (see, for example, *McFarlane v McFarlane* [2009] EWHC 891 and *Hvorostovsky v Hvorostovsky* [2009] EWCA Civ 791).

Unlike remarriage, the payee's cohabitation with another partner will not automatically terminate periodical payments. However, it will be one of the 'circumstances of the case' and will be taken into account. The effect such cohabitation will have on the award will depend on the facts of the case. The court will take into account the financial resources of the new partner and will ask what that partner *ought* to contribute to the household (*Grey v Grey* [2009] EWCA Civ 1424).

Where the party against whom the order was made has died, 'all the circumstances of the case' include the change in circumstances as a result of his death. This will generally be relevant only in the case of secured PPOs.

The court must also consider on a variation application (even if it decides not to vary the amount of the order) whether the term of any payments ordered could be limited without causing undue hardship to the payee.

The court will need to take into account the 'package' made by the original order for financial relief. For example, perhaps the wife received less maintenance than she otherwise would have done in return for a greater share in the home. This must be taken into consideration on the variation application in order to maintain the balance achieved by the original order.

Lastly, remember that it is possible to record in a side-letter the reasons why a particular order has been made (see **10.13.12**). Any side-letter should be drawn to the court's attention on a later variation application and, although it will not bind the court, it is likely that the court will uphold its terms (see N v N (*Consent Order: Variation*) [1993] 2 FLR 868).

11.7.4 Procedure

A shorter procedure set out in FPR 2010, Pt 9, Ch 5 applies to proceedings to vary a financial order. This includes the use of financial statements, which are a simplified version of Form E rather than Form E itself. These should be exchanged within 14 days of issue of the application. A first hearing will be listed between four and eight weeks after the application is issued. The matter should then be dealt with at this first hearing if possible. If not possible, directions can be given and a final hearing held. In *Joy-Morancho v Joy* [2017] EWHC 2086 (Fam) the court adopted an abbreviated treatment of the variation application. The judge made it clear that the court needed to further the overriding objective by identifying the issues and confining its consideration to facts relevant to those. The court must have regard to all the circumstances of the case, but this did not require the court to undertake the s 25 exercise all over again; instead it should act proportionately and in accordance with the overriding objective.

11.7.5 Undertakings

In *Birch v Birch* [2017] UKSC 53, the husband transferred the former family home into the wife's sole name on the basis that the wife gave an undertaking that she would indemnify the husband for all mortgage payments and use her best endeavours to release him from the mortgage. Had she not procured his release by September 2012, she further undertook that the property would be sold. The wife could not procure the husband's release and so applied to 'vary' the undertaking. The Supreme Court emphasised that the court had no power to vary an undertaking. However, it did have power to discharge an undertaking. As the relevant undertaking was equivalent to an order for sale, the court should apply the factors under s 31(7) when deciding whether to discharge it. The court could always apply conditions to the discharge if necessary. Thus, for example, in this case, as a condition for discharging the undertaking, the wife could be required to compensate the husband for any prejudice he may suffer from the undertaking being discharged by giving him a share in the proceeds of sale.

In A *v* A [2018] EWHC 340 (Fam) the judge stated that when deciding whether to discharge an undertaking, the court was not constrained by the conditions in *Barder v Barder* (**11.6** above). However, a finding that there had been a significant change of circumstances would not lead to a discharge of the undertaking without more. For example, factors such as the fact that the parties had intended their agreement to effect a clean break are likely to mean that the original undertaking should be replaced with another undertaking.

SUMMARY

(1) The following methods of enforcement are available in the Family Court:

    (a) attachment of earnings;

    (b) warrant of control;

    (c) third party debt order proceedings;

    (d) s 24A of the MCA 1973;

    (e) charging order;

    (f) judgment summons.

(2) The Child Maintenance Service will enforce payments of child maintenance where a maintenance assessment has been made.

(3) The Family Court can execute documents to transfer property where the respondent fails to do so.

(4) It may be possible to appeal an order for financial relief, but this must be done without delay.

(5) In exceptional circumstances the court may set aside an order. This may happen if, for example, the respondent did not disclose the existence of certain of his assets and this led to a substantially different order being made.

(6) Orders for maintenance can be varied, as can instalments of a lump sum and lump sum orders made in relation to a pension.

(7) Other lump sum orders, pension sharing orders and property adjustment orders cannot be varied.

CHAPTER 12

PRE-MARITAL AGREEMENTS AND SEPARATION AGREEMENTS

12.1	Introduction	177
12.2	Pre-marital agreements	177
12.3	Postnuptial and separation agreements	179
12.4	Reform	182
Summary		182

LEARNING OUTCOMES

After reading this chapter you will be able to:

- explain to what extent the court may take a pre-marital agreement into account when making financial orders on divorce
- explain what postnuptial and separation agreements are
- describe the contents of postnuptial and separation agreements
- set out the advantages and disadvantages of postnuptial and separation agreements compared with a court order
- describe the court's power to vary a separation agreement.

12.1 INTRODUCTION

This chapter looks at the ways in which married couples can achieve a binding agreement to cover maintenance and other matters without starting court proceedings. It looks at the validity of agreements entered into before marriage. It then examines how a spouse can enter into a maintenance or separation agreement as an alternative to starting divorce proceedings or obtaining an order under the DPMCA 1978.

12.2 PRE-MARITAL AGREEMENTS

12.2.1 General

An increasing number of cohabiting couples are entering into 'cohabitation agreements' governing the ownership of property and chattels (see **Chapter 16**). The general consensus is that, subject to general contractual principles, cohabitation agreements are binding.

What if a couple wish to enter a pre-marital agreement? The Supreme Court in *Radmacher v Granatino* [2010] UKSC 42 stated that the old rule that postnuptial and pre-marital agreements were contrary to public policy was obsolete and should be swept away. If parties who have made such an agreement should then decide to live apart, they should be entitled to enforce their agreement. However, such an agreement would not oust the jurisdiction of the court and would not prevent one party from arguing in financial order proceedings that he or she should not be held to the terms of the agreement.

In financial order proceedings, the court may take pre-marital agreements into account as 'one of the circumstances of the case', or as 'conduct which it would be inequitable to disregard' under s 25 of the MCA 1973.

In recent years the courts have been willing to place an increasing amount of weight on such agreements, provided certain safeguards are met. In *Radmacher v Granatino* (above) the court held that if a pre-nuptial (or indeed postnuptial) agreement is to carry full weight, both the husband and the wife must enter into it of their own free will, without undue influence or pressure, and be informed of its implications. Each party would need to have all the information that is material to his or her decision, and each party should intend that the agreement should govern the financial consequences of the marriage coming to an end. In some situations, the absence of legal advice before entering such an agreement would be critical. However, such advice is not always essential and each case will turn on its facts (*Versteegh v Versteegh* [2018] EWCA Civ 1050).

The principle for the court to apply in deciding whether to uphold the agreement is that '[t]he court should give effect to a nuptial agreement that is freely entered into by each party with a full appreciation of its implications unless in the circumstances prevailing it would not be fair to hold the parties to their agreement' (para 75). The reason for this is that there should be respect for individual autonomy. An agreement is likely to be upheld where it is motivated by a wish to make provision for existing property owned by one of the parties, or anticipated to be received.

However, a pre-marital agreement would not be upheld if this would prejudice the reasonable requirements of any child of the family. It would also be unfair to hold the parties to their agreement where circumstances had changed in a way that was not envisaged when the agreement was entered. It may well be unfair to hold the parties to their pre-marital agreement where the needs of one of the parties would not be met by doing so, or he or she would not be compensated under the second strand indentified in *Miller v Miller; McFarlane v McFarlane* [2006] UKHL 24.

In *Crossley v Crossley* [2007] EWCA Civ 1491, which followed a short, childless marriage of wealthy parties in their 50s and 60s who had entered into a pre-nuptial agreement, the Court of Appeal decided that the judge had a discretionary power to require a party to show cause why the pre-nuptial agreement should not rule the outcome of a claim for financial orders. The Court stated that if ever there was to be a paradigm case in which the court would look to the pre-nuptial agreement not simply as one of the peripheral factors in the case but as a factor of magnetic importance, the instant case was such. In *Radmacher v Granatino* (above), the Supreme Court gave decisive weight to the pre-marital contract which had been entered into by the parties. The Court of Appeal in *Brack v Brack* [2018] EWCA Civ 1306 stated that, where a pre-nuptial agreement was upheld, this was likely to mean that fairness would result in a needs-only award. However, the court was not restricted to this, and, in appropriate circumstances, it may be fair to award an amount in excess of needs.

Thus it can be seen that the weight that will be accorded to a pre-marital agreement will be very fact-specific. For example, in *Z v Z (No 2)* [2011] EWHC 2878 (Fam), the parties had entered a pre-marital agreement in France. This was upheld to the extent that it excluded the sharing approach. Instead, the judge applied the needs approach, generously interpreted, which resulted in the applicant receiving 40% of the assets. In *V v V* [2011] EWHC 3230 (Fam) the court again gave weight to the pre-nuptial agreement. The needs approach was applied, but a *Mesher* order was awarded and the husband given a charge back of one-third to reflect the pre-marital agreement and the fact that this was a short marriage. Conversely, in *B v S (Financial Remedy: Marital Property Regime)* [2012] EWHC 265 (Fam), the pre-marital agreement was given no weight on the basis that the parties had entered it without 'full appreciation of its implications'.

In *AH v PH (Scandinavian Marriage Settlement)* [2013] EWHC 3873 (Fam), the parties had entered a nuptial agreement in Scandinavia after legal advice. However, the agreement made no provision for spousal or child maintenance, and expert evidence indicated that it was not valid in the jurisdiction in which it was entered into. In addition, it seemed that the wife did not fully appreciate the agreement's implications. The court made it clear that it was not a question of either giving full effect to the agreement or ignoring it entirely. The court could decide what weight to give it as one of 'the circumstances of the case'. In this case, the agreement was entered to protect the husband's inherited wealth, and so this should be invaded only to the extent necessary to provide housing and maintenance for the wife.

In H v H [2016] EWFC B81, the wife had entered a pre-nuptial agreement against her solicitors' advice and the marriage was very short (12 weeks). The court held that the wife was experienced and knew what she was doing. The agreement should be upheld.

In these circumstances, an increasing number of couples choose to use pre-marital agreements, and there are precedents available to use (see, for example, *Precedents for separation, pre-marriage and pre-civil partnership* (Resolution) and *Consensus* (Class Legal)). Such an agreement would assist in resolving matters if the breakdown was amicable.

Note that a pre-marital agreement will need to comply with general contract principles. There will need to be offer and acceptance, intention to create legal relations, certainty and consideration. In *Radmacher v Granatino* (above), the court held that it should no longer be a problem to prove intention to create legal relations, which would be presumed. Unless the contract is by deed, there could be a problem in establishing consideration. The agreement would also be set aside if a party could show that undue influence was exerted over him or her when the agreement was entered into.

12.2.2 Law of Property (Miscellaneous Provisions) Act 1989, s 2

Section 2 of the Law of Property (Miscellaneous Provisions) Act 1989 provides that all the terms of any contract for the disposition of any interest in land must be in writing and signed by all the parties. This means that any informal agreement between spouses relating to ownership of the home will not be enforceable unless it is properly recorded.

12.3 POSTNUPTIAL AND SEPARATION AGREEMENTS

12.3.1 General

Once the couple are married, it is open to them to enter into a postnuptial agreement to regulate their financial arrangements, both during the marriage and after separation, and such agreements will be valid and enforceable, subject to the court's power of variation (see **12.3.5**) (*MacLeod v MacLeod* [2008] UKPC 64, endorsed in *Radmacher v Granatino* (above)).

If spouses separate, they can, as an alternative to divorce or other court proceedings, enter into an agreement that provides for maintenance, care of the children and division of any property (for precedents, see *Precedents for separation, pre-marriage and pre-civil partnership* (Resolution)). These agreements are known as either separation agreements or maintenance agreements. The only distinction is that a separation agreement will always include a clause in which the parties agree to an immediate separation. If one party has deserted the other, it is important that, if the parties have agreed on financial matters, a maintenance agreement is used. This will ensure that there is no suggestion that the other spouse is agreeing to the separation, which would end the desertion and the possibility of obtaining a divorce using Fact C (see **3.4.4**).

A separation agreement, like any other contract, must be formed in accordance with contract principles. A vital element is an intention to create legal relations. The agreement can be challenged by a party on the grounds of fraud, mistake, duress or undue influence. It is therefore important that both parties have independent legal advice before entering into this type of agreement. Just as for a consent order, it is important that there is full and frank disclosure before such an agreement is entered. Any agreement should be made conditional upon such disclosure being given. In *Briers v Briers* [2017] EWCA Civ 15, the wife had made it a condition of agreeing to the proposed settlement that the husband had given full disclosure. The Court held that lack of full disclosure had prevented a binding agreement.

12.3.2 Contents

The matters that typically are covered by a postnuptial or separation agreement are as follows.

12.3.2.1 Agreement to separate

In a separation agreement the parties can state that they are going to live apart. Their agreement effectively prevents either party being in desertion and is evidence that the parties are treating the marriage as at an end, so that a period of separation can begin to run for the purposes of divorce on the grounds of two or five years' separation (Facts D or E: see **3.4.5** and **3.4.6**).

12.3.2.2 Periodical payments

The agreement can contain provision, on separation, for the payment of maintenance to the parties and any children. In relation to children, any agreement to pay money will be binding. However, a separation agreement cannot oust the jurisdiction of the Child Maintenance Service (CMS) under the CSA 1991, so either party can at any later time apply to the CMS to determine the amount of maintenance payable. Any agreement to pay maintenance to a spouse cannot prevent either party applying to the court for financial orders as part of divorce, nullity or judicial separation proceedings. However, were this to happen, the separation agreement would be one of the factors that the court would consider under s 25 of the MCA 1973 in the financial order proceedings and may well carry significant weight. Care must also be taken to draft maintenance provisions for spouse and child clearly, making provision for how long the maintenance is to last and what will happen if the parties resume cohabitation.

12.3.2.3 Property

If appropriate, an agreement about the home and/or other property can be included.

12.3.2.4 Children

There is no need for any arrangements to be included relating to the children. Both parents still share parental responsibility and can make decisions jointly or alone relating to the children. However, if the parents wish, any agreement about where the children should live and how much contact is to be given to the parent with whom they do not live can be included. This would not prevent either parent from making an application under the CA 1989 at any later date.

12.3.3 Advantages of a postnuptial or separation agreement

The parties' decision to enter into a postnuptial or separation agreement will usually be based largely on a desire to avoid court proceedings, including applying to court for a consent order. They should also take into account the following factors.

12.3.3.1 Speed

A postnuptial or separation agreement may be entered into quickly; a contested court order may not be made for a considerable time. A postnuptial or separation agreement is, therefore, cheaper. It may also assist the parties by avoiding the confrontation and bitterness that is often caused by protracted court proceedings.

12.3.3.2 Flexibility

Anything can be agreed and included in a postnuptial or separation agreement. So, for example, a husband could agree to pay the outgoings and repairs on the home in which the wife and family remained living, or to pay off outstanding hire-purchase debts. Neither of these matters can be ordered by the divorce courts under the MCA 1973, even if the parties apply for a consent order.

12.3.4 Disadvantages of a postnuptial or separation agreement

12.3.4.1 Enforceability

A postnuptial or separation agreement is enforced in the same way as any other contract. The usual remedies for breach of contract must, therefore, be sought, ie damages to cover any loss from arrears of maintenance payments and the equitable remedies of specific performance or an injunction to force the other party to carry it out. This means that in comparison with a court order (see **Chapter 11**), a postnuptial or separation agreement is much more difficult to enforce.

12.3.4.2 Finality

A court order for a 'clean break' can prevent either party from applying to court again and achieves a once-and-for-all settlement. A postnuptial or separation agreement can never be a guaranteed final solution. A party to a postnuptial or separation agreement can always apply at a later date, for example on divorce, for further provision from the court. However, on a later application the postnuptial or separation agreement will be taken into account under s 25 of the MCA 1973, and may be followed. In *Edgar v Edgar* [1980] 3 All ER 887, the court laid down the principle that formal agreements properly and fairly arrived at, with competent advice, should not be displaced unless there are good and substantial grounds for concluding that an injustice will be done by holding the parties to the terms of their agreement. In *MacLeod v MacLeod* [2008] UKPC 64 the Privy Council stated that when deciding what weight to give such an agreement in financial order proceedings, the court should, by analogy, start with the statutory provisions relating to whether such an agreement should be varied. Thus, the agreement should be upheld unless there had been a change of circumstances that would make the arrangements manifestly unjust or a failure to make proper provision for a child of the family. However, whilst the Supreme Court in *Radmacher v Granatino* (above) stated that the tests in *Edgar v Edgar* (above) and *MacLeod v MacLeod* (above) were appropriate for separation agreements and may be appropriate for postnuptial agreements entered well into a marriage, they were not appropriate for all postnuptial agreements. They gave as an example of a time when they would not be appropriate that of a young couple entering a postnuptial agreement shortly after marriage. In such circumstances the effect to be given to the postnuptial agreement would depend on wider considerations.

12.3.4.3 Variation

A court order for periodical payments can always be varied by the court by an application by either party at a later date. All written separation agreements can also be varied by the court (see **12.3.5**). However, if the agreement is not in writing it can be varied only by agreement between the parties.

12.3.5 MCA 1973, ss 34–36

Despite the fact that separation agreements are made between the parties and do not involve the court, the MCA 1973 does contain provisions giving the court power to vary them.

The court will have jurisdiction if the agreement comes within the wide definition of 'maintenance agreement' under s 34(2) of the MCA 1973. This will include any written agreement containing financial arrangements, or any written agreement to separate which does not contain any financial arrangements (where no other document exists that does contain such arrangements).

12.3.5.1 The court's jurisdiction

Any provision in a maintenance agreement that restricts the right of either party to apply to court for financial provision is void. However, any other provision in the agreement will still be binding.

12.3.5.2 Variation

If the parties can agree a variation, the original separation agreement can be varied by them without application to the court. If they cannot agree, either party can apply to court, and the court has jurisdiction to vary or to insert financial arrangements in a written maintenance agreement during the lives of the parties under s 35 of the MCA 1973. It will vary the agreement only if there has been a change in circumstances justifying this, or the agreement did not make proper financial arrangements for any child of the family (MCA 1973, s 35(2); **Appendix 1(A)**). The court can then make such order as it thinks just having regard to all the circumstances.

The court can also in certain circumstances vary a written maintenance agreement after the death of one of the parties (MCA 1973, s 36).

12.4 REFORM

The Law Commission published its report *Matrimonial Property Needs and Agreements* (HC 1089) on 27 February 2014. In it, the Commission recommends the introduction of 'qualifying nuptial agreements', which would enable couples to contract out of the sharing element of financial provision but not out of making provision for their children or each other's needs. Certain procedural safeguards would need to be satisfied to bring an agreement within the definition of a 'qualifying nuptial agreement'. These are that:

(1)   the agreement must be a valid contract made by deed;

(2)   it must contain a statement signed by both parties stating that they understand the legal effect of the agreement;

(3)   it must not have been made within 28 days before the wedding or civil partnership ceremony;

(4)   both parties must have received independent legal advice at the time the agreement was formed; and

(5)   both parties must have received disclosure of material information about the other party's financial situation.

The report also contains a draft Nuptial Agreements Bill, which would introduce qualifying nuptial agreements. To date there have been no moves by the Government to introduce such a Bill. However, Baroness Shackleton has introduced the Divorce (Financial Provision) Bill into the House of Lords, which makes nuptial agreements binding and incorporates similar procedural requirements to the Law Commission proposals. However, this Bill goes further in that it would make all pre- and post-nuptial agreements complying with the relevant procedure binding as to all their terms.

SUMMARY

(1)   Pre-marital agreements (ie agreements made *before* marriage dealing with what will happen on divorce) are not necessarily binding, although they may carry significant weight depending on the circumstances of the case.

(2)   Postnuptial and separation agreements (ie agreements made when a couple *actually* separate) *can* be binding contracts.

(3)   A separation agreement may be made as an alternative to a court order.

(4)   The advantages of a separation agreement are:

    (a)   speed;

    (b)   flexibility.

(5)   The disadvantages of a separation agreement: are

    (a)   difficult to enforce;

    (b)   not final;

    (c)   variation by court.

CHAPTER 13

CHILDREN

13.1	Introduction	183
13.2	Parental responsibility	184
13.3	Section 8 orders	189
13.4	Welfare principle	204
13.5	Checklist of factors to be taken into account in applying welfare principle	206
13.6	The 'no order' presumption	209
13.7	Avoiding delay	209
13.8	Procedure for s 8 orders	210
13.9	Protection of children	220
13.10	Financial provision and property orders for children	224
Summary		227

LEARNING OUTCOMES

After reading this chapter you will be able to:

- describe what parental responsibility is and how it is acquired
- explain what s 8 orders are available and how the court exercises its powers on an application for a s 8 order
- describe the procedure on an application for a s 8 order
- explain what financial orders are available for children under s 15 and Sch 1.

13.1 INTRODUCTION

The Children Act 1989 (CA 1989), which came into force in 1991, has been described as 'the most comprehensive and far reaching reform of child law ... in living memory' (Lord Mackay, *Hansard*, House of Lords, 6 December 1988). The aim of the Act was to simplify the law relating to children, making it more consistent and more flexible, and to make the law more appropriate to the needs of children by making it more child-centred. The 1989 Act deals with both public and private law.

The Children and Families Act 2014 amended many parts of the CA 1989, and made some substantial changes to the areas of private children law and public children law (see **Chapter 14**). In private children law, the most significant change was the replacing of 'residence' and 'contact' orders under s 8 with 'child arrangements' orders. The changes were brought about following the recommendations of the Family Justice Review, and the reasoning behind the new child arrangements orders was that they should focus the minds of the parties on sorting out suitable arrangements for the children, rather than focusing on labels such as 'residence', and should remove the tendency for there to be a winning and a losing party when deciding on where the children should live and whom they should see.

The Children and Families Act 2014 also inserted a new s 1(2A) into the CA 1989, to be considered when deciding on a s 8 or parental responsibility order, which states that a court is to presume, unless the contrary is shown, that involvement of each parent in the life of the child will further the child's welfare.

Section 10 of the Children and Families Act 2014 also makes attending a Mediation Information and Assessment Meeting (MIAM) compulsory before issuing most private children law applications (see **Chapter 2**).

Children are sometimes described as a solicitor's invisible clients in divorce proceedings. The client is usually the parent, not the child, but a solicitor must consider the effect of their client's actions on the child involved. A solicitor may often feel that the client would be helped by mediation in relation to decisions about the children, and should recommend that an appropriate agency is consulted (see **1.3.2**).

The CA 1989 enables a child to apply for an order himself. The requirements involved are considered in this chapter. Provisions dealing with financial orders for children are summarised at **13.10**.

13.1.1 Cafcass

The Children and Family Court Advisory and Support Service (Cafcass) was established by the Criminal Justice and Court Services Act 2000. Cafcass is an executive body sponsored by the Ministry of Justice. In respect of family proceedings in which the welfare of children is in question, the Service has the principal function of safeguarding and promoting the welfare of the children, giving advice to any court about any application made to it in such proceedings, making provision for the children to be represented in such proceedings, and providing information, advice and other support for the children and their families. Cafcass officers, known as Family Court Advisers, now fulfil the roles of children and family reporters (in private law proceedings: see **13.3.5** and **13.8.5.6**) and children's guardians (in public law proceedings: see **14.11.3.1**).

13.2 PARENTAL RESPONSIBILITY

13.2.1 What is parental responsibility?

The CA 1989 introduced the concept of parental responsibility, which was a deliberate shift away from the idea that parents have 'rights' over their child towards the idea that they have 'responsibilities' towards their child. Parental power to control a child is not for the benefit of the parents but for that of the child. The Act defines this term as 'all the rights, duties, powers, responsibilities and authority which by law a parent of a child has in relation to the child and his property' (CA 1989, s 3(1) – see **Appendix 1(E)**). In reality, it gives the parent responsibility for taking all the important decisions in the child's life, for example, education, religion and medical care. It also enables a parent to take day-to-day decisions, for example, in relation to nutrition, recreation and outings. The duties involved in parental responsibility will change from time to time with differing needs and circumstances, and vary with the age and maturity of the child. It is important to bear in mind that a child will gradually become mature enough to take decisions himself. The House of Lords, in *Gillick v West Norfolk and Wisbech Area Health Authority* [1986] AC 112, said that 'parental authority ceases in respect of any aspect of a child's upbringing about which the child himself is sufficiently mature to make decisions for himself'.

13.2.2 Who has parental responsibility?

Married parents have joint parental responsibility; if parents are not married, only the mother has parental responsibility.

13.2.3 How can you acquire parental responsibility?

13.2.3.1 Unmarried fathers

An unmarried father can acquire parental responsibility in any one of six ways:

(a)   by being registered as the father on the child's birth certificate with the consent of the mother (after 1 December 2003) (CA 1989, s 4(1)(a));

(b)   by entering into a 'parental responsibility agreement' with the mother (CA 1989, s 4(1)(b)): this must be on a prescribed printed form (see below);

(c)   by applying to the court for a parental responsibility order (CA 1989, s 4(1)(c)) (see below for the courts' approach on such applications);

(d)   by being appointed a guardian either by the mother or by the court, although in these cases he will assume parental responsibility only on the mother's death (see below);

(e)   by obtaining a child arrangements order from the court (see **13.3.1**);

(f)   by marrying the mother.

Parental responsibility agreement

Many unmarried parents will be living together and will be happy to acknowledge their shared responsibility for their children. In this case, if they have not acquired parental responsibility by being registered on the birth certificate, they are able to enter into an agreement that will give the father joint parental responsibility with the mother. It will put them into the same position as if a parental responsibility order had been made.

Regulations provide that the agreement must be in a prescribed form, signatures of the parents must be witnessed by a Justice of the Peace, a justices' clerk or a court official who is authorised by the judge to administer oaths (not by a solicitor), and the agreement must be recorded by sending it together with two copies to the Central Family Court. No fee is payable. The Registry will seal the copies and send one to the mother and one to the father. Agreements are open to public inspection (Parental Responsibility Agreement Regulations 1991 (SI 1991/1478)).

Even though a parental responsibility agreement was entered into with the agreement of the parents, it cannot be ended by agreement. It will end only when the child reaches 18 years of age, unless a court order ending it has been obtained (see **13.2.4**) either on the application of anyone with parental responsibility, or on the application of the child (with leave).

Parental responsibility agreements are likely to be less common now that parental responsibility can be obtained by registration on the birth certificate.

Parental responsibility order

If the father without parental responsibility wants to share parental responsibility with the mother and she is not willing to agree to this, the father can apply to court for a parental responsibility order. Such an order will give him joint parental responsibility with the mother and place him in virtually the same position legally as if he were married.

If there is a dispute about paternity, s 20(1) of the Family Law Reform Act 1969 can be used to obtain a court direction for blood tests. The court has a discretion to give such a direction (*Re F (A Minor) (Blood Tests)* [1993] 1 FLR 598).

In deciding whether to grant the parental responsibility order, the court will use the welfare principle (see **13.4**) (but not, specifically, the statutory checklist (see **13.5**)). The court will also have regard to the non-intervention principle (see **13.6**), although it will generally be necessary to intervene when this order is sought as the parents will be in dispute.

In *Re H (Minors) (Local Authority: Parental Rights) (No 3)* [1991] 2 WLR 763, the court looked at which factors would be important in this situation and concluded that it was important to look at:

(a)   the father's degree of commitment to the child;

(b)   the state of the father's current relationship with the child; and

(c)   his reasons for making the application.

In *Re C and V (Contact and Parental Responsibility)* [1998] 1 FLR 392 the court emphasised that the factors listed in *Re H* were some, though not all of the factors that might be material in answering a much more general question as to whether or not a father has shown a genuine concern for the child and a genuine wish to assume the responsibility in law which nature had already thrust on him.

Re C and V also made clear that applications for parental responsibility and contact were quite separate applications and that a court should not refuse an application for parental responsibility just because it has decided not to order contact.

The court will not automatically refuse an order just because at the present time there is no likelihood of the order resulting in the father being able to exercise any of his responsibilities. A committed father could be granted the order if it would ultimately be in the best interests of the child's welfare to make it (*Re C (Minors) (Parental Rights)* [1992] 1 FLR 1). In *Re A (Minors) (Parental Responsibility)* [1993] Fam Law 464, the father, who had lived with the mother, was present at the child's birth and whose name was entered on the birth certificate (this case pre-dated the changes to the CA 1989, which would mean this automatically gave him parental responsibility), was granted a parental responsibility order (despite the mother's resistance and the fact that he had not seen the child for one year) as he had shown considerable commitment.

Case law has shown that the court is willing to make a parental responsibility order to give a father a recognised legal status, and objections, such as a mother's hostility to a father's involvement in the child's life, do not necessarily prevent the parental responsibility order being made (*Re G (A Minor) (Parental Responsibility Order)* [1994] 1 FLR 504) (and see *B v A and Others (Parental Responsibility)* [2006] EWHC 2 (Fam), where unusually the court made a parental responsibility order in favour of the father on the basis that the father would not contact the child's school or any healthcare professional involved in her care without the consent of the child's mother or her female partner, who had a shared residence order in respect of the child).

However, the court may still refuse a parental responsibility order where the father has shown a high degree of commitment if it is clear that the father may abuse his parental responsibility. Thus in *Re P (Parental Responsibility)* [1998] 2 FLR 96, the Court of Appeal refused to grant a parental responsibility order where the father had been very critical of the mother's care and made it clear that he would use his parental responsibility order as an excuse to monitor the arrangements for the child's care. In another case, *M v M (Parental Responsibility)* [1999] 2 FLR 737, the court declined to make a parental responsibility order where the unmarried father had been involved in an accident, causing him serious, permanent brain injuries. Although there had been a significant degree of commitment and attachment to the child, the father was incapable of exercising parental responsibility (and, in fact, required something akin to parental responsibility to be exercised by others over him).

A parental responsibility order, once made, will end automatically on the following events:

(a)   the majority of the child;
(b)   the marriage of the father to the mother during the minority of the child. The marriage will give the father parental responsibility for his child;
(c)   a court order discharging the parental responsibility order. An application to discharge the original order can be made by anyone who has parental responsibility for the child, for example the mother, or by the child himself, provided the court is satisfied that the child has sufficient understanding to make the application.

The application for a parental responsibility order can be made to the Family Court using a standard application form, which sets out details of the child and the applicant, including his reasons for applying. Parental responsibility orders, like parental responsibility agreements, will be less frequent now that parental responsibility can be obtained by registration on the birth certificate.

Child arrangements order

Section 12(1) of the CA 1989 provides that when the court makes a child arrangements order naming the father as a person with whom the child is to live then it must also make a parental responsibility order in favour of the father if he does not already have parental responsibility. If the court makes a child arrangements order naming the father as a person with whom the child should spend time or otherwise have contact, but not as a person with whom a child should live, then the court must decide whether it would be appropriate to make a parental responsibility order (CA 1989, s 12(1A)).

Guardianship (CA 1989, s 5)

A mother with sole parental responsibility could appoint the father as a guardian in her will. On her death, the father would then acquire parental responsibility because he is a guardian, even if he had never obtained parental responsibility during the mother's lifetime. If the mother had not appointed a guardian on her death, the court has the power to appoint a guardian, and it could decide to appoint the father. Alternatively, in these circumstances the father could apply to the court to be appointed guardian (CA 1989, s 5(1)(a); see **Appendix 1(E)**).

If a mother with sole parental responsibility has appointed someone other than the child's father as guardian, this appointment will take effect on her death and give the guardian sole parental responsibility, which the father could challenge only by applying for a child arrangements order and/or a parental responsibility order.

If the father has acquired parental responsibility during the mother's lifetime, any appointment by her of a guardian will be postponed while the surviving parent has parental responsibility. The only way a mother in this situation could ensure that the appointment of a guardian had immediate effect would be for her to seek a child arrangements order naming her as the person with whom the child is to live. In this case, on her death, the guardian and the father would share parental responsibility. This could be of great importance to a mother who is no longer cohabiting with the father of her child and who is anxious to safeguard a child after her death by making, for example, her mother a joint guardian with the father.

13.2.3.2 Step-parents and civil partners

Section 4A of the CA 1989 allows step-parents and civil partners to obtain parental responsibility agreements with the consent of all parents with parental responsibility, or to apply to the court for a parental responsibility order.

In the case of *Re R (Parental Responsibility)* [2011] EWHC 1535 (Fam), the court stated that while the court's power to grant parental responsibility to the step-parent is not limited to this 'paradigm case' of an incoming step-parent who will be living with both the parent providing primary care and the child, and who will be centrally participating in the upbringing of the child in the future, the other situations in which a parental responsibility order will be made under s 4A(1)(b) are likely to be limited. It said in that case, notwithstanding the husband's considerable commitment to the child, that it was not in the child's interests to grant him parental responsibility, as this would place him at the heart of all future important decisions about the child in a way that was very likely to lead to conflict with the mother. However, in *R v C and another* [2013] EWHC 1295 (Fam), the court made a parental responsibility order in favour of a step-parent who was separated from the child's mother and said that while in normal circumstances the beneficiary of such an order will be a person who might be described as an incoming step-parent who wishes to bring up a child together with the parent with parental responsibility, the power to confer parental responsibility is a flexible one and what is important is what is in the child's best interests for the future

Step-parents can also acquire parental responsibility if the court makes a child arrangements order in their favour (see **13.2.3.1**, **13.2.3.3**, **13.3.1** and **13.3.2**).

13.2.3.3   Others

Various other people may also acquire parental responsibility towards the child. A local authority will acquire parental responsibility if a care order is made in relation to the child, or anyone who is granted a residence order in relation to the child, or even the court if the child is made a ward of court. Also anyone obtaining a new special guardianship order will acquire parental responsibility (see **13.3.6**).

The Human Fertilisation and Embryology Act 2008, which came into force in April 2009, allows, in the case of female same sex couples who have not entered into a civil partnership and who are having a child conceived at a licensed clinic by IVF or artificial insemination, for the natural mother to nominate her same sex partner as the 'parent' of the child. Under s 4ZA of the CA 1989, the parent will then be able to apply for parental responsibility by being registered as a parent on the register of births, by making a parental responsibility agreement with the mother or by obtaining a parental responsibility order from the court. The provisions allowing the court to make parental responsibility orders to fathers when making child arrangements orders in their favour (see **13.2.3.1**) apply equally to second female parents.

In addition, when the court makes a child arrangements order in favour of a person who is not a parent or guardian of a child, naming him or her as a person with whom the child shall live, that person shall have parental responsibility for the child for the duration of the order. If the child arrangements order names a non-parent or non-guardian as a person with whom a child should spend time or otherwise have contact, but not live with, then the court may provide for that person to have parental responsibility for the duration of the order (see **13.3.3.1**). See *Re B (No 2) (A Child) (Welfare: Child Arrangements Order) (Inherent Jurisdiction)* [2017] EWHC 488 (Fam) for an example of this.

13.2.4   How can you lose parental responsibility?

There is no limit to the number of people who can have parental responsibility at any one time, and no one will lose parental responsibility just because another person acquires it (CA 1989, s 2(5)). If, on divorce, a child arrangements order is made with a provision that the child is to live with a grandparent, this will mean that the child's mother, father and grandparent will all have parental responsibility. The parents 'lose' the responsibility of having the child living with either of them because of the child arrangements order but retain all other responsibilities. If a care order is made, the local authority acquires parental responsibility but the parents still, in theory, retain parental responsibility. However, in practice the local authority is given the discretion to determine the extent to which a parent may meet his or her parental responsibility (CA 1989, s 33(3)).

Two situations in which parents will lose parental responsibility are:

(a)   the parent's death; and

(b)   the child's adoption. Section 46 of the Adoption and Children Act 2002 provides that an adoption order will automatically extinguish the parental responsibility that any person had before the making of the order.

An unmarried father or second female parent who has acquired parental responsibility by a parental responsibility order or parental responsibility agreement, or by registration on the birth certificate, can lose it if the court makes a further order ending it. (See *Re P (Terminating Parental Responsibility)* [1995] 1 FLR 1048, where an unmarried father who had acquired parental responsibility then lost it under a court order, having inflicted serious injury on the child, and a more recent case, *Re child X and another; A mother v A father* [2021] All ER (D) 92 (Apr), where the father attempted to murder the mother in front of one of the children.)

Similarly, a step-parent or civil partner who acquires parental responsibility under s 4A of the 1989 Act (see **13.2.2** above) can have it removed by the court.

Anyone other than an unmarried father or second female parent, who has acquired parental responsibility by being granted a child arrangements order, will lose it automatically when the child arrangements order terminates.

The acquisition and loss of parental responsibility in the case of unmarried fathers raises potential issues of discrimination under the HRA 1998. However, in *McMichael v UK* (1995) 20 EHRR 205, the European Court of Human Rights accepted that discrimination between married and unmarried fathers could be justified as identifying 'meritorious' fathers who might be accorded parental rights, thereby protecting the interests of the child and the mother.

13.2.5　Exercising parental responsibility

Even though several people may have parental responsibility for a child, in theory it is possible for each to act alone with no duty to consult anyone else (CA 1989, s 2(7)). However, in *Re C (Change of Surname)* [1998] 1 FLR 549, the court held that when there was joint parental responsibility, this did not confer the right unilaterally to change the child's surname, and suggested that good practice is to refer to the court all disputed issues regarding change of surname regardless of who has parental responsibility. Also, in *Re J (Child's Religious Upbringing and Circumcision)* [2000] 1 FLR 571, the court held that there is a small group of important decisions made on behalf of a child which, in the absence of agreement by all those with parental responsibility, ought not to be carried out or arranged by the one-parent carer, notwithstanding s 2(7). Instead, they should be referred to the court for the court's determination, on the facts of the case each time, by way of a specific issue order. As well as change of a child's surname, the court gave sterilisation and circumcision as examples of such decisions. *Re C (Welfare of child: Immunisation)* [2003] EWCA Civ 1148 added immunisations, where the parents were not in agreement, to this small group of decisions. In *Re H (Parental Responsibility)* [1998] 1 FLR 855, the court also said that a parent with parental responsibility would have the right to be consulted on schooling.

In *B v A and Others (Parental Responsibility)* [2006] EWHC 2 (Fam), the father had responded to an advertisement by the mother and her lesbian partner, to father a child. The court made a parental responsibility order in favour of the father on the basis the father would not contact the child's school or any health care professional involved in her care without the consent of the child's mother or her female partner, who had a shared residence order in respect of the child.

Subject to these exceptions, one parent can determine questions such as medical treatment and religion without consulting the other. The only way to challenge a decision is to make an application to court, for example, for a specific issue order or a prohibited steps order (see **13.3.3** and **13.3.4**). If a child is being adopted, or taken out of the UK, there are specific provisions requiring both parents' consent, or the consent of the court.

It is not possible to transfer or surrender parental responsibility (CA 1989, s 2(9)). However, parents can delegate responsibility for a child on a temporary basis, for example, to a school for a school trip, or to a nanny or childminder. Temporary carers do not acquire parental responsibility but 'may do what is reasonable in all the circumstances of the case for the purpose of safeguarding or promoting the child's welfare' (CA 1989, s 3(5)). This could cover emergency medical treatment for the child if needed when the parent is absent, for example during a school trip, or when the parent is at work during the day and a nanny is in charge.

13.3　SECTION 8 ORDERS

Under s 8 of the CA 1989 (see **Appendix 1(E)**), three different types of orders can be made in relation to children:

(a)   child arrangements orders;

(b)   prohibited steps orders;

(c)   specific issue orders.

Each of these orders will determine a particular matter relating to the child's upbringing. A s 8 order lasts until the child reaches the age of 16 (or 18, in exceptional circumstances) (CA 1989, s 91(10)).

Child arrangements orders have been introduced by the Children and Families Act 2014 and they replace residence and contact orders. Residence orders were used before April 2014 to settle the arrangements as to with whom a child should live, and contact orders required the person with whom the child lived to allow the child to visit or otherwise have contact with the person named in the order.

A child arrangements order means an order regulating arrangements relating to:

(a)   with whom a child is to live, spend time or otherwise have contact; and

(b)   when a child is to live, spend time or otherwise have contact with any person.

A child arrangements order can therefore deal with both issues of 'residence' and 'contact'. The distinction is made in terms of terminology of the order itself, which can be: (a) a child arrangements order which names the person with whom the child is to live; and (b) a child arrangements order which specifies the person with whom the child is to spend time or otherwise have contact with.

The transitional provisions provide for all pre-existing residence orders to be deemed as child arrangements orders regulating with whom a child is to live, and a pre-existing contact order is deemed as a child arrangements order regulating with whom and when a child is to spend time or otherwise have contact.

At the time of writing there is still very little reported case law on the child arrangements order, but it is envisaged that when the court is deciding on with whom the child shall live with or whom the child shall spend time or otherwise have contact with, it will rely on the volume of case law relevant to residence and contact order applications.

13.3.1   Child arrangements order regulating with whom and when a child shall live with any person

Following a divorce, parents will share parental responsibility and, therefore, the making of a child arrangements order can decide where a child will live.

A child arrangements order can be made in favour of non-parents and, if this is done, the non-parent will automatically have parental responsibility as well, but only for so long as the child arrangements order is in force (CA 1989, s 12(2)). The parental responsibility acquired in this way also has two limitations as, first, no agreement or refusal to an adoption order or freeing for adoption can be given and, secondly, no guardian can be appointed by the non-parent.

When deciding an application for a child arrangements order to regulate with whom the child should live, the child's welfare is the paramount concern (see **13.4**). In *Re B (a child) (residence order)* [2009] UKSC 5 the court awarded residence of a four-year-old child to the child's grandmother with whom he had lived all his life, rather than to his father. The Court said that:

> All consideration of the importance of parenthood in private law disputes about residence must be firmly rooted in an examination of what is in the child's best interests. This is the paramount consideration. It is only as a contributor to the child's welfare that parenthood assumes any significance.

A child arrangements order for shared living arrangements can be made in favour of two or more persons who do not all live together. The order can specify the periods during which the child is to live in the different households involved. This means that a court could order that a child lives alternate weeks with each parent, or lives during term-time with one parent and during the holidays with the other, or spends a fixed period (say, the summer holidays) with one parent. A child arrangements order is therefore a flexible power which can be adapted to the needs of a particular family. Obviously, the court will make an order for shared living arrangements only if it feels that it is in the welfare of the child to do so. It is not the case that orders for shared living arrangements can be made only in exceptional circumstances (as was once thought) (*Re D (Children) (Shared Residence Orders)* [2001] 1 FLR 495), and in recent years such orders have increasingly been used. In *Re K (A Child) (Shared Residence Order)* [2008] EWCA Civ 526 it was stated that the approach when deciding whether to make a shared residence order is to decide first how the children are to divide their time and then to decide how it should best be expressed in an order.

In *Re G (Residence: Same Sex Partners)* [2005] EWCA Civ 462, the biological mother of two children conceived by artificial insemination by donor and her same sex partner separated, leaving the children with the biological mother. The mother tried to marginalise the applicant's contact with the children. The applicant was granted a shared residence order. As this case pre-dated the provisions of the Children and Families Act 2014, the only way the non-biological mother could obtain parental responsibility was through obtaining a shared residence order which would prevent such marginalisation. This could now be achieved by the court granting a child arrangements order for the children to spend time with the applicant and exercising its discretion under s 12(2A) of the CA 1989 to grant parental responsibility to the applicant (see **13.2.3.3**).

The court is given wide powers to attach directions, conditions, and incidental and supplementary provisions to the child arrangements order. These could, for example, direct where the child is to be educated, or impose a ban on removing the child from the country; or could direct that the non-resident parent be informed if the child requires medical treatment in circumstances where the parent with whom the child is living has religious objections to blood transfusions.

When a child arrangements order has been made regulating with whom the child should live, two aspects of parental responsibility are automatically affected, as follows.

13.3.1.1 Change of surname

Where a child arrangements order that regulates with whom the child shall live is in force, the order will provide that no person can cause the child to be known by a new surname without either:

(a) the written consent of every person who has parental responsibility; or

(b) the leave of the court (CA 1989, s 13(1)).

However, following *Re C* (see **13.2.5**), it seems that where there is joint parental responsibility, regardless of whether there is a residence order, the same conditions will apply and the consent of the other person with personal responsibility should be sought. In *Re C* it was further suggested this would be good practice even if the father did not have parental responsibility.

If a mother wants to change her child's surname, perhaps following remarriage or reverting to a maiden surname herself, she will have to obtain the permission of the child's father; and if this is not given, she will have to apply to court. The court will base any decision on the welfare principle (see **13.4**). The court is generally reluctant to authorise a change of surname unless it is in the interests of the child to do so. Factors to weigh up include embarrassment to the child and parent of having different surnames, the child's wishes, and the extent to which the child's original surname is important to maintain links with the parent and other relations with whom he does not live. In *W v A (Child: Surname)* [1981] 1 All ER 100, both parents had remarried. The mother wanted to emigrate to Australia with her second husband who was

Australian, and take the two children (aged 12 and 14) from her first marriage with her. The mother wanted to change the children's surnames to the new husband's surname. The children, who were interviewed by the judge, also wanted to change their surname. The judge decided that the children should keep their natural father's name. He stressed that change of name was a serious issue and, in this case, it had not been shown that it was in the children's best interests to change their name. He did not place great weight on the children's wishes in this case as he felt that they had been influenced by their mother and were merely reflecting her view.

This case was followed in *Re F (Child: Surname)* [1993] 2 FLR 837, where it was stated that allowing a child to be known by a different surname is an important matter which is not to be undertaken lightly. In *Dawson v Wearmouth* [1999] 1 FLR 1167, the majority of the House of Lords considered that there had to be particular circumstances to justify a change of name; effectively, there is a presumption in favour of the status quo. *Re W, Re A, Re B (Change of Name)* [1999] 3 FCR 337, following the decision of the House of Lords in *Dawson v Wearmouth*, set out a list of factors to be considered when an application is made for a change of name.

In *Re B and C (Change of Names: Parental Responsibility: Evidence)* [2017] EWHC 3250 (Fam), the court allowed the mother to change the forenames and surnames of children who had been abducted by their father and take to Iran. The children had been rescued by their mother and were taken back to the UK, but they lived in constant fear of being abducted again. The reason for the change of name was to make it more difficult for the father to find the children and abduct them. In *Re child X and another; A mother v A father* [2021] All ER (D) 92 (Apr) where the father had tried to murder the mother in front of one of the children and where the father continued to present a risk to the mother and children from prison, the court allowed a change of the children's surname.

13.3.1.2   Leaving the UK

Child arrangements order regulating with whom the child shall live in force

Where a child arrangements order that regulates with whom the child shall live is in force, no person may remove the child from the UK without either:

(a)   the written consent of every person who has parental responsibility; or

(b)   leave of the court (CA 1989, s 13(1)).

The Act does allow the person named in the child arrangements order as a person with whom the child shall live to take the child out of the UK for periods of less than one month without such consent.

Thus, the parent with whom the child lives can take the child abroad as many times as he or she likes, provided each individual trip does not last more than one month. The parent who is not named in the child arrangements order as a person with whom the child shall live needs to seek consent every time he or she wants to take the child abroad for whatever period. However, at the time that the child arrangements order is granted, the court can add a direction authorising removal to avoid repeated applications to court. This would be sensible in a situation where the non-residential parent lives abroad, so that regular trips to stay with the parent will be permitted without consent being needed.

No child arrangements order regulating with whom the child shall live in force

If no such child arrangements order is in force, either parent can (in theory) take the child abroad without any restriction or need for consent under the CA 1989. However, the parent proposing the trip could be prevented from going by the other parent obtaining a prohibited steps or specific issue order forbidding the child being taken abroad. Additionally, a criminal offence under the Child Abduction Act 1984 will be committed by the parent taking the child if the permission of the other parent, or the court, is not obtained (see **13.9.1.3**).

Application to court to remove

If a parent needs to apply to court to seek permission to take the child abroad, the court will again base its decision on the welfare principle. If the parent wishes to remove the child for a temporary period for a holiday abroad, the court will usually find that a holiday abroad is in the best interests of the child unless, for example, it is a cover for abduction. Where there are legitimate concerns that the child might not be returned from a temporary trip abroad, the court will need to consider three elements set out in *Re K* [1999] 3 FCR 673:

(a) the magnitude of the risk of breach of the order if permission is given;

(b) the magnitude of the consequences of breach if it occurs; and

(c) the level of security that may be achieved by building in to the arrangements all of the available safeguards.

If the child is to be taken to a non-Hague Convention country then it will be usual to obtain expert evidence on the law of the jurisdiction in question to assess the risk and to establish what safeguards can be put in place.

In cases where emigration is intended, *Re F (A Child) (International Relocation Cases)* [2015] EWCA Civ 882 confirmed that the welfare of the child is paramount. This decision brought clarification to the law to be applied in these cases which had been confused following the case of *Payne v Payne* [2001] EWCA Civ 166. In *Payne*, the Court of Appeal stressed that there is no presumption in law in favour of the applicant parent wishing to move the child abroad. The welfare of the child is the paramount consideration, and the court must apply the principles and factors set out in s 1 of the CA 1989 (see **13.5**). Thorpe LJ also gave the following guidance:

(a) Pose the question: is the mother's application genuine in the sense that it is not motivated by some selfish desire to exclude the father from the child's life? Then ask is the mother's application realistic, by which I mean founded on practical proposals both well researched and investigated? If the application fails either of these tests refusal will inevitably follow.

(b) If however the application passes these tests then there must be a careful appraisal of the father's opposition: is it motivated by genuine concern for the future of the child's welfare or is it driven by some ulterior motive? What would be the extent of the detriment to him and his future relationship with the child were the application granted? To what extent would that be offset by extension of the child's relationships with the maternal family and homeland?

(c) What would be the impact on the mother, either as the single parent or as a new wife, of a refusal of her realistic proposal?

(d) The outcome of the second and third appraisals must then be brought into an overriding review of the child's welfare as the paramount consideration, directed by the statutory checklist insofar as appropriate.

Following *Payne*, some cases were decided on the application of the *Payne* guidance, rather than on the application of the welfare principle and the welfare checklist, and this led to criticism of the interpretation of the judgment in *Payne*. A series of cases questioned the applicability of the *Payne* guidance, such as *K v K (children) (removal from jurisdiction)* [2011] EWCA Civ 793.

The position was confirmed in the case of *Re F (A Child) (International Relocation Cases)* [2015] EWCA Civ 882, which was a father's appeal against a judgment allowing a mother to remove their 12-year-old daughter to Germany. The Court of Appeal allowed the appeal, as the judge at first instance had based her decision on 'the four point discipline' in *Payne v Payne*, without a clear overall welfare analysis of the proposals for the child. The Court said that '[t]he questions identified in *Payne* may or may not be relevant on the facts of an individual case and the court will be better placed if it concentrates not on assumptions or preconceptions but on the statutory welfare question which is before it', and that '[s]elective or partial legal citation from *Payne* without any wider legal analysis is likely to be regarded as an error of law'. The Court advised that a 'holistic' approach was required and that '[e]ach realistic option for the welfare of a child should be validly considered on its own internal merits (ie an analysis of the welfare factors relating to each option should be undertaken)'. Further, the Court stated, 'Not only is it necessary to consider both parents' proposals on their own merits and by reference to what the child has to say but it is also necessary to consider the options side by side in a comparative evaluation.' The case also reaffirmed that ECHR, Articles 6 and 8 rights were likely to be engaged in such applications, and that might necessitate a proportionality evaluation because of the likely severance of the relationship between the child and one of her parents.

The case of *Re C (Internal Relocation)* [2015] EWCA Civ 1305 was an application for internal relocation by a mother from London to Cumbria. However, the Court took the opportunity to re-examine the law in relation to both external and internal relocation. It confirmed the decisions of *K v K (children) (removal from jurisdiction)* and *Re F (A Child) (International Relocation Cases)*, and restated that the welfare principle dictates the result of external and internal relocation cases. The Court said that a court could rely on the *Payne* factors, where this is of assistance as part of the analysis of the evidence before determining what is in the child's best interests, if they were useful, but they were not part of the applicable test or applicable principles. The Court also confirmed the need to consider the proportionality of any proposed interference with the parents' rights under Article 8 of the ECHR.

Where there is concern over future contact arrangements, the court could impose conditions. For example, in *Re S (Removal from Jurisdiction)* [1999] 1 FLR 850, prior to authorising removal, the court required the resident parent to deposit a large sum of money pending authentication of the English contact order by the Chilean Supreme Court.

Relocation within the UK

Relocation within the UK does not require the consent of the court. However, if a resident parent's plans to relocate are opposed by the non-resident parent, an application may be made to the court. The resident parent would apply for a specific issue order (see **13.3.4**) and a non-resident parent would apply for a prohibited steps order (see **13.3.3**) or a child arrangements order providing that the child live with him (rather than applying for conditions to be attached under s 11(7) to an existing child arrangements order in favour of the resident parent; *Re F (children) (internal relocation)* [2010] EWCA Civ 1348). In *Re E (Residence: Imposition of Conditions)* [1997] 2 FLR 638 the court stated that it would be possible in 'exceptional cases' to attach conditions to a residence order preventing relocation, but that that did not sit easily with the general understanding of a residence order and had not been what Parliament had intended. Instead the court should consider where the children will live as one of the relevant factors in cross-applications for residence. The use of the term 'exceptional' in the above case had led courts to apply a test of 'exceptionality' when refusing a request to relocate internally, ie it would be refused only where there are 'exceptional' circumstances. However, in *Re C (Internal Relocation)* the court made clear that there was no extra requirement of 'exceptionality' in internal relocation cases, and that there is no difference in basic approach between external and internal relocation. The decision in either type of case hinges ultimately on the welfare of the child, with a consideration of the proportionality of any proposed interference with the parents' Article 8 ECHR rights.

13.3.2 Child arrangements order regulating with whom a child is to spend time or otherwise have contact

A child arrangements order can regulate with whom a child spends time or otherwise has contact, and when. These matters were dealt with in contact orders before April 2014.

Such an order can authorise physical contact, but can also cover contact by letter, e-mail or by telephone (or even by video). The amount of time can either be specified in the order, to cover weekend visits or holidays, or the order could be for 'reasonable contact', in which case the arrangements can be made by the parents. The latter is obviously preferable, as the parents can make and alter arrangements to suit the circumstances.

The order can be made in respect of a parent or any other person, for example it could enable contact to be maintained with more distant relatives or other friends of the child.

All s 8 orders can contain conditions and directions. These could be used to build up contact gradually between a young child and a parent who had not seen the child for a while, or to ensure supervised contact to protect the child. This could take place at a local Child Contact Centre. These centres have been set up across the country to provide an opportunity and setting for contact to take place in circumstances where arranging contact might otherwise be difficult. Only some centres can offer fully supervised contact, but most can provide 'supported' contact, whereby contact can take place in the centre or children can be handed from one parent to another.

Section 1(2A) of the CA 1989 requires the court to presume that involvement of each parent in the child's life is in the child's best interests, unless the contrary is shown (see **13.4.2**).

The court's approach has traditionally been that the child has a right to know both parents, and therefore the starting point is that a child should have contact with the non-resident parent. The right of mutual enjoyment by parent and child of each other's company constitutes a fundamental element of family life under Article 8 of the ECHR.

The position has been summarised recently in the case of *Re Q (A Child)* [2015] EWCA Civ 991, which confirmed the principles set out in *Re C (A Child) (Suspension of Contact)* [2011] 2 FLR 912:

- Contact between parent and child is a fundamental element of family life and is almost always in the interests of the child.
- Contact between parent and child is to be terminated only in exceptional circumstances, with cogent reasons for doing so and when there is no alternative. Contact is to be terminated only if it will be detrimental to the child's welfare.
- There is a positive obligation on the state, to attempt to promote contact. The judge must grapple with all the available alternatives before abandoning hope of achieving some contact. They must be careful not to come to a premature decision, for contact is to be stopped only as a last resort and only once it has become clear that the child will not benefit from continuing the attempt.
- The court should take both a medium-term and long-term view, and should not accord excessive weight to what appear likely to be short-term or transient problems.
- The court must consider if has taken all necessary steps to facilitate contact as can reasonably be demanded in the circumstances of the particular case.

However, the court will always consider all the circumstances, and may decide that because of factors such as the parent's conduct, the emotional welfare and stability of the child, or even the attitude and behaviour of a step-parent, it is in the best interests of the child not to allow contact (*Re T (A Minor) (Parental Responsibility: Contact)* [1993] 2 FLR 450).

Re M (Children) [2017] EWCA Civ 2164 was the appeal by the father against the court's refusal of the father's application for direct contact in *J v B (Ultra-Orthodox Judaism: Transgender)* [2017] EWFC 4. In *J v B*, the father of a family of five children who were part of an ultra-orthodox Jewish community left them to live as a transgender person outside the community. The father sought direct contact with the children which was opposed by the mother. The court reluctantly refused to order direct contact because it was concerned that it would result in the mother and the children being marginalised or excluded by the ultra-orthodox community with consequences so great for the children that this fact had to prevail over the advantages of contact. In *Re M*, the Court of Appeal allowed the father's appeal against refusal of direct contact and drew attention to two principles:

60.   The first is the core principle that the function of the judge in a case like this is to act as the 'judicial reasonable parent,' judging the child's welfare by the standards of reasonable men and women today, 2017, having regard to the ever changing nature of our world including, crucially for present purposes, *changes in social attitudes*, and always remembering that the reasonable man or woman is receptive to change, broadminded, tolerant, easy-going and slow to condemn. We live, or strive to live, in a tolerant society. We live in a democratic society subject to the rule of law. We live in a society whose law requires people to be treated equally and where their human rights are respected. We live in a plural society, in which the family takes many forms, some of which would have been thought inconceivable well within living memory.

61.   The second ... is the principle that the judge has a *positive* duty to attempt to promote contact; that the judge must grapple with all the available alternatives before abandoning hope of achieving some contact; that the judge must be careful not to come to a premature decision; and that 'contact is to be stopped only as a last resort and only once it has become clear that the child will not benefit from continuing the attempt'.

The Court also considered the human rights issues of discrimination under the Equality Act 2010 and Article 14 ECHR, as well as the right to religious belief under Article 9 ECHR, before reaching its decision.

Although it is a well-established principle that a child should have contact with both parents (unless there are cogent reasons to the contrary), that is not necessarily the approach towards any other member of the family, such as a grandparent. In *Re A (Section 8 Order: Grandparent Application)* [1995] 2 FLR 153, the Court of Appeal stressed that just because the grandmother had succeeded in obtaining leave to apply for a contact order, that did not mean that there was a presumption that she should actually be granted a contact order; the court had to consider what was in the child's best interests (although see also the case of *Re W* [1997] 1 FLR 793).

In *Re O (A Minor) (Contact: Imposition of Conditions)* [1995] 2 FLR 124, the Court of Appeal confirmed that the court had a wide and comprehensive jurisdiction to make contact orders, including for indirect contact, such as the non-resident parent being sent school progress reports, and any cards or letters sent by him being read to the child. The court rejected the mother's argument that it was wrong in principle to compel her to read the father's communications when she was unwilling and hostile to such contact, saying that would mean that the mother was being given a power of veto. She was subject to an enforceable duty to promote contact if the court considered that that promoted the child's welfare: that was a decision for the court, not for the mother. However, a contact order could not include a condition that the resident parent vacate the home where he lived to allow the non-resident parent who lived abroad to have contact with the child there (*Re K (A Child) (Contact: Ouster Injunction)* [2011] EWCA Civ 1075).

Domestic abuse

A distinction must be made between cases where a parent is opposed to contact for no good reason, when the court will be very slow to conclude contact would harm the child, and those where there are genuine and rational reasons for opposing contact. A particular difficulty arises where, during the relationship, the resident parent has been subjected to violence by the other parent. In *Re H (Contact: Domestic Violence)* [1998] 2 FLR 42, the Court of Appeal stated that domestic violence was not, of itself, a bar to contact but one factor in a very complex equation. However, for a long time there has been concern that the risks associated with domestic abuse have not been considered fully when making orders for a child to spend time with a parent in cases where violence is alleged. See, for example, *Re M (Contact: Violent Parent)* [1999] 2 FLR 321, where Wall J stated:

Too often, notwithstanding that domestic violence had been found, the mother was none the less ordered to arrange for contact with the father, the courts neglecting the other side of the equation which was that such a father should first demonstrate by changing his behaviour, that he was a fit person to have contact and would not destabilise or upset the children.

See also *Re K (Contact: Mother's Anxiety)* [1999] Fam Law 527, where the court found that the mother had been so traumatised by the father's behaviour that direct contact would bring about a state of heightened anxiety and fear, which would inevitably be conveyed to the boy, causing him significant emotional harm.

There has been increasing research into and awareness of the harm domestic abuse causes children who are exposed to an environment where there is abusive behaviour between adults. Although these provisions are not completely in force at the time of writing, the Domestic Abuse Act 2021 specifically describes a child who sees, hears or experiences domestic abuse by or against a parent as a victim of domestic abuse. The Domestic Abuse Act 2021 also contains a statutory definition of domestic abuse, which is the same as that contained in FPR 2010, Practice Direction 12J (below) and includes physical or sexual abuse; violent or threatening behaviour; controlling or coercive behaviour; economic abuse; and psychological, emotional or other abuse.

There has also been a growing awareness of the need for children to have relationships with both parents following separation. So, the courts have to deal with the importance for children of having an ongoing relationship with each parent, whilst ensuring that children are not exposed to harm in cases where there has been domestic abuse between their parents.

The issue came before the Court of Appeal in 2000 in four cases, heard together, where, in each case, the father's application for direct contact was refused because of a background of domestic abuse between the parents (*Re L (Contact: Domestic Violence)* [2000] 2 FLR 334). The Court of Appeal eschewed any presumption either for or against direct contact in cases involving domestic abuse. The balancing exercise required to determine what was best for a child's welfare had to be carried out in the usual way. However, the court should particularly consider the following points:

(a) the past and present conduct of both parties;

(b) the effect of the violence on the child and the residential parent;

(c) the motivation of the parent seeking contact; and

(d) in cases of serious domestic violence, the ability of the offending parent to recognise his past conduct, be aware of the need to change and to make genuine efforts to do so.

The Court of Appeal also pointed out the need for family judges and magistrates to have a heightened awareness of the effects on children of being exposed to domestic abuse by one parent against the other.

In the recent case of *H-N and others (Children) (Domestic Abuse: Finding of Fact Hearings) (Rev 2)* [2021] EWCA Civ 448, the Court of Appeal heard four appeals from orders made in private law children proceedings brought by mothers who had raised allegations of rape and domestic abuse. The Court confirmed that Practice Direction 12J (see below) remains fit for the purpose of providing the court with a structure to recognise all forms of domestic abuse and a mechanism for approaching such allegations in private law children proceedings. However, the Court found that the proper implementation of Practice Direction 12J is a challenge. The case also highlighted the concept of coercive and controlling behaviour, which can cause harm to a child living in a household. Courts need to consider whether there has been a pattern of coercive and controlling behaviour as part of their approach to domestic abuse cases.

FPR 2010, Practice Direction 12J deals with cases where domestic abuse is alleged. Following concerns in recent years that the previous Practice Direction 12J was not being fully complied with, the recently revised Practice Direction 12J – Child Arrangements and Contact Order: Domestic Abuse and Harm – came into force in October 2017. This is a detailed Practice Direction that applies where there are allegations or suspicions of domestic violence or abuse. The new definition of domestic abuse in the Practice Direction includes controlling, coercive or threatening behaviour as well as violence and abuse. The Practice Direction requires the court to consider at all stages of the proceedings whether domestic violence is raised as an issue, and if so, what those issues are and the extent to which they are relevant to deciding whether to make a child arrangements order, and the court should give directions to determine these issues as soon as possible and fairly.

The court is required to consider in every domestic abuse case whether the presumption of parental involvement in s 1 of the CA 1989 should apply.

The Practice Direction requires extensive steps to be taken, including detailed consideration of the need for an initial fact-finding hearing to determine the issue of violence. The court should also consider whether the child should be separately represented.

The court should not make an interim child arrangements order unless it is in the child's interests and would not expose the child or other parent to an 'unmanageable' risk of harm.

The court is also required under Practice Direction 12J to ensure that, where violence or abuse is admitted or proven, any child arrangements order in place protects the safety and well-being of the child and the parent with whom the child is living, and does not expose them to the risk of further harm. In particular, the court must be satisfied and must make clear how any contact ordered with a parent who has perpetrated violence or abuse is safe and in the best interests of the child.

Further, where domestic violence is found, the court should consider whether it would be assisted by any type of assessment of any party or the child or if any party should seek advice, treatment or other intervention as a pre-condition to any child arrangements order being made, and it may (with the consent of that party) give directions for such attendance and the filing of any consequent report. Further, or as an alternative to the advice, treatment or other intervention, the court may make an activity direction under ss 11A and 11B of the CA 1989 see (**13.3.2.1**).

When considering making a child arrangements order in cases where domestic violence has occurred, the Practice Direction requires the court to have regard to a list of factors similar to those in *Re L (Contact: Domestic Violence)*, above. On the making of a contact order where domestic violence has been proved, the court should consider what directions or conditions should be attached, such as whether the contact should be supervised and whether the order should be reviewed by the court at a later date. Where a risk assessment concludes that a parent poses a risk to a child or to the other parent, contact via a supported contact centre or supported by a parent or relative is not appropriate. In its reasons the court should also make clear how its findings have influenced its decision on the issue of residence or contact, and why it considers the order made is in the best interests of the child.

Following concerns that the risk of harm to children was not being given enough weight in private children cases, the Ministry of Justice published a report in March 2020, 'Assessing Risk of Harm to Children and Parents in Private Law Children Cases'. The report highlights the problems with the current private law system and identifies areas for change which include: the pro-contact culture of the family courts, their adversarial nature, the limited resources available to the courts and how they are used, and the way the family court works in a silo system, lacking coordination with other courts and organisations dealing with domestic abuse. The report made several recommendations for change.

13.3.2.1 Activity directions and conditions

Sections 11A–11H of the CA 1989 (recently amended by the Children and Families Act 2014) give the court powers to make activity directions and conditions with the aim of establishing, maintaining or improving the involvement in the life of the child of that individual or another individual who is a party.

Directions

Activity directions can be made when the court is *considering* making, varying or discharging a child arrangements order, or when considering whether a person has failed to comply with a provision of a child arrangements order or what steps to take in consequence of a person's failure to comply with a child arrangements order. An activity direction is a direction to a party to the proceedings to take part in a specified activity.

Conditions

When the court makes (or varies) a child arrangements order that provides for a child to live with different persons, or to spend time or otherwise have contact with a person, it can impose an activity condition requiring participation in an activity.

Activities

The activities that can be made the subject of directions and conditions include: programmes, classes, counselling or guidance sessions to establish, maintain or promote contact, or to address violent behaviour to enable or facilitate contact and information meetings regarding the making of arrangements for contact, including making arrangements by mediation. At the time of writing, Cafcass offers the following activities: one-off mediation assessment meetings; parenting courses consisting of two, two-hour sessions; and domestic violence perpetrator programmes lasting over 60 hours.

Before making activity directions or conditions, the court must be satisfied that the activity proposed is appropriate in the circumstances of the case, that the specified provider of the activity is suitable to provide it and that it is provided at a place to which the individual can reasonably be expected to travel.

Monitoring

When making the activity direction or condition, the court can require a Cafcass Family Court Adviser to monitor compliance with the direction or condition and report to the court on any failure to comply. The court can also ask Cafcass to monitor compliance with the child arrangements order itself by the individuals with whom the child lives or spends time, and to report to the court on the individual's compliance.

13.3.2.2 Enforcement of child arrangements orders

A practical problem with child arrangements orders providing for a child to spend time or otherwise have contact with someone is how to enforce them if the parent with day-to-day care is determined that contact will not occur. The court has power to enforce orders (FLA 1986, s 34). In practice, though, this is often ineffective in contact disputes.

The court can penalise in costs the party who is breaching the order (*Re B (Contact Application: Costs)* [1995] Fam Law 650). Ultimately, contempt proceedings may be used, or at least threatened, as a measure of last resort, when a parent with whom the child lives consistently and unreasonably refuses contact. However, these proceedings are often inappropriate and could cause the child added trauma, especially if the unfortunate result is the imprisonment of the parent with whom the child lives. Nevertheless, in *A v N (Committal: Refusal of Contact)* [1997] 1 FLR 533 the Court of Appeal upheld a decision to commit to prison a mother who had breached a suspended order for imprisonment.

Intractable cases

Cases where the resident parent (or a child) is refusing contact without any objective justification are referred to as 'intractable'. This resistance is also referred to as 'implacable hostility'. This is often linked to cases of 'parental alienation' which Cafcass has identified as 'when a child's resistance or hostility towards one parent is not justified and is the result of psychological manipulation by the other parent'.

The courts are becoming increasingly alert to cases of implacable hostility and parental alienation, and in *Re S (parental alienation: cult)* [2020] EWCA Civ 568, the Court said:

> In a situation of parental alienation the obligation on the court is to respond with exceptional diligence and take whatever effective measures are available. The situation calls for judicial resolve because the line of least resistance is likely to be less stressful for the child and for the court in the short term. But it does not represent a solution to the problem. Inaction will probably reinforce the position of the stronger party at the expense of the weaker party ...

Cafcass has recently released new guidance to support Family Court Advisers in identifying and assessing private law cases which feature parental alienation.

In these cases, the court is able to transfer residence of the child from the parent with care who is obstructing contact with the other parent (*V v V (Contact: Implacable Hostility)* [2004] 2 FLR 851). Until recently, it was understood that the case of *Re A* [2009] EWCA Civ 1141 required that transfer of residence in these cases should only be used as a 'last resort'. However, in *Re L (A child)* [2019] EWHC 867 (Fam), the President of the Family Division stated that this was not the meaning of the judgment in *Re A* and that to interpret it as such would put a gloss on the paramountcy principle and indicate an enhanced welfare test. He explained that the test is the child's welfare, based on an application of the welfare checklist (see **13.4**).

Another way of dealing with intractable cases was highlighted in *Re M (Intractable Contact Dispute: Interim Care Order)* [2003] EWHC 1024 (Fam), [2003] 2 FLR 636, where Wall J directed the local authority to investigate the case under s 37 of the CA 1989 (see **13.3.7**), with a view to taking care proceedings when faced with a mother who repeatedly frustrated contact. This resulted in the children being removed from the care of their mother under an interim care order, followed by a residence order in favour of the father.

This and a series of other cases highlighted the difficulties in enforcement of contact orders. In *Re A (A Child) (Intractable Contact Dispute: Human Rights Violations)* [2013] EWCA Civ 1104, where a father had faced almost 12 years of litigation to obtain contact with his 14-year-old daughter whose mother was implacably opposed to contact, the court at first instance refused direct contact based on the daughter's recent opposition. The Court of Appeal found that the family justice system had failed the father and daughter, and the entirety of the proceedings had violated the father's rights under Article 8 of the ECHR.

More recent provisions for the enforcement of contact

As a result of concerns raised in the above cases, the Children and Adoption Act 2006 also inserted new ss 11I–11P in the CA 1989, which came into force in 2008 and gave the court additional powers to deal with breaches of contact orders as follows:

(a) *Warning notices.* Where the court makes or varies a child arrangements order, it is to attach to the order a notice warning of the consequences of failing to comply with the order. The warning notice warns that non-compliance with the order may result in the individual being held in contempt of court and imprisoned or fined, and/or an order requiring him to undertake unpaid work (an enforcement order) or pay financial compensation.

(b) *Enforcement orders.* Where the court is satisfied beyond reasonable doubt that a person has failed to comply with a child arrangements order regulating contact, it may make an enforcement order imposing an unpaid work requirement of up to 200 hours. The breach of an activity condition or of a condition attached to a child arrangements order also constitutes a breach of a main child arrangements order. The court may not make an enforcement order if it is satisfied that the person had a reasonable excuse for failing to comply with the order.

The court must be satisfied that making the enforcement order is necessary to ensure compliance with the contact order, and that the effect of the enforcement order is proportionate to the seriousness of the breach of the contact order. The court must also be satisfied that the work can be done in the area where the person lives, and must obtain and consider information about the person and the likely effect of the enforcement on him, including as to any conflict with his religious beliefs and interference with his work or study times.

The court must take into account the welfare of the child who is the subject of the contact order when making an enforcement order.

When making an enforcement order, the court must attach a notice warning of the consequence of failure to comply. When making the enforcement order, the court may also ask Cafcass to monitor compliance with the order and report to the court as required.

(c) *Compensation for financial loss.* If the court is satisfied that a person has breached a child arrangements order without reasonable excuse and this has caused financial loss, then the court may order that person to pay compensation in respect of the financial loss (which may not exceed the amount of the applicant's financial loss). So, for example, if a father booked a holiday for himself and his child to take during a contact visit, and the mother refused to allow the child to go without reasonable excuse, then the mother could be ordered to pay the father compensation.

The case of *Re L-W (children) (contact order: committal)* [2010] EWCA Civ 1253 dealt with an appeal against the making of enforcement and compensation orders and of a committal order for several breaches by a father of contact orders. The Court overturned the majority of the orders on the basis that that whilst the father had not encouraged the child to go on the visits, he was required by the orders only to 'allow' contact and to 'make (the child) available' for contact, and this was not an obligation to 'make sure' that the child went and that contact took place if the child himself refused to attend contact.

13.3.3 Prohibited steps order

A prohibited steps order is an order that no step that could be taken by a parent in meeting his or her parental responsibilities for a child and which is of a kind specified in the order, shall be taken by any person without the consent of the court. This order deals with a specific problem that has arisen. However, it cannot overlap with a child arrangements order. Section 9(5) of the CA 1989 provides that the court cannot make a prohibited steps order or a specific issue order with a view to achieving a result that could be achieved by a child arrangements order. For example, the court could not grant an order prohibiting the child from living with anyone other than the applicant, as this would in effect be a child arrangements order. It can be used to restrict anyone, not just a parent. So, it could be used to prevent a grandparent with whom the child lived from removing the child from the jurisdiction.

Another situation in which the overlap between the various s 8 orders must be considered is child abduction. If, in an abduction case, the result that is required is for the abducted child to be returned to live with the non-abducting parent, the correct order for this parent to seek is a child arrangements order (with appropriate conditions and directions) and not a specific issue order ordering return of the child coupled with a prohibited steps order to prevent further removal (*Re W (A Minor) (Residence Order)* [1992] 2 FLR 332). If the required result is to obtain the return of the child to the UK and prevent further removal, but the child is to remain living with the abducting parent, then a prohibited steps order is the correct order to obtain (*Re D (A Minor) (Child: Removal from Jurisdiction)* [1992] 1 FLR 637).

If no child arrangements order were in force, which includes arrangements relating to with whom the child should live, a prohibited steps order could be used to prohibit the removal of the child from the country, or to prevent a change of surname.

In the past, if it were desired to prevent someone having contact with the child, it was possible to make a contact order providing for no contact. Therefore, the person with whom a child lives could be prevented from allowing contact with an abusing parent or anyone else who the court considered was harming the child in any way. However, in *Re H (Prohibited Steps Order)* [1995] 1 FLR 638, where the mother's cohabitee had abused the children, the court decided that a 'negative' contact order preventing the mother from allowing contact would afford only partial protection. Instead, the court made a prohibited steps order against the cohabitee, even though he was not a party to the proceedings and had not been given notice.

An important restriction on a prohibited steps order is that it can relate only to matters that are included within parental responsibility. If an order is needed to restrict publicity, for example, the wider powers of wardship are needed, as this is not one of the matters included within parental responsibility.

13.3.4 Specific issue order

A specific issue order is an order giving directions for the purpose of determining a specific question that has arisen, or which may arise in connection with any aspect of parental responsibility for a child.

It does not give a parent a general power, it just makes a decision on one issue over which there is a disagreement that cannot be resolved. It could be used to decide which school a child should attend, whether a child should have a particular operation (including, for example, sterilisation or circumcision) or course of treatment or immunisation (such as the MMR vaccination), or the religion a child should adopt.

In *Re JS (Disposal of Body)* [2016] EWHC 2859 (Fam), a 14-year-old girl who was suffering from terminal cancer wished to have her body cryo-preserved following her death. The child's mother agreed but the father was originally opposed. The court made a specific issue order permitting the mother to continue to make arrangements for the preservation of the child's body.

It can be used by non-parents, for example the local authority, or doctor or relation, to resolve issues involving the child, for example over abortion or life-saving medical decisions. In *Re R (A Minor) (Blood Transfusion)* [1993] 2 FLR 757, a specific issue order was used to deal with a situation where a child needed a blood transfusion and his parents refused to give consent due to their religious beliefs.

Again, it cannot be used to achieve a 'back-door' child arrangements order, for example by ordering a child to attend a particular school thereby necessitating a change of residence (see **13.3.3**).

13.3.5 Family assistance order

A family assistance order is not a s 8 order at all, although it is closely connected. Section 16 of the CA 1989 allows the court, in any family proceedings where it has power to make a s 8 order, to make an order requiring, for example, a Cafcass Family Court Adviser or local authority officer to be made available to advise, assist and befriend any person named in the order. The aim of the family assistance order is to support the family in the immediate aftermath of a family breakdown and to help everyone to adjust to the changed circumstances. The order can only be made by the court of its own motion, and is likely to be made in conjunction with one or more s 8 orders. It can last for a maximum of 12 months.

Before making a family assistance order, the court must obtain the opinion of the appropriate officer, as to whether it will be in the best interests of the child to have such an order and how the order might operate. The court can only make a family assistance order if it has obtained the consent of every person (except the child) to be named in the order.

Where a child arrangements order containing a contact provision is in force, the family assistance order can provide that the officer give advice and assistance to establish, improve and maintain contact. Also, where a family assistance order is in force at the same time as a s 8 order, the family assistance order may direct the officer to report to the court on matters relating to the s 8 order, as the court requires, including whether to vary or discharge the s 8 order. Also, the duty under s 16A of the CA 1989, to carry out a risk assessment and report to the court where the officer has cause to suspect the child is at risk of harm, applies for the duration of any family assistance order.

13.3.6 Special guardianship order

Sections 14A to 14F of the CA 1989 provide for special guardianship orders, a type of order that appoints one or more individuals to be a child's special guardian or special guardians.

13.3.6.1 Effect of order

The special guardianship order gives the holder parental responsibility, which he is entitled to exercise to the exclusion of any other person with parental responsibility. However, it does not extinguish the parents' parental responsibility.

Where a special guardianship order is in force, no one can cause the child to be known by a new surname or remove him from the UK (except for the special guardian who can remove the child for a period of less than three months) without the written consent of everyone with parental responsibility or the permission of the court.

It is a private law order, but is increasingly being used in cases where the local authority is or has been involved (see **Chapter 14**). It provides permanence without the legal separation involved in adoption. For example, it may be used in the case of an older child in long-term foster care, or for a child being looked after permanently by a member of his extended family.

In A *Local Authority v YZ and Others* [2006] 2 FLR 41, on the local authority's application for care orders in respect of five children, the court made special guardianship orders in respect of the three eldest of five children. The two eldest had lived with an aunt and uncle for two years, and the third child, aged 5, had lived with another aunt and her partner for almost two years. The two youngest were made subject to care orders with a care plan for adoption.

In *Re S (Adoption Order or Special Guardianship Order)* [2007] EWCA Civ 54 the Court gave examples of some circumstances in which a special guardianship order may be appropriate:

(a) older children who do not wish to be legally separated from their birth families;

(b) children being cared for on a permanent basis by members of their wider birth family;

(c) children in some minority ethnic communities, who have religious and cultural difficulties with adoption as it is set out in law;

(d) unaccompanied asylum-seeking children who need secure, permanent homes but have strong attachments to their families.

13.3.6.2 Who can apply?

A special guardian must be 18 or over and must not be a parent of the child.

Those able to apply for the order are:

(a) any guardian of the child;

(b) anyone named in a child arrangements order as a person with whom the child is to live, or anyone listed within s 10(5)(b) or (c) of the CA 1989;

(c) a relative or local authority foster carer with whom the child has lived for one year preceding the application; and

(d) anyone who has obtained leave of the court to make the application.

The court can also make a special guardianship order of its own motion, even if no application has been made.

13.3.6.3 Procedure

Before applying, the applicant must give the local authority three months' written notice of his intention to apply (s 14A(7)). On receipt of the notice, the local authority must investigate and prepare a report for the court dealing with matters such as the suitability of the applicant to be a special guardian. The court cannot make a special guardianship order unless this report has been received.

The court must consider the welfare principle (s 1(1)), the welfare checklist (s 1(3)) and the no order principle (s 1(5)) when deciding whether to make a special guardianship order. In *Re S* (**13.3.6.1** above), the Court said that a special guardianship order was only appropriate if, in the particular circumstances of the particular case, it was best fitted to meet the needs of the child concerned, and that each case would be decided on its facts.

Before making the order, the court must also consider whether to make a child arrangements order containing a contact provision, whether any s 8 order in force with respect to the child should be varied or discharged, and whether to discharge any enforcement orders or activity directions in force.

On making a special guardianship order, the court may also:

(a) give leave for the child to be known by a new surname;

(b) grant leave for the child to be removed from the UK either generally or for specified purposes.

13.3.6.4 Special guardian support services

The local authority must provide special guardian support services, including counselling, advice and financial support. Financial support can be used to facilitate a person becoming a special guardian, or to facilitate the continuation of the special guardianship order. Examples of financial assistance provided are payment of the prospective special guardian's legal fees to apply for the order, payment for the provision of furniture or equipment, and for adaptation of the home or the additional cost of buying a larger home.

13.3.7 Local authority investigation

If exceptional circumstances are revealed in family proceedings, for example on an application for a s 8 order serious neglect is discovered, which makes it unlikely that either parent should look after the children, the court may not be prepared to grant either parent a s 8 order. The court does not have the power to make a care order relating to a child without an application from the local authority, and what it will have to do is to make an order under s 37 of the CA 1989 to direct the local authority to investigate the child's circumstances. It is then for the local authority to decide whether or not to bring care or supervision proceedings, depending on the outcome of its inquiries. The court can, when making a s 37 order, make an interim care order to protect a child pending the investigation (see **14.9.1**).

13.4 WELFARE PRINCIPLE

Section 1(1) of CA 1989 states:

> When a court determines any question with respect to—
>
> (a)   the upbringing of a child; or
>
> (b)   the administration of the child's property or the application of any income arising from it,
>
> the child's welfare shall be the court's paramount consideration.

The welfare principle will determine any contested proceedings under s 8 of the CA 1989, and it will also extend to care proceedings (CA 1989, s 31) and related public law orders.

It is a concept that has been used for many years in cases concerning children, and is summarised by the words of Lord MacDermott in *J and Another v C and Others* [1969] 1 All ER 788:

> More than that the child's welfare is to be treated as the top item in a list of items relevant to the matter in question, [the words] connote a process whereby, when all the relevant facts, relationships, claims and wishes of parents, risks, choices and their circumstances are taken into account and weighed, the course to be followed will be that which is most in the interest of the child's welfare as that term has now to be understood ... [It is] the paramount consideration because it rules upon or determines the course to be followed.

13.4.1 Human Rights Act 1998

Article 8 of the ECHR provides that 'everyone has the right to respect for his private and family life, his home and his correspondence'. Although the welfare of the child is paramount under CA 1989, under Article 8 the starting point is that each family member is on an equal footing.

There has been debate as to whether the welfare principle is incompatible with Article 8 and an individual's right to respect for family life. In other words, placing the child's welfare as paramount does not involve balancing the family rights of the other relevant individuals. In the past, the European Court of Human Rights has tended to adopt more of a straightforward balancing exercise and the idea of paramountcy has not been supported.

Any inconsistency between the approach of the English courts and the minimum standards required by the Convention needed to be reconciled. For example, in contact applications, it could be argued that the court must consider the right of the parent and other family members to contact, as opposed to this being the right of the child.

Similarly, where an application is made to remove a child from the jurisdiction, the welfare of the child is paramount. If this means that the resident parent is allowed to leave with the child, the other parent's right to family life has been infringed. On the other hand, if the resident parent's application is refused, this inhibits his right to a private life. Nevertheless, in *Payne v Payne* [2001] EWCA Civ 166, [2001] 1 FLR 1052, the Court of Appeal held that the Convention had not affected the longstanding underlying principles (focusing on the welfare of the child) to be applied when dealing with such applications.

The position was confirmed by the case of *Hoppe v Germany* [2003] 1 FLR 384, where the European Court of Human Rights finally made plain its acceptance of the primacy of the interests of the child where a balance was required to be struck between competing Convention rights.

13.4.2 Parental involvement

The Children and Families Act 2014 introduced a new presumption, when considering making, varying or discharging s 8 orders or special guardianship orders and when making parental responsibility orders, that involvement of each parent in the life of the child will further the child's welfare. The 2014 Act inserted a new s 1(2A) and (2B) into the CA 1989 as follows:

> (2A) A court, in the circumstances mentioned in subsection (4)(a) or (7), is as respects each parent within subsection (6)(a) to presume, unless the contrary is shown, that involvement of that parent in the life of the child concerned will further the child's welfare.
>
> (2B) In subsection (2A) 'involvement' means involvement of some kind, either direct or indirect, but not any particular division of a child's time.

And it also inserted a new s 1(6) and (7) as follows:

> (6) In subsection (2A) 'parent' means parent of the child concerned; and, for the purposes of that subsection, a parent of the child concerned—
>
> (a) is within this paragraph if that parent can be involved in the child's life in a way that does not put the child at risk of suffering harm; and

(b)   is to be treated as being within paragraph (a) unless there is some evidence before the court in the particular proceedings to suggest that involvement of that parent in the child's life would put the child at risk of suffering harm whatever the form of the involvement.

(7)   The circumstances referred to are that the court is considering whether to make an order under section 4(1)(c) or (2A) or 4ZA(1)(c) or (5) (parental responsibility of parent other than mother).

13.5   CHECKLIST OF FACTORS TO BE TAKEN INTO ACCOUNT IN APPLYING WELFARE PRINCIPLE

Section 1(3) of CA 1989 (see **Appendix 1(E)**) directs the court to pay particular attention to seven factors when it is applying the welfare principle in contested s 8 proceedings and any proceedings for care and supervision orders.

The aim of the checklist is to promote a consistent approach by providing a framework to use when solicitors are preparing evidence and when courts are making decisions. It could sometimes be a very useful tool to use to explain to clients the approach that they should, and that the court certainly will, take in making a decision.

It provides a minimum that must be considered in every case. The Act gives no indication of the relative importance of the factors, so the court is left to assess the relative importance of each factor in the circumstances of each case. The checklist is not exhaustive and the court can also take any other relevant factors into account. For example, in *Re R (Residence Order: Finance)* [1995] 2 FLR 612 it was confirmed that a judge was entitled to look at the case in the round, which could include taking into account financial considerations, such as a possible assessment by the Child Support Agency.

13.5.1   The ascertainable wishes and feelings of the child concerned (considered in the light of his age and understanding)

This factor reflects the importance of allowing the child's wishes to be given a place in deciding what is in his or her welfare (see the *Gillick* case at **13.2.1**). Lord Justice Butler-Sloss (as she was then) in the Cleveland Report made the point that 'a child is a person, not an object of concern'.

There are a number of cases where, on the particular facts, the court not only considered but also followed the wishes of children. In M v M *(Transfer of Custody: Appeal)* [1987] 1 WLR 404, the trial judge said that it was wrong to order that a 12-year-old girl should live with her father instead of her mother without taking proper account of her adamant and strong opposition to this. In another case, the wishes of a 'sensible and mature' boy aged 14 years were the deciding factor in ordering that he should go to a local day school, enabling him to live with his father, rather than go away to a boarding school. The boy was very anxious to build a relationship with his father with whom he had not lived for five years (see *Re P (A Minor) (Education: Child's Views)* [1992] 1 FLR 316). In S v S *(Child Abduction: Child's Views)* [1992] 2 FLR 492, the Court of Appeal said that there was no age below which a child was to be considered as not having attained sufficient maturity for his views to be taken automatically into account.

A child's wishes do not necessarily always take precedence and the court may sometimes feel that the children's wishes are not in their best interests (*Re DW (A Minor)* [1984] Fam Law 17).

However, in *Re S (Contact: Children's Views)* [2002] EWHC 540 (Fam), [2002] 1 FLR 1156, the court expressed the view that if young people (here a 14- and a 16-year-old) are to respect the law, the law has to respect them and their wishes, even to the extent of allowing them, as occasionally they may do, to make mistakes.

There are a number of ways in which the child's wishes and feelings can be made known. The court will place great importance on the welfare report prepared by the children and family reporter, which will consider the child's wishes as well as the maturity of the child and the extent to which the parents may have exerted influence over the child in forming any views.

In some cases, a judge may interview a child privately during the case to form their own opinion. A child may also give evidence in the case, and following *Re W (Children)* [2010] UKSC 12 (see **13.8.5.6**), this is more usual.

Alternatively, the child may need separate legal representation. This may happen in difficult cases, with disputed facts, and where the child's views are perhaps not sufficiently dealt with in the welfare report (see *Re A (Contact: Separate Representation)* [2001] 1 FLR 715, CA and **13.8.3**).

A wider issue involving a child's wishes is the extent to which a child can consent to or refuse medical treatment (see *Re W (A Minor) (Consent to Medical Treatment)* [1993] 1 FLR 1). If a child is sufficiently mature, he can consent to treatment and only the court can override his consent. If such a child refuses consent to treatment then either the court or anyone with parental responsibility can give consent.

13.5.2 The child's physical, emotional and educational needs

This factor focuses on the child and will look at accommodation, medical needs and education, as well as how close the child is to brothers and sisters and others with whom he may lose touch if a particular order is made.

When the court has to decide between placing a child with a parent or another carer, there is a strong supposition that, other things being equal, it is in the interests of the child that he shall remain with his natural parents (*Re H (A Minor) (Custody: Interim Care and Control)* [1991] 2 FLR 109). In *In re G (Children)* [2006] UKHL 43, Baroness Hale identified three ways in which a person may be or may become the natural parent of a child: the genetic parent; the gestational parent; or the social and psychological parent. In most cases, the natural mother combines all three. This was a case that involved former lesbian partners. One of the partners (CG) had had two children by artificial insemination, whom both partners raised. The court said that the fact that CG was the natural mother, in every sense of the term, whilst raising no presumption in her favour, was undoubtedly an important and significant factor in determining what was best for the children.

The court will not equate welfare with material advantages, and the fact that one parent can offer more is of little weight, particularly because the court could compensate for this when making financial orders.

The court will consider the circumstances very carefully before splitting brothers and sisters (*C v C (Minors: Custody)* [1988] 2 FLR 291). This will mean that it will be unusual to separate siblings, especially when they are close in age, although the larger the age gap, especially if linked with the fact that one child is at boarding school, could mean that children might be happier separated, with generous contact during holidays.

13.5.3 The likely effect on the child of any change in circumstances

If the current arrangements for a child are working satisfactorily the court will be very unlikely to change them. This attitude, which is often referred to as maintaining the status quo, was explained in *Allington v Allington* [1985] FLR 586:

> It is generally accepted by those who are professionally concerned with children that particularly in the early years, continuity of care is a most important part of a child's sense of security and that disruption of established bonds is to be avoided whenever it is possible to do so.

A result of this attitude is that the person with whom the child is living is at a considerable advantage, and it may encourage them to increase this advantage by delaying the proceedings. This problem is tackled by the Act, where it provides that any delay is 'likely to prejudice the welfare of the child' (CA 1989, s 1(2)), and it further discourages delay by its imposition of a litigation timetable (CA 1989, s 11(1) and see **13.8.5.6**).

13.5.4   The child's age, sex, background and any characteristics of the child which the court considers relevant

Age may be important, as very young babies tend to need to live with their mothers, whereas a 15-year-old child can generally cope with living with either parent. Also, age has a decisive influence on the importance a court will attach to a child's wishes, but there is no presumption of law that a child of any age should be with one parent or the other (*Re W (A Minor) (Residence Order)* [1992] 2 FLR 332).

The sex of the child can be taken into account. In *Re H (A Minor)* (1990) *The Times*, 20 June, the court agreed that a 2-year-old girl should live with her father, and stated that '[i]t may be natural for young children to be with their mothers but this is merely one consideration not a presumption'. Obviously, the needs of a teenager might best be met by living with a parent of the same sex. The factor also refers to the background of the child. This can cover race, culture and religion. The needs of a mixed-race child are of particular difficulty when deciding where a child should live. The court will look at how the child has been brought up and the influence of each culture, and make appropriate arrangements for with whom the child shall live and spend time (see *Re P (A Minor) (Adoption)* [1990] 1 FLR 96).

13.5.5   Any harm that the child has suffered or is at risk of suffering

This factor will cover any past or future harm to the child. Harm is a very broad term that will cover both physical and psychological injury.

The court will also consider the harm caused to a child by him not seeing both parents. In the case of *Re S (Minors: Access)* [1990] 2 FLR 166, the court said that contact 'is the right of the child not of the parent ... The child has a right to know his other parent'.

13.5.6   How capable of meeting the child's needs is each of the child's parents and any other person in relation to whom the court considers the question relevant

This factor involves the court in looking at the parents or other proposed carers to assess their ability to care for the child. The parents' conduct will be relevant to the extent that it may affect their suitability as parents. Any criminal record, say, for violence or dishonesty, will be relevant.

In disputes between a natural parent and another, for example a grandparent, there is no presumption as such that it is better for the child to live with his natural parent (*Re G* [2006] UKHL 43). The welfare test is the paramount consideration, and it should be able to encompass any special contribution natural parents can make to the emotional needs of their child, in particular to his sense of identity and self-esteem, as well as the added commitment that knowledge of their parenthood may bring.

Whether a parent works will influence the care of the child. A parent's lifestyle and sexual orientation may also be relevant. Issues of homosexuality and lesbianism can affect the child, especially if this causes problems, for example teasing or bullying, at school. However, the courts' attitudes to homosexual parenting are now very different from what they were several years ago, and these issues are now likely to carry less weight.

A parent who suffers from a mental or physical illness that could mean sudden or long-term stays in hospital might also be less suitable as a full-time carer. Religion, too, may have an influence on a court's decision, especially if it may adversely affect a child's health, or have a harmful influence on the child's development. In *Re R (A Minor) (Residence: Religion)* [1993] 2 FLR 163, the court said that there was no rule of law or legal principle that it could never be right to force a child to abandon his religious beliefs. The court made a residence order that a child of 9 years of age live with his father, even though the child had been brought up in a strict religious sect from which the father had been excluded. The court took the religious issue into account but felt that it was in the child's best interests to be with his father.

If a parent is proposing to share care with someone else, that person's capabilities will also be considered. This means that new partners or spouses, relatives and friends may be relevant, as well as nannies and childminders.

13.5.7 The range of powers available to the court under this Act in the proceedings in question

This factor encourages the court to think laterally and consider every option open to it, including that of not making an order at all (see **13.6**).

The court has the power to make any order in favour of any person, irrespective of who has applied and for what. Thus, in the course of an application for a child arrangements order by a parent for a child to live with him or her, the court may decide that the child would be better off living with a grandparent. It can make this order even though the grandparents were not parties to the application. The deciding factor is the welfare of the child.

The court could also adjourn s 8 proceedings brought by a parent if it felt that a care or supervision order would be the best thing for the child (CA 1989, s 37(1)). This section enables the court to direct the local authority to investigate the circumstances of the child and, following this, the local authority could start care proceedings. (See **14.3.1**.)

13.6 THE 'NO ORDER' PRESUMPTION

Section 1(5) of the CA 1989 states:

> Where a court is considering whether or not to make one or more orders under this Act with respect to a child, it shall not make the order or any of the orders unless it considers that doing so would be better for the child than making no order at all.

This means that there is a policy that the court will not intervene and make an order unless it can be shown that there is a positive need and benefit to the child in doing so.

So, on relationship breakdown, including divorce, the courts will not routinely be asked to make orders concerning the children. If the parties agree on where a child is to live after the divorce and when the other parent should see him, no court will make an order.

The aim of this presumption is to try to reduce the bitterness felt by a parent who may consider that he has 'lost' if a court order is imposed ordering the child to live with the other parent, or allowing him contact only at defined times. The long-term damage to a child following divorce is greatly reduced if bitterness can be minimised, and the absence of unnecessary court intervention will help this. If parents are in dispute from the outset, or if agreed arrangements break down, the court can always be asked to make appropriate orders.

Other circumstances when the court will be likely to consider that an order is necessary include where there is a real danger that one parent may abduct the child and it is, therefore, an advantage to have in operation the restrictions on removal from the UK contained in a child arrangements order, or, perhaps, where both parents agree that an order is preferable. Another situation where the court made an order despite the fact that all parties were in agreement was where parents agreed with the maternal grandmother that the child should live with her. The court said that there was a reason to grant a residence order (now a child arrangements order providing that the child live with her) to the grandmother, as it would give her parental responsibility for the child and give her important rights, for example it would enable her to give consent to medical treatment and authorise school trips. The granting of a (now) child arrangements order also gave the arrangement more stability, as the parents could not change their minds without going back to court (*B v B (A Minor) (Residence Order)* [1992] 2 FLR 327).

13.7 AVOIDING DELAY

Section 1(2) of the CA 1989 states:

> In any proceedings in which any question with respect to the upbringing of a child arises, the court shall have regard to the general principle that any delay in determining the question is likely to prejudice the welfare of the child.

Delay can be particularly damaging in children cases, as a child's timescale is different from that of an adult. Six months is half a lifetime to a 1-year-old child. The object is to avoid drift or delay for no reason, which can be very damaging to a child. Note, though, that sometimes delay can be positively beneficial, for example an adjournment to see how the child is settling down in new arrangements.

Inappropriate delay may also now be a breach of Article 6 of the ECHR (the right to a hearing within a reasonable time).

13.8   PROCEDURE FOR s 8 ORDERS

The procedure for making s 8 applications is governed by the FPR 2010. The rules are largely contained in Pt 12, which is supplemented by Practice Direction 12B.

The new Practice Direction 12B – Child Arrangements Programme came into effect on 22 April 2014 and has modified parts of the procedure for private children law applications. It is now a requirement under s 10 of the Children and Families Act 2014 to attend a MIAM before issuing most private children law applications, and so Practice Direction 3A – Family Mediation Information and Assessment Meetings (MIAMS) also applies.

13.8.1   Legal aid

Legal aid is now only available for private Children Act proceedings where domestic violence can be show (see **2.2.1**).

13.8.2   Jurisdiction

Applications for s 8 orders can be made within any family proceedings; in fact the court can make an order of its own motion in such proceedings. Family proceedings are defined in the Act and cover divorce, nullity or judicial separation, financial orders applications (MCA 1973 and DPMCA 1978) and domestic abuse applications under the FLA 1996. Alternatively, 'freestanding' applications can be made where no order other than under the CA 1989 is needed.

13.8.3   Is leave of the court needed?

13.8.3.1   Who can apply for a s 8 order?

The following may apply for *any* s 8 order without permission of the court:

(a)   a parent;

(b)   a step-parent or civil partner who has parental responsibility for the child;

(c)   a guardian or special guardian; or

(d)   any person who is named in a child arrangements order as a person with whom the child is to live.

The following may apply for a child arrangements order *only* without permission:

(a)   a step-parent or civil partner who has treated the child as a child of the family;

(b)   any person with whom the child has lived for at least three years out of the last five years (but the period must not have ended more than three months before the application is made);

(c)   any person who has obtained the consent of all those people whose legal position would be affected, ie anyone with parental responsibility, or anyone who is named in a child arrangements order as someone with whom the child is to live, or the local authority if the child is in care; or

(d)   any person who has been awarded parental responsibility by virtue of the court's discretion in s 12(2A) (a person who is named in a child arrangements order as someone the child should spend time or otherwise have contact with).

A relative or foster parent of a child can apply for a child arrangements order only in relation to with whom and when the child should live, if the child has been living with that person for at least one year immediately preceding the application.

All other people not within the above require permission.

Therefore, for example, grandparents will require permission unless the child has been living with them for one year or they have the necessary consents. An application for permission must be made in writing.

It is unlikely that the requirement for certain categories of parties to apply for permission violates Article 6(1) of the ECHR, as it is not a blanket denial of access to the court but rather a hurdle to overcome.

13.8.3.2   Application by the child

A child can apply on his own behalf for a s 8 order, but permission of the court is required (see CA 1989, s 10). There have been several cases where teenage children have been granted permission to apply for and have gone on to obtain s 8 orders (see *Re AD (A Minor) (Child's Wishes)* [1993] 1 FCR 573). Even if a child obtains a child arrangements order allowing him to live apart from his parents, his parents will still retain parental responsibility. Orders have been sought to enable a child to live with grandparents or the parents of the child's boyfriend, and could also be used where a pregnant teenager did not want an abortion which her parents were forcing her to undergo.

If a child wants to obtain a s 8 order, there are four hurdles to overcome:

(a)   *To obtain a solicitor to act for him.* A minor can start proceedings without a litigation friend, provided the court gives permission to proceed without a litigation friend or a solicitor considers that the child has sufficient understanding to give instructions in relation to proceedings (FPR 2010, r 16.6). If the permission of the court is sought, it will base its decision on whether the child is mature enough to exercise a wise choice in his own interests in the circumstances that exist (*Re S (A Minor) (Independent Representation)* [1993] 3 All ER 36). However, in *CS v SBH and Others* [2019] EWHC 634 (Fam), the court suggested that following a shift away from a paternalistic approach in favour of an approach which gives significantly more weight to the autonomy of the child in the evaluation of whether they have sufficient understanding, the earlier authorities need to be approached with a degree of caution in terms of the level at which they set the 'bar' of understanding. The court set out a list of factors which should be considered when determining whether a child has sufficient understanding to give instructions.

In complex cases, the court is likely to recommend that a third party, such as an officer of Cafcass Legal (in a role formerly carried out by the Official Solicitor) or a children's guardian, acts for the child.

If a child approaches a solicitor direct, that solicitor can take the decision whether to act for the child. The Resolution guidelines (Section F: Assessing Understanding) point out that initially it is the solicitor's duty to assess the child's understanding. (See *Re CT (A Minor) (Wardship: Representation)* [1993] 2 FLR 278.) The solicitor must also be sensitive to their duty of confidentiality to the child.

(b)   *To obtain public funding.* A child will usually need public funding and will have to convince the Legal Services Commission that his application has merit. The means test will usually not be a problem, as it is the child's resources that are relevant when assessing financial eligibility. Legal Help is also available to a child to cover the cost of the initial interview.

(c)   *To obtain the court's permission.* The child will need to obtain permission of the court to start s 8 proceedings (CA 1989, s 10(8)). Permission will be given only if the court is satisfied that the child has sufficient understanding to make the application.

In *Re H (Residence Order: Child's Application For Leave)* [2000] 1 FLR 781, a 12-year-old boy was refused leave to apply for a residence order in the course of his parents' divorce proceedings. The boy wished to live with his father and was worried that the court would not attach enough weight to his wishes unless he made his own application. The court decided that, although he had sufficient understanding to instruct a solicitor independently, the boy did not have a separate argument to make that would not be made on the father's behalf. The judge also said that the boy must be assured that experienced judges would take full account of his wishes and are conscious that it is not usually a good idea to impose a result contrary to a child's wishes, even though those wishes are not decisive.

(d)   *To show that the merits of the case justify the order sought.* At the eventual hearing the court will consider the child's welfare and the statutory checklist (see **13.5**) when deciding whether to grant the order sought.

13.8.4 The Family Court

The Family Court came into existence on 22 April 2014 and replaced the jurisdiction of the family proceedings court, county court and High Court to hear family matters. Applications for s 8 orders will be made to the Family Court and will be allocated to a judge of the appropriate level.

13.8.5 The Child Arrangements Programme – FPR 2010, Practice Direction 12B

Practice Direction 12B – Child Arrangements Programme (CAP) contains much of the procedure for application, issue, service and listing, and conduct of the first hearing. It is designed to provide a framework for a consistent approach to the issues of private family law nationally.

13.8.5.1 The application

The applicant must file Form C100 (see **Appendix 3(H)**) (or Form C2 if there are already existing family proceedings), together with sufficient copies for service (and a fee). If the applicant alleges that the child has suffered or is at risk of suffering harm, he must also file a completed Form C1A (see **Appendix 3(I)**). Form C100 requires the applicant to give details of his address and that of the respondent during the previous five years to enable Cafcass to carry out safeguarding checks. Form C100 also requires the applicant to confirm he has attended a MIAM, or claim an exception applies, or include confirmation from a mediator that mediation is not suitable. The form also enables the applicant to include the details of the order needed and the reasons for applying. Form C100 (and all other documents used in the proceedings) should be simply worded using non-inflammatory language. Form C100 also refers parents to a Parenting Plan booklet, which offers guidance to parents on making arrangements for their children on relationship breakdown and asks about the parties' attempts to mediate. If a parenting plan has been drawn up, it should be attached to the form.

Under the CAP, the court must issue the application on the day of receipt, and within 24 hours of issue (48 hours in courts where applications are first considered on paper) the court must send (or hand) to the applicant:

(a)   a copy of Application Form C100 (together with Supplemental Information Form C1A if provided);

(b)   the Notice of Hearing C6;

(c)   the Acknowledgment Form C7;

(d)   a blank Form C1A; and

(e)   information leaflets for the parties.

The court also will send a copy of Forms C100, C1A and C6 to Cafcass within 48 hours of issue.

The application will be considered and allocated to an appropriate level of judge within the Family Court in accordance with the Family Court (Composition and Distribution of Business) Rules 2014 and the President's Guidance on Allocation and Gatekeeping. The court may at the same time give directions on allocation in limited circumstances, including where it finds the exemption from attending a MIAM has not been validly claimed or where an urgent issue requires determination.

The court will list the case for a First Hearing Dispute Resolution Appointment (FHDRA) to take place in week 5 following the issue of the application and no later than six weeks from the date of the application.

The applicant must join as a party every person whom he believes to have parental responsibility for the child. This would not always cover a step-parent or putative father. However, any person may apply to be joined, and the court has power to direct that anyone else be joined as a party. Therefore, all people with a genuine interest and active role in the child's upbringing can be involved in court proceedings.

The court may make a child a party to proceedings if it is in the best interests of the child to do so. Practice Direction 16A sets out guidance on what the court should consider before making a child a party and states that it will happen only in cases that involve an issue of significant difficulty, and consequently will occur only in a minority of cases.

13.8.5.2 Service

Unless the applicant requests to do so, or the court directs the applicant to do so, the court will serve the respondent(s) with:

(a)   copies of the application Form C100 (together with Form C1A if provided);

(b)   Notice of Hearing (Form C6);

(c)   a blank Acknowledgement (Form C7); and

(d)   a blank Form C1A.

The FPR 2010, Practice Direction 12C also provides that notice of the application must be given to a number of other interested people, so that they are given the chance to decide whether they want to be joined as a party. This will include anyone caring for the child, anyone who is a party to other proceedings that affect the child, or anyone with whom the child has lived for at least three years prior to the application.

13.8.5.3 Without notice applications

Urgent s 8 orders can be made without notice, and may be made without the requirement to attend a MIAM. The FPR 2010, Practice Direction 12.3 provides that without notice orders should be made only exceptionally, and where:

(a)   if the applicant were to give notice to the respondent(s), this would enable the respondent(s) to take steps to defeat the purpose of the injunction; cases where the application is brought without notice in order to conceal the step from the respondent(s) are very rare indeed; or

(b)   the case is one of exceptional urgency; that is to say, that there has been literally no time to give notice (either by telephone, text or email or otherwise) before the injunction is required to prevent the threatened wrongful act; or

(c)   if the applicant gives notice to the respondent(s), this would be likely to expose the applicant or relevant child to unnecessary risk of physical or emotional harm.

For example, a without notice application would be justified in a 'snatch' situation, where no order was made at the time of the divorce but a crisis arose when the parent failed to return the child to the other parent following a day's contact, or where an urgent medical problem arose and the parents were in dispute over a life-threatening decision. In *Re G (Minors) (Ex parte Interim Residence Order)* [1993] 1 FLR 910, the Court of Appeal granted an interim residence order to a father because of evidence that the mother was taking drugs and that the children needed to be removed from her care immediately.

Any order that follows an emergency 'without notice' hearing should specify:

(a)   the reason(s) why the order has been made without notice to the respondent(s);

(b)   the outline facts alleged which have been relied upon by the court in making the order, unless the facts are clearly contained in the statement in support; and

(c)   the right of the respondent(s) to apply to vary or discharge the order.

13.8.5.4   Acknowledgement

No later than 10 working days before the FHDRA, the respondent must complete the Acknowledgement (Form C7) (and Form C1A if appropriate) and file it at court, and serve a copy on the other party.

13.8.5.5   Cafcass, safety checks and risk assessments

The CAP (and in line with Practice Direction 12J – Child Arrangements and Contact Order: Domestic Violence and Harm (see **13.3.2**)) requires the court to send the documents listed at **13.8.5.1** to Cafcass to enable Cafcass to carry out its initial safeguarding checks. Cafcass is required by the CAP and in accordance with its safeguarding framework to make enquiries of local authorities and the police, and to carry out risk identification interviews by telephone with the parties. The purpose of these checks is to identify any issues of domestic violence, social services involvement or other issues that might pose a risk of harm to the child. Cafcass must report to the court the outcome of risk identification in a safeguarding letter or report at least three working days before the FHDRA.

Section 16A of the CA 1989 requires Cafcass to carry out a risk assessment in relation to any child whom it is given cause to suspect is at risk of harm and to provide the risk assessment to the court. The above initial safeguarding checks will enable Cafcass and the court to identify cases where a s 16A risk assessment is required.

13.8.5.6   First Hearing Dispute Resolution Appointment

The CAP sets out the procedure at the FHDRA. The parties and a Cafcass Family Court Adviser are required to attend the hearing, and a mediator may attend where available. The Cafcass Family Court Adviser, where practicable, will speak to each party at court individually before the hearing.

Conciliation will take place in court with a Cafcass Family Court Adviser and with a mediator, if available, to assist the parties in conciliation and resolution of the issues between them. The CAP provides for the attendance of mediators but leaves the detailed arrangements to be decided at a local level by courts, which means that different courts may have different coverage.

The CAP provides that at the FHDRA the following matters will be considered.

Safeguarding

The court will inform the parties of the outcome of the safeguarding enquiries carried out by Cafcass and decide whether a risk assessment should be carried out. The court should also decide whether a fact-finding hearing is needed to determine allegations that are likely to affect the decision of the court, for example to determine if there has been domestic violence within the family where this is being denied.

MIAM

The court will consider if any exemption for attendance at a MIAM has been validly claimed, and if the respondent has attended a MIAM. If the court decides that an exemption has not been validly claimed, it will direct the applicant or both parties to attend a MIAM.

Dispute resolution

The court will, with the assistance of the Cafcass Family Court Adviser and any mediator present, seek to conciliate and to resolve all or some of the issues between the parties. The court will identify any remaining issues and consider what other options are available to resolve them, for example further intervention by Cafcass; mediation; collaborative law; use of a parenting plan or attendance at a Parenting Information Programme.

Consent orders

Where agreement is reached at the hearing or submitted in writing to the court, no order shall be made without scrutiny by the court. So if safeguarding checks or risk assessment work remain outstanding, the making of the order will be deferred until completion of such work.

Reports

The court shall decide if a report is necessary under s 7 of the CA 1989 to address any welfare issues or other specific considerations. Before ordering a report, the court should consider alternative ways of working with the parties, as stated above. If a report is ordered, it should be directed specifically towards and limited to those issues, and the court should state in the order the specific factual and other issues which are to be addressed in a focused report. The s 7 report is usually prepared by a Cafcass Family Court Adviser, but it can be prepared by a local authority if it has had involvement with the family. The court will consider the evidence Cafcass provides about the extent and nature of the local authority's recent involvement with the family before deciding who should prepare the report. The reporter will have access to the court file and, depending on the nature of the report ordered, will interview the parties and/or the child, may visit the parties' homes and interview anyone else who appears relevant, such as a grandparent or a school teacher. A written report will be prepared, which will often include conclusions and recommendations, for example as to what order should be made. The report should be filed with the court at least 14 days before the final hearing and should be made available to the parties.

Expert evidence

The court is also required to consider if any expert evidence is required.

Section 13 of the Children and Families Act 2014 provides that a person may not instruct a person to provide expert evidence for use in children proceedings without permission of the court, and may not cause a child to be examined or assessed for the purposes of providing evidence in children proceedings without the permission of the court. No expert evidence can be placed before the court in these proceedings without the court's permission. The court will only give its permission for any of the above if it considers that the expert opinion is necessary to assist the court to resolve the matters fairly.

In practice, the court tends to prefer to rely on the s 7 report.

In addition, if the parties wish to instruct an expert, they will need to comply with the FPR 2010, Pt 25 and Practice Directions 25A–25F (see **14.11.6.2**).

Wishes and feelings of the child

The CAP states that the child should be at the centre of all proceedings and should feel that his needs, wishes and feelings have been considered in the court process. Therefore each decision should be assessed on its impact on the child.

The court must consider the wishes and feelings of the child as far as they are ascertainable in light of his age and understanding and circumstances, and so must therefore consider at the FHDRA if the child is aware of the proceedings, and if and how the child's wishes and feelings are to be ascertained. In addition, the court must consider if and how the child is to be involved in the proceedings; for example should he write to the court, have his views reported by Cafcass or a local authority, or meet the judge. There are guidelines for judges meeting children, drawn up by the Family Justice Council in 2010, whose aim is to encourage children to feel more involved and connected with the proceedings, and to give them the opportunities to satisfy themselves that the judge has understood their wishes and feelings and to understand the nature of the judge's task. These guidelines are currently under review by the Vulnerable Witnesses and Children Working Group, which has recommended their replacement by a new practice direction, currently in draft form.

Case management

The court is to establish what issues are agreed and what issues remain to be determined.

The court must also consider making any interim orders that may be useful, such as indirect or supervised contact, and also what directions it should make to ensure the application is ready for the next hearing.

Witness statements

The court must make directions to actively case manage the application and to ensure it is ready for final hearing. This will include directing the preparation and filing of witness statements. It is usual for the parties to file witness statements and, as no document can be filed or served without the court's leave, the court will have to make directions for this.

A witness statement must be signed and dated, and must include a statement of truth (FPR 2010, r 17.2).

Hearsay evidence may be included (as in other civil proceedings). So, for example, a children and family reporter can include in his report a remark made in a conversation with the child's schoolteacher that 'the child was always upset on the Mondays following a visit to his father'. The court can decide what weight to give to such evidence.

It was not usual for a child to be called to give evidence, but in *Re W (Children)* [2010] UKSC 12, which was a public law application, it was held that the existing presumption against a child giving evidence, which needed to be rebutted by anyone seeking to put questions to the child, could not be reconciled with the approach of the European Court of Human Rights and that, in deciding to call a child to give evidence, the court would have to carry out a balancing exercise between the advantages that that would bring to the determination of the truth and the damage it could do to the welfare of that child or any other child. Following a request from the Court of Appeal in *Re W*, guidelines in relation to children giving evidence were published in January 2012 ([2012] FLR 456). These include guidance on how to carry out the balancing exercise referred to in *Re W* and practical considerations in relation to the child giving evidence. These guidelines have been reviewed, however, by the Vulnerable Witnesses and Children Working Group (see above), which has recommended the insertion of a new rule in FPR 2010 in respect of children giving evidence, supplemented by new practice directions and guidance. At the time of writing, no new rule has been drafted.

However, in recent cases such as *Re E* [2016] EWCA Civ 473, the Court of Appeal observed that the guidance given in *Re W* had gone unheeded since it was given.

Timetabling further hearings

The judge shall at all times consider the impact the court timetable will have on the welfare and development of the child.

In accordance with the 'no delay' principle, the court will need to consider listing the next hearing date, which would be a Dispute Resolution Appointment. The court must also consider listing the case for final hearing.

Allocation

The court will consider if the case has been allocated to the correct level of judge, and shall also consider if it needs to be transferred to another court within or outside the area.

The order

The CAP specifies what matters should be set out in the order made at the FHDRA. In 2018 the President of the Family Division issued a set of standard orders and guidance for their use in children cases. The use of these standard orders is not mandatory but is strongly encouraged. The orders consist of clauses to cover most scenarios likely to arise, and so those clauses which are not relevant should be deleted.

13.8.5.7   The Dispute Resolution Appointment

The CAP requires the application to be listed for a Dispute Resolution Appointment (DRA) to follow the preparation of the s 7 or other expert report if it is considered likely to be helpful or in the interests of the child.

At the DRA the court will:

(a)   identify the key issue(s) (if any) to be determined and the extent to which those issues can be resolved or narrowed at the DRA;

(b)   consider whether the DRA can be used as a final hearing;

(c)   resolve or narrow the issues by hearing evidence;

(d)   identify the evidence to be heard on the issues which remain to be resolved at the final hearing;

(e)   give final case management directions including:

   (i)   filing of further evidence;

   (ii)   filing of a statement of facts/issues remaining to be determined;

   (iii) filing of a witness template and/or skeleton arguments;

   (iv)   ensuring compliance with Practice Direction 27A (the Bundles Practice Direction);

   (v)   listing the Final Hearing.

13.8.6   Judgment

The Final Hearing will be held in chambers before the appropriate judge. The relevant bundle of documents should be prepared and lodged with the court at least two working days before the hearing, in accordance with FPR 2010, Practice Direction 27A. This is the responsibility of the applicant. However, if the applicant is a litigant in person, it is the responsibility of the first listed respondent who is not a litigant in person. If all parties are unrepresented then none is obliged to file a bundle unless the court directs. Sanctions are available for failure to comply with this Practice Direction, such as costs orders or removing the case from the list.

Judgment must be delivered as soon as possible after the Final Hearing. Orders must be in writing, and a record of any finding of fact and the reasons for the decision will be kept on the file. A copy of the order must be served on each party and on any person with whom the child is living.

13.8.6.1   Section 91(14) order

In addition to deciding on the s 8 application, the court also can order that no further application is made without leave of the court (see also **14.5.4**). This can be ordered, for example, when there have been repeated and protracted Children Act proceedings, and the court feels it is in the best interests of the child to have a break from them. In the case of *Re P (Section 91(14) Guidelines) (Residence and Religious Heritage)* [1999] 2 FLR 573, the Court of Appeal set out guidelines extracted from earlier cases on the making of orders under s 91(14). These guidelines include that on the making of such an order, the child's welfare is the paramount consideration and that the power should be used sparingly and be the exception, not the rule.

Following concerns that perpetrators of domestic abuse were able to continue their abuse by making applications under the Children Act, s 67 of the Domestic Abuse Act 2021 inserts a new s 91A into the CA 1989, which is not in force at the time of writing. Section 91A clarifies that s 91(14) orders are available where the making of a Children Act application would put the child concerned or another individual at risk of harm. It also makes clear that the court can make a s 91(14) order of its own motion. Further, it provides that where a person who is named in a s 91(14) order applies for leave to make an application, the court must, in determining whether to grant leave, consider whether there has been a material change of circumstances since the order was made.

13.8.6.2   Costs

The public law case of *Re S (Children)* [2015] UKSC 20 (see **14.11.5**) reviewed the principles of costs in children cases. The principles include that the general rule that costs follow the event does not apply to most proceedings concerning children in the Family Court; the approach applies equally to public as well as private proceedings; two exceptions to the general approach that there should be no order for costs as identified in *Re T (Care Proceedings: Costs)* [2012] UKSC 36 are reprehensible conduct and an unreasonable stance in the litigation, but there may be other circumstances where, exceptionally, an order for costs may be justified.

It is therefore general practice not to order costs in children cases, although it may be appropriate to do so if the parent goes beyond what is reasonable. This means unreasonableness in relation to the conduct of the litigation, rather than unreasonableness in relation to the child. In *Re G (Costs: Child Case)* [1999] 2 FLR 250, the court drew a distinction between 'hopeless' and 'unreasonable' applications. In that case, although the court considered the father's application for a residence order was hopeless, it was not in itself unreasonable. In *Re T (A Child) (Order for Costs)* [2005] EWCA Civ 311 the court made an order for costs against a mother who, it found, was behaving unreasonably in obstructing contact, and in *Re J (Costs of Fact Finding Hearing)* [2009] EWCA Civ 1350 a father was ordered to pay two-thirds of the mother's costs of a fact-finding hearing where many of the allegations of domestic violence, which were denied by the father, were proved.

However, in the case of *MG v JF (Child Maintenance: Costs Allowance)* [2015] EWHC 564 (Fam), the court made an order under Sch 1 to the CA 1989 (see **13.10**) that the father fund a large proportion of the costs of the mother and her partner on s 8 applications (see **2.4.2**), even though the father had not been unreasonable in the proceedings. The mother and her partner were of limited means and could no longer afford to pay their own costs. In the absence of availability of legal aid, the court found it was impossible for them to be expected to represent themselves having regard to the factual and legal issues involved, and there would be a gross inequality of arms and arguably a violation of their rights under Articles 6 and 8 of the ECHR and Article 47 of the European Charter of Fundamental Rights. The court therefore found that even though the father had not behaved reprehensibly or unreasonably, he was the only realistic source of costs funding.

13.8.7 Duration of s 8 orders

Section 8 orders, except for child arrangements orders that regulate the child's living arrangements, will normally be expressed to cease to have effect when the child reaches 16 years of age (CA 1989, s 91(10)). The court has power in exceptional circumstances to make or extend a specific issue, contact or prohibited steps order beyond the child's 16th birthday (CA 1989, s 9(6)). In any event, all s 8 orders will end when the child reaches 18 years of age (CA 1989, s 91(11)).

If a child arrangements order that provides for a child to have contact with a parent is made in favour of a parent, it will automatically end if the child's parents live together for a continuous period of more than six months (CA 1989, s 11(5) and (6)). A child arrangements order that provides for a child to live with one of his parents will automatically end in the same circumstances only if both parents have parental responsibility.

Checklist for the procedure for a contested s 8 application in the Family Court

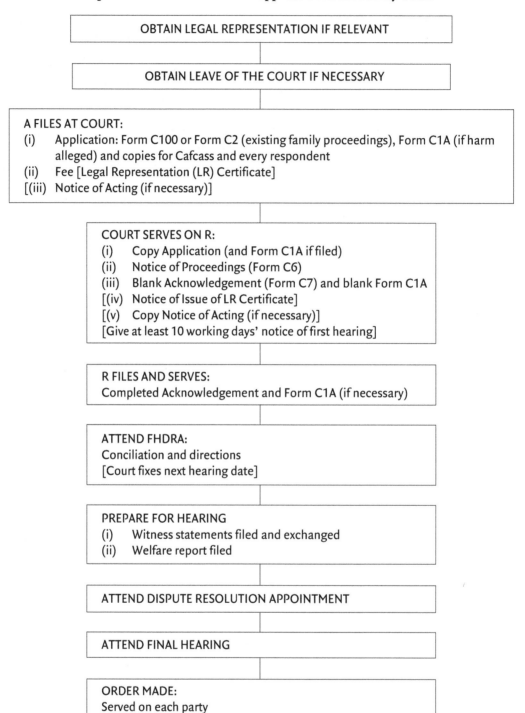

OBTAIN LEGAL REPRESENTATION IF RELEVANT

OBTAIN LEAVE OF THE COURT IF NECESSARY

A FILES AT COURT:
(i)   Application: Form C100 or Form C2 (existing family proceedings), Form C1A (if harm alleged) and copies for Cafcass and every respondent
(ii)   Fee [Legal Representation (LR) Certificate]
[(iii) Notice of Acting (if necessary)]

COURT SERVES ON R:
(i)   Copy Application (and Form C1A if filed)
(ii)   Notice of Proceedings (Form C6)
(iii) Blank Acknowledgement (Form C7) and blank Form C1A
[(iv) Notice of Issue of LR Certificate]
[(v)   Copy Notice of Acting (if necessary)]
[Give at least 10 working days' notice of first hearing]

R FILES AND SERVES:
Completed Acknowledgement and Form C1A (if necessary)

ATTEND FHDRA:
Conciliation and directions
[Court fixes next hearing date]

PREPARE FOR HEARING
(i)   Witness statements filed and exchanged
(ii)   Welfare report filed

ATTEND DISPUTE RESOLUTION APPOINTMENT

ATTEND FINAL HEARING

ORDER MADE:
Served on each party

13.9 PROTECTION OF CHILDREN

This section deals with emergency situations concerning children. It covers the threatened abduction of the child, recovering a child already removed from the UK, general emergency protection of a child by a parent or other interested person and, lastly, an outline of how a local authority may protect children.

13.9.1 Abduction of children

If a child is not returned to the parent with whom he lives following an agreed visit to the other parent and abduction is suspected, a legal adviser needs to assess the situation quickly and obtain such protection as the law offers to try to ensure that the child is returned as soon as possible. A list of relevant considerations is set out at **13.9.1.1** to **13.9.1.7** below.

13.9.1.1 Has a s 8 order already been made?

If the parent with whom the child normally lives already has a child arrangements order providing for the child to live with him or her, this will contain a provision preventing the other parent from removing the child from the UK without the consent of the resident parent or the consent of the court (CA 1989, s 13(1) and see **13.3.1**). This provision can be enforced by the court by an order that the child be produced to the parent with the child arrangements order in his or her favour (CA 1989, s 14; FLA 1986, s 34).

If there is no s 8 order in force, a without notice application for a child arrangements order to provide for the child to live with the applicant or a prohibited steps order could be applied for and then enforced by the court.

A court has the power, in proceedings for or relating to an order under s 8, to order any person who may have information as to the child's whereabouts to disclose it to the court (FLA 1986, s 33). This could be used to force relations or friends of the abductor to disclose addresses or likely destinations.

13.9.1.2 Family Law Act 1986

If a child has been removed from the jurisdiction of the English courts to another part of the UK, for example to Scotland or Northern Ireland, this Act enables a s 8 order to be recognised and enforced by the local court. So that this can be done, the s 8 order must first be registered with the appropriate court in the other part of the UK.

13.9.1.3 Child Abduction Act 1984

The Child Abduction Act 1984 (CAA 1984) (see **Appendix 1(D)**) contains criminal offences that will be committed if a child is removed without the appropriate consents, irrespective of whether any residence order is in force:

(a) It is an offence for a parent of a child, or any person with parental responsibility for a child, to take or send that child out of the UK without either the consent of all persons with parental responsibility, or the leave of the court (CAA 1984, s 1).

However, no offence is committed by a person named in a child arrangements order as a person with whom a child shall live who takes or sends the child out of the UK for a period of less than a month. There are also provisions in the Act, which apply where no such child arrangements order has been made, that provide a defence if the person who removes the child either reasonably believes that he has consent, or has taken all reasonable steps to obtain it.

If, following divorce, no s 8 order has been made, neither parent will be in contempt of court if he or she removes the child without the consent of the other under the CA 1989, as each has parental responsibility. However, neither can take the child out of the UK for any time whatsoever without committing a criminal offence under the CAA 1984, unless he or she obtains the appropriate consents.

(b) It is also an offence for any person, except a person with parental responsibility for a child, to take that child from any other person who has lawful control of the child without lawful authority or reasonable excuse (CAA 1984, s 2).

This will not affect married parents. However, a putative father who has not obtained parental responsibility will commit the s 2 offence, but has a defence if he can show that he had reasonable grounds for believing that he was the child's father. He will nevertheless be liable under s 1 (above) if he takes the child abroad, unless he has the mother's consent.

In the case of R v *Kayani*; R v *Solliman* [2011] EWCA Crim 2871, the Court refused two appeals against sentence for offences under the CAA 1984. The fathers in these cases had abducted the children and held them abroad for many years, depriving them of any relationship with the mothers. The sentences of five and three years' imprisonment respectively were upheld.

Difficult ethical problems can arise for a solicitor if a client informs him that he intends to abduct his child from the mother. There is a duty of confidentiality towards a client, but a solicitor cannot ignore the interests of the child and must decide which duty prevails. A solicitor in this situation should discuss the issue with the SRA's Professional Ethics Department (see the Law Society's Family Law Protocol, para 3.4.10). It is important that a solicitor ensures that a client is made fully aware of the consequences of the crime he is proposing to commit, and that the solicitor does not assist him to commit it.

13.9.1.4 'Port alert' procedure

The provisions in both the CA 1989 and the CAA 1984 may deter a potential abductor but do not contain any practical safeguards to actually prevent a determined abductor from removing the child. The 'port alert' procedure is designed to physically prevent a child from being taken abroad. The detail of this procedure is set out in *Practice Direction (Minor: Preventing Removal Abroad)* [1986] 1 WLR 475.

It is operated by the police on a 24-hour basis. If instituted, the police will liaise with immigration or security officials at ports and airports to try to find and stop the child from being taken abroad. The police have the power to arrest without warrant. There is no need for a s 8 order to have been obtained if the child is under 16, although if there is an order it should be produced to the police. The system is available for children over 16 only if, unusually, a s 8 order exists. The police will operate the port alert procedure only if they are satisfied that there is a real and imminent risk that a child will be taken out of the UK. 'Imminent' is taken to mean within 24 to 48 hours, and 'real' means that the system is not being used just as insurance. The port alert will last for 28 days.

Application should be made to a police station (preferably the applicant's local station) with full details of the grounds for applying, the child, the person likely to remove the child, the applicant, the likely destination, and the likely time of travel and port of embarcation. Any other helpful information should also be given, as well as recent photographs of the child and the abductor. If the police feel that the requirements are satisfied, they will put the child's name on a stop list, which is circulated to all ports and airports. The child will remain on this list for four weeks, and will then be removed unless a further application is made.

The court also has power to make a port alert order, either in conjunction with other orders or as a freestanding order.

13.9.1.5 Passports

Preventing issue of a passport

If the child does not have a passport already, it is possible for an interested party to give written notice to the Identity and Passport Service that a passport should not be issued to a child without the consent of the court, or of both parents or others (*Practice Direction (Minor: Preventing Removal Abroad)* [1986] 1 All ER 983). In *Hamilton Jones v David & Snape (A Firm)* [2003] EWHC 3147 (Ch), solicitors were found negligent in failing to re-register children with the passport agency or advising the mother to do so.

Surrender of passports

If the above provision is not applicable as the child already has a passport, an order can be obtained for the surrender of the relevant passport. This can be done only if there is in existence an order prohibiting or restricting the removal of the child from the UK. A without notice application for a residence order or a prohibited steps order may therefore need to be made. If a residence order or other s 8 order (eg a prohibited steps order) has been obtained, the court that made the order can order any person to surrender the child's passport, or any other passport that includes details of the child.

If a child arrangements order with a contact provision has been made, it is possible to include a direction that the parent exercising contact must lodge his passport with his solicitor during contact visits. Care must be taken by a solicitor acting for the parent with contact in these circumstances, as if this involves giving an undertaking to the court, there will be a conflict of interest if the client subsequently requests the return of the passport in breach of any undertaking given. If the solicitor returns the passport to their client, this will be a matter of professional misconduct, as well as a contempt of court, which could lead to a fine or imprisonment. If the client has given an undertaking to the court to lodge his passport with his solicitor, again the solicitor should not aid or abet their client to disobey a lawful court order (see para 2.5 of the SRA Code of Conduct for Solicitors).

13.9.1.6 Recovering a child abducted abroad

If the child has been removed from the UK, the abductor will have committed a criminal offence under the CAA 1984, but this by itself will not bring about the return of the child. Provisions do exist to obtain an order from the country to which the child has been taken to return the child. The Child Abduction and Custody Act 1985 (CACA 1985) brought the provisions of the Hague Convention on the Civil Aspects of International Child Abduction 1980 (the Hague Convention 1980) into force in this country. If a child is taken to a country which is a party to this Convention, it is possible to request the return of the child. This will usually be ordered if less than one year has elapsed since the removal. After this time the child will still be returned, unless settled in his new environment. There is in addition the European Convention on Recognition and Enforcement of Custody Decisions, which, however, has largely been superseded by Brussels IIa (Regulation 2201/2003). Brussels IIa supplements the Hague Convention 1980, but its terms prevail over the Hague Convention in relation to its signatory States. This means that provided the country to which the child has been taken is a party to either Convention or subject to Brussels IIa, an order can be obtained for the return of the child, although there are certain grounds on which the court in the country to which the child has been taken can decide that it is in the child's best interests to remain there.

Reference should be made to the CACA 1985 and specialist textbooks for the detail of this area.

International child abduction is a specialist area and solicitors should take specialist advice. Solicitors should discuss all such cases with the International Child Abduction and Contact Unit, based within the office of the Official Solicitor and Public Trustee. A source of general advice and support for clients with problems in this area is an organisation called Reunite International Child Abduction Centre.

13.9.1.7 Practical advice

In considering the legal steps that can be taken in this area, the solicitor must remind the client of the practical steps that can be taken to prevent an abduction occurring. These could include notifying the child's school to ensure that the child will not be collected by the potential abductor, in serious cases refusing to allow unsupervised contact and ensuring that the child's passport is kept safe.

13.9.2 General protection of children

The protection a child needs may relate to a wide range of issues. It might concern a medical issue, an abortion, a proposed marriage, a change of name or religion, or protection from a violent parent. Those with parental responsibility may not be prepared to make a decision, or may have made a decision with which another interested party disagrees. In this situation, a s 8 order may be used by parents and others to obtain a court decision. In urgent cases, all s 8 orders can be obtained without notice.

The availability and flexibility of s 8 orders means that there is less need to resort to the High Court's wardship jurisdiction. However, there is no restriction on anyone (other than a local authority) making a child a ward of court. If this is done, parental responsibility will vest in the High Court. The High Court will also have the power to make any s 8 order, unless the child is also subject to a care order.

13.9.3   Protection of a child by the local authority

The CA 1989 introduced a new legal framework for care and supervision orders (see **Chapter 14**).

A care or supervision order can be applied for only by the local authority, or by the NSPCC. The effect of a care order will be to vest parental responsibility in the local authority, who will then take over responsibility for the child from his parents or other carers, including deciding where he lives. A supervision order gives someone, usually a social worker, the duty to oversee the child, who will generally remain living in his home.

The 1989 Act also introduced orders for the emergency protection of children. These are:

(a)   emergency protection orders (EPOs): these are usually obtained by the local authority to protect the child in an urgent case where, because of some neglect or abuse, it is essential to remove the child from his home immediately;

(b)   child assessment orders: these can be used by the local authority to ensure that an essential examination or other assessment of the child, for example a medical examination, can be undertaken in circumstances where the parents are unco-operative and where the local authority suspects some harm is occurring but does not have enough evidence to bring care proceedings.

13.10   FINANCIAL PROVISION AND PROPERTY ORDERS FOR CHILDREN

The law relating to financial provision and property orders for children is complex and is scattered throughout a number of statutes. This section summarises and cross-refers the main provisions, as well as dealing with the financial provisions contained in the CA 1989.

The following jurisdictions are relevant:

(a)   maintenance under the CSA 1991;

(b)   maintenance and property orders in matrimonial proceedings under the MCA 1973;

(c)   maintenance and lump sums during marriage under the DPMCA 1978;

(d)   financial relief under the CA 1989.

13.10.1   Maintenance under the Child Support Act 1991

The CSA 1991 ousted the court's jurisdiction to make maintenance orders in the majority of cases (see **Chapter 7**). The Child Maintenance Service (CMS) currently has the responsibility for dealing with most new child maintenance cases.

The CMS will have jurisdiction whether the parents are married or unmarried, but can make a maintenance calculation only if the parents are no longer living together. Maintenance calculations can be made in favour of children under 16 years of age, and those under 19 years of age who are in full-time education. The CMS does not have jurisdiction to deal with step-children or children over 19 years still in full-time education, and in these cases application will have to be made to the courts to determine maintenance. Other situations where the courts can still be used include payment of school fees and, in wealthy families, when an amount exceeding the maximum figure payable by the CMS's calculation is sought, and also where the child lives abroad.

13.10.2 Maintenance and property orders in matrimonial proceedings

If a parent is involved in divorce, judicial separation or nullity proceedings, he could apply for a lump sum or property adjustment order for a child of the family as part of these proceedings (see **Chapter 4**). However, in practice, unless the family is wealthy, relatively few orders of this type are made in favour of children.

Apart from the situations mentioned above (see **13.10.1**), maintenance will generally be dealt with by the CMS.

13.10.3 Maintenance and lump sums during marriage

A married parent can apply during marriage for a maintenance order and a lump sum order of up to £1,000 for a child of the family from the other parent. This can be done using the DPMCA 1978 in the family proceedings court (see **4.9.2**), or s 27 of the MCA 1973 in the county court (see **4.9.1**). However, in most cases, maintenance will be dealt with by the CMS under the CSA 1991 as the courts will have no jurisdiction.

13.10.4 Financial relief under the Children Act 1989

Section 15 of and Sch 1 to the CA 1989 enable a parent (for these purposes, 'parent' includes an unmarried parent, a parent with whom the child does not reside (*Re S (Child: Financial Provision)* [2004] EWCA Civ 1685), a step-parent and a civil partner), guardian, special guardian, anyone with a residence order in their favour or a child to apply for the following orders against one or both parents of a child:

(a)   periodical payments to the applicant for the benefit of the child, or to the child direct;

(b)   lump sum to the applicant for the benefit of the child, or to the child direct;

(c)   settlement of property for the benefit of the child;

(d)   transfer of property to the applicant for the benefit of the child or to the child direct.

If the child lives abroad with one parent and the other parent lives in the UK, the court can make orders for periodical payments only.

There is no limit to the amount of orders for periodical payments or lump sum orders, but the court can make only one order for either a settlement of property or a transfer of property for the child. In *Phillips v Peace* [2004] EWHC 3180 (Fam), where a settlement of property order had already been made for the child, the mother, who wanted capital to buy a larger home, was precluded from applying for a further settlement of property or property adjustment order. She therefore applied for a lump sum to fund the rehousing, on conditions including that it was to be repaid to the father when the child was older. The court stated that a lump sum was not intended to revert to the payer and that the proposals would produce an effect so close to a settlement that it would be tantamount to varying the settlement or ordering a second settlement, which it could not do.

In deciding whether to exercise its powers under s 15 and Sch 1, and if so in what manner, the court (under CA 1989, Sch 1, para 4(1)) shall have regard to all the circumstances including—

    (a)   the income, earning capacity, property and other financial resources which each person mentioned in sub-paragraph (4) has or is likely to have in the foreseeable future;

    (b)   the financial needs, obligations and responsibilities which each person [parent, applicant for the order or any other person in whose favour the court proposes to make the order] has or is likely to have in the foreseeable future;

    (c)   the financial needs of the child;

    (d)   the income, earning capacity (if any), property and other financial resources of the child;

    (e)   any physical or mental disability of the child;

    (f)   the manner in which the child was being, or was expected to be, educated or trained.

The principles the court must use in deciding whether to make an order are broadly similar to s 25 of the MCA 1973. This means that the child's welfare is not paramount when deciding financial provision (*K v K (Minors: Property Transfer)* [1992] 2 FLR 220). In very wealthy families, standard of living is to be considered as part of all the circumstances, even though it is not included specifically in the checklist in Sch 1 (*F v G (Child: Financial Provision)* [2005] 1 FLR 261).

The provisions in the CA 1989 are rarely needed by married parents as they will normally apply only on marriage breakdown, when the MCA 1973 can be used for lump sums and property adjustment orders, and the CSA 1991 will be used for maintenance. However, the CA 1989 can be very important to an unmarried parent, as it can be used to obtain property orders for the benefit of the child, which could secure the right for the child and the caring parent to occupy the home (*J v J (A Minor: Property Transfer)* [1993] 2 FLR 56).

In *Re P (Child Financial Provision)* [2003] EWCA Civ 837, which involved a very wealthy father, the Court of Appeal gave guidance on how applications involving very wealthy parents should be dealt with. The Court said that the starting point should be to determine the home that needed to be provided, and then to decide the lump sum needed, usually to furnish the home and to provide a car. Then the court should determine what budget the carer required and, in assessing this, should recognise the responsibility and often the sacrifice of the carer. The Court of Appeal said that the budget should reflect the social and financial position of the carer and the absent parent. However, Thorpe LJ stated in obiter that there 'can be no slack to enable the recipient to fund a pension or an endowment policy or otherwise to put money away for a rainy day'. This principle was tested in *CA v DR (Schedule 1 Children Act 1989: Pension Claim)* [2021] EWFC 21 when the mother asked the court to award her periodical payments for the benefit of the child to include the build-up of a pension fund. The court refused to include a sum for pension provision as the 'claim amounts to an entitlement to build up personal savings over many years of [the child's] dependency to fund ongoing income needs at a time when the child's claims have come to an end as a matter of law ...'. The court said this was outside the provisions of the CA 1989 which could only be changed by Parliament or a higher court.

The order must be for the benefit of the child and can include money to pay a parent's legal costs. See *Re S (Child: Financial Provision)* [2004] EWCA Civ 1685, where the court was asked to make financial orders in favour of a mother whose child had been wrongfully retained by the father in Sudan after a contact visit. The money was to be used by the mother to travel to the Sudan to have contact with the child and to enforce the child's return through the Sudanese courts. The Court of Appeal did not finally decide the matter, but indicated that the courts should give the term 'for the benefit of the child' a wide construction.

More recently in *MG v JF (Child Maintenance: Costs Allowance)* (see **13.8.6.2**), the court made orders under Sch 1 to the CA 1989 for a father in s 8 proceedings to pay the litigation costs of a mother and her partner on the basis that the father was the only realistic source of funding if proceedings were to be conducted fairly. The court can make any s 8 order it considers necessary in the financial proceedings.

13.10.5 Summary of financial orders for children

13.10.5.1 Parties divorcing

(a)   CSA 1991 for maintenance;

(b)   MCA 1973 for lump sum/property adjustment order.

13.10.5.2 Parties staying married

(a)   CSA 1991 for maintenance;

(b)   DPMCA 1978 for £1,000 maximum lump sum;

(c)   MCA 1973, s 27 for lump sum;

(d)   CA 1989 for lump sum/property adjustment order.

13.10.5.3   Parties never married

(a)   CSA 1991 for maintenance;

(b)   CA 1989 for lump sum/property adjustment order.

SUMMARY

(1)   Issues concerning children are dealt with under the CA 1989.

(2)   Married parents have joint parental responsibility for their child. An unmarried mother has parental responsibility but an unmarried father does not, although he can acquire it by:

    (a)   registration on the child's birth certificate;

    (b)   court order;

    (c)   child arrangements order;

    (d)   parental responsibility agreement;

    (e)   guardianship;

    (f)   marriage to mother.

Other persons can also acquire parental responsibility.

(3)   The court can make s 8 orders. These are:

    (a)   child arrangements orders;

    (b)   prohibited steps orders; and

    (c)   specific issue orders.

(4)   When making any order, the court must consider:

    (a)   the welfare principle;

    (b)   the 'no order' presumption; and

    (c)   the principle of avoiding delay.

(5)   When applying the welfare principle, the court must pay attention to the factors in s 1(3):

    (a)   the ascertainable wishes and feelings of the child;

    (b)   the child's physical, emotional and educational needs;

    (c)   the likely effect on the child of any change in circumstances;

    (d)   the child's age, sex, background, etc;

    (e)   any harm the child has suffered/may suffer;

    (f)   the capability of the parents (and other relevant people) to care for the child; and

    (g)   the range of powers available to the court.

(6)   A checklist for the procedure for a contested s 8 application is set out at **13.8.7** above.

(7)   There are various procedures available to try to prevent the abduction of a child. The CAA 1984 is also relevant.

(8)   Financial provision for children can be obtained under several different jurisdictions, including the CA 1989.

CHAPTER 14

CHILDREN: PUBLIC LAW

14.1	Introduction	229
14.2	Local authority support for children and families (CA 1989, Pt III)	231
14.3	Preventing neglect or abuse	234
14.4	Care and supervision orders (CA 1989, Pt IV)	236
14.5	Contact (s 34)	241
14.6	Discharge of care orders (s 39)	243
14.7	Effect of a supervision order	243
14.8	Care or supervision order	244
14.9	Interim orders (s 38)	244
14.10	Emergency protection and assessment (CA 1989, Pt V)	246
14.11	Procedure for care and supervision orders	249
14.12	Human rights implications	256
14.13	Compensation for local authority failings	258
Summary and checklists		259

LEARNING OUTCOMES

After reading this chapter you will be able to:

- describe what duties and responsibilities the local authority has to children in its area
- understand what care and supervision orders are and how the court exercises its powers on such applications
- explain the significance of an emergency protection order
- describe the procedure on an application for a care or supervision order.

14.1 INTRODUCTION

The CA 1989 contains most of the statutory provisions relevant to public law proceedings as well as private law proceedings. The Act followed a number of reviews and reports, notably the Cleveland Report, which expressed concern that the local authority had acted too precipitately in removing children from their parents. Paradoxically, in other cases, the concern was that the authority had not acted promptly enough. One of the aims of the Act was to achieve a more balanced approach to the protection of children. Central to this is the concept of partnership: partnership between the local authority and parents, and co-operation between all the agencies relevant to the child's well-being. To this end, the Act is supplemented by guidance in a document called 'Working Together to Safeguard Children: A guide to inter-agency working to safeguard and promote the welfare of children' (July 2018) (together with various regulations). Although 'Working Together to Safeguard Children' does not have the force of statute, the guidance must be complied with, and can be departed from only if good reasons can be shown.

However, tragic cases have highlighted that there is still much progress to be made in the area of child protection. Following the death of Victoria Climbie at the hands of her great aunt and the man they lived with in 2001, Lord Laming, who chaired the inquiry into her death, made specific recommendations to improve the implementation of the child protection system, which had failed adequately to protect her.

Sadly, the death of Baby Peter in 2007 revealed continuing inadequacies in the implementation of the child protection system, and in 2008 the Government asked Lord Laming to undertake an independent progress report on child protection in England following that tragic death.

Lord Laming's report led to the Family Justice Review, and following the final report of the Review in 2011, the Government announced its intention to introduce legislation in the areas of private and public children law. The Children and Families Act 2014 made several changes to public children law. The most notable was a reduction of the time limit in which care applications are to be concluded to 26 weeks. Until then, the time limit had been 40 weeks, so this was a significant reduction. The average length of time in 2019 was 33 weeks, so this was a significant reduction. However, between April and June 2021 that had increased to 43 weeks which may be partly attributable to the difficulties caused by the pandemic. In addition, a new Public Law Outline (PLO), which governs procedure for applications for care and supervision orders, was implemented.

Another innovation was the Family Drug and Alcohol Court (FDAC), which was launched in 2008 in London. It offers an alternative form of care proceedings for families where substance misuse is a key factor. A specialised multi-disciplinary team independent of children's services (consisting of social workers, substance misuse experts, mental health workers, domestic violence experts, and chaired by a child and adolescent psychiatrist) assesses the parents and devises a programme, known as an intervention plan, for the parents. The programme includes detoxification, rehabilitation, regular screening for drugs, cognitive behavioural therapy, domestic violence groups and any other treatment appropriate to the family. Parents are also supported by a parent mentor, who is a parent who has successfully completed the process. The parents attend court every two weeks to monitor their progress, and the same judge will deal with the case throughout. The statistics show that FDAC is getting 46% of mothers clean, compared with 30% in normal care proceedings. Thirty-seven per cent of mothers recovered their children, compared with 25% in normal care proceedings. The FDAC has been rolled out in other courts outside London, and as of April 2021 there were 14 FDAC teams servicing 35 local authorities and 20 family courts

A more recent development is the current piloting of 'settlement conferences' by some family judges since 2016. In a settlement conference, a family judge adopts an inquisitorial approach in order to encourage cooperation between parties with a view to helping them identify solutions and reach an agreement that is in their children's best interests. Settlement conferences take place with the consent of all the parties. The judge hearing a settlement conference will be different to the judge that may hear the final hearing. They will be specially trained in facilitating settlement conferences. The judge should not impose any duress or pressure on any parties. Settlement implies that all parties will be in agreement to fully resolve some or all issues.

This has been a time of great change in the practice of family law, and in the practice of public children law in particular, and it has occurred against a backdrop of an escalating number of care applications (between 2008 and 2016 the number of applications almost doubled). This increase imposes a great strain on local authorities and courts and has inevitably had major consequences for the children and their families. In 2016, the then President of the Family Division referred to this as a 'crisis', following which the Care Crisis Review report was published in June 2018, identifying a number of contributing factors. The report found that the legislative framework is basically sound, but made a number of other recommendations for change. In 2019 Isobelle Trowler, first Chief Social Worker for Children and Families, published a research report: 'Care Proceedings in England: the Case for Clear Blue Water' which investigated the cause of the increase in the number of care applications brought. Part of her conclusion was that many families were being involved in court proceedings who could be diverted from court if they received more effective pre-proceedings input. The report made recommendations to the government to remedy this. Following this, the Public Law Working Group was set up by the President of the Family Division to address the operation of the child protection and family justice systems. The Public Law Working Group reported in March 2021 and made a series of recommendations. Since then, a series of resources in the form of Best Practice Guides have been published by the Public Law Working Group to help professionals and address some of the concerns raised in the report.

Currently, the digitalisation of public children law proceedings is underway, with compulsory issuing of applications and filing of documents gradually being rolled out across the country.

14.2 LOCAL AUTHORITY SUPPORT FOR CHILDREN AND FAMILIES (CA 1989, Pt III)

14.2.1 Introduction

The Act imposes responsibilities on local authorities to provide certain services, in particular for 'children in need' (see **14.2.3**). The local authority has to make an assessment as to whether a child is a 'child in need'. The local authority then has to decide how to discharge its responsibilities to that child, either by providing services directly or by facilitating their provision by, for example, voluntary organisations.

14.2.2 Prevention of harm

Every local authority must take reasonable steps through the provision of services to prevent children in its area suffering ill-treatment or neglect. There is also a related duty to take reasonable steps to reduce the need to bring care or supervision proceedings.

14.2.3 Children in need

14.2.3.1 Definition of a child 'in need'

A child is to be taken to be 'in need' if:

(a)   he is unlikely to achieve or maintain, or to have the opportunity of achieving or maintaining, a reasonable standard of health or development without the provision for him of services by a local authority; or

(b)   his health or development is likely to be significantly impaired, or further impaired, without the provision for him of such services; or

(c)   he is disabled (s 17(10)).

The definition therefore includes not just those children who are suffering, but also those who may be prejudiced in the future, if assistance is not provided for them.

'Development' is defined as physical, intellectual, emotional, social or behavioural development; 'health' as meaning physical or mental health; and 'disabled' as blind, deaf, dumb, suffering from mental disorder, or substantially and permanently handicapped by illness, injury or congenital deformity.

The definition of 'in need' is therefore very wide and reflects the Act's emphasis on local authorities taking preventative action through the provision of support services to families and commencing court proceedings only where absolutely necessary to protect the child.

The linking of 'need' to the provision of 'services' means that an authority could not identify a child as 'in need' and at the same time refuse to provide any service to meet that need. However, although the authority is obliged to provide some service to meet the child's needs, it has a discretion in deciding what service to provide and at what level. In *R v London Borough of Barnet, ex p B* [1994] 1 FLR 592, the court held that the obligations placed on a local authority to provide services must be subject to the ability to do so within its own budget restraints.

14.2.3.2 Duty to children in need (s 17)

It is the duty of every local authority:

(a)   to safeguard and promote the welfare of children within its area who are in need; and

(b)   so far as is consistent with that duty, to promote the upbringing of such children by their families,

by providing a range and level of services appropriate to those children's needs.

Any service provided by the authority to the child can also be provided to the child's family or any member of the family, if it is provided with a view to safeguarding or promoting the child's welfare. 'Family' is widely defined to include any person with parental responsibility and any other person with whom the child is living.

A local authority could provide a range of services to help the parents cope with a child with disabilities, for example: a home help, day-care provision (whether for the disabled child or another child in the household) and a short-term placement for the child to relieve the carers.

In support of the general duty under s 17 to provide services, local authorities are given a number of specific duties, such as to provide day-care services for pre-school children in need and to provide family centres. The definition of a family centre in Sch 2, para 9 is a centre that family members may attend for, among other things, advice, guidance or counselling, and where they may be provided with accommodation while receiving advice, guidance or counselling.

14.2.4 Provision of accommodation (s 20)

A local authority must provide accommodation for any child in need within its area if there is no person who has parental responsibility for him, he is lost or abandoned, or the person who has been caring for him is prevented (whether or not permanently and for whatever reason) from providing him with suitable accommodation or care.

14.2.4.1 Limits on providing accommodation

Recent cases have given guidance on obtaining parental consent for accommodation under s 20. In *Coventry City Council v C, B, CA and CH* [2012] EWHC 2190 (Fam) the court said that the consent should be 'fully informed'. In addition to that guidance, in *Re N (Adoption: Jurisdiction)* [2015] EWCA Civ 112, the Court said that, wherever possible, parental consent must be properly recorded and evidenced by the parent's signature, as well as being in clear, precise, simple and straightforward language, and should spell out that the parent can remove the child at any time.

A local authority may not provide accommodation if anyone with parental responsibility, who is willing and able to provide accommodation, objects. This means that if both parents have parental responsibility and one places the child in accommodation, the other parent can remove him.

The right of a person with parental responsibility to object does not apply if a person or persons named in a child arrangements order as a person with whom the child is to live agree to the child being accommodated.

Also, the right of a person with parental responsibility to remove a child in these circumstances does not apply where the child is aged 16 or over and the child agrees to being accommodated by the local authority (s 20(11)). This is a reflection of the principle of allowing the mature child more say in important decisions, such as where he or she should live.

There is no statutory time limit on the provision of s 20 accommodation. Each case has to be considered on its own facts, and active consideration should be given to whether care proceedings should be issued where s 20 accommodation is provided for a significant length of time. There have been several recent cases where courts have highlighted the misuse of s 20 by some local authorities, where children have been accommodated under s 20 for many years, depriving them (and the parents) of the planning and other safeguards that exist for children who are the subject of care proceedings. In the case of *Kent County Council v M and K* [2016] EWFC 28, the court awarded a 14-year-old girl damages for breach of her rights under Articles 6 and 8 of the ECHR, as she had remained in s 20 accommodation for three and a half years before the local authority issued care proceedings.

14.2.4.2 Preventing removal from accommodation

The local authority should ensure that all those with parental responsibility are involved in the initial negotiations and agree on the provision of accommodation to avoid any subsequent problems. However, it is always open to a person with parental responsibility to remove the child at any time without notice.

If there is a risk that one parent may seek to remove the child, the authority may suggest that the other seeks a child arrangements order naming him or her as a person with whom the child is to live (which may be granted without notice) to prevent the removal (a local authority cannot itself apply for a residence order (s 9(2)).

If that is not appropriate, or if both parents are seeking the child's return, which the authority does not consider to be in the child's best interests, it could apply for an EPO or interim care order.

14.2.5 Children 'looked after' by a local authority

Children who are in care (pursuant to a care order) or provided with accommodation (for a continuous period of more than 24 hours) are 'looked after' by the authority. This also includes children accommodated by a local authority under an EPO, or in police protection (see **14.10**).

When an authority is 'looking after' a child, it is acting in a parental role. It is under a duty to safeguard and promote the child's welfare, and to make use of services available for children (ie under Pt III).

It is central to the philosophy of the Act that an authority should seek to act in consultation (and, it is hoped, agreement) with all interested parties. Before making any decision with regard to the child it must find out, if reasonably practicable, the wishes and feelings of the child, parents and other relevant persons. Any decision should give due consideration to those wishes and to the child's religious persuasion, racial origin, and cultural and linguistic background.

Where the child is accommodated is of crucial importance. To foster the prospect of rehabilitation, the authority should first consider whether it is practicable for the child to live with a member of his family or other persons connected with him. If it is not practicable, consideration should be given to placing the child near to the family home.

14.2.6 Significance of the provision of services

As already seen, so far as it is consistent with the child's welfare, the local authority's duty under s 17 is to promote the upbringing of the child by his family through the provision of services. The authority should not initiate care proceedings unless there is clear evidence that the provision of services has failed to meet the child's needs, or is unlikely to be successful in meeting them.

In most cases, it is better to advise the parents to co-operate and throw the onus onto the local authority to show it has done everything reasonable to assist the child and his parents.

Accordingly, in appropriate circumstances, a local authority should be required to explain:

(a)   what steps it took to identify the child as being in need;

(b)   what its plans are if a care order is made; in particular, what services it would then provide that it could not provide without a court order;

(c)   what evidence there is that what the authority is seeking to achieve by means of a court order could not be more satisfactorily achieved by the provision of appropriate services, with the child remaining at home.

In *Re K (Supervision Orders)* [1999] 2 FLR 303, the court said it was wrong to make a supervision order where the duties imposed on the local authority (under Pt III) would sufficiently meet the child's needs.

14.2.7   Challenging the local authority

There is no provision in Pt III for compelling a local authority to provide services. Neither can a specific issue order be used for that purpose. The courts have said that a local authority's powers and duties under Pt III should not be subject to judicial scrutiny except by way of judicial review (*Re J (Specific Issue Order: Leave to Apply)* [1995] 1 FLR 669).

14.2.7.1   Complaints procedure (s 26)

Every local authority must establish a procedure for considering representations about the discharge of any of its functions under Pt III.

If dissatisfied with the local authority's response, the complainant can require that the matter is referred to a review panel, which must then make a recommendation. Although the ultimate decision remains with the local authority, if it ignores the panel's findings, or fails to give satisfactory reasons for not implementing the recommendation, its actions may be subject to judicial review. In *Re T (Accommodation by Local Authority)* [1995] 1 FLR 159, the court quashed the refusal of the authority to ratify the recommendation of the panel on the basis that it had failed to take into account the correct considerations in deciding that the child's welfare would not be seriously prejudiced by not being accommodated.

14.2.7.2   Judicial review

Only in exceptional circumstances will the court consider an application for judicial review where the statutory right of appeal under the complaints procedure has not been exhausted (*R v London Borough of Brent, ex p S* [1994] 1 FLR 203). Even if the statutory procedures have been exhausted, judicial review is unlikely to be successful if there has been a genuine and fair consultation. In *R v London Borough of Barnet, ex p B* [1994] 1 FLR 592, the court said that it is essentially a matter for the local authority, not the court, to decide what consideration and what weight should be given to the circumstances of any given child. In *Re T (Judicial Review: Local Authority Decisions Concerning Child in Need)* [2003] EWHC 2515 (Admin), the court confirmed it could only direct the local authority to reconsider the services it should provide by quashing the local authority's decision and directing reconsideration; it could not direct the local authority to take a particular course.

In *R (CD) v Isle of Anglesey County Council* [2005] 1 FLR 59, the court found that the local authority's care plan for a 15-year-old girl with cerebral palsy, who was being accommodated under s 20 of the CA 1989, was unlawful, as it failed to provide services appropriate to her needs and did not give due consideration to her wishes.

14.3   PREVENTING NEGLECT OR ABUSE

A central feature of the provisions for the protection of children is that this should be done in partnership with the family and in full consultation with other relevant agencies and professionals. Any assessment of the child should, wherever possible, be done following consultation and with the family's co-operation. The authority should seek to agree any protection plan for the child with the parents.

14.3.1 Court-directed investigation (s 37)

The court has no power to direct a local authority to commence proceedings for a care or supervision order. However, if in any 'family proceedings' where the court is considering the child's welfare, it appears to the court that it may be appropriate for a care or supervision order to be made, the court may direct the authority to investigate the child's circumstances. In deciding whether to make a direction under s 37 (see **Appendix 1(E)**), the child's welfare must be the court's paramount consideration.

'Family proceedings' include divorce, judicial separation, financial relief applications, domestic abuse applications under FLA 1996 and all Children Act proceedings other than emergency provisions (see **14.11.1**).

When undertaking the investigation, the local authority must consider whether it should apply for a care or supervision order, provide services or assistance for the child or his family, or take any other action with respect to the child. If the authority decides not to apply for a care or supervision order, it must inform the court within eight weeks (unless otherwise directed) of its reasons and other action, if any, it intends to take.

When directing an investigation, as an exception to the general rule, the court may make an interim care or supervision order without a formal application if satisfied as to the criteria in s 38 (see **14.9**). It would be usual in such circumstances for a children's guardian to be appointed for the child.

14.3.2 Local authority investigation (s 47)

When a child is subject to an emergency protection order, in police protection or where the authority suspects the child is suffering or likely to suffer significant harm, it must investigate the child's circumstances. (See **Appendix 1(E)**.)

The enquiries should involve a detailed assessment of the needs of the child and his family, and may lead to the provision of services under Pt III, including an offer of accommodation. Alternatively, the authority may decide it is necessary to commence proceedings for a care or supervision order (or an EPO if the child's immediate protection is in issue).

As part of its investigation, the authority should normally see the child. If access is refused, or it is denied information as to the child's whereabouts, the authority must make an application to the court unless satisfied that his welfare can be safeguarded without such an order (s 47(6)).

14.3.3 Child protection conferences

Where, following an investigation, the local authority considers that there might be a risk of significant harm to the child, the local authority will consider convening a child protection conference.

This is a formal meeting that brings together family members (and the child, where appropriate) with the supporters, advocates and professionals most involved with the child and the family, ie social services, police, health and education. Its purpose is to gather together and evaluate all the relevant information about the child and make decisions about his future safety, health and development.

Parents should be encouraged to attend, and may bring a solicitor or other person to support them. Certainly, in the case of *R v Cornwall County Council, ex p LH* [2000] 1 FLR 234, the court made it clear that it would be unlawful for a local authority to have a policy of a blanket refusal of attendance of solicitors.

The conference has to decide whether the child should be the subject of a child protection plan. It must do this if it decides that the child is at continuing risk of significant harm under the category of either physical, emotional or sexual abuse, or neglect. If the conference decides that a child protection plan is necessary, it must also formulate an outline child protection plan.

If a child becomes the subject of a child protection plan, this must be reviewed after three months and thereafter at no more than six-monthly intervals at child protection review conferences.

Even if the decision is that the child does not require a child protection plan, the conference may decide what further support and services may be offered to the family.

14.4 CARE AND SUPERVISION ORDERS (CA 1989, Pt IV)

A care order is an order placing the child in the care of a designated local authority.

A supervision order is an order putting the child under the supervision of a designated local authority, or of a probation officer.

14.4.1 Application

An application for a care order or supervision order can be made only by a local authority (or NSPCC). The court has no power to require a local authority to commence proceedings, nor can it make an order unless there has been an application (*Nottinghamshire County Council v P* [1993] 1 FLR 115).

14.4.2 Grounds for a care or supervision order (s 31)

A court may make a care order or supervision order in respect of a child under 17 only if it is satisfied that:

(a)   the child concerned is suffering, or is likely to suffer, significant harm; and

(b)   the harm or likelihood of harm is attributable to –

    (i)   the care given to the child, or likely to be given to him if the order were not made, not being what it would be reasonable to expect a parent to give to him; or

    (ii)   the child's being beyond parental control.

These conditions have become known as the 'threshold criteria', because they are not in themselves grounds for making a care or supervision order but the minimum circumstances that must be found before the court could be justified in making such an order.

Accordingly, in considering an application, the court must approach the matter in two distinct stages. First, it must establish whether the threshold criteria are satisfied and, secondly, if the criteria are satisfied, whether an order should be made and, if so, what type of order, bearing in mind the welfare principle (see **13.4**). Note, however, that the court has power to make a s 8 order (eg a residence order) whether or not the threshold criteria are satisfied (see **13.3**).

14.4.3 Interpreting the criteria

14.4.3.1 Significant harm

The central concept is whether there is harm which is significant. 'Harm' is defined as ill-treatment, or the impairment of health or development, including, for example, impairment suffered from seeing or hearing the ill-treatment of another. These terms are further defined:

(a)   'ill-treatment' includes sexual abuse and forms of ill-treatment which are not physical;

(b)   'health' means physical or mental health;

(c)   'development' covers physical, intellectual, emotional, social or behavioural development.

Where the question of whether the harm suffered by a child is significant turns on the child's health or development, it is necessary to compare his health or development with what could reasonably be expected of a similar child (s 31(10)). In *Re O (A Minor) (Care Order: Education:*

Procedure) [1992] 2 FLR 7, it was held that, in relation to a truant child, the comparison should be made with a child attending school rather than one who was not. Where the child has learning difficulties or medical problems, it would seem appropriate to compare with a child suffering similar difficulties.

In *Re L (Care: Threshold Criteria)* [2007] EWHC 3527 (Fam), the court made clear that society must be willing to tolerate very diverse standards of parenting, including the eccentric, the barely adequate and the inconsistent. It follows, therefore, that children will inevitably have both very different experiences of parenting and very unequal consequences flowing from it. It means that some children will experience disadvantage and harm, whilst others flourish in atmospheres of loving security and emotional stability. It was not the provenance of the state to spare children all the consequences of defective parenting.

Cases of neglect, physical or sexual abuse have commonly been found to pass the threshold of significant harm; however, more recently the courts have increasingly had to deal with cases of 'radicalisation' where harm might arise. These cases involved children planning, attempting or being groomed to travel abroad to become involved or associate with terrorist organisations; children at risk of being radicalised and children at risk of direct involvement in terrorist cases. Such was the frequency of these cases that the President of the Family Division issued guidance, 'Radicalisation Cases in the Family Court', in October 2015. These cases now include the assessment of risk to children who are returning with parents in such cases from abroad.

The court must be satisfied that the child is suffering, or is likely to suffer harm.

14.4.3.2 'Is suffering'

In *Re M (A Minor) (Care Order: Threshold Conditions)* [1994] 2 FLR 577, the House of Lords held that the relevant date for ascertaining whether the child is suffering significant harm is either at the hearing of the application for a care or supervision order, or the date on which the local authority initiated 'protective arrangements' for the child, provided there has been no lapse in those arrangements before the hearing of the application. Protective arrangements could, for example, be an EPO, an interim care order or being 'looked after' by the local authority. Accordingly, the court can find that the child is suffering significant harm at the date of the hearing, or alternatively, looking backwards, was so suffering when steps were taken to protect the child, provided these steps have continued in place until the hearing.

14.4.3.3 'Is likely to suffer'

This allows the court to consider whether a child is likely to suffer significant harm in the future, and would enable the court to protect a child where, for example, an acknowledged abuser returns to the household, or where another child has suffered in the same family.

If the facts which form the basis for concern over likely harm in the future are disputed (eg the alleged abuser disputes having previously abused another child), the court will have to make a finding as to whether the facts took place. The standard of proof when assessing the evidence is the balance of probabilities.

In *Re H and R (Child Sexual Abuse: Standard of Proof)* [1996] 1 FLR 80, the court held that 'likely to suffer' meant 'a real possibility, a possibility that cannot sensibly be ignored having regard to the nature and gravity of the feared harm in the particular case'.

The approach which should therefore be adopted is that, first, the local authority must prove the disputed facts on the balance of probabilities. Secondly, on the strength of such facts as are proved, the authority must ask: is there a real possibility that future significant harm will occur?

In *CL v East Riding Yorkshire Council and Others* [2006] EWCA Civ 49, injuries were caused to a child whilst in the care of both parents, which could not be proved to be non-accidental. The

Court of Appeal said that if non-accidental injury cannot be proved then the court should not use that injury as a basis for submitting that the threshold criteria are established in relation to that injury and that one or both of the parents are responsible. But the court is allowed to use the parents' behaviour in failing to ensure the child received immediate medical treatment and lying over how the injury occurred, as a basis for reaching the conclusion that a child is likely to suffer significant harm.

However, if non-accidental injuries are proved to have been caused to a child (and this is the only basis for seeking a care order), and a parent has been found to be in the pool of perpetrators (ie, where there is shared care of the child, the court has identified the persons who could have caused the injury but not been able to make a finding of fact as to which of those individuals was actually responsible) (see **14.4.3.4**), that finding is not sufficient to establish that a future child in a new family where the parent now lives is likely to suffer significant harm, as confirmed in *Re J (Children) (non-accidental injury: past possible perpetrator in new family)* [2013] UKSC 9. This has provoked concern that the result may be that unharmed children may be at risk. For example, if there are two possible perpetrators of serious injury or death to a child, and they both move on and live in different households where there are children, then the children in one of the houses will be living with the actual perpetrator, but the court will not be able to take this into account when considering if those children are at risk of suffering significant harm in any proceedings taken to protect them from the possible perpetrator.

14.4.3.4 Causation of the harm

A finding of significant harm or its likelihood is not sufficient. There must be a link between that finding and either the standard of parental care, or the child being beyond parental control.

The standard of care against which parental care is judged is not what it would be reasonable to expect this parent to give, but what a hypothetical reasonable parent would give to meet the child's needs. Accordingly, the fact that the parents have their own particular problems (eg low intelligence, addiction, mental or physical disability) does not justify their providing a lower standard of care.

Where the care of the child is shared between a number of individuals and the child has suffered serious harm through lack of proper care, there is no need to prove that it was due to a failure by one or more identified individuals before the court can make a care order. See *Lancashire County Council v B* [2000] 1 FLR 583, where a baby had suffered non-accidental head injuries. The House of Lords held that the threshold criteria were met (and a care order was made), even though it was not possible to make a definitive finding of fact on whether the injuries were caused by the parents or the child minder. The court acknowledged that this might mean that innocent parents might face the possibility of losing their child, but held that the factor that outweighed all others was the prospect that any unidentified, and unidentifiable, carers might inflict further damage on the child.

In *Re D (Care Proceedings: Preliminary Hearing)* [2009] EWCA Civ 472 the Court said that if identification of a perpetrator, for example between one of two parents, was not possible, it was a judge's duty to state that as his conclusion and not strain to identify the perpetrator of non-accidental injuries to children. If an individual perpetrator could be properly identified on the balance of probabilities, it was a judge's duty to identify him, but a judge should not start from the premise that it would only be in an exceptional case that it would not be possible to make such an identification. If the judge is not able to identify the perpetrator or perpetrators on the balance of probabilities, it is still important to identify the pool of possible perpetrators (*Re S-B (children) (non-accidental injury)* [2009] UKSC 17).

14.4.3.5 Concurrent applications

Where there has been an application for a care order, the court may be faced with a competing application for a child arrangements order in respect of with whom the child shall live. Before considering the merits of making such a child arrangements order, the court should decide whether the criteria for a care order are satisfied, and therefore whether the full range of orders is available to the court (see **14.4.5** and *Re* M (at **14.4.3.2**)).

14.4.4 Welfare principle (s 1)

If the court is satisfied that the threshold criteria are met, it must then decide what order, if any, to make. This stage of the proceedings is often referred to as the 'disposal' stage in practice. In making its decision, the court must apply the principle contained in s 1 (that the welfare of the child is the paramount consideration and that delaying a decision is likely to prejudice the child: see **13.4**), consider the checklist (see **13.5**) and not make an order unless it considers that doing so would be better for the child than making no order at all (see **13.6**). See also **14.4.5**.

14.4.5 Orders available to the court

Even if the threshold criteria are satisfied and the court considers that it is in the child's interests to make an order, as applications under Pt IV are 'family proceedings' it is not merely a question of whether to make a care or supervision order.

Under s 1(3)(g), the court is required to have regard to the range of orders available to it. On hearing an application for a care or supervision order, the court may make, amongst others:

(a)   a care order *or* supervision order if the threshold criteria are satisfied;

(b)   a child arrangements or other s 8 order, whether or not the criteria are satisfied, (however, a child arrangements order cannot be made in favour of a local authority);

(c)   a s 8 order in combination with a supervision order if the criteria are satisfied;

(d)   a special guardianship order (with or without a supervision order or a care order if the criteria are satisfied);

(e)   a family assistance order under s 16, with the agreement of all the persons (other than the child) named in the order, whether or not the criteria are satisfied.

When deciding what order, if any, to make, the court must conduct a balancing exercise, evaluating the pros and cons of the available orders. There has been a lot of recent case law on the approach to be taken by courts when performing welfare evaluations in deciding what order, if any, to make. In *Re* G (*a child*) [2013] EWCA Civ 965, the Court advised against the danger of the judge exercising a linear approach to the available options, whereby each option, starting with the least draconian, is looked at in isolation and then rejected because of its deficits, with the result that at the end of the line the only option left is the most draconian and that is therefore chosen without evaluation of its own merits or de-merits.

The court must also consider the principle of proportionality with reference to Article 8 of the ECHR when considering an application for a care order. In *Re* B (*A Child*) (*care order: proportionality: criterion for review*) [2013] UKSC 33, the Court said that when considering an order that will result in permanent separation between a child and his parents, the court must actively consider proportionality under Article 8 of making such an order, and do so only as 'a last resort' and where 'nothing else will do'.

In *Re* B-S (*Adoption: Application of s 47(5)*) [2013] EWCA Civ 1146, the Court drew on the cases of *Re* G and *Re* B, above, setting out good practice in care cases, and confirmed the need for proper evidence from the local authority and from the guardian addressing all the realistically possible options and containing an analysis of the arguments for and against each option. It was essential that these cases should be followed by an adequately reasoned judgment by the judge, evaluating all the options, undertaking a global holistic and faceted evaluation of the child's welfare, and taking into account all the negatives and positives of each option.

14.4.6 Care plans

In the application for a care order, the authority should outline what plans it has if a care order is made.

Guidelines on the structure, content and format of care plans for use in court proceedings are set out in Local Authority Circular LAC (99) 29 (12 August 1999) 'Care Plans and Care Proceedings under the Children Act 1989'.

Examples of some of the typical matters to be covered in the care plan are:

(a) the child's identified needs (including needs arising from race, culture, religion or language, special education or health needs) and how those needs might be met;

(b) the aim of the plan and the time-scale;

(c) the proposed placement (type and details) and a contingency plan if the placement breaks down;

(d) other services to be provided to the child and/or the family;

(e) arrangements for contact and reunification; and

(f) the extent to which the wishes of the child, his or her parents and anyone else relevant have been obtained and acted upon, or the reasons why such wishes have been discounted.

Section 31A of the CA 1989 requires the local authority to prepare a care plan for the future care of the child in every case in which it seeks a care order. The court will not be able to make a care order until it has considered such a 's 31A care plan'.

Any care plan is considered by the court. Since April 2014, s 31(3A) of the CA 1989 requires the court, when deciding on whether to make a care order, to consider the permanence provisions for the child only and not the remainder of the care plan, apart from plans for contact (the previous version of s 31(3A) required the court to scrutinise the care plan as a whole). The permanence provisions are the long-term plan for the upbringing of the child, which provide for care with the parent, wider family or friends, adoption or other long-term care. If it is not satisfied about material aspects of the care plan (eg where it is proposed to place the child with identified foster-parents, failure to give details as to the foster-parents and the proposed placement) the court may refuse to make a care order, or adjourn and invite the local authority to reconsider its care plan (Re S (Children) and W (A Child) [2007] EWCA Civ 232). Alternatively, it seems that the court may choose to make an interim order instead, until satisfied about the details of the care plan (Re W and B, Re W (Care Plan) [2001] EWCA Civ 757, [2001] 2 FLR 582).

Before making a care order the court must also consider the authority's arrangements for contact, and invite the parties to comment (s 34(11)).

14.4.7 Effect of a care order

The order remains in force until the child reaches 18, unless it is brought to an end earlier.

The local authority must receive the child into its care and provide accommodation and maintain the child for the duration of the order. However, a care order may be justified even if the care plan is for the child to remain at home (Re T (A Minor) (Care or Supervision Order) [1994] 1 FLR 103).

The care order gives the local authority parental responsibility jointly with any other holder. However, it is not an equal partnership. The authority has the power to determine the extent to which a parent may exercise parental responsibility, provided it is necessary to do so in the child's welfare. However, before making any decision, the authority should take into account the wishes and feelings of the child and parents.

While a care order is in force, no person may change the child's surname without the written consent of every person with parental responsibility, or leave of the court. In addition, the child may not be removed from the UK without similar consent or leave. This does not prevent the authority arranging for the child's temporary removal for a period of less than one month.

Most other court orders are incompatible with a care order and, accordingly, the making of a care order automatically discharges any s 8 order (but not a s 4 parental responsibility order). Interestingly, however, the fact that the local authority has a care order in relation to a child does not mean that it can prevent the mother from entering into a parental responsibility agreement with the father (*Re X (Parental Responsibility Agreement: Children in Care)* [2000] 1 FLR 517).

On the making of a final care order, the court is effectively handing over responsibility for the child to the local authority. The court cannot impose any conditions on the local authority, nor seek to keep the implementation of the care plan by the local authority under review. This has meant that the local authority can either change the care plan, or simply fail to deliver aspects of the plan without being challenged. There was a significant, but ultimately unsuccessful, challenge to this position using Articles 6 and 8 of the ECHR in *Re S (Minors) (Care Order: Implementation of Care Plan); Re W (Minors) (Care Order: Adequacy of Care Plan)* [2002] UKHL 10, [2002] 1 FLR 815, where the local authority had promised support and therapy for the mother, leading to rehabilitation with the children. This support was not provided, mostly due to a funding crisis at the local authority. The House of Lords stressed the pressing need for the Government to consider whether some court supervision might improve the quality of child care provided by local authorities.

Following this, the Adoption and Children Act 2002 amended s 26 of the CA 1989 and, since 2004, local authorities are required to appoint an Independent Reviewing Officer (IRO) in connection with each child subject to a care order. The care plans for these children must be kept under review, and the IRO must monitor the local authority's performance, make sure the child's views are understood and taken into account, ensure that any matters of concern are brought to the attention of an appropriately senior member of the local authority and, in necessary cases, refer the matter to Cafcass, who will have the power to bring the case back to court for directions. So far, IROs have not made significant use of this referral system, and recent cases have highlighted apparent weaknesses in the effectiveness of the current IRO system (see **14.12.2**).

14.5 CONTACT (s 34)

Regular contact with parents and other relatives can be important in enabling the child to adjust to his new environment, and is essential if there is to be a successful rehabilitation with the family.

Section 34 (see **Appendix 1(E)**) is a self-contained section and provides a completely different structure from private law proceedings. Any s 8 child arrangements order relating to arrangements for with whom the child spends time or otherwise has contact is discharged upon the making of a care order.

14.5.1 Initial considerations

Before making a care order, including an interim order, the court must consider the local authority's arrangements for contact and invite the parties to comment.

As contact is so important for a child, the local authority should, if possible, place the child with a member of his family or, if that is not appropriate, in accommodation near to the child's home. The local authority may also give assistance in travel and other expenses incurred in visiting the child to any person to whom there is a duty to promote contact.

14.5.2 Local authority duties

There is a general duty on the local authority, subject to its duty to safeguard and promote the welfare of the child, to promote contact between a child 'looked after' and his parents, others with parental responsibility and relatives, friends and other persons connected with him, unless it is not reasonably practicable or consistent with the child's welfare.

By s 34(1), the authority is also under a *positive* duty to allow a child in care reasonable contact with his parents (including a father without parental responsibility) and any person with whom the child previously lived by virtue of a court order, for example a child arrangements order. The courts have said that reasonable contact is not the same as contact at the discretion of the local authority. 'Reasonable' means contact which is agreed, or, in the absence of agreement, contact which the authority can demonstrate is objectively reasonable.

14.5.3 Application to the court

Any person mentioned in s 34(1), for example parents, can apply as of right to be allowed contact with the child. As there is a presumption of reasonable contact in this case, usually contact will be by agreement. It would be necessary for the parents to apply only if they were dissatisfied with the level of contact offered.

In *Re G (Domestic Violence: Direct Contact)* [2000] 2 FLR 865 the court stated that *Re L (Contact: Domestic Violence)* [2000] 2 FLR 334 (see **13.3.2**) applied equally in public law cases when parents were applying for contact with their child, and made an order allowing the local authority to terminate direct contact.

Any other person, for example grandparents, can apply with permission. On an application for permission the court should apply the criteria set out in s 10(9) (*Re M (Care: Contact: Grandmother's Application for Leave)* [1995] 2 FLR 86). In particular, it should consider the nature of the contact sought, the connection of the applicant to the child, the risk of harm to the child, and the wishes of the local authority and the parents.

A child in care has a right to apply for contact under s 34 with any named person. However, where contact is sought in relation to another child then, unless the local authority is opposing contact, the application should be under s 8 (requiring permission) rather than s 34, and it is the respondent child's welfare that is paramount (*Re F (Contact: Child in Care)* [1995] 1 FLR 510).

In *Re P-B (Children) (Contact: Committal)* [2009] EWCA Civ 143 it was held that a contact order under s 34 of the CA 1989 was capable of being enforced by committal.

14.5.4 Refusal of contact

Where an application for a contact order under s 34 is refused, no further application can be made by the applicant for six months, without permission. Furthermore, on disposing of *any* application for an order, the court may direct that no application for any specified order may be made by a person without permission (s 91(14)) (see also **13.8.6.1**). Such a direction would be made only in exceptional circumstances (*F v Kent County Council and Others* [1993] 1 FLR 432). Although the most likely reason for granting a restriction is where the applicant has made repeated and unreasonable applications with no hope of success, the court could make such an order, in the absence of repeated applications, if the welfare of the child requires it. In *Re M (Section 91(14) Order)* [1999] 2 FLR 553, the court imposed a restriction because it considered that the children urgently needed to settle down and make a permanent home away from their mother, and that a premature application by her could disrupt them and hinder their permanent placement. Such a restriction is unlikely to infringe the HRA 1998, as it does not restrict access to the courts but just imposes a requirement for leave.

The local authority cannot refuse contact with persons to whom the presumption of reasonable contact applies. However, the authority can apply to the court for an order authorising it to refuse contact between the child and any person mentioned in s 34(1). In an emergency, the local authority can temporarily suspend contact without an order, for a period of not more than seven days.

Although the court can authorise the refusal of contact by a local authority, it cannot, on the other hand, use its jurisdiction under s 34 to prohibit the local authority from allowing parental contact that the local authority considers to be advantageous to a child's welfare (*Re W (Section 34(2) Orders)* [2000] 1 FLR 502).

A contact order may be varied or discharged on the application of the child, local authority or the person named in the order. If the order is discharged, the presumption of reasonable contact with persons mentioned in s 34(1) still applies.

14.6   DISCHARGE OF CARE ORDERS (s 39)

A care order remains in force until the child reaches 18, unless it is brought to an end earlier. The order may be brought to an end by the making of a child arrangements order in respect of living arrangements for the child (the only s 8 order which can be applied for), the substitution of a supervision order, or by the making of an adoption order or a discharge order.

The application for a discharge can be made by any person with parental responsibility, the child or the local authority. There is no requirement for a child to seek leave before making an application.

On hearing an application to discharge the care order, the court may substitute a supervision order. The court must apply the welfare principle in s 1, but there is no requirement to find that the threshold criteria are still satisfied.

Where there has been a previous application to discharge a care order (other than an interim order) or to substitute a supervision order, no further application can be made for six months without leave.

If the care order is discharged without any other order being made, care of the child reverts to those having parental responsibility. A pre-care child arrangements order relating to the living arrangements of the child will not be revived, although on discharge the court has power to make any s 8 order.

There was an increasing trend for children in the care of local authorities (either under care orders, or being accommodated by voluntary agreement) to leave care early (ie between the ages of 16 and 18), with very little support provided for them. Research carried out by the Department of Health showed that the future for these children was often bleak. As a result, the Government introduced the Children (Leaving Care) Act 2000. It amended ss 22–24 of the CA 1989 to provide that it is the duty of the local authority looking after children to advise, assist and befriend them with a view to promoting their welfare when it has ceased to look after them. Each child must have a 'pathway plan' to cover the period from age 16 to independence (whether they remain in care until then or not) and to look beyond the age of 18 to 21. The plan will be reviewed at least every six months. The local authority must also arrange for each child to have a personal adviser (who does not necessarily have to be a social worker). With regard to education and training, the local authority has a power, but not a duty, to assist with the cost of this up to the age of 24 (CA 1989, s 24B).

14.7   EFFECT OF A SUPERVISION ORDER

Although the criteria are the same as for a care order (see **14.4.2**), the effect of a supervision order is very different. The order places the child under the supervision of a local authority, but the supervisor does not acquire parental responsibility.

The basic duties of the supervisor are to advise, assist and befriend the child, and to take steps to give effect to the order. Other powers of the supervisor depend on the order.

The order could include:

(a)   a requirement for the child to live at a specified place, or participate in specified activities;

(b)   with the consent of any 'responsible person' (any person with parental responsibility and any other person with whom the child lives), a requirement for that person to take all reasonable steps to ensure the child complies with any direction and also to comply with any directions to take part in specified activities. This has been used to require the responsible person to undergo treatment, for example in relation to sexual offences;

(c)   a requirement that the child submits to specified medical or psychiatric examination or treatment. Where the child has sufficient understanding to make an informed decision, he may refuse to submit to the examination or assessment. However, it has been held that under its inherent jurisdiction, the High Court has power to override a child's refusal (*South Glamorgan County Council v W and B* [1993] 1 FLR 574).

The court decides on the broad structure of the supervision to take place, but the detailed implementation of any requirement in the order is left to the supervisor (ie the local authority). If the supervisor's directions are not complied with, the supervisor can only seek a variation or discharge of the order. The directions cannot be directly enforced either by the supervisor, or by the court.

A supervision order is normally made for up to one year, but it can be extended for a further period of up to three years from the date of the original order. An application to extend the supervision order is governed by the principles in s 1, but there is no need to consider whether the threshold criteria are satisfied.

14.8   CARE OR SUPERVISION ORDER

The protection of the child is the decisive factor when the court is deciding whether to make a care or supervision order. The court must weigh the likelihood of future harm to the child against the potential harm of removing the child from his parents under a care order. Note, however, that a care order may still be justified where the local authority intends for the child to remain at home (*Re T (A Minor) (Care or Supervision Order)* [1994] 1 FLR 103).

With a care order, the authority acquires parental responsibility and has an obligation to safeguard the child's welfare. In an emergency it can remove the child without recourse to a court.

In contrast, a supervision order is made to help and assist the child; responsibility for safeguarding the child's welfare rests with his parents. In an emergency, the local authority would have to apply to the court to remove the child. However, a supervision order does give the court a degree of control over the upbringing of the child.

The courts have emphasised that, when deciding whether to make a care order or a supervision order, the order that represents the most proportionate response to the risks involved should be made. When the balance between the two orders is equal, the court should adopt the least interventionist approach (see *Re C and B (Care Order: Future Harm)* [2001] 1 FLR 611 and *Re C (Care Order or Supervision Order)* [2001] 2 FLR 466).

14.9   INTERIM ORDERS (s 38)

14.9.1   The court's powers to make interim orders

Once care proceedings have been instituted, the court has the power to make:

(a)   an interim care order;

(b)   an interim supervision order;

(c)   a child arrangements or other s 8 order for a limited period.

See **Appendix 1(E)**.

Where care or supervision proceedings are adjourned, or the court in any proceedings (eg divorce proceedings) gives a direction to a local authority under s 37 to investigate the child's circumstances (see **14.3.1**), the court may make an interim care or supervision order.

It may not make the order unless satisfied that there are reasonable grounds for believing that the threshold criteria (s 31: see **14.4.2**) are satisfied. At this stage, 'reasonable grounds' means that the court is likely to be relying to a large extent on the child's version of events, or on medical evidence that certain symptoms are consistent with abuse. The fact that belief suffices at the interim stage should be contrasted with the position at the Final Hearing, where the court must be satisfied by proof that the threshold criteria are met.

Alternatively, if the court makes a child arrangements order with respect to the living arrangements of the child pending the outcome of the care/supervision application, it must also make an interim supervision order (unless satisfied that the child's welfare will be satisfactorily safeguarded without it).

An interim order has the same effect as a final care or supervision order, except that the order can include directions as to the examination or assessment of the child and will be of limited duration.

In *Re G (Minors) (Interim Care Order)* [1993] 2 FLR 839, the court stated that an interim care order was an impartial step to preserve the status quo pending the Final Hearing and did not give a tactical advantage to the local authority. However, in *Re H (A Child) (Interim Care Order)* [2002] EWCA Civ 1932 the Court held that the rights of parents protected by Articles 6 and 8 of the ECHR required the judge in the instant case to abstain from premature determination of the case unless the welfare of the child demanded it. Where the effect of an interim care order would result in separation from a child's parents, it was only to be contemplated if the child's safety demanded immediate separation, and it must be a necessary and proportionate response.

It may be appropriate to delay making a final decision pending the outcome of an assessment of the child or a parent, or until the court is in possession of all material facts. The court must also be satisfied the local authority care plan is in the child's best interest. In *Re W and B, Re W (Care Plan)* [2001] EWCA Civ 757, [2001] 2 FLR 582, the Court of Appeal held that trial judges should have a wide discretion to make use of interim care orders where the proposed care plan seems uncertain or incomplete, or could be clarified after a relative brief adjournment.

When the court makes an interim care or supervision order, it may direct a medical or psychiatric examination or other assessment of the child under s 38(6) of the CA 1989. Since 22 April 2014, a direction under s 38(6) can only be made if the court is of the opinion that the examination or assessment is necessary to assist the court to resolve the proceedings justly. In deciding whether to make a direction under s 38(6), the court has a list of matters it must have regard to in s 38(7B) and which include:

(a)   the likely impact on the child's welfare;

(b)   the issues it would assist the court with and the questions it would enable the court to answer;

(c)   other available evidence;

(d)   the impact on the timetable, conduct and duration of proceedings; and

(e)   the cost of the examination or assessment.

This can include a residential assessment of the child with his family. These assessments are often very expensive, and in the past the Legal Aid Agency funded a significant proportion of these costs. Since 2007 the Agency has been increasingly reluctant to do so, which means that funding of such assessment is often problematic.

The case of *Re C (A Minor) (Interim Care Order: Residential Assessment)* [1996] 4 All ER 871, established that it was for the court to determine whether an assessment under s 38(6) would provide the court with the relevant material it required to make a decision at the Final Hearing. In *Re G (Interim Care Order: Residential Assessment)* [2005] UKHL 68, the House of Lords held that, to come within s 38(6), the assessment must be of 'the child' and the main focus must be on the child. It may include an assessment of the child's relationship with his or her parents, the risk the parents may present to him or her, and ways in which those risks may be avoided or managed, all with a view to enabling the court to make decisions under the Act. Any services that are provided for the child and his family must be ancillary to that end; they must not be an end in themselves.

Recent cases have given further guidance on the ordering of residential assessments under s 38(6). In *Re L and H (Residential Assessment)* [2007] EWCA Civ 213, the Court of Appeal stated that where there was some evidence that a residential assessment would be useful, the court should give serious consideration on an application for a s 38(6) assessment, in the interests of fairness, to the importance of having before it all the relevant evidence to make a decision at the Final Hearing.

14.9.2 Exclusion requirements

If the court makes an interim care order, it may include an 'exclusion requirement', provided there is reasonable cause to believe that if a person is excluded from the house where the child lives, the child will no longer suffer, or be likely to suffer, significant harm (s 38A(2)).

Before including such a requirement, another person (whether or not a parent) living in the house with the child must be able to look after the child and consent to the requirement being made. The 'exclusion requirement' may require the person to leave the dwelling house, or not to enter the dwelling house. It can also require the person not to enter an area surrounding the house. A power of arrest can be attached to the exclusion requirement. The requirement will cease to have effect if the local authority removes the child to other accommodation for a continuous period of more than 24 hours.

14.9.3 Contact

The provisions regarding contact with a child in care (see **14.5**) apply equally on the making of an interim care order. However, as the issue is only being considered pending a Final Hearing, contact between a parent and child should be maintained unless there are exceptional circumstances.

14.10 EMERGENCY PROTECTION AND ASSESSMENT (CA 1989, Pt V)

14.10.1 Emergency protection order (s 44)

An emergency protection order (EPO) is an order, initially limited to eight days, to protect a child in an emergency where he is otherwise likely to suffer significant harm (see **Appendix 1(E)**). Recent cases have emphasised that the draconian nature of an EPO in removing a child from his parent requires exceptional circumstances and proof of imminent danger (*X Council v B (Emergency Protection Orders)* [2004] EWHC 2015 (Fam)).

14.10.2 Grounds

The court may make an EPO on the application of any person, if it is satisfied that there is reasonable cause to believe that the child is likely to suffer significant harm if he:

(a)   is not removed to accommodation provided by or on behalf of the applicant; or

(b)   does not remain in the place where he is being accommodated.

The application will usually be made by a local authority, but anyone (such as a police officer or a relative) can apply. If the local authority is not the applicant, it has power to take over the order.

A local authority can also apply for an order where it is making enquiries because, for example, it suspects the child may be suffering significant harm and believes access is required as a matter of urgency, which is being unreasonably refused.

If the court finds that either condition applies, before making an order it must consider the welfare principle (s 1(1): see **14.4.4**) and the no order presumption (s 1(5): see **13.6**), although there is no requirement to apply the checklist under s 1(3) (see **13.5**).

If the court makes an order under s 44, it may include an 'exclusion requirement' if there is reasonable cause to believe that if a person is excluded from the dwelling house in which the child lives, the child is unlikely to suffer significant harm (s 44A(2)). The exclusion requirements and conditions are the same as when made in conjunction with an interim care order (see **14.9.2**).

14.10.3 Application

The application to the Family Court can be made on one day's notice. The application may also be made without notice with the consent of the justices' clerk and may be heard by a single justice. However, due consideration must be given to parents' rights under Articles 6 and 8 of the ECHR, and notice of the hearing should generally be given, unless it is genuinely an emergency or a case of great urgency. A copy of the application and order must be served on each party (every person with parental responsibility and the child) within 48 hours of the order.

In X Council v B (see **14.10.1**) the court gave detailed guidance on EPOs generally and also on the use of without notice applications, stating that, save in wholly exceptional cases, parents must be given notice. The case also stated the need for courts hearing without notice applications to keep a note of the evidence received, of its reasons and any findings of fact. This guidance was endorsed in Re X (Emergency Protection Orders) [2006] EWHC 510 (Fam), which said it is the duty of an applicant in an EPO to ensure that the guidance in X Council v B is brought to the court's attention, ie, following a without notice hearing, the parents should be given a copy of the clerk's notes, a copy of any material submitted to the court and a copy of the justices' reasons. Re X (Emergency Protection Orders) also stated that, on a without notice application, the court needed to determine whether or not the hearing should proceed on a without notice basis and to give reasons for that decision.

The court will normally appoint a children's guardian for the child (see **14.11.6.1**). The court may take account of any statement contained in any report made to the court, or any evidence given during the hearing which is relevant to the application.

14.10.4 Effect of the order

The order operates as a direction to any person who is in a position to do so to comply with any request to produce the child to the applicant, and authorises the removal or prevention of removal of the child from his present accommodation. The order may authorise the applicant to enter specified premises and search for the child. If the applicant is likely to be refused entry, the court can issue a warrant authorising the police to assist, using reasonable force if necessary.

The order also gives the applicant parental responsibility for the child, but this is limited to doing what is necessary to safeguard and promote the child's welfare.

The local authority should return the child to his parents as soon as it appears safe to do so, thus it should review the case regularly to ensure that the parents and child are separated for no longer than is necessary.

14.10.5 Contact

During the currency of the order, the applicant must, subject to any direction of the court, allow the child reasonable contact with his parents, any other person with parental responsibility, any person with whom he was living prior to the order and any person named in a child arrangements order as a person with whom the child is to spend time or otherwise have contact.

The court can give such directions and impose such conditions as it considers appropriate in relation to contact. However, where the applicant is a local authority, the court will usually leave contact to be negotiated between the parties unless the issue is clearly disputed. In *X Council v B (Emergency Protection Orders)* (see **14.10.1**), Mumby J emphasised that arrangements for contact must be driven by the needs of the family, not stunted by lack of resources.

14.10.6 Examination or assessment

The court may give directions as to a medical, or psychiatric examination or other assessment of the child, or may alternatively direct that there be no such examination or assessment. However, in an emergency, where the examination is required for medical reasons, this could be undertaken without the need for a court order under the applicant's parental responsibility.

A child of sufficient understanding to make an informed decision may refuse to submit to an examination or assessment, but it has been held that the High Court may overrule the child and give consent under its inherent jurisdiction (*South Glamorgan County Council v W and B* [1993] 1 FLR 574).

14.10.7 Duration

An EPO may be granted for up to eight days, although it should not be granted for any longer than is necessary to protect the child. The court can grant one extension for up to seven days on the application of the local authority, if it has reasonable cause to believe the child is likely to suffer significant harm if the order is not extended.

An application to discharge the order can be made on one day's notice. The application can be made by the child, a parent, any other person with parental responsibility or any person with whom the child was living prior to the order, unless that person was present at the hearing. As an application to extend the duration must be on notice, no one can apply for a discharge once the order has been extended.

14.10.8 Police protection (s 46)

A child may be taken into 'police protection' for up to 72 hours if a constable has reasonable cause to believe that the child is likely to suffer significant harm if he does not remove the child to suitable accommodation, or take steps to prevent removal from his present accommodation (these are the same criteria on which the *court* must be satisfied to make an EPO: see **14.10.2**). This power could be used, for example, where a child has run away, been abandoned or is found in unsuitable home circumstances, or alternatively to prevent his removal from, say, a hospital. (See **Appendix 1(E)**.)

The police do not acquire parental responsibility but must do what is reasonable in the circumstances to safeguard or promote the child's welfare. They must inform the local authority who, if requested, must provide accommodation for the child. Following investigation, the police or local authority could, if appropriate, apply for an EPO.

In *Langley v Liverpool City Council* [2005] EWCA Civ 1173 the Court of Appeal held that, where an EPO is in force, the police can remove a child under s 46 only if there are 'compelling reasons' to do so. If the police, knowing that an EPO was in force, removed a child under s 46 without compelling reasons, the police would be acting unlawfully and in breach of the family's rights under Article 8 of the ECHR.

14.10.9 Child assessment order (s 43)

This is an order for the assessment of the child's health or development, or of the way in which he has been treated. It is intended to deal with the situation where there is a suspicion that the child is suffering and there has been a denial of co-operation on the part of the child's carers. It is part of the 'planned responses' by a local authority, rather than a device to provide emergency protection.

The grounds for the order are very specific. Essentially, the local authority must have reasonable cause to suspect the child is suffering, or is likely to suffer, significant harm. The court must be satisfied that an assessment is necessary to confirm or dismiss those suspicions and that the child's carers are unlikely to co-operate with such an assessment. Although the checklist in s 1(3) need not be applied, the court must have regard to the welfare principle (s 1(1)) and no order presumption (s 1(5)).

The case of *Re I (Children: Child Assessment Order)* [2020] EWCA Civ 281 was a recent example of the use of a child assessment order. The father of four children had been imprisoned for an offence under the Terrorism Act 2000, and the local authority had concerns about the impact of his beliefs and activities on the children, and the parents were not cooperating with the local authority's attempts to assess the situation.

Under s 43(3), the court may make an EPO on an application for a child assessment order.

14.11 PROCEDURE FOR CARE AND SUPERVISION ORDERS

The procedure for making applications is mostly contained in the FPR 2010, Pt 12 and supporting practice directions. The Public Law Outline (PLO) contained in Practice Direction 12A also governs the procedure on applications for care and supervision orders. HM Courts and Tribunals Service is, at the time of writing, researching and piloting the launch of an online service for public law applications. It plans that, by autumn 2018, the application form will be completed online and that the court bundle will be available online. The aim of the project is that the majority of the court process will be digitalised by the second half of 2019.

14.11.1 Legal aid

Legal Representation is available for public law proceedings under the Children Act, but is based on a special regime that depends on the nature of the proceedings and the status of the party.

14.11.1.1 Family Help (Lower)

Family Help (Lower) is available only to parents and those with parental responsibility, and only once the local authority has given written notification of its intention to issue proceedings (see **14.11.2.2**). It is non means-tested and has a low merits test, which is likely to be met if the local authority intends to take proceedings. It will cover liaison and negotiations with the local authority before proceedings are issued.

14.11.1.2 Legal Representation

Family Help (Higher) is not available in public law family proceedings. Legal Representation is available to the child, his parents and those with parental responsibility once the local authority has issued its application. For these parties it is non means-tested and subject only to a merits test in respect of the need for parents to be separately represented.

Any other person who applies to be joined as a party can apply for Legal Representation but it will be means- and merits-tested.

Legal Representation is not available to a children's guardian, but Cafcass is responsible for paying for the services of the guardian.

14.11.1.3 Other applications

Applications by anyone for s 34 contact orders, s 39 discharge orders or any s 8 order are subject to a means and merits test.

14.11.2 Pre-proceedings action

The PLO requires local authorities to prepare the case thoroughly before proceedings are issued in all but extremely urgent cases, and the publication, *Court orders and pre-proceedings*, April 2014 (published by the Department of Education) is statutory guidance that sets out the steps expected. The effect is to 'front-load' investigations following a referral, and to bring the assessment carried out by the local authority to the fore of the proceedings. The PLO contains a pre-proceedings checklist, which details all the documents that need to be prepared before proceedings are issued.

14.11.2.1 Kinship assessments

Before deciding to issue proceedings, the local authority should have explored, possibly through a family group conference or other family meeting, whether the child could safely be cared for by a relative or friend, and should have assessed the suitability of such arrangements and considered the appropriate legal status of such arrangements.

14.11.2.2 Letter before proceedings

When the local authority decides it is going to issue proceedings, it must consider if it is appropriate to write to the parents to inform them and explain that they should seek legal advice. If it decides that there is time to work with the family to avoid proceedings, a letter should be sent to the family. This written notification is known as the 'letter before proceedings'. The letter before proceedings should set out a summary of the local authority's concerns, the steps the local authority has taken, what needs to be addressed by the parents and what support will be provided to them, as well as what will happen if the problems are not addressed. It should invite the parents to a meeting to discuss these concerns, and invite them to bring a solicitor. Details of how to obtain free legal advice and details of local solicitors should also be given.

The letter before proceedings should entitle the parents to Family Help (Lower) (see **14.11.1.1**).

14.11.2.3 The pre-proceedings meeting

The meeting with the parents that takes place as a result of the letter before proceedings should be followed by a letter and written revised plan for the child, setting out what the parents and local authority are to do to safeguard the child and what steps will be taken if this action is not effective. If the local authority continues to be concerned, following the meeting, that the child is suffering or is likely to suffer significant harm, it remains responsible for issuing an application to the court for a care or supervision order.

14.11.3 The FPR 2010, Pt 12 and Practice Direction 12A

The new PLO is in force from 22 April 2014. The PLO divides care proceedings into three major stages:

(1) Issue and Allocation;
(2) Case Management Hearing (CMH); and
(3) Issues Resolution Hearing (IRH).

For each stage, the PLO specifies time limits and, where necessary, checklists and standard forms.

14.11.3.1   Stage 1: Issue and Allocation

The PLO envisages that Stage 1 will be Day 1 of issue and Day 2.

On Day 1, when the local authority issues the application, it files an application form. This is Form C110A (see **Appendix 3(J)**). HMCTS is rolling out an online system to provide a paperless platform for all stages of public children applications. At the time of writing, it is anticipated that all applications for public children orders by local authorities will be made online by the end of 2021.

Form C110A contains an annex with a list of documents which need to be filed with the application at the time of issue. These are known as the annex documents and are:

(a)   social work chronology;

(b)   social work statement and genogram;

(c)   current assessments;

(d)   care plan; and

(e)   index of checklist documents.

The local authority will also need to pay a fee.

The PLO also makes provision for other documents, known as checklist documents. These are divided into checklist (a) documents, such as previous court orders, or s 7 or s 37 reports, which are to be served with the application form but not filed at court; and checklist (b) documents, such as records of key discussions with the family and pre-existing care plans, which are only to be disclosed on request by any party.

The applicant must join as a party the child and every person whom he believes to have parental responsibility. In public law proceedings, unlike private law proceedings, the child is automatically a party. This is because public law proceedings are based on the concept of significant harm attributable to the standard of parental care. This can create a conflict of interest between the child and his parents and between the child and the local authority, and therefore requires the child to be separately represented. In the case of parents, consideration should always be given as to whether separate representation is appropriate because of a potential conflict of interest.

In addition, any person who is not automatically a respondent may apply to be joined. A distinction is drawn between a putative father and other applicants. In the case of a putative father, his application should be granted unless there is some justifiable reason for not doing so (see *Re K (Care Proceedings: Notification of Father without Parental Responsibility)* [1999] 2 FLR 408). In the case of other applicants, the court will not join someone (other than a parent) where their interests and views are the same as those of an existing party. In *Re M (Minors) (Sexual Abuse: Evidence)* [1993] 1 FLR 822, the court held that, where the grandparents were offering a 'fall back' position to that of the mother, and were presenting the same case as her, there was no purpose in their separate representation, and they should not have been made parties unless they had a separate point to advance.

The local authority will notify the court if it is expected that there will be a need for a contested interim care order hearing or urgent preliminary CMH.

By Day 2 the local authority will serve the application, together with annex documents and evidential checklist documents, on the parties with the notice of the CMH.

The court will:

(a)   consider allocation to a specified level of judge in accordance with the Family Court (Composition and Distribution of Business) Rules 2014 and the President's Guidance on Allocation and Gatekeeping for Care, Supervision and other Proceedings under Pt IV of the CA 1989;

(b)   give standard directions on issue and allocation including:

   (i)   checking compliance with pre-proceedings checklist;

   (ii)   appointing a children's guardian;

   (iii)   appointing a solicitor for the child, if necessary;

   (iv)   filing and service of the case summary by the local authority, of case analysis by the children's guardian, and of the Parents' Response;

   (v)   listing the CMH; and

   (vi)   directing the children's solicitor to arrange an advocates' meeting two days before the CMH;

(c)   send notice of the CMH to Cafcass; and

(d)   make arrangements for a contested interim care order hearing or other preliminary hearing if necessary.

Service

As well as serving the respondents, the applicant must also give notice of the proceedings (C6A) to anyone caring for the child, an unmarried father who does not have parental responsibility and anyone who is a party to other relevant proceedings, so that they can consider whether to apply to be joined as a party.

In relation to a child, service must be on the solicitor acting for the child, or, if none, on the children's guardian. The court has power to direct that a requirement as to service on anyone shall not apply, or shall be effected in such manner as the court directs.

Appointment of a children's guardian

By Day 2, the court must appoint a children's guardian for the child, unless the court considers it is not necessary to safeguard the child's interests.

Children's guardians are usually experienced social workers who are contracted to Cafcass as officers of the service. They operate through regional offices around the country.

It is important to appreciate that the guardian is 'for the child', rather than to 'represent' the child. Accordingly, the guardian's role is to put forward what he considers to be in the best interests of the child, even though that may not coincide with the child's views.

Duties of the children's guardian

The duties of the children's guardian are contained in the FPR 2010, Chapter 16 and Practice Direction 16A. If the court has not already appointed a solicitor to represent the child (see below), the guardian will need to appoint one.

The guardian must give instructions to the solicitor representing the child, give the child appropriate advice, investigate the case and file a written report advising on the interests of the child in accordance with the timetable set by the court.

In addition, the guardian must attend all directions appointments and hearings (unless excused) and advise the court, amongst other things, on:

(a)   whether the child is of sufficient understanding for any purpose;

(b)   the wishes of the child in respect of any relevant matter;

(c)   the appropriate timing of the proceedings;

(d)   the options available to the court in respect of the child;

(e)   any other appropriate matter.

Under r 12 and Practice Direction 12A, the children's guardian is also required to prepare an initial case analysis document for the CMH and later hearings as directed. This document will set out a summary of the alleged harm, of the proposed solutions, and any further assessments, investigations and directions the guardian feels are appropriate. It will include details of the parties' views on the key issues, including those of the child. Therefore the guardian will need to have read the local authority evidence, carry out his own further enquiries and have ascertained the views of the child by the CMH. Thereafter the guardian is required to file an interim case analysis for each of the hearings, and a final case analyses in advance of the Final Hearing.

Appointment of solicitor for the child

Under the FPR 2010, r 12 and Practice Direction 12A, and pursuant to s 41(3) of the CA 1989, the court can appoint a solicitor for the child on issue of the application.

Duties of the solicitor

Where a children's guardian has been appointed, the solicitor must follow the instructions given by the guardian. However, in some cases it becomes apparent that the views of the child do not coincide with what the guardian considers to be in his best interests. In circumstances where the child wishes to give instructions that conflict with those of the guardian and the solicitor considers that the child is able, having regard to his understanding, to give such instructions, the solicitor must follow the child's instructions. Where this happens, the guardian must notify the court, and may seek leave to have separate legal representation.

14.11.3.2   Stage 2: Case Management Hearing

On the filing of the application, the court must fix a date for the CMH. According to the PLO, this CMH should take place between Day 12 and Day 18 following the issue of the application. By then the court should have been notified of the need for any contested hearing (for example for an interim care order) and should have made arrangements for the hearing to take place.

The purpose of waiting until Day 12 for the CMH to take place is so that it can be a more effective hearing as it should be clearer what the issues are and what evidence and assessments are necessary. This allows for more robust case management and timetabling of the case.

Advocates' meeting

No later than two days before the CMH, the advocates' meeting must take place. At this meeting the advocates will consider the information in the documents and identify the parties' positions. They will also deal with such matters as experts, disclosure and whether there will be a need for an interim care order hearing. The parties will prepare a draft case management order (on a prescribed form), and this will be filed with the court by the local authority advocate on the working day before the CMH.

Case Management Hearing

At the CMH the main objectives are, in line with the strong emphasis of the FPR 2010 on robust case management by the court, to confirm that the case has been allocated to the right level of court and to give initial case management directions having regard to the PLO.

The court will give detailed case management directions, including:

(a)   drawing up the Timetable for the Child. The Timetable for the Child is the timetable for the proceedings set by the court and shall take into account dates of the significant steps (including legal, social, care, health and education steps) in the life of the child and shall be appropriate for the child. This timetable should be considered at every stage of the proceedings and reviewed regularly;

(b)   confirming allocation;

(c)   identifying additional parties and representation, including allocation of a children's guardian;

(d)   identifying key issues and the evidence necessary to resolve them;

(e)   deciding if there is a real issue on the threshold criteria (see **14.4.2**);

(f)   determining any application for expert evidence;

(g)   directing filing of any threshold agreement, final evidence, care plan and responses to those documents and Case Analysis for the IRH;

(h)   directing advocates' meeting for the IRH;

(i)   listing further hearings: the IRH and Final Hearing;

(j)   issuing the case management order.

The court can make an interim care or supervision order if the conditions in s 38 are met, or a s 8 child arrangements order providing for with whom the child shall live, together with a supervision order, or list the application for an urgent contested interim hearing.

Attendance

The parties must attend any court appointments unless otherwise directed.

The court has power to direct that a child does not, or need not, attend. The general tendency is to allow the child's attendance only if satisfied that it would clearly be in his interests, and in practice the courts tend to assume that the child will not attend without the need to make a formal direction.

Evidence

Admissibility

As in private law children proceedings, the general rules as to the admissibility of evidence are relaxed.

Of particular relevance is that any statement contained in a children's guardian's report, and any evidence given in respect of matters referred to in it, is admissible. This provision is very wide in that 'any statement' is not restricted to one made by the guardian himself and could include a statement made by, for example, a home help or a school teacher. Further, the court may allow 'any evidence' from any witness to be admitted if it relates to a matter referred to in the report.

A children's guardian has the right to examine and take copies of records held by a local authority. However, the local authority may claim, for example in relation to social work records, that public interest requires that the evidence should be excluded. In that case, the guardian would have to apply to the court for a direction as to its admissibility.

Witness statements

Each party must file and serve on the other parties and on the children's guardian written statements of the oral evidence it intends to use, together with copies of any documents, including expert reports, which will be relied on, at or by such time as the court directs. Failure to do so means the evidence can be admitted only with leave.

Expert evidence

Expert witnesses such as doctors or psychologists are often used in CA 1989 cases to assist the court in its decision-making. However, s 13 of the Children and Families Act 2014 provides, in children proceedings, that the court's permission is required to instruct an expert and to put expert evidence before the court. Further, the court's leave is needed under s 13 for any medical or psychiatric examination, or other assessment of the child, for the purpose of preparing expert evidence, and, where leave has not been given, no evidence arising from the examination or assessment of the child can be produced without the court's leave.

The court will only give its permission for any of the above if it considers the expert opinion is 'necessary' to assist the court to resolve the matters fairly, and s 13(7) lists matters the court is to have regard to when deciding whether to grant permission. The old test was that a court would restrict expert evidence to that which was 'reasonably required' to resolve proceedings, and the new test is intended to raise the bar significantly and to reduce the number of experts instructed.

Section 13 of the Children and Families Act 2014 is supplemented by Pt 25 of the FPR 2010 and supporting practice directions, which set out the procedure and timing for obtaining the court's permission, as well as the contents of the letter of instruction to the expert and the contents of the expert's report. This is supplemented by the PLO, which requires the issue of expert evidence to be finalised at the CMH, which includes the form of the letter of instruction and the form of the questions to be put to the expert.

Disclosure

Although privilege from disclosure applies to solicitor/client communications, it does not apply in children cases to reports and other documents prepared for the purpose of the proceedings. Accordingly, where a party obtains an expert report, with or without the court's leave, no privilege will attach to the report, and it must be disclosed to the court and to the other parties (*Re L (Police Investigation: Privilege)* [1996] 1 FLR 731).

14.11.3.3 Stage 3: Issues Resolution Hearing

The IRH is likely to be the hearing before the Final Hearing. Again, Practice Direction 12A requires the advocates to meet at least seven days before the IRH to review the evidence and the position of the parties, and to identify the advocates' views of the remaining key issues and whether these can be resolved or narrowed at the IRH and, if so, what evidence would be required and arrangements made for hearing that evidence. They will also consider what evidence and witnesses will be required at a Final Hearing if it should proceed that far. The local authority advocate will draft the Case Management Order, which must be filed with the court by 11am one working day before the IRH.

At the IRH, the court is to identify the key issues that are to be determined and the extent to which they can be resolved or narrowed at the IRH. Under the PLO, the court is to consider whether the IRH can be used as a Final Hearing. If that is not possible, the court identifies what evidence is to be heard on the remaining issues at the Final Hearing. It will also give final case management directions. The court will issue a Case Management Order.

14.11.3.4 Stage 4: The Final Hearing

In advance of the Final Hearing all case management documents and bundles must be filed and served in accordance with FPR 2010, Practice Direction 27A (see **13.8.6**).

Where all the parties are agreed that a care order should be made, the court's consideration may be limited to a perusal of the documentation and approval of the agreed order. On the other hand, where there are unresolved issues, for example as to physical or sexual abuse, the court may order a split hearing (*Re S (Care Proceedings: Split Hearing)* [1996] 2 FLR 773) – the first hearing to resolve these issues; the second, substantive hearing to concentrate on what is in the child's best interests. *Re S (a child) (care proceedings: challenge to findings of fact)* [2014] EWCA Civ 25 gave guidance that a split hearing was appropriate in care proceedings only in those cases where there is a stark or discrete issue to be determined and an early conclusion on that issue will enable the substantive determination (ie whether a statutory order is necessary) to be made more expeditiously. Split hearings are only appropriate for the most simple cases where there is only one factual issue to be decided and where the threshold for jurisdiction in s 31 of the CA 1989 would not be satisfied if a finding could not be made thereby concluding the proceedings, or for the most complex medical causation cases where death or very serious medical issues had arisen and where an accurate medical diagnosis was integral to the future care of the child concerned.

14.11.4 Judgment

Judgment must be given as soon as practicable after the hearing. The court must state any findings of fact and the reasons for its decision.

The order must be in writing and a copy served on each party and on any person with whom the child is living.

14.11.5 Costs

The case of *Re S (Children)* [2015] UKSC 20 reviewed the principles of costs in children cases. The principles include: the general rule that costs follow the event does not apply to most proceedings concerning children in the Family Court; this approach applies equally to public as well as private proceedings; there are two exceptions to the general approach that there should be no order for costs, as identified in *Re T (Care Proceedings: Costs)* [2012] UKSC 36, which are reprehensible conduct and an unreasonable stance in the litigation, but there may be other circumstances where, exceptionally, an order for costs may be justified; and that a local authority should be in no better nor worse position than any other party on the question of costs.

It is unusual to order costs in children cases. In *Re T (Care Proceedings : Costs)* [2012] UKSC 36 the Supreme Court confirmed the general principle that costs should not be awarded against a party, including a local authority in a children case, in the absence of reprehensible behaviour or an unreasonable stance.

14.11.6 After a care order is made

Once a final care order has been made, the local authority has control over decisions relating to the child's welfare. The local authority should review its care plan on a regular basis; and before conducting such reviews, it should seek and take into account the wishes and views of the child and his parents.

The court has no future role in monitoring the local authority or the execution of its care plan unless some substantive issue comes before the court, such as an application for contact or discharge of the care order. This is a situation that has caused increasing judicial concern over the years, especially since enactment of the HRA 1998. As a result, s 25A–25C of the CA 1989 now require local authorities to appoint a named Independent Reviewing Officer (IRO) in connection with each looked-after child. The care plan for any such child must be kept under review, and the IRO must monitor the local authority's performance, make sure the child's views are understood and taken into account, ensure that any matters of concern are brought to the attention of an appropriately senior member of the local authority and, in necessary cases, refer the matter to Cafcass, which may seek to resolve issues by mediation or by issuing proceedings such as judicial review or under the HRA 1998. The effectiveness of the IRO system has been put under the spotlight following the case of *A and S v Lancashire County Council* [2012] EWHC 1689 (see **14.13**).

14.12 HUMAN RIGHTS IMPLICATIONS

Taking a child into care clearly constitutes an interference with family life under Article 8 of the ECHR. The local authority, as a public body, must act in a way that is compatible with Convention rights. Taking a child into care will not breach Article 8 provided the interference is in accordance with the law, it pursues a legitimate aim (namely, the protection of children) and is necessary.

In the context of public law proceedings, the European Court of Human Rights has repeatedly emphasised that interference in the right to family life by taking a child into care should be regarded as a temporary measure to be discontinued as soon as circumstances permit (*Johansen v Norway* (1996) 23 EHRR 33).

The manner in which a child is taken into care may also be open to challenge. The European Court of Human Rights has emphasised that it is important to involve parents in the decision-making process leading to care proceedings. This would include being involved in child protection conferences. In addition, in *P, C and S v United Kingdom* [2002] 2 FLR 631, the European Court of Human Rights stated that it is essential that parents involved in care proceedings have effective and competent legal representation. If they do not, Article 6 and the procedural guarantees inherent in Article 8 of the ECHR are breached.

14.12.1   The welfare principle

As mentioned in **Chapter 13**, there is a debate as to whether the welfare principle in s 1(1) of the CA 1989 is incompatible with Article 8 of the ECHR and an individual's right to respect for family life. In other words, placing the child's welfare as paramount does not involve balancing the family rights of the other relevant individuals. But the decisions of the European Court of Human Rights make it clear that the rights of the parent may have to defer to the interests of the child. In *Johansen v Norway* (see **14.12** above), the Court said that 'the parent cannot be entitled under Article 8 ... to have such measures taken as would harm the child's health and development'.

In the domestic case of *Dawson v Wearmouth* [1999] 1 FLR 1167 the court said:

> It is submitted that the father's rights under Article 8 are infringed. There is no basis for this submission. The present case is concerned with the welfare of the child, not with the rights of the father. There is nothing in the Convention which requires the courts of this country to act otherwise than in the interests of the child.

Also, in *KD (A Minor) (Access: Principles)* [1998] 2 FLR 139, there was an argument between the local authority and the parent as to contact. The mother relied on Article 8 of the ECHR and submitted that contact was a parental right and not a child's right. Lord Oliver said it would not be inappropriate to describe a parent's claim to contact as a 'right' It was also a normal assumption that a child will benefit from continuing contact with his natural parents:

> But both the 'right' and the assumption will always be displaced if the interests of the child dictate otherwise.

These cases suggest that there is no conflict between s 1(1) and Article 8, because Article 8(2) contains the important qualification of the right to respect for family life that 'there shall be no interference except such as in accordance with the law and is necessary in a democratic society for the protection of health or morals or for the protection of the rights and freedoms of others' (ie the child involved).

14.12.2   The care plan

One significant impact of the HRA 1998 in public law cases is how it has been used to highlight the courts' inability to maintain some judicial control over the implementation of a care plan by the local authority.

If the court makes a care order, it then has no further control over the care plan for the child and the local authority can change that plan at any time. If the parents are unhappy about the care plan, all they can do is apply to discharge the care order, or apply for contact if the arrangements are unreasonable.

This position has been criticised by many for some time as conflicting with the principle that the interests of the parent and of the child in the decision-making process should be given sufficient procedural protection. It has also been argued that the inability of the parents to question or call for any review of the care plan can lead to breaches of Articles 6 and 8 of the ECHR, and is incompatible with the 1998 Act.

As a result, the Government introduced the role of IRO (see **14.4.7**), who will review the care plan and, if necessary, refer the matter to Cafcass, which can seek to resolve problems through mediation or by issuing proceedings.

14.13 COMPENSATION FOR LOCAL AUTHORITY FAILINGS

In *D v East Berkshire Community Health NHS Trust, K and Another v Dewsbury Healthcare NHS Trust and Another, K and Another v Oldham NHS Trust and Another* [2005] UKHL 23, the House of Lords held that the local authority owed a duty of care to a child in relation to investigating abuse and commencing care proceedings, but not to the parent who is suspected of abusing the child. An example of this was *NXS v Camden London Borough Council* [2009] EWHC 1786 (QB), where the court awarded the claimant £60,000 damages for the local authority's failure to properly investigate and monitor allegations of violence by the mother towards the claimant as a baby and young child, as a result of which the abuse continued until she was 14 years old.

However, the more recent case of *Poole BC v GN* [2019] UKSC 25 has changed the position regarding cases brought against the local authority for breach of duty of care for failure to investigate under s 47 or to commence care proceedings. *Poole BC v GN* decided that public authorities could owe a duty of care in circumstances where the principles applicable to private individuals would impose such a duty, unless such a duty would be inconsistent with, and was therefore excluded by, the legislation from which their powers or duties were derived. They did not owe a duty of care at common law merely because they had statutory powers or duties, even if, by exercising their statutory functions, they could prevent a person from suffering harm. Several cases have followed this decision including *DFX (A Protected Party) v Coventry City Council* [2021] EWHC 1382 (QB) and *YXA v Wolverhampton City Council* [2021] EWHC 1444 (QB) and decided against claimants, stating that knowledge of a risk of significant harm and the power to intervene was not sufficient to amount to an assumption of responsibility so as to create a duty of care. It seems that claimants will now have a very high bar to clear to succeed in claims that local authorities owe a duty of care to children in the community when exercising their functions under the CA 1989.

Compensation can be awarded to children and parents where breaches of the ECHR are found. In *A and S v Lancashire County Council* [2012] EWHC 1689 (Fam), two brothers, who were made subject to care orders when they were 3 years and 1 year old in 1998, were subsequently freed for adoption, which severed links with their birth family, including all contact. In 2004 the local authority abandoned its plan for adoption; however, it never applied to revoke the freeing orders, which remained in place until 2012. During that time the older boy experienced a total of 77 moves between carers and the younger boy a total of 96. They had been subjected to abuse by more than one set of foster carers. If the freeing orders had been revoked, the boys' legal status would have been such that the local authority would have been obliged to permit and promote reasonable contact with their mother and siblings. The boys had repeatedly requested such contact but no action was taken. As a result of their experience, both boys had suffered lifelong damage. The court declared that the local authority had breached the boys' rights under Articles 8, 6 and 3 of the ECHR, and the IRO had breached the boys' Articles 6 and 8 rights by his failure to take appropriate action.

SUMMARY AND CHECKLISTS

(1)   There is a duty on local authorities to take reasonable steps through the provision of services to avoid the need for court proceedings.

(2)   A care or supervision order can be made only on application by a local authority (or NSPCC).

(3)   In contrast to private law proceedings, the child is always a party.

(4)   Before making a care or supervision order, the court must be satisfied both that the threshold criteria are met and that such an order is in the child's best interests.

(5)   Legal Representation for the main respondents is automatic.

(6)   There is a presumption of reasonable contact for parents.

(7)   In an emergency, anyone can apply for an EPO.

(8)   Checklists detailing grounds for a care or supervision order and the procedure are set out below.

Grounds for a care or supervision order – checklist

THRESHOLD CRITERIA:
(a)   The child is suffering, or likely to suffer, significant harm;
      AND
(b)   it is attributable to:
      (i)   the care given, or likely to be given, if the order is not made, not being what it
            would be reasonable to expect a parent to give; OR
      (ii) the child being beyond parental control

SHOULD AN ORDER BE MADE? IF SO, WHAT TYPE?
(a)   child's welfare paramount
(b)   welfare checklist
(c)   no order presumption
(d)   contact arrangement (if considering care order)

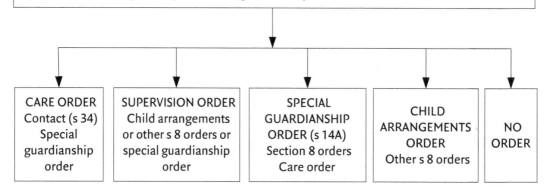

CARE ORDER Contact (s 34) Special guardianship order	SUPERVISION ORDER Child arrangements or other s 8 orders or special guardianship order	SPECIAL GUARDIANSHIP ORDER (s 14A) Section 8 orders Care order	CHILD ARRANGEMENTS ORDER Other s 8 orders	NO ORDER

Procedural checklist for a care order

1.	Applicant	Local authority (or NSPCC)
2.	Application	Form C110A
3.	Children's guardian	Appointed by the court. Court appoints solicitor for child
4.	Respondents	Every person with parental responsibility and the child
5.	Notice	Parent without parental responsibility Person with whom child living
6.	Legal Representation	As of right for child, parents and others with parental responsibility
7.	Service	By Day 2 (day after issue)
8.	Case Management Hearing	Detailed case management directions and confirming allocation
9.	Interim order	Care/supervision orders if criteria satisfied or s 8 child arrangements order with supervision order
10.	Issues Resolution Hearing	To narrow remaining issues and final case management and to consider if IRH can be used as a Final Hearing
11.	Final Hearing	Findings of fact/reasons

CHAPTER 15

DOMESTIC ABUSE

15.1	Introduction	261
15.2	Protection under Pt IV of the Family Law Act 1996	263
15.3	Human rights implications	277
15.5	Coercive and controlling behaviour	278
15.4	Protection from Harassment Act 1997	277
15.6	Forced Marriage (Civil Protection) Act 2007	278
Summary		279

LEARNING OUTCOMES

After reading this chapter you will be able to:

- explain what orders are available to protect victims of abuse under the Family Law Act 1996
- understand what the court must consider on applications for non-molestation and occupation orders and how the court exercises its powers
- describe the procedure to apply for non-molestation and occupation orders
- understand what orders are available under the Protection from Harassment Act 1997
- describe what protection is offered to victims of forced marriage by the Forced Marriage (Civil Protection) Act 2007.

15.1 INTRODUCTION

In January 2019 the Government published a report into the economic and social cost of domestic abuse, which revealed that the cost in the year ending March 2017 in England and Wales was an estimated £66 billion. It is estimated that 2 million adults (6% of adults) experience domestic abuse each year in England and Wales. Evidence suggests that those figures have risen since then, especially during the pandemic.

The Domestic Abuse Act (DAA) 2021 is part of the Government's attempt to tackle the issue of domestic abuse. When it is fully in force, it will introduce a raft of measures intended to help victims of domestic abuse.

The DAA 2021 introduces a statutory definition of domestic abuse from 1 October 2021 which includes:

- physical or sexual abuse;
- violent or threatening behaviour;
- controlling or coercive behaviour;
- economic abuse; and
- psychological, emotional or other abuse;

The DAA 2021 also describes any child who sees, hears or experiences the effects of domestic abuse as a victim of domestic abuse. It will also prohibit the cross-examination of victims by their alleged abuser in court proceedings.

The Act will create, when it is fully in force, new police powers in the form of new versions of domestic abuse protection notices to replace the current pilots and newer versions of domestic abuse protection orders which can be applied for in criminal, civil and family courts by victims and third parties. Such orders are similar in their scope to the Family Law Act 1996 non-molestation and occupation orders (see **15.2** below) but will also include electronic monitoring requirements and positive obligation orders such as a requirement to attend a particular course. The Government has said that these notices and orders will be piloted before being implemented.

The DAA 2021 has also established the office of Domestic Abuse Commissioner. The first Commissioner is already in place and is calling for increased funding and specialist court support for victims of domestic abuse.

This legislation follows a Government announcement on 25 June 2020 that there was to be a major overhaul of how the family courts deal with domestic abuse. The announcement said that there would be a reform of how the courts hear cases, through a new investigative approach, to be trialled as part of a new Integrated Domestic Abuse Courts pilot – which considers family and criminal matters in parallel in order to provide more consistent support for victims. Emphasis will be placed on getting to the root of an issue and ensuring all parties are safe and able to provide evidence on an equal footing – without the re-traumatising effects of being in court with an abusive ex-partner. The Government says that more victims will receive special protections in court and there will be stronger powers for judges to prevent abusers repeatedly bringing a victim back to court. At the time of writing, further details on when and how this new approach is to take place are still awaited.

Particular sensitivity needs to be employed by the solicitor in such cases, as the client is likely to be distressed and may be reluctant to talk about the abuse. Any children who are with the victim can usually be protected at the same time as their carer. However, if protection is needed specifically for the children alone, this should generally be dealt with by using the procedures outlined in **Chapter 13** or **Chapter 14**.

Although there is a variety of potential remedies available in situations of domestic abuse, the solicitor must be careful not to raise the client's expectations too high. A court order may give limited protection, but much will depend on the personality of the respondent. When the respondent is served with a court order, or arrested by the police (and later released), further violence may result. It is therefore crucial for the solicitor to adapt their advice to the particular circumstances of the applicant, taking into account the personalities of the parties, and to avoid giving the applicant a false sense of security.

The main emphasis here is on how to proceed in the civil courts, but the solicitor should be aware that court action is not the only possible remedy, and may not be the most appropriate one. For example, a solicitor's letter warning the perpetrator to desist from his behaviour or face court action may act as a deterrent. However, this would not be appropriate in cases of serious violence. In these cases, the victim may consider going to the police. Police forces are now becoming more involved in cases of domestic violence, and many have their own domestic violence unit.

If the client is in such fear that they do not want to return home, the solicitor should consider the possibility of finding a place for them in a women's refuge or in temporary local authority housing (see **6.11**).

If the appropriate course of action is to apply to the court for an order or orders to protect your client, currently the application will in most cases be made under Pt IV of the FLA 1996, which codified the law in this area, making the same remedies available in any level of court and extending protection to a wider group of people than before.

Another relevant statute in this area is the Protection from Harassment Act 1997 (PHA 1997). This Act will be considered briefly at **15.4**.

15.2 PROTECTION UNDER Pt IV OF THE FAMILY LAW ACT 1996

The FLA 1996 is likely to provide the remedies that will be most frequently utilised by the family law practitioner. Its provisions are therefore dealt with in some detail.

15.2.1 Types of order available

The types of order available fall into two main categories:

(a) 'Non-molestation orders' for the protection of parties and any children. These can be applied for by a wide range of 'associated persons'.

(b) 'Occupation orders', which exclude the other party from occupation of the home. They can extend to excluding that party from a specified area around the home if necessary. Occupation orders can be applied for by spouses and cohabitants. Other 'associated persons' can apply only in specified circumstances.

15.2.2 Who can apply?

One of the most important changes brought about by FLA 1996 was the extension of the right to apply for non-molestation and (sometimes) occupation orders to a wide group of associated persons. Section 62 states that a person is associated with another if:

(a) they are or have been married to each other, or they are or have been civil partners of each other;

(b) they are cohabitants or former cohabitants (ie they are or have been living together as husband and wife or civil partners);

(c) they live or have lived in the same household, otherwise than by reason of one of them being the other's employee, tenant, lodger or boarder;

(d) they are relatives (this term includes immediate relations and other close relations such as grandparents, grandchildren, aunts, uncles, nieces, nephews, cousins, step-parents and step-children) of the applicant or of the applicant's former or current spouse, civil partner or cohabitant (but this does not include a step-nephew: *M v D (Family Law Act 1996: Meaning of Associated Person)* [2021] EWHC 1351 (Fam));

(e) they have agreed to marry or enter into a civil partnership with one another (whether or not that agreement has been terminated – however, where the agreement has been terminated, any application must be made within three years of the termination date), or they have or have had an intimate personal relationship with each other which was of significant duration;

(f) in relation to a child, they are both parents or have, or have had, parental responsibility (where a child has been adopted, two people will be associated if one is the natural parent and the other is the child or adoptive parent of the child);

(g) they are parties to the same family proceedings (other than proceedings under Pt IV of the FLA 1996 itself).

In addition, children (ie those under 18) can apply for non-molestation and/or occupation orders in their own right. However, if they are under 16 they will require leave of the court, which will be given only if the court is satisfied that the child has sufficient understanding to make the application (s 43).

15.2.3 Non-molestation orders (s 42)

The court can grant an order prohibiting the respondent from molesting the applicant or a child. The word 'molestation' covers not only violence and threats of violence, but also pestering. Thus, such an order could be granted against a respondent who sends abusive letters to his wife, or who persistently telephones his former partner in the middle of the night.

The court can grant a non-molestation order on the application of any associated person within any family proceedings, or the applicant may make a 'free standing' application under the FLA 1996. The court can also make such an order of its own motion in family proceedings, which it did in *Re T (A Child) (Non-molestation Orders)* [2017] EWCA Civ 1889 when it made a non-molestation order against the parents of a 10-year-old girl who was placed with foster parents under a care order. Since 1 July 2007, the court is required, when considering making an occupation order, also to consider making a non-molestation order.

15.2.3.1 Factors that the court must consider

Section 42(5) specifies that the court must have regard to all circumstances, including the need to secure the health, safety and well-being of the applicant and any child. Thus, provided the applicant can show a genuine need for protection, a non-molestation order will be granted.

15.2.3.2 Duration

Section 42(7) states that the order may be made for a specified period or until further order. Thus, such an order may be made for an indefinite period (*Re B-J (Power of Arrest)* [2000] 2 FLR 443), but see Practice Guidance: Family Court – Duration of Ex Parte (Without Notice) Orders (**15.2.5**) for the duration of without notice non-molestation orders.

15.2.4 Occupation orders (ss 33 and 35–38)

The provisions relating to occupation orders are quite detailed and complex. The status of the applicant (ie whether they have a right to occupy the home, or is a former spouse, cohabitant or former cohabitant) will determine:

(a)   whether the proposed applicant can apply for an order;

(b)   the provisions of any order granted;

(c)   the factors that the court will take into account in deciding whether to grant any order; and

(d)   the duration of any occupation order.

An application for an occupation order can be made in the course of other family proceedings, or the applicant can make a 'free standing' application under FLA 1996.

15.2.4.1 Applicant has an existing right to occupy the home (s 33)

An applicant will have a right to occupy the home for the purposes of this section if they are entitled to occupy by virtue of a beneficial estate, or interest, or contract or statutory entitlement (eg under s 30 of the FLA 1996). The home in question must be, have been or have been intended to be the home of the applicant and the person with whom they are associated (the respondent). Thus *any* associated person can apply under s 33 where they have an existing legal right to occupy the home.

Where the above conditions are satisfied, the applicant can apply for an occupation order, which may:

(a)   require the respondent to permit the applicant to enter and remain in the home or part of the home;

(b)   regulate the occupation of the home by either or both parties;

(c)   prohibit, suspend or restrict the respondent's exercise of his right to occupy the home;

(d)   require the respondent to leave the home; or

(e)   exclude the respondent from a defined area in which the home is situated.

Where the applicant has a right of occupation under s 30 of the FLA 1996 and the respondent is the other spouse, the occupation order may further provide that those rights will not be brought to an end by the death of the other spouse or dissolution of the marriage. Unless such a provision is included in the order, it will cease to have effect on the death of either party or dissolution of the marriage.

Factors that the court must consider

Section 33(6) provides that in deciding whether to grant the order sought, the court must take into account all circumstances, including:

(a) the respective housing needs and housing resources of the parties and any child;

(b) the respective financial resources of the parties;

(c) the likely effect of any order, or of any decision by the court not to make such an order, on the health, safety or well-being of the parties and any relevant child; and

(d) the conduct of the parties in relation to each other and otherwise.

However, s 33(6) is subject to the 'balance of harm' test contained in s 33(7). This provides that if it appears to the court that the applicant or any child is likely to suffer significant harm attributable to the conduct of the respondent if an occupation order is not made, then the court *shall* make such an order unless it appears to the court that:

(a) the respondent or any child is likely to suffer significant harm if the order is made; and

(b) the harm likely to be suffered by the respondent or child is as great as or greater than the harm attributable to the conduct of the respondent which is likely to be suffered by the applicant or child if the order is not made.

The case of *Chalmers v Johns* [1999] 1 FLR 392 makes it clear that the applicant must show that she would suffer significant harm attributable to the respondent's conduct before the court applies the balance of harm test. Where such harm was not shown, the case would be determined on the basis of the factors in s 33(6) alone. Therefore, if the balance of harm test is made out in the applicant's favour, the court must make the order. If the test is not made out then the court has a discretion to make the order by applying the factors in s 33(6).

The case of *B v B (Occupation Order)* [1999] 1 FLR 715 illustrates the interrelationship of s 33(6) and s 33(7) and the balance of harm test. The wife moved out of the matrimonial home with the couple's 2-year-old daughter due to the husband's violence. They were then temporarily rehoused by the local authority. The husband remained in the matrimonial home with his son (aged 6) from a previous relationship. Should the wife be granted an occupation order under FLA 1996, s 33? The Court of Appeal held that she should not. Although the wife and child would suffer significant harm attributable to the husband's conduct if an order were not made, the harm that the husband's child would be likely to suffer if an order were made was greater. This was on the basis of the housing needs of both parties and children. Whereas the wife was entitled to be rehoused by the local authority as she was not intentionally homeless, the husband would not be so entitled, since he would be considered to be intentionally homeless on account of his violence. If the husband were forced to move out, his son would also need to change schools.

Recent case law has shown that it is not necessary for violence to have taken place for an occupation order to be granted. In *Grubb v Grubb* [2009] EWCA Civ 976 the Court of Appeal refused leave to appeal against an occupation order granted in the absence of violence between the parties. The order had been made under s 33(6) as the balance of harm test was not made out. The judge found that the husband had been verbally abusive and domineering, and that both parties were suffering from stress as a result of their continuing to live together. In this case the husband was in a position to arrange alternative accommodation for himself relatively easily and the occupation order was only made for a period of three months. In *Dolan v Corby* [2011] EWCA Civ 1664, the Court of Appeal upheld an occupation order against Mr Corby, who it found had been verbally abusive but not violent towards Miss Dolan. In *Re L (Children)* [2012] EWCA Civ 2012, a decision was upheld where the court found, in a case where there was no physical violence, that the children were suffering significant harm caused by the arguments between the parties, but that this harm was not attributable solely to the father's conduct, and so the balance of harm test in s 33(7) was not made out. However, the court made an occupation order after applying s 33(6).

Duration

An occupation order made under s 33 may be for a specified period, until the occurrence of a specified event (for example until the conclusion of the financial remedy proceedings following divorce – *PF v CF* [2016] EWHC 3117 (Fam)) or until further order. Thus, such an order can be for an indefinite period. In practice it is likely, at least initially, to be for a specified period, probably six months.

15.2.4.2   Applicant has no existing right to occupy the home and respondent has such a right (s 35 and s 36)

Applicant is former spouse or former civil partner (s 35)

An applicant under s 35 must be the former spouse of the respondent. The respondent must be entitled to occupy the home (by virtue of a beneficial estate, or interest, or contract or by statute). The home must be, or have been or have been intended to be, the matrimonial home.

Where these conditions are satisfied, the applicant can apply for an occupation order. Any order granted under s 35 *must* contain a provision (an 'occupation provision') stating:

(a)   if the applicant is in occupation, that the applicant has a right not to be excluded from the home or part of it by the respondent for a specified period and prohibiting the respondent from excluding the applicant during that period;

(b)   if the applicant is not in occupation, that the applicant be given a right to enter and occupy the home for a specified period and requiring the respondent to permit the exercise of that right.

In addition, the order *may* contain one or more provisions ('exclusion provisions'):

(a)   regulating the occupation of the home by either party;

(b)   prohibiting, suspending or restricting the respondent's right to occupy;

(c)   requiring the respondent to leave the home or part of it;

(d)   excluding the respondent from a defined area in which the home is situated.

Factors that the court must consider

Note that the factors are slightly different for occupation provisions and exclusion provisions.

In deciding whether to make an *occupation provision*, the court must take into account all circumstances, including:

(a)   the respective housing needs and housing resources of the parties and any child;

(b)   the respective financial resources of the parties;

(c)   the likely effect of any order, or of any decision by the court not to make such an order, on the health, safety or well-being of the parties and any relevant child;

(d)   the conduct of the parties in relation to each other and otherwise;

(e)   the length of time that has elapsed since the parties ceased to live together;

(f)   the length of time that has elapsed since the marriage ended; and

(g)   the existence of any pending proceedings between the parties under s 23A or s 24 of the MCA 1973 and Sch 1 to the CA 1989 (financial orders relating to children), or relating to the legal or beneficial ownership of the home (s 35(6)).

The factors the court must take into account when making an *exclusion provision* are the same as (a)–(e) above for an occupation provision. However, for an exclusion provision, the balance of harm test mentioned in **15.2.4.1** in relation to s 33 applies.

Duration

An occupation order made under s 35 must be made for a specified period not exceeding six months. The order can be extended any number of times, but any extension must be for a further specified period not exceeding six months. In addition, any order shall cease to have effect on the death of either party.

Applicant is cohabitant or former cohabitant (s 36)

An applicant under s 36 must be the cohabitant or former cohabitant of the respondent. Thus, other associated persons may not apply under this section. For example, a niece may not apply for an occupation order against her uncle under s 36. The respondent must be entitled to occupy the home (by virtue of a beneficial estate, or interest, or contract or by statute). The home must be, or have been or have been intended to be, the couple's home.

Where these conditions are satisfied, the applicant can apply for an occupation order. Any order granted *must* contain the same occupation provision as an order under s 35. In addition, it *may* contain any of the same exclusion provisions as an order under s 35.

Factors that the court must consider

In deciding whether to make an *occupation provision*, the relevant factors are in many ways similar to those under s 35. The court must take into account all circumstances, including:

(a)   the respective housing needs and housing resources of the parties and any child;

(b)   the respective financial resources of the parties;

(c)   the likely effect of any order, or of any decision by the court not to make such an order, on the health, safety or well-being of the parties and any relevant child;

(d)   the conduct of the parties in relation to each other and otherwise;

(e)   the nature of the parties' relationship, and in particular the level of commitment involved in it;

(f)   the length of time that they have lived together as husband and wife;

(g)   whether there are or have been any children who are children of both parties, or for whom both parties have or have had parental responsibility;

(h)   the length of time that has elapsed since the parties ceased to live together; and

(i)   the existence of any pending proceedings between the parties under Sch 1 to CA 1989 (financial orders relating to children), or relating to the legal or beneficial ownership of the home (s 36(6)).

In deciding whether to make an *exclusion provision*, the court must take into account all circumstances, including the factors (a)–(d) above in relation to an occupation provision. In addition, the court must consider the following balance of harm questions:

(a)   whether the applicant or any relevant child is likely to suffer significant harm attributable to the conduct of the respondent if the exclusion provision is not made; and

(b)   whether the harm likely to be suffered by the respondent or child if the provision is included is as great or greater than the harm attributable to the conduct of the respondent which is likely to be suffered by the applicant or child if the provision is not included.

This is similar to the balance of harm test in ss 33 and 35. However, there is no duty on the court to make an order where the greater harm to the applicant or child is established, it is just one question to be considered.

Once an order has been made and for so long as it is in force, s 36(13) provides that the applicant will be afforded the same protection as a spouse under s 30(3)–(6). This means that a mortgagee or landlord must accept payments towards the mortgage or rent made by the applicant.

Duration

An occupation order made under s 36 must be for a specified period not exceeding six months. The order can be extended only once, for a further specified period not exceeding six months.

Thus the longest period for which a cohabitant or former cohabitant can obtain an occupation order is one year. In addition, any order shall cease to have effect on the death of either party.

15.2.4.3 Neither party has a right to occupy the home (ss 37 and 38)

These sections enable one spouse or civil partner, a former spouse or former civil partner, cohabitant or former cohabitant to obtain an occupation order against the other in relation to a home in which they both live or lived together but which neither of them has a right to occupy. These sections could be used, for example, to give the applicant a licence to occupy a home that is owned by the respondent's parents. Section 37 applies to spouses or former spouses; s 38 to cohabitants or former cohabitants.

As with ss 33, 35 and 36, such an order may, amongst other things, exclude the respondent from the home or an area in which the home is situated.

Factors that the court must consider

In deciding whether to grant an order under this section, the court must take into account similar factors to those under s 33 (where a spouse or former spouse is applying) or s 36 (where a cohabitant or former cohabitant is applying).

Duration

Any order granted will last for a specified period not exceeding six months. Where the applicant is a spouse or former spouse, the order can be extended on one or more occasions, each time for a specified period not exceeding six months. Where the applicant is a cohabitant or former cohabitant, the order can be extended once only for a further specified period not exceeding six months.

15.2.4.4 Examples

The following examples illustrate the above provisions. You may also find the flowchart at **15.2.4.6** helpful.

EXAMPLES

(a) Eric and Nicola are married. They live in a house left to Eric by his parents. Eric has begun drinking heavily recently and been very violent towards Nicola.

Nicola would apply under s 33. As she is married, she would have a right to occupy the matrimonial home under s 30 of the FLA 1996 as Eric owns it.

(b) Lillian and John cohabit in John's flat, which he bought years ago. John has told Lillian the relationship is over and that she must leave. She is unable to do so, as she is totally financially dependent on him and is not well at the moment. This has made John very angry, and he has used violence against Lillian to try to make her leave.

Lillian would apply under s 36, as she is a cohabitant and she has no right to occupy the home but John does.

(c) Jenny and Agnes live in flat, which is a tenancy in their joint names. Agnes, who is suffering from depression, has been using violence against Jenny, who is now frightened to return home.

Jenny will apply under s 33, as she is entitled to occupy the home by virtue of her tenancy.

(d) Katie and Steve live in Steve's parents' holiday home as they cannot afford to live elsewhere. They are not married. Katie has recently become pregnant and Steve is furious as he does not want the baby; he has been violent towards Katie almost every day since he found out.

Katie will apply under s 38, as neither of them has a right to occupy the home and they are cohabitants.

15.2.4.5 Additional provisions in occupation orders made under s 33, s 35 or s 36 (s 40)

Section 40 enables the court, when making an occupation order under s 33, s 35 or s 36, to make an ancillary order dealing with such matters as the payment of the mortgage or other outgoings, and payment for repair and maintenance of the home. The court can also order the occupying party to pay the excluded party rent where the excluded party would (but for the occupation order) have a right to occupy the home. In addition, the court can grant either party use of the furniture or other contents of the home and order either party to take reasonable care of the furniture or other contents. In deciding whether to make such an ancillary order and in what terms, the court shall have regard to all circumstances of the case, including the financial needs, resources and obligations of the parties. Any ancillary order made will last for the same length of time as the occupation order itself.

There is, however, a problem of enforcement of any order for payments made under s 40. In *Nwogbe v Nwogbe* [2000] 2 FLR 744, the husband was ordered to pay rent, council tax and water rates but did not do so. The Court of Appeal held that it had no power to commit him. The payments did not fall within any of the exceptions to the Debtors Act 1869 (which abolished imprisonment for debt), neither did they come within the Attachment of Earnings Act 1971. Since payments were made to a third party, the wife did not become a judgment creditor and so none of the usual methods of enforcement were available to her. The court accepted that there was a clear lacuna in the law, which would need to be filled by Parliament.

15.2.4.6   Flowchart

The flowchart set out below explains who can apply for occupation orders and the appropriate section of the FLA 1996 to use.

Occupation orders – who can apply?

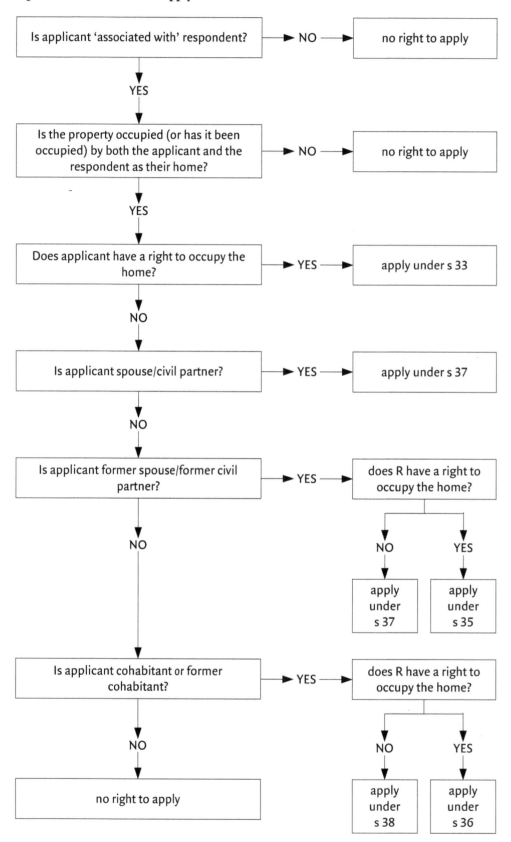

15.2.5 Emergency applications (s 45)

In urgent cases, it may be possible for the solicitor to protect an applicant or a child on the same day that they come to see the solicitor, or at least on the next day. Under s 45 of the FLA 1996, the court can make both non-molestation and occupation orders without notice to the respondent (or 'ex parte') where it considers that it is 'just and convenient' to do so. In deciding whether to allow an application to proceed without notice, the court will take into account all circumstances, including:

(a)   any risk of significant harm to the applicant or child if the order is not made immediately;

(b)   whether it is likely that the applicant will be deterred or prevented from pursuing the application if the order is not made immediately; and

(c)   whether there is reason to believe that the respondent is evading service and delay in effecting service will seriously prejudice the applicant or child.

However, the courts are generally reluctant to grant orders where the respondent has been given no notice. Therefore, where it is not possible to give the respondent the full two clear days' notice required, the applicant's solicitor should consider whether to apply to abridge the notice period instead of applying without notice. Where the respondent has been given some notice (however short), he may be able to attend court to give his version of events. This will mean that the court will be in a better position to assess the situation, and may therefore be persuaded to grant more wide-ranging relief than where the respondent has been given no notice at all. However, if the respondent has not had an opportunity to instruct a solicitor then the court is likely to make an interim (rather than final) order to allow the respondent time to seek legal advice before the final hearing.

Occupation orders are more rarely granted without notice, especially where they would involve ousting the respondent from his home.

It must be stressed that any order obtained without notice will be temporary only (an interim order). The solicitor must obtain a hearing date for the return hearing and give the respondent the required notice. In January 2017 the President of the Family Division reissued the Practice Guidance: Family Court – Duration of Ex Parte (Without Notice) Orders from October 2013, following concern that courts were making without notice non-molestation orders of unlimited duration. The Practice Guidance states:

(a)   A without notice injunctive order must never be made without limit of time. There must be a fixed end date.

(b)   It is not sufficient merely to specify a return day. The order must specify on its face and in clear terms precisely when it expires.

(c)   The duration of the order should not normally exceed 14 days.

(d)   The order must also specify the date, time and place of the hearing on the return day. It is usually convenient for this date to coincide with the expiry date of the order.

(e)   The order must contain a statement of the right to make an application to set aside or vary the order under FPR 2010, r 18.11. The phrase 'liberty to apply on 24 hours' notice' is not sufficient for this purpose. The order must spell out that the respondent is entitled, without waiting for the return day, to apply on notice to set aside or vary the order.

15.2.6 Undertakings (s 46)

In the past, the necessity for a full hearing was often avoided by the respondent offering to give an undertaking, ie a promise to the court on similar terms to the proposed order. This avoided a court order being made against the respondent. The applicant was often prepared to accept the undertaking since, as it was made voluntarily, it was more likely to be complied with.

Under s 46 of the FLA 1996, the court may still accept an undertaking in any case where it has power to make an occupation or non-molestation order. However, no power of arrest can be attached to an undertaking, and the court will not accept an undertaking in a case where it would otherwise attach a power of arrest to an occupation order. The court will not accept an undertaking on an application for a non-molestation order where the respondent has used or threatened violence or a non-molestation order is necessary so that any breach can be punishable under s 42A as a criminal offence (see **15.2.9.1**)).

15.2.7 Procedure

Applications for non-molestation and occupation orders will be made to the Family Court and will be allocated in accordance with the Family Court (Composition and Distribution of Business) Rules 2014 (SI 2014/840).

15.2.7.1 Legal aid

Provided that the client is eligible, initial advice and assistance will be covered by Legal Help.

Once the decision has been taken to bring proceedings for a non-molestation order and/or an occupation order, Legal Representation should be applied for immediately. If the situation is urgent, there is no need to apply for Level 2 or 3 funding first. Note that where the Legal Aid Agency considers that it would be appropriate to write a warning letter to the respondent and/or to try to enlist the assistance of the police, it will not grant funding until these steps have been taken and proved ineffective. In addition, funding is likely to be refused unless the conduct complained of took place within the last two to three weeks, or if the conduct complained of is not likely to be repeated or is of a 'trivial nature'.

In most cases, it will also be necessary to apply for Emergency Legal Representation. Family solicitors can themselves grant Emergency Legal Representation under the terms of their contract if they have devolved powers. If they do not have devolved powers, they will need to apply to the Legal Aid Agency by telephone or fax if it is an emergency.

The procedure set out below assumes that the applicant is entitled to legal aid. For a privately paying client, simply omit all steps relating to legal aid and remember that a court fee must be paid.

15.2.7.2 Obtaining a non-molestation or an occupation order without notice (ex parte)

(a) Grant Emergency Legal Representation. Emergency cover should only be granted for without notice proceedings where the applicant or child is in imminent danger of significant harm (ie there is a real risk that it will occur before a substantive application can be processed and brought before the court).

(b) Telephone the court to make an appointment if necessary.

(c) Telephone a process server so that he can be at court at the end of the hearing to collect the without notice order to serve it on the respondent. The order must be served personally, and it is not usually thought wise for the solicitor to do this.

(d) Draft the following:

    (i) application in Form FL401 (see **Appendix 3(K)**);

    (ii) statement in support. This must give details of the respondent's behaviour and both parties' housing needs and financial resources. It should also explain why the application is made without notice. The statement must be signed by the applicant and contain a statement of truth. Form FL401T is a new template witness statement which parties can now use if they wish;

    (iii) notice of issue of Emergency Legal Representation.

(e) It is not essential to draft the order sought. Generally, however, the court would find it helpful to have a draft and so, if time permits, draft the without notice order(s) on Form FL404 (occupation order) or Form FL404a (non-molestation order).

(f) File at court notice of issue of Emergency Legal Representation, the application in duplicate and the statement in support in duplicate, and notice of acting (if appropriate).

(g) Attend the hearing before the judge, who will read the statement in support and listen to the applicant's oral evidence. Hand any draft order to the judge.

(h) Any occupation order made will be issued in Form FL404 and any non-molestation order in Form FL404a. Where a power of arrest is attached to any of the provisions of an occupation order, those provisions shall be set out in Form FL406. A record of the hearing will be made on Form FL405. On filing, the court fixes a date for the on notice hearing, which will be inserted in a notice of proceedings (Form FL402). The respondent must be given two clear days' notice of this date.

(i) Hand the process server the without notice order(s), sealed copy application, copy statement in support, notice of proceedings and notice of issue of Emergency Legal Representation. Ask the process server to serve these documents on the respondent personally and then to swear a statement of service in the form required by s 9 of the Criminal Law Act 1967 so that it can be relied upon in a criminal court. The Family Procedure (Amendment No 2) Rules 2021, which came into force on 1 October 2021, allow the court to order service by means other than personal service where there is a good reason to: the court may direct that service is effected by an alternative method or at an alternative place.

(j) If the court has made an occupation order, serve a copy of the application and the order on any mortgagee or landlord, together with a notice in Form FL416 informing him that he has a right to make representations in writing or at any hearing. These documents should be served by first-class post.

(k) If the court has made a non-molestation order or attached a power of arrest to an occupation order (see **15.2.9**), take a copy of Form FL404a or Form FL406 to the police station nearest to where the applicant lives and a statement showing that the respondent has been served with the order or informed of its terms. The police will not be prepared to exercise any power of arrest unless they have notice of it. Many breaches of orders occur shortly after they are made, so it is important to give the police notice of the order or the power of arrest as soon as possible.

Remember that any hearing without notice must be followed by a hearing on notice so that the respondent has an opportunity to put his side of the story.

The President of the Family Division issued Practice Guidance, 'Family Court – Duration of Ex Parte (Without Notice) Orders' on 18 January 2017, which states that the order must make clear that it was made in the absence of the respondent and the court has considered only the applicant's evidence and has made no finding of fact. The order must also contain a statement of the right to set aside or vary it without waiting for the return day.

15.2.7.3 Obtaining a non-molestation or an occupation order on notice

If a without notice order has been obtained, many of these steps may already have been completed:

(a) Grant Emergency Legal Representation.

(b) Draft the following:
  (i) application in Form FL401;
  (ii) statement in support. It must give details of the respondent's behaviour and both parties' housing needs and financial resources. The statement must be signed by

the applicant and contain a statement of truth. Form FL401T is a new template witness statement which parties can now use if they wish. Where a without notice order has been obtained, the statement will probably already have been drafted. The same statement is generally used for both without notice and on notice hearings. However, where further instances of violence have occurred, or the initial statement has been hurriedly drafted, a further statement should be drafted;

(iii)   notice of issue of Legal Representation.

(c)   File the application in duplicate, statement in duplicate, notice of issue of Legal Representation, notice of acting (where appropriate) and Emergency Legal Representation certificate (where appropriate).

(d)   On filing, the court fixes a hearing date, which will be inserted in a notice of proceedings (Form FL402). The respondent must be given two clear days' notice of this date. Hand to a process server sealed copy application, copy statement in support, notice of hearing, notice of issue of Emergency Legal Representation and notice of acting (where appropriate). Ask him to serve these documents on the respondent personally and to swear an affidavit to confirm service.

(e)   If the FL401 includes an application for an occupation order, serve any mortgagee or landlord with a copy of the application and a notice in Form FL416 informing him that he has a right to make representations in writing or at the hearing. These documents should be served by first-class post.

(f)   Once the respondent (and mortgagee/landlord) has been served, file a statement confirming that this has been done in Form FL415.

(g)   Prepare the draft order(s) required on Form FL404 or Form FL404a. This is not essential, but the court will find it useful.

(h)   Attend the hearing before the judge. If the respondent fails to attend, service can be proved using the affidavit. The court can then make an order in the absence of the respondent.

Hand any order(s) drafted to the judge. The judge will read any statements filed by the parties and may hear oral evidence from the applicant and respondent. If either of the parties has witnesses (eg a neighbour or relative), they may then give evidence. Any occupation order made will be issued on Form FL404 and any non-molestation order on Form FL404a. Where a power of arrest is attached to any of the provisions of an occupation order, those provisions will be set out on Form FL406. A record of the hearing will be made on Form FL405. The court may direct a further hearing to hear representations from any mortgagee or landlord.

(i)   The respondent must be served personally with the order (even if he was present when it was made). Again, this is usually done by a process server who should swear a statement of service in the form required by s 9 of the Criminal Justice Act 1967 so that it can be relied upon in the criminal court. The Family Procedure (Amendment No 2) Rules 2021, which came into force on 1 October 2021, allow the court to order service by means other than personal service where there is a good reason to: the court may direct that service is effected by an alternative method or at an alternative place.

(j)   If the court has made a non-molestation order or attached a power of arrest to an occupation order (see **15.2.9**), take a copy of Form FL404a or Form FL406 and sworn statement of service to the police station nearest to where the applicant lives.

15.2.8   Procedural checklist

A checklist of the appropriate procedure may be helpful. One is set out below.

On notice procedure checklist

```
┌─────────────────────────────────────────────────────────────────────┐
│            OBTAIN LEGAL REPRESENTATION IF RELEVANT                    │
└─────────────────────────────────────────────────────────────────────┘
                                  │
┌─────────────────────────────────────────────────────────────────────┐
│ FILE:                                                                 │
│ (i)     Application (Form FL 401) in duplicate                        │
│ (ii)    Statement in support in duplicate                             │
│ (iii)   Legal Representation Certificate and Notice of Issue          │
│ (iv)    Notice of Acting (if client in divorce under Legal Help)      │
└─────────────────────────────────────────────────────────────────────┘
                                  │
┌─────────────────────────────────────────────────────────────────────┐
│ SERVE ON R:                                                           │
│ (i)     Copy Application                                              │
│ (ii)    Copy Statement                                               │
│ [(iii)  Notice of Issue of LR Certificate]                            │
│ (iv)    Notice of Hearing (Form FL 402)                               │
│ [(v)    Copy Notice of Acting]                                        │
│ [Give two clear days' notice]                                         │
└─────────────────────────────────────────────────────────────────────┘
                                  │
┌─────────────────────────────────────────────────────────────────────┐
│ SERVE ON MORTGAGEE/LANDLORD:                                          │
│ Notice in Form FL 416                                                 │
└─────────────────────────────────────────────────────────────────────┘
                                  │
┌─────────────────────────────────────────────────────────────────────┐
│ FILE:                                                                 │
│ Statement of Service                                                  │
└─────────────────────────────────────────────────────────────────────┘
                                  │
┌─────────────────────────────────────────────────────────────────────┐
│ ATTEND FIRST HEARING:                                                 │
│ Present case                                                          │
│ Produce draft order (if drafted)                                      │
└─────────────────────────────────────────────────────────────────────┘
                                  │
┌─────────────────────────────────────────────────────────────────────┐
│ SERVE order on R and mortgagee/landlord                               │
│ LODGE copy at police station of Form FL404a or Form FL406 with        │
│ statement of service                                                  │
└─────────────────────────────────────────────────────────────────────┘
```

15.2.9   Enforcement

Since 1 July 2007 breach of a non-molestation order is a criminal offence (FLA 1996, s 42A). Before 1 July 2007 the basic method of enforcement where a respondent had breached a non-molestation order or an occupation order was committal for contempt of court. How the respondent came before the court depended generally on whether or not the order had a power of arrest attached to it. This position remains the same for breaches of an occupation order, but for non-molestation orders made after 1 July 2007 breach will be a criminal offence and dealt with differently.

15.2.9.1   Breach of a non-molestation order

Section 42A of the FLA 1996 makes breach of a non-molestation order a criminal offence punishable by up to five years' imprisonment on indictment and 12 months' imprisonment on conviction in the magistrates' court. Where a respondent breaches a non-molestation order, he will be arrested for the crime of breaching the order and can be charged and brought before a criminal court. The prosecution will be handled by the CPS and the solicitors for the complainant will not play any role.

A respondent cannot, however, be punished for the same offence twice, so if he is convicted of an offence under s 42A, he cannot be punished for contempt of court for the same conduct.

15.2.9.2 Breach of an occupation order

Power of arrest

Under s 47 of the FLA 1996, where the court makes an occupation order (or, before 1 July 2007, where it made a non-molestation order) and it appears to the court that the respondent has used or threatened violence against the applicant (ie any associated person) or a child, then it shall attach a power of arrest to one or more provisions of the order. The only exception to this is where the court is satisfied that the applicant or child will be adequately protected without such a power of arrest.

The court can attach a power of arrest to one or more provisions of the order. Any power of arrest will be drafted on Form FL406, which will set out which provisions the power of arrest will apply to.

A power of arrest can also be attached to one or more provisions of a without notice order, but only where it appears to the court that the respondent has used or threatened violence against the applicant or child and that there is a risk of significant harm to the applicant or child if the power of arrest is not attached immediately.

Any power of arrest granted will usually be expressed to last for the same period as the provisions of the order to which it is attached (although this will not always be the case). This period can be extended any number of times.

A police officer will have the power to arrest the respondent without warrant if he has reasonable cause to suspect the respondent of being in breach of any of the terms of the order set out in the power of arrest. Once arrested, the respondent must be brought before a judge, district judge or magistrate within 24 hours.

Warrant of arrest

Where the court has not attached a power of arrest, or the respondent's breach is not covered by the power of arrest, or an undertaking is breached, the applicant may apply for a warrant of arrest. The applicant will need to give evidence on oath to satisfy the judge, district judge or magistrate that there are reasonable grounds for believing that the respondent has breached the order. The judge, district judge or magistrate can then issue a warrant of arrest.

Penalty

The penalty available will depend upon whether the respondent is brought before a judge in the county court, or a magistrate in the family proceedings court. In the county court, the judge can commit the respondent for up to two years (and/or impose an unlimited fine). In the family proceedings court, the respondent can be fined up to £5,000 or committed for up to two months.

In the case of *Hammerton v Hammerton* [2007] EWCA Civ 248, the Court of Appeal said proceedings for committal were a criminal charge for the purposes of Article 6 of the European Convention on Human Rights, so a defendant had the right to representation. Where a defendant to committal proceedings was unrepresented, the judge should enquire as to the circumstances in which he was unrepresented and consider, at the outset of the hearing, whether there should be an adjournment to enable the defendant to be represented.

In both the county court and the family proceedings court, immediate committal was a remedy of last resort and was unlikely to be ordered save in exceptional situations. General guidelines on committal were given by the Court of Appeal in *Hale v Tanner* [2000] 2 FLR 879. These include:

(a)   that imprisonment is not the automatic consequence of the breach of an order but there was no principle that imprisonment should not be imposed on a first breach;

(b)   that the court should bear in mind the context – there could be aggravating or mitigating factors;

(c)   that the length of committal had to bear some reasonable relationship to the maximum available;

(d)   that suspension was available in a much wider range of circumstances than in a criminal case and should usually be used initially where committal is contemplated to try to secure compliance with the order.

Since the Protection from Harassment Act 1997 (see **15.4** below), which provides greater sentencing powers, cases have seemed to indicate that courts are willing to impose longer custodial sentences for breaches of FLA 1996 orders than in the past. In *Lomas v Parle* [2003] EWCA Civ 1804, the Court of Appeal increased a sentence of imprisonment from four months to eight months, and said care must be taken that sentences for breach of FLA 1996 orders are not manifestly discrepant with those under the Protection from Harassment Act 1997. In *H v O (Contempt of Court: Sentencing)* [2004] EWCA Civ 1691, the Court of Appeal, whilst reducing a sentence of imprisonment from 12 months to nine months, stated that it felt that Parliament and society now demanded more deterrent punishment than in the past for domestic violence. In *Robinson v Murray* [2005] EWCA Civ 935, where the Court of Appeal upheld a sentence of eight months' imprisonment, it suggested if a case warranted a sentence near the top of the range, the appropriate course is to bring proceedings under the Protection from Harassment Act 1997 so that the greater powers of punishment are available to the court.

Finally, if the order had no power of arrest attached, the judge or magistrate may attach a power of arrest.

15.3 HUMAN RIGHTS IMPLICATIONS

Non-molestation or occupation orders may raise issues under Article 6 of the ECHR. Public funding is often denied to respondents to such orders, who may be advised to give undertakings on the basis of no admissions. Consideration may have to be given as to whether legal aid should be provided, given that undertakings can be the first step in committal proceedings which may result in imprisonment or a fine. One of the Article 6 guarantees is that the proceedings are fair and that each party has 'equality of arms' with the other. Yet if a respondent is not represented on an application, can he be said to have 'equality of arms'?

Occupation orders may also raise issues under Article 8 (the right to respect for family life and home). Interference with this right must be necessary and proportionate. Courts must therefore give careful consideration to the duration and scope of such orders.

15.4 PROTECTION FROM HARASSMENT ACT 1997

In the past, when an applicant did not come within the ambit of the relevant domestic abuse legislation, for example if they were the partner of the abuser but they had not cohabited, they would have to bring an action for an appropriate tort, for example, assault. However, until quite recently there was no tort of harassment, so protection could be obtained only where the conduct complained of amounted to an established tort (see, eg, *Burris v Azadani* [1995] 4 All ER 802).

The PHA 1997 plugged this gap in the law. Section 3 of the Act created a statutory tort where a person pursues a course of conduct that amounts to harassment of another and which he knows or ought to know amounts to harassment of the other. There is no definition of harassment, save that the PHA 1997 states that this includes 'alarming the person or causing them distress' (s 7). A 'course of conduct' must include conduct on at least two occasions.

Section 3 provides that where the statutory tort has been committed or is apprehended, the victim may claim damages and/or an injunction. Should the injunction be breached, then the victim may apply for a warrant of arrest in the same way as under the FLA 1996. Also, breach of the injunction may be a criminal offence, punishable by up to five years' imprisonment on conviction on indictment (s 3(6) and (9)).

The PHA 1997 also created new criminal offences: the offence of criminal harassment and the more serious offence of putting someone in fear of violence (ss 2 and 4 respectively). Since November 2012 the criminal offences of stalking (s 2A) and stalking involving fear of violence or serious alarm or distress (s 4A) have been in force. In addition, s 5 gives the criminal courts power to make restraining orders prohibiting the perpetrator from engaging in further harassment on conviction of any offence, and s 5A allows the criminal courts to make restraining orders on the acquittal of a defendant if they consider it necessary to protect a person from harassment by the defendant.

15.5 COERCIVE AND CONTROLLING BEHAVIOUR

The family solicitor should be aware of the new criminal offence of coercive and controlling behaviour, which was created by s 76 of the Serious Crime Act 2015. It came into force on 29 December 2015 to plug a gap in the law that meant that repeated patterns of non-physical behaviour were not recognised as domestic abuse in a criminal context. Although it does not provide for any civil orders, it may provide a solution for clients who are willing to involve the police.

This offence is constituted by behaviour on the part of the perpetrator that takes place 'repeatedly or continuously'. The victim and alleged perpetrator must be 'personally connected' at the time the behaviour takes place. The behaviour must have had a 'serious effect' on the victim, meaning that it has caused the victim to fear that violence will be used against them on 'at least two occasions', or it has had a 'substantial adverse effect on the victims' day to day activities'. The alleged perpetrator must have known that their behaviour would have a serious effect on the victim, or the behaviour must have been such that they 'ought to have known' it would have that effect.

The cross-Government definition of domestic violence and abuse outlines controlling or coercive behaviour as follows:

> Controlling behaviour is: a range of acts designed to make a person subordinate and/or dependent by isolating them from sources of support, exploiting their resources and capacities for personal gain, depriving them of the means needed for independence, resistance and escape and regulating their everyday behaviour.
>
> Coercive behaviour is: an act or a pattern of acts of assault, threats, humiliation and intimidation or other abuse that is used to harm, punish, or frighten their victim.

On conviction on indictment a person can be imprisoned for up to five years.

The Home Office has issued statutory guidance, 'Statutory Guidance Framework: Controlling or Coercive Behaviour in an Intimate Family Relationship', which contains examples of controlling or coercive behaviour.

15.6 FORCED MARRIAGE (CIVIL PROTECTION) ACT 2007

The Forced Marriage (Civil Protection) Act 2007, which came into force in November 2008, inserted a new Pt IVA into the FLA 1996, which allows the court to make a forced marriage protection order under s 63A to protect a person from being forced into marriage, or an attempt being made to force a person into marriage, or to protect a person who has been forced into marriage. The order can contain such prohibitions, restrictions or requirements and other terms as the court considers appropriate for the purposes of the order, and it may cover conduct outside England and Wales.

An application may be made by the victim or by a relevant third party (the local authority) or by another person with leave of the court (this envisages including friends, boyfriends and girlfriends, or teachers of the victim). An order may alternatively be made without application in existing family proceedings. The respondent need not be the other party to the forced marriage and can include additional third parties beyond those who are forcing the victim to marry, such as those who are, amongst other behaviour, aiding and abetting or encouraging or assisting those who are forcing or attempting to force the victim to marry.

In deciding whether to exercise its powers under this section and, if so, in what manner, the court must have regard to all the circumstances, including the need to secure the health, safety and well-being of the person to be protected. In ascertaining that person's well-being, the court must, in particular, have such regard to the person's wishes and feelings (so far as they are reasonably ascertainable) as the court considers appropriate in the light of the person's age and understanding.

Orders can be made without notice where it is 'just and convenient' to do so, and a power of arrest can be attached to an order. If the respondent breaches the order it is contempt of court, which is punishable by a maximum of two years' imprisonment.

The Anti-social Behaviour, Crime and Policing Act 2014 has since 16 June 2014 made it a criminal offence to breach a forced marriage protection order under s 63CA of the FLA 1996, and (in s 121 of the 2014 Act) has created a new criminal offence of forcing another person to marry if a person uses violence, threats or any other form of coercion for the purpose of causing another person to enter into a marriage, and they believe, or ought reasonably to believe, that the conduct may cause the other person to enter into the marriage without free and full consent. The offences are punishable by terms of imprisonment of up to five and seven years respectively.

SUMMARY

(1) In cases of domestic abuse, a solicitor will have to decide whether to take action in the civil courts, or whether other remedies, for example writing a warning letter, involving the police or removing the victim to a safe environment, may be more appropriate.

(2) The FLA 1996 allows applicants to apply for two main types of relief:

  (a) non-molestation orders;

  (b) occupation orders.

(3) Non-molestation orders can be obtained by a wide range of 'associated persons'.

(4) Occupation orders can be applied for by a more limited range of people. Whether a person has a right to occupy the home, or is a former spouse, cohabitant or former cohabitant, will determine whether they can apply at all and the relief they can obtain.

(5) In urgent cases, it may be possible to obtain orders under the FLA 1996 without notice.

(6) The respondent may give an undertaking instead of having an order made against him.

(7) A power of arrest must generally be attached to an occupation order unless the court is satisfied that the applicant will be adequately protected without it.

(8) Where a non-molestation order is breached it is a criminal offence.

(9) Where an occupation order is breached it can be enforced by applying for committal of the respondent for contempt of court.

(10) The PHA 1997 created a statutory tort of harassment, which may be used where the applicant does not fall within the provisions of the FLA 1996.

(11) The Forced Marriage (Civil Protection) Act 2007 protects a person being forced into marriage or who has been forced into marriage.

CHAPTER 16

THE COHABITING FAMILY

16.1	Introduction	281
16.2	Setting up home together	282
16.3	Breaking up	285
16.4	Children	290
16.5	Bankruptcy	292
16.6	Death	292
Summary		294

LEARNING OUTCOMES

After reading this chapter you will be able to:

- consider what action may be taken by couples before setting up home together
- explain the issues regarding ownership of the home when cohabiting couples separate and how the court deals with them
- describe what happens to a deceased cohabitant's property on death and what provisions are available for the surviving cohabitant.

16.1 INTRODUCTION

In this chapter the terms 'cohabiting family' and 'cohabiting couples' are used to refer to couples who live together without marrying (or entering into a civil partnership).

The number of couples who are living together has dramatically increased in recent years to 3.5 million families in 2020. Family lawyers have traditionally been consulted by such couples when their relationship breaks down; but increasingly nowadays, they are being instructed by couples who want advice on setting up home together.

In July 2004 the (then) Department for Constitutional Affairs launched a public information campaign, 'Living Together'. This had the aim of making cohabiting couples more aware of their legal status and providing them with practical advice on how they could protect themselves and their families, as survey results had shown there was a common public misconception that cohabiting couples enjoy similar rights to married couples. Unfortunately, research published in 2008 showed that 51% of people still believed that there is a status of 'common law marriage' that gives cohabitants the same rights as married couples, and results of the 2019 British Attitudes Survey reveal that 46% of people believe in the concept of 'common law marriage' (including 48% of those in cohabiting couples).

The financial orders available under the MCA 1973 do not apply to cohabiting couples, and to date English law has developed piecemeal to deal with the problems of such couples.

The Civil Partnership Act 2004 arose as a result of pressure for reform in this area. However, this dealt with the position of same sex couples only. The Government's reason for not extending it to opposite sex couples was that they already had the option of marriage available to them, but following the decision in R (on the application of Steinfeld and Keidan) v Secretary of State for International Development [2018] UKSC 32 (see **3.1.2**), the Civil Partnerships, Marriages and Deaths (Registration etc) Act 2019 was passed, and since December 2019 the right to enter civil partnerships has been extended to opposite sex couples.

During the passage of the Civil Partnership Act 2004 through Parliament, concerns were expressed about the lack of a coherent scheme of remedies to relieve the potential financial hardship of cohabiting couples on relationship breakdown. As a result of this the Law Commission was asked to review the law in this area and to suggest possible reforms. In July 2007 the Law Commission published its report, 'Cohabitation: The Financial Consequences of Relationship Breakdown', which proposed a scheme to provide remedies for eligible applicants (such as those with children or who have lived together for a specified time), so long as they had not agreed to disapply the scheme and only if the applicant had made qualifying contributions to the relationship giving rise to enduring consequences at the point of separation (such as giving up a career to care for the couple's children). In March 2008 the Government announced that it would delay acting on the Law Commission's proposals, as it wanted to examine research on the Family Law (Scotland) Act 2006, which came into force in Scotland in 2007 and contains provisions similar to those recommended by the Law Commission. In 2011 the Coalition Government announced that it did not intend to take forward the Law Commission's recommendations.

In April 2018, and again in November 2018, the junior Justice Minister said that the Government would consider how to proceed in relation to proposals made by the Law Commission in the context of any further reforms to the family justice system. To date, the Government has not given any further indication of what might happen next. In April 2021, the parliamentary Women and Equalities Committee launched an enquiry into the equalities issues around cohabitation, how cohabitation rights could be strengthened and what legal protection for cohabitants could look like and how this might be introduced.

For several years Resolution has been actively considering the question of comprehensive reform in this area, and several private Cohabitation Bills have been introduced into Parliament, which have not succeeded. Resolution publishes a Guidance note on cohabitation, which is only available to its members and which offers a comprehensive guide to advising clients on this area.

This chapter summarises the current legal position both during the time when the couple are living together, including advice on how to avoid problems in the first place, and when the relationship breaks down.

16.2 SETTING UP HOME TOGETHER

16.2.1 Ownership of the home

16.2.1.1 Duty of the buyers' solicitor

When a solicitor acts for joint buyers, they have a duty to advise on the relative merits of owning as joint tenants and tenants in common, and may be sued in negligence if they fail to do this (see *Walker v Hall* [1984] FLR 126, *Taylor v Warners* (1988) 85(25) LSG 26).

It is also important to consider when advising joint buyers whether there is any conflict, or potential conflict, of interest between them, in which case a solicitor should not act for both of them.

16.2.1.2 Declaration as to beneficial interests

An effective way to clarify beneficial interests in a jointly-owned property is by using a declaration of trust. Section 53(1)(b) of the Law of Property Act 1925 requires that a declaration must be in writing signed by the buyers. This will generally be conclusive evidence as to the ownership (*Pettit v Pettit* [1970] AC 777). Since there is no equivalent to s 25 of the

MCA 1973 (see **4.5**) for an unmarried couple, the arrangement cannot be undone by the court at a later stage. Therefore, the buyers must both understand the position and be in agreement as to their respective shares at the time of purchase.

The declaration can either be included in the purchase deed, or be contained in a separate deed. On balance, it is preferable to prepare a separate document, especially if the property is registered, because Land Registry will not return the transfer after registration.

A further advantage is that some other important matters can be dealt with in a separate document, for example division of outgoings such as repairs, insurance and the mortgage repayments; circumstances in which a sale may take place or be postponed; and, if necessary, provisions giving one party an option to buy the other's share.

16.2.2 Life insurance

It is important that couples living together make provision for life insurance to cover each of them against the financial consequences of the death of the other.

There is a legal requirement that provides that the person for whom the benefit of a life assurance policy is made must have an insurable interest in the life of the assured, otherwise the policy will be void and illegal (Life Assurance Act 1774, s 1). This interest must be of a financial nature. This can be a problem because, whilst marriage is recognised as giving the parties an insurable interest in each others' lives without the need to prove financial loss, cohabitation is not so recognised. It is therefore essential that where couples are living together, mutual financial support can be shown.

Most couples are concerned with life insurance in relation to an endowment or repayment mortgage upon their home. Clear advice must be given to them on the validity of the policy and the consequences if they split up. Insurance is also relevant in the guise of death benefit paid as part of an employment contract. Often the employee can nominate to whom the money should be paid by giving instructions to the trustees of the scheme.

16.2.3 Wills

The vast majority of people die intestate. This is not advisable, especially for a cohabiting couple (see **16.6.2**). When a couple decide to live together, they should discuss whether provisions should be made for the survivor if one of them should die. Wills that contain complementary provisions could then be made. A solicitor acting on a house purchase can explain the problems and encourage the buyers to make a will. A will might appoint a guardian for any children and deal with the division of assets.

16.2.4 Cohabitation agreements

A cohabiting couple can enter into an agreement setting out arrangements that will apply while they are living together, as well as establishing rights on the breakdown of the relationship. This is a developing area of the law and as yet there is no modern decision on the validity of such agreements. However, in *Sutton v Mischon De Reya and Gower & Co* [2003] EWHC 3166 (Ch), [2004] 1 FLR 837, the court gave the strongest indication yet that there was nothing contrary to public policy in a cohabitation agreement. It is clear that solicitors are increasingly being asked to advise on and draft agreements in this field. The Law Commission, in its report (see **16.1**), recommends legislation to make clear that cohabitation agreements are not contrary to public policy.

16.2.4.1 Validity of cohabitation agreements

In the absence of modern authority, cohabitation agreements are governed by general principles of the law of contract. The following issues could therefore be relevant.

Illegality on grounds of public policy

To avoid challenge on the ground of illegality on grounds of public policy, an agreement must avoid any implication that cohabitation is part of the obligations of the agreement. It is therefore safer to enter into the agreement after, rather than before, the couple have started living together.

Undue influence

Undue influence may arise if the agreement is unduly favourable to one party and that party cannot show that it was entered into freely or following independent advice (see *Zamet and Others v Hyman and Another* [1961] 3 All ER 933).

A related issue for a solicitor is to bear in mind that it is likely to be impossible to act for both parties due to the potential conflict of interest. For example, one party may be contributing all the finance for a house purchase, which would mean that the other party, in agreeing to this in a cohabitation agreement, would give up any chance of obtaining a share if the relationship broke down. As a general principle, The Law Society's Family Law Protocol (para 11.2.4) says that solicitors should advise clients that they can only act for one party in drawing up such an agreement and that the other party should be separately represented.

Intention to create legal relations

In domestic circumstances there is a rebuttable presumption that the parties did not intend to enter into a contract. Where the couple have a written agreement, especially if they received separate legal advice upon it, it should not be difficult to rebut the presumption (see *Balfour v Balfour* [1919] 2 KB 571 and *Merritt v Merritt* [1970] 1 WLR 1121).

Certainty

Any arrangements proposed must be set out clearly, otherwise the agreement may fail through lack of certainty.

Consideration

Any potential problem arising from a failure of consideration can be avoided by making the agreement a deed.

16.2.4.2   Matters to be covered in a cohabitation agreement

The main issues which could usefully be covered in a cohabitation agreement are as follows:

(a)   ownership of real and personal property (see **16.2.1**);

(b)   finances, for example, how to divide bills and resolve ownership of joint accounts;

(c)   children, for example, their maintenance and surnames. Any agreement made in relation to children will be limited by the CA 1989 and the CSA 1991 and will be open to review by the court (see **16.4**);

(d)   other matters: here it is important not to include matters that are too trivial, or personal matters, for example housework or division of chores, because this could make it more likely that a court would hold that the parties did not intend to create legal relations.

16.2.4.3   Enforcement of cohabitation agreements

The general rules of contract will apply to the enforcement of cohabitation agreements. It might also be advisable to include an arbitration clause in the agreement for dealing with disputes between the parties. The Family Law Bar Association Conciliation Board's conciliation procedure is available to unmarried couples who have lived together.

16.3 BREAKING UP

When cohabiting couples split up, neither party has any right to claim maintenance from the other. Maintenance can nevertheless be claimed for children of the relationship (see **16.4.2**). Major disputes are therefore likely to centre around the ownership or occupation of their home. It is possible to bring the dispute before the court by seeking a declaration of ownership of the home under s 14 of the Trusts of Land and Appointment of Trustees Act 1996 (TLATA 1996) (see **Appendix 1(H)**).

If the couple were engaged within three years before the dispute, it might be possible to use s 17 of the Married Women's Property Act 1882. This Act enables property disputes to be determined summarily by the county court; generally it is used only by married couples. The Act confers no jurisdiction to vary property rights and so the court's powers are purely declaratory (*Mossop v Mossop* [1988] 2 All ER 20).

16.3.1 Ownership of the home

16.3.1.1 Jointly-owned property

If the correct procedure was adopted when the property was purchased, the couple's intentions as to ownership should be clear from the purchase deed or declaration of trust. If the couple purchased as joint tenants, either could apply to the court for an order of sale under s 14 of the TLATA 1996 and the proceeds would then be divided equally. If the couple purchased as tenants in common, or if the joint tenancy was severed, only a declaration of trust made by them will be decisive (see **16.2.1.2**).

If they own as tenants in common and there is no declaration of trust, it will be presumed they own in equal shares unless the contrary can be proved (*Stack v Dowden* [2007] UKHL 17). The onus is on the party who wishes to show that the beneficial interest is divided other than equally. In *Stack v Dowden*, the House of Lords said it would look at many factors as well as the financial contributions the parties made, such as how the parties conducted their finances and why the house was acquired, to determine whether they intended to own it in unequal shares. It also said that cases where the joint legal owners were to be taken to have intended that their beneficial interests should be different from their legal interests would be very unusual.

In *Stack v Dowden*, the House of Lords said that when determining the size of a claimant's share, where there had been no express agreement, the court had to determine what the parties' intentions had been, actual or inferred, with respect to the property in the light of their whole course of conduct in relation to it.

This was further clarified and expanded on in *Jones v Kernott* [2011] UKSC 53, where the following principles were set out:

(a) the starting point is that they are joint tenants in law and equity;

(b) that presumption can be displaced by showing that they had a different common intention when they acquired the home, or they later formed the common intention that their shares would change;

(c) their common intention is to be inferred or deduced objectively from their conduct;

(d) where it is clear the parties did not intend a joint tenancy at the outset, or had changed their original intention, but it is not possible to ascertain by direct evidence or inference what they intended their shares to be, each party will be entitled to the share the court considers fair having regard to the whole course of dealing between them in relation to the property. Thus the court will impute an intention to the parties as to their beneficial shares.

It is therefore a two-stage test. The first stage is to establish if there was an agreement (actual or inferred) to hold the property other than as joint tenants in equal beneficial shares. If this is established, the second stage is to decide the size of the shares. This may be inferred from the parties' conduct, but if this is not possible, the court can impute an intention as to the size of the shares. Imputation is not open to the court at the first stage.

It is open to one partner to buy out the other's interest. If this is done, the prior permission of any lender must be sought. In contrast to divorcing couples, any transfer will be liable to stamp duty land tax on the consideration paid plus the amount of any mortgage debt assumed (see Stamp Act 1891, s 57, Inland Revenue SP 27 April 1990, Finance Act 1985, s 83(1), and Stamp Duty (Exempt Instruments) Regulations 1987 (SI 1987/516), Category H).

16.3.1.2 Legal estate in one name only

If a property is in the sole legal ownership of one party, the presumption is that that party also owns all the beneficial interest. In this situation the other party will have to establish a claim in equity. This will involve establishing a resulting or constructive trust, or making a successful claim under the doctrine of proprietary estoppel. The court cannot alter an unmarried partner's share to reflect MCA 1973, s 25 principles as it is able to do with a married couple.

If a claim is successful and a trust is established, the non-legal owner will be entitled to a share in the property equal to his beneficial interest as determined by the court in accordance with land law principles. If proprietary estoppel is established then one of the remedies available is to give the claimant an interest in the property.

Resulting trusts

Resulting trusts can be established only by a direct contribution to the purchase price by the partner who is not the legal owner. *Curley v Parkes* [2004] EWCA Civ 1515 suggested that the contribution must be made at the time of purchase and that subsequent payments, such as mortgage payments, would not suffice. However, a direct contribution to the purchase price will not establish a trust if given by way of gift or loan. The successful claimant will be awarded a share to reflect the initial contribution made (contrast this with the position under constructive trusts (below) where, in the absence of any express agreement as to the size of the share, the court will decide what shares the parties intended by looking at their whole course of conduct in relation to the property). *Stack v Dowden* suggests that, in domestic cases of cohabitants, resulting trusts are no longer the appropriate approach, and that these cases should be decided under the principle of constructive trusts (see below). This was confirmed more recently in *Jones v Kernott* [2011] UKSC 53.

Constructive trusts

In *Lloyds Bank plc v Rosset* [1990] 2 WLR 867, [1990] 1 All ER 1111, the House of Lords considered the law in this area in detail, and the case contains a clear analysis of the circumstances where equity will impose a trust on the legal owner.

For a constructive trust to arise the claimant must show there was a common intention to share ownership and that the claimant acted in reliance on this to his detriment.

The common intention can be established by an express agreement. In *H v M (Property: Beneficial Interest)* [1992] 1 FLR 229, the parties lived together for 11 years, had two children, but never married. The assets included two bungalows in Essex and a property in Spain, all in the legal ownership of the man. The woman claimed a beneficial interest in the property. The court looked very closely at exactly what had been said by the parties as to how any assets would be divided. The man had said to the woman, 'Don't worry about the future because when we are married it will be half yours anyway and I'll always look after you and the boy'. The man also made an excuse that the property was in his name alone for 'tax reasons'. As on the facts there was an express common intention (his statements to her), the woman had to show only that she had acted on this to her detriment. The court accepted that her detrimental action was the execution of a mortgage deed by her 'as occupier' postponing any rights she might have to the lender, thus prejudicing her domestic security. On this basis, the court awarded her an equal share in the English property, but dismissed her claim for a share of the Spanish house as no similar conversation had taken place.

The court will generally find an agreement to create a trust from discussions in the course of which the legal owner gives an excuse why legal ownership is not to be shared. In *Eves v Eves* [1975] 1 WLR 1338, a man told the woman that the property was only in his name as she was under 21 years of age. Subsequently, she worked on various structural alterations to it. She was held to be entitled to a 25% share (see also *Grant v Edwards* [1986] Ch 638). However, in *Curran v Collins* [2015] EWCA Civ 404, the court said that such cases do not establish the proposition that the mere giving of a 'specious excuse' necessarily or even usually leads to an inference that the person to whom the excuse is given can reasonably regard herself as having an immediate entitlement to an interest in the property in question.

If there is no evidence of an express agreement, a common intention to share the property can be inferred from the parties' conduct. In *Lloyds Bank plc v Rosset* [1990] 2 WLR 867, [1990] 1 All ER 1111, Lord Bridge said that '... direct contributions to the purchase price by the partner who is not the legal owner, whether initially or by payment of mortgage instalments, will readily justify the inference necessary to the creation of a constructive trust. But as I read the authorities, it is at least extremely doubtful whether anything less will do.' So conduct such as payment of mortgage instalments and financial contributions to improvements to the property can be used to infer the common intention to share the property.

Contributions by labour may also count. In *Cooke v Head* [1972] 1 WLR 518, the woman non-legal owner made a small contribution to the mortgage payments as well as contributions by manual labour in helping to build a bungalow on land owned by the man. She was entitled to a one-third share for their 'joint efforts'. However, in the *Lloyds Bank* case (above) it was pointed out that a common intention by the parties to renovate a house as a joint venture did not throw any light on their intentions with respect to the beneficial ownership of the property. The work done by the wife in supervising and helping with work and decorating was not enough on its own in this case to justify the inference of a common intention to share.

Generally, contributions to household expenses other than the mortgage are much less likely to establish a trust. In *Burns v Burns* [1984] Ch 317, an unmarried couple with two children occupied for 17 years a house bought in the man's name. The woman made no contribution towards deposit or mortgage repayments, but fully performed the tasks expected of a wife and mother and, when able to return to work, was content to meet the household expenses out of her earnings. At no time did the man depend on her financial help. In that case, it was held that the necessary common intention could not be inferred from her natural concern with the well-being of the household. More recently, however, in *Le Foe v Le Foe and Woolwich plc; Woolwich plc v Le Foe and Le Foe* [2001] 2 FLR 970, the court decided that it was entitled to infer that the parties commonly intended that the wife should have a beneficial interest as a result of her indirect contributions to the mortgage.

However, in addition there must be detrimental reliance. The court appears to take a wide view of this, as illustrated above in *H v M*. Nevertheless, in *Midland Bank v Dobson and Dobson* [1986] 1 FLR 171, the performance by the woman of normal household duties and the purchase by her of household items were 'quite consistent with the man's absolute ownership of the house'. Unless followed by conduct of a sacrificial nature, the expression of intention was at best an unenforceable declaration of trust lacking the written evidence required by Law of Property Act 1925, s 53(1)(b).

Determining the size of the share

In *Jones v Kernott* [2011] UKSC 53, which was a case of jointly-owned property, the Court said that in situations where the property is in the sole name of one party, the first issue is to determine whether the other party has any beneficial interest in the property at all. If that is established then the court has to decide what that interest is. There is no presumption of joint beneficial ownership. The parties' common intention had to be deduced objectively from their conduct, but if this is not possible then the court will impute an intention to the parties, who will receive a share the court considers fair having regard to the whole course of dealing between them in relation to the property.

Proprietary estoppel

The doctrine of estoppel has been used to give rights of ownership: see *Pascoe v Turner* [1979] 1 WLR 431 (although remedies also include granting a licence to occupy (see **16.3.2**) or payment of money to the claimant, as in *Southwell v Blackburn* [2014] EWCA Civ 1347). Three elements are required:

(a)   an assurance of an interest in the property;

(b)   reliance on that assurance;

(c)   detriment suffered as a result.

In addition, the above three elements must exist to the extent that it would be unconscionable to deny the claimant relief.

Proprietary estoppel is wider and more flexible than a constructive trust, which requires common intention to be shown rather than just an assurance.

16.3.2   Occupation of home

If a non-legal owner does not have any beneficial interest in the property under the principles discussed above, he or she will have no right to remain there and may be excluded by the owner at any time on giving reasonable notice. However, in these circumstances the following ways of protecting the non-legal owner must be considered:

(a)   contractual licence;

(b)   licence by estoppel;

(c)   FLA 1996, Pt IV;

(d)   CA 1989, s 15 and Sch 1.

16.3.2.1   Contractual licence

It is necessary to establish the existence of a contract creating a licence. This means that a party will have to show that there was an intention to create legal relations, offer and acceptance, and consideration.

In *Tanner v Tanner* [1975] 3 All ER 776, a woman gave up a rent-controlled flat to occupy a house bought by the man, in which she brought up their children. The court found a licence for her to occupy the property did exist, which would last until the children grew up.

Each case must depend on the particular circumstances, and often the necessary elements for a contract will not be established (see *Coombes v Smith* [1986] 1 WLR 808).

16.3.2.2   Licence by estoppel

If there is insufficient evidence to establish a contract, the doctrine of estoppel has sometimes been invoked to give rise to rights of occupation rather than ownership.

Three elements are required:

(a)   assurance of the right to occupy;

(b)   reliance on that assurance;

(c)   detriment suffered as a result.

In *Greasley v Cooke* [1980] 3 All ER 710, the woman was engaged initially as a maid, but subsequently cohabited with the son of the family for 30 years. The woman looked after the children and was led to believe she could remain in the property for as long as she wished. The court held that an equity had been raised that could only be satisfied by allowing her to remain in the house for as long as she wished (see also *Maharaj v Chand* [1986] AC 898).

16.3.2.3 Family Law Act 1996

Provided the man and woman are cohabitants or former cohabitants, an unmarried partner may either obtain an order under the FLA 1996 to protect her and any children living with her from further violence from her partner, or, in certain circumstances, an order to remove her partner from the home (see **Chapter 15**).

Even if the FLA 1996 is used, it will provide only short-term protection, as the order will give no long-term right to remain in the home.

Reference should be made to the Housing Act 1996 (see **6.10**) to establish whether the local authority has any duty to provide alternative housing.

16.3.2.4 Children Act 1989, s 15 and Sch 1

An unmarried parent could apply on behalf of a child for financial orders from the other parent (see **13.10.4**). The orders that can be obtained include a property adjustment order or a settlement. It would be possible for a child to be granted a transfer of property order (which will include a tenancy), or a *Mesher* order to provide the child with a home until he is no longer dependent. The non-owning partner looking after the child would, therefore, be able to occupy the property as he would be looking after the child (see J v J (*A Minor: Property Transfer*) [1993] 2 FLR 56).

16.3.3 Sale of the property

If the property is jointly owned, or if it is established that a trust of land does exist by virtue of a resulting or constructive trust, one partner can apply to the court for an order to deal with any dispute. The most likely dispute is that one partner will want to sell the house and the other will wish to remain living there. The application will now be made under the TLATA 1996 (see **Appendix 1(H)**).

Sections 14 and 15 of the TLATA 1996 give the court wide powers to deal with any disputes concerning land subject to a trust. Section 14 gives the court power to make an order that reflects the underlying nature and purpose of the trust. Section 15 sets out the matters to which the court must have regard in determining any application for an order under s 14. They include:

(a) the intention of the person or persons who created the trust;

(b) the purpose for which the property subject to the trust is held;

(c) the welfare of any minor who occupies, or might reasonably be expected to occupy any trust property as his home; and

(d) the interests of any secured creditor (eg a mortgagee) of any beneficiary.

If the court finds that the home is still needed as a family home it will delay a sale. This could be until the children grow up. Even where there are no children, the court could postpone the sale of the house for a specified period, for example to give the occupier time to buy out the non-occupier, or until the occupier finds alternative accommodation. This will only be a postponement for a few months at the most.

The effect of the TLATA 1996 is to combine the old legal provisions in the Law of Property Act 1925, s 30 and the existing case law under that section (*Re Ever's Trust* [1980] 1 WLR 1327; *Bernard v Josephs* [1983] 4 FLR 178) to ensure that the court has broad and flexible powers.

If the client is in receipt of legal aid, the statutory charge will apply to proceedings under s 14 of the TLATA 1996 (see **2.9**). However, the Legal Services Commission has power, at its discretion, to postpone enforcement of the statutory charge in any case where the home is recovered or preserved under s 14 proceedings, or the proceedings result in the payment of a lump sum to the applicant which is to be used to purchase a home.

16.3.4 Tenancies

The FLA 1996 has altered the position of cohabitants in relation to certain tenancies. The basic position before the Act (which will still be the position if the FLA 1996 does not apply) is that if a tenancy is in the name of one partner, the other has no protection and will be a bare licensee who can be evicted on 'reasonable notice'. An occupation order may give protection under the FLA 1996 for a limited period (see **Chapter 15**). If the couple are joint tenants, both will be entitled to occupy the property. If one gives up occupation, the other's continued occupation ensures the continuance of the tenancy.

Schedule 7 to the FLA 1996 introduced for the first time the right, in some circumstances, for a cohabitant to obtain a tenancy transfer order in relation to certain tenancies. The right to apply for a transfer order will apply irrespective of whether the tenancy is held jointly by the couple or by one of them alone, and will only be available on separation where the tenancy was of a dwelling house the couple occupied together as husband and wife. The court's powers are available only in relation to tenancies specified in the Act, including protected and statutory tenancies within the Rent Act 1977, some agricultural tenancies, a secure tenancy (Housing Act 1985, s 79) and an assured tenancy (Housing Act 1988, Pt VII).

When deciding whether to make a tenancy transfer order the court must have regard to all the circumstances of the case, including the circumstances in which the tenancy was granted or in which either party became the tenant, similar factors to those relevant when granting occupation orders (see **Chapter 15**) and the suitability of the parties as tenants. Schedule 7 contains detailed provisions specifying the transfer orders that can be made, and also gives the court a discretion to award compensation to the transferor. Orders under Sch 7 take effect without the need for any further document transferring the tenancy. The power to transfer tenancies could, therefore, be used as an alternative to an occupation order.

16.4 CHILDREN

There is an increasing number of children born each year to parents who are not married to each other. This makes no difference to the day-to-day care of the child while they are cohabiting, but there are legal differences that will alter the legal position if the parents separate. This section looks at the differences in the legal position where a child's parents are not married.

16.4.1 Parental responsibility

Where the parents of a child are not married at the time of the child's birth, the mother will have sole parental responsibility for the child (CA 1989, s 2(2)(a) (see **Appendix 1(E)**)). The father will not have parental responsibility unless he acquires it in accordance with the provisions of the Act (see **13.2.2**). Strictly, only the mother will have the right to sign a form of consent to an operation, decide where the child should be educated, or appoint a guardian for the child if the father does not have parental responsibility.

Not having parental responsibility does not cut the father off completely, because the Act allows even a father without parental responsibility to apply for any s 8 order without leave, as he will come within the definition of 'parent' for the purposes of the Act. So, if he is unhappy about any aspect of the child's upbringing, he could apply for a specific issue order to determine the dispute with the mother. He could also apply for a child arrangements order, so the child could live with him. If his child is in care, he can apply for contact with the child (CA

1989, s 34). However, in any event he may still prefer formally to share parental responsibility. This could be reassuring for him if, for example, the child's mother has religious objections to blood transfusions, and parental responsibility will give him more rights if the child is taken into care or put up for adoption.

The ways in which an unmarried father can acquire parental responsibility for his child are examined in detail at **13.2.2.**

Also, in the case of children born to female same sex couples and conceived by IVF or artificial insemination at a licensed clinic, the Human Fertilisation and Embryology Act 2008 allows a mother to nominate her female partner as the 'parent' of the child in certain circumstances (see **13.2.3.3** above), which will enable the female 'parent' to obtain parental responsibility in similar ways to an unmarried father.

16.4.1.1 Human Rights Act 1998

The fact that some unmarried fathers (currently) have to apply for parental responsibility, unlike all mothers and married fathers, has not been found to violate their rights under the HRA 1998. In the Scottish case of *McMichael v UK* (1995) 20 EHRR 205, the child of unmarried parents was placed in care and then freed for adoption. The parents were denied access to essential documents and the mother brought a successful complaint under Article 6 of the ECHR. The father complained that, as an unmarried father without parental rights, he was discriminated against as he had no right to the legal custody of his son or to participate in the care proceedings. The European Court of Human Rights held that the relevant legislation, which distinguished between married and unmarried fathers, had the legitimate aim of providing a mechanism for identifying meritorious fathers. The conditions imposed on natural fathers for obtaining recognition of their parental rights were proportionate to that aim.

What is of perhaps greater concern is the fact that the court can remove parental responsibility from unmarried fathers but not from mothers or married fathers. In *Smallwood v UK* (1999) 2 EHRLR 221, a father whose contact order had been revoked then lost parental responsibility after the court considered that he would use it to disrupt the children. The father's application to the Commission was declared inadmissible on the basis that differences in treatment between married and unmarried men had an objective and reasonable justification. The Commission also said it was compatible with the Convention to have a system whereby the rights of unmarried fathers concerning care or custody over their children were more limited than those of the mother.

Removal of parental responsibility is clearly a serious interference with a father's right to family life under Article 8. Yet, on the basis of Convention cases, it seems likely that applications under the HRA 1998 may similarly fail on the basis that interference with this particular Convention right is justifiable and necessary.

In addition, there are other areas of potential disadvantage to unmarried fathers without parental responsibility where they may be able to argue a breach of Article 8 and Article 14 (the right not to be discriminated against in the delivery of Convention rights). For example, a child may not be removed from the jurisdiction without either the consent of everyone with parental responsibility or the leave of the court, which means that an unmarried father without parental responsibility has no right to object.

16.4.2 Financial provision and property orders

The ways of applying for maintenance and property orders for the benefit of children of unmarried parents are much more limited than those available for children of married parents (see **Chapter 13**). The two methods available are, first, to apply for maintenance using the CSA 1991 (this Act applies to all absent parents irrespective of their marital status) and, secondly, to apply under the CA 1989.

The CA 1989 expressly provides that a father's obligation to maintain his children does not depend on his having parental responsibility. The financial provisions contained in s 15 of and Sch 1 to the CA 1989 apply to both married and unmarried parents. The most useful provisions for an unmarried parent are those enabling lump sum orders and property transfer and settlement orders (see **13.10.4** and **16.3.2.4**).

16.5 BANKRUPTCY

A bankrupt's property vests in the trustee in bankruptcy. A partner remaining in the home may be a joint owner or have a beneficial interest. The trustee in bankruptcy can apply for an order for sale of the home and is likely to be successful. If the application for sale is made more than one year after the bankruptcy, the court must assume that the interests of the creditors outweigh all other considerations, unless the circumstances of the case are exceptional (see **9.9.1**).

16.6 DEATH

16.6.1 Ownership rights

If the home was jointly owned as beneficial joint tenants, on the death of one party the survivor will become the sole owner. If the home was jointly owned as beneficial tenants in common, the deceased's share will pass in accordance with his will, or under the intestacy rules. In both cases there are inheritance tax problems because, as the parties were not married, the spouse exemption does not apply.

The sole legal owner of the home may die without leaving it by will to the other partner. If the survivor wishes to obtain a share, he will either have to establish that he had a beneficial interest in the property, or successfully bring a claim under the I(PFD)A 1975 (see **16.6.3).** If the survivor is not successful, he will be a bare licensee. The licence can be terminated by the deceased's personal representatives on giving notice to the surviving partner.

If the survivor was the sole legal owner, there could still be complications if the deceased had a beneficial interest in the property that has passed by his will or on intestacy to someone other than the survivor.

16.6.2 Intestacy

The intestacy rules do not make any provision for an unmarried partner. However, any children of the couple will have rights on their parents' intestacy. It is therefore essential that an unmarried couple make wills.

16.6.3 Family provision

If the survivor can establish that, before the deceased's death, he was being maintained by the deceased, he is likely to be able to bring a claim under the I(PFD)A 1975 (see **Appendix 1(B)**). Periodical payments, lump sum and transfer or settlement of property orders can be made by the court.

A change to the I(PFD)A 1975 introduced by the Law Reform (Succession) Act 1995 extended the circumstances in which a claim can be made. It is possible for an unmarried cohabitee to claim financial provision out of the deceased partner's estate if he or she lived with the deceased as husband and wife throughout a period of two years prior to the death, irrespective of whether he or she was financially dependent upon the deceased. The CPA 2004 has extended this provision to include same sex partners. In addition to the common guidelines (I(PFD)A 1975, s 3) there are special guidelines for the court to consider in an application by an unmarried partner. The court must have regard to the age of the applicant, the length of the cohabitation with the deceased and the contributions made by the applicant to the welfare of the family of the deceased, including contributions made by looking after the home or caring for the family.

Despite these changes, an unmarried partner is still not treated as generously as a surviving spouse. First, the court can award an unmarried partner only such financial provision as it would be reasonable to receive for maintenance. A surviving spouse can be awarded such financial provision as it would be reasonable to receive whether or not the provision is required for maintenance. However, in the case of *Negus v Bahouse and Another* [2007] EWHC 2628 (Ch), the court awarded Ms Negus the transfer of a flat free of mortgage, plus a sum of £200,000 in addition to the £459,000 she had received from her former cohabitant's (the deceased's) pension policy and the half share of a flat in Spain he had left her. The court said that 'maintenance' did not mean just enough to enable a person to get by; lifestyle or 'tone' should be taken into account. Secondly, on an application by a spouse, the court will have regard to the provision that would have been awarded had the marriage ended with a divorce rather than with death. There is no similar provision for unmarried partners.

16.6.4 Pensions

Recent cases have ruled that refusal by a deceased's pension authority to pay the survivor of an unmarried cohabiting couple a share of their deceased partner's pension is discriminatory and unlawful in certain circumstances. In *Re an application by Denise Brewster for Judicial Review* [2017] UKSC 8, the Supreme Court was concerned with the position of a cohabitant in relation to her entitlement to her deceased partner's pension under the Local Government Pension Scheme (Benefits, Membership and Contributions) Regulations (Northern Ireland) 2009. The appellant and her partner had lived together for about 10 years before the partner died in December 2009. The pension administrators required a form of nomination for payment under the scheme to unmarried partners, but not for married partners, and in the absence of such a form refused payment. The appellant sought judicial review that this requirement was incompatible with Article 14 of the ECHR, and the Supreme Court found that the appellant was entitled to receive a survivor's pension under the scheme. There was no rational connection between the objective and the imposition of the nomination requirement, and it also failed to meet the test for justification for a difference in treatment.

16.6.5 Widowed parent's allowance and bereavement support payment

Payments of some benefits on death have been available to married couples only. However, in *Re an application by Siobhan McLaughlin for Judicial Review (Child Poverty Action Group and another intervening)* [2018] UKSC 48, the applicant and her partner had four children and had lived together for 23 years prior to his death. The appellant's claim for widowed parent's allowance under the Social Security Contributions and Benefits (Northern Ireland) Act 1992 was refused. The Supreme Court found that the relevant legislation was incompatible with Article 14, read in conjunction with Article 8 of the ECHR, as it was not a proportionate means of achieving the legitimate aim of privileging marriage to deny the appellant and her children the benefit of the deceased's contributions because they had not been married.

More recently, the case of *Jackson v Secretary of State for Work and Pensions* [2020] EWHC 183 (Admin) dealt with a claim for higher rate bereavement support payment (HRBSP), payable under s 30 of the Pensions Act 2014 which might be payable to the surviving parent if their spouse or civil partner died and there was one or more dependent child or children. However, it could not be paid to the surviving parent if their non-married cohabitee or non-civil partner died, no matter how long or settled the cohabitation. The court found that this was incompatible with Article 14 of the ECHR read with Article 8.

Following these cases, in July 2021, the Department for Work and Pensions published a draft proposal for a remedial order regarding widowed parent's allowance (WPA) and bereavement support payment (BSP), extending their coverage to cohabiting couples with dependent children. The draft order would have retroactive effect from 30 August 2018.

SUMMARY

(1)   When couples decide to cohabit the following issues should be clarified:

    (a)   how any property (especially the home) is owned as between the couple;

    (b)   life insurance cover;

    (c)   wills.

    The couple should be advised to enter into a cohabitation agreement.

(2)   When a cohabiting couple split up:

    (a)   neither party can claim maintenance from the other;

    (b)   maintenance for any children of the relationship can usually be claimed from the Child Maintenance Service;

    (c)   ownership of the home will be determined by land law principles and an order for sale may be obtained;

    (d)   occupation of the home may be obtained by establishing a contractual licence, or by obtaining a property order in favour of a child under the CA 1989 or, temporarily, by obtaining an occupation order under the FLA 1996;

    (e)   transfer of tenancy orders can be made in some circumstances under the FLA 1996;

    (f)   as regards children of an unmarried couple:

        (i)   mother has sole parental responsibility,

        (ii)   father can obtain parental responsibility;

    (g)   if partner is bankrupt, sale of home can be delayed only if there are dependent children, and then only for 12 months;

    (h)   if a cohabiting partner dies intestate there is no provision under the intestacy rules for the other partner to obtain any part of the estate. Any children of the couple will have a claim;

    (i)   the I(PFD)A 1975 may be available to a cohabiting partner.

(3)   There are various proposals for reform of the law relating to cohabiting couples.

APPENDICES

		Page
Appendix 1	**Legislation**	297
(A)	Matrimonial Causes Act 1973	297
(B)	Inheritance (Provision for Family and Dependants) Act 1975	315
(C)	Domestic Proceedings and Magistrates' Courts Act 1978	318
(D)	Child Abduction Act 1984	320
(E)	Children Act 1989	322
(F)	Child Support Act 1991	380
(G)	Family Law Act 1996	390
(H)	Trusts of Land and Appointment of Trustees Act 1996	407
(I)	Family Procedure Rules 2010	408
Appendix 2	**Code of Practice for Resolution Members**	435
Appendix 3	**Court Forms**	437
(A)	Divorce application	437
(B)	Form A (Application for a financial order)	453
(C)	Form E (Statement for a financial order)	469
(D)	Form D81 (Statement of information for a consent order)	497
(E)	Parental responsibility agreement (1)	503
(F)	Parental responsibility agreement (2)	505
(G)	Form C1 (Children Act application)	507
(H)	Form C100 (Application for a s 8 order)	517
(I)	Form C1A (Allegations of harm and domestic violence)	541
(J)	Form C110A (Application for a care or supervision order)	553
(K)	Form FL401 (Family Law Act application)	575

Appendix 1 – Legislation

(A)   Matrimonial Causes Act 1973

1   Divorce on breakdown of marriage

(1)   Subject to section 3 below, a petition for divorce may be presented to the court by either party to a marriage on the ground that the marriage has broken down irretrievably.

(2)   The court hearing a petition for divorce shall not hold the marriage to have broken down irretrievably unless the petitioner satisfies the court of one or more of the following facts, that is to say—

    (a)   that the respondent has committed adultery and the petitioner finds it intolerable to live with the respondent;

    (b)   that the respondent has behaved in such a way that the petitioner cannot reasonably be expected to live with the respondent;

    (c)   that the respondent has deserted the petitioner for a continuous period of at least two years immediately preceding the presentation of the petition;

    (d)   that the parties of the marriage have lived apart for a continuous period of at least two years immediately preceding the presentation of the petition (hereafter in this Act referred to as 'two years' separation') and the respondent consents to a decree being granted;

    (e)   that the parties to the marriage have lived apart for a continuous period of at least five years immediately preceding the presentation of the petition (hereafter in this Act referred to as 'five years' separation').

(3)   On a petition for divorce it shall be the duty of the court to inquire, so far as it reasonably can, into the facts alleged by the petitioner and into any facts alleged by the respondent.

(4)   If the court is satisfied on the evidence of any such fact as is mentioned in subsection (2) above, then, unless it is satisfied on all the evidence that the marriage has not broken down irretrievably, it shall, subject to section 5 below, grant a decree of divorce.

(5)   Every decree of divorce shall in the first instance be a decree nisi and shall not be made absolute before the expiration of six months from its grant unless the High Court by general order from time to time fixes a shorter period, or unless in any particular case the court in which the proceedings are for the time being pending from time to time by special order fixes a shorter period than the period otherwise applicable for the time being by virtue of this subsection.

(6)   Only conduct between the respondent and a person of the opposite sex may constitute adultery for the purposes of this section.

[(1)   Subject to section 3, either or both parties to a marriage may apply to the court for an order (a "divorce order") which dissolves the marriage on the ground that the marriage has broken down irretrievably.

(2)   An application under subsection (1) must be accompanied by a statement by the applicant or applicants that the marriage has broken down irretrievably.

(3)   The court dealing with an application under subsection (1) must—

    (a)   take the statement to be conclusive evidence that the marriage has broken down irretrievably, and

    (b)   make a divorce order.

(4)   A divorce order—

    (a)   is, in the first instance, a conditional order, and

    (b)   may not be made final before the end of the period of 6 weeks from the making of the conditional order.

(5)   The court may not make a conditional order unless—

    (a)   in the case of an application that is to proceed as an application by one party to the marriage only, that party has confirmed to the court that they wish the application to continue, or

    (b)   in the case of an application that is to proceed as an application by both parties to the marriage, those parties have confirmed to the court that they wish the application to continue;

and a party may not give confirmation for the purposes of this subsection before the end of the period of 20 weeks from the start of proceedings.

(6)   The Lord Chancellor may by order made by statutory instrument amend this section so as to shorten or lengthen the period for the purposes of subsection (4)(b) or (5).

(7)   But the Lord Chancellor may not under subsection (6) provide for a period which would result in the total number of days in the periods for the purposes of subsections (4)(b) and (5) (taken together) exceeding 26 weeks.

(8)   In a particular case the court dealing with the case may by order shorten the period that would otherwise be applicable for the purposes of subsection (4)(b) or (5).

(9)   A statutory instrument containing an order under subsection (6) may not be made unless a draft of the instrument has been laid before and approved by a resolution of each House of Parliament.

(10)   Without prejudice to the generality of section 75 of the Courts Act 2003, Family Procedure Rules may make provision as to the procedure for an application under subsection (1) by both parties to a marriage to become an application by one party to the marriage only (including provision for a statement made under subsection (2) in connection with the application to be treated as made by one party to the marriage only).]

Note. This section is substituted for specified purposes by the Divorce, Dissolution and Separation Act 2020, ss. 1, 8(3)(a), 8(4).

2   Supplemental provisions as to facts raising presumption of breakdown

(1)   One party to a marriage shall not be entitled to rely for the purposes of section 1(2)(a) above on adultery committed by the other if, after it became known to him that the other had committed that adultery, the parties have lived with each other for a period exceeding, or periods together exceeding, six months.

(2)   Where the parties to a marriage have lived with each other after it became known to one party that the other had committed adultery, but subsection (1) above does not apply, in any proceedings for divorce in which the petitioner relies on that adultery the fact that the parties have lived with each other after that time shall be disregarded in determining for the purposes of section 1(2)(a) above whether the petitioner finds it intolerable to live with the respondent.

(3)   Where in any proceedings for divorce the petitioner alleges that the respondent has behaved in such a way that the petitioner cannot reasonably be expected to live with him, but the parties to the marriage have lived with each other for a period or periods after the date of the occurrence of the final incident relied on by the petitioner and held by the court to support his allegation, that fact shall be disregarded in determining for the purposes of section 1(2)(b) above whether the petitioner cannot reasonably be expected to live with the respondent if the length of that period or of those periods together was six months or less.

(4)   For the purposes of section 1(2)(c) above the court may treat a period of desertion as having continued at a time when the deserting party was incapable of continuing the necessary intention if the evidence before the court is such that, had that party not been so incapable, the court would have inferred that his desertion continued at that time.

(5)   In considering for the purposes of section 1(2) above whether the period for which the respondent has deserted the petitioner or the period for which the parties to a marriage have lived apart has been continuous, no account shall be taken of any one period (not exceeding six months) or of any two or more periods (not exceeding six months in all) during which the parties resumed living with each other, but no period during which the parties lived with each other shall count as part of the period of desertion or of the period for which the parties to the marriage lived apart, as the case may be.

(6)   For the purposes of section 1(2)(d) and (e) above and this section a husband and wife shall be treated as living apart unless they are living with each other in the same household, and references in this section to the parties to a marriage living with each other shall be construed as references to their living with each other in the same household.

(7)   Provision shall be made by rules of court for the purpose of ensuring that where in pursuance of section 1(2)(d) above the petitioner alleges that the respondent consents to a decree being granted the respondent has been given such information as will enable him to understand the consequences to him of his consenting to a decree being granted and the steps which he must take to indicate that he consents to the grant of a decree.

3   Bar on petitions for divorce within one year of marriage

(1)   No petition for divorce shall be presented to the court before the expiration of the period of one year from the date of the marriage.

(2)   Nothing in this section shall prohibit the presentation of a petition based on matters which occurred before the expiration of that period.

5   Refusal of decree in five year separation cases on grounds of grave hardship to respondent

(1)   The respondent to a petition for divorce in which the petitioner alleges five years' separation may oppose the grant of a decree on the ground that the dissolution of the marriage will result in grave financial or other hardship to him and that it would in all the circumstances be wrong to dissolve the marriage.

(2)   Where the grant of a decree is opposed by virtue of this section, then—

(a)   if the court finds that the petitioner is entitled to rely in support of his petition on the fact of five years' separation and makes no such finding as to any other fact mentioned in section 1(2) above, and

(b)   if apart from this section the court would grant a decree on the petition,

the court shall consider all the circumstances, including the conduct of the parties to the marriage and the interests of those parties and of any children or other persons concerned, and if of opinion that the dissolution of the marriage will result in grave financial or other hardship to the respondent and that it would in all the circumstances be wrong to dissolve the marriage it shall dismiss the petition.

(3)   For the purposes of this section hardship shall include the loss of the chance of acquiring any benefit which the respondent might acquire if the marriage were not dissolved.

6   Attempts at reconciliation of parties to marriage

(1)   Provision shall be made by rules of court for requiring the legal representative acting for a petitioner for divorce to certify whether he has discussed with the petitioner the possibility of a reconciliation and given him the names and addresses of persons qualified to help effect a reconciliation between parties to a marriage who have become estranged.

(2)   If at any stage of proceedings for divorce it appears to the court that there is a reasonable possibility of a reconciliation between the parties to the marriage, the court may adjourn the proceedings for such period as it thinks fit to enable attempts to be made to effect such a reconciliation.

The power conferred by the foregoing provision is additional to any other power of the court to adjourn proceedings.

10   Proceedings after decree nisi: special protection for respondent in separation cases

(1)   Where in any case the court has granted a decree of divorce on the basis of a finding that the petitioner was entitled to rely in support of his petition on the fact of two years' separation coupled with the respondent's consent to a decree being granted and has made no such finding as to any other fact mentioned in section 1(2) above, the court may, on an application made by the respondent at any time before the decree is made absolute, rescind the decree if it is satisfied that the petitioner misled the respondent (whether intentionally or unintentionally) about any matter which the respondent took into account in deciding to give his consent.

(2)   The following provisions of this section apply where—

(a)   the respondent to a petition for divorce in which the petitioner alleged two years' or five years' separation coupled, in the former case, with the respondent's consent to a decree being granted, has applied to the court for consideration under subsection (3) below of his financial position after the divorce; and

(b)   the court has granted a decree on the petition on the basis of a finding that the petitioner was entitled to rely in support of his petition on the fact of two years' or five years' separation (as the case may be) and has made no such finding as to any other fact mentioned in section 1(2) above.

(3)   The court hearing an application by the respondent under subsection (2) above shall consider all the circumstances, including the age, health, conduct, earning capacity, financial resources and financial

obligations of each of the parties, and the financial position of the respondent as, having regard to the divorce, it is likely to be after the death of the petitioner should the petitioner die first; and, subject to subsection (4) below, the court shall not make the decree absolute unless it is satisfied—

    (a)   that the petitioner should not be required to make any financial provision for the respondent, or

    (b)   that the financial provision made by the petitioner for the respondent is reasonable and fair or the best that can be made in the circumstances.

(4)   The court may if it thinks fit make the decree absolute notwithstanding the requirements of subsection (3) above if—

    (a)   it appears that there are circumstances making it desirable that the decree should be made absolute without delay, and

    (b)   the court has obtained a satisfactory undertaking from the petitioner that he will make such financial provision for the respondent as the court may approve.

10A   Proceedings after decree nisi: religious marriage

(1)   This section applies if a decree of divorce has been granted but not made absolute and the parties to the marriage concerned -

    (a)   were married in accordance with—

        (i)   the usages of the Jews, or

        (ii)   any other prescribed religious usages; and

    (b)   must co-operate if the marriage is to be dissolved in accordance with those usages.

(2)   On the application of either party, the court may order that a decree of divorce is not to be made absolute until a declaration made by both parties that they have taken such steps as are required to dissolve the marriage in accordance with those usages is produced to the court.

(3)   An order under subsection (2)—

    (a)   may be made only if the court is satisfied that in all the circumstances of the case it is just and reasonable to do so; and

    (b)   may be revoked at any time.

(4)   A declaration of a kind mentioned in subsection (2)—

    (a)   must be in a specified form;

    (b)   must, in specified cases, be accompanied by such documents as may be specified; and

    (c)   must, in specified cases, satisfy such other requirements as may be specified.

(5)   The validity of a decree of divorce made by reference to such a declaration is not to be affected by any inaccuracy in that declaration.

(6)   'Prescribed' means prescribed in an order made by the Lord Chancellor after consulting the Lord Chief Justice and such an order—

    (a)   must be made by statutory instrument;

    (b)   shall be subject to annulment in pursuance of a resolution of either House of Parliament.

(7)   'Specified' means specified in rules of court.

(8)   The Lord Chief Justice may nominate a judicial office holder (as defined in section 109(4) of the Constitutional Reform Act 2005) to exercise his functions under this section.

17   Judicial separation

(1)   A petition for judicial separation may be presented to the court by either party to a marriage on the ground that any such fact as is mentioned in section 1(2) above exists, and the provisions of section 2 above shall apply accordingly for the purposes of a petition for judicial separation alleging any such fact, as they apply in relation to a petition for divorce alleging that fact.

(2)   On a petition for judicial separation it shall be the duty of the court to inquire, so far as it reasonably can, into the facts alleged by the petitioner and into any facts alleged by the respondent, but the court shall not be concerned to consider whether the marriage has broken down irretrievably, and if it is satisfied on the evidence of any such fact as is mentioned in section 1(2) above it shall ... grant a decree of judicial separation.

(3)   Sections 6 and 7 above shall apply for the purpose of encouraging the reconciliation of parties to proceedings for judicial separation and of enabling the parties to a marriage to refer to the court for its

opinion an agreement or arrangement relevant to actual or contemplated proceedings for judicial separation, as they apply in relation to proceedings for divorce.

18 Effects of judicial separation

(1) Where the court grants a decree of judicial separation it shall no longer be obligatory for the petitioner to cohabit with the respondent.

(2) If while a decree of judicial separation is in force and the separation is continuing either of the parties to the marriage dies intestate as respects all or any of his or her real or personal property, the property as respects which he or she died intestate shall devolve as if the other party to the marriage had then been dead.

(3) (Not reproduced)

22 Maintenance pending suit

(1) On a petition for divorce, nullity of marriage or judicial separation, the court may make an order for maintenance pending suit, that is to say, an order requiring either party to the marriage to make to the other such periodical payments for his or her maintenance and for such term, being a term beginning not earlier than the date of the presentation of the petition and ending with the date of the determination of the suit, as the court thinks reasonable.

(2) An order under this section may not require a party to a marriage to pay to the other party any amount in respect of legal services for the purposes of the proceedings.

(3) In subsection (2) 'legal services' has the same meaning as in section 22ZA.

23 Financial provision orders in connection with divorce proceedings etc

(1) On granting a decree of divorce, a decree of nullity of marriage or a decree of judicial separation or at any time thereafter (whether, in the case of a decree of divorce or of nullity of marriage, before or after the decree is made absolute), the court may make any one or more of the following orders, that is to say—

  (a) an order that either party to the marriage shall make to the other such periodical payments, for such term, as may be specified in the order;

  (b) an order that either party to the marriage shall secure to the other to the satisfaction of the court such periodical payments, for such term, as may be so specified;

  (c) an order that either party to the marriage shall pay to the other such lump sum or sums as may be so specified;

  (d) an order that a party to the marriage shall make to such person as may be specified in the order for the benefit of a child of the family, or to such a child, such periodical payments, for such term, as may be so specified;

  (e) an order that a party to the marriage shall secure to such person as may be so specified for the benefit of such a child, or to such a child, to the satisfaction of the court, such periodical payments, for such term, as may be so specified;

  (f) an order that a party to the marriage shall pay to such person as may be so specified for the benefit of such a child, or to such a child, such lump sum as may be so specified;

subject, however, in the case of an order under paragraph (d), (e) or (f) above, to the restrictions imposed by section 29(1) and (3) below on the making of financial provision orders in favour of children who have attained the age of eighteen.

(2) The court may also, subject to those restrictions, make any one or more of the orders mentioned in subsection (1)(d), (e) and (f) above—

  (a) in any proceedings for divorce, nullity of marriage or judicial separation, before granting a decree; and

  (b) where any such proceedings are dismissed after the beginning of the trial, either forthwith or within a reasonable period after the dismissal.

(3) Without prejudice to the generality of subsection (1)(c) or (f) above—

  (a) an order under this section that a party to a marriage shall pay a lump sum to the other party may be made for the purpose of enabling that other party to meet any liabilities or expenses reasonably incurred by him or her in maintaining himself or herself or any child of the family before making an application for an order under this section in his or her favour;

(b)   an order under this section for the payment of a lump sum to or for the benefit of a child of the family may be made for the purpose of enabling any liabilities or expenses reasonably incurred by or for the benefit of that child before the making of an application for an order under this section in his favour to be met; and

(c)   an order under this section for the payment of a lump sum may provide for the payment of that sum by instalments of such amount as may be specified in the order and may require the payment of the instalments to be secured to the satisfaction of the court.

(4)   The power of the court under subsection (1) or (2)(a) above to make an order in favour of a child of the family shall be exercisable from time to time; and where the court makes an order in favour of a child under subsection (2)(b) above, it may from time to time, subject to the restrictions mentioned in subsection (1) above, make a further order in his favour of any of the kinds mentioned in subsection (1)(d), (e) or (f) above.

(5)   Without prejudice to the power to give a direction under section 30 below for the settlement of an instrument by conveyancing counsel, where an order is made under subsection (1)(a), (b) or (c) above on or after granting a decree of divorce or nullity of marriage, neither the order nor any settlement made in pursuance of the order shall take effect unless the decree has been made absolute.

(6)   Where the court—

(a)   makes an order under this section for the payment of a lump sum; and

(b)   directs—

(i)   that payment of that sum or any part of it shall be deferred; or

(ii)   that the sum or any part of it shall be paid by instalments,

the court may order that the amount deferred or the instalments shall carry interest at such rate as may be specified by the order from such date, not earlier than the date of the order, as may be so specified, until the date when payment of it is due.

24   Property adjustment orders in connection with divorce proceedings etc

(1)   On granting a decree of divorce, a decree of nullity of marriage or a decree of judicial separation or at any time thereafter (whether, in the case of a decree of divorce or of nullity of marriage, before or after the decree is made absolute), the court may make any one or more of the following orders, that is to say—

(a)   an order that a party to the marriage shall transfer to the other party, to any child of the family or to such person as may be specified in the order for the benefit of such a child such property as may be so specified, being property to which the first-mentioned party is entitled, either in possession or reversion;

(b)   an order that a settlement of such property as may be so specified, being property to which a party to the marriage is so entitled, be made to the satisfaction of the court for the benefit of the other party to the marriage and of the children of the family or either or any of them;

(c)   an order varying for the benefit of the parties to the marriage and of the children of the family or either or any of them any ante-nuptial or post-nuptial settlement (including such a settlement made by will or codicil) made on the parties to the marriage, other than one in the form of a pension arrangement (within the meaning of section 25D below);

(d)   an order extinguishing or reducing the interest of either of the parties to the marriage under any such settlement, other than one in the form of a pension arrangement (within the meaning of section 25D below);

subject, however, in the case of an order under paragraph (a) above, to the restrictions imposed by section 29(1) and (3) below on the making of orders for a transfer of property in favour of children who have attained the age of eighteen.

(2)   The court may make an order under subsection (1)(c) above notwithstanding that there are no children of the family.

(3)   Without prejudice to the power to give a direction under section 30 below for the settlement of an instrument by conveyancing counsel, where an order is made under this section on or after granting a decree of divorce or nullity of marriage, neither the order nor any settlement made in pursuance of the order shall take effect unless the decree has been made absolute.

24A   Orders for sale of property

(1)   Where the court makes an order under section 22ZA or makes under section 23 or 24 of this Act a secured periodical payments order, an order for the payment of a lump sum or a property adjustment order, then, on making that order or at any time thereafter, the court may make a further order for the sale of such property as may be specified in the order, being property in which or in the proceeds of sale of which either or both of the parties to the marriage has or have a beneficial interest, either in possession or reversion.

(2)   Any order made under subsection (1) above may contain such consequential or supplementary provisions as the court thinks fit and, without prejudice to the generality of the foregoing provision, may include—

    (a)   provision requiring the making of a payment out of the proceeds of sale of the property to which the order relates, and

    (b)   provision requiring any such property to be offered for sale to a person, or class of persons, specified in the order.

(3)   Where an order is made under subsection (1) above on or after the grant of a decree of divorce or nullity of marriage, the order shall not take effect unless the decree has been made absolute.

(4)   Where an order is made under subsection (1) above, the court may direct that the order, or such provision thereof as the court may specify, shall not take effect until the occurrence of an event specified by the court or the expiration of a period so specified.

(5)   Where an order under subsection (1) above contains a provision requiring the proceeds of sale of the property to which the order relates to be used to secure periodical payments to a party to the marriage, the order shall cease to have effect on the death or re-marriage of, or formation of a civil partnership by, that person.

(6)   Where a party to a marriage has a beneficial interest in any property, or in the proceeds of sale thereof, and some other person who is not a party to the marriage also has a beneficial interest in that property or in the proceeds of sale thereof, then, before deciding whether to make an order under this section in relation to that property, it shall be the duty of the court to give that other person an opportunity to make representations with respect to the order; and any representations made by that other person shall be included among the circumstances to which the court is required to have regard under section 25(1) below.

24B   Pension sharing orders in connection with divorce proceedings etc

(1)   On granting a decree of divorce or a decree of nullity of marriage or at any time thereafter (whether before or after the decree is made absolute), the court may, on an application made under this section, make one or more pension sharing orders in relation to the marriage.

(2)   A pension sharing order under this section is not to take effect unless the decree on or after which it is made has been made absolute.

(3)   A pension sharing order under this section may not be made in relation to a pension arrangement which—

    (a)   is the subject of a pension sharing order in relation to the marriage, or

    (b)   has been the subject of pension sharing between the parties to the marriage.

(4)   A pension sharing order under this section may not be made in relation to shareable state scheme rights if—

    (a)   such rights are the subject of a pension sharing order in relation to the marriage, or

    (b)   such rights have been the subject of pension sharing between the parties to the marriage.

(5)   A pension sharing order under this section may not be made in relation to the rights of a person under a pension arrangement if there is in force a requirement imposed by virtue of section 25B or 25C below which relates to benefits or future benefits to which he is entitled under the pension arrangement.

24C   Pension sharing orders: duty to stay

(1)   No pension sharing order may be made so as to take effect before the end of such period after the making of the order as may be prescribed by regulations made by the Lord Chancellor.

(2)   The power to make regulations under this section shall be exercisable by statutory instrument which shall be subject to annulment in pursuance of a resolution of either House of Parliament.

24D   Pension sharing orders: apportionment of charges

If a pension sharing order relates to rights under a pension arrangement, the court may include in the order provision about the apportionment between the parties of any charge under section 41 of the Welfare Reform and Pensions Act 1999 (charges in respect of pension sharing costs), or under corresponding Northern Ireland legislation.

25   Matters to which court is to have regard in deciding how to exercise its powers under ss 23, 24, 24A, 24B and 24E

(1)   It shall be the duty of the court in deciding whether to exercise its powers under section 23, 24, 24A, 24B or 24E above and, if so, in what manner, to have regard to all the circumstances of the case, first consideration being given to the welfare while a minor of any child of the family who has not attained the age of eighteen.

(2)   As regards the exercise of the powers of the court under section 23(1)(a), (b) or (c), 24, 24A, 24B or 24E above in relation to a party to the marriage, the court shall in particular have regard to the following matters—

(a)   the income, earning capacity, property and other financial resources which each of the parties to the marriage has or is likely to have in the foreseeable future, including in the case of earning capacity any increase in that capacity which it would in the opinion of the court be reasonable to expect a party to the marriage to take steps to acquire;

(b)   the financial needs, obligations and responsibilities which each of the parties to the marriage has or is likely to have in the foreseeable future;

(c)   the standard of living enjoyed by the family before the breakdown of the marriage;

(d)   the age of each party to the marriage and the duration of the marriage;

(e)   any physical or mental disability of either of the parties to the marriage;

(f)   the contributions which each of the parties has made or is likely in the foreseeable future to make to the welfare of the family, including any contribution by looking after the home or caring for the family;

(g)   the conduct of each of the parties, if that conduct is such that it would in the opinion of the court be inequitable to disregard it;

(h)   in the case of proceedings for divorce or nullity of marriage, the value to each of the parties to the marriage of any benefit ... which, by reason of the dissolution or annulment of the marriage, that party will lose the chance of acquiring.

(3)   As regards the exercise of the powers of the court under section 23(1)(d), (e) or (f), (2) or (4), 24 or 24A above in relation to a child of the family, the court shall in particular have regard to the following matters—

(a)   the financial needs of the child;

(b)   the income, earning capacity (if any), property and other financial resources of the child;

(c)   any physical or mental disability of the child;

(d)   the manner in which he was being and in which the parties to the marriage expected him to be educated or trained;

(e)   the considerations mentioned in relation to the parties to the marriage in paragraphs (a), (b), (c) and (e) of subsection (2) above.

(4)   As regards the exercise of the powers of the court under section 23(1)(d), (e) or (f), (2) or (4), 24 or 24A above against a party to a marriage in favour of a child of the family who is not the child of that party, the court shall also have regard—

(a)   to whether that party assumed any responsibility for the child's maintenance, and, if so, to the extent to which, and the basis upon which, that party assumed such responsibility and to the length of time for which that party discharged such responsibility;

(b)   to whether in assuming and discharging such responsibility that party did so knowing that the child was not his or her own;

(c)   to the liability of any other person to maintain the child.

25A   Exercise of court's powers in favour of party to marriage on decree of divorce or nullity of marriage

(1)   Where on or after the grant of a decree of divorce or nullity of marriage the court decides to exercise its powers under section 23(1)(a), (b) or (c), 24, 24A, 24B or 24E above in favour of a party to the marriage, it shall be the duty of the court to consider whether it would be appropriate so to exercise those powers that the financial obligations of each party towards the other will be terminated as soon after the grant of the decree as the court considers just and reasonable.

(2)   Where the court decides in such a case to make a periodical payments or secured periodical payments order in favour of a party to the marriage, the court shall in particular consider whether it would be appropriate to require those payments to be made or secured only for such term as would in the opinion of the court be sufficient to enable the party in whose favour the order is made to adjust without undue hardship to the termination of his or her financial dependence on the other party.

(3)   Where on or after the grant of a decree of divorce or nullity of marriage an application is made by a party to the marriage for a periodical payments or secured periodical payments order in his or her favour, then, if the court considers that no continuing obligation should be imposed on either party to make or secure periodical payments in favour of the other, the court may dismiss the application with a direction that the applicant shall not be entitled to make any future application in relation to that marriage for an order under section 23(1)(a) or (b) above.

25B   Pensions

(1)   The matters to which the court is to have regard under section 25(2) above include—

   (a)   in the case of paragraph (a), any benefits under a pension arrangement which a party to the marriage has or is likely to have, and

   (b)   in the case of paragraph (h), any benefits under a pension arrangement which, by reason of the dissolution or annulment of the marriage, a party to the marriage will lose the chance of acquiring,

and, accordingly, in relation to benefits under a pension arrangement, section 25(2)(a) above shall have effect as if 'in the foreseeable future' were omitted.

(2)   ...

(3)   The following provisions apply where, having regard to any benefits under a pension arrangement, the court determines to make an order under section 23 above.

(4)   To the extent to which the order is made having regard to any benefits under a pension arrangement, the order may require the person responsible for the pension arrangement in question, if at any time any payment in respect of any benefits under the arrangement becomes due to the party with pension rights, to make a payment for the benefit of the other party.

(5)   The order must express the amount of any payment required to be made by virtue of subsection (4) above as a percentage of the payment which becomes due to the party with pension rights.

(6)   Any such payment by the person responsible for the arrangement—

   (a)   shall discharge so much of his liability to the party with pension rights as corresponds to the amount of the payment, and

   (b)   shall be treated for all purposes as a payment made by the party with pension rights in or towards the discharge of his liability under the order.

(7)   Where the party with pension rights has a right of commutation under the arrangement, the order may require him to exercise it to any extent; and this section applies to any payment due in consequence of commutation in pursuance of the order as it applies to other payments in respect of benefits under the arrangement.

(7A)   The power conferred by subsection (7) above may not be exercised for the purpose of commuting a benefit payable to the party with pension rights to a benefit payable to the other party.

(7B)   The power conferred by subsection (4) or (7) above may not be exercised in relation to a pension arrangement which—

   (a)   is the subject of a pension sharing order in relation to the marriage, or

   (b)   has been the subject of pension sharing between the parties to the marriage.

(7C)   In subsection (1) above, references to benefits under a pension arrangement include any benefits by way of pension, whether under a pension arrangement or not.

25C   Pensions: lump sums

(1)   The power of the court under section 23 above to order a party to a marriage to pay a lump sum to the other party includes, where the benefits which the party with pension rights has or is likely to have under a pension arrangement include any lump sum payable in respect of his death, power to make any of the following provision by the order.

(2)   The court may—

    (a)   if the person responsible for the pension arrangement in question has power to determine the person to whom the sum, or any part of it, is to be paid, require him to pay the whole or part of that sum, when it becomes due, to the other party,

    (b)   if the party with pension rights has power to nominate the person to whom the sum, or any part of it, is to be paid, require the party with pension rights to nominate the other party in respect of the whole or part of that sum,

    (c)   in any other case, require the person responsible for the pension arrangement in question to pay the whole or part of that sum, when it becomes due, for the benefit of the other party instead of to the person to whom, apart from the order, it would be paid.

(3)   Any payment by the person responsible for the arrangement under an order made under section 23 above by virtue of this section shall discharge so much of his liability in respect of the party with pension rights as corresponds to the amount of the payment.

(4)   The powers conferred by this section may not be exercised in relation to a pension arrangement which—

    (a)   is the subject of a pension sharing order in relation to the marriage, or

    (b)   has been the subject of pension sharing between the parties to the marriage.

27   Financial provision orders etc in case of neglect by party to marriage to maintain other party or child of the family

(1)   Either party to a marriage may apply to the court for an order under this section on the ground that the other party to the marriage (in this section referred to as the respondent)—

    (a)   has failed to provide reasonable maintenance for the applicant, or

    (b)   has failed to provide, or to make a proper contribution towards, reasonable maintenance for any child of the family.

(2)   The court may not entertain an application under this section unless—

    (a)   the applicant or the respondent is domiciled in England and Wales on the date of the application;

    (b)   the applicant has been habitually resident there throughout the period of one year ending with that date; or

    (c)   the respondent is resident there on that date.

(2A)   If the application or part of it relates to a matter in relation to which Article 18 of the 2007 Hague Convention applies, the court may not entertain that application or part of it except where permitted by Article 18.

(2B)   In subsection (2A), "the 2007 Hague Convention" means the Convention on the International Recovery of Child Support and Other Forms of Family Maintenance concluded on 23 November 2007 at The Hague.

(3)   Where an application under this section is made on the ground mentioned in subsection (1)(a) above then, in deciding—

    (a)   whether the respondent has failed to provide reasonable maintenance for the applicant, and

    (b)   what order, if any, to make under this section in favour of the applicant,

the court shall have regard to all the circumstances of the case including the matters mentioned in section 25(2) above, and where an application is also made under this section in respect of a child of the family who has not attained the age of eighteen, first consideration shall be given to the welfare of the child while a minor.

(3A)   Where an application under this section is made on the ground mentioned in subsection (1)(b) above then, in deciding—

(a)   whether the respondent has failed to provide, or to make a proper contribution towards, reasonable maintenance for the child of the family to whom the application relates, and

(b)   what order, if any, to make under this section in favour of the child,

the court shall have regard to all the circumstances of the case including the matters mentioned in section 25(3)(a) to (e) above, and where the child of the family to whom the application relates is not the child of the respondent, including also the matters mentioned in section 25(4) above.

(3B)   In relation to an application under this section on the ground mentioned in subsection (1)(a) above, section 25(2)(c) above shall have effect as if for the reference therein to the breakdown of the marriage there were substituted a reference to the failure to provide reasonable maintenance for the applicant, and in relation to an application under this section on the ground mentioned in subsection (1)(b) above, section 25(2)(c) above (as it applies by virtue of section 25(3)(e) above) shall have effect as if for the reference therein to the breakdown of the marriage there were substituted a reference to the failure to provide, or to make a proper contribution towards, reasonable maintenance for the child of the family to whom the application relates.

(4)   ...

(5)   Where on an application under this section it appears to the court that the applicant or any child of the family to whom the application relates is in immediate need of financial assistance, but it is not yet possible to determine what order, if any, should be made on the application, the court may make an interim order for maintenance, that is to say, an order requiring the respondent to make to the applicant until the determination of the application such periodical payments as the court thinks reasonable.

(6)   Where on an application under this section the applicant satisfies the court of any ground mentioned in subsection (1) above, the court may make any one or more of the following orders, that is to say—

(a)   an order that the respondent shall make to the applicant such periodical payments, for such term, as may be specified in the order;

(b)   an order that the respondent shall secure to the applicant, to the satisfaction of the court, such periodical payments, for such term, as may be so specified;

(c)   an order that the respondent shall pay to the applicant such lump sum as may be so specified;

(d)   an order that the respondent shall make to such person as may be specified in the order for the benefit of the child to whom the application relates, or to that child, such periodical payments, for such term, as may be so specified;

(e)   an order that the respondent shall secure to such person as may be so specified for the benefit of that child, or to that child, to the satisfaction of the court, such periodical payments, for such term, as may be so specified;

(f)   an order that the respondent shall pay to such person as may be so specified for the benefit of that child, or to that child, such lump sum as may be so specified;

subject, however, in the case of an order under paragraph (d), (e) or (f) above, to the restrictions imposed by section 29(1) and (3) below on the making of financial provision orders in favour of children who have attained the age of eighteen.

(6A)   An application for the variation under section 31 of this Act of a periodical payments order or secured periodical payments order made under this section in favour of a child may, if the child has attained the age of sixteen, be made by the child himself.

(6B)   Where a periodical payments order made in favour of a child under this section ceases to have effect on the date on which the child attains the age of sixteen or at any time after that date but before or on the date on which he attains the age of eighteen, then, if, on an application made to the court for an order under this subsection, it appears to the court that—

(a)   the child is, will be or (if an order were made under this subsection) would be receiving instruction at an educational establishment or undergoing training for a trade, profession or vocation, whether or not he also is, will be or would be in gainful employment; or

(b)   there are special circumstances which justify the making of an order under this subsection,

the court shall have power by order to revive the first-mentioned order from such date as the court may specify, not being earlier than the date of the making of the application, and to exercise its powers under section 31 of this Act in relation to any order so revived.

(7)   Without prejudice to the generality of subsection (6)(c) or (f) above, an order under this section for the payment of a lump sum—

(a)   may be made for the purpose of enabling any liabilities or expenses reasonably incurred in maintaining the applicant or any child of the family to whom the application relates before the making of the application to be met;

(b)   may provide for the payment of that sum by instalments of such amount as may be specified in the order and may require the payment of the instalments to be secured to the satisfaction of the court.

(8)   ...

28   Duration of continuing financial provision orders in favour of party to marriage, and effect of remarriage or formation of civil partnership

(1)   Subject in the case of an order made on or after the grant of a decree of a divorce or nullity of marriage to the provisions of sections 25A(2) above and 31(7) below, the term to be specified in a periodical payments or secured periodical payments order in favour of a party to a marriage shall be such term as the court thinks fit, except that the term shall not begin before or extend beyond the following limits, that is to say—

(a)   in the case of a periodical payments order, the term shall begin not earlier than the date of the making of an application for the order, and shall be so defined as not to extend beyond the death of either of the parties to the marriage or, where the order is made on or after the grant of a decree of divorce or nullity of marriage, the remarriage of, or formation of a civil partnership by, the party in whose favour the order is made; and

(b)   in the case of a secured periodical payments order, the term shall begin not earlier than the date of the making of an application for the order, and shall be so defined as not to extend beyond the death or, where the order is made on or after the grant of such a decree, the remarriage of the party, or formation of a civil partnership by, in whose favour the order is made.

(1A)   Where a periodical payments or secured periodical payments order in favour of a party to a marriage is made on or after the grant of a decree of divorce or nullity of marriage, the court may direct that that party shall not be entitled to apply under section 31 below for the extension of the term specified in the order.

(2)   Where a periodical payments or secured periodical payments order in favour of a party to a marriage is made otherwise than on or after the grant of a decree of divorce or nullity of marriage, and the marriage in question is subsequently dissolved or annulled but the order continues in force, the order shall, notwithstanding anything in it, cease to have effect on the remarriage of, or formation of the civil partnership by, that party, except in relation to any arrears due under it on the date of the remarriage or formation of the civil partnership.

(3)   If after the grant of a decree dissolving or annulling a marriage either party to that marriage remarries whether at any time before or after the commencement of this Act or forms a civil partnership, that party shall not be entitled to apply, by reference to the grant of that decree, for a financial provision order in his or her favour, or for a property adjustment order, against the other party to that marriage.

29   Duration of continuing financial provision orders in favour of children, and age limit on making certain orders in their favour

(1)   Subject to subsection (3) below, no financial provision order and no order for a transfer of property under section 24(1)(a) above shall be made in favour of a child who has attained the age of eighteen.

(2)   The term to be specified in a periodical payments or secured periodical payments order in favour of a child may begin with the date of the making of an application for the order in question or any later date or a date ascertained in accordance with subsection (5) or (6) below but—

(a)   shall not in the first instance extend beyond the date of the birthday of the child next following his attaining the upper limit of the compulsory school age (construed in accordance with section 8 of the Education Act 1996) unless the court considers that in the circumstances of the case the welfare of the child requires that it should extend to a later date; and

(b)   shall not in any event, subject to subsection (3) below, extend beyond the date of the child's eighteenth birthday.

(3)   Subsection (1) above, and paragraph (b) of subsection (2), shall not apply in the case of a child, if it appears to the court that—

    (a)   the child is, or will be, or if an order were made without complying with either or both of those provisions would be, receiving instruction at an educational establishment or undergoing training for a trade, profession or vocation, whether or not he is also, or will also be, in gainful employment; or

    (b)   there are special circumstances which justify the making of an order without complying with either or both of those provisions.

(4)   Any periodical payments order in favour of a child shall, notwithstanding anything in the order, cease to have effect on the death of the person liable to make payments under the order, except in relation to any arrears due under the order on the date of the death.

(5)   Where—

    (a)   a maintenance calculation ('the current calculation') is in force with respect to a child; and

    (b)   an application is made under Part II of this Act for a periodical payments or secured periodical payments order in favour of that child—

        (i)   in accordance with section 8 of the Child Support Act 1991, and

        (ii)   before the end of the period of 6 months beginning with the making of the current calculation,

    the term to be specified in any such order made on that application may be expressed to begin on, or at any time after, the earliest permitted date.

(6)   For the purposes of subsection (5) above, 'the earliest permitted date' is whichever is the later of—

    (a)   the date 6 months before the application is made; or

    (b)   the date on which the current calculation took effect or, where successive maintenance calculations have been continuously in force with respect to a child, on which the first of those calculations took effect.

(7)   Where—

    (a)   a maintenance calculation ceases to have effect ... by or under any provision of the Child Support Act 1991; and

    (b)   an application is made, before the end of the period of 6 months beginning with the relevant date, for a periodical payments or secured periodical payments order in favour of a child with respect to whom that maintenance calculation was in force immediately before it ceased to have effect,

    the term to be specified in any such order made on that application may begin with the date on which that maintenance calculation ceased to have effect, ... or any later date.

(8)   In subsection (7)(b) above—

    (a)   where the maintenance calculation ceased to have effect, the relevant date is the date on which it so ceased;

    (b)   ...

30 Direction for settlement of instrument for securing payments or effecting property adjustment

Where the court decides to make a financial provision order requiring any payments to be secured or a property adjustment order—

(a)   it may direct that the matter be referred to one of the conveyancing counsel of the court for him to settle a proper instrument to be executed by all necessary parties; and

(b)   where the order is to be made in proceedings for divorce, nullity of marriage or judicial separation it may, if it thinks fit, defer the grant of the decree in question until the instrument has been duly executed.

31 Variation, discharge etc of certain orders for financial relief

(1)   Where the court has made an order to which this section applies, then, subject to the provisions of this section and of section 28(1A) above, the court shall have power to vary or discharge the order or to suspend any provision thereof temporarily and to revive the operation of any provision so suspended.

(2)   This section applies to the following orders, that is to say—

    (a)   any order for maintenance pending suit and any interim order for maintenance;

    (b)   any periodical payments order;

    (c)   any secured periodical payments order;

    (d)   any order made by virtue of section 23(3)(c) or 27(7)(b) above (provision for payment of a lump sum by instalments);

    (dd)   any deferred order made by virtue of section 23(1)(c) (lump sums) which includes provision made by virtue of—

        (i)   section 25B(4), ...

        (ii)   section 25C, or

        (iii)   section 25F(2),

        (provision in respect of pension rights or pension compensation rights);

    (e)   any order for a settlement of property under section 24(1)(b) or for a variation of settlement under section 24(1)(c) or (d) above, being an order made on or after the grant of a decree of judicial separation;

    (f)   any order made under section 24A(1) above for the sale of property.

    (g)   a pension sharing order under section 24B above, or a pension compensation sharing order under section 24E above, which is made at a time before the decree has been made absolute.

(2A)   Where the court has made an order referred to in subsection (2)(a), (b) or (c) above, then, subject to the provisions of this section, the court shall have power to remit the payment of any arrears due under the order or of any part thereof.

(2B)   Where the court has made an order referred to in subsection (2)(dd)(ii) above, this section shall cease to apply to the order on the death of either of the parties to the marriage.

(3)   The powers exercisable by the court under this section in relation to an order shall be exercisable also in relation to any instrument executed in pursuance of the order.

(4)   The court shall not exercise the powers conferred by this section in relation to an order for a settlement under section 24(1)(b) or for a variation of settlement under section 24(1)(c) or (d) above except on an application made in proceedings—

    (a)   for the rescission of the decree of judicial separation by reference to which the order was made, or

    (b)   for the dissolution of the marriage in question.

(4A)   In relation to an order which falls within paragraph (g) of subsection (2) above ('the subsection (2) order')—

    (a)   the powers conferred by this section may be exercised—

        (i)   only on an application made before the subsection (2) order has or, but for paragraph (b) below, would have taken effect; and

        (ii)   only if, at the time when the application is made, the decree has not been made absolute; and

    (b)   an application made in accordance with paragraph (a) above prevents the subsection (2) order from taking effect before the application has been dealt with.

(4B)   No variation of a pension sharing order, or a pension compensation sharing order, shall be made so as to take effect before the decree is made absolute.

(4C)   The variation of a pension sharing order, or a pension compensation sharing order, prevents the order taking effect before the end of such period after the making of the variation as may be prescribed by regulations made by the Lord Chancellor.

(5)   Subject to subsections (7A) to (7G) below and without prejudice to any power exercisable by virtue of subsection (2)(d), (dd), (e) or (g) above or otherwise than by virtue of this section, no property adjustment order or pension sharing order or a pension compensation sharing order shall be made on an application for the variation of a periodical payments or secured periodical payments order made (whether in favour of a party to a marriage or in favour of a child of the family) under section 23 above, and no order for the payment of a lump sum shall be made on an application for the variation of a periodical payments or secured periodical payments order in favour of a party to a marriage (whether made under section 23 or under section 27 above).

(6)   Where the person liable to make payments under a secured periodical payments order has died, an application under this section relating to that order (and to any order made under section 24A(1) above which requires the proceeds of sale of property to be used for securing those payments) may be made

by the person entitled to payments under the periodical payments order or by the personal representatives of the deceased person, but no such application shall, except with the permission of the court, be made after the end of the period of six months from the date on which representation in regard to the estate of that person is first taken out.

(7)   In exercising the powers conferred by this section the court shall have regard to all the circumstances of the case, first consideration being given to the welfare while a minor of any child of the family who has not attained the age of eighteen, and the circumstances of the case shall include any change in any of the matters to which the court was required to have regard when making the order to which the application relates, and—

    (a)   in the case of a periodical payments or secured periodical payments order made on or after the grant of a decree of divorce or nullity of marriage, the court shall consider whether in all the circumstances and after having regard to any such change it would be appropriate to vary the order so that payments under the order are required to be made or secured only for such further period as will in the opinion of the court be sufficient (in the light of any proposed exercise by the court, where the marriage has been dissolved, of its powers under subsection (7B) below) to enable the party in whose favour the order was made to adjust without undue hardship to the termination of those payments;

    (b)   in a case where the party against whom the order was made has died, the circumstances of the case shall also include the changed circumstances resulting from his or her death.

(7A)   Subsection (7B) below applies where, after the dissolution of a marriage, the court—

    (a)   discharges a periodical payments order or secured periodical payments order made in favour of a party to the marriage; or

    (b)   varies such an order so that payments under the order are required to be made or secured only for such further period as is determined by the court.

(7B)   The court has power, in addition to any power it has apart from this subsection, to make supplemental provision consisting of any of—

    (a)   an order for the payment of a lump sum in favour of a party to the marriage;

    (b)   one or more property adjustment orders in favour of a party to the marriage;

    (ba)   one or more pension sharing orders;

    (bb)   a pension compensation sharing order;

    (c)   a direction that the party in whose favour the original order discharged or varied was made is not entitled to make any further application for—

        (i)   a periodical payments or secured periodical payments order, or

        (ii)   an extension of the period to which the original order is limited by any variation made by the court.

(7C)   An order for the payment of a lump sum made under subsection (7B) above may—

    (a)   provide for the payment of that sum by instalments of such amount as may be specified in the order; and

    (b)   require the payment of the instalments to be secured to the satisfaction of the court.

(7D)   Section 23(6) above applies where the court makes an order for the payment of a lump sum under subsection (7B) above as it applies where the court makes such an order under section 23 above.

(7E)   If under subsection (7B) above the court makes more than one property adjustment order in favour of the same party to the marriage, each of those orders must fall within a different paragraph of section 21(2) above.

(7F)   Sections 24A and 30 above apply where the court makes a property adjustment order under subsection (7B) above as they apply where it makes such an order under section 24 above.

(7G)   Subsections (3) to (5) of section 24B above apply in relation to a pension sharing order under subsection (7B) above as they apply in relation to a pension sharing order under that section.

(7H)   Subsections (3) to (10) of section 24E above apply in relation to a pension compensation sharing order under subsection (7B) above as they apply in relation to a pension compensation sharing order under that section.

(8)   The personal representatives of a deceased person against whom a secured periodical payments order was made shall not be liable for having distributed any part of the estate of the deceased after the expiration of the period of six months referred to in subsection (6) above on the ground that they ought

to have taken into account the possibility that the court might permit an application under this section to be made after that period by the person entitled to payments under the order; but this subsection shall not prejudice any power to recover any part of the estate so distributed arising by virtue of the making of an order in pursuance of this section.

(9)   The following are to be left out of account when considering for the purposes of subsection (6) above when representation was first taken out—

(a)   a grant limited to settled land or to trust property,

(b)   any other grant that does not permit any of the estate to be distributed,

(c)   a grant limited to real estate or to personal estate, unless a grant limited to the remainder of the estate has previously been made or is made at the same time,

(d)   a grant, or its equivalent, made outside the United Kingdom (but see subsection (9A) below).

...

(10)   Where the court, in exercise of its powers under this section, decides to vary or discharge a periodical payments or secured periodical payments order, then, subject to section 28(1) and (2) above, the court shall have power to direct that the variation or discharge shall not take effect until the expiration of such period as may be specified in the order.

(11)   Where—

(a)   a periodical payments or secured periodical payments order in favour of more than one child ('the order') is in force;

(b)   the order requires payments specified in it to be made to or for the benefit of more than one child without apportioning those payments between them;

(c)   a maintenance calculation ('the calculation') is made with respect to one or more, but not all, of the children with respect to whom those payments are to be made; and

(d)   an application is made, before the end of the period of 6 months beginning with the date on which the calculation was made, for the variation or discharge of the order,

the court may, in exercise of its powers under this section to vary or discharge the order, direct that the variation or discharge shall take effect from the date on which the calculation took effect or any later date.

(12)   Where—

(a)   an order ('the child order') of a kind prescribed for the purposes of section 10(1) of the Child Support Act 1991 is affected by a maintenance calculation;

(b)   on the date on which the child order became so affected there was in force a periodical payments or secured periodical payments order ('the spousal order') in favour of a party to a marriage having the care of the child in whose favour the child order was made; and

(c)   an application is made, before the end of the period of 6 months beginning with the date on which the maintenance calculation was made, for the spousal order to be varied or discharged,

the court may, in exercise of its powers under this section to vary or discharge the spousal order, direct that the variation or discharge shall take effect from the date on which the child order became so affected or any later date.

(13)   For the purposes of subsection (12) above, an order is affected if it ceases to have effect or is modified by or under section 10 of the Child Support Act 1991.

(14)   Subsections (11) and (12) above are without prejudice to any other power of the court to direct that the variation of discharge of an order under this section shall take effect from a date earlier than that on which the order for variation or discharge was made.

(15)   The power to make regulations under subsection (4C) above shall be exercisable by statutory instrument which shall be subject to annulment in pursuance of a resolution of either House of Parliament.

35   Alteration of agreements by court during lives of parties

(1)   Where a maintenance agreement is for the time being subsisting and each of the parties to the agreement is for the time being either domiciled or resident in England and Wales, then ... either party may apply to the court ... for an order under this section.

(2)   If the court ... is satisfied either—

(a) that by reason of a change in the circumstances in the light of which any financial arrangements contained in the agreement were made or, as the case may be, financial arrangements were omitted from it (including a change foreseen by the parties when making the agreement), the agreement should be altered so as to make different, or, as the case may be, so as to contain, financial arrangements, or

(b) that the agreement does not contain proper financial arrangements with respect to any child of the family,

then subject to subsections (4) and (5) below, the court may by order make such alterations in the agreement—

(i) by varying or revoking any financial arrangements contained in it, or

(ii) by inserting in it financial arrangements for the benefit of one of the parties to the agreement or of a child of the family,

as may appear to the court to be just having regard to all the circumstances, including, if relevant, the matters mentioned in section 25(4) above; and the agreement shall have effect thereafter as if any alteration made by the order had been made by agreement between the parties and for valuable consideration.

(3)–(6) (Not reproduced)

37 Avoidance of transactions intended to prevent or reduce financial relief

(1) For the purposes of this section 'financial relief' means relief under any of the provisions of sections 22, 23, 24, 24B, 27, 31 (except subsection (6)) and 35 above, and any reference in this section to defeating a person's claim for financial relief is a reference to preventing financial relief from being granted to that person, or to that person for the benefit of a child of the family, or reducing the amount of any financial relief which might be so granted, or frustrating or impeding the enforcement of any order which might be or has been made at his instance under any of those provisions.

(2) Where proceedings for financial relief are brought by one person against another, the court may, on the application of the first-mentioned person—

(a) if it is satisfied that the other party to the proceedings is, with the intention of defeating the claim for financial relief, about to make any disposition or to transfer out of the jurisdiction or otherwise deal with any property, make such order as it thinks fit for restraining the other party from so doing or otherwise for protecting the claim;

(b) if it is satisfied that the other party has, with that intention, made a reviewable disposition and that if the disposition were set aside financial relief or different financial relief would be granted to the applicant, make an order setting aside the disposition;

(c) if it is satisfied, in a case where an order has been obtained under any of the provisions mentioned in subsection (1) above by the applicant against the other party, that the other party has, with that intention, made a reviewable disposition, make an order setting aside the disposition;

and an application for the purposes of paragraph (b) above shall be made in the proceedings for the financial relief in question.

(3) Where the court makes an order under subsection (2)(b) or (c) above setting aside a disposition it shall give such consequential directions as it thinks fit for giving effect to the order (including directions requiring the making of any payments or the disposal of any property).

(4) Any disposition made by the other party to the proceedings for financial relief in question (whether before or after the commencement of those proceedings) is a reviewable disposition for the purposes of subsection (2)(b) and (c) above unless it was made for valuable consideration (other than marriage) to a person who, at the time of the disposition, acted in relation to it in good faith and without notice of any intention on the part of the other party to defeat the applicant's claim for financial relief.

(5) Where an application is made under this section with respect to a disposition which took place less than three years before the date of the application or with respect to a disposition or other dealing with property which is about to take place and the court is satisfied—

(a) in a case falling within subsection (2)(a) or (b) above, that the disposition or other dealing would (apart from this section) have the consequence, or

(b) in a case falling within subsection (2)(c) above, that the disposition has had the consequence, of defeating the applicant's claim for financial relief, it shall be presumed, unless the contrary is shown, that the person who disposed of or is about to dispose of or deal with the property did so or, as the case may be, is about to do so, with the intention of defeating the applicant's claim for financial relief.

(6)   In this section 'disposition' does not include any provision contained in a will or codicil but, with that exception, includes any conveyance, assurance or gift of property of any description, whether made by an instrument or otherwise.

(7)   This section does not apply to a disposition made before 1st January 1968.

(B) Inheritance (Provision for Family and Dependants) Act 1975

1 Application for financial provision from deceased's estate

(1) Where after the commencement of this Act a person dies domiciled in England and Wales and is survived by any of the following persons—

    (a) the spouse or civil partner of the deceased;

    (b) a former spouse or former civil partner of the deceased, but not one who has formed a subsequent marriage or civil partnership;

    (ba) any person (not being a person included in paragraph (a) or (b) above) to whom subsection (1A) … below applies;

    (c) a child of the deceased;

    (d) any person (not being a child of the deceased) who in relation to any marriage or civil partnership to which the deceased was at any time a party, or otherwise in relation to any family in which the deceased at any time stood in the role of a parent, was treated by the deceased as a child of the family;

    (e) any person (not being a person included in the foregoing paragraphs of this subsection) who immediately before the death of the deceased was being maintained, either wholly or partly, by the deceased;

that person may apply to the court for an order under section 2 of this Act on the ground that the disposition of the deceased's estate effected by his will or the law relating to intestacy, or the combination of his will and that law, is not such as to make reasonable financial provision for the applicant.

(1A) This subsection applies to a person if the deceased died on or after 1st January 1996 and, during the whole of the period of two years ending immediately before the date when the deceased died, the person was living—

    (a) in the same household as the deceased, and

    (b) as if that person and the deceased were a married couple or civil partners.

(1B) …

(2) In this Act 'reasonable financial provision'—

    (a) in the case of an application made by virtue of subsection (1)(a) above by the husband or wife of the deceased (except where the marriage with the deceased was the subject of a decree of judicial separation and at the date of death the decree was in force and the separation was continuing), means such financial provision as it would be reasonable in all the circumstances of the case for a husband or wife to receive, whether or not that provision is required for his or her maintenance;

    (aa) in the case of an application made by virtue of subsection (1)(a) above by the civil partner of the deceased (except where, at the date of death, a separation order under Chapter 2 of Part 2 of the Civil Partnership Act 2004 was in force in relation to the civil partnership and the separation was continuing), means such financial provision as would be reasonable in all the circumstances of the case for a civil partner to receive, whether or not that provision is required for his or her maintenance;

    (b) in the case of any other application made by virtue of subsection (1) above, means such financial provision as it would be reasonable in all the circumstances of the case for the applicant to receive for his maintenance.

(2A) The reference in subsection (1)(d) above to a family in which the deceased stood in the role of a parent includes a family of which the deceased was the only member (apart from the applicant).

(3) For the purposes of subsection (1)(e) above, a person is to be treated as being maintained by the deceased (either wholly or partly, as the case may be) only if the deceased was making a substantial contribution in money or money's worth towards the reasonable needs of that person, other than a contribution made for full valuable consideration pursuant to an arrangement of a commercial nature.

2 Powers of court to make orders

(1) Subject to the provisions of this Act, where an application is made for an order under this section, the court may, if it is satisfied that the disposition of the deceased's estate effected by his will or the law

relating to intestacy, or the combination of his will and that law, is not such as to make reasonable financial provision for the applicant, make any one or more of the following orders—

(a)   an order for the making to the applicant out of the net estate of the deceased of such periodical payments and for such term as may be specified in the order;

(b)   an order for the payment to the applicant out of that estate of a lump sum of such amount as may be so specified;

(c)   an order for the transfer to the applicant of such property comprised in that estate as may be so specified;

(d)   an order for the settlement for the benefit of the applicant of such property comprised in that estate as may be so specified;

(e)   an order for the acquisition out of property comprised in that estate of such property as may be so specified and for the transfer of the property so acquired to the applicant or for the settlement thereof for his benefit;

(f)   an order varying any ante-nuptial or post-nuptial settlement (including such a settlement made by will) made on the parties to a marriage to which the deceased was one of the parties, the variation being for the benefit of the surviving party to that marriage, or any child of that marriage, or any person who was treated by the deceased as a child of the family in relation to that marriage;

(g)   an order varying any settlement made—

(i)   during the subsistence of a civil partnership formed by the deceased, or

(ii)   in anticipation of the formation of a civil partnership by the deceased, on the civil partners (including such a settlement made by will), the variation being for the benefit of the surviving civil partner, or any person who was treated by the deceased as a child of the family in relation to the civil partnership;

(h)   an order varying for the applicant's benefit the trusts on which the deceased's estate is held (whether arising under the will, or the law relating to intestacy, or both).

(2)–(4)   (not reproduced)

15   Restriction imposed in divorce proceedings etc on application under this Act

(1)   On the grant of a decree of divorce, a decree of nullity of marriage or a decree of judicial separation or at any time thereafter the court, if it considers it just to do so, may, on the application of either party to the marriage, order that the other party to the marriage shall not on the death of the applicant be entitled to apply for an order under section 2 of this Act.

In this subsection 'the court' means the High Court or the family court.

(2)   In the case of a decree of divorce or nullity of marriage an order may be made under subsection (1) above before or after the decree is made absolute, but if it is made before the decree is made absolute it shall not take effect unless the decree is made absolute.

(3)   Where an order made under subsection (1) above on the grant of a decree of divorce or nullity of marriage has come into force with respect to a party to a marriage, then, on the death of the other party to that marriage, the court shall not entertain any application for an order under section 2 of this Act made by the first-mentioned party.

(4)   Where an order made under subsection (1) above on the grant of a decree of judicial separation has come into force with respect to any party to a marriage, then, if the other party to that marriage dies while the decree is in force and the separation is continuing, the court shall not entertain any application for an order under section 2 of this Act made by the first-mentioned party.

15ZA   Restriction imposed in proceedings for the dissolution etc. of a civil partnership on application under this Act

(1)   On making a dissolution order, nullity order, separation order or presumption of death order under Chapter 2 of Part 2 of the Civil Partnership Act 2004, or at any time after making such an order, the court if it considers it just to do so, may, on the application of either of the civil partners, order that the other civil partner shall not on the death of the applicant be entitled to apply for an order under section 2 of this Act.

(2)   In subsection (1) above 'the court' means the High Court, or the family court.

(3)   In the case of a dissolution order, nullity order or presumption of death order ('the main order') an order may be made under subsection (1) above before (as well as after) the main order is made final, but if made before the main order is made final it shall not take effect unless the main order is made final.

(4)   Where an order under subsection (1) above made in connection with a dissolution order, nullity order or presumption of death order has come into force with respect to a civil partner, then, on the death of the other civil partner, the court shall not entertain any application for an order under section 2 of the Act made by the surviving civil partner.

(5)   Where an order under subsection (1) above made in connection with a separation order has come into force with respect to a civil partner, then, if the other civil partner dies while the separation order is in force and the separation is continuing, the court shall not entertain any application for an order under section 2 of this Act made by the surviving civil partner.

(C)   Domestic Proceedings and Magistrates' Courts Act 1978

1   Grounds of application for financial provision

Either party to a marriage may apply to the family court for an order under section 2 of this Act on the ground that the other party to the marriage ...—

(a)   has failed to provide reasonable maintenance for the applicant; or

(b)   has failed to provide, or to make a proper contribution towards, reasonable maintenance for any child of the family; or

(c)   has behaved in such a way that the applicant cannot reasonably be expected to live with the respondent; or

(d)   has deserted the applicant.

2   Powers of court to make orders for financial provision

(1)   Where on an application for an order under this section the applicant satisfies the court of any ground mentioned in section 1 of this Act, the court may, subject to the provisions of this Part of this Act, make any one or more of the following orders, that is to say—

    (a)   an order that the respondent shall make to the applicant such periodical payments, and for such term, as may be specified in the order;

    (b)   an order that the respondent shall pay to the applicant such lump sum as may be so specified;

    (c)   an order that the respondent shall make to the applicant for the benefit of a child of the family to whom the application relates, or to such a child, such periodical payments, and for such term, as may be so specified;

    (d)   an order that the respondent shall pay to the applicant for the benefit of a child of the family to whom the application relates, or to such a child, such lump sum as may be so specified.

(2)   Without prejudice to the generality of subsection (1)(b) or (d) above, an order under this section for the payment of a lump sum may be made for the purpose of enabling any liability or expenses reasonably incurred in maintaining the applicant, or any child of the family to whom the application relates, before the making of the order to be met.

(3)   The amount of any lump sum required to be paid by an order under this section shall not exceed £1,000 or such larger amount as the Lord Chancellor may from time to time by order fix for the purposes of this subsection.

    ...

(4)   An order made by the Lord Chancellor under this section—

    (a)   shall be made only after consultation with the Lord Chief Justice;

    (b)   shall be made by statutory instrument and be subject to annulment in pursuance of a resolution of either House of Parliament.

(5)   The Lord Chief Justice may nominate a judicial office holder (as defined in section 109(4) of the Constitutional Reform Act 2005) to exercise his functions under this section.

3   Matters to which court is to have regard in exercising its powers under s 2

(1)   Where an application is made for an order under section 2 of this Act, it shall be the duty of the court, in deciding whether to exercise its powers under that section and, if so, in what manner, to have regard to all the circumstances of the case, first consideration being given to the welfare while a minor of any child of the family who has not attained the age of eighteen.

(2)   As regards the exercise of its powers under subsection (1)(a) or (b) of section 2, the court shall in particular have regard to the following matters—

    (a)   the income, earning capacity, property and other financial resources which each of the parties to the marriage has or is likely to have in the foreseeable future, including in the case of earning capacity any increase in that capacity which it would in the opinion of the court be reasonable to expect a party to the marriage to take steps to acquire;

    (b)   the financial needs, obligations and responsibilities which each of the parties to the marriage has or is likely to have in the foreseeable future;

(c)   the standard of living enjoyed by the parties to the marriage before the occurrence of the conduct which is alleged as the ground of the application;

(d)   the age of each party to the marriage and the duration of the marriage;

(e)   any physical or mental disability of either of the parties to the marriage;

(f)   the contributions which each of the parties has made or is likely in the foreseeable future to make to the welfare of the family, including any contribution by looking after the home or caring for the family;

(g)   the conduct of each of the parties, if that conduct is such that it would in the opinion of the court be inequitable to disregard it.

(3)   As regards the exercise of its power under subsection (1)(c) or (d) of section 2, the court shall in particular have regard to the following matters—

(a)   the financial needs of the child;

(b)   the income, earning capacity (if any), property and other financial resources of the child;

(c)   any physical or mental disability of the child;

(d)   the standard of living enjoyed by the family before the occurrence of the conduct which is alleged as the ground of the application;

(e)   the manner in which the child was being and in which the parties to the marriage expected him to be educated or trained;

(f)   the matters mentioned in relation to the parties to the marriage in paragraphs (a) and (b) of subsection (2) above.

(4)   As regards the exercise of its power under section 2 in favour of a child of the family who is not the child of the respondent, the court shall also have regard—

(a)   to whether the respondent has assumed any responsibility for the child's maintenance and, if he did, to the extent to which, and the basis on which, he assumed that responsibility and to the length of time during which he discharged that responsibility;

(b)   to whether in assuming and discharging that responsibility the respondent did so knowing that the child was not his own child;

(c)   to the liability of any other person to maintain the child.

(D)   Child Abduction Act 1984

1   Offence of abduction of child by parent, etc

(1)   Subject to subsections (5) and (8) below, a person connected with a child under the age of sixteen commits an offence if he takes or sends the child out of the United Kingdom without the appropriate consent.

(2)   A person is connected with a child for the purposes of this section if—

(a)   he is a parent of the child; or

(b)   in the case of a child whose parents were not married to, or civil partners of, each other at the time of his birth, there are reasonable grounds for believing that he is the father of the child; or

(c)   he is a guardian of the child; or

(ca)   he is a special guardian of the child; or

(d)   he is a person named in a child arrangements order as a person with whom the child is to live; or

(e)   he has custody of the child.

(3)   In this section 'the appropriate consent', in relation to a child, means—

(a)   the consent of each of the following—

(i)   the child's mother;

(ii)   the child's father, if he has parental responsibility for him;

(iii)   any guardian of the child;

(iiia)   any special guardian of the child;

(iv)   any person named in a child arrangements order as a person with whom the child is to live;

(v)   any person who has custody of the child; or

(b)   the leave of the court granted under or by virtue of any provision of Part II of the Children Act 1989; or

(c)   if any person has custody of the child, the leave of the court which awarded custody to him.

(4)   A person does not commit an offence under this section by taking or sending a child out of the United Kingdom without obtaining the appropriate consent if—

(a)   he is a person named in a child arrangements order as a person with whom the child is to live and he takes or sends him out of the United Kingdom for a period of less than one month; or

(b)   he is a special guardian of the child and he takes or sends the child out of the United Kingdom for a period of less than three months.

(4A)   Subsection (4) above does not apply if the person taking or sending the child out of the United Kingdom does so in breach of an order under Part II of the Children Act 1989.

(5)   A person does not commit an offence under this section by doing anything without the consent of another person whose consent is required under the foregoing provisions if—

(a)   he does it in the belief that the other person—

(i)   has consented; or

(ii)   would consent if he was aware of all the relevant circumstances; or

(b)   he has taken all reasonable steps to communicate with the other person but has been unable to communicate with him; or

(c)   the other person has unreasonably refused to consent, ...

(5A)   Subsection (5)(c) above does not apply if—

(a)   the person who refused to consent is a person—

(i)   named in a child arrangements order as a person with whom the child is to live;

(ia)   who is a special guardian of the child; or

(ii)   who has custody of the child; or

(b)   the person taking or sending the child out of the United Kingdom is, by so acting, in breach of an order made by a court in the United Kingdom.

(6)   Where, in proceedings for an offence under this section, there is sufficient evidence to raise an issue as to the application of subsection (5) above, it shall be for the prosecution to prove that that subsection does not apply.

(7) For the purposes of this section—

    (a) 'guardian of a child', 'special guardian', 'child arrangements order' and 'parental responsibility' have the same meaning as in the Children Act 1989; and

    (b) a person shall be treated as having custody of a child if there is in force an order of a court in the United Kingdom awarding him (whether solely or jointly with another person) custody, legal custody or care and control of the child.

(8) This section shall have effect subject to the provisions of the Schedule to this Act in relation to a child who is in the care of a local authority detained in a place of safety, remanded otherwise than on bail or the subject of proceedings or an order relating to adoption.

2 Offence of abduction of child by other persons

(1) Subject to subsection (3) below, a person, other than one mentioned in subsection (2) below, commits an offence if, without lawful authority or reasonable excuse, he takes or detains a child under the age of sixteen—

    (a) so as to remove him from the lawful control of any person having lawful control of the child; or

    (b) so as to keep him out of the lawful control of any person entitled to lawful control of the child.

(2) The persons are—

    (a) where the father and mother of the child in question were married to, or civil partners of, each other at the time of his birth, the child's father and mother;

    (b) where the father and mother of the child in question were not married to, or civil partners of, each other at the time of his birth, the child's mother; and

    (c) any other person mentioned in section 1(2)(c) to (e) above.

(3) In proceedings against any person for an offence under this section, it shall be a defence for that person to prove—

    (a) where the father and mother of the child in question were not married to, or civil partners of, each other at the time of his birth—

        (i) that he is the child's father; or

        (ii) that, at the time of the alleged offence, he believed, on reasonable grounds, that he was the child's father; or

    (b) that, at the time of the alleged offence, he believed that the child had attained the age of sixteen.

3 Construction of references to taking, sending and detaining

For the purposes of this Part of this Act—

(a) a person shall be regarded as taking a child if he causes or induces the child to accompany him or any other person or causes the child to be taken;

(b) a person shall be regarded as sending a child if he causes the child to be sent; ...

(c) a person shall be regarded as detaining a child if he causes the child to be detained or induces the child to remain with him or any other person; and

(d) references to a child's parents and to a child whose parents were (or were not) married to, or civil partners of, each other at the time of his birth shall be construed in accordance with section 1 of the Family Law Reform Act 1987 (which extends their meaning).

(E)   Children Act 1989

1   Welfare of the child

(1)   When a court determines any question with respect to—

    (a)   the upbringing of a child; or

    (b)   the administration of a child's property or the application of any income arising from it,

the child's welfare shall be the court's paramount consideration.

(2)   In any proceedings in which any question with respect to the upbringing of a child arises, the court shall have regard to the general principle that any delay in determining the question is likely to prejudice the welfare of the child.

(2A)   A court, in the circumstances mentioned in subsection (4)(a) or (7), is as respects each parent within subsection (6)(a) to presume, unless the contrary is shown, that involvement of that parent in the life of the child concerned will further the child's welfare.

(2B)   In subsection (2A) 'involvement' means involvement of some kind, either direct or indirect, but not any particular division of a child's time.

(3)   In the circumstances mentioned in subsection (4), a court shall have regard in particular to—

    (a)   the ascertainable wishes and feelings of the child concerned (considered in the light of his age and understanding);

    (b)   his physical, emotional and educational needs;

    (c)   the likely effect on him of any change in his circumstances;

    (d)   his age, sex, background and any characteristics of his which the court considers relevant;

    (e)   any harm which he has suffered or is at risk of suffering;

    (f)   how capable each of his parents, and any other person in relation to whom the court considers the question to be relevant, is of meeting his needs;

    (g)   the range of powers available to the court under this Act in the proceedings in question.

(4)   The circumstances are that—

    (a)   the court is considering whether to make, vary or discharge a section 8 order, and the making, variation or discharge of the order is opposed by any party to the proceedings; or

    (b)   the court is considering whether to make, vary or discharge a special guardianship order or an order under Part IV.

(5)   Where a court is considering whether or not to make one or more orders under this Act with respect to a child, it shall not make the order or any of the orders unless it considers that doing so would be better for the child than making no order at all.

(6)   In subsection (2A) 'parent' means parent of the child concerned; and, for the purposes of that subsection, a parent of the child concerned—

    (a)   is within this paragraph if that parent can be involved in the child's life in a way that does not put the child at risk of suffering harm; and

    (b)   is to be treated as being within paragraph (a) unless there is some evidence before the court in the particular proceedings to suggest that involvement of that parent in the child's life would put the child at risk of suffering harm whatever the form of the involvement.

(7)   The circumstances referred to are that the court is considering whether to make an order under section 4(1)(c) or (2A) or 4ZA(1)(c) or (5) (parental responsibility of parent other than mother).

2   Parental responsibility for children

(1)   Where a child's father and mother were married to, or civil partners of, each other at the time of his birth, they shall each have parental responsibility for the child.

(1A)   Where a child—

    (a)   has a parent by virtue of section 42 of the Human Fertilisation and Embryology Act 2008; or

    (b)   has a parent by virtue of section 43 of that Act and is a person to whom section 1(3) of the Family Law Reform Act 1987 applies,

the child's mother and the other parent shall each have parental responsibility for the child.

(2) Where a child's father and mother were not married to, or civil partners of, each other at the time of his birth—

(a) the mother shall have parental responsibility for the child;

(b) the father shall have parental responsibility for the child if he has acquired it (and has not ceased to have it) in accordance with the provisions of this Act.

(2A) Where a child has a parent by virtue of section 43 of the Human Fertilisation and Embryology Act 2008 and is not a person to whom section 1(3) of the Family Law Reform Act 1987 applies—

(a) the mother shall have parental responsibility for the child;

(b) the other parent shall have parental responsibility for the child if she has acquired it (and has not ceased to have it) in accordance with the provisions of this Act.

(3) References in this Act to a child whose father and mother were, or (as the case may be) were not, married to, or civil partners of, each other at the time of his birth must be read with section 1 of the Family Law Reform Act 1987 (which extends their meaning).

(4) The rule of law that a father is the natural guardian of his legitimate child is abolished.

(5) More than one person may have parental responsibility for the same child at the same time.

(6) A person who has parental responsibility for a child at any time shall not cease to have that responsibility solely because some other person subsequently acquires parental responsibility for the child.

(7) Where more than one person has parental responsibility for a child, each of them may act alone and without the other (or others) in meeting that responsibility; but nothing in this Part shall be taken to affect the operation of any enactment which requires the consent of more than one person in a matter affecting the child.

(8) The fact that a person has parental responsibility for a child shall not entitle him to act in any way which would be incompatible with any order made with respect to the child under this Act.

(9) A person who has parental responsibility for a child may not surrender or transfer any part of that responsibility to another but may arrange for some or all of it to be met by one or more persons acting on his behalf.

(10) The person with whom any such arrangement is made may himself be a person who already has parental responsibility for the child concerned.

(11) The making of any such arrangement shall not affect any liability of the person making it which may arise from any failure to meet any part of his parental responsibility for the child concerned.

3 Meaning of 'parental responsibility'

(1) In this Act 'parental responsibility' means all the rights, duties, powers, responsibilities and authority which by law a parent of a child has in relation to the child and his property.

(2) It also includes the rights, powers and duties which a guardian of the child's estate (appointed, before the commencement of section 5, to act generally) would have had in relation to the child and his property.

(3) The rights referred to in subsection (2) include, in particular, the right of the guardian to receive or recover in his own name, for the benefit of the child, property of whatever description and wherever situated which the child is entitled to receive or recover.

(4) The fact that a person has, or does not have, parental responsibility for a child shall not affect—

(a) any obligation which he may have in relation to the child (such as a statutory duty to maintain the child); or

(b) any rights which, in the event of the child's death, he (or any other person) may have in relation to the child's property.

(5) A person who—

(a) does not have parental responsibility for a particular child; but

(b) has care of the child,

may (subject to the provisions of this Act) do what is reasonable in all the circumstances of the case for the purpose of safeguarding or promoting the child's welfare.

4   Acquisition of parental responsibility by father

(1)   Where a child's father and mother were not married to, or civil partners of, each other at the time of his birth, the father shall acquire parental responsibility for the child if—

(a)   he becomes registered as the child's father under any of the enactments specified in subsection (1A);

(b)   he and the child's mother make an agreement (a 'parental responsibility agreement') providing for him to have parental responsibility for the child; or

(c)   the court, on his application, orders that he shall have parental responsibility for the child.

(1A)   The enactments referred to in subsection (1)(a) are—

(a)   paragraphs (a), (b) and (c) of section 10(1) and of section 10A(1) of the Births and Deaths Registration Act 1953;

(b)   paragraphs (a), (b)(i) and (c) of section 18(1), and sections 18(2)(b) and 20(1)(a) of the Registration of Births, Deaths and Marriages (Scotland) Act 1965; and

(c)   sub-paragraphs (a), (b) and (c) of Article 14(3) of the Births and Deaths Registration (Northern Ireland) Order 1976.

(1B)   The Secretary of State may by order amend subsection (1A) so as to add further enactments to the list in that subsection.

(2)   No parental responsibility agreement shall have effect for the purposes of this Act unless—

(a)   it is made in the form prescribed by regulations made by the Lord Chancellor; and

(b)   where regulations are made by the Lord Chancellor prescribing the manner in which such agreements must be recorded, it is recorded in the prescribed manner.

(2A)   A person who has acquired parental responsibility under subsection (1) shall cease to have that responsibility only if the court so orders.

(3)   The court may make an order under subsection (2A) on the application—

(a)   of any person who has parental responsibility for the child; or

(b)   with the leave of the court, of the child himself,

subject, in the case of parental responsibility acquired under subsection (1)(c), to section 12(4).

(4)   The court may only grant leave under subsection (3)(b) if it is satisfied that the child has sufficient understanding to make the proposed application.

4ZA   Acquisition of parental responsibility by second female parent

(1)   Where a child has a parent by virtue of section 43 of the Human Fertilisation and Embryology Act 2008 and is not a person to whom section 1(3) of the Family Law Reform Act 1987 applies, that parent shall acquire parental responsibility for the child if—

(a)   she becomes registered as a parent of the child under any of the enactments specified in subsection (2);

(b)   she and the child's mother make an agreement providing for her to have parental responsibility for the child; or

(c)   the court, on her application, orders that she shall have parental responsibility for the child.

(2)   The enactments referred to in subsection (1)(a) are—

(a)   paragraphs (a), (b) and (c) of section 10(1B) and of section 10A(1B) of the Births and Deaths Registration Act 1953;

(b)   paragraphs (a), (b) and (d) of section 18B(1) and sections 18B(3)(a) and 20(1)(a) of the Registration of Births, Deaths and Marriages (Scotland) Act 1965; and

(c)   sub-paragraphs (a), (b) and (c) of Article 14ZA(3) of the Births and Deaths Registration (Northern Ireland) Order 1976.

(3)   The Secretary of State may by order amend subsection (2) so as to add further enactments to the list in that subsection.

(4)   An agreement under subsection (1)(b) is also a 'parental responsibility agreement', and section 4(2) applies in relation to such an agreement as it applies in relation to parental responsibility agreements under section 4.

(5) A person who has acquired parental responsibility under subsection (1) shall cease to have that responsibility only if the court so orders.

(6) The court may make an order under subsection (5) on the application—

(a) of any person who has parental responsibility for the child; or

(b) with the leave of the court, of the child himself,

subject, in the case of parental responsibility acquired under subsection (1)(c), to section 12(4).

(7) The court may only grant leave under subsection (6)(b) if it is satisfied that the child has sufficient understanding to make the proposed application.

4A Acquisition of parental responsibility by step-parent

(1) Where a child's parent ('parent A') who has parental responsibility for the child is married to, or a civil partner of, a person who is not the child's parent ('the step-parent')—

(a) parent A, or if the other parent of the child also has parental responsibility for the child, both parents may by agreement with the step-parent provide for the step-parent to have parental responsibility for the child; or

(b) the court may, on the application of the step-parent, order that the step-parent shall have parental responsibility for the child.

(2) An agreement under subsection (1)(a) is also a 'parental responsibility agreement', and section 4(2) applies in relation to such agreements as it applies in relation to parental responsibility agreements under section 4.

(3) A parental responsibility agreement under subsection (1)(a), or an order under subsection (1)(b), may only be brought to an end by an order of the court made on the application—

(a) of any person has parental responsibility for the child; or

(b) with the leave of the court, of the child himself.

(4) The court may only grant leave under subsection (3)(b) if it is satisfied that the child has sufficient understanding to make the proposed application.

5 Appointment of guardians

(1) Where an application with respect to a child is made to the court by any individual, the court may by order appoint that individual to be the child's guardian if—

(a) the child has no parent with parental responsibility for him; or

(b) a parent, guardian or special guardian of the child's was named in a child arrangements order as a person with whom the child was to live and has died while the order was in force; or

(c) paragraph (b) does not apply, and the child's only or last surviving special guardian dies.

(2) The power conferred by subsection (1) may also be exercised in any family proceedings if the court considers that the order should be made even though no application has been made for it.

(3) A parent who has parental responsibility for his child may appoint another individual to be the child's guardian in the event of his death.

(4) A guardian of a child may appoint another individual to take his place as the child's guardian in the event of his death; and a special guardian of a child may appoint another individual to be the child's guardian in the event of his death.

(5) An appointment under subsection (3) or (4) shall not have effect unless it is made in writing, is dated and is signed by the person making the appointment or—

(a) in the case of an appointment made by a will which is not signed by the testator, is signed at the direction of the testator in accordance with the requirements of section 9 of the Wills Act 1837; or

(b) in any other case, is signed at the direction of the person making the appointment, in his presence and in the presence of two witnesses who each attest the signature.

(6) A person appointed as a child's guardian under this section shall have parental responsibility for the child concerned.

(7) Where—

(a) on the death of any person making an appointment under subsection (3) or (4), the child concerned has no parent with parental responsibility for him; or

(b)   immediately before the death of any person making such an appointment, a child arrangements order was in force in which the person was named as a person with whom the child was to live or the person was the child's only (or last surviving) special guardian,

the appointment shall take effect on the death of that person.

(8)   Where, on the death of any person making an appointment under subsection (3) or (4)—

(a)   the child concerned has a parent with parental responsibility for him; and

(b)   subsection (7)(b) does not apply,

the appointment shall take effect when the child no longer has a parent who has parental responsibility for him.

(9)   Subsections (1) and (7) do not apply if the child arrangements order referred to in paragraph (b) of those subsections also named a surviving parent of the child as a person with whom the child was to live.

(10)   Nothing in this section shall be taken to prevent an appointment under subsection (3) or (4) being made by two or more persons acting jointly.

(11)   Subject to any provision made by rules of court, no court shall exercise the High Court's inherent jurisdiction to appoint a guardian of the estate of any child.

(12)   Where the rules of court are made under subsection (11) they may prescribe the circumstances in which, and conditions subject to which, an appointment of such a guardian may be made.

(13)   A guardian of a child may only be appointed in accordance with the provisions of this section.

7   Welfare reports

(1)   A court considering any question with respect to a child under this Act may—

(a)   ask an officer of the Service or a Welsh family proceedings officer; or

(b)   ask a local authority to arrange for—

(i)   an officer of the authority; or

(ii)   such other person (other than an officer of the Service or a Welsh family proceedings officer) as the authority considers appropriate,

to report to the court on such matters relating to the welfare of that child as are required to be dealt with in the report.

(2)   The Lord Chancellor may, after consulting the Lord Chief Justice, make regulations specifying matters which, unless the court orders otherwise, must be dealt with in any report under this section.

(3)   The report may be made in writing, or orally, as the court requires.

(4)   Regardless of any enactment or rule of law which would otherwise prevent it from doing so, the court may take account of—

(a)   any statement contained in the report; and

(b)   any evidence given in respect of the matters referred to in the report,

in so far as the statement or evidence is, in the opinion of the court, relevant to the question which it is considering.

(5)   It shall be the duty of the authority or officer of the Service or a Welsh family proceedings officer to comply with any request for a report under this section.

(6)   The Lord Chief Justice may nominate a judicial office holder (as defined in section 109(4) of the Constitutional Reform Act 2005) to exercise his functions under subsection (2).

8   Child arrangements orders and other orders with respect to children

(1)   In this Act—

'child arrangements order' means an order regulating arrangements relating to any of the following—

(a)   with whom a child is to live, spend time or otherwise have contact, and

(b)   when a child is to live, spend time or otherwise have contact with any person;

...

'a prohibited steps order' means an order that no step which could be taken by a parent in meeting his parental responsibility for a child, and which is of a kind specified in the order, shall be taken by any person without the consent of the court;

...; and

'a specific issue order' means an order giving directions for the purpose of determining a specific question which has arisen, or which may arise, in connection with any aspect of parental responsibility for a child.

(2) In this Act 'a section 8 order' means any of the orders mentioned in subsection (1) and any order varying or discharging such an order.

(3) For the purposes of this Act 'family proceedings' means any proceedings—

    (a) under the inherent jurisdiction of the High Court in relation to children; and

    (b) under the enactments mentioned in subsection (4),

but does not include proceedings on an application for leave under section 100(3).

(4) The enactments are—

    (a) Parts I, II and IV of this Act;

    (b) the Matrimonial Causes Act 1973;

    (ba) Schedule 5 to the Civil Partnership Act 2004;

    (c) ...

    (d) the Adoption and Children Act 2002;

    (e) the Domestic Proceedings and Magistrates' Courts Act 1978;

    (ea) Schedule 6 to the Civil Partnership Act 2004;

    (f) ...

    (g) Part III of the Matrimonial and Family Proceedings Act 1984;

    (h) the Family Law Act 1996;

    (i) sections 11 and 12 of the Crime and Disorder Act 1998;

    (j) Part 1 of Schedule 2 to the Female Genital Mutilation Act 2003 (other than paragraph 3 of that Schedule).

9 Restrictions on making section 8 orders

(1) No court shall make any section 8 order, other than a child arrangements order to which subsection (6B) applies, with respect to a child who is in the care of a local authority.

(2) No application may be made by a local authority for a child arrangements order and no court shall make such an order in favour of a local authority.

(3) A person who is, or was at any time within the last six months, a local authority foster parent of a child may not apply for leave to apply for a section 8 order with respect to the child unless—

    (a) he has the consent of the authority;

    (b) he is relative of the child; or

    (c) the child has lived with him for at least one year preceding the application.

(4) ...

(5) No court shall exercise its powers to make a specific issue order or prohibited steps order—

    (a) with a view to achieving a result which could be achieved by making a child arrangements order or an order under section 51A of the Adoption and Children Act 2002 (post-adoption contact); or

    (b) in any way which is denied to the High Court (by section 100(2)) in the exercise of its inherent jurisdiction with respect to children.

(6) No court shall make a section 8 order which is to have effect for a period which will end after the child has reached the age of sixteen unless it is satisfied that the circumstances of the case are exceptional.

(6A) Subsection (6) does not apply to a child arrangements order to which subsection (6B) applies.

(6B) This subsection applies to a child arrangements order if the arrangements regulated by the order relate only to either or both of the following—

    (a) with whom the child concerned is to live, and

    (b) when the child is to live with any person.

(7) No court shall make any section 8 order, other than one varying or discharging such an order, with respect to a child who has reached the age of sixteen unless it is satisfied that the circumstances of the case are exceptional.

10   Power of court to make section 8 orders

(1)   In any family proceedings in which a question arises with respect to the welfare of any child, the court may make a section 8 order with respect to the child if—

(a)   an application for the order has been made by a person who—

(i)   is entitled to apply for a section 8 order with respect to the child; or

(ii)   has obtained the leave of the court to make the application; or

(b)   the court considers that the order should be made even though no such application has been made.

(2)   The court may also make a section 8 order with respect to any child on the application of a person who—

(a)   is entitled to apply for a section 8 order with respect to the child; or

(b)   has obtained the leave of the court to make the application.

(3)   This section is subject to the restrictions imposed by section 9.

(4)   The following persons are entitled to apply to the court for any section 8 order with respect to a child—

(a)   any parent, guardian or special guardian of the child;

(aa)   any person who by virtue of section 4A has parental responsibility for the child;

(b)   any person who is named, in a child arrangements order that is in force with respect to the child, as a person with whom the child is to live.

(5)   The following persons are entitled to apply for a child arrangements order with respect to a child—

(a)   any party to a marriage (whether or not subsisting) in relation to whom the child is a child of the family;

(aa)   any civil partner in a civil partnership (whether or not subsisting) in relation to whom the child is a child of the family;

(b)   any person with whom the child has lived for a period of at least three years;

(c)   any person who—

(i)   in any case where a child arrangements order in force with respect to the child regulates arrangements relating to with whom the child is to live or when the child is to live with any person, has the consent of each of the persons named in the order as a person with whom the child is to live;

(ii)   in any case where the child is in the care of a local authority, has the consent of that authority; or

(iii)   in any other case, has the consent of each of those (if any) who have parental responsibility for the child;

(d)   any person who has parental responsibility for the child by virtue of provision made under section 12(2A).

(5A)   A local authority foster parent is entitled to apply for a child arrangements order to which subsection (5C) applies with respect to a child if the child has lived with him for a period of at least one year immediately preceding the application.

(5B)   A relative of a child is entitled to apply for a child arrangements order to which subsection (5C) applies with respect to the child if the child has lived with the relative for a period of at least one year immediately preceding the application.

(5C)   This subsection applies to a child arrangements order if the arrangements regulated by the order relate only to either or both of the following—

(a)   with whom the child concerned is to live, and

(b)   when the child is to live with any person.

(6)   A person who would not otherwise be entitled (under the previous provisions of this section) to apply for the variation or discharge of a section 8 order shall be entitled to do so if—

(a)   the order was made on his application; or

(b)   in the case of a child arrangements order, he is named in provisions of the order regulating arrangements relating to—

(i)   with whom the child concerned is to spend time or otherwise have contact, or

(ii)   when the child is to spend time or otherwise have contact with any person.

(7)   Any person who falls within a category of person prescribed by rules of court is entitled to apply for any such section 8 order as may be prescribed in relation to that category of person.

(7A)   If a special guardianship order is in force with respect to a child, an application for a child arrangements order to which subsection (7B) applies may only be made with respect to him, if apart from this subsection the leave of the court is not required, with such leave.

(7B)   This subsection applies to a child arrangements order if the arrangements regulated by the order consist of, or include, arrangements which relate to either or both of the following—

(a)   with whom the child concerned is to live, and

(b)   when the child is to live with any person.

(8)   Where the person applying for leave to make an application for a section 8 order is the child concerned, the court may only grant leave if it is satisfied that he has sufficient understanding to make the proposed application for the section 8 order.

(9)   Where the person applying for leave to make an application for a section 8 order is not the child concerned, the court shall, in deciding whether or not to grant leave, have particular regard to—

(a)   the nature of the proposed application for the section 8 order;

(b)   the applicant's connection with the child;

(c)   any risk there might be of that proposed application disrupting the child's life to such an extent that he would be harmed by it; and

(d)   where the child is being looked after by a local authority—

(i)   the authority's plans for the child's future; and

(ii)   the wishes and feelings of the child's parents.

(10)   The period of three years mentioned in subsection (5)(b) need not be continuous but must not have begun more than five years before, or ended more than three months before, the making of the application.

11   General principles and supplementary provisions

(1)   In proceedings in which any question of making a section 8 order, or any other question with respect to such an order, arises, the court shall (in the light of any provision in rules of court that is of the kind mentioned in subsection (2)(a) or (b))—

(a)   draw up a timetable with a view to determining the question without delay; and

(b)   give such directions as it considers appropriate for the purpose of ensuring, so far as is reasonably practicable, that that timetable is adhered to.

(2)   Rules of court may—

(a)   specify periods within which specified steps must be taken in relation to proceedings in which such questions arise; and

(b)   make other provision with respect to such proceedings for the purpose of ensuring, so far as is reasonably practicable, that such questions are determined without delay.

(3)   Where a court has power to make a section 8 order, it may do so at any time during the course of the proceedings in question even though it is not in a position to dispose finally of those proceedings.

(4)   ...

(5)   Where—

(a)   a child arrangements order has been made with respect to a child; and

(b)   the child has two parents who each have parental responsibility for him,

the order, so far as it has the result that there are times when the child lives or is to live with one of the parents, shall cease to have effect if the parents live together for a continuous period of more than six months.

(6)   A child arrangements order made with respect to a child, so far as it provides for the child to spend time or otherwise have contact with one of the child's parents at times when the child is living with the child's other parent, shall cease to have effect if the parents live together for a continuous period of more than six months.

(7)   A section 8 order may—

(a)   contain directions about how it is to be carried into effect;

(b)   impose conditions which must be complied with by any person—

(i) who is named in the order as a person with whom the child concerned is to live, spend time or otherwise have contact;

(ii) who is a parent of the child ...;

(iii) who is not a parent of his but who has parental responsibility for him; or

(iv) with whom the child is living,

and to whom the conditions are expressed to apply;

(c) be made to have effect for a specified period, or contain provisions which are to have effect for a specified period;

(d) make such incidental, supplemental or consequential provision as the court thinks fit.

11A   ... Activity directions

(1) Subsection (2) applies in proceedings in which the court is considering whether to make provision about one or more of the matters mentioned in subsection (1A) by making—

(a) a child arrangements order with respect to the child concerned, or

(b) an order varying or discharging a child arrangements order with respect to the child concerned.

(1A) The matters mentioned in this subsection are—

(a) with whom a child is to live,

(b) when a child is to live with any person,

(c) with whom a child is to spend time or otherwise have contact, and

(d) when a child is to spend time or otherwise have contact with any person.

(2) The court may make an activity direction in connection with the provision that the court is considering whether to make.

(2A) Subsection (2B) applies in proceedings in which subsection (2) does not apply and in which the court is considering—

(a) whether a person has failed to comply with a provision of a child arrangements order, or

(b) what steps to take in consequence of a person's failure to comply with a provision of a child arrangements order.

(2B) The court may make an activity direction in connection with that provision of the child arrangements order.

(3) An activity direction is a direction requiring an individual who is a party to the proceedings concerned to take part in an activity that would, in the court's opinion, help to establish, maintain or improve the involvement in the life of the child concerned of—

(a) that individual, or

(b) another individual who is a party to the proceedings.

(4) The direction is to specify the activity and the person providing the activity.

(5) The activities that may be so required include, in particular—

(a) programmes, classes and counselling or guidance sessions of a kind that—

(i) may assist a person as regards establishing, maintaining or improving involvement in a child's life;

(ii) may, by addressing a person's violent behaviour, enable or facilitate involvement in a child's life;

(b) sessions in which information or advice is given as regards making or operating arrangements for involvement in a child's life, including making arrangements by means of mediation.

(6) No individual may be required by an activity direction—

(a) to undergo medical or psychiatric examination, assessment or treatment;

(b) to take part in mediation.

(7) A court may not on the same occasion—

(a) make an activity direction under subsection (2), and

(b) dispose finally of the proceedings as they relate to the matters mentioned in subsection (1A) in connection with which the activity direction is made.

(7A) A court may not on the same occasion—

(a) make an activity direction under subsection (2B), and

(b)   dispose finally of the proceedings as they relate to failure to comply with the provision in connection with which the activity direction is made.

(8)   Each of subsections (2) and (2B) has effect subject to the restrictions in sections 11B and 11E.

(9)   In considering whether to make an activity direction, the welfare of the child concerned is to be the court's paramount consideration.

11B   ... Activity directions: further provision

(1)   A court may not make an activity direction under section 11A(2) in connection with any matter mentioned in section 11A(1A) unless there is a dispute as regards the provision about that matter that the court is considering whether to make in the proceedings.

(2)   A court may not make an activity direction requiring an individual who is a child to take part in an activity unless the individual is a parent of the child in relation to whom the court is considering provision about a matter mentioned in section 11A(1A).

(3)   A court may not make an activity direction in connection with the making, variation or discharge of a child arrangements order, if the child arrangements order is, or would if made be, an excepted order.

(4)   A child arrangements order with respect to a child is an excepted order if—

(a)   it is made in proceedings that include proceedings on an application for a relevant adoption order in respect of the child; or

(b)   it makes provision as regards contact between the child and a person who would be a parent or relative of the child but for the child's adoption by an order falling within subsection (5).

(5)   An order falls within this subsection if it is—

(a)   a relevant adoption order;

(b)   an adoption order, within the meaning of section 72(1) of the Adoption Act 1976, other than an order made by virtue of section 14 of that Act on the application of a married couple one of whom is the mother or the father of the child;

(c)   a Scottish adoption order, within the meaning of the Adoption and Children Act 2002, other than an order made—

(i)   by virtue of section 14 of the Adoption (Scotland) Act 1978 on the application of a married couple one of whom is the mother or the father of the child, or

(ii)   by virtue of section 15(1)(aa) of that Act; or

(iii)   by virtue of an application under section 30 of the Adoption and Children (Scotland) Act 2007 where subsection (3) of that section applies; or

(d)   a Northern Irish adoption order, within the meaning of the Adoption and Children Act 2002, other than an order made by virtue of Article 14 of the Adoption (Northern Ireland) Order 1987 on the application of a married couple one of whom is the mother or the father of the child.

(6)   A relevant adoption order is an adoption order, within the meaning of section 46(1) of the Adoption and Children Act 2002, other than an order made—

(a)   on an application under section 50 of that Act by a couple (within the meaning of that Act) one of whom is the mother or the father of the person to be adopted, or

(b)   on an application under section 51(2) of that Act.

(7)   A court may not make an activity direction in relation to an individual unless the individual is habitually resident in England and Wales; and a direction ceases to have effect if the individual subject to the direction ceases to be habitually resident in England and Wales.

11C   ... Activity conditions

(1)   This section applies if in any family proceedings the court makes—

(a)   a child arrangements order containing—

(i)   provision for a child to live with different persons at different times,

(ii)   provision regulating arrangements relating to with whom a child is to spend time or otherwise have contact, or

(iii)   provision regulating arrangements relating to when a child is to spend time or otherwise have contact with any person; or

(b)   an order varying a child arrangements order so as to add, vary or omit provision of a kind mentioned in paragraph (a)(i), (ii) or (iii).

(2)   The child arrangements order may impose, or the child arrangements order may be varied so as to impose, a condition (an 'activity condition') requiring an individual falling within subsection (3) to take part in an activity that would, in the court's opinion, help to establish, maintain or improve the involvement in the life of the child concerned of—

(a)   that individual, or

(b)   another individual who is a party to the proceedings.

(3)   An individual falls within this subsection if he is—

(a)   for the purposes of the child arrangements order so made or varied, a person with whom the child concerned lives or is to live;

(b)   a person whose contact with the child concerned is provided for in that order; or

(c)   a person upon whom that order imposes a condition under section 11(7)(b).

(4)   The condition is to specify the activity and the person providing the activity.

(5)   Subsections (5) and (6) of section 11A have effect as regards the activities that may be required by an activity condition as they have effect as regards the activities that may be required by an activity direction.

(6)   Subsection (2) has effect subject to the restrictions in sections 11D and 11E.

11D   ... Activity conditions: further provision

(1)   A child arrangements order may not impose an activity condition on an individual who is a child unless the individual is a parent of the child concerned.

(2)   If a child arrangements order is an excepted order (within the meaning given by section 11B(4)), it may not impose (and it may not be varied so as to impose) an activity condition.

(3)   A child arrangements order may not impose an activity condition on an individual unless the individual is habitually resident in England and Wales; and a condition ceases to have effect if the individual subject to the condition ceases to be habitually resident in England and Wales.

11E   ... Activity directions and conditions: making

(1)   Before making an activity direction (or imposing an activity condition by means of a child arrangements order), the court must satisfy itself as to the matters falling within subsections (2) to (4).

(2)   The first matter is that the activity proposed to be specified is appropriate in the circumstances of the case.

(3)   The second matter is that the person proposed to be specified as the provider of the activity is suitable to provide the activity.

(4)   The third matter is that the activity proposed to be specified is provided in a place to which the individual who would be subject to the direction (or the condition) can reasonably be expected to travel.

(5)   Before making such a direction (or such an order), the court must obtain and consider information about the individual who would be subject to the direction (or the condition) and the likely effect of the direction (or the condition) on him.

(6)   Information about the likely effect of the direction (or the condition) may, in particular, include information as to—

(a)   any conflict with the individual's religious beliefs;

(b)   any interference with the times (if any) at which he normally works or attends an educational establishment.

(7)   The court may ask an officer of the Service or a Welsh family proceedings officer to provide the court with information as to the matters in subsections (2) to (5); and it shall be the duty of the officer of the Service or Welsh family proceedings officer to comply with any such request.

(8)   In this section 'specified' means specified in an activity direction (or in an activity condition).

11F ... Activity directions and conditions: financial assistance

(1) The Secretary of State may by regulations make provision authorising him to make payments to assist individuals falling within subsection (2) in paying relevant charges or fees.

(2) An individual falls within this subsection if he is required by an activity direction or condition to take part in an activity that is expected to help to establish, maintain or improve the involvement of that or another individual in the life of a child, not being a child ordinarily resident in Wales.

(3) The National Assembly for Wales may by regulations make provision authorising it to make payments to assist individuals falling within subsection (4) in paying relevant charges or fees.

(4) An individual falls within this subsection if he is required by an activity direction or condition to take part in an activity that is expected to help to establish, maintain or improve the involvement of that or another individual in the life of a child who is ordinarily resident in Wales.

(5) A relevant charge or fee, in relation to an activity required by an activity direction or condition, is a charge or fee in respect of the activity payable to the person providing the activity.

(6) Regulations under this section may provide that no assistance is available to an individual unless—

(a) the individual satisfies such conditions as regards his financial resources as may be set out in the regulations;

(b) the activity in which the individual is required by an activity direction or condition to take part is provided to him in England or Wales;

(c) where the activity in which the individual is required to take part is provided to him in England, it is provided by a person who is for the time being approved by the Secretary of State as a provider of activities required by an activity direction or condition;

(d) where the activity in which the individual is required to take part is provided to him in Wales, it is provided by a person who is for the time being approved by the National Assembly for Wales as a provider of activities required by an activity direction or condition.

(7) Regulations under this section may make provision—

(a) as to the maximum amount of assistance that may be paid to or in respect of an individual as regards an activity in which he is required by an activity direction or condition to take part;

(b) where the amount may vary according to an individual's financial resources, as to the method by which the amount is to be determined;

(c) authorising payments by way of assistance to be made directly to persons providing activities required by an activity direction or condition.

11G ... Activity directions and conditions: monitoring

(1) This section applies if in any family proceedings the court—

(a) makes an activity direction in relation to an individual, or

(b) makes a child arrangements order that imposes, or varies a child arrangements order so as to impose, an activity condition on an individual.

(2) The court may on making the direction (or imposing the condition by means of a child arrangements order) ask an officer of the Service or a Welsh family proceedings officer—

(a) to monitor, or arrange for the monitoring of, the individual's compliance with the direction (or the condition);

(b) to report to the court on any failure by the individual to comply with the direction (or the condition).

(3) It shall be the duty of the officer of the Service or Welsh family proceedings officer to comply with any request under subsection (2).

11H Monitoring contact and shared residence

(1) This section applies if in any family proceedings the court makes—

(a) a child arrangements order containing provision of a kind mentioned in section 11C(1)(a)(i), (ii) or (iii), or

(b) an order varying a child arrangements order so as to add, vary or omit provision of any of those kinds.

(2) The court may ask an officer of the Service or a Welsh family proceedings officer—

(a)   to monitor whether an individual falling within subsection (3) complies with each provision of any of those kinds that is contained in the child arrangements order (or in the child arrangements order as varied);

(b)   to report to the court on such matters relating to the individual's compliance as the court may specify in the request.

(3)   An individual falls within this subsection if the child arrangements order so made (or the child arrangements order as so varied)—

(za)   provides for the child concerned to live with different persons at different times and names the individual as one of those persons;

(a)   imposes requirements on the individual with regard to the child concerned spending time or otherwise having contact with some other person;

(b)   names the individual as a person with whom the child concerned is to spend time or otherwise have contact; or

(c)   imposes a condition under section 11(7)(b) on the individual.

(4)   If the child arrangements order (or the child arrangements order as varied) includes an activity condition, a request under subsection (2) is to be treated as relating to the provisions of the order other than the activity condition.

(5)   The court may make a request under subsection (2)—

(a)   on making the child arrangements order (or the order varying the child arrangements order), or

(b)   at any time during the subsequent course of the proceedings as they relate to contact with the child concerned or to the child's living arrangements.

(6)   In making a request under subsection (2), the court is to specify the period for which the officer of the Service or Welsh family proceedings officer is to monitor compliance with the order; and the period specified may not exceed twelve months.

(7)   It shall be the duty of the officer of the Service or Welsh family proceedings officer to comply with any request under subsection (2).

(8)   The court may order any individual falling within subsection (3) to take such steps as may be specified in the order with a view to enabling the officer of the Service or Welsh family proceedings officer to comply with the court's request under subsection (2).

(9)   But the court may not make an order under subsection (8) with respect to an individual who is a child unless he is a parent of the child with respect to whom the order falling within subsection (1) was made.

(10)   A court may not make a request under subsection (2) in relation to a child arrangements order that is an excepted order (within the meaning given by section 11B(4)).

11I   Child arrangements

Where the court makes (or varies) a child arrangements order, it is to attach to the child arrangements order (or the order varying the child arrangements order) a notice warning of the consequences of failing to comply with the child arrangements order.

11J   Enforcement orders

(1)   This section applies if a child arrangements order with respect to a child has been made.

(2)   If the court is satisfied beyond reasonable doubt that a person has failed to comply with a provision of the child arrangements order, it may make an order (an 'enforcement order') imposing on the person an unpaid work requirement.

(3)   But the court may not make an enforcement order if it is satisfied that the person had a reasonable excuse for failing to comply with the provision.

(4)   The burden of proof as to the matter mentioned in subsection (3) lies on the person claiming to have had a reasonable excuse, and the standard of proof is the balance of probabilities.

(5)   The court may make an enforcement order in relation to the child arrangements order only on the application of—

(a)   a person who is, for the purposes of the child arrangements order, a person with whom the child concerned lives or is to live;

(b)   a person whose contact with the child concerned is provided for in the child arrangements order;

(c)   any individual subject to a condition under section 11(7)(b) or an activity condition imposed by the child arrangements order; or

(d)   the child concerned.

(6)   Where the person proposing to apply for an enforcement order in relation to a child arrangements order is the child concerned, the child must obtain the leave of the court before making such an application.

(7)   The court may grant leave to the child concerned only if it is satisfied that he has sufficient understanding to make the proposed application.

(8)   Subsection (2) has effect subject to the restrictions in sections 11K and 11L.

(9)   The court may suspend an enforcement order for such period as it thinks fit.

(10)   Nothing in this section prevents a court from making more than one enforcement order in relation to the same person on the same occasion.

(11)   Proceedings in which any question of making an enforcement order, or any other question with respect to such an order, arises are to be regarded for the purposes of section 11(1) and (2) as proceedings in which a question arises with respect to a section 8 order.

(12)   In Schedule A1—

(a)   Part 1 makes provision as regards an unpaid work requirement;

(b)   Part 2 makes provision in relation to the revocation and amendment of enforcement orders and failure to comply with such orders.

(13)   ...

11K   Enforcement orders: further provision

(1)   A court may not make an enforcement order against a person in respect of a failure to comply with a provision of a child arrangements order unless it is satisfied that before the failure occurred the person had been given (in accordance with rules of court) a copy of, or otherwise informed of the terms of—

(a)   in the case of a failure to comply with a provision of a child arrangements order where the order was varied before the failure occurred, a notice under section 11I relating to the order varying the child arrangements order or, where more than one such order has been made, the last order preceding the failure in question;

(b)   in any other case, a notice under section 11I relating to the child arrangements order.

(2)   A court may not make an enforcement order against a person in respect of any failure to comply with a provision of a child arrangements order occurring before the person attained the age of 18.

(3)   A court may not make an enforcement order against a person in respect of a failure to comply with a provision of a child arrangements order where the child arrangements order is an excepted order (within the meaning given by section 11B(4)).

(4)   A court may not make an enforcement order against a person unless the person is habitually resident in England and Wales; and an enforcement order ceases to have effect if the person subject to the order ceases to be habitually resident in England and Wales.

11L   Enforcement orders: making

(1)   Before making an enforcement order as regards a person in breach of a provision of a child arrangements order, the court must be satisfied that—

(a)   making the enforcement order proposed is necessary to secure the person's compliance with the child arrangements order or any child arrangements order that has effect in its place;

(b)   the likely effect on the person of the enforcement order proposed to be made is proportionate to the seriousness of the breach ....

(2)   Before making an enforcement order, the court must satisfy itself that provision for the person to work under an unpaid work requirement imposed by an enforcement order can be made in the local justice area in which the person in breach resides or will reside.

(3)   Before making an enforcement order as regards a person in breach of a provision of a child arrangements order, the court must obtain and consider information about the person and the likely effect of the enforcement order on him.

(4)   Information about the likely effect of the enforcement order may, in particular, include information as to—

    (a)   any conflict with the person's religious beliefs;

    (b)   any interference with the times (if any) at which he normally works or attends an educational establishment.

(5)   A court that proposes to make an enforcement order may ask an officer of the Service or a Welsh family proceedings officer to provide the court with information as to the matters in subsections (2) and (3).

(6)   It shall be the duty of the officer of the Service or Welsh family proceedings officer to comply with any request under this section.

(7)   In making an enforcement order in relation to a child arrangements order, a court must take into account the welfare of the child who is the subject of the child arrangements order.

11M   Enforcement orders: monitoring

(1)   On making an enforcement order in relation to a person, the court is to ask an officer of the Service or a Welsh family proceedings officer—

    (a)   to monitor, or arrange for the monitoring of, the person's compliance with the unpaid work requirement imposed by the order;

    (b)   to report to the court if a report under paragraph 8 of Schedule A1 is made in relation to the person;

    (c)   to report to the court on such other matters relating to the person's compliance as may be specified in the request;

    (d)   to report to the court if the person is, or becomes, unsuitable to perform work under the requirement.

(2)   It shall be the duty of the officer of the Service or Welsh family proceedings officer to comply with any request under this section.

11N   Enforcement orders: warning notices

Where the court makes an enforcement order, it is to attach to the order a notice warning of the consequences of failing to comply with the order.

11O   Compensation for financial loss

(1)   This section applies if a child arrangements order with respect to a child has been made.

(2)   If the court is satisfied that—

    (a)   an individual has failed to comply with a provision of the child arrangements order, and

    (b)   a person falling within subsection (6) has suffered financial loss by reason of the breach,

    it may make an order requiring the individual in breach to pay the person compensation in respect of his financial loss.

(3)   But the court may not make an order under subsection (2) if it is satisfied that the individual in breach had a reasonable excuse for failing to comply with the particular provision of the child arrangements order.

(4)   The burden of proof as to the matter mentioned in subsection (3) lies on the individual claiming to have had a reasonable excuse.

(5)   An order under subsection (2) may be made only on an application by the person who claims to have suffered financial loss.

(6)   A person falls within this subsection if he is—

    (a)   a person who is, for the purposes of the child arrangements order, a person with whom the child concerned lives or is to live;

    (b)   a person whose contact with the child concerned is provided for in the child arrangements order;

    (c)   an individual subject to a condition under section 11(7)(b) or an activity condition imposed by the child arrangements order; or

    (d)   the child concerned.

(7)   Where the person proposing to apply for an order under subsection (2) is the child concerned, the child must obtain the leave of the court before making such an application.

(8)   The court may grant leave to the child concerned only if it is satisfied that he has sufficient understanding to make the proposed application.

(9)   The amount of compensation is to be determined by the court, but may not exceed the amount of the applicant's financial loss.

(10)   In determining the amount of compensation payable by the individual in breach, the court must take into account the individual's financial circumstances.

(11)   An amount ordered to be paid as compensation may be recovered by the applicant as a civil debt due to him.

(12)   Subsection (2) has effect subject to the restrictions in section 11P.

(13)   Proceedings in which any question of making an order under subsection (2) arises are to be regarded for the purposes of section 11(1) and (2) as proceedings in which a question arises with respect to a section 8 order.

(14)   In exercising its powers under this section, a court is to take into account the welfare of the child concerned.

11P   Orders under section 11O(2): further provision

(1)   A court may not make an order under section 11O(2) requiring an individual to pay compensation in respect of a failure by him to comply with a provision of a child arrangements order unless it is satisfied that before the failure occurred the individual had been given (in accordance with rules of court) a copy of, or otherwise informed of the terms of—

(a)   in the case of a failure to comply with a provision of a child arrangements order where the order was varied before the failure occurred, a notice under section 11I relating to the order varying the child arrangements order or, where more than one such order has been made, the last order preceding the failure in question;

(b)   in any other case, a notice under section 11I relating to the child arrangements order.

(2)   A court may not make an order under section 11O(2) requiring an individual to pay compensation in respect of a failure by him to comply with a provision of a child arrangements order where the failure occurred before the individual attained the age of 18.

(3)   A court may not make an order under section 11O(2) requiring an individual to pay compensation in respect of a failure by him to comply with a provision of a child arrangements order where the child arrangements order is an excepted order (within the meaning given by section 11B(4)).

12   Child arrangements orders and parental responsibility

(1)   Where—

(a)   the court makes a child arrangements order with respect to a child,

(b)   the father of the child, or a woman who is a parent of the child by virtue of section 43 of the Human Fertilisation and Embryology Act 2008, is named in the order as a person with whom the child is to live, and

(c)   the father, or the woman, would not otherwise have parental responsibility for the child,

the court must also make an order under section 4 giving the father, or under section 4ZA giving the woman, that responsibility.

(1A)   Where—

(a)   the court makes a child arrangements order with respect to a child,

(b)   the father of the child, or a woman who is a parent of the child by virtue of section 43 of the Human Fertilisation and Embryology Act 2008, is named in the order as a person with whom the child is to spend time or otherwise have contact but is not named in the order as a person with whom the child is to live, and

(c)   the father, or the woman, would not otherwise have parental responsibility for the child,

the court must decide whether it would be appropriate, in view of the provision made in the order with respect to the father or the woman, for him or her to have parental responsibility for the child and, if it decides that it would be appropriate for the father or the woman to have that responsibility, must also make an order under section 4 giving him, or under section 4ZA giving her, that responsibility.

(2)   Where the court makes a child arrangements order and a person who is not a parent or guardian of the child concerned is named in the order as a person with whom the child is to live, that person shall have parental responsibility for the child while the order remains in force so far as providing for the child to live with that person.

(2A)   Where the court makes a child arrangements order and—

(a)   a person who is not the parent or guardian of the child concerned is named in the order as a person with whom the child is to spend time or otherwise have contact, but

(b)   the person is not named in the order as a person with whom the child is to live,

the court may provide in the order for the person to have parental responsibility for the child while paragraphs (a) and (b) continue to be met in the person's case.

(3)   Where a person has parental responsibility for a child as a result of subsection (2) or (2A), he shall not have the right—

(a)   ...

(b)   to agree, or refuse to agree, to the making of an adoption order, or an order under section 84 of the Adoption and Children Act 2002, with respect to the child; or

(c)   to appoint a guardian for the child.

(4)   Where subsection (1) ... requires the court to make an order under section 4 or 4ZA in respect of a parent of a child, the court shall not bring that order to an end at any time while the child arrangements order concerned remains in force so far as providing for the child to live with that parent.

(5), (6)   ...

13   Change of child's name or removal from jurisdiction

(1)   Where a child arrangements order to which subsection (4) applies is in force with respect to a child, no person may—

(a)   cause the child to be known by a new surname; or

(b)   remove him from the United Kingdom;

without either the written consent of every person who has parental responsibility for the child or the leave of the court.

(2)   Subsection (1)(b) does not prevent the removal of a child, for a period of less than one month, by a person named in the child arrangements order as a person with whom the child is to live.

(3)   In making a child arrangements order to which subsection (4) applies, the court may grant the leave required by subsection (1)(b), either generally or for specified purposes.

(4)   This subsection applies to a child arrangements order if the arrangements regulated by the order consist of, or include, arrangements which relate to either or both of the following—

(a)   with whom the child concerned is to live, and

(b)   when the child is to live with any person.

14A   Special guardianship orders

(1)   A 'special guardianship order' is an order appointing one or more individuals to be a child's 'special guardian' (or special guardians).

(2)   A special guardian—

(a)   must be aged eighteen or over; and

(b)   must not be a parent of the child in question,

and subsections (3) to (6) are to be read in that light.

(3)   The court may make a special guardianship order with respect to any child on the application of an individual who—

(a)   is entitled to make such an application with respect to the child; or

(b)   has obtained the leave of the court to make the application,

or on the joint application of more than one such individual.

(4)   Section 9(3) applies in relation to an application for leave to apply for a special guardianship order as it applies in relation to an application for leave to apply for a section 8 order.

(5)   The individuals who are entitled to apply for a special guardianship order with respect to a child are—

(a)   any guardian of the child;

(b)   any individual who is named in a child arrangements order as a person with whom the child is to live;

(c)   any individual listed in subsection (5)(b) or (c) of section 10 (as read with subsection (10) of that section);

(d)   a local authority foster parent with whom the child has lived for a period of at least one year immediately preceding the application;

(e)   a relative with whom the child has lived for a period of at least one year immediately preceding the application.

(6)   The court may also make a special guardianship order with respect to a child in any family proceedings in which a question arises with respect to the welfare of the child if—

(a)   an application for the order has been made by an individual who falls within subsection (3)(a) or (b) (or more than one such individual jointly); or

(b)   the court considers that a special guardianship order should be made even though no such application has been made.

(7)   No individual may make an application under subsection (3) or (6)(a) unless, before the beginning of the period of three months ending with the date of the application, he has given written notice of his intention to make the application—

(a)   if the child in question is being looked after by a local authority, to that local authority, or

(b)   otherwise, to the local authority in whose area the individual is ordinarily resident.

(8)   On receipt of such a notice, the local authority must investigate the matter and prepare a report for the court dealing with—

(a)   the suitability of the applicant to be a special guardian;

(b)   such matters (if any) as may be prescribed by the Secretary of State; and

(c)   any other matter which the local authority consider to be relevant.

(9)   The court may itself ask a local authority to conduct such an investigation and prepare such a report, and the local authority must do so.

(10)   The local authority may make such arrangements as they see fit for any person to act on their behalf in connection with conducting an investigation or preparing a report referred to in subsection (8) or (9).

(11)   The court may not make a special guardianship order unless it has received a report dealing with the matters referred to in subsection (8).

(12)   Subsections (8) and (9) of section 10 apply in relation to special guardianship orders as they apply in relation to section 8 orders.

(13)   This section is subject to section 29(5) and (6) of the Adoption and Children Act 2002.

14B   Special guardianship orders: making

(1)   Before making a special guardianship order, the court must consider whether, if the order were made—

(a)   a child arrangements order containing contact provision should also be made with respect to the child, ...

(b)   any section 8 order in force with respect to the child should be varied or discharged,

(c)   where provision contained in a child arrangements order made with respect to the child is not discharged, any enforcement order relating to that provision should be revoked, and

(d)   where an activity direction has been made—

(i)   in proceedings for the making, variation or discharge of a child arrangements order with respect to the child, or

(ii)   in other proceedings that relate to such an order,

that direction should be discharged.

(1A)   In subsection (1) "contact provision" means provision which regulates arrangements relating to—

(a)   with whom a child is to spend time or otherwise have contact, or

(b)   when a child is to spend time or otherwise have contact with any person;

but in paragraphs (a) and (b) a reference to spending time or otherwise having contact with a person is to doing that otherwise than as a result of living with the person.

(2)   On making a special guardianship order, the court may also—

    (a)   give leave for the child to be known by a new surname;

    (b)   grant the leave required by section 14C(3)(b), either generally or for specified purposes.

14C   Special guardianship orders: effect

(1)   The effect of a special guardianship order is that while the order remains in force—

    (a)   a special guardian appointed by the order has parental responsibility for the child in respect of whom it is made; and

    (b)   subject to any other order in force with respect to the child under this Act, a special guardian is entitled to exercise parental responsibility to the exclusion of any other person with parental responsibility for the child (apart from another special guardian).

(2)   Subsection (1) does not affect—

    (a)   the operation of any enactment or rule of law which requires the consent of more than one person with parental responsibility in a matter affecting the child; or

    (b)   any rights which a parent of the child has in relation to the child's adoption or placement for adoption.

(3)   While a special guardianship order is in force with respect to a child, no person may—

    (a)   cause the child to be known by a new surname; or

    (b)   remove him from the United Kingdom,

without either the written consent of every person who has parental responsibility for the child or the leave of the court.

(4)   Subsection (3)(b) does not prevent the removal of a child, for a period of less than three months, by a special guardian of his.

(5)   If the child with respect to whom a special guardianship order is in force dies, his special guardian must take reasonable steps to give notice of that fact to—

    (a)   each parent of the child with parental responsibility; and

    (b)   each guardian of the child,

but if the child has more than one special guardian, and one of them has taken such steps in relation to a particular parent or guardian, any other special guardian need not do so as respects that parent or guardian.

(6)   This section is subject to section 29(7) of the Adoption and Children Act 2002.

14D   Special guardianship orders: variation and discharge

(1)   The court may vary or discharge a special guardianship order on the application of—

    (a)   the special guardian (or any of them, if there are more than one);

    (b)   any parent or guardian of the child concerned;

    (c)   any individual who is named in a child arrangements order as a person with whom the child is to live;

    (d)   any individual not falling within any of paragraphs (a) to (c) who has, or immediately before the making of the special guardianship order had, parental responsibility for the child;

    (e)   the child himself; or

    (f)   a local authority designated in a care order with respect to the child.

(2)   In any family proceedings in which a question arises with respect to the welfare of a child with respect to whom a special guardianship order is in force, the court may also vary or discharge the special guardianship order if it considers that the order should be varied or discharged, even though no application has been made under subsection (1).

(3)   The following must obtain the leave of the court before making an application under subsection (1)—

    (a)   the child;

    (b)   any parent or guardian of his;

(c) any step-parent of his who has acquired, and has not lost, parental responsibility for him by virtue of section 4A;

(d) any individual falling within subsection (1)(d) who immediately before the making of the special guardianship order had, but no longer has, parental responsibility for him.

(4) Where the person applying for leave to make an application under subsection (1) is the child, the court may only grant leave if it is satisfied that he has sufficient understanding to make the proposed application under subsection (1).

(5) The court may not grant leave to a person falling within subsection (3)(b)(c) or (d) unless it is satisfied that there has been a significant change in circumstances since the making of the special guardianship order.

15   Orders for financial relief with respect to children

(1) Schedule 1 (which consists primarily of the re-enactment, with consequential amendments and minor modifications, of provisions of section 6 of the Family Law Reform Act 1969, the Guardianship of Minors Acts 1971 and 1973, the Children Act 1975 and of sections 15 and 16 of the Family Law Reform Act 1987) makes provision in relation to financial relief for children.

(2) ...

16   Family assistance orders

(1) Where, in any family proceedings, the court has power to make an order under this Part with respect to any child, it may (whether or not it makes such an order) make an order requiring—

(a) an officer of the Service or a Welsh family proceedings officer to be made available; or

(b) a local authority to make an officer of the authority available,

to advise, assist and (where appropriate) befriend any person named in the order.

(2) The persons who may be named in an order under this section ('a family assistance order') are—

(a) any parent, guardian or special guardian of the child;

(b) any person with whom the child is living or who is named in a child arrangements order as a person with whom the child is to live, spend time or otherwise have contact;

(c) the child himself.

(3) No court may make a family assistance order unless—

(a) ...

(b) it has obtained the consent of every person to be named in the order other than the child.

(4) A family assistance order may direct—

(a) the person named in the order; or

(b) such of the persons named in the order as may be specified in the order,

to take such steps as may be so specified with a view to enabling the officer concerned to be kept informed of the address of any person named in the order and to be allowed to visit any such person.

(4A) If the court makes a family assistance order with respect to a child and the order is to be in force at the same time as contact provision contained in a child arrangements order made with respect to the child, the family assistance order may direct the officer concerned to give advice and assistance as regards establishing, improving and maintaining contact to such of the persons named in the order as may be specified in the order.

(4B) In subsection (4A) "contact provision" means provision which regulates arrangements relating to—

(a) with whom a child is to spend time or otherwise have contact, or

(b) when a child is to spend time or otherwise have contact with any person.

(5) Unless it specifies a shorter period, a family assistance order shall have effect for a period of twelve months beginning with the day on which it is made.

(6) If the court makes a family assistance order with respect to a child and the order is to be in force at the same time as a section 8 order made with respect to the child, the family assistance order may direct the officer concerned to report to the court on such matters relating to the section 8 order as the court may require (including the question whether the section 8 order ought to be varied or discharged).

(7) A family assistance order shall not be made so as to require a local authority to make an officer of theirs available unless—

(a)   the authority agree; or

(b)   the child concerned lives or will live within their area.

(8), (9) ...

17   Provision of services for children in need, their families and others

(1)   It shall be the general duty of every local authority (in addition to the other duties imposed on them by this Part)—

(a)   to safeguard and promote the welfare of children within their area who are in need; and

(b)   so far as is consistent with that duty, to promote the upbringing of such children by their families,

by providing a range and level of services appropriate to those children's needs.

(2)   For the purpose principally of facilitating the discharge of their general duty under this section, every local authority shall have the specific duties and powers set out in Part I of Schedule 2.

(3)   Any service provided by an authority in the exercise of functions conferred on them by this section may be provided for the family of a particular child in need or for any member of his family, if it is provided with a view to safeguarding or promoting the child's welfare.

(4)   The Secretary of State may by order amend any provision of Part I of Schedule 2 or add any further duty or power to those for the time being mentioned there.

(4A)   Before determining what (if any) services to provide for a particular child in need in the exercise of functions conferred on them by this section, a local authority shall, so far as is reasonably practicable and consistent with the child's welfare—

(a)   ascertain the child's wishes and feelings regarding the provision of those services; and

(b)   give due consideration (having regard to his age and understanding) to such wishes and feelings of the child as they have been able to ascertain.

(5)   Every local authority—

(a)   shall facilitate the provision by others (including in particular voluntary organisations) of services which it is a function of the authority to provide by virtue of this section, or section 18, 20, 22A to 22C, 23B to 23D, 24A or 24B; and

(b)   may make such arrangements as they see fit for any person to act on their behalf in the provision of any such service.

(6)   The services provided by a local authority in the exercise of functions conferred on them by this section may include providing accommodation and giving assistance in kind or ... in cash.

(7)   Assistance may be unconditional or subject to conditions as to the repayment of the assistance or of its value (in whole or in part).

(8)   Before giving any assistance or imposing any conditions, a local authority shall have regard to the means of the child concerned and of each of his parents.

(9)   No person shall be liable to make any repayment of assistance or of its value at any time when he is in receipt of universal credit (except in such circumstances as may be prescribed), of income support under Part VII of the Social Security Contributions and Benefits Act 1992, of any element of child tax credit other than the family element, of working tax credit, of an income-based jobseeker's allowance or of an income-related employment and support allowance.

(10)   For the purposes of this Part a child shall be taken to be in need if—

(a)   he is unlikely to achieve or maintain, or to have the opportunity of achieving or maintaining, a reasonable standard of health or development without the provision for him of services by a local authority under this Part;

(b)   his health or development is likely to be significantly impaired, or further impaired, without the provision for him of such services; or

(c)   he is disabled,

and 'family,' in relation to such a child, includes any person who has parental responsibility for the child and any other person with whom he has been living.

(11)   For the purposes of this Part, a child is disabled if he is blind, deaf or dumb or suffers from mental disorder of any kind or is substantially and permanently handicapped by illness, injury or congenital deformity or such other disability as may be prescribed; and in this Part—

'development' means physical, intellectual, emotional, social or behavioural development; and

'health' means physical or mental health.

(12) The Treasury may by regulations prescribe circumstances in which a person is to be treated for the purposes of this Part (or for such of those purposes as are prescribed) as in receipt of any element of child tax credit other than the family element or of working tax credit.

(13) The duties imposed on a local authority by virtue of this section do not apply in relation to a child in the authority's area who is being looked after by a local authority in Wales in accordance with Part 6 of the Social Services and Well-being (Wales) Act 2014.

20 Provision of accommodation for children: general

(1) Every local authority shall provide accommodation for any child in need within their area who appears to them to require accommodation as a result of—

    (a) there being no person who has parental responsibility for him;

    (b) his being lost or having been abandoned; or

    (c) the person who has been caring for him being prevented (whether or not permanently, and for whatever reason) from providing him with suitable accommodation or care.

(2) Where a local authority provide accommodation under subsection (1) for a child who is ordinarily resident in the area of another local authority, that other local authority may take over the provision of accommodation for the child within—

    (a) three months of being notified in writing that the child is being provided with accommodation; or

    (b) such other longer period as may be prescribed in regulations made by the Secretary of State.

(2A) Where a local authority in Wales provide accommodation under section 76(1) of the Social Services and Well-being (Wales) Act 2014 (accommodation for children without parents or who are lost or abandoned etc) for a child who is ordinarily resident in the area of a local authority in England, that local authority in England may take over the provision of accommodation for the child within—

    (a) three months of being notified in writing that the child is being provided with accommodation; or

    (b) such other longer period as may be prescribed in regulations made by the Secretary of State.

(3) Every local authority shall provide accommodation for any child in need within their area who has reached the age of sixteen and whose welfare the authority consider is likely to be seriously prejudiced if they do not provide him with accommodation.

(4) A local authority may provide accommodation for any child within their area (even though a person who has parental responsibility for him is able to provide him with accommodation) if they consider that to do so would safeguard or promote the child's welfare.

(5) A local authority may provide accommodation for any person who has reached the age of sixteen but is under twenty-one in any community home which takes children who have reached the age of sixteen if they consider that to do so would safeguard or promote his welfare.

(6) Before providing accommodation under this section, a local authority shall, so far as is reasonably practicable and consistent with the child's welfare—

    (a) ascertain the child's wishes and feelings regarding the provision of accommodation; and

    (b) give due consideration (having regard to his age and understanding) to such wishes and feelings of the child as they have been able to ascertain.

(7) A local authority may not provide accommodation under this section for any child if any person who—

    (a) has parental responsibility for him; and

    (b) is willing and able to—

        (i) provide accommodation for him; or

        (ii) arrange for accommodation to be provided for him,

objects.

(8) Any person who has parental responsibility for a child may at any time remove the child from accommodation provided by or on behalf of the local authority under this section.

(9) Subsections (7) and (8) do not apply while any person—

    (a) who is named in a child arrangements order as a person with whom the child is to live;

(aa)   who is a special guardian of the child; or

(b)   who has care of the child by virtue of an order made in the exercise of the High Court's inherent jurisdiction with respect to children,

agrees to the child being looked after in accommodation provided by or on behalf of the local authority.

(10)   Where there is more than one such person as is mentioned in subsection (9), all of them must agree.

(11)   Subsections (7) and (8) do not apply where a child who has reached the age of sixteen agrees to being provided with accommodation under this section.

22   General duty of local authority in relation to children looked after by them

(1)   In this section, any reference to a child who is looked after by a local authority is a reference to a child who is—

(a)   in their care; or

(b)   provided with accommodation by the authority in the exercise of any functions (in particular those under this Act) which are social services functions within the meaning of the Local Authority Social Services Act 1970, apart from functions under sections 17, 23B and 24B.

(2)   In subsection (1) 'accommodation' means accommodation which is provided for a continuous period of more than 24 hours.

(3)   It shall be the duty of a local authority looking after any child—

(a)   to safeguard and promote his welfare; and

(b)   to make such use of services available for children cared for by their own parents as appears to the authority reasonable in his case.

(3A)   The duty of a local authority under subsection (3)(a) to safeguard and promote the welfare of a child looked after by them includes in particular a duty to promote the child's educational achievement.

(3B)   A local authority ... must appoint at least one person for the purpose of discharging the duty imposed by virtue of subsection (3A).

(3C)   A person appointed by a local authority under subsection (3B) must be an officer employed by that authority or another local authority ....

(4)   Before making any decision with respect to a child whom they are looking after, or proposing to look after, a local authority shall, so far as is reasonably practicable, ascertain the wishes and feelings of—

(a)   the child;

(b)   his parents;

(c)   any person who is not a parent of his but who has parental responsibility for him; and

(d)   any other person whose wishes and feelings the authority consider to be relevant,

regarding the matter to be decided.

(5)   In making any such decision a local authority shall give due consideration—

(a)   having regard to his age and understanding, to such wishes and feelings of the child as they have been able to ascertain;

(b)   to such wishes and feelings of any person mentioned in subsection (4)(b) to (d) as they have been able to ascertain; and

(c)   to the child's religious persuasion, racial origin and cultural and linguistic background.

(6)   If it appears to a local authority that it is necessary, for the purposes of protecting members of the public from serious injury, to exercise their powers with respect to a child whom they are looking after in a manner which may not be consistent with their duties under this section, they may do so.

(7)   If the Secretary of State considers it necessary, for the purpose of protecting members of the public from serious injury, to give directions to a local authority with respect to the exercise of their powers with respect to a child whom they are looking after, the Secretary of State may give such directions to the authority.

(8)   Where any such directions are given to an authority they shall comply with them even though doing so is inconsistent with their duties under this section.

22A   Provision of accommodation for children in care

When a child is in the care of a local authority, it is their duty to provide the child with accommodation.

22B   Maintenance of looked after children

It is the duty of a local authority to maintain a child they are looking after in other respects apart from the provision of accommodation.

22C   Ways in which looked after children are to be accommodated and maintained

(1)   This section applies where a local authority are looking after a child ('C').

(2)   The local authority must make arrangements for C to live with a person who falls within subsection (3) (but subject to subsection (4)).

(3)   A person ('P') falls within this subsection if—

　　(a)   P is a parent of C;

　　(b)   P is not a parent of C but has parental responsibility for C; or

　　(c)   in a case where C is in the care of the local authority and there was a child arrangements order in force with respect to C immediately before the care order was made, P was a person named in the child arrangements order as a person with whom C was to live.

(4)   Subsection (2) does not require the local authority to make arrangements of the kind mentioned in that subsection if doing so—

　　(a)   would not be consistent with C's welfare; or

　　(b)   would not be reasonably practicable.

(5)   If the local authority are unable to make arrangements under subsection (2), they must place C in the placement which is, in their opinion, the most appropriate placement available.

(6)   In subsection (5) 'placement' means—

　　(a)   placement with an individual who is a relative, friend or other person connected with C and who is also a local authority foster parent;

　　(b)   placement with a local authority foster parent who does not fall within paragraph (a);

　　(c)   placement in a children's home in respect of which a person is registered under Part 2 of the Care Standards Act 2000 or Part 1 of the Regulation and Inspection of Social Care (Wales) Act 2016 (anaw 2); or

　　(d)   subject to section 22D, placement in accordance with other arrangements which comply with any regulations made for the purposes of this section.

(7)   In determining the most appropriate placement for C, the local authority must, subject to subsection (9B) and the other provisions of this Part (in particular, to their duties under section 22)—

　　(a)   give preference to a placement falling within paragraph (a) of subsection (6) over placements falling within the other paragraphs of that subsection;

　　(b)   comply, so far as is reasonably practicable in all the circumstances of C's case, with the requirements of subsection (8); and

　　(c)   comply with subsection (9) unless that is not reasonably practicable.

(8)   The local authority must ensure that the placement is such that—

　　(a)   it allows C to live near C's home;

　　(b)   it does not disrupt C's education or training;

　　(c)   if C has a sibling for whom the local authority are also providing accommodation, it enables C and the sibling to live together;

　　(d)   if C is disabled, the accommodation provided is suitable to C's particular needs.

(9)   The placement must be such that C is provided with accommodation within the local authority's area.

(9A)   Subsection (9B) applies (subject to subsection (9C)) where the local authority ...—

　　(a)   are considering adoption for C, or

　　(b)   are satisfied that C ought to be placed for adoption but are not authorised under section 19 of the Adoption and Children Act 2002 (placement with parental consent) or by virtue of section 21 of that Act (placement orders) to place C for adoption.

(9B)   Where this subsection applies—

　　(a)   subsections (7) to (9) do not apply to the local authority,

　　(b)   the local authority must consider placing C with an individual within subsection (6)(a), and

(c)   where the local authority decide that a placement with such an individual is not the most appropriate placement for C, the local authority must consider placing C with a local authority foster parent who has been approved as a prospective adopter.

(9C)   Subsection (9B) does not apply where the local authority have applied for a placement order under section 21 of the Adoption and Children Act 2002 in respect of C and the application has been refused.

(10)   The local authority may determine—

(a)   the terms of any arrangements they make under subsection (2) in relation to C (including terms as to payment); and

(b)   the terms on which they place C with a local authority foster parent (including terms as to payment but subject to any order made under section 49 of the Children Act 2004).

(11)   The Secretary of State may make regulations for, and in connection with, the purposes of this section.

(12)   For the meaning of 'local authority foster parent' see section 105(1).

22F   Regulations as to children looked after by local authorities

Part 2 of Schedule 2 has effect for the purposes of making further provision as to children looked after by local authorities and in particular as to the regulations which may be made under section 22C(11).

22G   General duty of local authority to secure sufficient accommodation for looked after children

(1)   It is the general duty of a local authority to take steps that secure, so far as reasonably practicable, the outcome in subsection (2).

(2)   The outcome is that the local authority are able to provide the children mentioned in subsection (3) with accommodation that—

(a)   is within the authority's area; and

(b)   meets the needs of those children.

(3)   The children referred to in subsection (2) are those—

(a)   that the local authority are looking after,

(b)   in respect of whom the authority are unable to make arrangements under section 22C(2), and

(c)   whose circumstances are such that it would be consistent with their welfare for them to be provided with accommodation that is in the authority's area.

(4)   In taking steps to secure the outcome in subsection (2), the local authority must have regard to the benefit of having—

(a)   a number of accommodation providers in their area that is, in their opinion, sufficient to secure that outcome; and

(b)   a range of accommodation in their area capable of meeting different needs that is, in their opinion, sufficient to secure that outcome.

(5)   In this section ' accommodation providers ' means—

local authority foster parents; and

children's homes in respect of which a person is registered under Part 2 of the Care Standards Act 2000.

26   Review of cases and inquiries into representations

(1)   The Secretary of State may make regulations requiring the case of each child who is being looked after by a local authority to be reviewed in accordance with the provisions of the regulations.

(2)   The regulations may, in particular, make provision—

(a)   as to the manner in which each case is to be reviewed;

(b)   as to the considerations to which the local authority are to have regard in reviewing each case;

(c)   as to the time when each case is first to be reviewed and the frequency of subsequent reviews;

(d)   requiring the authority, before conducting any review, to seek the views of—

(i)   the child;

(ii)   his parents;

(iii)   any person who is not a parent of his but who has parental responsibility for him; and

(iv)   any other person whose views the authority consider to be relevant,

including, in particular, the views of those persons in relation to any particular matter which is to be considered in the course of the review;

(e)   requiring the authority ..., in the case of a child who is in their care—

(i)   to keep the section 31A plan for the child under review and, if they are of the opinion that some change is required, to revise the plan, or make a new plan, accordingly,

(ii)   to consider whether an application should be made to discharge the care order;

(f)   requiring the authority ..., in the case of a child in accommodation provided by the authority—

(i)   if there is no plan for the future care of the child, to prepare one,

(ii)   if there is such a plan for the child, to keep it under review and, if they are of the opinion that some change is required, to revise the plan or make a new plan, accordingly,

(iii)   to consider whether the accommodation accords with the requirements of this Part;

(g)   requiring the authority to inform the child, so far as is reasonably practicable, of any steps he may take under this Act;

(h)   requiring the authority to make arrangements, including arrangements with such other bodies providing services as it considers appropriate, to implement any decision which they propose to make in the course, or as a result, of the review;

(i)   requiring the authority to notify details of the result of the review and of any decision taken by them in consequence of the review to—

(i)   the child;

(ii)   his parents;

(iii)   any person who is not a parent of his but who has parental responsibility for him; and

(iv)   any other person whom they consider ought to be notified;

(j)   requiring the authority to monitor the arranangements which they have made with a view to ensuring that they comply with the regulations;

(k)   ...

(2A)–(2D) ...

(3)   Every local authority shall establish a procedure for considering any representations (including any complaint) made to them by—

(a)   any child who is being looked after by them or who is not being looked after by them but is in need;

(b)   a parent of his;

(c)   any person who is not a parent of his but who has parental responsibility for him;

(d)   any local authority foster parent;

(e)   such other person as the authority consider has a sufficient interest in the child's welfare to warrant his representations being considered by them,

about the discharge by the authority of any of their qualifying functions in relation to the child.

(3A)   The following are qualifying functions for the purposes of subsection (3)—

(a)   functions under this Part,

(b)   such functions under Part 4 or 5 as are specified by the Secretary of State in regulations.

(3B)   The duty under subsection (3) extends to representations (including complaints) made to the authority by—

(a)   any person mentioned in section 3(1) of the Adoption and Children Act 2002 (persons for whose needs provision is made by the Adoption Service) and any other person to whom arrangements for the provision of adoption support services (within the meaning of that Act) extend,

(b)   such other person as the authority consider has sufficient interest in a child who is or may be adopted to warrant his representations being considered by them,

about the discharge by the authority of such functions under the Adoption and Children Act 2002 as are specified by the Secretary of State in regulations.

(3C)   The duty under subsection (3) extends to any representations (including complaints) which are made to the authority by—

(a)   a child with respect to whom a special guardianship order is in force,

(b)   a special guardian or a parent of such a child,

(c)   any other person the authority consider has a sufficient interest in the welfare of such a child to warrant his representations being considered by them, or

(d)   any person who has applied for an assessment under section 14F(3) or (4),

about the discharge by the authority of such functions under section 14F as may be specified by the Secretary of State in regulations.

(4)   The procedure shall ensure that at least one person who is not a member or officer of the authority takes part in—

(a)   the consideration; and

(b)   any discussions which are held by the authority about the action (if any) to be taken in relation to the child in the light of the consideration,

but this subsection is subject to subsection (5A).

(4A)   Regulations may be made by the Secretary of State imposing time limits on the making of representations under this section.

(5)   In carrying out any consideration of representations under this section a local authority shall comply with any regulations made by the Secretary of State for the purpose of regulating the procedure to be followed.

(5A)   Regulations under subsection (5) may provide that subsection (4) does not apply in relation to any consideration or discussion which takes place as part of a procedure for which provision is made by the regulations for the purpose of resolving informally the matters raised in the representations.

(6)   The Secretary of State may make regulations requiring local authorities to monitor the arrangements that they have made with a view to ensuring that they comply with any regulations made for the purposes of subsection (5).

(7)   Where any representation has been considered under the procedure established by a local authority under this section, the authority shall—

(a)   have due regard to the findings of those considering the representation; and

(b)   take such steps as are reasonably practicable to notify (in writing)—

(i)   the person making the representation;

(ii)   the child (if the authority consider that he has sufficient understanding); and

(iii)   such other persons (if any) as appear to the authority to be likely to be affected,

of the authority's decision in the matter and their reasons for taking that decision and of any action which they have taken, or propose to take.

(8)   Every local authority shall give such publicity to their procedure for considering representations under this section as they consider appropriate.

31   Care and supervision orders

(1)   On the application of any local authority or authorised person, the court may make an order—

(a)   placing the child with respect to whom the application is made in the care of a designated local authority; or

(b)   putting him under the supervision of a designated local authority. ...

(2)   A court may only make a care order or supervision order if it is satisfied—

(a)   that the child concerned is suffering, or is likely to suffer, significant harm; and

(b)   that the harm, or likelihood of harm, is attributable to—

(i)   the care given to the child, or likely to be given to him if the order were not made, not being what it would be reasonable to expect a parent to give to him; or

(ii)   the child's being beyond parental control.

(3)   No care order or supervision order may be made with respect to a child who has reached the age of seventeen (or sixteen, in the case of a child who is married).

(3A)   A court deciding whether to make a care order—

(a)   is required to consider the permanence provisions of the section 31A plan for the child concerned, but

(b)   is not required to consider the remainder of the section 31A plan, subject to section 34(11).

(3B)   For the purposes of subsection (3A), the permanence provisions of a section 31A plan are—

    (a)   such of the plan's provisions setting out the long-term plan for the upbringing of the child concerned as provide for any of the following—

        (i)   the child to live with any parent of the child's or with any other member of, or any friend of, the child's family;

        (ii)   adoption;

        (iii)   long-term care not within sub-paragraph (i) or (ii);

    (b)   such of the plan's provisions as set out any of the following—

        (i)   the impact on the child concerned of any harm that he or she suffered or was likely to suffer;

        (ii)   the current and future needs of the child (including needs arising out of that impact);

        (iii)   the way in which the long-term plan for the upbringing of the child would meet those current and future needs.

(3C)   The Secretary of State may by regulations amend this section for the purpose of altering what for the purposes of subsection (3A) are the permanence provisions of a section 31A plan.

(4)   An application under this section may be made on its own or in any other family proceedings.

(5)   The court may—

    (a)   on an application for a care order, make a supervision order;

    (b)   on an application for a supervision order, make a care order.

(6)   Where an authorised person proposes to make an application under this section he shall—

    (a)   if it is reasonably practicable to do so; and

    (b)   before making the application,

consult the local authority appearing to him to be the authority in whose area the child concerned is ordinarily resident.

(7)   An application made by an authorised person shall not be entertained by the court if, at the time when it is made, the child concerned is—

    (a)   the subject of an earlier application for a care order, or supervision order, which has not been disposed of; or

    (b)   subject to—

        (i)   a care order or supervision order;

        (ii)   a youth rehabilitation order within the meaning of Part 1 of the Criminal Justice and Immigration Act 2008;

        (iii)   (applies to Scotland only)

(8)   The local authority designated in a care order must be—

    (a)   the authority within whose area the child is ordinarily resident; or

    (b)   where the child does not reside in the area of a local authority, the authority within whose area any circumstances arose in consequence of which the order is being made.

(9)   In this section—

'authorised person' means—

    (a)   the National Society for the Prevention of Cruelty to Children and any of its officers; and

    (b)   any person authorised by order of the Secretary of State to bring proceedings under this section and any officer of a body which is so authorised;

'harm' means ill-treatment or the impairment of health or development including, for example, impairment suffered from seeing or hearing the ill-treatment of another;

'development' means physical, intellectual, emotional, social or behavioural development;

'health' means physical or mental health; and

'ill-treatment' includes sexual abuse and forms of ill-treatment which are not physical.

(10)   Where the question of whether harm suffered by a child is significant turns on the child's health or development, his health or development shall be compared with that which could reasonably be expected of a similar child.

(11)   In this Act—

'a care order' means (subject to section 105(1)) an order under subsection (1)(a) and (except where express provision to the contrary is made) includes an interim care order made under section 38; and

'a supervision order' means an order under subsection (1)(b) and (except where express provision to the contrary is made) includes an interim supervision order made under section 38.

31A   Care orders: care plans

(1)   Where an application is made on which a care order might be made with respect to a child, the appropriate local authority must, within such time as the court may direct, prepare a plan ('a care plan') for the future care of the child.

(2)   While the application is pending, the authority must keep any care plan prepared by them under review and, if they are of the opinion some change is required, revise the plan, or make a new plan, accordingly.

(3)   A care plan must give any prescribed information and do so in the prescribed manner.

(4)   For the purposes of this section, the appropriate local authority, in relation to a child in respect of whom a care order might be made, is the local authority proposed to be designated in the order.

(5)   In section 31(3A) and this section, references to a care order do not include an interim care order.

(6)   A plan prepared, or treated as prepared, under this section is referred to in this Act as a 'section 31A care plan'.

33   Effect of care order

(1)   Where a care order is made with respect to a child it shall be the duty of the local authority designated by the order to receive the child into their care and to keep him in their care while the order remains in force.

(2)   Where—

(a)   a care order has been made with respect to a child on the application of an authorised person; but

(b)   the local authority designated by the order was not informed that that person proposed to make the application,

the child may be kept in the care of that person until received into the care of the authority.

(3)   While a care order is in force with respect to a child, the local authority designated by the order shall—

(a)   have parental responsibility for the child; and

(b)   have the power (subject to the following provisions of this section) to determine the extent to which—

(i)   a parent, guardian or special guardian of the child; or

(ii)   a person who by virtue of section 4A has parental responsibility for the child,

may meet his parental responsibility for him.

(4)   The authority may not exercise the power in subsection (3)(b) unless they are satisfied that it is necessary to do so in order to safeguard or promote the child's welfare.

(5)   Nothing in subsection (3)(b) shall prevent a person mentioned in that provision who has care of the child from doing what is reasonable in all the circumstances of the case for the purpose of safeguarding or promoting his welfare.

(6)   While a care order is in force with respect to a child, the local authority designated by the order shall not—

(a)   cause the child to be brought up in any religious persuasion other than that in which he would have been brought up if the order had not been made; or

(b)   have the right—

(i)   ...

(ii)   to agree or refuse to agree to the making of an adoption order, or an order under section 84 of the Adoption and Children Act 2002, with respect to the child; or

(iii)   to appoint a guardian for the child.

(7)   While a care order is in force with respect to a child, no person may—

(a)   cause the child to be known by a new surname; or

(b)   remove him from the United Kingdom,

without either the written consent of every person who has parental responsibility for the child or the leave of the court.

(8)   Subsection (7)(b) does not—

(a)   prevent the removal of such a child, for a period of less than one month, by the authority in whose care he is; or

(b)   apply to arrangements for such a child to live outside England and Wales (which are governed by paragraph 19 of Schedule 2 in England, and section 124 of the Social Services and Well-being (Wales) Act 2014 in Wales).

(9)   The power in subsection (3)(b) is subject (in addition to being subject to the provisions of this section) to any right, duty, power, responsibility or authority which a person mentioned in that provision has in relation to the child and his property by virtue of any other enactment.

34   Parental contact etc with children in care

(1)   Where a child is in the care of a local authority, the authority shall (subject to the provisions of this section and their duty under section 22(3)(a) or, where the local authority is in Wales, under section 78(1)(a) of the Social Services and Well-being (Wales) Act 2014) allow the child reasonable contact with—

(a)   his parents;

(b)   any guardian or special guardian of his;

(ba)   any person who by virtue of section 4A has parental responsibility for him;

(c)   where there was a child arrangements order in force with respect to the child immediately before the care order was made, any person named in the child arrangements order as a person with whom the child was to live; and

(d)   where, immediately before the care order was made, a person had care of the child by virtue of an order made in the exercise of the High Court's inherent jurisdiction with respect to children, that person.

(2)   On an application made by the authority or the child, the court may make such order as it considers appropriate with respect to the contact which is to be allowed between the child and any named person.

(3)   On an application made by—

(a)   any person mentioned in paragraphs (a) to (d) of subsection (1); or

(b)   any person who has obtained the leave of the court to make the application,

the court may make such order as it considers appropriate with respect to the contact which is to be allowed between the child and that person.

(4)   On an application made by the authority or the child, the court may make an order authorising the authority to refuse to allow contact between the child and any person who is mentioned in paragraphs (a) to (d) of subsection (1) and named in the order.

(5)   When making a care order with respect to a child, or in any family proceedings in connection with a child who is in the care of a local authority, the court may make an order under this section, even though no application for such an order has been made with respect to the child, if it considers that the order should be made.

(6)   An authority may refuse to allow the contact that would otherwise be required by virtue of subsection (1) or an order under this section if—

(a)   they are satisfied that it is necessary to do so in order to safeguard or promote the child's welfare; and

(b)   the refusal—

(i)   is decided upon as a matter of urgency; and

(ii)   does not last for more than seven days.

(6A)   Where (by virtue of an order under this section, or because subsection (6) applies) a local authority in England are authorised to refuse to allow contact between the child and a person mentioned in any of paragraphs (a) to (c) of paragraph 15(1) of Schedule 2, paragraph 15(1) of that Schedule does not require the authority to endeavour to promote contact between the child and that person.

(6B)   Where (by virtue of an order under this section, or because subsection (6) applies) a local authority in Wales is authorised to refuse contact between the child and a person mentioned in any of paragraphs

(a) to (c) of section 95(1) of the Social Services and Well-being (Wales) Act 2014, section 95(1) of that Act does not require the authority to promote contact between the child and that person.

(7) An order under this section may impose such conditions as the court considers appropriate.

(8) The Secretary of State may by regulations make provision as to—

  (za) what a local authority in England must have regard to in considering whether contact between a child and a person mentioned in any of paragraphs (a) to (d) of subsection (1) is consistent with safeguarding and promoting the child's welfare;

  (a) the steps to be taken by a local authority who have exercised their powers under subsection (6);

  (b) the circumstances in which, and conditions subject to which, the terms of any order under this section may be departed from by agreement between the local authority and the person in relation to whom the order is made;

  (c) notification by a local authority of any variation or suspension of arrangements made (otherwise than under an order under this section) with a view to affording any person contact with a child to whom this section applies.

(9) The court may vary or discharge any order made under this section on the application of the authority, the child concerned or the person named in the order.

(10) An order under this section may be made either at the same time as the care order itself or later.

(11) Before making, varying or discharging an order under this section or making a care order with respect to any child the court shall—

  (a) consider the arrangements which the authority have made, or propose to make, for affording any person contact with a child to whom this section applies; and

  (b) invite the parties to the proceedings to comment on those arrangements.

35 Supervision orders

(1) While a supervision order is in force it shall be the duty of the supervisor—

  (a) to advise, assist and befriend the supervised child;

  (b) to take such steps as are reasonably necessary to give effect to the order; and

  (c) where—

    (i) the order is not wholly complied with; or

    (ii) the supervisor considers that the order may no longer be necessary,

    to consider whether or not to apply to the court for its variation or discharge.

(2) Parts I and II of Schedule 3 make further provision with respect to supervision orders.

37 Powers of court in certain family proceedings

(1) Where, in any family proceedings in which a question arises with respect to the welfare of any child, it appears to the court that it may be appropriate for a care or supervision order to be made with respect to him, the court may direct the appropriate authority to undertake an investigation of the child's circumstances.

(2) Where the court gives a direction under this section the local authority concerned shall, when undertaking the investigation, consider whether they should—

  (a) apply for a care order or for a supervision order with respect to the child;

  (b) provide services or assistance for the child or his family; or

  (c) take any other action with respect to the child.

(3) Where a local authority undertake an investigation under this section, and decide not to apply for a care order or supervision order with respect to the child concerned, they shall inform the court of—

  (a) their reasons for so deciding;

  (b) any service or assistance which they have provided, or intend to provide, for the child and his family; and

  (c) any other action which they have taken, or propose to take, with respect to the child.

(4) The information shall be given to the court before the end of the period of eight weeks beginning with the date of the direction, unless the court otherwise directs.

(5) The local authority named in a direction under subsection (1) must be—

(a) the authority in whose area the child is ordinarily resident; or

(b) where the child is not ordinarily resident in the area of a local authority, the authority within whose area any circumstances arose in consequence of which the direction is being given.

(6) If, on the conclusion of any investigation or review under this section, the authority decide not to apply for a care order or supervision order with respect to the child—

(a) they shall consider whether it would be appropriate to review the case at a later date; and

(b) if they decide that it would be, they shall determine the date on which that review is to begin.

38 Interim orders

(1) Where—

(a) in any proceedings on an application for a care order or supervision order, the proceedings are adjourned; or

(b) the court gives a direction under section 37(1),

the court may make an interim care order or an interim supervision order with respect to the child concerned.

(2) A court shall not make an interim care order or interim supervision order under this section unless it is satisfied that there are reasonable grounds for believing that the circumstances with respect to the child are as mentioned in section 31(2).

(3) Where, in any proceedings on an application for a care order or supervision order, a court makes a child arrangements order with respect to the living arrangements of the child concerned, it shall also make an interim supervision order with respect to him unless satisfied that his welfare will be satisfactorily safeguarded without an interim order being made.

(3A) For the purposes of subsection (3), a child arrangements order is one made with respect to the living arrangements of the child concerned if the arrangements regulated by the order consist of, or include, arrangements which relate to either or both of the following—

(a) with whom the child is to live, and

(b) when the child is to live with any person.

(4) An interim order made under or by virtue of this section shall have effect for such period as may be specified in the order, but shall in any event cease to have effect on whichever of the following events first occurs—

(a), (b) ...

(c) in a case which falls within subsection (1)(a), the disposal of the application;

(d) in a case which falls within subsection (1)(b), the disposal of an application for a care order or supervision order made by the authority with respect to the child;

(da) in a case which falls within subsection (1)(b) and in which—

(i) no direction has been given under section 37(4), and

(ii) no application for a care order or supervision order has been made with respect to the child,

the expiry of the period of eight weeks beginning with the date on which the order is made;

(e) in a case which falls within subsection (1)(b) and in which—

(i) the court has given a direction under section 37(4), but

(ii) no application for a care order or supervision order has been made with respect to the child,

the expiry of the period fixed by that direction.

(5) ...

(6) Where the court makes an interim care order, or interim supervision order, it may give such directions (if any) as it considers appropriate with regard to the medical or psychiatric examination or other assessment of the child; but if the child is of sufficient understanding to make an informed decision he may refuse to submit to the examination or other assessment.

(7) A direction under subsection (6) may be to the effect that there is to be—

(a) no such examination or assessment; or

(b) no such examination or assessment unless the court directs otherwise.

(7A)   A direction under subsection (6) to the effect that there is to be a medical or psychiatric examination or other assessment of the child may be given only if the court is of the opinion that the examination or other assessment is necessary to assist the court to resolve the proceedings justly.

(7B)   When deciding whether to give a direction under subsection (6) to that effect the court is to have regard in particular to—

(a)   any impact which any examination or other assessment would be likely to have on the welfare of the child, and any other impact which giving the direction would be likely to have on the welfare of the child,

(b)   the issues with which the examination or other assessment would assist the court,

(c)   the questions which the examination or other assessment would enable the court to answer,

(d)   the evidence otherwise available,

(e)   the impact which the direction would be likely to have on the timetable, duration and conduct of the proceedings,

(f)   the cost of the examination or other assessment, and

(g)   any matters prescribed by Family Procedure Rules.

(8)   A direction under subsection (6) may be—

(a)   given when the interim order is made or at any time while it is in force; and

(b)   varied at any time on the application of any person falling within any class of person prescribed by rules of court for the purposes of this subsection.

(9)   Paragraphs 4 and 5 of Schedule 3 shall not apply in relation to an interim supervision order.

(10)   Where a court makes an order under or by virtue of this section it shall, in determining the period for which the order is to be in force, consider whether any party who was, or might have been, opposed to the making of the order was in a position to argue his case against the order in full.

38A   Power to include exclusion requirement in interim care order

(1)   Where—

(a)   on being satisfied that there are reasonable grounds for believing that the circumstances with respect to a child are as mentioned in section 31(2)(a) and (b)(i), the court makes an interim care order with respect to a child, and

(b)   the conditions mentioned in subsection (2) are satisfied,

the court may include an exclusion requirement in the interim care order.

(2)   The conditions are—

(a)   that there is reasonable cause to believe that, if a person ('the relevant person') is excluded from a dwelling-house in which the child lives, the child will cease to suffer, or cease to be likely to suffer, significant harm, and

(b)   that another person living in the dwelling-house (whether a parent of the child or some other person)—

(i)   is able and willing to give to the child the care which it would be reasonable to expect a parent to give him, and

(ii)   consents to the inclusion of the exclusion requirement.

(3)   For the purposes of this section an exclusion requirement is any one or more of the following—

(a)   a provision requiring the relevant person to leave a dwelling-house in which he is living with the child,

(b)   a provision prohibiting the relevant person from entering a dwelling-house in which the child lives, and

(c)   a provision excluding the relevant person from a defined area in which a dwelling-house in which the child lives is situated.

(4)   The court may provide that the exclusion requirement is to have effect for a shorter period than the other provisions of the interim care order.

(5)   Where the court makes an interim care order containing an exclusion requirement, the court may attach a power of arrest to the exclusion requirement.

(6)   Where the court attaches a power of arrest to an exclusion requirement of an interim care order, it may provide that the power of arrest is to have effect for a shorter period than the exclusion requirement.

(7)   Any period specified for the purposes of subsection (4) or (6) may be extended by the court (on one or more occasions) on an application to vary or discharge the interim care order.

(8)   Where a power of arrest is attached to an exclusion requirement of an interim care order by virtue of subsection (5), a constable may arrest without warrant any person whom he has reasonable cause to believe to be in breach of the requirement.

(9)   Sections 47(7), (11) and (12) and 48 of, and Schedule 5 to, the Family Law Act 1996 shall have effect in relation to a person arrested under subsection (8) of this section as they have effect in relation to a person arrested under section 47(6) of that Act.

(10)   If, while an interim care order containing an exclusion requirement is in force, the local authority have removed the child from the dwelling-house from which the relevant person is excluded to other accommodation for a continuous period of more than 24 hours, the interim care order shall cease to have effect in so far as it imposes the exclusion requirement.

38B   Undertakings relating to interim care orders

(1)   In any case where the court has power to include an exclusion requirement in an interim care order, the court may accept an undertaking from the relevant person.

(2)   No power of arrest may be attached to any undertaking given under subsection (1).

(3)   An undertaking given to a court under subsection (1)—

(a)   shall be enforceable as if it were an order of the court, and

(b)   shall cease to have effect if, while it is in force, the local authority have removed the child from the dwelling-house from which the relevant person is excluded to other accommodation for a continuous period of more than 24 hours.

(4)   This section has effect without prejudice to the powers of the High Court and family court apart from this section.

(5)   In this section 'exclusion requirement' and 'relevant person' have the same meaning as in section 38A.

39   Discharge and variation etc of care orders and supervision orders

(1)   A care order may be discharged by the court on the application of—

(a)   any person who has parental responsibility for the child;

(b)   the child himself; or

(c)   the local authority designated by the order.

(2)   A supervision order may be varied or discharged by the court on the application of—

(a)   any person who has parental responsibility for the child;

(b)   the child himself; or

(c)   the supervisor.

(3)   On the application of a person who is not entitled to apply for the order to be discharged, but who is a person with whom the child is living, a supervision order may be varied by the court in so far as it imposes a requirement which affects that person.

(3A)   On the application of a person who is not entitled to apply for the order to be discharged, but who is a person to whom an exclusion requirement contained in the order applies, an interim care order may be varied or discharged by the court in so far as it imposes the exclusion requirement.

(3B)   Where a power of arrest has been attached to an exclusion requirement of an interim care order, the court may, on the application of any person entitled to apply for the discharge of the order so far as it imposes the exclusion requirement, vary or discharge the order in so far as it confers a power of arrest (whether or not any application has been made to vary or discharge any other provision of the order).

(4)   Where a care order is in force with respect to a child the court may, on the application of any person entitled to apply for the order to be discharged, substitute a supervision order for the care order.

(5)   When a court is considering whether to substitute one order for another under subsection (4) any provision of this Act which would otherwise require section 31(2) to be satisfied at the time when the proposed order is substituted or made shall be disregarded.

44 Orders for emergency protection of children

(1) Where any person ('the applicant') applies to the court for an order to be made under this section with respect to a child, the court may make the order if, but only if, it is satisfied that—

   (a) there is reasonable cause to believe that the child is likely to suffer significant harm if—

      (i) he is not removed to accommodation provided by or on behalf of the applicant; or

      (ii) he does not remain in the place in which he is then being accommodated;

   (b) in the case of an application made by a local authority—

      (i) enquiries are being made with respect to the child under section 47(1)(b); and

      (ii) those enquiries are being frustrated by access to the child being unreasonably refused to a person authorised to seek access and that the applicant has reasonable cause to believe that access to the child is required as a matter of urgency; or

   (c) in the case of an application made by an authorised person—

      (i) the applicant has reasonable cause to suspect that a child is suffering, or is likely to suffer, significant harm;

      (ii) the applicant is making enquiries with respect to the child's welfare; and

      (iii) those enquiries are being frustrated by access to the child being unreasonably refused to a person authorised to seek access and the applicant has reasonable cause to believe that access to the child is required as a matter of urgency.

(2) In this section—

   (a) 'authorised person' means a person who is an authorised person for the purposes of section 31; and

   (b) 'a person authorised to seek access' means—

      (i) in the case of an application by a local authority, an officer of the local authority or a person authorised by the authority to act on their behalf in connection with the enquiries; or

      (ii) in the case of an application by an authorised person, that person.

(3) Any person—

   (a) seeking access to a child in connection with enquiries of a kind mentioned in subsection (1); and

   (b) purporting to be a person authorised to do so,

shall, on being asked to do so, produce some duly authenticated document as evidence that he is such a person.

(4) While an order under this section ('an emergency protection order') is in force it—

   (a) operates as a direction to any person who is in a position to do so to comply with any request to produce the child to the applicant;

   (b) authorises—

      (i) the removal of the child at any time to accommodation provided by or on behalf of the applicant and his being kept there; or

      (ii) the prevention of the child's removal from any hospital, or other place, in which he was being accommodated immediately before the making of the order; and

   (c) gives the applicant parental responsibility for the child.

(5) Where an emergency protection order is in force with respect to a child, the applicant—

   (a) shall only exercise the power given by virtue of subsection (4)(b) in order to safeguard the welfare of the child;

   (b) shall take, and shall only take, such action in meeting his parental responsibility for the child as is reasonably required to safeguard or promote the welfare of the child (having regard in particular to the duration of the order); and

   (c) shall comply with the requirements of any regulations made by the Secretary of State for the purposes of this subsection.

(6) Where the court makes an emergency protection order, it may give such directions (if any) as it considers appropriate with respect to—

   (a) the contact which is, or is not, to be allowed between the child and any named person;

(b)   the medical or psychiatric examination or other assessment of the child.

(7)   Where any direction is given under subsection (6)(b), the child may, if he is of sufficient understanding to make an informed decision, refuse to submit to the examination or other assessment.

(8)   A direction under subsection (6)(a) may impose conditions and one under subsection (6)(b) may be to the effect that there is to be—

(a)   no such examination or assessment; or

(b)   no such examination or assessment unless the court directs otherwise.

(9)   A direction under subsection (6) may be—

(a)   given when the emergency protection order is made or at any time while it is in force; and

(b)   varied at any time on the application of any person falling within any class of person prescribed by rules of court for the purposes of this subsection.

(10)   Where an emergency protection order is in force with respect to a child and—

(a)   the applicant has exercised the power given by subsection (4)(b)(i) but it appears to him that it is safe for the child to be returned; or

(b)   the applicant has exercised the power given by subsection (4)(b)(ii) but it appears to him that it is safe for the child to be allowed to be removed from the place in question,

he shall return the child or (as the case may be) allow him to be removed.

(11)   Where he is required by subsection (10) to return the child the applicant shall—

(a)   return him to the care of the person from whose care he was removed; or

(b)   if that is not reasonably practicable, return him to the care of—

(i)   a parent of his;

(ii)   any person who is not a parent of his but who has parental responsibility for him; or

(iii)   such other person as the applicant (with the agreement of the court) considers appropriate.

(12)   Where the applicant has been required by subsection (10) to return the child, or to allow him to be removed, he may again exercise his powers with respect to the child (at any time while the emergency protection order remains in force) if it appears to him that a change in the circumstances of the case makes it necessary for him to do so.

(13)   Where an emergency protection order has been made with respect to a child, the applicant shall, subject to any direction given under subsection (6), allow the child reasonable contact with—

(a)   his parents;

(b)   any person who is not a parent of his but who has parental responsibility for him;

(c)   any person with whom he was living immediately before the making of the order;

(d)   any person named in a child arrangements order as a person with whom the child is to spend time or otherwise have contact;

(e)   any person who is allowed to have contact with the child by virtue of an order under section 34; and

(f)   any person acting on behalf of any of those persons.

(14)   Wherever it is reasonably practicable to do so, an emergency protection order shall name the child; and where it does not name him it shall describe him as clearly as possible.

(15)   A person shall be guilty of an offence if he intentionally obstructs any person exercising the power under subsection (4)(b) to remove, or prevent the removal of, a child.

(16)   A person guilty of an offence under subsection (15) shall be liable on summary conviction to a fine not exceeding level 3 on the standard scale.

46   Removal and accommodation of children by police in cases of emergency

(1)   Where a constable has reasonable cause to believe that a child would otherwise be likely to suffer significant harm, he may—

(a)   remove the child to suitable accommodation and keep him there; or

(b)   take such steps as are reasonable to ensure that the child's removal from any hospital, or other place, in which he is then being accommodated is prevented.

(2)   For the purposes of this Act, a child with respect to whom a constable has exercised his powers under this section is referred to as having been taken into police protection.

(3)   As soon as is reasonably practicable after taking a child into police protection, the constable concerned shall—

(a)   inform the local authority within whose area the child was found of the steps that have been, and are proposed to be, taken with respect to the child under this section and the reasons for taking them;

(b)   give details to the authority within whose area the child is ordinarily resident ('the appropriate authority') of the place at which the child is being accommodated;

(c)   inform the child (if he appears capable of understanding)—

(i)   of the steps that have been taken with respect to him under this section and of the reasons for taking them; and

(ii)   of the further steps that may be taken with respect to him under this section;

(d)   take such steps as are reasonably practicable to discover the wishes and feelings of the child;

(e)   secure that the case is inquired into by an officer designated for the purposes of this section by the chief officer of the police area concerned; and

(f)   where the child was taken into police protection by being removed to accommodation which is not provided—

(i)   by or on behalf of a local authority; or

(ii)   as a refuge, in compliance with the requirements of section 51,

secure that he is moved to accommodation which is so provided.

(4)   As soon as is reasonably practicable after taking a child into police protection, the constable concerned shall take such steps as are reasonably practicable to inform—

(a)   the child's parents;

(b)   every person who is not a parent of his but who has parental responsibility for him; and

(c)   any other person with whom the child was living immediately before being taken into police protection,

of the steps that he has taken under this section with respect to the child, the reasons for taking them and the further steps that may be taken with respect to him under this section.

(5)   On completing any inquiry under subsection (3)(e), the officer conducting it shall release the child from police protection unless he considers that there is still reasonable cause for believing that the child would be likely to suffer significant harm if released.

(6)   No child may be kept in police protection for more than 72 hours.

(7)   While a child is being kept in police protection, the designated officer may apply on behalf of the appropriate authority for an emergency protection order to be made under section 44 with respect to the child.

(8)   An application may be made under subsection (7) whether or not the authority know of it or agree to its being made.

(9)   While a child is being kept in police protection—

(a)   neither the constable concerned nor the designated officer shall have parental responsibility for him; but

(b)   the designated officer shall do what is reasonable in all the circumstances of the case for the purpose of safeguarding or promoting the child's welfare (having regard in particular to the length of the period during which the child will be so protected).

(10)   Where a child has been taken into police protection, the designated officer shall allow—

(a)   the child's parents;

(b)   any person who is not a parent of the child but who has parental responsibility for him;

(c)   any person with whom the child was living immediately before he was taken into police protection;

(d)   any person named in a child arrangements order as a person with whom the child is to spend time or otherwise have contact;

(e)   any person who is allowed to have contact with the child by virtue of an order under section 34; and

(f) any person acting on behalf of any of those persons,

to have such contact (if any) with the child as, in the opinion of the designated officer, is both reasonable and in the child's best interests.

(11) Where a child who has been taken into police protection is in accommodation provided by, or on behalf of, the appropriate authority, subsection (10) shall have effect as if it referred to the authority rather than to the designated officer.

47 Local authority's duty to investigate

(1) Where a local authority—

    (a) are informed that a child who lives, or is found, in their area—

        (i) is the subject of an emergency protection order; or

        (ii) is in police protection; ...

        (iii) ...

    (b) have reasonable cause to suspect that a child who lives, or is found, in their area is suffering, or is likely to suffer, significant harm,

the authority shall make, or cause to be made, such enquiries as they consider necessary to enable them to decide whether they should take any action to safeguard or promote the child's welfare.

...

(2) Where a local authority have obtained an emergency protection order with respect to a child, they shall make, or cause to be made, such enquiries as they consider necessary to enable them to decide what action they should take to safeguard or promote the child's welfare.

(3) The enquiries shall, in particular, be directed towards establishing—

    (a) whether the authority should—

        (i) make any application to court under this Act;

        (ii) exercise any of their other powers under this Act;

        (iii) exercise any of their powers under section 11 of the Crime and Disorder Act 1998 (child safety orders); or

        (iv) (where the authority is a local authority in Wales) exercise any of their powers under the Social Services and Well-being (Wales) Act 2014;

    with respect to the child;

    (b) whether, in the case of a child—

        (i) with respect to whom an emergency protection order has been made; and

        (ii) who is not in accommodation provided by or on behalf of the authority,

    it would be in the child's best interests (while an emergency protection order remains in force) for him to be in such accommodation; and

    (c) whether, in the case of a child who has been taken into police protection, it would be in the child's best interests for the authority to ask for an application to be made under section 46(7).

(4) Where enquiries are being made under subsection (1) with respect to a child, the local authority concerned shall (with a view to enabling them to determine what action, if any, to take with respect to him) take such steps as are reasonably practicable—

    (a) to obtain access to him; or

    (b) to ensure that access to him is obtained, on their behalf, by a person authorised by them for the purpose,

unless they are satisfied that they already have sufficient information with respect to him.

(5) Where, as a result of any such enquiries, it appears to the authority that there are matters connected with the child's education which should be investigated, they shall consult the local authority (as defined in section 579(1) of the Education 1996), if different, specified in subsection (5ZA).

(5ZA) The local authority referred to in subsection (5) is—

    (a) the local authority who—

        (i) maintain any school at which the child is a pupil, or

        (ii) make arrangements for the provision of education for the child otherwise than at school pursuant to section 19 of the Education Act 1996, or

      (b)   in a case where the child is a pupil at a school which is not maintained by a local authority, the local authority in whose area the school is situated.

(5A)   For the purposes of making a determination under this section as to the action to be taken with respect to a child, a local authority shall, so far as is reasonably practicable and consistent with the child's welfare—

      (a)   ascertain the child's wishes and feelings regarding the action to be taken with respect to him; and

      (b)   give due consideration (having regard to his age and understanding) to such wishes and feelings of the child as they have been able to ascertain.

(6)   Where, in the course of enquiries made under this section—

      (a)   any officer of the local authority concerned; or

      (b)   any person authorised by the authority to act on their behalf in connection with those enquiries—

            (i)   is refused access to the child concerned; or

            (ii)   is denied information as to his whereabouts,

the authority shall apply for an emergency protection order, a child assessment order, a care order or a supervision order with respect to the child unless they are satisfied that his welfare can be satisfactorily safeguarded without their doing so.

(7)   If, on the conclusion of any enquiries or review made under this section, the authority decide not to apply for an emergency protection order, a care order, a child assessment order or a supervision order they shall—

      (a)   consider whether it would be appropriate to review the case at a later date; and

      (b)   if they decide that it would be, determine the date on which that review is to begin.

(8)   Where, as a result of complying with this section, a local authority conclude that they should take action to safeguard or promote the child's welfare they shall take that action (so far as it is both within their power and reasonably practicable for them to do so).

(9)   Where a local authority are conducting enquiries under this section, it shall be the duty of any person mentioned in subsection (11) to assist them with those enquiries (in particular by providing relevant information and advice) if called upon by the authority to do so.

(10)   Subsection (9) does not oblige any person to assist a local authority where doing so would be unreasonable in all the circumstances of the case.

(11)   The persons are—

      (a)   any local authority;

      (b)   ...

      (c)   any local housing authority;

      (ca)   the National Health Service Commissioning Board;

      (d)   any clinical commissioning group, Local Health Board, Special Health Authority, ... National Health Service trust or NHS foundation trust; and

      (e)   any person authorised by the Secretary of State for the purposes of this section.

(12)   Where a local authority are making enquiries under this section with respect to a child who appears to them to be ordinarily resident within the area of another authority, they shall consult that other authority, who may undertake the necessary enquiries in their place.

SCHEDULE 1
FINANCIAL PROVISION FOR CHILDREN

Section 15(1)

Orders for financial relief against parents

1.— (1)   On an application made by a parent, guardian or special guardian of a child, or by any person who is named in a child arrangements order as a person with whom a child is to live, the court may make one or more of the orders mentioned in sub-paragraph (2) ....

    (2)   The orders referred to in sub-paragraph (1) are—

      (a)   an order requiring either or both parents of a child—

        (i)   to make to the applicant for the benefit of the child; or

        (ii)   to make to the child himself,

        such periodical payments, for such term, as may be specified in the order;

  (b)   an order requiring either or both parents of a child—

        (i)   to secure to the applicant for the benefit of the child; or

        (ii)   to secure to the child himself,

        such periodical payments, for such term, as may be so specified;

  (c)   an order requiring either or both parents of a child—

        (i)   to pay to the applicant for the benefit of the child; or

        (ii)   to pay to the child himself,

        such lump sum as may be so specified;

  (d)   an order requiring a settlement to be made for the benefit of the child, and to the satisfaction of the court, of property—

        (i)   to which either parent is entitled (either in possession or in reversion); and

        (ii)   which is specified in the order;

  (e)   an order requiring either or both parents of a child—

        (i)   to transfer to the applicant, for the benefit of the child; or

        (ii)   to transfer to the child himself,

        such property to which the parent is, or the parents are, entitled (either in possession or in reversion) as may be specified in the order.

(3)   The powers conferred by this paragraph may be exercised at any time.

(4)   An order under sub-paragraph (2)(a) or (b) may be varied or discharged by a subsequent order made on the application of any person by or to whom payments were required to be made under the previous order.

(5)   Where a court makes an order under this paragraph—

  (a)   it may at any time make a further such order under sub-paragraph (2)(a), (b) or (c) with respect to the child concerned if he has not reached the age of eighteen;

  (b)   it may not make more than one order under sub-paragraph (2)(d) or (e) against the same person in respect of the same child.

(6)   On making, varying or discharging ... a special guardianship order, or on making, varying or discharging provision in a child arrangements order with respect to the living arrangements of a child, the court may exercise any of its powers under this Schedule even though no application has been made to it under this Schedule.

(6A) For the purposes of sub-paragraph (6) provision in a child arrangements order is with respect to the living arrangements of a child if it regulates arrangements relating to—

  (a)   with whom the child is to live, or

  (b)   when the child is to live with any person.

(7)   Where a child is a ward of court, the court may exercise any of its powers under this Schedule even though no application has been made to it.

Orders for financial relief for persons over eighteen

2.— (1)   If, on an application by a person who has reached the age of eighteen, it appears to the court—

  (a)   that the applicant is, will be or (if an order were made under this paragraph) would be receiving instruction at an educational establishment or undergoing training for a trade, profession or vocation, whether or not while in gainful employment; or

  (b)   that there are special circumstances which justify the making of an order under this paragraph, the court may make one or both of the orders mentioned in sub-paragraph (2).

  (2)   The orders are—

  (a)   an order requiring either or both of the applicant's parents to pay to the applicant such periodical payments, for such term, as may be specified in the order;

  (b)   an order requiring either or both of the applicant's parents to pay to the applicant such lump sum as may be so specified.

(3)   An application may not be made under this paragraph by any person if, immediately before he reached the age of sixteen, a periodical payments order was in force with respect to him.

(4)   No order shall be made under this paragraph at a time when the parents of the applicant are living with each other in the same household.

(5)   An order under sub-paragraph (2)(a) may be varied or discharged by a subsequent order made on the application of any person by or to whom payments were required to be made under the previous order.

(6)   In sub-paragraph (3) 'periodical payments order' means an order made under—

(a)   this Schedule;

(b)   ...

(c)   section 23 or 27 of the Matrimonial Causes Act 1973;

(d)   Part I of the Domestic Proceedings and Magistrates' Courts Act 1978;

(e)   Part 1 or 9 of Schedule 5 to the Civil Partnership Act 2004 (financial relief in the High Court or a county court etc);

(f)   Schedule 6 to the 2004 Act (financial relief in the magistrates' courts etc),

for the making or securing of periodical payments.

(7)   The powers conferred by this paragraph shall be exercisable at any time.

(8)   Where the court makes an order under this paragraph it may from time to time while that order remains in force make a further such order.

Duration of orders for financial relief

3.—   (1)   The term to be specified in an order for periodical payments made under paragraph 1(2)(a) or (b) in favour of a child may begin with the date of the making of an application for the order in question or any later date or a date ascertained in accordance with sub-paragraph (5) or (6) but—

(a)   shall not in the first instance extend beyond the child's seventeenth birthday unless the court thinks it right in the circumstances of the case to specify a later date; and

(b)   shall not in any event extend beyond the child's eighteenth birthday.

(2)   Paragraph (b) of sub-paragraph (1) shall not apply in the case of a child if it appears to the court that—

(a)   the child is, or will be or (if an order were made without complying with that paragraph) would be receiving instruction at an educational establishment or undergoing training for a trade, profession or vocation, whether or not while in gainful employment; or

(b)   there are special circumstances which justify the making of an order without complying with that paragraph.

(3)   An order for periodical payments made under paragraph 1(2)(a) or 2(2)(a) shall, notwithstanding anything in the order, cease to have effect on the death of the person liable to make payments under the order.

(4)   Where an order is made under paragraph 1(2)(a) or (b) requiring periodical payments to be made or secured to the parent of a child, the order shall cease to have effect if—

(a)   any parent making or securing the payments; and

(b)   any parent to whom the payments are made or secured,

live together for a period of more than six months.

(5)   Where—

(a)   a maintenance assessment ('the current assessment') is in force with respect to a child; and

(b)   an application is made for an order under paragraph 1(2)(a) or (b) of this Schedule for periodical payments in favour of that child—

(i)   in accordance with section 8 of the Child Support Act 1991; and

(ii)   before the end of the period of 6 months beginning with the making of the current assessment,

the term to be specified in any such order made on that application may be expressed to begin on, or at any time after, the earliest permitted date.

(6)   For the purposes of subsection (5) above, 'the earliest permitted date' is whichever is the later of—

(a)   the date 6 months before the application is made; or

(b)   the date on which the current assessment took effect or, where successive maintenance assessments have been continuously in force with respect to a child, on which the first of those assessments took effect.

(7)   Where—

(a)   a maintenance assessment ceases to have effect or is cancelled by or under any provision of the Child Support Act 1991, and

(b)   an application is made, before the end of the period of 6 months beginning with the relevant date, for an order for periodical payments under paragraph 1(2)(a) or (b) in favour of a child with respect to whom that maintenance assessment was in force immediately before it ceased to have effect or was cancelled,

the term to be specified in any such order, or in any interim order under paragraph 9, made on that application may begin with the date on which that maintenance assessment ceased to have effect or, as the case may be, the date with effect from which it was cancelled, or any later date.

(8)   In sub-paragraph (7)(b)—

(a)   where the maintenance assessment ceased to have effect, the relevant date is the date on which it so ceased; and

(b)   where the maintenance assessment was cancelled, the relevant date is the later of—

(i)   the date on which the person who cancelled it did so, and

(ii)   the date from which the cancellation first had effect.

Matters to which court is to have regard in making orders for financial relief

4.— (1)   In deciding whether to exercise its powers under paragraph 1 or 2, and if so in what manner, the court shall have regard to all the circumstances including—

(a)   the income, earning capacity, property and other financial resources which each person mentioned in sub-paragraph (4) has or is likely to have in the foreseeable future;

(b)   the financial needs, obligations and responsibilities which each person mentioned in sub-paragraph (4) has or is likely to have in the foreseeable future;

(c)   the financial needs of the child;

(d)   the income, earning capacity (if any), property and other financial resources of the child;

(e)   any physical or mental disability of the child;

(f)   the manner in which the child was being, or was expected to be, educated or trained.

(2)   In deciding whether to exercise its powers under paragraph 1 against a person who is not the mother or father of the child, and if so in what manner, the court shall in addition have regard to—

(a)   whether that person has assumed responsibility for the maintenance of the child and, if so, the extent to which and basis on which he assumed that responsibility and the length of the period during which he met that responsibility;

(b)   whether he did so knowing that the child was not his child;

(c)   the liability of any other person to maintain the child.

(3)   Where the court makes an order under paragraph 1 against a person who is not the father of the child, it shall record in the order that the order is made on the basis that the person against whom the order is made is not the child's father.

(4)   The persons mentioned in sub-paragraph (1) are—

(a)   in relation to a decision whether to exercise its powers under paragraph 1, any parent of the child;

(b)   in relation to a decision whether to exercise its powers under paragraph 2, the mother and father of the child;

(c)   the applicant for the order;

(d)   any other person in whose favour the court proposes to make the order.

(5)   In the case of a child who has a parent by virtue of section 42 or 43 of the Human Fertilisation and Embryology Act 2008, any reference in sub-paragraph (2), (3) or (4) to the child's father is a reference to the woman who is a parent of the child by virtue of that section.

Provisions relating to lump sums

5.— (1)   Without prejudice to the generality of paragraph 1, an order under that paragraph for the payment of a lump sum may be made for the purpose of enabling any liabilities or expenses—

(a)   incurred in connection with the birth of the child or in maintaining the child; and

(b)   reasonably incurred before the making of the order,

to be met.

(2)   ...

(3)   The power of the court under paragraph 1 or 2 to vary or discharge an order for the making or securing of periodical payments by a parent shall include power to make an order under that provision for the payment of a lump sum by that parent.

(4)   ...

(5)   An order made under paragraph 1 or 2 for the payment of a lump sum may provide for the payment of that sum by instalments.

(6)   Where the court provides for the payment of a lump sum by instalments the court, on an application made either by the person liable to pay or the person entitled to receive that sum, shall have power to vary that order by varying—

(a)   the number of instalments payable;

(b)   the amount of any instalment payable;

(c)   the date on which any instalment becomes payable.

(7)   The Lord Chief Justice may nominate a judicial office holder (as defined in section 109(4) of the Constitutional Reform Act 2005) to exercise his functions under this paragraph.

Variation etc of orders for periodical payments

6.— (1)   In exercising its powers under paragraph 1 or 2 to vary or discharge an order for the making or securing of periodical payments the court shall have regard to all the circumstances of the case, including any change in any of the matters to which the court was required to have regard when making the order.

(2)   The power of the court under paragraph 1 or 2 to vary an order for the making or securing of periodical payments shall include power to suspend any provision of the order temporarily and to revive any provision so suspended.

(3)   Where on an application under paragraph 1 or 2 for the variation or discharge of an order for the making or securing of periodical payments the court varies the payments required to be made under that order, the court may provide that the payments as so varied shall be made from such date as the court may specify, except that, subject to sub-paragraph (9), the date shall not be earlier than the date of the making of the application.

(4)   An application for the variation of an order made under paragraph 1 for the making or securing of periodical payments to or for the benefit of a child may, if the child has reached the age of sixteen, be made by the child himself.

(5)   Where an order for the making or securing of periodical payments made under paragraph 1 ceases to have effect on the date on which the child reaches the age of sixteen, or at any time after that date but before or on the date on which he reaches the age of eighteen, the child may apply to the court which made the order for an order for its revival.

(6)   If on such an application it appears to the court that—

(a)   the child is, will be or (if an order were made under this sub-paragraph) would be receiving instruction at an educational establishment or undergoing training for a trade, profession or vocation, whether or not while in gainful employment; or

(b)   there are special circumstances which justify the making of an order under this paragraph,

the court shall have power by order to revive the order from such date as the court may specify, not being earlier than the date of the making of the application.

(7)   Any order which is revived by an order under sub-paragraph (5) may be varied or discharged under that provision, on the application of any person by whom or to whom payments are required to be made under the revived order.

(8)   An order for the making or securing of periodical payments made under paragraph 1 may be varied or discharged, after the death of either parent, on the application of a guardian or special guardian of the child concerned.

(9)   Where—

    (a)   an order under paragraph 1(2)(a) or (b) for the making or securing of periodical payments in favour of more than one child ('the order') is in force;

    (b)   the order requires payments specified in it to be made to or for the benefit of more than one child without apportioning those payments between them;

    (c)   a maintenance assessment ('the assessment') is made with respect to one or more, but not all, of the children with respect to whom those payments are to be made; and

    (d)   an application is made, before the end of the period of 6 months beginning with the date on which the assessment was made, for the variation or discharge of the order,

the court may, in exercise of its powers under paragraph 1 to vary or discharge the order, direct that the variation or discharge shall take effect from the date on which the assessment took effect or any later date.

Variation of orders for periodical payments etc made by magistrates' courts

6A.— (1)   Subject to sub-paragraph (7), the power of the family court—

    (a)   under paragraph 1 or 2 to vary an order for the making of periodical payments, or

    (b)   under paragraph 5(6) to vary an order for the payment of a lump sum by instalments,

shall include power, if the court is satisfied that payment has not been made in accordance with the order, to exercise one of its powers under section 1(4) and (4A) of the Maintenance Enforcement Act 1991.

(2)–(5) ...

(6)   Subsection (6) of section 1 of the Maintenance Enforcement Act 1991 (power of court to order that account be opened) shall apply for the purposes of sub-paragraph (1) as it applies for the purposes of that section.

(7)   Before varying the order by exercising one of its powers under section 1(4) and (4A) of the Maintenance Enforcement Act 1991, the court shall have regard to any representations made by the parties to the application.

(8)   ...

(9)   None of the powers of the court ... conferred by this paragraph shall be exercisable in relation to an order under this Schedule for the making of periodical payments, or for the payment of a lump sum by instalments, unless at the time when the order was made the person required to make the payments was ordinarily resident in England and Wales.

(10)   ...

Variation of orders for secured periodical payments after death of parent

7.— (1)   Where the parent liable to make payments under a secured periodical payments order has died, the persons who may apply for the variation or discharge of the order shall include the personal representatives of the deceased parent.

(2)   No application for the variation of the order shall, except with the permission of the court, be made after the end of the period of six months from the date on which representation in regard to the estate of that parent is first taken out.

(3)   The personal representatives of a deceased person against whom a secured periodical payments order was made shall not be liable for having distributed any part of the estate of the deceased after the end of the period of six months referred to in sub-paragraph (2) on the ground that they ought to have taken into account the possibility that the court might permit an application for variation to be made after that period by the person entitled to payments under the order.

(4)   Sub-paragraph (3) shall not prejudice any power to recover any part of the estate so distributed arising by virtue of the variation of an order in accordance with this paragraph.

(5)   Where an application to vary a secured periodical payments order is made after the death of the parent liable to make payments under the order, the circumstances to which the court is required to have regard under paragraph 6(1) shall include the changed circumstances resulting from the death of the parent.

(6)   The following are to be left out of account when considering for the purposes of sub-paragraph (2) when representation was first taken out—

(a)   a grant limited to settled land or to trust property,

(b)   any other grant that does not permit any of the estate to be distributed,

(c)   a grant limited to real estate or to personal estate, unless a grant limited to the remainder of the estate has previously been made or is made at the same time,

(d)   a grant, or its equivalent, made outside the United Kingdom (but see sub-paragraph (6A)).

...

(7)   In this paragraph 'secured periodical payments order' means an order for secured periodical payments under paragraph 1(2)(b).

Financial relief under other enactments

8.— (1)   This paragraph applies where a child arrangements order to which sub-paragraph (1A) applies or a special guardianship order is made with respect to a child at a time when there is in force an order ('the financial relief order') made under any enactment other than this Act and requiring a person to contribute to the child's maintenance.

(1A)   This sub-paragraph applies to a child arrangements order if the arrangements regulated by the order consist of, or include, arrangements which relate to either or both of the following—

(a)   with whom the child concerned is to live, and

(b)   when the child is to live with any person.

(2)   Where this paragraph applies, the court may, on the application of—

(a)   any person required by the financial relief order to contribute to the child's maintenance; or

(b)   any person who is named in a child arrangements order as a person with whom the child is to live or in whose favour ... a special guardianship order with respect to the child is in force,

make an order revoking the financial relief order, or varying it by altering the amount of any sum payable under the order or by substituting the applicant for the person to whom any such sum is otherwise payable under that order.

Interim orders

9.— (1)   Where an application is made under paragraph 1 or 2 the court may, at any time before it disposes of the application, make an interim order—

(a)   requiring either or both parents to make such periodical payments, at such times and for such term as the court thinks fit; and

(b)   giving any direction which the court thinks fit.

(2)   An interim order made under this paragraph may provide for payments to be made from such date as the court may specify, except that, subject to paragraph 3(5) and (6), the date shall not be earlier than the date of the making of the application under paragraph 1 or 2.

(3)   An interim order made under this paragraph shall cease to have effect when the application is disposed of or, if earlier, on the date specified for the purposes of this paragraph in the interim order.

(4)   An interim order in which a date has been specified for the purposes of sub-paragraph (3) may be varied by substituting a later date.

Alteration of maintenance agreements

10.— (1)   In this paragraph and in paragraph 11 'maintenance agreement' means any agreement in writing made with respect to a child, whether before or after the commencement of this paragraph, which—

(a)   is or was made between the father and mother of the child; and (b)　contains provision with respect to the making or securing of payments, or the disposition or use of any property, for the maintenance or education of the child,

and any such provisions are in this paragraph, and paragraph 11, referred to as 'financial arrangements'.

(2)　Subject to sub-paragraph (2A), where a maintenance agreement is for the time being subsisting and each of the parties to the agreement is for the time being either domiciled or resident in England and Wales, then, either party may apply to the court for an order under this paragraph.

(2A)　If an application or part of an application relates to a matter in relation to which Article 18 of the 2007 Hague Convention applies, the court may not entertain the application or that part of it except where permitted by Article 18.

(2B)　In sub-paragraph (2A), 'the 2007 Hague Convention' means the Convention on the International Recovery of Child Support and Other Forms of Family Maintenance concluded on 23 November 2007 at The Hague.

(3)　If the court to which the application is made is satisfied either—

(a)　that, by reason of a change in the circumstances in the light of which any financial arrangements contained in the agreement were made (including a change foreseen by the parties when making the agreement), the agreement should be altered so as to make different financial arrangements; or

(b)　that the agreement does not contain proper financial arrangements with respect to the child,

then that court may by order make such alterations in the agreement by varying or revoking any financial arrangements contained in it as may appear to it to be just having regard to all the circumstances.

(4)　If the maintenance agreement is altered by an order under this paragraph, the agreement shall have effect thereafter as if the alteration had been made by agreement between the parties and for valuable consideration.

(5)　Where a court decides to make an order under this paragraph altering the maintenance agreement—

(a)　by inserting provision for the making or securing by one of the parties to the agreement of periodical payments for the maintenance of the child; or

(b)　by increasing the rate of periodical payments required to be made or secured by one of the parties for the maintenance of the child,

then, in deciding the term for which under the agreement as altered by the order the payments or (as the case may be) the additional payments attributable to the increase are to be made or secured for the benefit of the child, the court shall apply the provisions of sub-paragraphs (1) and (2) of paragraph 3 as if the order were an order under paragraph 1(2)(a) or (b).

(6)　...

(7)　For the avoidance of doubt it is hereby declared that nothing in this paragraph affects any power of a court before which any proceedings between the parties to a maintenance agreement are brought under any other enactment to make an order containing financial arrangements or any right of either party to apply for such an order in such proceedings.

(8)　In the case of a child who has a parent by virtue of section 42 or 43 of the Human Fertilisation and Embryology Act 2008, the reference in sub-paragraph (1)(a) to the child's father is a reference to the woman who is a parent of the child by virtue of that section.

11.— (1)　Where a maintenance agreement provides for the continuation, after the death of one of the parties, of payments for the maintenance of a child and that party dies domiciled in England and Wales, the surviving party or the personal representatives of the deceased party may apply to the High Court or the family court for an order under paragraph 10.

(2)　If a maintenance agreement is altered by a court on an application under this paragraph, the agreement shall have effect thereafter as if the alteration had been made, immediately before the death, by agreement between the parties and for valuable consideration.

(3)　An application under this paragraph shall not, except with leave of the High Court or the family court, be made after the end of the period of six months beginning with the day on which representation in regard to the estate of the deceased is first taken out.

(4)   The following are to be left out of account when considering for the purposes of sub-paragraph (3) when representation was first taken out—

(a)   a grant limited to settled land or to trust property,

(b)   any other grant that does not permit any of the estate to be distributed,

(c)   a grant limited to real estate or to personal estate, unless a grant limited to the remainder of the estate has previously been made or is made at the same time,

(d)   a grant, or its equivalent, made outside the United Kingdom (but see sub-paragraph (4A)).

...

(5)   ...

(6)   The provisions of this paragraph shall not render the personal representatives of the deceased liable for having distributed any part of the estate of the deceased after the expiry of the period of six months referred to in sub-paragraph (3) on the ground that they ought to have taken into account the possibility that a court might grant leave for an application by virtue of this paragraph to be made by the surviving party after that period.

(7)   Sub-paragraph (6) shall not prejudice any power to recover any part of the estate so distributed arising by virtue of the making of an order in pursuance of this paragraph.

Enforcement of orders for maintenance

12.— (1)   Any person for the time being under an obligation to make payments in pursuance of any order for the payment of money made by the family court under this Act shall give notice of any change of address to such person (if any) as may be specified in the order.

(2)   Any person failing without reasonable excuse to give such a notice shall be guilty of an offence and liable on summary conviction to a fine not exceeding level 2 on the standard scale.

(3)   ...

Direction for settlement of instrument by conveyancing counsel

13.   Where the High Court or the family court decides to make an order under this Act for the securing of periodical payments or for the transfer or settlement of property, it may direct that the matter be referred to one of the conveyancing counsel of the court to settle a proper instrument to be executed by all necessary parties.

Jurisdiction ...

14.— (1)   The court has jurisdiction in relation to an application under paragraph 1 in respect of a child if any of the following persons are habitually resident or domiciled in England and Wales on the date of the application—

(a)   a parent of the child;

(b)   a guardian or special guardian of the child;

(c)   a person who is named in a child arrangements order as a person with whom the child is to live;

(d)   the child.

(2)   The court has jurisdiction in relation to an application under paragraph 2 if the applicant or a parent against whom the order is sought or made is habitually resident or domiciled in England and Wales on the date of the application

Local authority contribution to child's maintenance

15.— (1)   Where a child lives, or is to live, with a person as the result of a child arrangements order, a local authority may make contributions to that person towards the cost of the accommodation and maintenance of the child.

(2)   Sub-paragraph (1) does not apply where the person with whom the child lives, or is to live, is a parent of the child or the husband or wife or civil partner of a parent of the child.

Interpretation

16.— (1)   In this Schedule 'child' includes, in any case where an application is made under paragraph 2 or 6 in relation to a person who has reached the age of eighteen, that person.

(2)   In this Schedule, except paragraphs 2 and 15, 'parent' includes—

(a)   any party to a marriage (whether or not subsisting) in relation to whom the child concerned is a child of the family, and

(b)   any civil partner in a civil partnership (whether or not subsisting) in relation to whom the child concerned is a child of the family;

and for this purpose any reference to either parent or both parents shall be read as a reference to any parent of his and to all of his parents.

(3)   In this Schedule, 'maintenance assessment' has the same meaning as it has in the Child Support Act 1991 by virtue of section 54 of that Act as read with any regulations in force under that section.

SCHEDULE 2
SUPPORT FOR CHILDREN AND FAMILIES PROVIDED BY LOCAL AUTHORITIES IN ENGLAND

Sections 17, 23, 29

PART I
PROVISION OF SERVICES FOR FAMILIES

Application to local authorities in England

A1.— (1)   This Schedule applies only in relation to local authorities in England.

(2)   Accordingly, unless the contrary intention appears, a reference in this Schedule to a local authority means a local authority in England.

Identification of children in need and provision of information

1.— (1)   Every local authority shall take reasonable steps to identify the extent to which there are children in need within their area.

(2)   Every local authority shall—

(a)   publish information—

(i)   about services provided by them under sections 17, 18, 20 and 23D; and

(ii)   where they consider it appropriate, about the provision by others (including, in particular, voluntary organisations) of services which the authority have power to provide under those sections; and

(b)   take such steps as are reasonably practicable to ensure that those who might benefit from the services receive the information relevant to them.

…

Maintenance of a register of disabled children

2.— (1)   Every local authority shall open and maintain a register of disabled children within their area.

(2)   The register may be kept by means of a computer.

Assessment of children's needs

3.   Where it appears to a local authority that a child within their area is in need, the authority may assess his needs for the purposes of this Act at the same time as any assessment of his needs is made under—

(a)   the Chronically Sick and Disabled Persons Act 1970;

(b)   Part IV of the Education Act 1996;

(ba)   Part 3 of the Children and Families Act 2014;

(c)   the Disabled Persons (Services, Consultation and Representation) Act 1986; or

(d)   any other enactment.

Prevention of neglect and abuse

4.— (1)   Every local authority shall take reasonable steps, through the provision of services under Part III of this Act, to prevent children within their area suffering ill-treatment or neglect.

(2)   Where a local authority believe that a child who is at any time within their area—

(a)   is likely to suffer harm; but

(b)   lives or proposes to live in the area of another local authority or in the area of a local authority in Wales,

they shall inform that other local authority or the local authority in Wales, as the case may be.

(3)   When informing that other local authority or the local authority in Wales they shall specify—

(a)   the harm that they believe he is likely to suffer; and

(b)   (if they can) where the child lives or proposes to live.

Provision of accommodation in order to protect child

5.— (1)   Where—

(a)   it appears to a local authority that a child who is living on particular premises is suffering, or is likely to suffer, ill treatment at the hands of another person who is living on those premises; and

(b)   that other person proposes to move from the premises,

the authority may assist that other person to obtain alternative accommodation.

(2)   Assistance given under this paragraph may be in cash.

(3)   Subsections (7) to (9) of section 17 shall apply in relation to assistance given under this paragraph as they apply in relation to assistance given under that section.

Provision for disabled children

6.— (1)   Every local authority shall provide services designed—

(a)   to minimise the effect on disabled children within their area of their disabilities; ...

(b)   to give such children the opportunity to lead lives which are as normal as possible; and

(c)   to assist individuals who provide care for such children to continue to do so, or to do so more effectively, by giving them breaks from caring.

(2)   The duty imposed by sub-paragraph (1)(c) shall be performed in accordance with regulations made by the Secretary of State.

Provision to reduce need for care proceedings etc

7.   Every local authority shall take reasonable steps designed—

(a)   to reduce the need to bring—

(i)   proceedings for care or supervision orders with respect to children within their area;

(ii)   criminal proceedings against such children;

(iii)   any family or other proceedings with respect to such children which might lead to them being placed in the authority's care; or

(iv)   proceedings under the inherent jurisdiction of the High Court with respect to children;

(b)   to encourage children within their area not to commit criminal offences; and

(c)   to avoid the need for children within their area to be placed in secure accommodation within the meaning given in section 25 and in section 119 of the Social Services and Well-being (Wales) Act 2014.

Provision for children living with their families

8.   Every local authority shall make such provision as they consider appropriate for the following services to be available with respect to children in need within their area while they are living with their families—

(a)   advice, guidance and counselling;

(b)   occupational, social, cultural, or recreational activities;

(c)   home help (which may include laundry facilities);

(d)   facilities for, or assistance with, travelling to and from home for the purpose of taking advantage of any other service provided under this Act or of any similar service;

(e)   assistance to enable the child concerned and his family to have a holiday.

Provision for accommodated children

8A.— (1)   Every local authority shall make provision for such services as they consider appropriate to be available with respect to accommodated children.

(2)   'Accommodated children' are those children in respect of whose accommodation the local authority have been notified under section 85 or 86 or under section 120 of the Social Services and Well-being (Wales) Act 2014 (assessment of children accommodated by health authorities and education authorities).

(3)   The services shall be provided with a view to promoting contact between each accommodated child and that child's family.

(4)   The services may, in particular, include—

    (a)   advice, guidance and counselling;

    (b)   services necessary to enable the child to visit, or to be visited by, members of the family;

    (c)   assistance to enable the child and members of the family to have a holiday together.

(5)   Nothing in this paragraph affects the duty imposed by paragraph 10.

Family centres

9.— (1)   Every local authority shall provide such family centres as they consider appropriate in relation to children within their area.

(2)   'Family centre' means a centre at which any of the persons mentioned in sub-paragraph (3) may—

    (a)   attend for occupational, social, cultural or recreational activities;

    (b)   attend for advice, guidance or counselling; or

    (c)   be provided with accommodation while he is receiving advice, guidance or counselling.

(3)   The persons are—

    (a)   a child;

    (b)   his parents;

    (c)   any person who is not a parent of his but who has parental responsibility for him;

    (d)   any other person who is looking after him.

Maintenance of the family home

10.   Every local authority shall take such steps as are reasonably practicable, where any child within their area who is in need and whom they are not looking after is living apart from his family—

    (a)   to enable him to live with his family; or

    (b)   to promote contact between him and his family,

if, in their opinion, it is necessary to do so in order to safeguard or promote his welfare.

Duty to consider racial groups to which children in need belong

11.   Every local authority shall, in making any arrangements—

    (a)   for the provision of day care within their area; or

    (b)   designed to encourage persons to act as local authority foster parents,

have regard to the different racial groups to which children within their area who are in need belong.

PART II
CHILDREN LOOKED AFTER BY LOCAL AUTHORITIES IN ENGLAND

Regulations as to conditions under which child in care is allowed to live with parent, etc

12A.   Regulations under section 22C may, in particular, impose requirements on a local authority as to—

    (a)   the making of any decision by a local authority to allow a child in their care to live with any person falling within section 22C(3) (including requirements as to those who must be consulted before the decision is made and those who must be notified when it has been made);

    (b)   the supervision or medical examination of the child concerned;

    (c)   the removal of the child, in such circumstances as may be prescribed, from the care of the person with whom the child has been allowed to live;

    (d)   the records to be kept by local authorities.

Regulations as to placements of a kind specified in section 22C(6)(d)

12B.   Regulations under section 22C as to placements of the kind specified in section 22C(6)(d) may, in particular, make provision as to—

    (a)   the persons to be notified of any proposed arrangements;

    (b)   the opportunities such persons are to have to make representations in relation to the arrangements proposed;

    (c)   the persons to be notified of any proposed changes in arrangements;

    (d)   the records to be kept by local authorities;

    (e)   the supervision by local authorities of any arrangements made.

Placements out of area

12C. Regulations under section 22C may, in particular, impose requirements which a local authority must comply with—

   (a) before a child looked after by them is provided with accommodation at a place outside the area of the authority; or

   (b) if the child's welfare requires the immediate provision of such accommodation, within such period of the accommodation being provided as may be prescribed.

Avoidance of disruption in education

12D.—(1) Regulations under section 22C may, in particular, impose requirements which a local authority must comply with before making any decision concerning a child's placement if he is in the fourth key stage.

   (2) A child is 'in the fourth key stage' if he is a pupil in the fourth key stage for the purposes of Part 6 or 7 of the Education 2002 (see section 82 and 103 of that Act).

Regulations as to placing of children with local authority foster parents

12E. Regulations under section 22C may, in particular, make provision—

   (a) with regard to the welfare of children placed with local authority foster parents;

   (b) as to the arrangements to be made by local authorities in connection with the health and education of such children;

   (c) as to the records to be kept by local authorities;

   (d) for securing that where possible the local authority foster parent with whom a child is to be placed is—

      (i) of the same religious persuasion as the child; or

      (ii) gives an undertaking that the child will be brought up in that religious persuasion;

   (e) for securing the children placed with local authority foster parents, and the premises in which they are accommodated, will be supervised and inspected by a local authority and that the children will be removed from those premises if their welfare appears to require it.

12F.—(1) Regulations under section 22C may, in particular, also make provision—

   (a) for securing that a child is not placed with a local authority foster parent unless that person is for the time being approved as a local authority foster parent by such local authority as may be prescribed in regulations made by the Secretary of State;

   (b) establishing a procedure under which any person in respect of whom a qualifying determination has been made may apply to the Secretary of State for a review of that determination by a panel constituted by the Secretary of State.

   (2) A determination is a qualifying determination if—

      (a) it relates to the issue of whether a person should be approved, or should continue to be approved, as a local authority foster parent; and

      (b) it is of a prescribed description.

   (3) Regulations made by virtue of sub-paragraph (1)(b) may include provision as to—

      (a) the duties and powers of a panel;

      (b) the administration and procedures of a panel;

      (c) the appointment of members of a panel (including the number, or any limit on the number, of members who may be appointed and any conditions for appointment);

      (d) the payment of fees to members of a panel;

      (e) the duties of any person in connection with a review conducted under the regulations;

      (f) the monitoring of any such reviews.

   (4) Regulations made by virtue of sub-paragraph (3)(e) may impose a duty to pay to the Secretary of State such sum as that national authority may determine; but such a duty may not be imposed upon a person who has applied for a review of a qualifying determination.

   (5) The Secretary of State must secure that, taking one financial year with another, the aggregate of the sums which become payable to it under regulations made by virtue of sub-paragraph (4) does not exceed the cost to it of performing its independent review functions.

(6) The Secretary of State may make an arrangement with an organisation under which independent review functions are performed by the organisation on the national authority's behalf.

(7) If the Secretary of State makes such an arrangement with an organisation, the organisation is to perform its functions under the arrangement in accordance with any general or special directions given by that national authority.

(8) The arrangement may include provision for payments to be made to the organisation by the Secretary of State.

(9) Payments made by the Secretary of State in accordance with such provision shall be taken into account in determining (for the purpose of sub-paragraph (5)) the cost to that national authority of performing its independent review functions.

(10) ...

(11) In this paragraph—

'financial year' means a period of twelve months ending with 31st March;

'independent review function' means a function conferred or imposed on a national authority by regulations made by virtue of sub-paragraph (1)(b);

'organisation' includes the Welsh Ministers, a public body and a private or voluntary organisation.

12G. Regulations under section 22C may, in particular, also make provision as to the circumstances in which local authorities may make arrangements for duties imposed on them by the regulations to be discharged on their behalf.

Promotion and maintenance of contact between child and family

15.— (1) Where a child is being looked after by a local authority, the authority shall, unless it is not reasonably practicable or consistent with his welfare, endeavour to promote contact between the child and—

(a) his parents;

(b) any person who is not a parent of his but who has parental responsibility for him; and

(c) any relative, friend or other person connected with him.

(2) Where a child is being looked after by a local authority—

(a) the authority shall take such steps as are reasonably practicable to secure that—

(i) his parents; and

(ii) any person who is not a parent of his but who has parental responsibility for him,

are kept informed of where he is being accommodated; and

(b) every such person shall secure that the authority are kept informed of his or her address.

(3) Where a local authority ('the receiving authority') take over the provision of accommodation for a child from another local authority or a local authority in Wales ('the transferring authority') under section 20(2)—

(a) the receiving authority shall (where reasonably practicable) inform—

(i) the child's parents; and

(ii) any person who is not a parent of his but who has parental responsibility for him;

(b) sub-paragraph (2)(a) shall apply to the transferring authority, as well as the receiving authority, until at least one such person has been informed of the change; and

(c) sub-paragraph (2)(b) shall not require any person to inform the receiving authority of his address until he has been so informed.

(4) Nothing in this paragraph requires a local authority to inform any person of the whereabouts of a child if—

(a) the child is in the care of the authority; and

(b) the authority has reasonable cause to believe that informing the person would prejudice the child's welfare.

(5) Any person who fails (without reasonable excuse) to comply with sub-paragraph (2)(b) shall be guilty of an offence and liable on summary conviction to a fine not exceeding level 2 on the standard scale.

(6)   It shall be a defence in any proceedings under sub-paragraph (5) to prove that the defendant was residing at the same address as another person who was the child's parent or had parental responsibility for the child and had reasonable cause to believe that the other person had informed the appropriate authority that both of them were residing at that address.

Visits to or by children: expenses

16.— (1)   This paragraph applies where—

(a)   a child is being looked after by a local authority; and

(b)   the conditions mentioned in sub-paragraph (3) are satisfied.

(2)   The authority may—

(a)   make payments to—

(i)   a parent of the child;

(ii)   any person who is not a parent of his but who has parental responsibility for him; or

(iii)   any relative, friend or other person connected with him,

in respect of travelling, subsistence or other expenses incurred by that person in visiting the child; or

(b)   make payments to the child, or to any person on his behalf, in respect of travelling, subsistence or other expenses incurred by or on behalf of the child in his visiting—

(i)   a parent of his;

(ii)   any person who is not a parent of his but who has parental responsibility for him; or

(iii)   any relative, friend or other person connected with him.

(3)   The conditions are that—

(a)   it appears to the authority that the visit in question could not otherwise be made without undue financial hardship; and

(b)   the circumstances warrant the making of the payments.

…

Power to guarantee apprenticeship deeds etc

18.— (1)   While a child is being looked after by a local authority, or is a person qualifying for advice and assistance, the authority may undertake any obligation by way of guarantee under any deed of apprenticeship or articles of clerkship which he enters into.

(2)   Where a local authority have undertaken any such obligation under any deed or articles they may at any time (whether or not they are still looking after the person concerned) undertake the like obligation under any supplemental deed or articles.

Arrangements to assist children to live abroad

19.— (1)   A local authority may only arrange for, or assist in arranging for, any child in their care to live outside England and Wales with the approval of the court.

(2)   A local authority may, with the approval of every person who has parental responsibility for the child arrange for, or assist in arranging for, any other child looked after by them to live outside England and Wales.

(3)   The court shall not give its approval under sub-paragraph (1) unless it is satisfied that—

(a)   living outside England and Wales would be in the child's best interests;

(b)   suitable arrangements have been, or will be, made for his reception and welfare in the country in which he will live;

(c)   the child has consented to living in that country; and

(d)   every person who has parental responsibility for the child has consented to his living in that country.

(4)   Where the court is satisfied that the child does not have sufficient understanding to give or withhold his consent, it may disregard sub-paragraph (3)(c) and give its approval if the child is to live in the country concerned with a parent, guardian, special guardian, or other suitable person.

(5)   Where a person whose consent is required by sub-paragraph (3)(d) fails to give his consent, the court may disregard that provision and give its approval if it is satisfied that that person—

(a)   cannot be found;

(b)   is incapable of consenting; or

(c)   is withholding his consent unreasonably.

(6)   Section 85 of the Adoption and Children Act 2002 (which imposes restrictions on taking children out of the United Kingdom) shall not apply in the case of any child who is to live outside England and Wales with the approval of the court given under this paragraph.

(7)   Where a court decides to give its approval under this paragraph it may order that its decision is not to have effect during the appeal period.

(8)   In sub-paragraph (7) 'the appeal period' means—

(a)   where an appeal is made against the decision, the period between the making of the decision and the determination of the appeal; and

(b)   otherwise, the period during which an appeal may be made against the decision.

(9)   This paragraph does not apply—

(a)   to a local authority placing a child in secure accommodation in Scotland under section 25, or

(b)   to a local authority placing a child for adoption with prospective adopters.

Preparation for ceasing to be looked after

19A.   It is the duty of the local authority looking after a child to advise, assist and befriend him with a view to promoting his welfare when they have ceased to look after him.

19B.—(1)   A local authority shall have the following additional functions in relation to an eligible child whom they are looking after.

(2)   In sub-paragraph (1) 'eligible child' means, subject to sub-paragraph (3), a child who—

(a)   is aged sixteen or seventeen; and

(b)   has been looked after by a local authority or by a local authority in Wales for a prescribed period, or periods amounting in all to a prescribed period, which began after he reached a prescribed age and ended after he reached the age of sixteen.

(3)   The Secretary of State may prescribe—

(a)   additional categories of eligible children; and

(b)   categories of children who are not to be eligible children despite falling within sub-paragraph (2).

(4)   For each eligible child, the local authority shall carry out an assessment of his needs with a view to determining what advice, assistance and support it would be appropriate for them to provide him under this Act—

(a)   while they are still looking after him; and

(b)   after they cease to look after him,

and shall then prepare a pathway plan for him.

(5)   The local authority shall keep the pathway plan under regular review.

(6)   Any such review may be carried out at the same time as a review of the child's case carried out by virtue of section 26.

(7)   The Secretary of State may by regulations make provision as to assessments for the purposes of sub-paragraph (4).

(8)   The regulations may in particular provide for the matters set out in section 23B(6).

Preparation for ceasing to be looked after: staying put arrangements

19BA.—(1)   This paragraph applies in relation to an eligible child (within the meaning of paragraph 19B) who has been placed by a local authority ... with a local authority foster parent.

(2)   When carrying out the assessment of the child's needs in accordance with paragraph 19B(4), the local authority must determine whether it would be appropriate to provide advice, assistance and support under this Act in order to facilitate a staying put arrangement, and with a view to maintaining such an arrangement, after the local authority cease to look after him or her.

(3)   The local authority must provide advice, assistance and support under this Act in order to facilitate a staying put arrangement if—

(a)   the local authority determine under sub-paragraph (2) that it would be appropriate to do so, and

(b)   the eligible child and the local authority foster parent wish to make a staying put arrangement.

(4)   In this paragraph, "staying put arrangement" has the meaning given by section 23CZA.

Personal advisers

19C.   A local authority shall arrange for each child whom they are looking after who is an eligible child for the purposes of paragraph 19B to have a personal adviser.

Death of children being looked after by local authorities

20.— (1)   If a child who is being looked after by a local authority dies, the authority—

(a)   shall notify the Secretary of State and Her Majesty's Chief Inspector of Education, Children's Services and Skills;

(b)   shall, so far as is reasonably practicable, notify the child's parents and every person who is not a parent of his but who has parental responsibility for him;

(c)   may, with the consent (so far as it is reasonably practicable to obtain it) of every person who has parental responsibility for the child, arrange for the child's body to be buried or cremated; and

(d)   may, if the conditions mentioned in sub-paragraph (2) are satisfied, make payments to any person who has parental responsibility for the child, or any relative, friend or other person connected with the child, in respect of travelling, subsistence or other expenses incurred by that person in attending the child's funeral.

(2)   The conditions are that—

(a)   it appears to the authority that the person concerned could not otherwise attend the child's funeral without undue financial hardship; and

(b)   that the circumstances warrant the making of the payments.

(3)   Sub-paragraph (1) does not authorise cremation where it does not accord with the practice of the child's religious persuasion.

(4)   Where a local authority have exercised their power under sub-paragraph (1)(c) with respect to a child who was under sixteen when he died, they may recover from any parent of the child any expenses incurred by them.

(5)   Any sums so recoverable shall, without prejudice to any other method of recovery, be recoverable summarily as a civil debt.

(6)   Nothing in this paragraph affects any enactment regulating or authorising the burial, cremation or anatomical examination of the body of a deceased person.

PART III

CONTRIBUTIONS TOWARDS MAINTENANCE OF CHILDREN LOOKED AFTER BY LOCAL AUTHORITIES IN ENGLAND

Liability to contribute

21.— (1)   Where a local authority are looking after a child (other than in the cases mentioned in sub-paragraph (7)) they shall consider whether they should recover contributions towards the child's maintenance from any person liable to contribute ('a contributor').

(2)   An authority may only recover contributions from a contributor if they consider it reasonable to do so.

(3)   The persons liable to contribute are—

(a)   where the child is under sixteen, each of his parents;

(b)   where he has reached the age of sixteen, the child himself.

(4)   A parent is not liable to contribute during any period when he is in receipt of universal credit (except in such circumstances as may be prescribed), of income support under Part VII of the Social Security Contributions and Benefits Act 1992, of any element of child tax credit other than the family element, of working tax credit, of an income-based jobseeker's allowance or of an income-related employment and support allowance.

(5) A person is not liable to contribute towards the maintenance of a child in the care of a local authority in respect of any period during which the child is living with, under arrangements made by the authority in accordance with section 22C, a parent of his.

(6) A contributor is not obliged to make any contribution towards a child's maintenance except as agreed or determined in accordance with this Part of this Schedule.

(7) The cases are where the child is looked after by a local authority under—

    (a) section 21;

    (b) an interim care order;

    (c) section 92 of the Powers of Criminal Courts (Sentencing) Act 2000 or section 260 of the Sentencing Code.

Agreed contributions

22.— (1) Contributions towards a child's maintenance may only be recovered if the local authority have served a notice ('a contribution notice') on the contributor specifying—

    (a) the weekly sum which they consider that he should contribute; and

    (b) arrangements for payment.

(2) The contribution notice must be in writing and dated.

(3) Arrangements for payment shall, in particular, include—

    (a) the date on which liability to contribute begins (which must not be earlier than the date of the notice);

    (b) the date on which liability under the notice will end (if the child has not before that date ceased to be looked after by the authority); and

    (c) the date on which the first payment is to be made.

(4) The authority may specify in a contribution notice a weekly sum which is a standard contribution determined by them for all children looked after by them.

(5) The authority may not specify in a contribution notice a weekly sum greater than that which they consider—

    (a) they would normally be prepared to pay if they had placed a similar child with local authority foster parents; and

    (b) it is reasonably practicable for the contributor to pay (having regard to his means).

(6) An authority may at any time withdraw a contribution notice (without prejudice to their power to serve another).

(7) Where the authority and the contributor agree—

    (a) the sum which the contributor is to contribute; and

    (b) arrangements for payment,

(whether as specified in the contribution notice or otherwise) and the contributor notifies the authority in writing that he so agrees, the authority may recover summarily as a civil debt any contribution which is overdue and unpaid.

(8) A contributor may, by serving a notice in writing on the authority, withdraw his agreement in relation to any period of liability falling after the date of service of the notice.

(9) Sub-paragraph (7) is without prejudice to any other method of recovery.

Contribution orders

23.— (1) Where a contributor has been served with a contribution notice and has—

    (a) failed to reach any agreement with the local authority as mentioned in paragraph 22(7) within the period of one month beginning with the day on which the contribution notice was served; or

    (b) served a notice under paragraph 22(8) withdrawing his agreement,

the authority may apply to the court for an order under this paragraph.

(2) On such an application the court may make an order ('a contribution order') requiring the contributor to contribute a weekly sum towards the child's maintenance in accordance with arrangements for payment specified by the court.

(3) A contribution order—

    (a) shall not specify a weekly sum greater than that specified in the contribution notice; and

(b)   shall be made with due regard to the contributor's means.

(4)   A contribution order shall not—

(a)   take effect before the date specified in the contribution notice; or

(b)   have effect while the contributor is not liable to contribute (by virtue of paragraph 21); or

(c)   remain in force after the child has ceased to be looked after by the authority who obtained the order.

(5)   An authority may not apply to the court under sub-paragraph (1) in relation to a contribution notice which they have withdrawn.

(6)   Where—

(a)   a contribution order is in force;

(b)   the authority serve another contribution notice; and

(c)   the contributor and the authority reach an agreement under paragraph 22(7) in respect of that other contribution notice,

the effect of the agreement shall be to discharge the order from the date on which it is agreed that the agreement shall take effect.

(7)   Where an agreement is reached under sub-paragraph (6) the authority shall notify the court—

(a)   of the agreement; and

(b)   of the date on which it took effect.

(8)   A contribution order may be varied or revoked on the application of the contributor or the authority.

(9)   In proceedings for the variation of a contribution order, the authority shall specify—

(a)   the weekly sum which, having regard to paragraph 22, they propose that the contributor should contribute under the order as varied; and

(b)   the proposed arrangements for payment.

(10)   Where a contribution order is varied, the order—

(a)   shall not specify a weekly sum greater than that specified by the authority in the proceedings for variation; and

(b)   shall be made with due regard to the contributor's means.

(11)   An appeal shall lie in accordance with rules of court from any order made under this paragraph.

Enforcement of contribution orders etc

24.— (1)   ...

(2)   Where a contributor has agreed, or has been ordered, to make contributions to a local authority, any other local authority within whose area the contributor is for the time being living may—

(a)   at the request of the local authority who served the contributions notice; and

(b)   subject to agreement as to any sum to be deducted in respect of services rendered,

collect from the contributor any contributions due on behalf of the authority who served the notice.

(3)   In sub-paragraph (2) the reference to any other local authority includes a reference to—

(aa)   a local authority in Wales;

(a)   a local authority within the meaning of section 1(2) of the Social Work (Scotland) Act 1968; and

(b)   a Health and Social Services Board established under Article 16 of the Health and Personal Social Services (Northern Ireland) Order 1972.

(4)   The power to collect sums under sub-paragraph (2) includes the power to—

(a)   receive and give a discharge for any contributions due; and

(b)   (if necessary) enforce payment of any contributions,

even though those contributions may have fallen due at a time when the contributor was living elsewhere.

(5)   Any contribution collected under sub-paragraph (2) shall be paid (subject to any agreed deduction) to the local authority who served the contribution notice.

(6)   In any proceedings under this paragraph, a document which purports to be—

      (a)   a copy of an order made by a court under or by virtue of paragraph 23; and

      (b)   certified as a true copy by the designated officer for the court,

shall be evidence of the order.

(7)   In any proceedings under this paragraph, a certificate which—

      (a)   purports to be signed by the clerk or some other duly authorised officer of the local authority who obtained the contribution order; and

      (b)   states that any sum due to the authority under the order is overdue and unpaid,

shall be evidence that the sum is overdue and unpaid.

Regulations

25.   The Secretary of State may make regulations—

    (a)   as to the considerations which a local authority must take into account in deciding—

      (i)   whether it is reasonable to recover contributions; and

      (ii)   what the arrangements for payment should be;

    (b)   as to the procedures they must follow in reaching agreements with—

      (i)   contributors (under paragraphs 22 and 23); and

      (ii)   any other local authority under paragraph 24(2).

(F)   Child Support Act 1991

1   The duty to maintain

(1)   For the purposes of this Act, each parent of a qualifying child is responsible for maintaining him.

(2)   For the purposes of this Act, a non-resident parent shall be taken to have met his responsibility to maintain any qualifying child of his by making periodical payments of maintenance with respect to the child of such amount, and at such intervals, as may be determined in accordance with the provisions of this Act.

(3)   Where a maintenance calculation made under this Act requires the making of periodical payments, it shall be the duty of the non-resident parent with respect to whom the calculation was made to make those payments.

2   Welfare of children: the general principle

Where, in any case which falls to be dealt with under this Act, the Secretary of State ... is considering the exercise of any discretionary power conferred by this Act, the Secretary of State shall have regard to the welfare of any child likely to be affected by the decision.

3   Meaning of certain terms used in this Act

(1)   A child is a 'qualifying child' if—

    (a)   one of his parents is, in relation to him, a non-resident parent; or

    (b)   both of his parents are, in relation to him, non-resident parents.

(2)   The parent of any child is a 'non-resident parent', in relation to him, if—

    (a)   that parent is not living in the same household with the child; and

    (b)   the child has his home with a person who is, in relation to him, a person with care.

(3)   A person is a 'person with care', in relation to any child, if he is a person—

    (a)   with whom the child has his home;

    (b)   who usually provides a day to day care for the child (whether exclusively or in conjunction with any other person); and

    (c)   who does not fall within a prescribed category of person.

(4)   The Secretary of State shall not, under subsection (3)(c), prescribe as a category—

    (a)   parents;

    (b)   guardians;

    (c)   persons named, in a child arrangements order under section 8 of the Children Act 1989, as persons with whom a child is to live;

    (d)   (not reproduced)

(5)   For the purposes of this Act there may be more than one person with care in relation to the same qualifying child.

(6)   Periodical payments which are required to be paid in accordance with a maintenance calculation are referred to in this Act as 'child support maintenance'.

(7)   Expressions are defined in this section only for the purposes of this Act.

4   Child support maintenance

(1)   A person who is, in relation to any qualifying child or any qualifying children, either the person with care or the non-resident parent may apply to the Secretary of State for a maintenance calculation to be made under this Act with respect to that child, or any of those children.

(2)   Where a maintenance calculation has been made in response to an application under this section the Secretary of State may, if the person with care ... applies to the Secretary of State under this subsection, arrange for—

    (a)   the collection of the child support maintenance payable in accordance with the calculation;

    (b)   the enforcement of the obligation to pay child support maintenance in accordance with the calculation.

(2A)   The Secretary of State may only make arrangements under subsection (2)(a) if—

(a)   the non-resident parent agrees to the arrangements, or

(b)   the Secretary of State is satisfied that without the arrangements child support maintenance is unlikely to be paid in accordance with the calculation.

(3)   Where an application under subsection (2) for the enforcement of the obligation mentioned in subsection (2)(b) authorises the Secretary of State to take steps to enforce that obligation whenever the Secretary of State considers it necessary to do so, the Secretary of State may act accordingly.

(4)   A person who applies to the Secretary of State under this section shall, so far as that person reasonably can, comply with such regulations as may be made by the Secretary of State with a view to the Secretary of State ... being provided with the information which is required to enable—

(a)   the non-resident parent to be identified or traced (where that is necessary);

(b)   the amount of child support maintenance payable by the non-resident parent to be calculated; and

(c)   that amount to be recovered from the non-resident parent.

(5)   Any person who has applied to the Secretary of State under this section may at any time request the Secretary of State to cease acting under this section.

(6)   It shall be the duty of the Secretary of State to comply with any request made under subsection (5) (but subject to any regulations made under subsection (8)).

(7)   The obligation to provide information which is imposed by subsection (4)—

(a)   shall not apply in such circumstances as may be prescribed; and

(b)   may, in such circumstances as may be prescribed, be waived by the Secretary of State.

(8)   The Secretary of State may by regulations make such incidental, supplemental or transitional provision as he thinks appropriate with respect to cases in which he is requested to cease to act under this under this section.

(9)   ...

(10)   No application may be made at any time under this section with respect to a qualifying child or any qualifying children if—

(a)   there is in force a written maintenance agreement made before 5 April 1993, or a maintenance order made before a prescribed date, in respect of that child or those children and the person who is, at that time, the non-resident parent; or

(aa)   a maintenance order made on or after the date prescribed for the purposes of paragraph (a) is in force in respect of them, but has been so for less than the period of one year beginning with the date on which it was made; or

(ab)   a maintenance agreement—

(i)   made on or after the date prescribed for the purposes of paragraph (a); and

(ii)   registered for execution in the Books of Council and Session or the sheriff court books,

is in force in respect of them, but has been so for less than the period of one year beginning with the date on which it was made; ...

(11)   ...

5   Child support maintenance: supplemental provisions

(1)   Where—

(a)   there is more than one person with care of a qualifying child; and

(b)   one or more, but not all, of them have parental responsibility for ... the child;

no application may be made for a maintenance calculation with respect to the child by any of those persons who do not have parental responsibility for ... the child.

(2)   Where more than one application for a maintenance calculation is made with respect to the child concerned, only one of them may be proceeded with.

(3)   The Secretary of State may by regulation make provision as to which of two or more applications for a maintenance calculation with respect to the same child is to be proceeded with.

8   Role of the courts with respect to maintenance for children

(1)   This subsection applies in any case where the Secretary of State would have jurisdiction to make a maintenance calculation with respect to a qualifying child and a non-resident parent of his on an application duly made ... by a person entitled to apply for such a calculation with respect to that child.

(2)   Subsection (1) applies even though the circumstances of the case are such that the Secretary of State would not make a calculation if it were applied for.

(3)   Except as provided in subsection (3A), in any case where subsection (1) applies, no court shall exercise any power which it would otherwise have to make, vary or revive any maintenance order in relation to the child and non-resident parent concerned.

(3A)   Unless a maintenance calculation has been made with respect to the child concerned, subsection (3) does not prevent a court from varying a maintenance order in relation to that child and the non-resident parent concerned—

(a)   if the maintenance order was made on or after the date prescribed for the purposes of section 4(10)(a) or 7(10)(a); or

(b)   where the order was made before then, in any case in which section 4(10) or 7(10) prevents the making of an application for a maintenance calculation with respect to or by that child.

(4)   Subsection (3) does not prevent a court from revoking a maintenance order.

(5)   The Lord Chancellor ... may by order provide that, in such circumstances as may be specified by the order, this section shall not prevent a court from exercising any power which it has to make a maintenance order in relation to a child if—

(a)   a written agreement (whether or not enforceable) provides for the making, or securing, by a non-resident parent of the child of periodical payments to or for the benefit of the child; and

(b)   the maintenance order which the court makes is, in all material respects, in the same terms as that agreement.

(5A)   The Lord Chancellor may make an order under subsection (5) only with the concurrence of the Lord Chief Justice.

(6)   This section shall not prevent a court from exercising any power which it has to make a maintenance order in relation to a child if—

(a)   a maintenance calculation is in force with respect to the child;

(b)   the non-resident parent's gross weekly income exceeds the figure referred to in paragraph 10(3) of Schedule 1 (as it has effect from time to time pursuant to regulations made under paragraph 10A(1)(b)); and

(c)   the court is satisfied that the circumstances of the case make it appropriate for the non-resident parent to make or secure the making of periodical payments under a maintenance order in addition to the child support maintenance payable by him in accordance with the maintenance calculation.

(7)   This section shall not prevent a court from exercising any power which it has to make a maintenance order in relation to a child if—

(a)   the child is, will be or (if the order were to be made) would be receiving instruction at an educational establishment or undergoing training for a trade, profession or vocation (whether or not while in gainful employment); and

(b)   the order is made solely for the purposes of requiring the person making or securing the making of periodical payments fixed by the order to meet some or all of the expenses incurred in connection with the provision of the instruction or training.

(8)   This section shall not prevent a court from exercising any power which it has to make a maintenance order in relation to a child if—

(a)   an allowance under Part 4 of the Welfare Reform Act 2012 (personal independence payment) or a disability living allowance is paid to or in respect of him; or

(b)   no such allowance is paid but he is disabled,

and the order is made solely for the purpose of requiring the person making or securing the making of periodical payments fixed by the order to meet some or all of any expenses attributable to the child's disability.

(9)   For the purposes of subsection (8), a child is disabled if he is blind, deaf or dumb or is substantially and permanently handicapped by illness, injury, mental disorder or congenital deformity or such other disability as may be prescribed.

(10)   This section shall not prevent a court from exercising any power which it has to make a maintenance order in relation to a child if the order is made against a person with care of the child.

(11)   In this Act 'maintenance order', in relation to any child, means an order which requires the making or securing of periodical payments to or for the benefit of the child and which is made under—

(a)   Part II of the Matrimonial Causes Act 1973;

(b)   the Domestic Proceedings and Magistrates' Courts Act 1978;

(c)   Part III of the Matrimonial and Family Proceedings Act 1984;

...

(e)   Schedule 1 to the Children Act 1989; ...

(ea)   Schedule 5, 6 or 7 of the Civil Partnership Act 2004; or

(f)   any other prescribed enactment,

and includes any order varying or reviving such an order.

(12)   The Lord Chief Justice may nominate a judicial office holder (as defined in section 109(4) of the Constitutional Reform Act 2005) to exercise his functions under this section.

9   Agreements about maintenance

(1)   In this section 'maintenance agreement' means any agreement for the making, or for securing the making, of periodical payments by way of maintenance, or in Scotland aliment, to or for the benefit of any child.

(2)   Nothing in this Act shall be taken to prevent any person from entering into a maintenance agreement.

(2A)   The Secretary of State may, with a view to reducing the need for applications under sections 4 and 7—

(a)   take such steps as the Secretary of State considers appropriate to encourage the making and keeping of maintenance agreements, and

(b)   in particular, before accepting an application under those sections, invite the applicant to consider with the Secretary of State whether it is possible to make such an agreement.

(3)   Subject to section 4(10)(a) and (ab) and section 7(10), the existence of a maintenance agreement shall not prevent any party to the agreement, or any other person, from applying for a maintenance calculation with respect to any child to or for whose benefit periodical payments are to be made or secured under the agreement.

(4)   Where any agreement contains a provision which purports to restrict the right of any person to apply for a maintenance calculation, that provision shall be void.

(5)   Where section 8 would prevent any court from making a maintenance order in relation to a child and a non-resident parent of his, no court shall exercise any power that it has to vary any agreement so as—

(a)   to insert a provision requiring that non-resident parent to make or secure the making of periodical payments by way of maintenance, or in Scotland aliment, to or for the benefit of that child; or

(b)   to increase the amount payable under such a provision.

(6)   In any case in which section 4(10) or 7(10) prevents the making of an application for a maintenance calculation, ...

subsection (5) shall have effect with the omission of paragraph (b).

10   Relationship between maintenance calculations and certain court orders and related matters

(1)   Where an order of a kind prescribed for the purposes of this subsection is in force with respect to any qualifying child with respect to whom a maintenance calculation is made, the order—

(a)   shall, so far as it relates to the making or securing of periodical payments, cease to have effect to such extent as may be determined in accordance with regulations made by the Secretary of State; or

(b)   where the regulations so provide, shall, so far as it so relates, have effect subject to such modifications as may be so determined.

(2)   Where an agreement of a kind prescribed for the purposes of this subsection is in force with respect to any qualifying child with respect to whom a maintenance calculation is made, the agreement—

   (a)   shall, so far as it relates to the making or securing of periodical payments, be unenforceable to such extent as may be determined in accordance with regulations made by the Secretary of State; or

   (b)   where the regulations so provide, shall, so far as it so relates, have effect subject to such modifications as may be so determined.

(3)   Any regulations under this section may, in particular, make such provision with respect to—

   (a)   any case where any person with respect to whom an order or agreement of a kind prescribed for the purposes of subsection (1) or (2) has effect applies to the prescribed court, before the end of the prescribed period, for the order or agreement to be varied in the light of the maintenance calculation and of the provisions of this Act;

   (b)   the recovery of any arrears under the order or agreement which fell due before the coming into force of the maintenance calculation,

as the Secretary of State considers appropriate and may provide that, in prescribed circumstances, an application to any court which is made with respect to an order of a prescribed kind relating to the making or securing of periodical payments to or for the benefit of a child shall be treated by the court as an application for the order to be revoked.

(4)   The Secretary of State may by regulations make provision for—

   (a)   notification to be given by the Secretary of State concerned to the prescribed person in any case where the Secretary of State considers that the making of a maintenance calculation has affected, or is likely to affect, any order of a kind prescribed for the purposes of this subsection; or

   (b)   notification to be given by the prescribed person to the Secretary of State in any case where a court makes an order which it considers has affected, or is likely to affect, a maintenance calculation.

(5)   Rules of court may require any person who, in prescribed circumstances, makes an application to the family court for a maintenance order to furnish the court with a statement in a prescribed form, and signed by an officer of the Secretary of State, as to whether or not, at the time when the statement is made, there is a maintenance calculation in force with respect to that person or the child concerned.

In this subsection—

'maintenance order' means an order of a prescribed kind for the making or securing of periodical payments to or for the benefit of a child; and

'prescribed' means prescribed by the rules.

11   Maintenance calculations

(1)   An application for a maintenance calculation made to the Secretary of State shall be dealt with by the Secretary of State in accordance with the provision made by or under this Act.

(2)   The Secretary of State shall (unless the Secretary of State decides not to make a maintenance calculation in response to the application, or makes a decision under section 12) determine the application by making a decision under this section about whether any child support maintenance is payable and, if so, how much.

(3)–(5)   ...

(6)   The amount of child support maintenance to be fixed by a maintenance calculation shall be determined in accordance with Part I of Schedule 1 unless an application for a variation has been made and agreed.

(7)   If the Secretary of State has agreed to a variation, the amount of child support maintenance to be fixed shall be determined on the basis determined under section 28F(4).

(8)   Part II of Schedule 1 makes further provision with respect to maintenance calculations.

44   Jurisdiction

(1)   The Secretary of State shall have jurisdiction to make a maintenance calculation with respect to a person who is—

   (a)   a person with care;

   (b)   a non-resident parent; or

(c)   a qualifying child,

only if that person is habitually resident in the United Kingdom, except in the case of a non-resident parent who falls within subsection (2A).

(2)   Where the person with care is not an individual, subsection (1) shall have effect as if paragraph (a) were omitted.

(2A)   A non-resident parent falls within this subsection if he is not habitually resident in the United Kingdom, but is—

(a)   employed in the civil service of the Crown, including Her Majesty's Diplomatic Service and Her Majesty's Overseas Civil Service;

(b)   a member of the naval, military or air forces of the Crown, including any person employed by an ssociation established for the purposes of Part XI of the Reserves Forces Act 1996;

(c)   employed by a company of a prescribed description registered under the Companies Act 2006; or

(d)   employed by a body of a prescribed description.

(3)   (not reproduced)

...

SCHEDULE 1
MAINTENANCE CALCULATIONS
PART I
CALCULATION OF WEEKLY AMOUNT OF CHILD SUPPORT MAINTENANCE

1   General rule

(1)   Subject to paragraph 5A, the weekly rate of child support maintenance is the basic rate unless a reduced rate, a flat rate or the nil rate applies.

(2)   Unless the nil rate applies, the amount payable weekly to a person with care is—

(a)   the applicable rate, if paragraph 6 does not apply; or

(b)   if paragraph 6 does apply, that rate as apportioned between the persons with care in accordance with paragraph 6,

as adjusted, in either case, by applying the rules about shared care in paragraph 7 or 8.

2   Basic rate

(1)   Subject to sub-paragraph (2), the basic rate is the following percentage of the non-resident parent's gross weekly income—

12% where the non-resident parent has one qualifying child;

16% where the non-resident parent has two qualifying children;

19% where the non-resident parent has three or more qualifying children.

(2)   If the gross weekly income of the non-resident parent exceeds £800, the basic rate is the aggregate of the amount found by applying sub-paragraph (1) in relation to the first £800 of that income and the following percentage of the remainder—

9% where the non-resident parent has one qualifying child;

12% where the non-resident parent has two qualifying children;

15% where the non-resident parent has three or more qualifying children.

(3)   If the non-resident parent also has one or more relevant other children, gross weekly income shall be treated for the purposes of sub-paragraphs (1) and (2) as reduced by the following percentage—

11% where the non-resident parent has one relevant other child;

14% where the non-resident parent has two relevant other children;

16% where the non-resident parent has three or more relevant other children.

3   Reduced rate

(1)   A reduced rate is payable if—

(a)   neither a flat rate nor the nil rate applies; and

(b)   the non-resident parent's gross weekly income is less than £200 but more than £100.

(2)   The reduced rate payable shall be prescribed in, or determined in accordance with, regulations.

(3)   The regulations may not prescribe, or result in, a rate of less than £7.

4   Flat rate

(1)   Except in a case falling within sub-paragraph (2), a flat rate of £7 is payable if the nil rate does not apply and—

(a)   the non-resident parent's gross weekly income is £100 or less; or

(b)   he receives any benefit, pension or allowance prescribed for the purposes of this paragraph of this sub-paragraph; or

(c)   he or his partner (if any) receives any benefit prescribed for the purposes of this paragraph of this sub-paragraph.

(2)   A flat rate of a prescribed amount is payable if the nil rate does not apply and—

(a)   the non-resident parent has a partner who is also a non-resident parent;

(b)   the partner is a person with respect to whom a maintenance calculation is in force; and

(c)   the non-resident parent or his partner receives any benefit prescribed under sub-paragraph (1)(c).

(3)   The benefits, pensions and allowances which may be prescribed for the purposes of sub-paragraph (1)(b) include ones paid to the non-resident parent under the law of a place outside the United Kingdom.

5   Nil rate

The rate payable is nil if the non-resident parent—

(a)   is of a prescribed description; or

(b)   has a gross weekly income of below £7.

5A   Non-resident parent party to other maintenance arrangement

(1)   This paragraph applies where—

(a)   the non-resident parent is a party to a qualifying maintenance arrangement with respect to a child of his who is not a qualifying child, and

(b)   the weekly rate of child support maintenance apart from this paragraph would be the basic rate or a reduced rate or calculated following agreement to a variation where the rate would otherwise be a flat rate or the nil rate.

(2)   The weekly rate of child support maintenance is the greater of £7 and the amount found as follows.

(3)   First, calculate the amount which would be payable if the non-resident parent's qualifying children also included every child with respect to whom the non-resident parent is a party to a qualifying maintenance arrangement.

(4)   Second, divide the amount so calculated by the number of children taken into account for the purposes of the calculation.

(5)   Third, multiply the amount so found by the number of children who, for purposes other than the calculation under sub-paragraph (3), are qualifying children of the non-resident parent.

(6)   For the purposes of this paragraph, the non-resident parent is a party to a qualifying maintenance arrangement with respect to a child if the non-resident parent is—

(a)   liable to pay maintenance or aliment for the child under a maintenance order, or

(b)   a party to an agreement of a prescribed description which provides for the non-resident parent to make payments for the benefit of the child,

and the child is habitually resident in the United Kingdom.

6   Apportionment

(1)   If the non-resident parent has more than one qualifying child and in relation to them there is more than one person with care, the amount of child support maintenance payable is (subject to paragraph 7 or 8) to be determined by apportioning the rate between the persons with care.

(2)   The rate of maintenance liability is to be divided by the number of qualifying children, and shared among the persons with care according to the number of qualifying children in relation to whom each is a person with care.

7   Shared care—basic and reduced rate

(1)   This paragraph applies where the rate of child support maintenance payable is the basic rate or a reduced rate or is determined under paragraph 5A.

(2)   If the care of a qualifying child is, or is to be, shared between the non-resident parent and the person with care, so that the non-resident parent from time to time has care of the child overnight, the amount of child support maintenance which he would otherwise have been liable to pay the person with care, as calculated in accordance with the preceding paragraphs of this Part of this Schedule, is to be decreased in accordance with this paragraph.

(3)   First, there is to be a decrease according to the number of such nights which the Secretary of State determines there to have been, or expects there to be, or both during a prescribed twelve-month period.

(4)   The amount of that decrease for one child is set out in the following Table—

Number of nights	Fraction to subtract
52 to 103	One-seventh
104 to 155	Two-sevenths
156 to 174	Three-sevenths
175 or more	One-half

(5)   If the person with care is caring for more than one qualifying child of the non-resident parent, the applicable decrease is the sum of the appropriate fractions in the Table divided by the number of such qualifying children.

(6)   If the applicable fraction is one-half in relation to any qualifying child in the care of the person with care, the total amount payable to the person with care is then to be further decreased by £7 for each such child.

(7)   If the application of the preceding provisions of this paragraph would decrease the weekly amount of child support maintenance (or the aggregate of all such amounts) payable by the non-resident parent to the person with care (or all of them) to less than £7, he is instead liable to pay child support maintenance at the rate of £7 a week, apportioned (if appropriate) in accordance with paragraph 6.

8   Shared care—flat rate

(1)   This paragraph applies only if—

    (a)   the rate of child support maintenance payable is a flat rate; and

    (b)   that rate applies because the non-resident parent falls within paragraph 4(1)(b) or (c) or 4(2).

(2)   If the care of a qualifying child is, or is to be, shared as mentioned in paragraph 7(2) for at least 52 nights during a prescribed 12-month period, the amount of child support maintenance payable by the non-resident parent to the person with care of that child is nil.

9   Regulations about shared care

(1)   The Secretary of State may by regulations provide—

    (za)   for how it is to be determined whether the care of a qualifying child is to be shared as mentioned in paragraph 7(2);

    (a)   for which nights are to count for the purposes of shared care under paragraphs 7 and 8 ...;

    (b)   for what counts, or does not count, as 'care' for those purposes;

    (ba)   for how it is to be determined how many nights count for those purposes; and

    (c)   for paragraph 7(3) or 8(2) to have effect, in prescribed circumstances, as if the period mentioned there were other than 12 months, and in such circumstances for the Table in paragraph 7(4) (or that Table as modified pursuant to regulations made under paragraph 10A(2)(a)), or the period mentioned in paragraph 8(2), to have effect with prescribed adjustments.

(2)   Regulations under sub-paragraph (1)(ba) may include provision enabling the Secretary of State to proceed for a prescribed period on the basis of a prescribed assumption.

10   Gross weekly income

(1)   For the purposes of this Schedule, gross weekly income is to be determined in such manner as is provided for in regulations.

(2)   The regulations may, in particular—

(a)   provide for determination in prescribed circumstances by reference to income of a prescribed description in a prescribed past period;

(b)   provide for the Secretary of State to estimate any income or make an assumption as to any fact where, in Secretary of State's view, the information at Secretary of State's disposal is unreliable or insufficient, or relates to an atypical period in the life of the non-resident parent.

(3)   Any amount of gross weekly income (calculated as above) over £3,000 is to be ignored for the purposes of this Schedule.

10A   Regulations about rates, figures, etc

(1)   The Secretary of State may by regulations provide that—

(a)   paragraph 2 is to have effect as if different percentages were substituted for those set out there;

(b)   paragraph 2(2), 3(1) or (3), 4(1), 5, 5A(2), 7(7) or 10(3) is to have effect as if different amounts were substituted for those set out there.

(2)   The Secretary of State may by regulations provide that—

(a)   the Table in paragraph 7(4) is to have effect as if different numbers of nights were set out in the first column and different fractions were substituted for those set out in the second column;

(b)   paragraph 7(6) is to have effect as if a different amount were substituted for that mentioned there, or as if the amount were an aggregate amount and not an amount for each qualifying child, or both.

10B   Regulations about income

The Secretary of State may by regulations provide that, in such circumstances and to such extent as may be prescribed—

(a)   where the Secretary of State is satisfied that a person has intentionally deprived himself of a source of income with a view to reducing the amount of his gross weekly income, his gross weekly income shall be taken to include income from that source of an amount estimated by the Secretary of State;

(b)   a person is to be treated as possessing income which he does not possess;

(c)   income which a person does possess is to be disregarded.

10C   References to various terms

(1)   References in this Part of this Schedule to 'qualifying children' are to those qualifying children with respect to whom the maintenance calculation falls to be made or with respect to whom a maintenance calculation in respect of the non-resident parent has effect.

(2)   References in this Part of this Schedule to 'relevant other children' are to—

(a)   children other than qualifying children in respect of whom the non-resident parent or his partner receives child benefit under Part IX of the Social Security Contributions and Benefits Act 1992; and

(b)   such other description of children as may be prescribed.

(3)   In this Part of this Schedule, a person 'receives' a benefit, pension, or allowance for any week if it is paid or due to be paid to him in respect of that week.

(4)   In this Part of this Schedule, a person's 'partner' is—

(a)   if they are a couple, the other member of that couple;

(b)   if the person is a husband or wife by virtue of a marriage entered into under a law which permits polygamy, another party to the marriage who is of the opposite sex and is a member of the same household.

(5)   In sub-paragraph (4)(a), 'couple' means—

(a)   two people who are married to, or civil partners of, each other and are members of the same household, or

(b)   two people who are not married to, or civil partners of, each other but are living together as a married couple or civil partners.

(6)   ...

PART II
GENERAL PROVISIONS ABOUT MAINTENANCE CALCULATIONS

11   Effective date of calculation

(1)   A maintenance calculation shall take effect on such date as may be determined in accordance with regulations made by the Secretary of State.

(2)   That date may be earlier than the date on which the calculation is made.

12   Form of calculation

Every maintenance calculation shall be made in such form and contain such information as the Secretary of State may direct.

13   (not reproduced)

14   Consolidated applications and calculations

The Secretary of State may by regulations provide—

(a)   for two or more applications for maintenance calculations to be treated, in prescribed circumstances, as a single application; and

(b)   for the replacement, in prescribed circumstances, of a maintenance calculation made on the application of one person by a later maintenance calculation made on the application of that or any other person.

15   Separate calculations for different periods

Where the Secretary of State is satisfied that the circumstances of a case require different amounts of child support maintenance to be calculated in respect of different periods, the Secretary of State may make separate maintenance calculations each expressed to have effect in relation to a different specified period.

16   Termination of calculations

(1)   A maintenance calculation shall cease to have effect—

(a)   on the death of the non-resident parent, or of the person with care, with respect to whom it was made;

(b)   on there no longer being any qualifying child with respect to whom it would have effect;

(c)   on the non-resident parent with respect to whom it was made ceasing to be a parent of—

(i)   the qualifying child with respect to whom it was made; or

(ii)   where it was made with respect to more than one qualifying child, all of the qualifying children with respect to whom it was made;

(d), (e) (not reproduced)

(2)–(9) (not reproduced)

(10)   A person with care with respect to whom a maintenance calculation is in force shall provide the Secretary of State with such information, in such circumstances, as may be prescribed, with a view to assisting the Secretary of State ... in determining whether the calculation has ceased to have effect ...

(11)   The Secretary of State may by regulations make such supplemental, incidental or transitional provision as he thinks necessary or expedient in consequence of the provisions of this paragraph.

(G)   Family Law Act 1996

30   Rights concerning home where one spouse or civil partner has no estate, etc.

(1)   This section applies if—

    (a)   one spouse or civil partner ('A') is entitled to occupy a dwelling-house by virtue of—

        (i)   a beneficial estate or interest or contract; or

        (ii)   any enactment giving A the right to remain in occupation; and

    (b)   the other spouse or civil partner ('B') is not so entitled.

(2)   Subject to the provisions of this Part, B has the following rights ('home rights')—

    (a)   if in occupation, a right not to be evicted or excluded from the dwelling-house or any part of it by A except with the leave of the court given by an order under section 33;

    (b)   if not in occupation, a right with the leave of the court so given to enter into and occupy the dwelling-house.

(3)   If B is entitled under this section to occupy a dwelling-house or any part of a dwelling-house, any payment or tender made or other thing done by B in or towards satisfaction of any liability of A in respect of rent, mortgage payments or other outgoings affecting the dwelling-house is, whether or not it is made or done in pursuance of an order under section 40, as good as if made or done by A.

(4)   B's occupation by virtue of this section—

    (a)   is to be treated, for the purposes of the Rent (Agriculture) Act 1976 and the Rent Act 1977 (other than Part V and sections 103 to 106 of that Act), as occupation by A as A's residence, and

    (b)   if B occupies the dwelling-house as B's only or principal home, is to be treated, for the purposes of the Housing Act 1985, Part I of the Housing Act 1988, Chapter 1 of Part 5 of the Housing Act 1996 and the Prevention of Social Housing Fraud Act 2013, as occupation by A as A's only or principal home.

(5)   If B—

    (a)   is entitled under this section to occupy a dwelling-house or any part of a dwelling-house, and

    (b)   makes any payment in or towards satisfaction of any liability of A in respect of mortgage payments affecting the dwelling-house,

  the person to whom the payment is made may treat it as having been made by A, but the fact that that person has treated any such payment as having been so made does not affect any claim of B against A to an interest in the dwelling-house by virtue of the payment.

(6)   If B is entitled under this section to occupy a dwelling-house or part of a dwelling-house by reason of an interest of A under a trust, all the provisions of subsections (3) to (5) apply in relation to the trustees as they apply in relation to A.

(7)   This section does not apply to a dwelling-house which—

    (a)   in the case of spouses, has at no time been, and which was at the time intended by them to be, a matrimonial home of theirs, and

    (b)   in the case of civil partners, has at no time been, and was at no time intended to be, a civil partnership home of theirs.

(8)   B's home rights continue—

    (a)   only so long as the marriage or civil partnership subsists, except to the extent that an order under section 33(5) otherwise provides; and

    (b)   only so long as A is entitled as mentioned in subsection (1) to occupy the dwelling-house, except where provision is made by section 31 for those rights to be a charge on an estate or interest in the dwelling-house.

(9)   It is hereby declared that a person—

    (a)   who has an equitable interest in a dwelling-house or in its proceeds of sale, but

    (b)   is not a person in whom there is vested (whether solely or as joint tenant) a legal estate in fee simple or a legal term of years absolute in the dwelling-house,

  is to be treated, only for the purpose of determining whether he has home rights, as not being entitled to occupy the dwelling-house by virtue of that interest.

33   Occupation orders where applicant has estate or interest etc or has home rights

(1)   If—

  (a)   a person ('the person entitled')—

    (i)   is entitled to occupy a dwelling-house by virtue of a beneficial estate or interest or contract or by virtue of any enactment giving him the right to remain in occupation, or

    (ii)   has home rights in relation to a dwelling-house, and

  (b)   the dwelling-house—

    (i)   is or at any time has been the home of the person entitled and of another person with whom he is associated, or

    (ii)   was at any time intended by the person entitled and any such other person to be their home,

  the person entitled may apply to the court for an order containing any of the provisions specified in subsections (3), (4) and (5).

(2)   If an agreement to marry is terminated, no application under this section may be made by virtue of section 62(3)(e) by reference to that agreement after the end of the period of three years beginning with the date on which it is terminated.

(2A)   If a civil partnership agreement (as defined by section 73 of the Civil Partnership Act 2004) is terminated, no application under this section may be made by virtue of section 62(3)(eza) by reference to that agreement after the period of three years beginning with the day on which it is terminated.

(3)   An order under this section may—

  (a)   enforce the applicant's entitlement to remain in occupation as against the other person ('the respondent');

  (b)   require the respondent to permit the applicant to enter and remain in the dwelling-house or part of the dwelling-house;

  (c)   regulate the occupation of the dwelling-house by either or both parties;

  (d)   if the respondent is entitled as mentioned in subsection (1)(a)(i), prohibit, suspend or restrict the exercise by him of his right to occupy the dwelling-house;

  (e)   if the respondent has home rights in relation to the dwelling-house and the applicant is the other spouse or civil partner, restrict or terminate those rights;

  (f)   require the respondent to leave the dwelling-house or part of the dwelling-house; or

  (g)   exclude the respondent from a defined area in which the dwelling-house is included.

(4)   An order under this section may declare that the applicant is entitled as mentioned in subsection (1)(a)(i) or has home rights.

(5)   If the applicant has home rights and the respondent is the other spouse or civil partner, an order under this section made during the marriage or civil partnership may provide that those rights are not brought to an end by—

  (a)   the death of the other spouse or civil partner; or

  (b)   the termination (otherwise than by death) of the marriage or civil partnership.

(6)   In deciding whether to exercise its powers under subsection (3) and (if so) in what manner, the court shall have regard to all the circumstances including—

  (a)   the housing needs and housing resources of each of the parties and of any relevant child;

  (b)   the financial resources of the parties;

  (c)   the likely effect of any order, or of any decision by the court not to exercise its powers under subsection (3), on the health, safety or well-being of the parties and of any relevant child; and

  (d)   the conduct of the parties in relation to each other and otherwise.

(7)   If it appears to the court that the applicant or any relevant child is likely to suffer significant harm attributable to conduct of the respondent if an order under this section containing one or more of the provisions mentioned in subsection (3) is not made, the court shall make the order unless it appears to the court that—

  (a)   the respondent or any relevant child is likely to suffer significant harm if the order is made; and

(b)   the harm likely to be suffered by the respondent or child in that event is as great as, or greater than, the harm attributable to conduct of the respondent which is likely to be suffered by the applicant or child if the order is not made.

(8)   The court may exercise its powers under subsection (5) in any case where it considers that in all the circumstances it is just and reasonable to do so.

(9)   An order under this section—

(a)   may not be made after the death of either of the parties mentioned in subsection (1); and

(b)   except in the case of an order made by virtue of subsection (5)(a), ceases to have effect on the death of either party.

(10)   An order under this section may, in so far as it has continuing effect, be made for a specified period, until the occurrence of a specified event or until further order.

34   Effect of order under s 33 where rights are charge on dwelling-house

(1)   If B's home rights are a charge on the estate or interest of A or of trustees for A—

(a)   an order under section 33 against A has, except so far as a contrary intention appears, the same effect against persons deriving title under A or under the trustees and affected by the charge, and

(b)   sections 33(1), (3), (4) and (10) and 30(3) to (6) apply in relation to any person deriving title under A or under the trustees and affected by the charge as they apply in relation to A.

(2)   The court may make an order under section 33 by virtue of subsection (1)(b) if it considers that in all the circumstances it is just and reasonable to do so.

35   One former spouse or former civil partner with no existing right to occupy

(1)   This section applies if—

(a)   one former spouse or former civil partner is entitled to occupy a dwelling-house by virtue of a beneficial estate or interest or contract, or by virtue of any enactment giving him the right to remain in occupation;

(b)   the other former spouse or former civil partner is not so entitled; and

(c)   the dwelling-house—

(i)   in the case of former spouses, was at any time their matrimonial home or was at any time intended by them to be their matrimonial home, or

(ii)   in the case of former civil partners, was at any time their civil partnership home or was at any time intended by them to be their civil partnership home.

(2)   The former spouse or former civil partner not so entitled may apply to the court for an order under this section against the other former spouse or former civil partner ('the respondent').

(3)   If the applicant is in occupation, an order under this section must contain provision—

(a)   giving the applicant the right not to be evicted or excluded from the dwelling-house or any part of it by the respondent for the period specified in the order; and

(b)   prohibiting the respondent from evicting or excluding the applicant during that period.

(4)   If the applicant is not in occupation, an order under this section must contain provision—

(a)   giving the applicant the right to enter into and occupy the dwelling-house for the period specified in the order; and

(b)   requiring the respondent to permit the exercise of that right.

(5)   An order under this section may also—

(a)   regulate the occupation of the dwelling-house by either or both of the parties;

(b)   prohibit, suspend or restrict the exercise by the respondent of his right to occupy the dwelling-house;

(c)   require the respondent to leave the dwelling-house or part of the dwelling-house; or

(d)   exclude the respondent from a defined area in which the dwelling-house is included.

(6)   In deciding whether to make an order under this section containing provision of the kind mentioned in subsection (3) or (4) and (if so) in what manner, the court shall have regard to all the circumstances including—

(a)   the housing needs and housing resources of each of the parties and of any relevant child;

(b)   the financial resources of each of the parties;

(c)   the likely effect of any order, or of any decision by the court not to exercise its powers under subsection (3) or (4), on the health, safety or well-being of the parties and of any relevant child;

(d)   the conduct of the parties in relation to each other and otherwise;

(e)   the length of time that has elapsed since the parties ceased to live together;

(f)   the length of time that has elapsed since the marriage or civil partnership was dissolved or annulled; and

(g)   the existence of any pending proceedings between the parties—

    (i)   for an order under section 23A or 24 of the Matrimonial Causes Act 1973 (property adjustment orders in connection with divorce proceedings etc);

    (ia)   for a property adjustment order under Part 2 of Schedule 5 to the Civil Partnership Act 2004;

    (ii)   for an order under paragraph 1(2)(d) or (e) of Schedule 1 to the Children Act 1989 (orders for financial relief against parents); or

    (iii)   relating to the legal or beneficial ownership of the dwelling-house.

(7)   In deciding whether to exercise its power to include one or more of the provisions referred to in subsection (5) ('a subsection (5) provision') and (if so) in what manner, the court shall have regard to all the circumstances including the matters mentioned in subsection (6)(a) to (e).

(8)   If the court decides to make an order under this section and it appears to it that, if the order does not include a subsection (5) provision, the applicant or any relevant child is likely to suffer significant harm attributable to conduct of the respondent, the court shall include the subsection (5) provision in the order unless it appears to the court that—

(a)   the respondent or any relevant child is likely to suffer significant harm if the provision is included in the order; and

(b)   the harm likely to be suffered by the respondent or child in that event is as great as or greater than the harm attributable to conduct of the respondent which is likely to be suffered by the applicant or child if the provision is not included.

(9)   An order under this section—

(a)   may not be made after the death of either of the former spouses or former civil partners; and

(b)   ceases to have effect on the death of either of them.

(10)   An order under this section must be limited so as to have effect for a specified period not exceeding six months, but may be extended on one or more occasions for a further specified period not exceeding six months.

(11)   A former spouse or former civil partner who has an equitable interest in the dwelling-house or in the proceeds of sale of the dwelling-house but in whom there is not vested (whether solely or as joint tenant) a legal estate in fee simple or a legal term of years absolute in the dwelling-house is to be treated (but only for the purpose of determining whether he is eligible to apply under this section) as not being entitled to occupy the dwelling-house by virtue of that interest.

(12)   Subsection (11) does not prejudice any right of such a former spouse or former civil partner to apply for an order under section 33.

(13)   So long as an order under this section remains in force, subsections (3) to (6) of section 30 apply in relation to the applicant—

(a)   as if he were B (the person entitled to occupy the dwelling-house by virtue of that section); and

(b)   as if the respondent were A (the person entitled as mentioned in subsection (1)(a) of that section).

36   One cohabitant or former cohabitant with no existing right to occupy

(1)   This section applies if—

(a)   one cohabitant or former cohabitant is entitled to occupy a dwelling-house by virtue of a beneficial estate or interest or contract or by virtue of any enactment giving him the right to remain in occupation;

(b)   the other cohabitant or former cohabitant is not so entitled; and

(c)   that dwelling-house is the home in which they cohabit or a home in which they at any time cohabited or intended to cohabit.

(2)   The cohabitant or former cohabitant not so entitled may apply to the court for an order under this section against the other cohabitant or former cohabitant ('the respondent').

(3)   If the applicant is in occupation, an order under this section must contain provision—

(a)   giving the applicant the right not to be evicted or excluded from the dwelling-house or any part of it by the respondent for the period specified in the order, and

(b)   prohibiting the respondent from evicting or excluding the applicant during that period.

(4)   If the applicant is not in occupation, an order under this section must contain provision—

(a)   giving the applicant the right to enter into and occupy the dwelling-house for the period specified in the order; and

(b)   requiring the respondent to permit the exercise of that right.

(5)   An order under this section may also—

(a)   regulate the occupation of the dwelling-house by either or both of the parties;

(b)   prohibit, suspend or restrict the exercise by the respondent of his right to occupy the dwelling-house;

(c)   require the respondent to leave the dwelling-house or part of the dwelling-house; or

(d)   exclude the respondent from a defined area in which the dwelling-house is included.

(6)   In deciding whether to make an order under this section containing provision of the kind mentioned in subsection (3) or (4) and (if so) in what manner, the court shall have regard to all the circumstances including—

(a)   the housing needs and housing resources of each of the parties and of any relevant child;

(b)   the financial resources of each of the parties;

(c)   the likely effect of any order, or of any decision by the court not to exercise its powers under subsection (3) or (4), on the health, safety or well-being of the parties and of any relevant child;

(d)   the conduct of the parties in relation to each other and otherwise;

(e)   the nature of the parties' relationship and in particular the level of commitment involved in it;

(f)   the length of time during which they have cohabited;

(g)   whether there are or have been any children who are children of both parties or for whom both parties have or have had parental responsibility;

(h)   the length of time that has elapsed since the parties ceased to live together; and

(i)   the existence of any pending proceedings between the parties—

(i)   for an order under paragraph 1(2)(d) or (e) of Schedule 1 to the Children Act 1989 (orders for financial relief against parents), or

(ii)   relating to the legal or beneficial ownership of the dwelling-house.

(7)   In deciding whether to exercise its powers to include one or more of the provisions referred to in subsection (5) ('a subsection (5) provision') and (if so) in what manner, the court shall have regard to all the circumstances including—

(a)   the matters mentioned in subsection (6)(a) to (d); and

(b)   the questions mentioned in subsection (8).

(8)   The questions are—

(a)   whether the applicant or any relevant child is likely to suffer significant harm attributable to conduct of the respondent if the subsection (5) provision is not included in the order; and

(b)   whether the harm likely to be suffered by the respondent or child if the provision is included is as great as or greater than the harm attributable to conduct of the respondent which is likely to be suffered by the applicant or child if the provision is not included.

(9)   An order under this section—

(a)   may not be made after the death of either of the parties; and

(b)   ceases to have effect on the death of either of them.

(10)   An order under this section must be limited so as to have effect for a specified period not exceeding six months, but may be extended on one occasion for a further specified period not exceeding six months.

(11) A person who has an equitable interest in the dwelling-house or in the proceeds of sale of the dwelling-house but in whom there is not vested (whether solely or as joint tenant) a legal estate in fee simple or a legal term of years absolute in the dwelling-house is to be treated (but only for the purpose of determining whether he is eligible to apply under this section) as not being entitled to occupy the dwelling-house by virtue of that interest.

(12) Subsection (11) does not prejudice any right of such a person to apply for an order under section 33.

(13) So long as the order remains in force, subsections (3) to (6) of section 30 apply in relation to the applicant—

    (a) as if he were B (the person entitled to occupy the dwelling-house by virtue of that section); and

    (b) as if the respondent were A (the person entitled as mentioned in subsection (1)(a) of that section).

37 Neither spouse or civil partner entitled to occupy

(1) This section applies if—

    (a) one spouse or former spouse and the other spouse or former spouse occupy a dwelling-house which is or was the matrimonial home; but

    (b) neither of them is entitled to remain in occupation—

        (i) by virtue of a beneficial estate or interest or contract; or

        (ii) by virtue of any enactment giving him the right to remain in occupation.

(1A) This section applies if—

    (a) the civil partner or former civil partner and the other civil partner or former civil partner occupy a dwelling-house which is or was the civil partnership home; but

    (b) neither of them is entitled to remain in occupation—

        (i) by virtue of a beneficial estate or contract; or

        (ii) by virtue of any enactment giving him the right to remain in occupation.

(2) Either of the parties may apply to the court for an order against the other under this section.

(3) An order under this section may—

    (a) require the respondent to permit the applicant to enter and remain in the dwelling-house or part of the dwelling-house;

    (b) regulate the occupation of the dwelling-house by either or both of the parties;

    (c) require the respondent to leave the dwelling-house or part of the dwelling-house; or

    (d) exclude the respondent from a defined area in which the dwelling-house is included.

(4) Subsections (6) and (7) of section 33 apply to the exercise by the court of its powers under this section as they apply to the exercise by the court of its powers under subsection (3) of that section.

(5) An order under this section must be limited so as to have effect for a specified period not exceeding six months, but may be extended on one or more occasions for a further specified period not exceeding six months.

38 Neither cohabitant or former cohabitant entitled to occupy

(1) This section applies if—

    (a) one cohabitant or former cohabitant and the other cohabitant or former cohabitant occupy a dwelling-house which is the home in which they cohabit or cohabited; but

    (b) neither of them is entitled to remain in occupation—

        (i) by virtue of a beneficial estate or interest or contract; or

        (ii) by virtue of any enactment giving him the right to remain in occupation.

(2) Either of the parties may apply to the court for an order against the other under this section.

(3) An order under this section may—

    (a) require the respondent to permit the applicant to enter and remain in the dwelling-house or part of the dwelling-house;

    (b) regulate the occupation of the dwelling-house by either or both of the parties;

    (c) require the respondent to leave the dwelling-house or part of the dwelling-house; or

    (d) exclude the respondent from a defined area in which the dwelling-house is included.

(4)   In deciding whether to exercise its powers to include one or more of the provisions referred to in subsection (3) ('a subsection (3) provision') and (if so) in what manner, the court shall have regard to all the circumstances including—

(a)   the housing needs and housing resources of each of the parties and of any relevant child;

(b)   the financial resources of each of the parties;

(c)   the likely effect of any order, or of any decision by the court not to exercise its powers under subsection (3), on the health, safety or well-being of the parties and of any relevant child;

(d)   the conduct of the parties in relation to each other and otherwise; and

(e)   the questions mentioned in subsection (5).

(5)   The questions are—

(a)   whether the applicant or any relevant child is likely to suffer significant harm attributable to conduct of the respondent if the subsection (3) provision is not included in the order; and

(b)   whether the harm likely to be suffered by the respondent or child if the provision is included is as great as or greater than the harm attributable to conduct of the respondent which is likely to be suffered by the applicant or child if the provision is not included.

(6)   An order under this section shall be limited so as to have effect for a specified period not exceeding six months, but may be extended on one occasion for a further specified period not exceeding six months.

39   Supplementary provisions

(1)   In this Part an 'occupation order' means an order under section 33, 35, 36, 37 or 38.

(2)   An application for an occupation order may be made in other family proceedings or without any other family proceedings being instituted.

(3)   If—

(a)   an application for an occupation order is made under section 33, 35, 36, 37 or 38, and

(b)   the court considers that it has no power to make the order under the section concerned, but that it has power to make an order under one of the other sections,

the court may make an order under that other section.

(4)   The fact that a person has applied for an occupation order under sections 35 to 38, or that an occupation order has been made, does not affect the right of any person to claim a legal or equitable interest in any property in any subsequent proceedings (including subsequent proceedings under this Part).

40   Additional provisions that may be included in certain occupation orders

(1)   The court may on, or at any time after, making an occupation order under section 33, 35 or 36—

(a)   impose on either party obligations as to—

(i)   the repair and maintenance of the dwelling-house; or

(ii)   the discharge of rent, mortgage payments or other outgoings affecting the dwelling-house;

(b)   order a party occupying the dwelling-house or any part of it (including a party who is entitled to do so by virtue of a beneficial estate or interest or contract or by virtue of any enactment giving him the right to remain in occupation) to make periodical payments to the other party in respect of the accommodation, if the other party would (but for the order) be entitled to occupy the dwelling-house by virtue of a beneficial estate or interest or contract or by virtue of any such enactment;

(c)   grant either party possession or use of furniture or other contents of the dwelling-house;

(d)   order either party to take reasonable care of any furniture or other contents of the dwelling-house;

(e)   order either party to take reasonable steps to keep the dwelling-house and any furniture or other contents secure.

(2)   In deciding whether and, if so, how to exercise its powers under this section, the court shall have regard to all the circumstances of the case including—

(a)   the financial needs and financial resources of the parties; and

(b)   the financial obligations which they have, or are likely to have in the foreseeable future, including financial obligations to each other and to any relevant child.

(3)   An order under this section ceases to have effect when the occupation order to which it relates ceases to have effect.

42   Non-molestation orders

(1)   In this Part a 'non-molestation order' means an order containing either or both of the following provisions—

(a)   provision prohibiting a person ('the respondent') from molesting another person who is associated with the respondent;

(b)   provision prohibiting the respondent from molesting a relevant child.

(2)   The court may make a non-molestation order—

(a)   if an application for the order has been made (whether in other family proceedings or without any other family proceedings being instituted) by a person who is associated with the respondent; or

(b)   if in any family proceedings to which the respondent is a party the court considers that the order should be made for the benefit of any other party to the proceedings or any relevant child even though no such application has been made.

(3)   In subsection (2) 'family proceedings' includes proceedings in which the court has made an emergency protection order under section 44 of the Children Act 1989 which includes an exclusion requirement (as defined in section 44A(3) of that Act).

(4)   Where an agreement to marry is terminated, no application under subsection (2)(a) may be made by virtue of section 62(3)(e) by reference to that agreement after the end of the period of three years beginning with the day on which it is terminated.

(4A)   A court considering whether to make an occupation order shall also consider whether to exercise the power conferred by subsection (2)(b).

(4B)   In this Part 'the applicant', in relation to a non-molestation order, includes (where the context permits) the person for whose benefit such an order would be or is made in exercise of the power conferred by subsection (2)(b).

(5)   In deciding whether to exercise its powers under this section and, if so, in what manner, the court shall have regard to all the circumstances including the need to secure the health, safety and well-being—

(a)   of the applicant ...; and

(b)   of any relevant child.

(6)   A non-molestation order may be expressed so as to refer to molestation in general, to particular acts of molestation, or to both.

(7)   A non-molestation order may be made for a specified period or until further order.

(8)   A non-molestation order which is made in other family proceedings ceases to have effect if those proceedings are withdrawn or dismissed.

42A   Offence of breaching non-molestation order

(1)   A person who without reasonable excuse does anything that he is prohibited from doing by a non-molestation order is guilty of an offence.

(2)   In the case of a non-molestation order made by virtue of section 45(1), a person can be guilty of an offence under this section only in respect of conduct engaged in at a time when he was aware of the existence of the order.

(3)   Where a person is convicted of an offence under this section in respect of any conduct, that conduct is not punishable as a contempt of court.

(4)   A person cannot be convicted of an offence under this section in respect of any conduct which has been punished as a contempt of court.

(5)   A person guilty of an offence under this section is liable—

(a)   on conviction on indictment, to imprisonment for a term not exceeding five years, or a fine, or both;

(b)   on summary conviction, to imprisonment for a term not exceeding 12 months, or a fine not exceeding the statutory maximum, or both.

(6)   A reference in any enactment to proceedings under this Part, or to an order under this Part, does not include a reference to proceedings for an offence under this section or to an order made in such proceedings.

45   Ex parte orders

(1)   The court may, in any case where it considers that it is just and convenient to do so, make an occupation order or a non-molestation order even though the respondent has not been given such notice of the proceedings as would otherwise be required by rules of court.

(2)   In determining whether to exercise its powers under subsection (1), the court shall have regard to all the circumstances including—

(a)   any risk of significant harm to the applicant or a relevant child, attributable to conduct of the respondent, if the order is not made immediately;

(b)   whether it is likely that the applicant will be deterred or prevented from pursuing the application if an order is not made immediately; and

(c)   whether there is reason to believe that the respondent is aware of the proceedings but is deliberately evading service and that the applicant or a relevant child will be seriously prejudiced by the delay involved in effecting substituted service.

(3)   If the court makes an order by virtue of subsection (1) it must afford the respondent an opportunity to make representations relating to the order as soon as just and convenient at a full hearing.

(4)   If, at a full hearing, the court makes an occupation order ('the full order'), then—

(a)   for the purposes of calculating the maximum period for which the full order may be made to have effect, the relevant section is to apply as if the period for which the full order will have effect began on the date on which the initial order first had effect; and

(b)   the provisions of section 36(10) or 38(6) as to the extension of orders are to apply as if the full order and the initial order were a single order.

(5)   In this section—

'full hearing' means a hearing of which notice has been given to all the parties in accordance with rules of court;

'initial order' means an occupation order made by virtue of subsection (1); and

'relevant section' means section 33(10), 35(10), 36(10), 37(5) or 38(6).

46   Undertakings

(1)   In any case where the court has power to make an occupation order or non-molestation order, the court may accept an undertaking from any party to the proceedings.

(2)   No power of arrest may be attached to any undertaking given under subsection (1).

(3)   The court shall not accept an undertaking under subsection (1) instead of making an occupation order in any case where apart from this section a power of arrest would be attached to the order.

(3A)   The court shall not accept an undertaking under subsection (1) instead of making a non-molestation order in any case where it appears to the court that—

(a)   the respondent has used or threatened violence against the applicant or a relevant child; and

(b)   for the protection of the applicant or child it is necessary to make a non-molestation order so that any breach may be punishable under section 42A.

(4)   An undertaking given to a court under subsection (1) is enforceable as if the court had made an occupation order or a non-molestation order in terms corresponding to those of the undertaking.

(5)   This section has effect without prejudice to the powers of the High Court and the family court apart from this section.

47   Arrest for breach of order

(1)   ...

(2)   If—

(a)   the court makes an occupation order; and

(b)   it appears to the court that the respondent has used or threatened violence against the applicant or a relevant child, it shall attach a power of arrest to one or more provisions of the order unless the court is satisfied that in all the circumstances of the case the applicant or child will be adequately protected without such a power of arrest.

(3) Subsection (2) does not apply in any case where the occupation order is made by virtue of section 45(1), but in such a case the court may attach a power of arrest to one or more provisions of the order if it appears to it—

(a) that the respondent has used or threatened violence against the applicant or a relevant child; and

(b) that there is a risk of significant harm to the applicant or child, attributable to conduct of the respondent, if the power of arrest is not attached to those provisions immediately.

(4) If, by virtue of subsection (3), the court attaches a power of arrest to any provisions of an occupation order, it may provide that the power of arrest is to have effect for a shorter period than the other provisions of the order.

(5) Any period specified for the purposes of subsection (4) may be extended by the court (on one or more occasions) on an application to vary or discharge the occupation order.

(6) If, by virtue of subsection (2) or (3), a power of arrest is attached to certain provisions of an order, a constable may arrest without warrant a person whom he has reasonable cause for suspecting to be in breach of any such provision.

(7) If a power of arrest is attached under subsection (2) or (3) to certain provisions of the order and the respondent is arrested under subsection (6)—

(a) he must be brought before the relevant judicial authority within the period of 24 hours beginning at the time of his arrest; and

(b) if the matter is not then disposed of forthwith, the relevant judicial authority before whom he is brought may remand him.

In reckoning for the purposes of this subsection any period of 24 hours, no account is to be taken of Christmas Day, Good Friday or any Sunday.

(8) If the court—

(a) has made a non-molestation order, or

(b) has made an occupation order but has not attached a power of arrest under subsection (2) or (3) to any provision of the order, or has attached that power only to certain provisions of the order,

then, if at any time the applicant considers that the respondent has failed to comply with the order, he may apply to the relevant judicial authority for the issue of a warrant for the arrest of the respondent.

(9) The relevant judicial authority shall not issue a warrant on an application under subsection (8) unless—

(a) the application is substantiated on oath; and

(b) the relevant judicial authority has reasonable grounds for believing that the respondent has failed to comply with the order.

(10) If a person is brought before a court by virtue of a warrant issued under subsection (9) and the court does not dispose of the matter forthwith, the court may remand him.

(11) Schedule 5 (which makes provision corresponding to that applying in magistrates' courts in civil cases under sections 128 and 129 of the Magistrates' Courts Act 1980) has effect in relation to the powers of the High Court and the family court to remand a person by virtue of this section.

(12) If a person remanded under this section is granted bail ... he may be required by the relevant judicial authority to comply, before release on bail or later, with such requirements as appear to that authority to be necessary to secure that he does not interfere with witnesses or otherwise obstruct the course of justice.

62 Meaning of 'cohabitants', 'relevant child' and 'associated persons'

(1) For the purposes of this Part—

(a) 'cohabitants' are two persons who are neither married to each other nor civil partners of each other but are living together as if they were a married couple or civil partners; and

(b) 'cohabit' and 'former cohabitants' are to be read accordingly, but the latter expression does not include cohabitants who have subsequently married each other or become civil partners of each other.

(2) In this Part, 'relevant child', in relation to any proceedings under this Part, means—

(a)   any child who is living with or might reasonably be expected to live with either party to the proceedings;

(b)   any child in relation to whom an order under the Adoption Act 1976, the Adoption and Children Act 2002 or the Children Act 1989 is in question in the proceedings; and

(c)   any other child whose interests the court considers relevant.

(3)   For the purposes of this Part, a person is associated with another person if—

(a)   they are or have been married to each other;

(aa)   they are or have been civil partners of each other;

(b)   they are cohabitants or former cohabitants;

(c)   they live or have lived in the same household, otherwise than merely by reason of one of them being the other's employee, tenant, lodger or boarder;

(d)   they are relatives;

(e)   they have agreed to marry one another (whether or not that agreement has been terminated);

(eza)   they have entered into a civil partnership agreement (as defined by section 73 of the Civil Partnership Act 2004) (whether or not that agreement has been terminated);

(ea)   they have or have had an intimate personal relationship with each other which is or was of significant duration;

(f)   in relation to any child, they are both persons falling within subsection (4); or

(g)   they are parties to the same family proceedings (other than proceedings under this Part).

(4)   A person falls within this subsection in relation to a child if—

(a)   he is a parent of the child; or

(b)   he has or has had parental responsibility for the child.

(5)   If a child has been adopted or falls within subsection (7), two persons are also associated with each other for the purpose of this Part if—

(a)   one is a natural parent of the child or a parent of such a natural parent; and

(b)   the other is the child or any person—

(i)   who has become a parent of the child by virtue of an adoption order or has applied for an adoption order, or

(ii)   with whom the child has at any time been placed for adoption.

(6)   A body corporate and another person are not, by virtue of subsection (3)(f) or (g), to be regarded for the purposes of this Part as associated with each other.

(7)   A child falls within this section if—

(a)   an adoption agency, within the meaning of section 2 of the Adoption and Children Act 2002, has power to place him for adoption under section 19 of that Act (placing children with parental consent) or he has become the subject of an order under section 21 of that Act (placement orders); or

(b)   he is freed for adoption by virtue of an order made—

(i)   in England and Wales, under section 18 of the Adoption Act 1976,

(ii)   ...

(iii)   in Northern Ireland, under Article 17(1) or 18(1) of the Adoption (Northern Ireland) Order 1987, or

(c)   he is the subject of a Scottish permanence order which includes provision granting authority to adopt.

(8)   In subsection (7)(c) 'Scottish permanence order' means a permanence order under section 80 of the Adoption and Children (Scotland) Act 2007 (asp 4) (including a deemed permanence order having effect by virtue of article 13(1), 14(2), 17(1) or 19(2) of the Adoption and Children (Scotland) Act 2007 (Commencement No. 4, Transitional and Savings Provisions) Order 2009 (SSI 2009/267)).

63   Interpretation of Part IV

(1)   In this Part—

'adoption order' means an adoption order within the meaning of section 72(1) of the Adoption Act 1976 or section 46(1) of the Adoption and Children Act 2002;

'associated', in relation to a person, is to be read with section 62(3) to (6);

'child' means a person under the age of eighteen years;

'cohabit', 'cohabitant' and 'former cohabitant' have the meaning given by section 62(1);

'the court' is to be read with section 57;

'development' means physical, intellectual, emotional, social or behavioural development;

'dwelling-house' includes (subject to subsection (4))—

(a)   any building or part of a building which is occupied as a dwelling,

(b)   any caravan, house-boat or structure which is occupied as a dwelling,

and any yard, garden, garage or outhouse belonging to it and occupied with it;

'family proceedings' means any proceedings—

(a)   under the inherent jurisdiction of the High Court in relation to children; or

(b)   under the enactments mentioned in subsection (2);

'harm'—

(a)   in relation to a person who has reached the age of eighteen years, means ill-treatment or the impairment of health; and

(b)   in relation to a child, means ill-treatment or the impairment of health or development;

'health' includes physical or mental health;

'home rights' has the meaning given by section 30;

'ill-treatment' includes forms of ill-treatment which are not physical and, in relation to a child, includes sexual abuse;

...

mortgage', 'mortgagor' and 'mortgagee' have the same meaning as in the Law of Property Act 1925;

'mortgage payments' includes any payments which, under the terms of the mortgage, the mortgagor is required to make to any person;

'non-molestation order' has the meaning given by section 42(1);

'occupation order' has the meaning given by section 39;

'parental responsibility' has the same meaning as in the Children Act 1989;

'relative', in relation to a person, means—

(a)   the father, mother, stepfather, stepmother, son, daughter, stepson, stepdaughter, grandmother, grandfather, grandson or granddaughter of that person or of that person's spouse, former spouse, civil partner or former civil partner, or

(b)   the brother, sister, uncle, aunt, niece, nephew or first cousin (whether of the full blood or of the half blood or by marriage or civil partnership) of that person or of that person's spouse, former spouse, civil partner or former civil partner,

and includes, in relation to a person who is cohabiting or has cohabited with another person, any person who would fall within paragraph (a) or (b) if the parties were married to each other or were civil partners of each other;

'relevant child', in relation to any proceedings under this Part, has the meaning given by section 62(2);

'the relevant judicial authority', in relation to any order under this Part, means—

(a)   where the order was made by the High Court, a judge of that court;

(aa)   where the order was made by the family court, a judge of that court.

(2)   The enactments referred to in the definition of 'family proceedings' are—

(a)   ...

(b)   this Part;

(ba)   Part 4A;

(c)   the Matrimonial Causes Act 1973;

(d)   the Adoption Act 1976;

(e)   the Domestic Proceedings and Magistrates' Courts Act 1978;

(f)   Part III of the Matrimonial and Family Proceedings Act 1984;

(g)   Parts I, II and IV of the Children Act 1989;

(h)   sections 54 and 54A of the Human Fertilisation and Embryology Act 2008;

(i)   the Adoption and Children Act 2002;

(ia)   Part 1 of Schedule 2 to the Female Genital Mutilation Act 2003, other than paragraph 3 of that Schedule;

(j)   Schedules 5 to 7 to the Civil Partnership Act 2004.

(3)   Where the question of whether harm suffered by a child is significant turns on the child's health or development, his health or development shall be compared with that which could reasonably be expected of a similar child.

(4)   For the purposes of sections 31, 32, 53 and 54 and such other provisions of this Part (if any) as may be prescribed, this Part is to have effect as if paragraph (b) of the definition of 'dwelling-house' were omitted.

(5)   It is hereby declared that this Part applies as between the parties to a marriage even though either of them is, or has at any time during the marriage been, married to more than one person.

PART IVA
FORCED MARRIAGE

Forced marriage protection orders

63A   Forced marriage protection orders

(1)   The court may make an order for the purposes of protecting—

(a)   a person from being forced into a marriage or from any attempt to be forced into a marriage; or

(b)   a person who has been forced into a marriage.

(2)   In deciding whether to exercise its powers under this section and, if so, in what manner, the court must have regard to all the circumstances including the need to secure the health, safety and well-being of the person to be protected.

(3)   In ascertaining that person's well-being, the court must, in particular, have such regard to the person's wishes and feelings (so far as they are reasonably ascertainable) as the court considers appropriate in the light of the person's age and understanding.

(4)   For the purposes of this Part a person ('A') is forced into a marriage if another person ('B') forces A to enter into a marriage (whether with B or another person) without A's free and full consent.

(5)   For the purposes of subsection (4) it does not matter whether the conduct of B which forces A to enter into a marriage is directed against A, B or another person.

(6)   In this Part—

'force' includes coerce by threats or other psychological means (and related expressions are to be read accordingly); and

'forced marriage protection order' means an order under this section.

63B   Contents of orders

(1)   A forced marriage protection order may contain—

(a)   such prohibitions, restrictions or requirements; and

(b)   such other terms;

as the court considers appropriate for the purposes of the order.

(2)   The terms of such orders may, in particular, relate to—

(a)   conduct outside England and Wales as well as (or instead of) conduct within England and Wales;

(b)   respondents who are, or may become, involved in other respects as well as (or instead of) respondents who force or attempt to force, or may force or attempt to force, a person to enter into a marriage;

(c)   other persons who are, or may become, involved in other respects as well as respondents of any kind.

(3)   For the purposes of subsection (2) examples of involvement in other respects are—

(a)   aiding, abetting, counselling, procuring, encouraging or assisting another person to force, or to attempt to force, a person to enter into a marriage; or

(b)   conspiring to force, or to attempt to force, a person to enter into a marriage.

63C   Applications and other occasions for making orders

(1)   The court may make a forced marriage protection order—

    (a)   on an application being made to it; or

    (b)   without an application being made to it but in the circumstances mentioned in subsection (6).

(2)   An application may be made by—

    (a)   the person who is to be protected by the order; or

    (b)   a relevant third party.

(3)   An application may be made by any other person with the leave of the court.

(4)   In deciding whether to grant leave, the court must have regard to all the circumstances including—

    (a)   the applicant's connection with the person to be protected;

    (b)   the applicant's knowledge of the circumstances of the person to be protected; and

    (c)   the wishes and feelings of the person to be protected so far as they are reasonably ascertainable and so far as the court considers it appropriate, in the light of the person's age and understanding, to have regard to them.

(5)   An application under this section may be made in other family proceedings or without any other family proceedings being instituted.

(6)   The circumstances in which the court may make an order without an application being made are where—

    (a)   any other family proceedings are before the court ('the current proceedings');

    (b)   the court considers that a forced marriage protection order should be made to protect a person (whether or not a party to the current proceedings); and

    (c)   a person who would be a respondent to any such proceedings for a forced marriage protection order is a party to the current proceedings.

(7)   In this section—

'family proceedings' has the same meaning as in Part 4 (see section 63(1) and (2)) but also includes—

    (a)   proceedings under the inherent jurisdiction of the High Court in relation to adults;

    (b)   proceedings in which the court has made an emergency protection order under section 44 of the Children Act 1989 which includes an exclusion requirement (as defined in section 44A(3) of that Act); and

    (c)   proceedings in which the court has made an order under section 50 of the Act of 1989 (recovery of abducted children etc); and

'relevant third party' means a person specified, or falling within a description of persons specified, by order of the Lord Chancellor.

(8)   An order of the Lord Chancellor under subsection (7) may, in particular, specify the Secretary of State.

63CA   Offence of breaching order

(1)   A person who without reasonable excuse does anything that the person is prohibited from doing by a forced marriage protection order is guilty of an offence.

(2)   In the case of a forced marriage protection order made by virtue of section 63D(1), a person can be guilty of an offence under this section only in respect of conduct engaged in at a time when the person was aware of the existence of the order.

(3)   Where a person is convicted of an offence under this section in respect of any conduct, that conduct is not punishable as a contempt of court.

(4)   A person cannot be convicted of an offence under this section in respect of any conduct which has been punished as a contempt of court.

(5)   A person guilty of an offence under this section is liable—

    (a)   on conviction on indictment, to imprisonment for a term not exceeding five years, or a fine, or both;

    (b)   on summary conviction, to imprisonment for a term not exceeding 12 months, or a fine, or both.

(6)   A reference in any enactment to proceedings under this Part, or to an order under this Part, does not include a reference to proceedings for an offence under this section or to an order made in proceedings for such an offence.

(7)   "Enactment" includes an enactment contained in subordinate legislation within the meaning of the Interpretation Act 1978.

Further provision about orders

63D   Ex parte orders: Part 4A

(1)   The court may, in any case where it considers that it is just and convenient to do so, make a forced marriage protection order even though the respondent has not been given such notice of the proceedings as would otherwise be required by rules of court.

(2)   In deciding whether to exercise its powers under subsection (1), the court must have regard to all the circumstances including—

(a)   any risk of significant harm to the person to be protected or another person if the order is not made immediately;

(b)   whether it is likely that an applicant will be deterred or prevented from pursuing an application if an order is not made immediately; and

(c)   whether there is reason to believe that—

(i)   the respondent is aware of the proceedings but is deliberately evading service; and

(ii)   the delay involved in effecting substituted service will cause serious prejudice to the person to be protected or (if a different person) an applicant.

(3)   The court must give the respondent an opportunity to make representations about any order made by virtue of subsection (1).

(4)   The opportunity must be—

(a)   as soon as just and convenient; and

(b)   at a hearing of which notice has been given to all the parties in accordance with rules of court.

63E   Undertakings instead of orders

(1)   In any case where the court has power to make a forced marriage protection order, the court may accept an undertaking from the respondent instead of making the order.

(2)   But a court may not accept an undertaking under subsection (1) if it appears to the court—

(a)   that the respondent has used or threatened violence against the person to be protected, and

(b)   that, for the person's protection, it is necessary to make a forced marriage protection order so that any breach of it by the respondent may be punishable under section 63CA.

(4)   An undertaking given to the court under subsection (1) is enforceable as if the court had made the order in terms corresponding to those of the undertaking.

(5)   This section is without prejudice to the powers of the court apart from this section.

63F   Duration of orders

A forced marriage protection order may be made for a specified period or until varied or discharged.

63G   Variation of orders and their discharge

(1)   The court may vary or discharge a forced marriage protection order on an application by—

(a)   any party to the proceedings for the order;

(b)   the person being protected by the order (if not a party to the proceedings for the order); or

(c)   any person affected by the order.

(2)   In addition, the court may vary or discharge a forced marriage protection order made by virtue of section 63C(1)(b) even though no application under subsection (1) above has been made to the court.

(3)   Section 63D applies to a variation of a forced marriage protection order as it applies to the making of such an order.

(4)   Section 63E applies to proceedings for a variation of a forced marriage protection order as it applies to proceedings for the making of such an order.

(5)   Accordingly, references in sections 63D and 63E to making a forced marriage protection order are to be read for the purposes of subsections (3) and (4) above as references to varying such an order.

(6), (7) ...

Arrest for breach of orders

63H   ...

63I   ...

63J   Arrest under warrant

(1)   ...

(2)   An interested party may apply to the relevant judge for the issue of a warrant for the arrest of a person if the interested party considers that the person has failed to comply with a forced marriage protection order or is otherwise in contempt of court in relation to the order.

(3)   The relevant judge must not issue a warrant on an application under subsection (2) unless—

(a)   the application is substantiated on oath; and

(b)   the relevant judge has reasonable grounds for believing that the person to be arrested has failed to comply with the order or is otherwise in contempt of court in relation to the order.

(4)   In this section 'interested party', in relation to a forced marriage protection order, means—

(a)   the person being protected by the order;

(b)   (if a different person) the person who applied for the order; or

(c)   any other person;

but no application may be made under subsection (2) by a person falling within paragraph (c) without the leave of the relevant judge.

63K   Remand: general

(1)   The court before which an arrested person is brought ... by virtue of a warrant issued under section 63J may, if the matter is not then disposed of immediately, remand the person concerned.

(2)   Schedule 5 has effect in relation to the powers of the court to remand a person by virtue of this section but as if the following modifications were made to the Schedule.

(3)   The modifications are that—

(a)   in paragraph 2(1) of Schedule 5, the reference to section 47 is to be read as a reference to this section; and

(b)   in paragraph 2(5)(b) of the Schedule, the reference to section 48(1) is to be read as a reference to section 63L(1).

(4)   Subsection (5) applies if a person remanded under this section is granted bail under Schedule 5 as modified above.

(5)   The person may be required by the relevant judge to comply, before release on bail or later, with such requirements as appear to the relevant judge to be necessary to secure that the person does not interfere with witnesses or otherwise obstruct the course of justice.

63L   Remand: medical examination and report

(1)   Any power to remand a person under section 63K(1) may be exercised for the purpose of enabling a medical examination and report to be made if the relevant judge has reason to consider that a medical report will be required.

(2)   If such a power is so exercised, the adjournment must not be for more than 4 weeks at a time unless the relevant judge remands the accused in custody.

(3)   If the relevant judge remands the accused in custody, the adjournment must not be for more than 3 weeks at a time.

(4)   Subsection (5) applies if there is reason to suspect that a person who has been arrested—

(a)   ...

(b)   under a warrant issued on an application made under section 63J(2);

is suffering from mental disorder within the meaning of the Mental Health Act 1983.

(5)   The relevant judge has the same power to make an order under section 35 of the Mental Health Act 1983 (remand for report on accused's mental condition as the Crown Court has under section 35 of that Act in the case of an accused person within the meaning of that section.

Jurisdiction and procedure

63M   Jurisdiction of courts: Part 4A

(1)   For the purposes of this Part 'the court' means the High Court or the family court.

(2)–(4)...

63O   Contempt proceedings: Part 4A

The powers of the court in relation to contempt of court arising out of a person's failure to comply with a forced marriage protection order or otherwise in connection with such an order may be exercised by the relevant judge.

63P   ...

Supplementary

63Q   Guidance

(1)   The Secretary of State may from time to time prepare and publish guidance to such descriptions of persons as the Secretary of State considers appropriate about—

(a)   the effect of this Part or any provision of this Part; or

(b)   other matters relating to forced marriages.

(2)   A person exercising public functions to whom guidance is given under this section must have regard to it in the exercise of those functions.

(3)   Nothing in this section permits the Secretary of State to give guidance to any court or tribunal.

63R   Other protection or assistance against forced marriage

(1)   This Part does not affect any other protection or assistance available to a person who—

(a)   is being, or may be, forced into a marriage or subjected to an attempt to be forced into a marriage; or

(b)   has been forced into a marriage.

(2)   In particular, it does not affect—

(a)   the inherent jurisdiction of the High Court;

(b)   any criminal liability;

(c)   any civil remedies under the Protection from Harassment Act 1997;

(d)   any right to an occupation order or a non-molestation order under Part 4 of this Act;

(e)   any protection or assistance under the Children Act 1989;

(f)   any claim in tort; or

(g)   the law of marriage.

63S   Interpretation of Part 4A

In this Part—

'the court' is to be read with section 63M;

'force' (and related expressions), in relation to a marriage, are to be read in accordance with section 63A(4) to (6);

'forced marriage protection order' has the meaning given by section 63A(6);

'marriage' means any religious or civil ceremony of marriage (whether or not legally binding); and

'the relevant judge', in relation to any order under this Part, means—

(a)   where the order was made by the High Court, a judge of that court; and

(b)   where the order was made by the family court, a judge of that court.

(H) Trusts of Land and Appointment of Trustees Act 1996

14 Applications for order

(1) Any person who is a trustee of land or has an interest in property subject to a trust of land may make an application to the court for an order under this section.

(2) On an application for an order under this section the court may make any such order—

(a) relating to the exercise by the trustees of any of their functions (including an order relieving them of any obligation to obtain the consent of, or to consult, any person in connection with the exercise of any of their functions), or

(b) declaring the nature or extent of a person's interest in property subject to the trust,

as the court thinks fit.

(3) The court may not under this section make any order as to the appointment or removal of trustees.

(4) The powers conferred on the court by this section are exercisable on an application whether it is made before or after the commencement of this Act.

15 Matters relevant in determining applications

(1) The matters to which the court is to have regard in determining an application for an order under section 14 include—

(a) the intentions of the person or persons (if any) who created the trust,

(b) the purposes for which the property subject to the trust is held,

(c) the welfare of any minor who occupies or might reasonably be expected to occupy any land subject to the trust as his home, and

(d) the interests of any secured creditor of any beneficiary.

(2) In the case of an application relating to the exercise in relation to any land of the powers conferred on the trustees by section 13, the matters to which the court is to have regard also include the circumstances and wishes of each of the beneficiaries who is (or apart from any previous exercise by the trustees of those powers would be) entitled to occupy the land under section 12.

(3) In the case of any other application, other than one relating to the exercise of the power mentioned in section 6(2), the matters to which the court is to have regard also include the circumstances and wishes of any beneficiaries of full age and entitled to an interest in possession in property subject to the trust or (in case of dispute) of the majority (according to the value of their combined interests).

(4) This section does not apply to an application if section 335A of the Insolvency Act 1986 (which is inserted by Schedule 3 and relates to applications by a trustee of a bankrupt) applies to it.

(I)   Family Procedure Rules 2010 (SI 2010/2955)

Part 1
Overriding Objective

1.1   The overriding objective

(1)   These rules are a new procedural code with the overriding objective of enabling the court to deal with cases justly, having regard to any welfare issues involved.

(2)   Dealing with a case justly includes, so far as is practicable—

    (a)   ensuring that it is dealt with expeditiously and fairly;

    (b)   dealing with the case in ways which are proportionate to the nature, importance and complexity of the issues;

    (c)   ensuring that the parties are on an equal footing;

    (d)   saving expense; and

    (e)   allotting to it an appropriate share of the court's resources, while taking into account the need to allot resources to other cases.

1.2   Application by the court of the overriding objective

The court must seek to give effect to the overriding objective when it—

(a)   exercises any power given to it by these rules; or

(b)   interprets any rule.

1.3   Duty of the parties

The parties are required to help the court to further the overriding objective.

1.4   Court's duty to manage cases

(1)   The court must further the overriding objective by actively managing cases.

(2)   Active case management includes—

    (a)   setting timetables or otherwise controlling the progress of the case;

    (b)   identifying at an early stage—

        (i)   the issues; and

        (ii)   who should be a party to the proceedings;

    (c)   deciding promptly—

        (i)   which issues need full investigation and hearing and which do not; and

        (ii)   the procedure to be followed in the case;

    (d)   deciding the order in which issues are to be resolved;

    (e)   controlling the use of expert evidence;

    (f)   encouraging the parties to use a non-court dispute resolution procedure if the court considers that appropriate and facilitating the use of such procedure;

    (g)   helping the parties to settle the whole or part of the case;

    (h)   encouraging the parties to co-operate with each other in the conduct of proceedings;

    (i)   considering whether the likely benefits of taking a particular step justify the cost of taking it;

    (j)   dealing with as many aspects of the case as it can on the same occasion;

    (k)   dealing with the case without the parties needing to attend at court;

    (l)   making use of technology; and

    (m)   giving directions to ensure that the case proceeds quickly and efficiently.

Part 3
Non-court Dispute Resolution

Chapter 1
Interpretation

3.1   In this Part—

'allocation' means allocation of proceedings other than appeal proceedings to a level of judge;

'authorised family mediator' means a person identified by the Family Mediation Council as qualified to conduct a MIAM;

'domestic violence' means any incident, or pattern of incidents, of controlling, coercive or threatening behaviour, violence or abuse (whether psychological, physical, sexual, financial or emotional) between the prospective applicant and another prospective party;

'family mediation information and assessment meeting' has the meaning given to it in section 10(3) of the 2014 Act.

'harm' has the meaning given to it in section 31 of the Children Act 1989;

'mediator's exemption' has the meaning given to it in Rule 3.8(2);

'MIAM' means a family mediation information and assessment meeting;

'MIAM exemption' has the meaning given to it in Rule 3.8(1);

'MIAM requirement' is the requirement in section 10(1) of the 2014 Act for a person to attend a MIAM before making a relevant family application;

'private law proceedings' has the meaning given to it in Rule 12.2;

'prospective applicant' is the person who is considering making a relevant family application;

'prospective party' is a person who would be likely to be a party to the proceedings in the relevant family application;

'prospective respondent' is a person who would be a likely respondent to the proceedings in the relevant family application; and

'relevant family application' has the meaning given to it in section 10(3) of the 2014 Act.

Chapter 2
The court's duty and powers generally

3.2   Scope of this Chapter

This Chapter contains the court's duty and powers to encourage and facilitate the use of non-court dispute resolution.

3.3   The court's duty to consider non-court dispute resolution

(1)   The court must consider, at every stage in proceedings, whether non-court dispute resolution is appropriate.

(2)   In considering whether non-court dispute resolution is appropriate in proceedings which were commenced by a relevant family application, the court must take into account—

(a)   whether a MIAM took place;

(b)   whether a valid MIAM exemption was claimed or mediator's exemption was confirmed; and

(c)   whether the parties attempted mediation or another form of non-court dispute resolution and the outcome of that process.

PRACTICE DIRECTION 3A

Family Mediation
Information and Assessment Meetings (MIAMS)

Summary

1   The purpose of this Practice Direction is to supplement the MIAM Rules in the Family Procedure Rules and to set out good practice to be followed by prospective respondents who are expected to also attend a MIAM.

2   Under section 10(1) of the Children and Families Act 2014, it is now a requirement for a person to attend a MIAM before making certain kinds of applications to obtain a court order. (A list of these applications is set out in Rule 3.6 and in paragraphs 12 and 13 below.) The person who would be the respondent to the application is expected to attend the MIAM. The court has a general power to adjourn proceedings in order for non-court dispute resolution to be attempted, including attendance at a MIAM to consider family mediation and other options.

3   A MIAM is a short meeting that provides information about mediation as a way of resolving disputes. A MIAM is conducted by a trained mediator who will assess whether mediation is appropriate in the circumstances. A MIAM should be held within 15 business days of contacting the mediator.

4   There are exemptions to the MIAM requirement. These are set out in the MIAM Rules (see Chapter 3 to Part 3 of the Family Procedure Rules), and are explained in more detail in this Practice Direction.

5   The effect of the MIAM requirement and accompanying Rules is that a person who wishes to make certain kinds of applications to the court must first attend a MIAM unless a 'MIAM exemption' or a 'mediator's exemption' applies. These exemptions are set out in Rule 3.8.

6   When making certain kinds of applications (see paragraphs 12 and 13 below), an applicant must therefore provide on the application form, or on a separate form, one of the following: (i) confirmation from a mediator that she or he has attended a MIAM; (ii) confirmation from a mediator that a 'mediator's exemption' applies; or (iii) a claim that a MIAM exemption applies. An applicant who claims an exemption from the MIAM requirement is not required to attach any supporting evidence with their application, but should bring any supporting evidence to the first hearing.

7   If an applicant claims a MIAM exemption, the court will issue proceedings but will inquire into the exemption claimed, either at the stage at which the case is allocated or at the first hearing. At the first hearing, the court may review any supporting evidence in order to ensure that the MIAM exemption was validly claimed. As set out in more detail below, if a MIAM exemption has not been validly claimed, the court may direct the applicant or the parties to attend a MIAM, and may adjourn proceedings for that purpose.

Background: Consideration of mediation and other non-court dispute resolution

8   The adversarial court process is not always best suited to the resolution of family disputes. Such disputes are often best resolved through discussion and agreement, where that can be managed safely and appropriately.

9   Family mediation is one way of settling disagreements. A trained mediator can help the parties to reach an agreement. A mediator who conducts a MIAM is a qualified independent facilitator who can also discuss other forms of dispute resolution if mediation is not appropriate.

10   Attendance at a MIAM provides an opportunity for the parties to a dispute to receive information about the process of mediation and to understand the benefits it can offer as a way to resolve disputes. At that meeting, a trained mediator will discuss with the parties the nature of their dispute and will explore with them whether mediation would be a suitable way to resolve the issues on which there is disagreement.

The applications to which the MIAM requirement applies

11   In accordance with section 10 of the 2014 Act, and Rule 3.6, the proceedings to which the MIAM requirement applies are the private law proceedings relating to children listed in paragraph 12 and the proceedings for a financial remedy listed in paragraph 13 below.

Private law proceedings relating to children

12   (1)   The private law proceedings relating to children referred to in paragraph 11 are proceedings for the following orders, unless one of the circumstances specified in sub-paragraph (2) applies—

     (a)   a child arrangements order and other orders with respect to a child or children under section 8 of the Children Act 1989;

     (b)   a parental responsibility order (under sections 4(1)(c), 4ZA(1)(c) or 4A(1)(b) of the Children Act 1989) or an order terminating parental responsibility (under sections 4(2A), 4ZA(5) or 4A(3) of that Act);

     (c)   an order appointing a child's guardian (under section 5(1) of the Children Act 1989) or an order terminating the appointment (under section 6(7) of that Act);

     (d)   an order giving permission to change a child's surname or remove a child from the United Kingdom (under sections 13(1) or 14C of the Children Act 1989);

     (e)   a special guardianship order; and

     (f)   an order varying or discharging such an order (under section 14D of the Children Act 1989).

   (2)   The circumstances referred to in sub-paragraph (1) are that the proceedings—

     (a)   are for a consent order;

     (b)   are for an order relating to a child or children in respect of whom there are ongoing emergency proceedings, care proceedings or supervision proceedings; or

     (c)   are for an order relating to a child or children who are the subject of an emergency protection order, a care order or a supervision order.

Proceedings for a financial remedy

13   (1)   The proceedings for a financial remedy referred to in paragraph 11 are proceedings for the following orders, unless one of the circumstances specified in sub-paragraph (2) applies—

     (a)   the following financial orders:

       (i)   an order for maintenance pending suit;

       (ii)   an order for maintenance pending outcome of proceedings;

       (iii)   an order for periodical payments or lump sum provision as mentioned in section 21(1) of the Matrimonial Causes Act 1973, except an order under section 27(6) of that Act;

       (iv)   an order for periodical payments or lump sum provision as mentioned in paragraph 2(1) of Schedule 5 to the Civil Partnership Act 2004, made under Part 1 of Schedule 5 to that Act;

       (v)   a property adjustment order;

       (vi)   a variation order;

       (vii)   a pension sharing order; or

       (viii)   a pension compensation sharing order;

     (b)   an order for financial provision for children (under Schedule 1 to the Children Act 1989);

     (c)   an order for financial provision in a case of neglect to maintain (under section 27 of the Matrimonial Causes Act 1973 or under Part 9 of Schedule 5 to the Civil Partnership Act 2004);

     (d)   an order for alteration of a maintenance agreement (under section 35 of the Matrimonial Causes Act 1973 or under paragraph 69 of Schedule 5 to the 2004 Act);

     (e)   an order for financial provision for failure to maintain for parties to a marriage and children of the family (under Part 1 of the Domestic Proceedings and Magistrates' Courts Act 1978 or an order under Schedule 6 to the Civil Partnership Act 2004); and

     (f)   an order for special protection for respondent in certain separation cases (under section 10(2) of the Matrimonial Causes Act 1973 or under section 48(2) of the Civil Partnership Act 2004).

   (2)   The circumstances referred to in sub-paragraph (1) are that the proceedings—

     (a)   are for a consent order; or

(b)   are for enforcement of any order made in proceedings for a financial remedy or of any agreement made in or in contemplation of proceedings for a financial remedy.

Making an application

14   An application to the court in any of the proceedings specified above must be on the relevant court form which must contain either: (a) a confirmation from a mediator that the applicant has attended a MIAM; (b) a claim by the applicant that a MIAM exemption applies (the list of MIAM exemptions is set out in Rule 3.8(1)); or (c) a confirmation from a mediator that a mediator's exemption applies (the list of circumstances that qualify for a mediator's exemption is in Rule 3.8(2)).

15   Relevant application forms are available from the HMCTS form finder service at www.justice.gov.uk/forms/hmcts. For matters concerning children you can find out which form to use by reading the leaflet CB1—Making an application—Children and the Family Courts. Leaflet CB7—Guide for separated parents: children and the family courts also provides guidance on the court process.

16   The relevant form can be completed either by the applicant or his or her legal representative. Any reference in this Practice Direction or in the Rules to completion of the form by an applicant includes a reference to completion by a legal representative.

MIAM exemptions

17   FPR Rule 3.8(1) sets out the circumstances in which the MIAM requirement does not apply. These are called MIAM exemptions.

18   In order to claim that a MIAM exemption applies, an applicant will need to tick the appropriate MIAM exemption boxes on the relevant form.

19   Applicants should note that some of the MIAM exemptions require that certain evidence is available. The next section of the Practice Direction specifies those forms of evidence. This evidence does not need to be provided with the application but applicants should bring such evidence to the first hearing because the court will inquire into such evidence in order to determine whether the MIAM exemption has been validly claimed.

MIAM exemption—Domestic violence

20   (1)   The forms of evidence referred to in Rule 3.8(1)(a) are—

    (a)   evidence that a prospective party has been arrested for a relevant domestic violence offence;

    (b)   evidence of a relevant police caution for a domestic violence offence;

    (c)   evidence of relevant criminal proceedings for a domestic violence offence which have not concluded;

    (d)   evidence of a relevant conviction for a domestic violence offence;

    (e)   a court order binding a prospective party over in connection with a domestic violence offence;

    (f)   a domestic violence protection notice issued under section 24 of the Crime and Security Act 2010 against a prospective party;

    (g)   a relevant protective injunction;

    (h)   an undertaking given in England and Wales under section 46 or 63E of the Family Law Act 1996 (or given in Scotland or Northern Ireland in place of a protective injunction) by a prospective party, provided that a cross-undertaking relating to domestic violence was not given by another prospective party;

    (i)   a copy of a finding of fact, made in proceedings in the United Kingdom, that there has been domestic violence by a prospective party;

    (j)   an expert report produced as evidence in proceedings in the United Kingdom for the benefit of a court or tribunal confirming that a person with whom a prospective party is or was in a family relationship, was assessed as being, or at risk of being, a victim of domestic violence by that prospective party;

    (k)   a letter or report from an appropriate health professional confirming that—

        (i)   that professional, or another appropriate health professional, has examined a prospective party in person; and

  (ii) in the reasonable professional judgment of the author or the examining appropriate health professional, that prospective party has, or has had, injuries or a condition consistent with being a victim of domestic violence;

(l) a letter or report from—

  (i) the appropriate health professional who made the referral described below;

  (ii) an appropriate health professional who has access to the medical records of the prospective party referred to below; or

  (iii) the person to whom the referral described below was made;

  confirming that there was a referral by an appropriate health professional of a prospective party to a person who provides specialist support or assistance for victims of, or those at risk of, domestic violence;

(m) a letter from any person who is a member of a multi-agency risk assessment conference (or other suitable local safeguarding forum) confirming that a prospective party, or a person with whom that prospective party is in a family relationship, is or has been at risk of harm from domestic violence by another prospective party;

(n) a letter from an independent domestic violence advisor confirming that they are providing support to a prospective party;

(o) a letter from an independent sexual violence advisor confirming that they are providing support to a prospective party relating to sexual violence by another prospective party;

(p) a letter from an officer employed by a local authority or housing association (or their equivalent in Scotland or Northern Ireland) for the purpose of supporting tenants containing—

  (i) a statement to the effect that, in their reasonable professional judgment, a person with whom a prospective party is or has been in a family relationship is, or is at risk of being, a victim of domestic violence by that prospective party;

  (ii) a description of the specific matters relied upon to support that judgment; and

  (iii) a description of the support they provided to the victim of domestic violence or the person at risk of domestic violence by that prospective party;

(q) a letter which—

  (i) is from an organisation providing domestic violence support services, or a registered charity, which letter confirms that it—

   (aa) is situated in England and Wales,

   (bb) has been operating for an uninterrupted period of six months or more; and

   (cc) provided a prospective party with support in relation to that person's needs as a victim, or a person at risk, of domestic violence; and

  (ii) contains—

   (aa) a statement to the effect that, in the reasonable professional judgment of the author of the letter, the prospective party is, or is at risk of being, a victim of domestic violence;

   (bb) a description of the specific matters relied upon to support that judgment;

   (cc) a description of the support provided to the prospective party; and

   (dd) a statement of the reasons why the prospective party needed that support;

(r) a letter or report from an organisation providing domestic violence support services in the United Kingdom confirming—

  (i) that a person with whom a prospective party is or was in a family relationship was refused admission to a refuge;

  (ii) the date on which they were refused admission to the refuge; and

  (iii) they sought admission to the refuge because of allegations of domestic violence by the prospective party referred to in paragraph (i);

(s) a letter from a public authority confirming that a person with whom a prospective party is or was in a family relationship, was assessed as being, or at risk of being, a victim of domestic violence by that prospective party (or a copy of that assessment);

(t)   a letter from the Secretary of State for the Home Department confirming that a prospective party has been granted leave to remain in the United Kingdom under paragraph 289B of the Rules made by the Home Secretary under section 3(2) of the Immigration Act 1971, which can be found at https://www.gov.uk/guidance/immigration-rules/immigration-rules-index;

(u)   evidence which demonstrates that a prospective party has been, or is at risk of being, the victim of domestic violence by another prospective party in the form of abuse which relates to financial matters.

MIAM exemption—Bankruptcy

21   The forms of evidence referred to in Rule 3.8(1)(h) are—

(a)   application by the prospective applicant for a bankruptcy order;

(b)   petition by a creditor of the prospective applicant for a bankruptcy order; or

(c)   a bankruptcy order in respect of the prospective applicant.

Finding an authorised family mediator

22   As set out in Rule 3.9, a MIAM must be conducted by an authorised family mediator. Under that rule, an authorised family mediator is a person identified by the Family Mediation Council as qualified to conduct a MIAM.

23   A list of authorised family mediators, including their location, can be found using the 'Find your local mediator' search engine at: www.familymediationcouncil.org.uk

24   The expectation is that a prospective applicant should be able to find an authorised family mediator within 15 miles of his or her home. As stated in Rule 3.8(1)(o) a MIAM exemption is available if—

(i)   the prospective applicant has contacted as many authorised family mediators as have an office within fifteen miles of his or her home (or three of them if there are three or more), and all of them have stated that they are not available to conduct a MIAM within fifteen business days of the date of contact; and

(ii)   the names, postal addresses and telephone numbers or e-mail addresses for such authorised family mediators, and the dates of contact, can be provided to the court if requested.

25   Rule 3.8(1)(p) also provides an exemption if there is no authorised family mediator with an office within fifteen miles of the prospective applicant's home.

26   To determine whether a mediator is within the distance of 15 miles from their home, applicants can use the 'Find your local mediator' search engine to type in their own post code and then use the distance option to display only family mediators within a 15 mile distance.

27   The applicant will need to be prepared to produce at the first hearing the names, contact information and details of the dates of contact with the authorised family mediators.

28   Information about the Family Mediation Council, including its code of conduct can also be found at www.familymediationcouncil.org.uk

Funding attendance at a MIAM

29   The cost of attending a MIAM will depend on whether the prospective parties attend separately or together and whether at least one of the prospective parties is eligible for Legal Aid. If at least one party is eligible for Legal Aid then the total cost of MIAM attendance can be met by the Legal Aid Agency, whether the parties attend the same MIAM or separate MIAMs.

30   If neither party is eligible for Legal Aid then the mediator will agree with the prospective parties how the cost of MIAM attendance is to be met.

31   Parties can find out whether they are eligible for Legal Aid by using the calculator tool available at www.gov.uk/legal-aid

Attending a MIAM

32   Prospective respondents are expected to attend a MIAM, either with the prospective applicant or separately. A respondent may choose to attend a MIAM separately but this should usually be with the same authorised family mediator.

33   The prospective applicant should provide contact details for the prospective respondent to an authorised family mediator for the purpose of the mediator contacting them to discuss their willingness to attend a MIAM and, if appropriate, to schedule their attendance at a MIAM.

34   If the mediator contacts the prospective respondent and determines that he or she is unwilling to attend a MIAM, a prospective applicant should ask the mediator to confirm this as a ground for MIAM exemption in the relevant section of the application form, which should then be returned signed to the applicant.

Family Procedure Rules 2010 (SI 2010/2955)

Part 7
Procedure for Applications in Matrimonial and Civil Partnership Proceedings

Chapter 2
Rules about Starting and Responding to Proceedings

7.8   Service of application

(1)   After an application for a matrimonial or civil partnership order has been issued by the court, a copy of it must be served on the respondent and on any co-respondent.

(Rule 6.5 provides for who may serve an application for a matrimonial or civil partnership order.)

(2)   When the application is served on a respondent or co-respondent it must be accompanied by—

(a)   a form for acknowledging service; and

(b)   a notice of proceedings.

7.12 What the respondent and co-respondent should do on receiving the application

(1)   The respondent, and any co-respondent, must file an acknowledgment of service within 7 days beginning with the date on which the application for a matrimonial or civil partnership order was served.

(2)   This rule is subject to rule 6.42 (which specifies how the period for filing an acknowledgment of service is calculated where the application is served out of the jurisdiction).

(3)   The acknowledgment of service must—

(a)   subject to paragraph (4), be signed by the respondent or the respondent's legal representative or, as the case may be, the co respondent or the co respondent's legal representative;

(b)   include the respondent's or, as the case may be, the co respondent's address for service; and

(c)   where it is filed by the respondent, indicate whether or not the respondent intends to defend the case.

(4)   Where paragraph (5) or (6) applies, the respondent must sign the acknowledgment of service personally.

(5)   This paragraph applies where—

(a)   the application for a matrimonial order alleges that the respondent has committed adultery; and

(b)   the respondent admits the adultery.

(6)   This paragraph applies where—

(a)   the application for a matrimonial or civil partnership order alleges that the parties to the marriage or civil partnership concerned have been separated for more than 2 years; and

(b)   the respondent consents to the making of the matrimonial or civil partnership order.

(7)   ...

(8)   A respondent who wishes to defend the case must file and serve an answer within 21 days beginning with the date by which the acknowledgment of service is required to be filed.

(9)   An answer is not required where the respondent does not object to the making of the matrimonial or civil partnership order but objects to paying the costs of the application ...

(10)   A respondent may file an answer even if the intention to do so was not indicated in the acknowledgment of service.

(11)   Paragraph (11A) applies where—

(a)   the application is for—

    (i)   nullity of marriage under section 12(1)(d) of the 1973 Act;

    (ii)   nullity of marriage under section 12A(3) of the 1973 Act in a case where section 12(1)(d) of the 1973 Act applies; or

    (iii) nullity of civil partnership under section 50(1)(b) of the 2004 Act; and

(b)   the respondent files an answer containing no more than a simple denial of the facts stated in the application.

(11A) The respondent must, if intending to rebut the matters stated in the application, give notice to the court of that intention when filing the answer.

(12)   A respondent to an application for a matrimonial or civil partnership order alleging 2 years' separation and the respondent's consent may—

(a)   indicate consent to the making of the matrimonial or civil partnership order in writing at any time after service of the application, whether in the acknowledgment of service or otherwise;

(b)   indicate lack of consent to the making of that order, or withdraw any such consent already given, by giving notice to the court.

(13)   Where a respondent gives a notice under paragraph (12)(b) and no other relevant fact is alleged, the proceedings must be stayed, and notice of the stay given to the parties by the court officer.

(14)   In this rule, a 'relevant fact' is—

(a)   in matrimonial proceedings, one of the facts mentioned in section (1)(2) of the 1973 Act; and

(b)   in civil partnership proceedings, one of the facts mentioned in section 44(5) of the 2004 Act.

(15)   In paragraphs (3)(c), (8), (9) and (10), any reference to a respondent is to be read as including a reference to a co-respondent where the context so requires.

(The form of the answer is referred to in Practice Direction 5A.)

(In relation to paragraph (11)(a)(ii), section 9(6) of the Marriage (Same Sex Couples) Act 2013 provides that where a civil partnership is converted into a marriage, the civil partnership ends on the conversion, and the resulting marriage is to be treated as having subsisted since the date the civil partnership was formed.)

Chapter 3
How the Court Determines Matrimonial and Civil Partnership Proceedings

7.19   Applications for a decree nisi or a conditional order

(1)   An application may be made to the court for it to consider the making of a decree nisi, a conditional order, a decree of judicial separation or a separation order in the proceedings—

(a)   at any time after the time for filing the acknowledgment of service has expired, provided that no party has filed an acknowledgment of service indicating an intention to defend the case; and

(b)   in any other case, at any time after the time for filing an answer to every application for a matrimonial or civil partnership order made in the proceedings has expired.

(2)   An application under paragraph (1) may be made—

(a)   in a case within paragraph (1)(a), by the applicant; and

(b)   in any other case, by either party to the marriage or civil partnership in question.

(3)   An application under this rule must, if the information which was required to be provided by the application form is no longer correct, be accompanied by a statement setting out particulars of the change.

(4)   If no party has filed an answer opposing the making of a decree nisi, a conditional order, a decree of judicial separation or a separation order on another party's application, then an application under this rule must be accompanied by a statement—

(a)   stating whether there have been any changes in the information given in the application ...;

(b)   confirming that, subject to any changes stated, the contents of the application ... are true; and

(c)   where the acknowledgment of service has been signed by the other party to the marriage or civil partnership, confirming that party's signature on the acknowledgment of service.

(5)   A statement under paragraph (4) must be verified by a statement of truth.

Chapter 4
Court Orders

7.32   Making decrees nisi absolute or conditional orders final by giving notice

(1)   Unless rule 7.33 applies—

- (a)   in matrimonial proceedings, a spouse in whose favour a decree nisi has been made may give notice to the court that he or she wishes the decree nisi to be made absolute; or

- (b)   in civil partnership proceedings, a civil partner in whose favour a conditional order has been made may give notice to the court that he or she wishes the conditional order to be made final.

(2)   Subject to paragraphs (3) and (4), where the court receives a notice under paragraph (1) it will make the decree nisi absolute or the conditional order final (as the case may be) if it is satisfied that—

- (a)   no application for rescission of the decree nisi or the conditional order is pending;

- (b)   no appeal against the making of the decree nisi or the conditional order is pending;

- (c)   no order has been made by the court extending the time for bringing an appeal of the kind mentioned in sub-paragraph (b), or if such an order has been made, that the time so extended has expired;

- (d)   no application for an order of the kind mentioned in sub-paragraph (c) is pending;

- (e)   no application to prevent the decree nisi being made absolute or the conditional order being made final is pending;

- (f)   ...

- (g)   the provisions of section 10(2) to (4) of the 1973 Act or section 48(2) to (4) of the 2004 Act do not apply or have been complied with;

- (h)   any order under section 10A(2) of the 1973 Act has been complied with; and

- (i)   where the decree nisi was made on the ground in section 12(1)(g) of, or paragraph 11(1)(e) of Schedule 1 to, the 1973 Act, or was made under section 12A(3) of the 1973 Act in a case where section 12(1)(g) of the 1973 Act applies, or the conditional order was made under section 50(1)(d) of the 2004 Act—

   - (i)   there is not pending a reference under section 8(5) of the Gender Recognition Act 2004, or an application under section 8(5A) of that Act, in respect of the application on which the interim gender recognition certificate to which the application relates was granted;

   - (ii)   that interim certificate has not been revoked under section 8(6)(b) of that Act; and

   - (iii)   no appeal is pending against an order under section 8(6)(a) of that Act.

(3)   Where the notice is received more than 12 months after the making of the decree nisi or the conditional order, it must be accompanied by an explanation in writing stating—

- (a)   why the application has not been made earlier;

- (b)   whether the applicant and respondent have lived together since the decree nisi or the conditional order was made, and, if so, between what dates;

- (c)   if the applicant is female, whether she has given birth to a child since the decree nisi or the conditional order was made and whether it is alleged that the child is or may be a child of the family;

- (d)   if the respondent is female, whether the applicant has reason to believe that she has given birth to a child since the decree nisi or the conditional order was made and whether it is alleged that the child is or may be a child of the family.

(4)   Where paragraph (3) applies, the court may—

- (a)   require the applicant to file an affidavit verifying the explanation or to verify the explanation with a statement of truth; and

- (b)   make such order on the application as it thinks fit, but where it orders the decree nisi to be made absolute or the conditional order to be made final that order is not to take effect until the court is satisfied that none of the matters mentioned in paragraph (2)(a) to (i) applies.

Part 9
Applications for a Financial Remedy

9.7   Application for interim orders

(1)   A party may apply at any stage of the proceedings for—

    (a)   an order for maintenance pending suit;

    (b)   an order for maintenance pending outcome of proceedings;

    (c)   an order for interim periodical payments;

    (d)   an interim variation order;

    (da)   an order for payment in respect of legal services; or

    (e)   any other form of interim order.

(2)   An application for an order mentioned in paragraph (1) shall be made using the Part 18 procedure.

(3)   Where a party makes an application before filing a financial statement, the written evidence in support must—

    (a)   explain why the order is necessary; and

    (b)   give up to date information about that party's financial circumstances.

(4)   Unless the respondent has filed a financial statement, the respondent must, at least 7 days before the court is to deal with the application, file a statement of his means and serve a copy on the applicant.

(5)   An application for an order mentioned in paragraph (1)(e) may be made without notice.

9.12   Duties of the court and the applicant upon issuing an application

(1)   When an application under this Part is issued, except where Chapter 5 of this Part applies—

    (a)   the court will fix a first appointment not less than 12 weeks and not more than 16 weeks after the date of the filing of the application; and

    (b)   subject to paragraph (2), within 4 days beginning with the date on which the application was filed, a court officer will—

        (i)   serve a copy of the application on the respondent; and

        (ii)   give notice of the date of the first appointment to the applicant and the respondent.

(2)   Where the applicant wishes to serve a copy of the application on the respondent and on filing the application so notifies the court—

    (a)   paragraph (1)(b) does not apply;

    (b)   a court officer will return to the applicant the copy of the application and the notice of the date of the first appointment; and

    (c)   the applicant must,—

        (i)   within 4 days beginning with the date on which the copy of the application is received from the court, serve the copy of the application and notice of the date of the first appointment on the respondent; and

        (ii)   file a certificate of service at or before the first appointment.

    (Rule 6.37 sets out what must be included in a certificate of service.)

(3)   The date fixed under paragraph (1), or for any subsequent appointment, must not be cancelled except with the court's permission and, if cancelled, the court must immediately fix a new date.

(4)   In relation to an application to which the 2007 Hague Convention applies, where the applicant does not already know the address of the respondent at the time the application is issued, paragraph (2) does not apply and the court will serve the application in accordance with paragraph (1).

9.13   Service of application on mortgagees, trustees etc

(1)   Where an application for a financial remedy includes an application for an order for a variation of settlement, the applicant must serve copies of the application on—

    (a)   the trustees of the settlement;

    (b)   the settlor if living; and

    (c)   such other persons as the court directs.

(2)   In the case of an application for an avoidance of disposition order, the applicant must serve copies of the application on the person in whose favour the disposition is alleged to have been made.

(3)   Where an application for a financial remedy includes an application relating to land, the applicant must serve a copy of the application on any mortgagee of whom particulars are given in the application.

(4)   Any person served under paragraphs (1), (2) or (3) may make a request to the court in writing, within 14 days beginning with the date of service of the application, for a copy of the applicant's financial statement or any relevant part of that statement.

(5)   Any person who—

    (a)   is served with copies of the application in accordance with paragraphs (1), (2) or (3); or

    (b)   receives a copy of a financial statement, or a relevant part of that statement, following an application made under paragraph (4),

    may within 14 days beginning with the date of service or receipt file a statement in answer.

(6)   Where a copy of an application is served under paragraphs (1), (2) or (3), the applicant must file a certificate of service at or before the first appointment.

(7)   A statement in answer filed under paragraph (5) must be verified by a statement of truth.

9.14   Procedure before the first appointment

(1)   Not less than 35 days before the first appointment both parties must simultaneously exchange with each other and file with the court a financial statement in the form referred to in Practice Direction 5A.

(2)   The financial statement must—

    (a)   be verified by a statement of truth; and

    (b)   accompanied by the following documents only—

        (i)   any documents required by the financial statement;

        (ii)   any other documents necessary to explain or clarify any of the information contained in the financial statement; and

        (iii)   any documents provided to the party producing the financial statement by a person responsible for a pension arrangement, either following a request under rule 9.30 or as part of a relevant valuation; and

        (iv)   any notification or other document referred to in rule 9.37(2), (4) or (5) which has been received by the party producing the financial statement.

(2ZA), (2A) (not reproduced)

(3)   Where a party was unavoidably prevented from sending any document required by the financial statement, that party must at the earliest opportunity—

    (a)   serve a copy of that document on the other party; and

    (b)   file a copy of that document with the court, together with a written explanation of the failure to send it with the financial statement.

(4)   No disclosure or inspection of documents may be requested or given between the filing of the application for a financial remedy and the first appointment, except—

    (a)   copies sent with the financial statement, or in accordance with paragraph (3); or

    (b)   in accordance with paragraphs (5) and (6).

    (Rule 21.1 explains what is meant by disclosure and inspection.)

(5)   Not less than 14 days before the hearing of the first appointment, each party must file with the court and serve on the other party—

    (a)   a concise statement of the issues between the parties;

    (b)   a chronology;

    (c)   a questionnaire setting out by reference to the concise statement of issues any further information and documents requested from the other party or a statement that no information and documents are required; and

    (d)   a notice stating whether that party will be in a position at the first appointment to proceed on that occasion to a FDR appointment.

(6)   Not less than 14 days before the hearing of the first appointment, the applicant must file with the court and serve on the respondent confirmation—

(a)   of the names of all persons served in accordance with rule 9.13(1) to (3); and

(b)   that there are no other persons who must be served in accordance with those paragraphs.

9.15   Duties of the court at the first appointment

(1)   The first appointment must be conducted with the objective of defining the issues and saving costs.

(2)   At the first appointment the court must determine—

(a)   the extent to which any questions seeking information under rule 9.14(5)(c) must be answered; and

(b)   what documents requested under rule 9.14(5)(c) must be produced,

and give directions for the production of such further documents as may be necessary.

(3)   The court must give directions where appropriate about—

(a)   the valuation of assets (including the joint instruction of joint experts);

(b)   obtaining and exchanging expert evidence, if required;

(c)   the evidence to be adduced by each party; and

(d)   further chronologies or schedules to be filed by each party.

(4)   The court must direct that the case be referred to a FDR appointment unless—

(a)   the first appointment or part of it has been treated as a FDR appointment and the FDR appointment has been effective; or

(b)   there are exceptional reasons which make a referral to a FDR appointment inappropriate.

(5)   If the court decides that a referral to a FDR appointment is not appropriate it must direct one or more of the following—

(a)   that a further directions appointment be fixed;

(b)   that an appointment be fixed for the making of an interim order;

(c)   that the case be fixed for a final hearing and, where that direction is given, the court must determine the judicial level at which the case should be heard.

(Under Part 3 the court may also direct that the case be adjourned if it considers that non-court dispute resolution is appropriate.)

(6)   In considering whether to make a costs order under rule 28.3(5), the court must have particular regard to the extent to which each party has complied with the requirement to send documents with the financial statement and the explanation given for any failure to comply.

(7)   The court may—

(a)   where an application for an interim order has been listed for consideration at the first appointment, make an interim order;

(b)   having regard to the contents of the notice filed by the parties under rule 9.14(5)(d), treat the appointment (or part of it) as a FDR appointment to which rule 9.17 applies;

(c)   in a case where a pension sharing order or a pension attachment order is requested, direct any party with pension rights to file and serve a Pension Inquiry Form, completed in full or in part as the court may direct; and

(d)   in a case where a pension compensation sharing order or a pension compensation attachment order is requested, direct any party with PPF compensation rights to file and serve a Pension Protection Fund Inquiry Form, completed in full or in part as the court may direct.

(8)   Both parties must personally attend the first appointment unless the court directs otherwise.

9.16   After the first appointment

(1)   Between the first appointment and the FDR appointment, a party is not entitled to the production of any further documents except—

(a)   in accordance with directions given under rule 9.15(2); or

(b)   with the permission of the court.

(2)   At any stage—

(a)   a party may apply for further directions or a FDR appointment;

(b)   the court may give further directions or direct that parties attend a FDR appointment.

9.17 The FDR appointment

(1) The FDR appointment must be treated as a meeting held for the purposes of discussion and negotiation.

(2) The judge hearing the FDR appointment must have no further involvement with the application, other than to conduct any further FDR appointment or to make a consent order or a further directions order.

(3) Not less than 7 days before the FDR appointment, the applicant must file with the court details of all offers and proposals, and responses to them.

(4) Paragraph (3) includes any offers, proposals or responses made wholly or partly without prejudice (GL), but paragraph (3) does not make any material admissible as evidence if, but for that paragraph, it would not be admissible.

(5) At the conclusion of the FDR appointment, any documents filed under paragraph (3), and any filed documents referring to them, must, at the request of the party who filed them, be returned to that party and not retained on the court file.

(6) Parties attending the FDR appointment must use their best endeavours to reach agreement on matters in issue between them.

(7) The FDR appointment may be adjourned from time to time.

(8) At the conclusion of the FDR appointment, the court may make an appropriate consent order.

(9) If the court does not make an appropriate consent order as mentioned in paragraph (8), the court must give directions for the future course of the proceedings including, where appropriate—

    (a) the filing of evidence, including up to date information; and

    (b) fixing a final hearing date.

(10) Both parties must personally attend the FDR appointment unless the court directs otherwise.

9.26 Applications for consent orders for financial remedy

(1) Subject to paragraph (5) and to rule 35.2, in relation to an application for a consent order—

    (a) the applicant must file two copies of a draft of the order in the terms sought, one of which must be endorsed with a statement signed by the respondent to the application signifying agreement; and

    (b) each party must file with the court and serve on the other party, a statement of information in the form referred to in Practice Direction 5A.

(2) Where each party's statement of information is contained in one form, it must be signed by both the applicant and respondent to certify that they have read the contents of the other party's statement.

(3) Where each party's statement of information is in a separate form, the form of each party must be signed by the other party to certify that they have read the contents of the statement contained in that form.

(4) Unless the court directs otherwise, the applicant and the respondent need not attend the hearing of an application for a consent order.

(5) Where all or any of the parties attend the hearing of an application for a financial remedy the court may—

    (a) dispense with the filing of a statement of information; and

    (b) give directions for the information which would otherwise be required to be given in such a statement in such a manner as it thinks fit.

(6) In relation to an application for a consent order under Part 3 of the 1984 Act or Schedule 7 to the 2004 Act, the application for permission to make the application may be heard at the same time as the application for a financial remedy if evidence of the respondent's consent to the order is filed with the application.

(The following rules contain provision in relation to applications for consent orders - rule 9.32 (pension sharing order), rule 9.34 (pension attachment order), rule 9.41 (pension compensation sharing orders) and rule 9.43 (pension compensation attachment orders.)

9.26B Adding or removing parties

(1) The court may direct that a person or body be added as a party to proceedings for a financial remedy if—

(a)   it is desirable to add the new party so that the court can resolve all the matters in dispute in the proceedings; or

(b)   there is an issue involving the new party and an existing party which is connected to the matters in dispute in the proceedings, and it is desirable to add the new party so that the court can resolve that issue.

(2)   The court may direct that any person or body be removed as a party if it is not desirable for that person or body to be a party to the proceedings.

(3)   If the court makes a direction for the addition or removal of a party under this rule, it may give consequential directions about—

(a)   the service of a copy of the application form or other relevant documents on the new party; and

(b)   the management of the proceedings.

(4)   The power of the court under this rule to direct that a party be added or removed may be exercised either on the court's own initiative or on the application of an existing party or a person or body who wishes to become a party.

(5)   An application for an order under this rule must be made in accordance with the Part 18 procedure and, unless the court directs otherwise, must be supported by evidence setting out the proposed new party's interest in or connection with the proceedings or, in the case of removal of a party, the reasons for removal.

9.26E   Enforcement and apportionment where periodical payments are made under more than one order

(1)   This rule applies where periodical payments are required to be made by a payer to a payee under more than one periodical payments order.

(2)   Proceedings for the recovery of payments under more than one order may be made in one application by the payee, which must indicate the payments due under each order.

(3)   Paragraphs (4) and (5) apply where any sum paid to the court on any date by a payer who is liable to make payments to the court under two or more periodical payments orders is less than the total sum that the payer is required to pay to the court on that date in respect of those orders.

(4)   The payment made will be apportioned between the orders in proportion to the amounts due under each order over a period of one year.

(5)   If, as a result of the apportionment referred to in paragraph (4), the payments under any periodical payments order are no longer in arrears, the residue shall be applied to the amount due under the other order or, if there is more than one other order, shall be apportioned between the other orders in accordance with paragraph (4).

(6)   In this rule—

'payee' means a person entitled to receive payments under a periodical payments order; and

'payer' means a person required to make payments under a periodical payments order.

Chapter 7
Estimates of Costs

9.27   Estimates of Costs

(1)   Except where paragraph (4) applies, not less than one day before every hearing or appointment, each party must file with the court and serve on each other party an estimate of the costs incurred by that party up to the date of that hearing or appointment.

(2)   Not less than one day before the first appointment, each party must file with the court and serve on each other party an estimate of the costs that party expects to incur up to the FDR appointment if a settlement is not reached.

(3)   Not less than one day before the FDR appointment, each party must file with the court and serve on each other party an estimate of the costs that party expects to incur up to the final hearing if a settlement is not reached.

(4)   Not less than 14 days before the date fixed for the final hearing of an application for a financial remedy, each party ('the filing party') must (unless the court directs otherwise) file with the court and serve on each other party a statement giving full particulars of all costs in respect of the proceedings which the

filing party has incurred or expects to incur, to enable the court to take account of the parties' liabilities for costs when deciding what order (if any) to make for a financial remedy.

(5)   A costs estimate filed and served in accordance with paragraph (1), (2) or (3) and particulars of costs filed and served in accordance with paragraph (4) must include confirmation—

    (a)   that they have been served on each other party; and

    (b)   in the case of a party who is legally represented, that they have been discussed with the party on whose behalf they are provided.

(6)   Each party must bring to a hearing or appointment a copy of any estimate of costs filed and served in accordance with paragraph (1), (2) or (3) and any particulars of costs filed and served in accordance with paragraph (4).

(7)   The amount of—

    (a)   a costs estimate filed and served in accordance with paragraph (1), (2) or (3); and

    (b)   particulars of costs filed and served in accordance with paragraph (4),must be recorded in a recital to the order made at the hearing or appointment before which the estimate or particulars were filed or served.

(8)   If a party fails to comply with paragraph (1), (2), (3) or (4)—

    (a)   this fact must be recorded in a recital to the order made at the hearing or appointment before which the costs estimate or particulars of costs should have been filed and served; and

    (b)   the court must direct that the relevant costs estimate or particulars of costs must be filed with the court and served on each other party within three days of the hearing or appointment or within such other time period as the court directs.

(Rule 28.3 makes provision for orders for costs in financial remedy proceedings.)

(Practice Direction 9A makes provision for statements of truth to be included in estimates of costs and particulars of costs filed and served in accordance with this rule.)

9.28   Duty to make open proposals

(1)   Not less than 14 days before the date fixed for the final hearing of an application for a financial remedy, the applicant must (unless the court directs otherwise) file with the court and serve on the respondent an open statement which sets out concise details, including the amounts involved, of the orders which the applicant proposes to ask the court to make.

(2)   Not more than 7 days after service of a statement under paragraph (1), the respondent must file with the court and serve on the applicant an open statement which sets out concise details, including the amounts involved, of the orders which the respondent proposes to ask the court to make.

Chapter 8
Pensions

9.29   Application and interpretation of this Chapter

(1)   This Chapter applies

    (a)   where an application for a financial remedy has been made; and

    (b)   the applicant or respondent is the party with pension rights.

(2)   In this Chapter—

    (a)   in proceedings under the 1973 Act and the 1984 Act, all words and phrases defined in sections 25D(3) and (4) of the 1973 Act have the meaning assigned by those subsections;

    (b)   in proceedings under the 2004 Act—

        (i)   all words and phrases defined in paragraphs 16(4) to (5) and 29 of Schedule 5 to that Act have the meanings assigned by those paragraphs; and

        (ii)   'the party with pension rights' has the meaning given to 'civil partner with pension rights' by paragraph 29 of Schedule 5 to the 2004 Act;

    (c)   all words and phrases defined in section 46 of the Welfare Reform and Pensions Act 1999 have the meanings assigned by that section.

9.30   What the party with pension rights must do when the court fixes a first appointment

(1)   Where the court fixes a first appointment as required by rule 9.12(1)(a) the party with pension rights must request the person responsible for each pension arrangement under which the party has or is likely to have benefits to provide the information referred to in regulation 2(2) of the Pensions on Divorce etc (Provision of Information) Regulations 2000.

(The information referred to in regulation 2 of the Pensions on Divorce etc (Provision of Information) Regulations 2000 relates to the valuation of pension rights or benefits.)

(2)   The party with pension rights must comply with paragraph (1) within 7 days beginning with the date on which that party receives notification of the date of the first appointment.

(3)   Within 7 days beginning with the date on which the party with pension rights receives the information under paragraph (1) that party must send a copy of it to the other party, together with the name and address of the person responsible for each pension arrangement.

(4)   A request under paragraph (1) need not be made where the party with pension rights is in possession of, or has requested, a relevant valuation of the pension rights or benefits accrued under the pension arrangement in question.

9.31   Applications for pension sharing orders

Where an application for a financial remedy includes an application for a pension sharing order, or where a request for such an order is added to an existing application for a financial remedy, the applicant must serve a copy of the application on the person responsible for the pension arrangement concerned.

9.32   Applications for consent orders for pension sharing

(1)   This rule applies where—

(a)   the parties have agreed on the terms of an order and the agreement includes a pension sharing order;

(b)   service has not been effected under rule 9.31; and

(c)   the information referred to in paragraph (2) has not otherwise been provided.

(2)   The party with pension rights must—

(a)   request the person responsible for the pension arrangement concerned to provide the information set out in Section C of the Pension Inquiry Form; and

(b)   on receipt, send a copy of the information referred to in sub-paragraph (a) to the other party.

9.33   Applications for pension attachment orders

(1)   Where an application for a financial remedy includes an application for a pension attachment order, or where a request for such an order is added to an existing application for a financial remedy, the applicant must serve a copy of the application on the person responsible for the pension arrangement concerned and must at the same time send—

(a)   an address to which any notice which the person responsible is required to serve on the applicant is to be sent;

(b)   an address to which any payment which the person responsible is required to make to the applicant is to be sent; and

(c)   where the address in sub-paragraph (b) is that of a bank, a building society or the Department of National Savings, sufficient details to enable the payment to be made into the account of the applicant.

(2)   A person responsible for a pension arrangement who receives a copy of the application under paragraph (1) may, within 21 days beginning with the date of service of the application, request the party with the pension rights to provide that person with the information disclosed in the financial statement relating to the party's pension rights or benefits under that arrangement.

(3)   If the person responsible for a pension arrangement makes a request under paragraph (2), the party with the pension rights must provide that person with a copy of the section of that party's financial statement that relates to that party's pension rights or benefits under that arrangement.

(4)   The party with the pension rights must comply with paragraph (3)—

(a)   within the time limited for filing the financial statement by rule 9.14(1); or

(b)   within 21 days beginning with the date on which the person responsible for the pension arrangement makes the request,

whichever is the later.

(5)   A person responsible for a pension arrangement who receives a copy of the section of a financial statement as required pursuant to paragraph (4) may, within 21 days beginning with the date on which that person receives it, send to the court, the applicant and the respondent a statement in answer.

(6)   A person responsible for a pension arrangement who files a statement in answer pursuant to paragraph (5) will be entitled to be represented at the first appointment, or such other hearing as the court may direct, and the court must within 4 days, beginning with the date on which that person files the statement in answer, give the person notice of the date of the first appointment or other hearing as the case may be.

9.34   Applications for consent orders for pension attachment

(1)   This rule applies where service has not been effected under rule 9.33(1).

(2)   Where the parties have agreed on the terms of an order and the agreement includes a pension attachment order, then they must serve on the person responsible for the pension arrangement concerned—

(a)   a copy of the application for a consent order;

(b)   a draft of the proposed order, complying with rule 9.35; and

(c)   the particulars set out in rule 9.33(1).

(3)   No consent order that includes a pension attachment order must be made unless either—

(a)   the person responsible for the pension arrangement has not made any objection within 21 days beginning with the date on which the application for a consent order was served on that person; or

(b)   the court has considered any such objection, and for the purpose of considering any objection the court may make such direction as it sees fit for the person responsible to attend before it or to furnish written details of the objection.

9.35   Pension sharing orders or pension attachment orders

An order for a financial remedy, whether by consent or not, which includes a pension sharing order or a pension attachment order, must—

(a)   in the body of the order, state that there is to be provision by way of pension sharing or pension attachment in accordance with the annex or annexes to the order; and

(b)   be accompanied by a pension sharing annex or a pension attachment annex as the case may require, and if provision is made in relation to more than one pension arrangement there must be one annex for each pension arrangement.

9.36   Duty of the court upon making a pension sharing order or a pension attachment order

(1)   A court which varies or discharges a pension sharing order or a pension attachment order, must send, or direct one of the parties to send—

(a)   to the person responsible for the pension arrangement concerned; or

(b)   where the Board has assumed responsibility for the pension scheme or part of it, the Board;

the documents referred to in paragraph (4).

(2)   A court which makes a pension sharing order or pension attachment order, must send, or direct one of the parties to send to the person responsible for the pension arrangement concerned, the documents referred to in paragraph (4).

(3)   Where the Board has assumed responsibility for the pension scheme or part of it after the making of a pension sharing order or attachment order but before the documents have been sent to the person responsible for the pension arrangement in accordance with paragraph (2), the court which makes the pension sharing order or the pension attachment order, must send, or direct one of the parties to send to the Board the documents referred to in paragraph (4).

(4)   The documents to be sent in accordance with paragraph (1) to (3) are—

    (a)   in the case of—

        (i)   proceedings under the 1973 Act, a copy of the decree of judicial separation;

        (ii)   proceedings under Schedule 5 to the 2004 Act, a copy of the separation order;

        (iii)   proceedings under Part 3 of the 1984 Act, a copy of the document of divorce, annulment or legal separation;

        (iv)   proceedings under Schedule 7 to the 2004 Act, a copy of the document of dissolution, annulment or legal separation;

    (b)   in the case of divorce or nullity of marriage, a copy of the decree absolute under rule 7.31 or 7.32; or

    (c)   in the case of dissolution or nullity of civil partnership, a copy of the order making the conditional order final under rule 7.31 or 7.32; and

    (d)   a copy of the pension sharing order or the pension attachment order, or as the case may be of the order varying or discharging that order, including any annex to that order relating to that pension arrangement but no other annex to that order.

(5)   The documents referred to in paragraph (4) must be sent—

    (a)   in proceedings under the 1973 Act and the 1984 Act, within 7 days beginning with the date on which—

        (i)   the relevant pension sharing or pension attachment order, or any order varying or discharging such an order, is made; or

        (ii)   the decree absolute of divorce or nullity or decree of judicial separation is made,

      whichever is the later; and

    (b)   in proceedings under the 2004 Act, within 7 days beginning with the date on which—

        (i)   the relevant pension sharing or pension attachment order, or any order varying or discharging such an order, is made; or

        (ii)   the final order of dissolution or nullity or separation order is made,

      whichever is the later.

PRACTICE DIRECTION 9A
APPLICATION FOR A FINANCIAL REMEDY

This Practice Direction supplements FPR Part 9

Introduction

1.1   Part 9 of the Family Procedure Rules sets out the procedure applicable to the financial proceedings that are included in the definition of a 'financial remedy'.

1.2   The fast-track procedure set out in Chapter 5 of Part 9 of the Family Procedure Rules applies to—

    (a)   any application where the financial remedy sought is only for an order for periodical payments (as defined in rule 9.9B(1));

    (b)   any application made under—

        (i)   the Domestic Proceedings and Magistrates' Courts Act 1978;

        (ii)   Schedule 6 to the Civil Partnership Act 2004;

        (iii)   ...

        (iv)   Article 10 of the 2007 Hague Convention;

    (c)   any application for the variation of an order for periodical payments, except where the applicant seeks the dismissal (immediate or otherwise) of the periodical payments order and its substitution with one or more of a lump sum order, a property adjustment order, a pension sharing order or a pension compensation sharing order.

1.2A   The standard procedure set out in Chapter 4 of Part 9 applies in respect of all other applications for a financial remedy. In a case to which the fast-track procedure applies any party may seek a direction from the court that the standard procedure should apply to the application. An applicant who seeks such a direction must include a request in the application for a financial remedy and give reasons; any such request by a respondent, or any representations about a request by the applicant, must be made, giving reasons, within 7 days after service of the application for a financial remedy. At any stage in the proceedings the court may order that an application proceeding under the fast-track procedure must proceed under the standard procedure.

1.3   Where an application for a financial remedy includes an application relating to land, details of any mortgagee must be included in the application.

Pre-application protocol

2.1   The 'pre-application protocol' annexed to this Direction outlines the steps parties should take to seek and provide information from and to each other prior to the commencement of any application for a financial remedy. The court will expect the parties to comply with the terms of the protocol.

Costs

3.1   Rule 9.27(1) requires each party to file with the court, and serve on each other party, not less than one day before a hearing or appointment, an estimate of the costs incurred by that party up to the date of that hearing or appointment. Rule 9.27(2) and (3) make provision for the filing and service of estimates of specified future costs not less than one day before a first appointment and a FDR appointment. The rule also makes provision for the filing and service of particulars of costs not less than 14 days before a final hearing of an application for a financial remedy. The rule makes provision to ensure that all parties are aware of all incurred and estimated future costs (including their own) and for the court to give directions as to compliance if these requirements are not satisfied.

3.1A   References in rule 9.27 (and any other rule) to a time period of a day or a number of days must be read by reference to rule 2.9 (computation of time).

3.2   The purpose of this rule is to enable the court and the parties to take account of the impact of each party's costs liability on their financial situations. Parties should ensure that the information contained in the estimate is as full and accurate as possible and that any sums already paid in respect of a party's financial remedy costs are clearly set out. Where relevant, any liability arising from the costs of other proceedings between the parties should continue to be referred to in the appropriate section of a party's financial statement; any such costs should not be included in the estimates under rule 9.27.

3.2A   An estimate of costs which is to be filed and served in accordance with rule 9.27(1), (2) or (3), and particulars of costs which are to be filed and served in accordance with rule 9.27(4) must be verified by a statement of truth.

...

3.3   Rule 28.3 provides that the general rule in financial remedy proceedings is that the court will not make an order requiring one party to pay the costs of another party. However the court may make such an order at any stage of the proceedings where it considers it appropriate to do so because of the conduct of a party in relation to the proceedings.

3.4   Any breach of this practice direction or the pre-application protocol annexed to it will be taken into account by the court when deciding whether to depart from the general rule as to costs.

Procedure before the first appointment

4.1   In addition to the matters listed at rule 9.14(5), the parties should, if possible, with a view to identifying and narrowing any issues between the parties, exchange and file with the court—

(a)   a summary of the case agreed between the parties;

(b)   a schedule of assets agreed between the parties; and

(c)   details of any directions that they seek, including, where appropriate, the name of any expert they wish to be appointed.

4.2   Where a party is prevented from sending the details referred to in (c) above, the party should make that information available at the first appointment.

Financial Statements and other documents

5.1   Practice Direction 22A (Written Evidence) applies to any financial statement filed in accordance with rules 9.14 or 9.19 and to any exhibits to a financial statement. In preparing a bundle of documents to be exhibited to or attached to a financial statement, regard must be had in particular to paragraphs 11.1 to 11.3 and 13.1 to 13.4 of that Direction. Where on account of their bulk, it is impracticable for the exhibits to a financial statement to be retained on the court file after the First Appointment, the court may give directions as to their custody pending further hearings.

5.2   Where the court directs a party to provide information or documents by way of reply to a questionnaire or request by another party, the reply must be verified by a statement of truth. Unless otherwise directed, a reply to a questionnaire or request for information and documents shall not be filed with the court.

(Part 17 and Practice Direction 17A make further provision about statements of truth)

Financial Dispute Resolution (FDR) Appointment

6.1   A key element in the procedure is the Financial Dispute Resolution (FDR) appointment. Rule 9.17 provides that the FDR appointment is to be treated as a meeting held for the purposes of discussion and negotiation. Such meetings have been developed as a means of reducing the tension which inevitably arises in family disputes and facilitating settlement of those disputes.

6.2   In order for the FDR to be effective, parties must approach the occasion openly and without reserve. Non-disclosure of the content of such meetings is vital and is an essential prerequisite for fruitful discussion directed to the settlement of the dispute between the parties. The FDR appointment is an important part of the settlement process. As a consequence of *Re D (Minors) (Conciliation: Disclosure of Information)* [1993] Fam 231, evidence of anything said or of any admission made in the course of an FDR appointment will not be admissible in evidence, except at the trial of a person for an offence committed at the appointment or in the very exceptional circumstances indicated in *Re D*.

6.3   Courts will therefore expect—

(a)   parties to make offers and proposals;

(b)   recipients of offers and proposals to give them proper consideration; and

(c)   (subject to paragraph 6.4), that parties, whether separately or together, will not seek to exclude from consideration at the appointment any such offer or proposal.

6.4   Paragraph 6.3(c) does not apply to an offer or proposal made during non-court dispute resolution.

6.5   In order to make the most effective use of the first appointment and the FDR appointment, the legal representatives attending those appointments will be expected to have full knowledge of the case.

6.6   ...

Consent orders

7.1   Rule 9.26 (1)(a) requires an application for a consent order to be accompanied by two copies of the draft order in the terms sought, one of which must be endorsed with a statement signed by the respondent to the application signifying the respondent's agreement. The rule is considered to have been properly complied with if the endorsed statement is signed by solicitors on record as acting for the respondent; but where the consent order applied for contains undertakings, it should be signed by the party giving the undertakings as well as by that party's solicitor.

(Provision relating to the enforcement of undertakings is contained in the Practice Direction 33A supplementing Part 33 of the FPR)

7.2   Rule 9.26(1)(b) requires each party to file with the court and serve on the other party a statement of information. Where this is contained in one form, both parties must sign the statement to certify that each has read the contents of the other's statement.

7.3   Rule 35.2 deals with applications for a consent order in respect of a financial remedy where the parties wish to have the content of a written mediation agreement to which the Mediation Directive applies made the subject of a consent order.

Annex
Pre-application protocol
Notes of guidance

Scope of the Protocol

1.   This protocol is intended to apply to all applications for a financial remedy as defined by rule 2.3. It is designed to cover all classes of case, ranging from a simple application for periodical payments to an

application for a substantial lump sum and property adjustment order. The protocol is designed to facilitate the operation of the procedure for financial remedy applications.

2. In considering the options of pre-application disclosure and negotiation, solicitors should bear in mind the advantage of having a court timetable and court managed process. There is sometimes an advantage in preparing disclosure before proceedings are commenced. However, solicitors should bear in mind the objective of controlling costs and in particular the costs of discovery and that the option of pre-application disclosure and negotiation has risks of excessive and uncontrolled expenditure and delay. This option should only be encouraged where both parties agree to follow this route and disclosure is not likely to be an issue or has been adequately dealt with in mediation or otherwise.

3. Solicitors should consider at an early stage and keep under review whether it would be appropriate to suggest mediation and/or collaborative law to the clients as an alternative to solicitor negotiation or court based litigation.

4. Making an application to the court should not be regarded as a hostile step or a last resort, rather as a way of starting the court timetable, controlling disclosure and endeavouring to avoid the costly final hearing and the preparation for it.

First letter

5. The circumstances of parties to an application for a financial remedy are so various that it would be difficult to prepare a specimen first letter. The request for information will be different in every case. However, the tone of the initial letter is important and the guidelines in paragraphs 14 and 15 should be followed. It should be approved in advance by the client. Solicitors writing to an unrepresented party should always recommend that he seeks independent legal advice and enclose a second copy of the letter to be passed to any solicitor instructed. A reasonable time limit for an answer may be 14 days.

Negotiation and Settlement

6. In the event of pre-application disclosure and negotiation, as envisaged in paragraph 12 an application should not be issued when a settlement is a reasonable prospect.

Disclosure

7. The protocol underlines the obligation of parties to make full and frank disclosure of all material facts, documents and other information relevant to the issues. Solicitors owe their clients a duty to tell them in clear terms of this duty and of the possible consequences of breach of the duty, which may include criminal sanctions under the Fraud Act 2006. This duty of disclosure is an ongoing obligation and includes the duty to disclose any material changes after initial disclosure has been given. Solicitors are referred to the Good Practice Guides available to Resolution members at www.resolution.org.uk and can also contact the Law Society's Practice Advice Service on 0870 606 2522.

The Protocol

General principles

8. All parties must always bear in mind the overriding objective set out at rules 1.1 to 1.4 and try to ensure that applications should be resolved and a just outcome achieved as speedily as possible without costs being unreasonably incurred. The needs of any children should be addressed and safeguarded. The procedures which it is appropriate to follow should be conducted with minimum distress to the parties and in a manner designed to promote as good a continuing relationship between the parties and any children affected as is possible in the circumstances.

9. The principle of proportionality must be borne in mind at all times. It is unacceptable for the costs of any case to be disproportionate to the financial value of the subject matter of the dispute.

10. Parties should be informed that where a court is considering whether to make an order requiring one party to pay the costs of another party, it will take into account pre-application offers to settle and conduct of disclosure.

Identifying the issues

11. Parties must seek to clarify their claims and identify the issues between them as soon as possible. So that this can be achieved, they must provide full, frank and clear disclosure of facts, information and

documents, which are material and sufficiently accurate to enable proper negotiations to take place to settle their differences. Openness in all dealings is essential.

Disclosure

12. If parties carry out voluntary disclosure before the issue of proceedings the parties should exchange schedules of assets, income, liabilities and other material facts, using the financial statement as a guide to the format of the disclosure. Documents should only be disclosed to the extent that they are required by the financial statement. Excessive or disproportionate costs should not be incurred.

Correspondence

13. Any first letter and subsequent correspondence must focus on the clarification of claims and identification of issues and their resolution. Protracted and unnecessary correspondence and 'trial by correspondence' must be avoided.

14. The impact of any correspondence upon the reader and in particular the parties must always be considered. Any correspondence which raises irrelevant issues or which might cause the other party to adopt an entrenched, polarised or hostile position is to be discouraged.

Summary

15. The aim of all pre-application proceedings steps must be to assist the parties to resolve their differences speedily and fairly or at least narrow the issues and, should that not be possible, to assist the court to do so.

Family Procedure Rules 2010 (SI 2010/2955)

Part 28
Costs

28.1 Costs

The court may at any time make such order as to costs as it thinks just.

28.3 Costs in financial remedy proceedings

(1) This rule applies in relation to financial remedy proceedings.

(2) Rule 44.2(1), (4) and (5) of the CPR do not apply to financial remedy proceedings.

(3) Rules 44.2(6) to (8) and 44.12 of the CPR apply to an order made under this rule as they apply to an order made under rule 44.3 of the CPR.

(4) In this rule—

    (a) 'costs' has the same meaning as in rule 44.1(1)(c) of the CPR; and

    (b) 'financial remedy proceedings' means proceedings for—

        (i) a financial order except an order for maintenance pending suit, an order for maintenance pending outcome of proceedings, an interim periodical payments order, an order for payment in respect of legal services or any other form of interim order for the purposes of rule 9.7(1)(a), (b), (c) and (e);

        (ii) an order under Part 3 of the 1984 Act;

        (iii) an order under Schedule 7 to the 2004 Act;

        (iv) an order under section 10(2) of the 1973 Act;

        (v) an order under section 48(2) of the 2004 Act.

(5) Subject to paragraph (6), the general rule in financial remedy proceedings is that the court will not make an order requiring one party to pay the costs of another party.

(6) The court may make an order requiring one party to pay the costs of another party at any stage of the proceedings where it considers it appropriate to do so because of the conduct of a party in relation to the proceedings (whether before or during them).

(7) In deciding what order (if any) to make under paragraph (6), the court must have regard to—

(a) any failure by a party to comply with these rules, any order of the court or any practice direction which the court considers relevant;

(b) any open offer to settle made by a party;

(c) whether it was reasonable for a party to raise, pursue or contest a particular allegation or issue;

(d) the manner in which a party has pursued or responded to the application or a particular allegation or issue;

(e) any other aspect of a party's conduct in relation to proceedings which the court considers relevant; and

(f) the financial effect on the parties of any costs order.

(8) No offer to settle which is not an open offer to settle is admissible at any stage of the proceedings, except as provided by rule 9.17.

(9) For the purposes of this rule 'financial remedy proceedings' do not include an application under rule 9.9A.

Part 30
Appeals

30.3 Permission

(1) Paragraphs (1B) and (2) of this rule set out when permission to appeal is, or is not, required under these rules to appeal against a decision or order of the family court.

(1A) This rule does not apply where the route of appeal from a decision or order of the family court is to the Court of Appeal, namely where the appeal is against a decision or order made by a circuit judge or Recorder—

(a) in proceedings under—

(i) Part 4 of the 1989 Act (care and supervision);

(ii) Part 5 of the 1989 Act (protection of children);

(iii) paragraph 19(1) of Schedule 2 to the 1989 Act (approval by the court of local authority arrangements to assist children to live abroad); or

(iv) the 2002 Act (adoption, placement etc);

(b) in exercise of the family court's jurisdiction in relation to contempt of court where that decision or order was made in, or in connection with, proceedings referred to in sub-paragraph (a); or

(c) where that decision or order was itself made on an appeal to the family court.

(Appeals in the cases referred to in this paragraph are outside the scope of these rules. The CPR make provision requiring permission to appeal in those cases.)

(1B) Permission to appeal is required under these rules—

(a) unless paragraph (2) applies, where the appeal is against a decision made by a circuit judge, Recorder, district judge or costs judge; or

(b) as provided by Practice Direction 30A.

(2) Permission to appeal is not required where the appeal is against—

(a) a committal order;

(b) a secure accommodation order under section 25 of the 1989 Act; or

(c) a refusal to grant habeas corpus for release in relation to a minor.

(3) An application for permission to appeal may be made—

(a) to the lower court at the hearing at which the decision to be appealed was made; or

(b) to the appeal court in an appeal notice.

(Rule 30.4 sets out the time limits for filing an appellant's notice at the appeal court. Rule 30.5 sets out the time limits for filing a respondent's notice at the appeal court. Any application for permission to appeal to the appeal court must be made in the appeal notice (see rules 30.4(1) and 30.5(3).)

(4) Where the lower court refuses an application for permission to appeal, a further application for permission to appeal may be made to the appeal court.

(5) Subject to paragraph (5A), where the appeal court, without a hearing, refuses permission to appeal, the person seeking permission may request the decision to be reconsidered at a hearing.

(5A)   Where a judge of the High Court or in the family court, a judge of the High Court or a Designated Family Judge refuses permission to appeal without a hearing and considers that the application is totally without merit, the judge may make an order that the person seeking permission may not request the decision to be reconsidered at a hearing.

(5B)   Rule 4.3(5) will not apply to an order that the person seeking permission may not request the decision to be reconsidered at a hearing made under paragraph (5A).

(6)   A request under paragraph (5) must be filed within 7 days beginning with the date on which the notice that permission has been refused was served.

(7)   Permission to appeal may be given only where—

(a)   the court considers that the appeal would have a real prospect of success; or

(b)   there is some other compelling reason why the appeal should be heard.

(8)   An order giving permission may—

(a)   limit the issues to be heard; and

(b)   be made subject to conditions.

30.4   Appellant's notice

(1)   Where the appellant seeks permission from the appeal court it must be requested in the appellant's notice.

(2)   Subject to paragraph (3), the appellant must file the appellant's notice at the appeal court within—

(a)   such period as may be directed by the lower court (which may be longer or shorter than the period referred to in sub-paragraph (b)); or

(b)   where the court makes no such direction, 21 days after the date of the decision of the lower court against which the appellant wishes to appeal.

(3)   Where the appeal is against—

(a)   a case management decision; or

(b)   an order under section 38(1) of the 1989 Act,

the appellant must file the appellant's notice within 7 days beginning with the date of the decision of the lower court

(4)   Unless the appeal court orders otherwise, an appellant's notice must be served on each respondent and the persons referred to in paragraph (5)—

(a)   as soon as practicable; and

(b)   in any event not later than 7 days,

after it is filed.

(5)   The persons referred to in paragraph (4) are—

(a)   any children's guardian, welfare officer, or children and family reporter;

(b)   a local authority who has prepared a report under section 14A(8) or (9) of the 1989 Act;

(c)   an adoption agency or local authority which has prepared a report on the suitability of the applicant to adopt a child;

(d)   a local authority which has prepared a report on the placement of the child for adoption; and

(e)   …

30.5   Respondent's notice

(1)   A respondent may file and serve a respondent's notice.

(2)   A respondent who—

(a)   is seeking permission to appeal from the appeal court; or

(b)   wishes to ask the appeal court to uphold the order of the lower court for reasons different from or additional to those given by the lower court,

must file a respondent's notice.

(3)   Where the respondent seeks permission from the appeal court it must be requested in the respondent's notice.

(4)   Subject to paragraph (4A), a respondent's notice must be filed within—

(a)   such period as may be directed by the lower court; or

(b)   where the court makes no such direction, 14 days beginning with the date referred to in paragraph (5).

(4A) Where the appeal is against a case management decision, a respondent's notice must be filed within—

(a)   such period as may be directed by the lower court; or

(b)   where the court makes no such direction, 7 days beginning with the date referred to in paragraph (5).

(5)   The date referred to in paragraph (4) is—

(a)   the date on which the respondent is served with the appellant's notice where—

(i)   permission to appeal was given by the lower court; or

(ii)   permission to appeal is not required;

(b)   the date on which the respondent is served with notification that the appeal court has given the appellant permission to appeal; or

(c)   the date on which the respondent is served with notification that the application for permission to appeal and the appeal itself are to be heard together.

(6)   Unless the appeal court orders otherwise, a respondent's notice must be served on the appellant, any other respondent and the persons referred to in rule 30.4(5)—

(a)   as soon as practicable; and

(b)   in any event not later than 7 days,

after it is filed.

(7)   Where there is an appeal against an order under section 38(1) of the 1989 Act—

(a)   a respondent may not, in that appeal, bring an appeal from the order or ask the appeal court to uphold the order of the lower court for reasons different from or additional to those given by the lower court; and

(b)   paragraphs (2) and (3) do not apply.

30.6   Grounds of appeal

The appeal notice must state the grounds of appeal.

30.7   Variation of time

(1)   An application to vary the time limit for filing an appeal notice must be made to the appeal court.

(2)   The parties may not agree to extend any date or time limit set by—

(a)   these rules;

(b)   Practice Direction 30A; or

(c)   an order of the appeal court or the lower court.

(Rule 4.1(3)(a) provides that the court may extend or shorten the time for compliance with a rule, practice direction or court order (even if an application for extension is made after the time for compliance has expired).)

(Rule 4.1(3)(c) provides that the court may adjourn or bring forward a hearing.)

30.11   Appeal court's powers

(1)   In relation to an appeal the appeal court has all the powers of the lower court.

(Rule 30.1(4) provides that this Part is subject to any enactment that sets out special provisions with regard to any particular category of appeal.)

(2)   The appeal court has power to—

(a)   affirm, set aside (GL) or vary any order or judgment made or given by the lower court;

(b)   refer any application or issue for determination by the lower court;

(c)   order a new hearing;

(d)   make orders for the payment of interest;

(e)   make a costs order.

(3)   The appeal court may exercise its powers in relation to the whole or part of an order of the lower court.

(Rule 4.1 contains general rules about the court's case management powers.)

(4)   If the appeal court—

    (a)   refuses an application for permission to appeal;

    (b)   strikes out an appellant's notice; or

    (c)   dismisses an appeal,

and it considers that the application, the appellant's notice or the appeal is totally without merit, the provisions of paragraph (5) must be complied with.

(5)   Where paragraph (4) applies—

    (a)   the court's order must record the fact that it considers the application, the appellant's notice or the appeal to be totally without merit; and

    (b)   the court must at the same time consider whether it is appropriate to make a civil restraint order.

30.12   Hearing of appeals

(1)   Every appeal will be limited to a review of the decision of the lower court unless—

    (a)   an enactment or practice direction makes different provision for a particular category of appeal; or

    (b)   the court considers that in the circumstances of an individual appeal it would be in the interests of justice to hold a re-hearing.

(2)   Unless it orders otherwise, the appeal court will not receive—

    (a)   oral evidence; or

    (b)   evidence which was not before the lower court.

(3)   The appeal court will allow an appeal where the decision of the lower court was—

    (a)   wrong; or

    (b)   unjust because of a serious procedural or other irregularity in the proceedings in the lower court.

(4)   The appeal court may draw any inference of fact which it considers justified on the evidence.

(5)   At the hearing of the appeal a party may not rely on a matter not contained in that party's appeal notice unless the appeal court gives permission.

Part 33
Enforcement

33.3   How to apply

(1)   Except where a rule or practice direction otherwise requires, an application for an order to enforce an order for the payment of money must be made in a notice of application accompanied by a statement which must—

    (a)   state the amount due under the order, showing how that amount is arrived at; and

    (b)   be verified by a statement of truth.

(2)   The notice of application may either—

    (a)   apply for an order specifying the method of enforcement; or

    (b)   apply for an order for such method of enforcement as the court may consider appropriate.

(3)   If an application is made under paragraph (2)(b), an order to attend court will be issued and rule 71.2 (6) and (7) of the CPR will apply as if the application had been made under that rule.

Appendix 2 – Code of Practice for Resolution Members

Resolution is a community of family justice professionals who work with families and individuals to resolve issues in a constructive way.

Resolution membership is about the approach we take to our work. This means that as a Resolution member, I will:

- Reduce or manage any conflict and confrontation; for example, by not using inflammatory language.
- Support and encourage families to put the best interests of any children first.
- Act with honesty, integrity and objectivity.
- Help clients understand and manage the potential long-term financial and emotional consequences of decisions.
- Listen to and treat everyone with respect and without judgment.
- Use my experience and knowledge to guide clients through the options available to them.
- Continually develop my knowledge and skills.
- Use the Resolution Guides to Good Practice in my day-to-day work.

And I will work with other Resolution members to uphold this Code and ensure it is at the heart of everything I do.

Reproduced with kind permission of Resolution.

Appendix 3 – Court Forms

(A) Divorce application

Application for a divorce, dissolution or (judicial) separation

To be completed by the court	
Name of court	
Case No.	
Date received by the court	
Date issued	
Time issued	

You can also apply for a divorce online at
www.gov.uk/apply-for-divorce

You can only make an application for divorce or dissolution if you have been in your marriage or civil partnership for at least one year. This does not apply to (judicial) separation applications.

The information you give will be used as evidence by the court to decide if you are entitled to legally end your marriage or civil partnership or to get a (judicial) separation order from your partner. A copy of this form will be sent to your spouse/civil partner by the court.

If there are exceptional reasons why your application should be dealt with urgently then please set those reasons out in a covering letter.

There is a court fee for making this application - see notes on page 15

Help with Fees –
Ref no. (if applicable)   H W F – ☐☐☐ – ☐☐☐

If you have to pay a fee indicate how you will pay

☐ **cheque**

☐ **debit/credit card** – The court will call you between 9am – 4pm Monday to Friday, using the contact details you provide later in the form to collect payment.

Section 1
Your application
(known as a petition in divorce and judicial separation)

At times in this form you will be referred to as the Petitioner or Applicant, and your spouse/civil partner will be referred to as the Respondent. These are the technical terms used in law.

1.1 What application do you wish to make?

☐ **Divorce** on the ground that the marriage has broken down irretrievably

☐ **Dissolution** on the ground that the civil partnership has broken down irretrievably

☐ **(Judicial) separation**

1.2 What documents are you supplying to support your application?

In cases of urgent applications it may be possible for you to make an application to allow you to deliver the original or a certified copy of the marriage/civil partnership certificate to the court at a later date.

☐ Your marriage or civil partnership certificate or a certified copy of the certificate from where you got married or entered into a civil partnership (a photocopy will **not** be accepted).

☐ A translation that has been certified by a notary public or authenticated by a statement of truth by the person who did the translation. This should be provided if your marriage or civil partnership certificate (or a similar document issued under the law in the country you registered your marriage or civil partnership) is not in English.

There is a separate fee for making an application to issue without your marriage certificate: see www.gov.uk/court-fees-what-they-are

For marriages/civil partnerships in England and Wales you can order a copy of the certificate at www.gro.gov.uk/gro/content/certificates. You will need to pay for each copy.

If you entered into a **religious marriage** as well as a civil marriage, these divorce proceedings may not dissolve the religious part of your marriage. It is important that you contact the relevant religious authority and seek further guidance if you are unsure.

Section 2
About you (the applicant/petitioner)

2.1   Your current name

First name(s)

Last name

Is this either your married name or the name shown on your marriage or civil partnership certificate?

☐ Yes

☐ No, please attach your change of name deed/statutory declaration or if this is not applicable, explain why your name has changed

This can be different to the one on your marriage or civil partnership certificate. This can be your last name, your spouse/civil partner's last name or a double barrelled last name that combines the two.

If you have changed your name , other than through your marriage, since you got married you must attach a copy of your change of name deed or otherwise explain why your name has changed.

2.2   Confidentiality

Can your contact details be shared with your spouse/civil partner?

☐ Yes

☐ No, please complete the separate **C8** form with your details in order to do this.

If you do not wish to disclose your contact details to your spouse/civil partner you should leave those details blank and complete **Form C8 Confidential contact details**.

2.3   What is your home address?

If you want to keep your contact details confidential, **do not** complete this question. Please complete **form C8**.

Building and street

Second line of address

Town or city

County (optional)

Postcode

You should give a home address in the UK, if you have one. If you have a solicitor acting for you, the court will send all papers to their address. If you do not have a solicitor, the court will send papers to your home address, or you can provide a business address in the UK in the next section. If you want to supply an address outside of the UK, different rules may apply about documents being sent to you. You may wish to seek legal advice.

Remember a copy of this form will be sent to your spouse/civil partner. If you do not want them to know your current contact details you should not enter them here or provide any details in the form which may give them information on how to contact you.

Phone no. (if you have one)

Email (if you have one)

2.4   Do you have a solicitor acting for you?

☐ Yes, please give their details below

☐ No, **go to question 2.9**

If you have a solicitor acting for you, the court will send all papers to their address.

2.5   Your solicitor's name (if applicable)

2.6   Your solicitor's reference number

2.7   Name of solicitor's firm

2.8   Solicitor's address

Building and street

Second line of address

Town or city

County (optional)

Postcode

DX address (if applicable)

If you want your court issued papers sent to a business address rather than your home then that address should also be in the UK. If you want to supply an address outside of the UK, different rules may apply about documents being sent to you. You may wish to seek legal advice.

Phone no.

Email

**2.9   If you do not have a solicitor acting for you, do you want the court
issued papers sent to your home address?**

☐ Yes, **go to Section 3**

☐ No, please send them to my business address below

Building and street

Second line of address

Town or city

County (optional)

Postcode

Section 3
About your spouse/civil partner (the respondent)

3.1   **Your spouse/civil partner's current name**

First name(s)

Last name

Is this their married name or the name shown on your marriage or civil partnership certificate?

☐ Yes

☐ No, if known, please explain why their name has changed

3.2   **Their home address**

Building and street

Second line of address

Town or city

County (optional)

Postcode

Phone no. (if known)

Email (if known)

Unless a different address is provided at section 3.7 court papers will be sent to the address at section 3.2.

If your spouse/ civil partner has a solicitor acting for them you should complete their details at sections 3.3 to 3.7 and the court papers will be sent to their solicitor.

If they do not have a solicitor but have provided a different address to their home address to send the papers, then please provide the details in sections 3.3 to 3.7.

If your spouse/ civil partner has not given you such an address, then the court papers will be sent to their last known or usual address provided in this section.

If you know that they no longer live at that address, you will need to take all reasonable steps to obtain a current address. Details on how you might do that can be found here: www.gov.uk/divorce-missing-husband-wife

If any of the addresses you provide are outside of the UK then different rules about sending papers to them apply. You may wish to seek further legal advice.

Page 5

3.3   Has your spouse/civil partner provided a different address for the court documents to be sent to?

☐ Yes, please use the address below

☐ No, **go to section 4**

3.4   Their solicitor's name (if applicable and if known)

```
[                                              ]
```

3.5   Their solicitor's reference number (if applicable and if known)

```
[                          ]
```

3.6   Name of their solicitor's firm (if applicable and if known)

```
[                                              ]
```

3.7   Their solicitor's or other address they have provided

The court will send documents to this address.

Building and street

```
[                                              ]
```

Second line of address

```
[                                              ]
```

Town or city

```
[                                ]
```

County (optional)

```
[                                ]
```

Postcode

```
[   |   |   |   |   |   |   ]
```

DX address (if applicable)

```
[                                              ]
```

Section 4
Details of marriage/civil partnership

You should attach your marriage or civil partnership certificate to this application, together with a certified translation in English if necessary (the court will usually keep your documents and not return them). If you do not have the original certificate and cannot get a copy of it, you will have to make a separate application, alongside this application, to issue this form without it.

If you are applying without your marriage/civil partnership certificate you will need to make a separate application on **Form D11** (Application notice) and pay another court fee. It is recommended that you seek legal advice if you are unsure of how to do this.

4.1 Did your marriage take place outside of the UK?

☐ Yes

☐ No

4.2 Are you making a separate application to issue without your marriage or civil partnership certificate?

☐ Yes

☐ No

If you answered 'Yes', to either question 4.1 or 4.2 above, please give the place where the marriage/civil partnership was formed, as it appears on your marriage/civil partnership certificate (if any)

4.3 Date of marriage or civil partnership

DAY   MONTH   YEAR

You can only apply for a divorce/dissolution if you have been in your marriage or civil partnership for at least one year.

4.4 Your full first name(s) and last name(s) – as shown on your certificate

Your spouse/civil partner's full first name(s) and last name(s) – as shown on your certificate

4.5 Are the details set out in your marriage or civil partnership certificate correct?

☐ Yes

☐ No, please explain why

Page 7

Section 5
Why this court can deal with your case
(Jurisdiction)

The court needs to understand why you think it has the legal power (jurisdiction) to deal with your application.

Please complete section 5.1 or if that section does not apply to you then complete section 5.2.

5.1   The court has legal power to deal with this application because one of the following applies:

Divorce – **Opposite Sex Couple** – Section 5(2) of the Domicile and Matrimonial Proceedings Act 1973

Divorce – **Same Sex Couple** – Marriage (Same Sex Couples) (Jurisdiction and Recognition of Judgments) Regulations 2014 and Schedule A1 to the Domicile and Matrimonial Proceedings Act 1973

Civil Partnerships – the Civil Partnership (Jurisdiction and Recognition of Judgments) Regulations 2005 and Section 221 of the Civil Partnership Act 2004

Please tick the reasons that apply:

☐ both parties to the marriage/civil partners are habitually resident in England and Wales;

☐ both parties to the marriage/civil partners were last habitually resident in England and Wales and one of them continues to reside there;

☐ the respondent is habitually resident in England and Wales;

☐ the applicant is habitually resident in England and Wales and has resided there for at least one year immediately before the application was made;

☐ the applicant is domiciled and habitually resident in England and Wales and has resided there for at least six months immediately before the application was made;

☐ both parties to the marriage/civil partners are domiciled in England and Wales; **or**

☐ the ☐ applicant or the ☐ respondent is domiciled in England and Wales.

OR (see section 5.2 over the page)

Habitual Residence
Your habitual residence is the place in which your life is mainly based. You must be settled there and intend to stay settled there. Some of the following may apply: you work there, own property, have your children in school there, and your main family life takes place there.

Domicile
Your domicile is the main permanent home in which you live, or to which you intend to return. When you were born you will have acquired your parents' domicile (either your father's if they were married, or your mother's if they weren't married or if your father died before you were born). If you have since moved to another country and made that your permanent home then your domicile may have moved there.

If you were born in England or Wales, lived your entire life here, and intend to stay here, then it is very likely that you'll be **both habitually resident and domiciled** here. You should get legal advice if you are not sure which reason(s) apply.

If you need help deciding which reasons apply to you then you should consider seeking legal advice, particularly if you live outside England and Wales.

5.2 If the options in section 5.1 do not apply to you, please consider if below is applicable:

☐ the Applicant and Respondent registered as civil partners of each other in England or Wales or, in the case of a same sex couple, married each other under the law of England and Wales and it would be in the interests of justice for the court to assume jurisdiction in this case.

Section 6
Give the reason for your divorce or dissolution
(the facts)

6.1   **If your application is for divorce or dissolution, you must choose one or more of the following reasons to support the fact that your marriage or civil partnership has broken down irretrievably (it can't be saved).**

If your application is for (judicial) separation you must choose one or more of the following reasons to support your application.

You will need to provide information (evidence) to support the reason(s) given.

☐ **Adultery**
The Respondent has committed adultery and the Petitioner finds it intolerable to live with the Respondent.

☐ **Behaviour**
The Respondent has behaved in such a way that the Petitioner/Applicant cannot reasonably be expected to live with the Respondent.

☐ **Desertion**
The Respondent has deserted the Petitioner/Applicant for a continuous period of at least two years immediately preceding the presentation of this petition/application.

☐ **Separated for 2 years and consent**
The parties to the marriage/civil partnership have lived apart for a continuous period of at least two years immediately preceding the presentation of the petition/application and the Respondent consents to a decree/order being granted.

☐ **Separated for 5 years**
The parties to the marriage/civil partnership have lived apart for a continuous period of at least five years immediately preceding the presentation of the petition or application.

Adultery is only available in relation to marriages and if the adultery was between your spouse and a member of the opposite sex. You cannot use adultery if, once you become aware of it, you lived together as a couple for a period, or combination of periods, exceeding 6 months.

Behaviour cannot be used if you lived together as a couple for a period, or periods, totalling more than 6 months after the date of last incident you want to rely on as evidence.

For 2 and 5 years' separation please make sure that you have been separated the right amount of time in order to make your application.

What if we lived together after we separated?

Living in the same residence while separated
You can still live in the same residence while separated, as long as you are not living together as a couple, for example, you do not eat, sleep or cook together.

Living together as a couple after separating
If you have lived together as a couple after separating, you cannot use the 2 years' separation with consent, 5 years' separation and desertion facts if it was for more than 6 months, during or after the separation period. This 6 month timescale can have been either in a single period or over several periods.

Section 7

Supporting information (Statement of case)

7.1   **If you are using 2 years' separation and consent or 5 years' separation, on what date did you reach the conclusion that your marriage or civil partnership was at an end?**

AND

On what date did you stop living together as a couple?

(both dates must be at least 2 or 5 years ago, plus any periods you lived together as couple in that time if less than 6 months, before the date you make this application)

AND

Has there been any period or periods during this time that you have lived together as a couple again?

☐   Yes, and the details and dates for those periods are as follows

(if necessary, continue on a separate sheet)

☐   No, **we have not been a couple again - go to section 9**

7.2   **If using adultery, behaviour or desertion you must give brief details to support the reasons for your application.**
(please refer to the notes on this page for guidance)

(if necessary, continue on a separate sheet)

If you are relying on adultery/ behaviour or desertion you must complete question 7.2

Adultery

Please give the date when you first become aware of the adultery and, if known, dates and places where the adultery happened.

It is not normally necessary to name the person your spouse committed adultery with; you should only consider doing so if the petition is likely to be disputed.

If you include them you must provide their address in section 8 and the court will send them a copy of your petition to give them a chance to respond.

Your petition could be delayed if they do not respond and it could cost you more money.

Behaviour

You should include examples of your spouse's/civil partner's behaviour which affected you the most, and the most recent incidents.

You can describe how they have behaved over a period of time or use particular incidents. Include dates if relevant. Provide enough detail to satisfy the court that you cannot reasonably be expected to live with them. Please remember that they will be sent a copy of this application.

Desertion

You should include the date when your spouse/civil partner left (deserted you) without your consent and describe why and how this came about. You should also confirm that you have lived separately since the date of desertion.

Page 11

Section 8

Adultery cases only – details of the person your partner committed adultery with (co-respondent)

People do not generally name the person their spouse committed adultery with. However, if you have named them in section 7 then you must give their details below so a copy of this petition can be sent to them. If you did not name them, you do not need to fill in these details.

8.1   Name of the person your spouse committed adultery with (co-respondent)

First name(s)

Last name

8.2   The address to send court papers to them

Building and street

Second line of address

Town or city

County (optional)

Postcode

If the other person is named, then they will usually become a party to the court case and be sent copies of the petition.

Your petition could be delayed if they do not respond and it could cost you more money to resolve that issue.

Section 9
Existing court cases

9.1 **Are there any existing or previous court proceedings relating to your marriage/civil partnership, property or children?**

☐ Yes, please give details below

☐ No

Case number(s)

Summary of the on-going or previous court proceedings

Section 10
Dividing your money and property –
Orders which are sought

If you disagree with your spouse or civil partner about how your property, money, pensions and other assets will be split, then you can ask the court to decide for you. Types of financial order include:

- an order for maintenance pending suit/outcome
- periodical payments order
- secured provision order
- lump sum order
- property adjustment order
- Pension sharing/ compensation sharing/ attachment order

These decisions are called 'financial orders'. You can apply for orders for yourself, and/or, if appropriate, for your children.

If you agree with your spouse or civil partner on how your money and property will be split, and want it to be legally binding, you can apply for a financial order to be made by consent.

10.1 Do you want to apply for a financial order?

☐ Yes, I want to apply for a financial order for (select all that apply)

☐ myself

☐ my children

☐ No

If you answer 'Yes' to question 10.1 the court will take no action at this stage. To formally start financial proceedings, you will also need to complete a separate application form and pay another court fee.

You can find more guidance on financial orders and how to get help agreeing on any issues at www.gov. uk/money-property-when-relationship-ends/apply-for-a-financial-order

If you answer 'No' to question 10.1 you can still apply for a financial order in the future, but only **until you remarry or form** another **civil partnership**. This restriction does not apply to pension sharing or pension compensation sharing orders.

If you are unsure what to do here it is recommended you seek legal advice.

The court will not start processing your request for a financial order until you submit the separate application and pay the fee. You can do this at the same time you apply for your divorce, dissolution or (judicial) separation or at any time after that. Please note that decisions regarding child maintenance are usually made by agreement or by the Child Maintenance Service and the court can only make these orders under certain circumstances.

Section 11
Summary of what is being applied for (the prayer) and **Statement of Truth**

11   The Petitioner/Applicant applies for the following:

11.1 The application

☐ That the   ☐ marriage be dissolved   ☐ civil partnership be dissolved

or

☐ That the Petitioner/Applicant be (judicially) separated from the Respondent.

11.2 Costs (if you wish to claim costs from the Respondent or Co-Respondent)

☐ That the ☐ Respondent ☐ Co-Respondent

shall be ordered to pay the costs of this application

You can ask the court to consider making an order that some or all of the costs of this application are paid for by your spouse/civil partner and/or, if applicable, the co-respondent. The court will not normally order costs where the application is based on 5 years' separation.

11.3 Financial Order
(if you ticked 'Yes' to the question at 10.1 and wish to make an application for a Financial Order)

That a financial order may be granted for:

☐ The **Petitioner/Applicant**

☐ For the **children**

This **statement of truth** must be completed by the person making this application (referred to as the Petitioner/Applicant), or by a solicitor acting for them.

[I believe]* [The Petitioner/Applicant believes]* that the facts stated in this application for a divorce/dissolution/(judicial) separation are true. *delete as applicable

*[I am duly authorised by the Petitioner/Applicant to sign this statement.]

PRINT full name

Signed

Dated

Name of solicitor's firm (if applicable)

Proceedings for contempt of court may be brought against a person who makes or causes to be made, a false statement in a document verified by a statement of truth.

When returning your form, you must include:

- **Three copies of your completed application form**
  (one will be sent back to you with the court seal and one will be kept on the court file and one will be sent to the Respondent).

- **One original or certified** copy of your marriage/civil partnership certificate or a similar document issued under the law in force in the country where the marriage or civil partnership registration took place (photocopies will not be accepted). If your certificate is not in English then a certified translation must also be provided. The court will keep the documents you send. If you want them back you will need to apply for their return.

- **The court fee**
  You can find the current fee in leaflet **EX50 Civil and Family Court Fees** which can be downloaded from: **https://hmctsformfinder.justice.gov.uk**

  If you cannot afford to pay a court fee, you may be eligible for a fee remission or a reduced fee. The form **EX160 Apply for help with fees** and the **EX160A guidance** booklet gives you further information - https://www.gov.uk/get-help-with-court-fees

  If you are paying by cheque please remember to include it with your application and make it payable to 'HM Courts & Tribunals Service'.

- If applicable, a completed **Form C8 Confidential contact details**

- If applicable, a completed **Form A Notice of [intention to proceed with] an application for a financial order**

Please send the items listed above to the HMCTS Divorce Centre for your area. You can find out your Divorce Centre by using the online HMCTS Courtfinder **https://courttribunalfinder.service.gov.uk/search/** or by contacting your local family court.

(B) Form A (Application for a financial order)

Notice of [intention to proceed with] **a financial application to which the standard procedure applies**

To be completed by the Applicant	
The Family Court sitting at	Case No.
Help with Fees – Ref no. (if applicable) **H W F** – ☐☐☐ – ☐☐☐	

This form should be completed if you are applying for financial provision (a financial order or other financial remedy) **except** an application:

- for a periodical payments order **only**, under section 23 of the Matrimonial Causes Act 1973, paragraph 2 of Schedule 5 to the Civil Partnership Act 2004 or paragraphs 1 or 2 of Schedule 1 to the Children Act 1989 – please complete Form A1.
- to vary or to discharge a periodical payments order **only** – please complete Form A1.
- for financial provision under Part 1 of the Domestic Proceedings and Magistrates' Courts Act 1978 or Schedule 6 to the Civil Partnership Act 2004 – please complete Form A1.
- after an overseas divorce etc (Form D50F) or for neglect or failure to maintain a party or child (Form D50C) or for alteration of a maintenance agreement during the lifetime of the parties (Form D50H)

Full name of applicant

Full name of respondent(s)

Nature of application

This application is for financial provision, including provision to be made to or for the benefit of the child(ren):

☐ in connection with matrimonial or civil partnership proceedings (divorce, dissolution etc), if so:

Has the court granted you a decree nisi or a conditional dissolution order?

☐ Yes, attach a copy to this form
☐ No

Has the court granted you a decree absolute or dissolution order?

☐ Yes, attach a copy to this form
☐ No

or

☐ under paragraphs 1 or 2 of Schedule 1 to the Children Act 1989

tick the statement that applies	**and**	tick one or more of the following orders
The applicant intends:		
☐ **to apply** to the Court for		☐ an order for maintenance pending suit/outcome of proceedings
or		☐ a lump sum order
☐ **to proceed with** the application in the		☐ a property adjustment order
☐ divorce		☐ a settlement or a transfer of property for the benefit of the child(ren)
☐ dissolution		☐ a periodical payments order **together with** other financial provision
☐ nullity		
☐ annulment		☐ a pension sharing order
☐ (judicial) separation		☐ a pension compensation sharing order
application for		
or		
☐ **to apply to vary**		
☐ **to apply to discharge** a periodical payments order **and** to substitute for it one or more orders opposite		☐ a lump sum order
		☐ a property adjustment order
		☐ a pension sharing order
		☐ a pension compensation sharing order

Additional information required

Are you applying for an order by consent in terms of written agreement (a consent order)?

☐ **Yes, attach the draft order to this form**
☐ No

2

1. Further details of the financial application

If your application includes an application for a property adjustment order in relation to land, please give the following details, if applicable

Address(es) of the property or properties

Name(s) and address(es) of any mortgagee(s)

If an application is made for any periodical payments or secured periodical payments for children, please complete this section.

- [ ] there is a written agreement made before 5 April 1993 about maintenance for the benefit of children

- [ ] there is a written agreement made on or after 5 April 1993 about maintenance for the benefit of children

- [ ] there is no agreement, but the applicant is applying for payments:

  - [ ] for a stepchild or stepchildren
  - [ ] in addition to child support maintenance already paid under a Child Support Agency assessment
  - [ ] to meet expenses arising from a child's disability
  - [ ] to meet expenses incurred by a child in being educated or training for work
  - [ ] when either the child **or** the person with care of the child **or** the absent parent of the child is not habitually resident in the United Kingdom

If none of the above applies, the court may not have jurisdiction to hear the application for periodical payments.

Has the Child Support Agency made any calculation of maintenance in respect of the child(ren)

- [ ] Yes   [ ] No

If Yes, state briefly your reasons for making this application to the court including any reasons why the Child Support Agency is no longer dealing with your claim or any reasons why you need additional maintenance to top up payments made through the Child Support Agency:

3

If your application includes an application in relation to one or more children, please complete the tables below for each child, continuing on additional sheets if necessary

Name of child 1	
Date of birth	☐☐ / ☐☐ / ☐☐☐☐
Gender	☐ Male ☐ Female
Relationship to Applicant	
Relationship to Respondent	
Country of residence (if not England or Wales)	

Name of child 2	
Date of birth	☐☐ / ☐☐ / ☐☐☐☐
Gender	☐ Male ☐ Female
Relationship to Applicant	
Relationship to Respondent	
Country of residence (if not England or Wales)	

4

Service details

☐ I am not represented by a solicitor in these proceedings (please give your address in the boxes below)

☐ I am not represented by a solicitor in these proceedings but am receiving advice from a solicitor (please give your address in the boxes below)

☐ I am represented by a solicitor in these proceedings, who has signed Section 5, and all documents for my attention should be sent to my solicitor whose details are as follows:

Solicitor's details

Name of solicitor

Name of firm

Address to which all documents should be sent for service

Building and street

Second line of address

Town or city

County (optional)

Country (optional)

Postcode

Phone number

Fax number

DX number

5

Your reference

Solicitor's fee account number

Email – only provide an email address if you consent to us contacting you via email about this application

Respondent's address for service - if you have appointed a solicitor, please give their details here

Respondent solicitor's name

Respondent solicitor's firm

Building and street

Second line of address

Town or city

County (optional)

Country (optional)

Postcode

2. Requirement to attend a Mediation, Information and Assessment Meeting (MIAM)

Before making an application for a financial order you must first attend a Mediation, Information and Assessment Meeting (MIAM). At the MIAM an authorised family mediator will consider with you (and the other party if present) whether family mediation, or another form of non-court dispute resolution, would be a more appropriate alternative to court. The mediator will also be able to sign post you to other help and support services.

You **must** have attended a MIAM before making this application **unless** the requirement to attend a MIAM does not apply because the financial order you are applying for:

- is for a consent order; **or**
- you are exempt from the requirement to attend a MIAM. (Some exemptions you can claim for yourself, others must be certified by an authorised family mediator).

In special circumstances such as where domestic violence is involved - you may not need to attend a MIAM. However, you will be asked to provide the judge with evidence (such as a police report to prove domestic violence has taken place) and should bring it to the first hearing.

All applicants must complete sections 1 and 2 and complete and sign section 5 of this form. **In addition**, you must tick one of the boxes below and ensure that you, your legal adviser or a family mediator completes and signs the relevant section(s) of this form as shown.

2a. Are you claiming exemption from the requirement to attend a MIAM?   ☐ Yes   ☐ No

If Yes, complete section 3.

If No, please **answer question 2b.**

2b. Has a family mediator informed you that a mediator's exemption applies, and you do not need to attend a MIAM?   ☐ Yes   ☐ No

If Yes, you must ensure that the family mediator completes and signs section 4a.

If No, please **answer question 2c.**

2c. Have you attended a MIAM?   ☐ Yes   ☐ No

If Yes, you must ensure that the **family mediator completes and signs section 4b.**

If No, you cannot make this application.

3.   Applicant claims exemption(s) from attendance at a Mediation, Information and Assessment Meeting (MIAM)

(To be completed by the person intending to make a court application or their legal representative)

The applicant has not attended a MIAM because the following MIAM exemption(s) applies:

☐ Domestic violence (you must complete **section 3a**)

☐ Urgency (you must complete **section 3b**)

☐ Previous MIAM attendance or previous MIAM exemption (you must complete **section 3c**)

☐ Other (you must complete **section 3d**)

Now complete the relevant section 3a, b, c or d by ticking the appropriate box(es)

Further details of MIAM exemption(s) claimed by the applicant

If you have claimed a MIAM exemption above you must also tick the relevant box(es), as shown below to confirm that you have the necessary evidence to support your ground(s) for exemption and should bring it to the first hearing. Where you are asked to provide additional details you must do so.

Section 3a - Domestic violence evidence

The applicant confirms that there is evidence of domestic violence, as specified below:

☐ evidence that a prospective party has been arrested for a relevant domestic violence offence;

☐ evidence of a relevant police caution for a domestic violence offence;

☐ evidence of relevant criminal proceedings for a domestic violence offence which have not concluded;

☐ evidence of a relevant conviction for a domestic violence offence;

☐ a court order binding a prospective party over in connection with a domestic violence offence;

☐ a domestic violence protection notice issued under section 24 of the Crime and Security Act 2010 against a prospective party;

☐ a relevant protective injunction;

☐ an undertaking given in England and Wales under section 46 or 63E of the Family Law Act 1996 (or given in Scotland or Northern Ireland in place of a protective injunction) by a prospective party, provided that a cross-undertaking relating to domestic violence was not given by another prospective party;

☐ a copy of a finding of fact, made in proceedings in the United Kingdom, that there has been domestic violence by a prospective party;

☐ an expert report produced as evidence in proceedings in the United Kingdom for the benefit of a court or tribunal confirming that a person with whom a prospective party is or was in a family relationship, was assessed as being, or at risk of being, a victim of domestic violence by that prospective party;

8

Section 3a - Domestic violence evidence - **continued**

☐ a letter or report from an appropriate health professional confirming that-

    (i) that professional, or another appropriate health professional, has examined a prospective party in person; and

    (ii) in the reasonable professional judgment of the author or the examining appropriate health professional, that prospective party has, or has had, injuries or a condition consistent with being a victim of domestic violence;

☐ a letter or report from-

    (i) the appropriate health professional who made the referral described below;

    (ii) an appropriate health professional who has access to the medical records of the prospective party referred to below; or

    (iii) the person to whom the referral described below was made;

    confirming that there was a referral by an appropriate health professional of a prospective party to a person who provides specialist support or assistance for victims of, or those at risk of, domestic violence;

☐ a letter from any person who is a member of a multi-agency risk assessment conference (or other suitable local safeguarding forum) confirming that a prospective party, or a person with whom that prospective party is in a family relationship, is or has been at risk of harm from domestic violence by another prospective party;

☐ a letter from an independent domestic violence advisor confirming that they are providing support to a prospective party;

☐ a letter from an independent sexual violence advisor confirming that they are providing support to a prospective party relating to sexual violence by another prospective party;

☐ a letter from an officer employed by a local authority or housing association (or their equivalent in Scotland or Northern Ireland) for the purpose of supporting tenants containing-

    (i) a statement to the effect that, in their reasonable professional judgment, a person with whom a prospective party is or has been in a family relationship is, or is at risk of being, a victim of domestic violence by that prospective party;

    (ii) a description of the specific matters relied upon to support that judgment; and

    (iii) a description of the support they provided to the victim of domestic violence or the person at risk of domestic violence by that prospective party;

☐ a letter which-

    (i) is from an organisation providing domestic violence support services, or a registered charity, which letter confirms that it-

        (a) is situated in England and Wales,

        (b) has been operating for an uninterrupted period of six months or more; and

        (c) provided a prospective party with support in relation to that person's needs as a victim, or a person at risk, of domestic violence; and

    (ii) contains-

        (a) a statement to the effect that, in the reasonable professional judgment of the author of the letter, the prospective party is, or is at risk of being, a victim of domestic violence;

9

Section 3a - Domestic violence evidence - continued

    (b) a description of the specific matters relied upon to support that judgment;

    (c) a description of the support provided to the prospective party; and

    (d) a statement of the reasons why the prospective party needed that support;

☐ a letter or report from an organisation providing domestic violence support services in the United Kingdom confirming-

    (i) that a person with whom a prospective party is or was in a family relationship was refused admission to a refuge;

    (ii) the date on which they were refused admission to the refuge; and

    (iii) they sought admission to the refuge because of allegations of domestic violence by the prospective party referred to in paragraph (i);

☐ a letter from a public authority confirming that a person with whom a prospective party is or was in a family relationship, was assessed as being, or at risk of being, a victim of domestic violence by that prospective party (or a copy of that assessment);

☐ a letter from the Secretary of State for the Home Department confirming that a prospective party has been granted leave to remain in the United Kingdom under paragraph 289B of the Rules made by the Home Secretary under section 3(2) of the Immigration Act 1971, which can be found at https://www.gov.uk/guidance/immigration-rules/immigration-rules-index;

☐ evidence which demonstrates that a prospective party has been, or is at risk of being, the victim of domestic violence by another prospective party in the form of abuse which relates to financial matters.

Section 3b – Urgency

The applicant confirms that the application must be made urgently because:

☐ there is risk to the life, liberty or physical safety of the prospective applicant or his or her family or his or her home; or

☐ any delay caused by attending a MIAM would cause—

    ☐ a significant risk of a miscarriage of justice; or

    ☐ unreasonable hardship to the prospective applicant; or

    ☐ irretrievable problems in dealing with the dispute (including the irretrievable loss of significant evidence); or

☐ there is a significant risk that in the period necessary to schedule and attend a MIAM, proceedings relating to the dispute will be brought in another state in which a valid claim to jurisdiction may exist, such that a court in that other State would be seized of the dispute before a court in England and Wales.

Section 3c – Previous MIAM attendance or MIAM exemption

The applicant confirms that one of the following applies:

☐ in the 4 months prior to making the application, the person attended a MIAM or participated in another form of non-court dispute resolution relating to the same or substantially the same dispute; or

☐ at the time of making the application, the person is participating in another form of non-court dispute resolution relating to the same or substantially the same dispute; or

☐ in the 4 months prior to making the application, the person filed a relevant family application confirming that a MIAM exemption applied and that application related to the same or substantially the same dispute; or

Section 3c – Previous MIAM
attendance or MIAM exemption -
continued

☐ the application would be made in existing proceedings which are continuing
and the prospective applicant attended a MIAM before initiating those
proceedings; or

☐ the application would be made in existing proceedings which are continuing
and a MIAM exemption applied to the application for those proceedings.

Section 3d – Other exemptions

**The applicant confirms that one of the following other grounds for
exemption applies:**

☐ evidence that the prospective applicant is bankrupt exists in one of the
following forms:

☐ application by the prospective applicant for a bankruptcy order;

☐ petition by a creditor of the prospective applicant for a bankruptcy
order; or

☐ a bankruptcy order in respect of the prospective applicant.

☐ the prospective applicant does not have sufficient contact details for any of
the prospective respondents to enable a family mediator to contact any of
the prospective respondents for the purpose of scheduling the MIAM.

☐ the application would be made without notice (Paragraph 5.1 of Practice
Direction 18A sets out the circumstances in which applications may be made
without notice.)

☐ (i) the prospective applicant is or all of the prospective respondents are
subject to a disability or other inability that would prevent attendance at a
MIAM unless appropriate facilities can be offered by an authorised mediator;
(ii) the prospective applicant has contacted as many authorised family
mediators as have an office within fifteen miles of his or her home (or three
of them if there are three or more), and all have stated that they are unable
to provide such facilities; and (iii)the names, postal addresses and telephone
numbers or e-mail addresses for such authorised family mediators, and the
dates of contact, can be provided to the court if requested.

☐ the prospective applicant or all of the prospective respondents cannot
attend a MIAM because he or she is, or they are, as the case may be (i) in
prison or any other institution in which he or she is or they are required to be
detained; (ii) subject to conditions of bail that prevent contact with the other
person; or (iii) subject to a licence with a prohibited contact requirement in
relation to the other person.

☐ the prospective applicant or all of the prospective respondents are not
habitually resident in England and Wales.

☐ a child is one of the prospective parties by virtue of Rule 12.3(1).

☐ (i) the prospective applicant has contacted as many authorised family
mediators as have an office within fifteen miles of his or her home (or three
of them if there are three or more), and all of them have stated that they are
not available to conduct a MIAM within fifteen business days of the date
of contact; and (ii) the names, postal addresses and telephone numbers
or e-mail addresses for such authorised family mediators, and the dates of
contact, can be provided to the court if requested.

☐ there is no authorised family mediator with an office within fifteen miles of
the prospective applicant's home.

Now complete Section 5.

4. Mediator certifies that the prospective applicant is exempt from attendance at Mediation Information and Assessment Meeting (MIAM) or confirms MIAM attendance

(To be completed and signed by the authorised family mediator) (tick the boxes that apply)

4a.

The following MIAM exemption(s) applies:

☐ An authorised family mediator confirms that he or she is satisfied that -

  ☐ (a) mediation is not suitable as a means of resolving the dispute because none of the respondents is willing to attend a MIAM; or

  ☐ (b) mediation is not suitable as a means of resolving the dispute because all of the respondents failed without good reason to attend a MIAM appointment; or

  ☐ (c) mediation is otherwise not suitable as a means of resolving the dispute.

4b.

The prospective applicant attended a MIAM:

☐ The prospective applicant only attended a MIAM.

☐ The prospective applicant and respondent party(s) attended the MIAM together.

☐ The prospective applicant and respondent(s) have each attended a separate MIAM.

☐ The prospective respondent party(s) has/have made or is/are making arrangements to attend a separate MIAM.

Mediation or other form of Dispute Resolution is not proceeding because:

☐ The applicant has attended a MIAM alone and

- the applicant does not wish to start or continue mediation; or
- the mediator has determined that mediation is unsuitable; or
- the respondent did not wish to attend a MIAM

☐ Both the applicant and respondent have attended a MIAM (separately or together) and

- the applicant does not wish to start or continue mediation; or
- the respondent does not wish to start or continue mediation; or
- the mediator has determined that mediation is unsuitable

☐ Mediation has started, but has:

- broken down; or
- concluded with some or all issues unresolved

Signed _____

Authorised Family Mediator
(a family mediator who is authorised to undertake MIAMs)

FMC Registration no. _____

Family Mediation Service name _____

Sole trader name _____

Address _____

Dated [D D / M M / Y Y Y Y]

12

5. Signature

I am duly authorised by the applicant to sign this statement.

Print full name

Name of applicant solicitors firm
(if applicable)

Address of solicitor's firm
(if applicable)

Signed   Dated D D / M M / Y Y Y Y

*delete as appropriate   *(Applicant) (Litigation friend)
(Applicant's solicitor)

Position or office held
(If signing on behalf of firm or
company)

Checklist for completing Form A

Page 1
- ☐ Write in your full name
- ☐ Tick the nature of the financial application you are making and the type(s) or order you are seeking
- ☐ Tick if you are applying for an order by consent in the terms of a written agreement (a consent order).

Page 2 and 3
- ☐ Tick the relevant box(es) to provide further details about the order you are applying for, and provide additional information where shown.

Page 4
- ☐ Complete the details for service for the applicant and for the respondent.

Page 5
- ☐ Answer questions 2a to 2c about whether a MIAM exemption applies or whether you have attended a MIAM.

- ☐ If you answered question 2a on page 5 with "yes" you must tick one of the first four boxes in section 3 to indicate the category of MIAM exemption that you are claiming. You must then complete section 3a, b, c or d as shown.

Page 10
- ☐ If a family mediator needs to certify that a mediator's exemption applies you must ask them to complete section 4a of this form and sign where shown.

- ☐ If you have attended a MIAM you must ask the family mediator who conducted it to complete section 4b of the form and sign where shown.

Page 11
- ☐ Check that you (or your solicitor if relevant) have completed and signed section 5.

What you do next
You should normally make your application to the Designated Family Centre for your area. You can find this, and a full list of courts and what type of work they do online at courttribunalfinder.service.gov.uk

Fees
You may need to pay a fee with your application. You should read leaflet **EX50 Civil and family court fees** to find out what fee, if any, you need to pay. This leaflet is available from your local court or online at hmctsformfinder.justice.gov.uk

General information for completing this form

1. You need to complete this form if you want to ask the court to make one or more of the orders shown on page 1. You must tick the relevant boxes on page 1 to indicate the nature of your application and the type(s) of order you are seeking.

2. Pages 1 to 3 set out the core information you need to provide if you wish to make an application to the court. You or your solicitor must also sign and date Section 5 of this form.

3. If you are applying for an order by consent you should tick the box on page 1 to make this clear and attach the draft order with this application.

Requirement to attend a Mediation, Information and Assessment Meeting

4. It is now a legal requirement that, unless an exemption applies, a person who wishes to apply to court for a financial order must first attend a Mediation, Information and Assessment Meeting (a MIAM). At the stage before proceedings the other party (the respondent) is expected to attend either the same MIAM or a separate MIAM.

5. At the MIAM, a trained family mediator will give you (the applicant) and the other person if present (the respondent) information about family mediation and other types of non-court dispute resolution. They will consider with you whether non-court dispute resolution would be an appropriate way to resolve the dispute. It is then for the applicant and respondent to decide whether or not to do so.

6. The requirement for the applicant to attend a MIAM does not apply if a financial order is being applied for and the other person (respondent) is in agreement about what you are asking the court to order (the order is a "consent order").

7. You or your solicitor must tick the relevant box in Section 2 of this form so that the court knows whether the MIAM requirement applies, whether an exemption applies (and why) or whether you have attended a MIAM.

MIAM exemptions and MIAM attendance

8. As the applicant you are expected to have contacted an authorised family mediator in order to make arrangements to attend a MIAM unless :
   - the MIAM requirement does not apply for the reason explained at paragraph 6 of these notes, or

   - you are claiming a MIAM exemption, or a family mediator certifies that a mediator's exemption applies.

9. You can find an authorised family mediator by using the 'Find your local mediator' search facility available at: www.familymediationcouncil.org.uk

10. You should give the mediator the contact details of the other person so that the family mediator can contact them to check their willingness to attend a MIAM. If the other persons (or none of the other persons if there is more than one respondent) are unwilling to attend a MIAM this is a ground for the family mediator to exempt you from attending a MIAM.

11. If you or your solicitor believe that you have grounds for claiming exemption from MIAM attendance you or your solicitor must tick the relevant box in Section 2 of this form and complete Section 3.

12. If a family mediator wishes to certify that a mediator's exemption applies, so that you do not need to attend a MIAM, you must ask the family mediator to complete Section 4a of this form and sign it where shown.

13. If you have attended a MIAM you must ask the family mediator who conducted the MIAM to complete Section 4b of this form and sign it where shown.

14. If you claim a MIAM exemption and make an application to the court, the court will inquire into the grounds for exemption. The court may ask you to produce written evidence (see Section 3 of this form for details against each exemption shown).

15. If the court determines that the exemption was not validly claimed it may direct you, or you and the other party, to attend a MIAM and, if the case has already progressed to the first hearing, may adjourn the case to enable you to make arrangements to attend a MIAM.

16. The detailed procedure relating to the MIAM requirement and MIAM exemptions and attendance is set out in Part 3 of the Family Procedure Rules and in supporting Practice Direction 3A (judicial guidance). These are available online at: www.justice.gov.uk/courts/procedure-rules/family/practice_directions/pd_part_03a

Paying for MIAM attendance or for family mediation

17. Legal aid is available for MIAMs and for family mediation. If you are eligible for legal aid you could receive both the MIAM and mediation sessions free of charge, as well as some advice from a solicitor to support you in the mediation process.

18. If you, or the prospective respondent, is eligible for Legal Aid then the total cost of MIAM attendance can be met by the Legal Aid Agency, whether you and the prospective respondent attend the same MIAM or separate MIAMs.

19. If neither you nor the respective respondent is eligible for Legal Aid then the mediator will agree with you how the cost of MIAM attendance is to be met.

20. Please refer to paragraph 29 for further details on how you can find out whether you are eligible for Legal Aid by using the calculator tool available at www.gov.uk/legal-aid

Safety and MIAM attendance

21. Please note: the family mediator will discuss with you and with the other person whether you wish to attend the MIAM separately or together. Family mediators have a responsibility to ensure the safety and security of all concerned and will always check with each of you that attending together is your individual choice and is safe.

Information about mediation

22. If suitable, mediation can be a better way of resolving issues about financial arrangements when you or your partner petition for a matrimonial or civil partnership order. Mediation can be less expensive than going to court and much less stressful for all the family.

23. Family Mediation is an impartial process that involves an independent third person who assists both parties involved in a family dispute to reach a resolution. Family mediation can be used to settle any or all of the following issues:

    • Financial arrangements and dividing up property
    • Arrangements for children
    • Any combination of these
    • Any other disputes to do with separation and divorce.

24. The family mediator helps the process of negotiation between the parties to agree their own arrangements by way of a Memorandum of Understanding. You can ask a solicitor, if you have one, to check the Memorandum of Understanding.

25. If both parties agree, you can ask the court to endorse what you have agreed by issuing a consent order. The mediator will help you to decide whether your case is complicated and does in fact need the court to consider your situation and make an order. The mediator should also tell you about other local services and options for resolving your dispute.

26. A statutory Mediation Information and Assessment Meeting (MIAM) is reserved for "authorised mediators" under the Family Procedure Rules. "Authorised family mediator" means a person identified by the Family Mediation Council as qualified to conduct a MIAM. "Qualified to conduct a MIAM" is interpreted as holding current Family Mediation Council accreditation (FMCA). FMCA mediators are issued with a unique FMC registration number. Authorised mediators are requested to enter this number in the box provided.

Further information and sources of help

27. General information about family mediation is available from the Family Mediation Council website at: www.familymediationcouncil.org.uk

28. The family mediator who undertakes the MIAM for you must be a member of a national mediation organisation which adheres to the Family Mediation Council's Code of Conduct and the mediator must be authorised to conduct MIAMs. The service finder will help you find such a local mediator.

29. You can find out more about legal aid for family matters, including whether you may eligible for legal aid on the Legal Aid Information Service on the Gov. UK site at: www.gov.uk/check-legal-aid or you can telephone the Civil Legal Advice direct helpline 0345 345 4345.

30. For general advice on separation services and options for resolving disputes: www.sortingoutseparation.org.uk

31. For help with taking a case to court without a lawyer, the Personal Support Unit: www.thepsu.org/

32. For guidance on representing yourself at court, including a list of commonly used terms that you may come across: http://www.barcouncil.org.uk/using-a-barrister/representing-yourself-in-court/

33. For advice about finding and using a family law solicitor see: Law Society www.lawsociety.org.uk, and Resolution (family law solicitors): www.resolution.org.uk

34. For advice about finding a family law barrister: see http://www.barcouncil.org.uk/using-a-barrister/find-a-barrister/ and for arrangements for using a barrister directly see http://www.barcouncil.org.uk/using-a-barrister/how-to-instruct-a-barrister/

(C) Form E (Statement for a financial order)

Financial statement

- For a financial order under the Matrimonial Causes Act 1973/ Civil Partnership Act 2004
- For financial relief after an overseas divorce etc under Part 3 of the Matrimonial and Family Proceedings Act 1984/Schedule 7 to the Civil Partnership Act 2004

To be completed by the relevant party	
Name of court	Case No.
Name of Applicant	
Name of Respondent	

of

_____

(please tick appropriate boxes)

☐ Spouse   ☐ Civil partner

Dated ☐ ☐ / ☐ ☐ / ☐ ☐ ☐ ☐

The parties are

_____ and _____

Who is the	Who is the
☐ Spouse ☐ civil partner	☐ Spouse ☐ civil partner
☐ Petitioner ☐ Applicant ☐ Respondent in the	☐ Petitioner ☐ Applicant ☐ Respondent in the
☐ divorce ☐ dissolution ☐ nullity	☐ divorce ☐ dissolution ☐ nullity
☐ (judicial) separation ☐ financial relief application	☐ (judicial) separation ☐ financial relief application
Applicant in this matter	Respondent in this matter

This form should only be completed in applications for a financial order (which can only be applied for as part of a divorce, dissolution, annulment or (judicial) separation in the High Court or family courts in England and Wales) or for applications for financial relief after an overseas divorce/dissolution etc. If the application is for any other financial remedy please complete Form E1. If the application is for a variation of an order for a financial remedy please complete Form E2.

Please fill in this form fully and accurately. Where any box is not applicable, write 'N/A'.

You have a duty to the court to give a full, frank and clear disclosure of all your financial and other relevant circumstances.

A failure to give full and accurate disclosure may result in any order the court makes being set aside.

If you are found to have been deliberately untruthful, criminal proceedings may be brought against you for fraud under the Fraud Act 2006.

The information given in this form must be confirmed by a statement of truth. **Proceedings for contempt of court may be brought against a person who makes or causes to be made, a false statement in a document verified by a statement of truth.**

You must attach documents to the form where they are specifically sought and you may attach other documents where it is necessary to explain or clarify any of the information that you give.

Essential documents that must accompany this statement are detailed in the form.

If there is not enough room on the form for any particular piece of information, you may continue on an attached sheet of paper.

If you are in doubt about how to complete any part of this form you should seek legal advice.

This statement is filed by _____

Solicitor's fee account no.	

Name and address of solicitor

1   General Information

1.1   Full name

1.2   Date of birth

Date	Month	Year

1.3   Date of the marriage/ civil partnership

Date	Month	Year

1.4   Occupation

1.5   Date of the separation

Date	Month	Year

Tick here if not applicable ☐

1.6   Date of the

Petition for divorce/ dissolution/nullity/ (judicial) separation			Decree nisi/ conditional order/ (judicial) separation order			Decree absolute/ final order (if applicable)		
Date	Month	Year	Date	Month	Year	Date	Month	Year

1.7   If you have subsequently married or formed a civil partnership, or will do so, state the date

Date	Month	Year

1.8   Are you living with a new partner?   Yes ☐   No ☐

1.9   Do you intend to live with a new partner within the next six months?   Yes ☐   No ☐

1.10   Details of any children of the family

Full names	Date of birth			With whom does the child live?
	Date	Month	Year	

1.11   Details of the state of health of yourself and the children if you think this should be taken into account

Yourself	Children

1.12 Details of the present and proposed future educational arrangements for the children.

Present arrangements	Future arrangements

1.13 Details of any child support maintenance calculation or any maintenance order or agreement made in respect of any children of the family. If no calculation, order or agreement has been made, give an estimate of the liability of the non-resident parent in respect of the children of the family under the Child Support Act 1991.

1.14 If this application is to vary an order, attach a copy of the order and give details of the part that is to be varied and the changes sought. You may need to continue on a separate sheet.

1.15 Details of any other court cases between you and your spouse/civil partner, whether in relation to money, property, children or anything else.

Case No	Court	Type of proceedings

1.16 Your present residence and the occupants of it and on what terms you occupy it (e.g. tenant, owner-occupier).

Address	Occupants	Terms of occupation

2 Financial Details

Part 1 Real Property (land and buildings) and Personal Assets

2.1 Complete this section in respect of the family home (the last family home occupied by you and your spouse/civil partner) if it remains unsold.

> Documentation required for attachment to this section:
>
> a) A copy of any valuation of the property obtained within the last six months. If you cannot provide this document, please give your own realistic estimate of the current market value
>
> b) A recent mortgage statement confirming the sum outstanding on **each** mortgage

Property name and address	
Land Registry title number	
Mortgage company name(s) and address(es) and account number(s)	
Type of mortgage	
Details of who owns the property and the extent of your legal and beneficial interest in it (i.e. state if it is owned by you solely or jointly owned with your spouse/civil partner or with others)	
If you consider that the legal ownership as recorded at the Land Registry does not reflect the true position, state why	
Current market value of the property	
Balance(s) outstanding on any mortgage(s)	
If a sale at this stage would result in penalties payable under the mortgage, state amount	
Estimate the costs of sale of the property	
Total equity in the property (i.e. market value less outstanding mortgage(s), penalties if any and the costs of sale)	

TOTAL value of your interest in the family home: Total A £

2.2 Details of your interest in any other property, land or buildings. Complete one page for each property you have an interest in.

> Documentation required for attachment to this section:
> a)   A copy of any valuation of the property obtained within the last six months. If you cannot provide this document, please give your own realistic estimate of the current market value
> b)   A recent mortgage statement confirming the sum outstanding on **each** mortgage

Property name and address	
Land Registry title number	
Mortgage company name(s) and address(es) and account number(s)	
Type of mortgage	
Details of who owns the property and the extent of your legal and beneficial interest in it (i.e. state if it is owned by you solely or jointly owned with your spouse/civil partner or with others)	
If you consider that the legal ownership as recorded at the Land Registry does not reflect the true position, state why	
Current market value of the property	
Balance outstanding on any mortgage(s)	
If a sale at this stage would result in penalties payable under the mortgage, state amount	
Estimate the costs of sale of the property	
Total equity in the property (i.e. market value less outstanding mortgage(s), penalties if any and the costs of sale)	
Total value of your interest in this property	

TOTAL value of your interest in ALL other property: Total B   £

2.3 Details of all personal bank, building society and National Savings Accounts that you hold or have held at any time in the last twelve months and which are or were either in your own name or in which you have or have had any interest. This applies whether any such account is in credit or in debit. For joint accounts give your interest and the name of the other account holder. If the account is overdrawn, show a minus figure.

> Documentation required for attachment to this section:
> For each account listed, all statements covering the last 12 months.

Name of bank or building society, including branch name	Type of account (e.g. current)	Account number	Name of other account holder (if applicable)	Balance at the date of this statement	Total current value of your interest

TOTAL value of your interest in ALL accounts: (C1) | £

2.4 Details of all investments, including shares, PEPs, ISAs, TESSAs, National Savings Investments (other than already shown above), bonds, stocks, unit trusts, investment trusts, gilts and other quoted securities that you hold or have an interest in. (Do not include dividend income as this will be dealt with separately later on.)

> Documentation required for attachment to this section:
> Latest statement or dividend counterfoil relating to each investment.

Name	Type of Investment	Size of Holding	Current value	Name of any other account holder (if applicable)	Total current value of your interest

TOTAL value of your interest in ALL holdings: (C2) | £

6

2.5 Details of all life insurance policies including endowment policies that you hold or have an interest in. Include those that do not have a surrender value. Complete one page for each policy.

Documentation required for attachment to this section: A surrender valuation of each policy that has a surrender value.

Name of company			
Policy type			
Policy number			
If policy is assigned, state in whose favour and amount of charge			
Name of any other owner and the extent of your interest in the policy			
Maturity date (if applicable)	Date	Month	Year
Current surrender value (if applicable)			
If policy includes life insurance, the amount of the insurance and the name of the person whose life is insured			
Total current surrender value of your interest in this policy			

TOTAL value of your interest in ALL policies: (C3) £

2.6 Details of all monies that are OWED TO YOU. Do not include sums owed in director's or partnership accounts which should be included at section 2.11.

Brief description of money owed and by whom	Balance outstanding	Total current value of your interest

TOTAL value of your interest in ALL debts owed to you: (C4) £

2.7   Details of all cash sums held in excess of £500. You must state where it is held and the currency it is held in.

Where held	Amount	Currency	Total current value of your interest

TOTAL value of your interest in ALL cash sums: (C5)	£

2.8   Details of personal belongings individually worth more than £500.

INCLUDE:

- Cars (gross value)
- Collections, pictures and jewellery
- Furniture and house contents

Brief description of item	Total current value of your interest

TOTAL value of your interest in ALL personal belongings: (C6)	£
Add together all the figures in boxes C1 to C6 to give the TOTAL current value of your interest in personal assets: TOTAL C	£

2 Financial Details   Part 2 Capital: Liabilities and Capital Gains Tax

2.9 Details of any liabilities you have.

EXCLUDE liabilities already shown such as:
- Mortgages
- Any overdrawn bank, building society or National Savings accounts

INCLUDE:
- Money owed on credit cards and store cards
- Bank loans
- Hire purchase agreements

List all credit and store cards held including those with a nil or positive balance. Where the liability is not solely your own, give the name(s) of the other account holder(s) and the amount of your share of the liability.

Liability	Name(s) of other account holder(s) (if applicable)	Total liability	Total current value of your interest in the liability

TOTAL value of your interest in ALL liabilities: (D1)	£

2.10 If any Capital Gains Tax would be payable on the disposal now of any of your real property or personal assets, give your estimate of the tax liability.

Asset	Total Capital Gains Tax liability

TOTAL value of ALL your potential Capital Gains Tax liabilities: (D2)	£
Add together D1 and D2 to give the TOTAL value of your liabilities: TOTAL D	£

2 Financial Details   Part 3 Capital: Business assets and directorships

2.11 Details of all your business interests. Complete one page for each business you have an interest in.

> Documentation required for attachment to this section:
> a) Copies of the business accounts for the last two financial years
> b) Any documentation, if available at this stage, upon which you have based your estimate of the current value of your interest in this business, for example a letter from an accountant or a formal valuation.
>   It is not essential to obtain a formal valuation at this stage

Name of the business	
Briefly describe the nature of the business	
Are you (please tick appropriate box)	☐ Sole trader ☐ Partner in a partnership with others ☐ Shareholder in a limited company
If you are a partner or a shareholder, state the extent of your interest in the business (i.e. partnership share or the extent of your shareholding compared to the overall shares issued)	
State when your next set of accounts will be available	
If any of the figures in the last accounts are not an accurate reflection of the current position, state why. For example, if there has been a material change since the last accounts, or if the valuations of the assets are not a true reflection of their value (e.g. because property or other assets have not been re-valued in recent years or because they are shown at a book value)	
Total amount of any sums owed to you by the business by way of a director's loan account, partnership capital or current accounts or the like. Identify where these appear in the business accounts	
Your estimate of the current value of your business interest. Explain briefly the basis upon which you have reached that figure	
Your estimate of any Capital Gains Tax that would be payable if you were to dispose of your business now	
Net value of your interest in this business after any Capital Gains Tax liability	

TOTAL value of ALL your interests in business assets: TOTAL E   £

2.12 List any directorships you hold or have held in the last 12 months (other than those already disclosed in Section 2.11).

2 Financial Details

Part 4 Capital: Pensions and Pension Protection Fund (PPF) Compensation

2.13 Give details of all your pension rights and all PPF compensation entitlements, including prospective entitlements. Complete a separate page for each pension or PPF compensation entitlement.

EXCLUDE:
- Basic State Pension

INCLUDE (complete a separate page for each one):
- Additional State Pension (SERPS and State Second Pension (S2P))
- Free Standing Additional Voluntary Contribution Schemes (FSAVC) separate from the scheme of your employer
- Membership of ALL pension plans or schemes
- PPF compensation entitlement for each scheme you were a member of which has transferred to PPF

Documentation required for attachment to this section:

a) A recent statement showing the cash equivalent (CE) provided by the trustees or managers of each pension arrangement; for the additional state pension, a valuation of these rights or for PPF a valuation of PPF compensation entitlement

b) If any valuation is not available, give the estimated date when it will be available and attach a copy of your letter to the pension company, administrators, or PPF Board from whom the information was sought and/or state the date on which an application for a valuation of an Additional State Pension was submitted to the Department of Work and Pensions

Name and address of pension arrangement or PPF Board	
Your National Insurance Number	
Number of pension arrangement or reference number or PPF compensation reference number	
Type of scheme e.g. occupational or personal, final salary, money purchase, additional state pension, PPF or other (if other, please give details)	

	Date	Month	Year
Date the CE, PPF compensation or additional state pension was calculated			

Is the pension in payment or drawdown? (please answer Yes or No)	☐ Yes ☐ No
State the CE quotation, the additional state pension valuation or PPF valuation of those rights	
If the arrangement is an occupational pension arrangement that is paying reduced CEs, please quote what the CE would have been if not reduced. If this is not possible, please indicate if the CE quoted is a reduced CE	
Is the PPF compensation capped? (please answer Yes or No)	☐ Yes ☐ No

TOTAL value of ALL your pension assets: TOTAL F £

2 Financial Details   Part 5 Capital: Other assets

2.14 Give details of any other assets not listed in Parts 1 to 4 above.

INCLUDE (the following list is not exhaustive):

- Any personal or business assets not yet disclosed
- Unrealisable assets
- Share option schemes, stating the estimated net sale proceeds of the shares if the options were capable of exercise now, and whether Capital Gains Tax or income tax would be payable
- Business expansion schemes
- Futures
- Commodities
- Trust interests (including interests under a discretionary trust), stating your estimate of the value of the interest and when it is likely to become realisable. If you say it will never be realisable, or has no value, give your reasons
- Any asset that is likely to be received in the foreseeable future
- Any asset held on your behalf by a third party
- Any asset not disclosed elsewhere on this form even if held outside England and Wales

You are reminded of your obligation to disclose all your financial assets and interests of ANY nature.

Type of asset	Value	Total NET value of your interest

TOTAL value of ALL your other assets: TOTAL G £

13

2   Financial Details   Part 6 Income: Earned income from employment

2.15 Details of earned income from employment. Complete one page for each employment.

Documentation required for attachment to this section:
a)   P60 for the last financial year (you should have received this from your employer shortly after the last 5th April)
b)   Your last three payslips
c)   Your last Form P11D if you have been issued with one

Name and address of your employer	
Job title and brief details of the type of work you do	
Hours worked per week in this employment	
How long have you been with this employer?	
Explain the basis of your income i.e. state whether it is based on an annual salary or an hourly rate of pay and whether it includes commissions or bonuses	
Gross income for the last financial year as shown on your P60	
Net income for the last financial year i.e. gross income less income tax and national insurance	
Average net income for the last three months i.e. total income less income tax and national insurance divided by three	
Briefly explain any other entries on the attached payslips other than basic income, income tax and national insurance	
If the payslips attached for the last three months are not an accurate reflection of your normal income briefly explain why	
Details and value of any bonuses or other occasional payments that you receive from this employment not otherwise already shown, including the basis upon which they are paid	
Details and value of any benefits in kind, perks or other remuneration received from this employer in the last year (e.g. provision of a car, payment of travel, accommodation, meal expenses, etc.)	
Your estimate of your net income from this employment for the next 12 months. If this differs significantly from your current income explain why in box 4.1.2	

Estimated TOTAL of ALL net earned income from employment for the next 12 months: TOTAL H   £

2 Financial Details

Part 7 Income: Income from self-employment or partnership

2.16 You will have already given details of your business and provided the last two years accounts at section 2.11. Complete this section giving details of your income from your business. Complete one page for each business.

Documentation required for attachment to this section:

a) A copy of your last tax assessment or, if that is not available, a letter from your accountant confirming your tax liability

b) If net income from the last financial year and estimated net income for the next 12 months is significantly different, a copy of management accounts for the period since your last account

Name of the business	
Date to which your last accounts were completed	
Your share of gross business profit from the last completed accounts	
Income tax and national insurance payable on your share of gross business profit above	
Net income for that year (using the two figures directly above, gross business profit less income tax and national insurance payable)	
Details and value of any benefits in kind, perks or other remuneration received from this business in the last year e.g. provision of a car, payment of travel, accommodation, meal expenses, etc.	
Amount of any regular monthly or other drawings that you take from this business	
If the estimated figure directly below is different from the net income as at the end date of the last completed accounts, briefly explain the reason(s)	
Your estimate of your net annual income for the next 12 months	

Estimated TOTAL of ALL net income from self-employment or partnership for the next 12 months: TOTAL I | £

15

2 Financial Details

Part 8 Income: Income from investments
e.g. dividends, interest or rental income

2.17 Details of income received in the last financial year (the year ended last 5th April), and your
estimate of your income for the current financial year. Indicate whether the income was paid gross
or net of income tax. You are not required to calculate any tax payable that may arise.

Nature of income and the asset from which it derived	Paid gross or net	Income received in the last financial year	Estimated income for the next 12 months

Estimated TOTAL investment income for the next 12 months: TOTAL J   **£**

2 Financial Details

Part 9 Income: Income from state benefits (including state pension and child benefit)

2.18 Details of all state benefits that you are currently receiving.

Name of benefit	Amount paid	Frequency of payment	Estimated income for the next 12 months

Estimated TOTAL benefit income for the next 12 months: TOTAL K	£

2 Financial Details   Part 10 Income: Any other income

2.19 Details of any other income not disclosed above.

INCLUDE:

Any source including a Pension (excluding State Pension), and Pension Protection Fund (PPF) compensation

- from which income has been received during the last 12 months (even if it has now ceased)
- from which income is likely to be received during the next 12 months

You are reminded of your obligation to give full disclosure of your financial circumstances

Nature of income	Paid gross or net	Income received in the last financial year	Estimated income for the next 12 months

Estimated TOTAL other income for the next 12 months: TOTAL L **£**

2 Financial Details   Summaries

2.20 Summary of your capital (Parts 1 to 5).

Description	Reference of the section on this statement	Value
Current value of your interest in the family home	A	
Current value of your interest in all other property	B	
Current value of your interest in personal assets	C	
Current value of your interest in business assets	E	
Current value of your pension and PPF compensation assets	F	
Current value of all your other assets	G	
Total value of your assets (Totals A+B+C+E+F+G)		£
Current value of your liabilities	D	
Value of your assets **LESS** the value of your liabilities (Totals A+B+C+E+F+G – D)		£

2.21 Summary of your estimated income for the next 12 months (Parts 6 to 10).

Description	Reference of the section on this statement	Value
Estimated net total of income from employment	H	
Estimated net total of income from self-employment or partnership	I	
Estimated net total of investment income	J	
Estimated state benefit receipts	K	
Estimated net total of all other income	L	
Estimated TOTAL income for the next 12 months (Totals H to L):		£

19

3 Financial Requirements   Part 1 Income needs

3.1   Income needs for yourself and for any children living with you or provided for by you. ALL figures should be annual, monthly or weekly (state which). You ***must not*** use a combination of these periods. State your current income needs and, if these are likely to change in the near future, explain the anticipated change and give an estimate of the future cost.

The income needs below are: (delete those not applicable)	Weekly	Monthly	Annual
I anticipate my income needs are going to change because			

3.1.1 Income needs for yourself.

INCLUDE:

- All income needs for yourself
- Income needs for any children living with you or provided for by you only if these form part of your total income needs (e.g. housing, fuel, car expenses, holidays, etc)

Item	Current cost	Estimated future cost
SUB-TOTAL your income needs	£	

3.1.2 Income needs for children living with you or provided for by you.

INCLUDE:
- Only those income needs that are different to those of your household shown above

Item	Current cost	Estimated future cost
SUB-TOTAL children's income needs:	£	
TOTAL of ALL income needs:	£	

20

3 Financial Requirements   Part 2 Capital needs

3.2 Set out below the reasonable future capital needs for yourself and for any children living with you or provided for by you.

3.2.1 Capital needs for yourself.

INCLUDE:
- All capital needs for yourself
- Capital needs for any children living with you or provided for by you only if these form part of your total capital needs (e.g. housing, car, etc.)

Item	Cost
SUB-TOTAL your capital needs:	£

3.2.2 Capital needs for children living with you or provided for by you.

INCLUDE:
- Only those capital needs that are different to those of your household shown above

Item	Cost
SUB-TOTAL your children's capital needs	£
TOTAL of ALL capital needs:	£

4 Other Information

4.1   Details of any significant changes in your assets or income.

At both sections 4.1.1 and 4.1.2, INCLUDE:
- ALL assets held both within and outside England and Wales
- The disposal of any asset

4.1.1 Significant changes in assets or income during the LAST 12 months.

4.1.2 Significant changes in assets or income likely to occur during the NEXT 12 months.

4.2   Brief details of the standard of living enjoyed by you and your spouse/civil partner during the marriage/civil partnership.

4.3 Are there any particular contributions to the family property and assets or outgoings, or to family life, or the welfare of the family that have been made by you, your partner or anyone else that you think should be taken into account? If there are any such items, briefly describe the contribution and state the amount, when it was made and by whom.

INCLUDE:

- Contributions already made
- Contributions that will be made in the foreseeable future

4.4 Bad behaviour or conduct by the other party will only be taken into account in very exceptional circumstances when deciding how assets should be shared after divorce/dissolution. If you feel it should be taken into account in your case, identify the nature of the behaviour or conduct below.

4.5 Give details of any other circumstances that you consider could significantly affect the extent of the financial provision to be made by or for you or any child of the family.

INCLUDE (the following list is not exhaustive):

- Earning capacity
- Disability
- Inheritance prospects
- Redundancy
- Retirement
- Any agreement made between you and your spouse/civil partner before or after your marriage/civil partnership stating whether or not you rely upon the agreement giving your reasons
- Any plans to marry, form a civil partnership or live with a new partner
- Any contingent liabilities

4.6   If you have subsequently married or formed a civil partnership (or intend to) or are living with another person (or intend to), give brief details, so far as they are known to you, of his or her income, assets and liabilities.

Annual Income		Assets and Liabilities	
Nature of income	Value (if known, state whether gross or net)	Item	Value (if known)
Total income: £		Total assets/liabilities: £	

24

5 Order Sought

5.1 If you are able at this stage, specify what kind of orders you are asking the court to make.
Even if you cannot be specific at this stage, if you are able to do so, indicate:

a) If the family home is still owned, whether you are asking for it to be transferred to yourself or your spouse/civil partner or whether you are saying it should be sold

b) Whether you consider this is a case for continuing spousal maintenance/maintenance for your civil partner or whether you see the case as being appropriate for a 'clean break' *(A 'clean break' means a settlement or order which provides amongst other things, that neither you nor your spouse/civil partner will have any further claim against the income or capital of the other party. A 'clean break' does not terminate the responsibility of a parent to a child.)*

c) Whether you are seeking a
   i) pension sharing order
   ii) pension attachment order
   iii) pension compensation sharing order
   iv) pension compensation attachment order

d) If you are seeking a transfer or settlement of any property or assets, identify the property or assets in question

5.2 If you are seeking a variation of an ante-nuptial or post-nuptial settlement or a relevant settlement made during, or in anticipation of, a civil partnership, identify the settlement, by whom it was made, its trustees and beneficiaries and state why you allege it is a settlement which the court can vary.

5.3 If you are seeking an avoidance of disposition order, or if you have already applied for such an order, identify the property to which the disposition relates and the person or body in whose favour the disposition is alleged to have been made.

Statement of Truth

*delete as appropriate

*[I believe] [the Applicant/Respondent believes] that the facts stated in this statement are true

*I am duly authorised by the Applicant/Respondent to sign this statement

and confirm that the information given above is a full, frank, clear and accurate disclosure of my financial and other relevant circumstances.

Print full name	
Address for service	
	Postcode
Name of Applicant's/ Respondent's solicitor's firm	

Signed		Dated D D / M M / Y Y Y Y

*(Applicant/Respondent) (Litigation friend)
*(Applicant's/Respondent's solicitor)

Position or office held
(if signing on behalf of
firm or company)

Proceedings for contempt of court may be brought against a person who makes or causes to be made, a false statement in a document verified by a statement of truth.

Address all communications to the Court Manager of the Court and quote the case number.
If you do not quote this number, your correspondence may be returned.

Schedule of Documents to accompany Form E

The following list shows the documents you must attach to your Form E if applicable. You may attach other documents where it is necessary to explain or clarify any of the information that you give in the Form E.

Form E paragraph	Document	Please tick		
		Attached	Not applicable	To follow
1.14	**Application to vary an order:** if applicable, attach a copy of the relevant order.	☐	☐	☐
2.1	**Matrimonial home valuation:** a copy of any valuation relating to the matrimonial home that has been obtained in the last six months.	☐	☐	☐
2.1	**Matrimonial home mortgage(s):** a recent mortgage statement in respect of each mortgage on the matrimonial home confirming the amount outstanding.	☐	☐	☐
2.2	**Any other property:** a copy of any valuation relating to each other property disclosed that has been obtained in the last six months.	☐	☐	☐
2.2	**Any other property:** a recent mortgage statement in respect of each mortgage on each other property disclosed confirming the amount outstanding.	☐	☐	☐
2.3	**Personal bank, building society and National Savings accounts:** copies of statements for the last 12 months for each account that has been held in the last twelve months, either in your own name or in which you have or have had any interest.	☐	☐	☐
2.4	**Other investments:** the latest statement or dividend counterfoil relating to each investment as disclosed in paragraph 2.4.	☐	☐	☐
2.5	**Life insurance (including endowment) policies:** a surrender valuation for each policy that has a surrender value as disclosed under paragraph 2.5.	☐	☐	☐
2.11	**Business interests:** a copy of the business accounts for the last two financial years for each business interest disclosed.	☐	☐	☐
2.11	**Business interests:** any documentation that is available to confirm the estimate of the current value of the business, for example, a letter from an accountant or formal valuation if that has been obtained.	☐	☐	☐
2.13	**Pension and PPF compensation:** a recent statement showing the cash equivalent (CE) provided by the trustees or managers of each pension arrangement or valuation of each PPF entitlement provided by the PPF Board that you have disclosed (or, in the case of the additional state pension, a valuation of these rights). If not yet available, attach a copy of the letter sent to the pension company, administrators or the PPF Board requesting the information.	☐	☐	☐
2.15	**Employment income:** your P60 for the last financial year in respect of each employment that you have.	☐	☐	☐
2.15	**Employment income:** your last three payslips in respect of each employment that you have.	☐	☐	☐
2.15	**Employment income:** your last form P11D if you have been issued with one.	☐	☐	☐
2.16	**Self-employment or partnership income:** a copy of your last tax assessment or if that is not available, a letter from your accountant confirming your tax liability.	☐	☐	☐
2.16	**Self-employment or partnership income:** if net income from the last financial year and the estimated income for the next twelve months is significantly different, a copy of the management accounts for the period since your last accounts.	☐	☐	☐
State relevant Form E paragraph	Description of other documents attached:	☐	☐	☐

(D)   Form D81 (Statement of information for a consent order)

Statement of information for a consent order in relation to a financial remedy

To be completed by the parties	
Name of court	Case No.
Name of Petitioner/Applicant	
Name of Respondent	

If completing this form by hand, please use **black ink and BLOCK CAPITAL LETTERS** and tick the boxes that apply.

You may complete separate forms if you wish. However both parties must confirm they have read the contents of each statement of information.

Details of the marriage/civil partnership

1. Please give the date of the ☐ marriage ☐ civil partnership   D D / M M / Y Y Y Y

2. On what date did you separate?   D D / M M / Y Y Y Y

3. On what date was your decree nisi/conditional order of divorce/ dissolution/nullity or (judicial) separation decree/order pronounced?   D D / M M / Y Y Y Y

    (Please note that a consent order cannot be made until the court has pronounced a decree nisi/conditional order unless it is a consent order for maintenance pending suit.)

4. On what date was your decree absolute/final order of divorce/ dissolution/nullity granted?   D D / M M / Y Y Y Y

    If this has not yet been pronounced please write 'not applicable'

Dates of birth of the parties

5. Please give the date of birth of the parties along with the date of birth of any child(ren) of the family aged under 18, or any other child(ren) dependant upon the family.

    Date of birth

    Petitioner/ Applicant   D D / M M / Y Y Y Y

    Respondent   D D / M M / Y Y Y Y

    Child(ren) (if applicable)   D D / M M / Y Y Y Y   D D / M M / Y Y Y Y   D D / M M / Y Y Y Y

    D D / M M / Y Y Y Y   D D / M M / Y Y Y Y   D D / M M / Y Y Y Y

Financial agreements

6. Please state how the attached proposed consent order was reached e.g. discussions between parties, negotiations through solicitors, Mediation, Collaborative Process or other out of court dispute resolution process.

Summary of means

The information in this section should so far as possible be correct as at the time this statement is signed.

The information should therefore be stated before implementation of the proposed consent order.

If the application is made only for an order for interim periodical payments or for variation of an order for periodical payments, you need only give details of 'net income'.

Capital

7. Please give the following information for each party and the child(ren) (if applicable). Use additional sheets if necessary. Jointly owned capital should be divided as appropriate and listed below. If no agreement has been reached regarding shares, it should be divided equally.

Type of capital	Petitioner/Applicant	Respondent	Child(ren) if applicable
a. Property (net of any mortgage(s))	£	£	£
b. Other capital e.g. savings, investments, ISAs etc	£	£	£
c. Gross capital (a. plus b.)	£	£	£
d. Liabilities (excluding mortgages deducted at a.) e.g. loans and overdrafts	£	£	£
e. Net capital excluding pensions and Pension Protection Fund (PPF) compensation (c. less d.)	£	£	£
f. Pensions valuation including the Additional State Pension (cash equivalent)	£	£	£
g. PPF compensation valuation	£	£	£
h. Total capital (e. plus f. plus g.)	£	£	£

Income

8. Please state for each party, their total **net** (after deductions for tax and NI contributions only) monthly income from all sources e.g. wages, state benefits, child support and maintenance payments, pension or PPF compensation payments, interest from bank accounts, tips etc.

Petitioner/Applicant	£
Respondent	£
Child(ren) (if applicable)	£

9. Are there any other matters relating to the proposed consent order that the court should consider e.g. medical conditions, change of employment, any significant change in circumstances, any prior agreement reached between the parties etc?

Where the parties and the children will live

10. Please give details of where the named parties will live and the basis on which you will occupy the property e.g. owner, tenant etc.

	Address	Basis of occupation in property
Petitioner/Applicant		
Respondent		
Child(ren) (if applicable)		

New relationships

11. Please tick the appropriate box below

Petitioner/Applicant

☐ I have no intention at present to remarry/enter into a new civil partnership or cohabit.

☐ I have remarried/formed a civil partnership.
The date of the marriage/civil partnership was [D D / M M / Y Y Y Y]

☐ I intend to remarry/form a civil partnership.
The date of the intended marriage/civil partnership is [D D / M M / Y Y Y Y]

☐ I am in a cohabiting relationship with another person.

☐ I intend to cohabit.

Respondent

☐ I have no intention at present to remarry/enter into a new civil partnership or cohabit.

☐ I have remarried/formed a civil partnership.
The date of the marriage/civil partnership was [D D / M M / Y Y Y Y]

☐ I intend to remarry/form a civil partnership.
The date of the intended marriage/civil partnership is [D D / M M / Y Y Y Y]

☐ I am in a cohabiting relationship with another person.

☐ I intend to cohabit.

continued over the page ⇨

3

Notice to mortgagee

These questions are to be answered by the Petitioner/Applicant where the terms of the order provide for a transfer of property.

12. Has every mortgagee (if any) of the property been served with notice of the application?

    ☐ Yes   ☐ No

13. Has any objection to a transfer of property been made by any mortgagee, within 14 days from the date when the notice of the application was served?

    ☐ Yes   ☐ No

Notice to pension arrangement/PPF Board

Question 14 is to be answered by the Petitioner/Applicant where the terms of an order include provision for a pension attachment order and/or a PPF pension compensation attachment order. Question 15 is to be answered by the Petitioner/Applicant only where the terms of the order include provision for a pension attachment order.

(Please note that if you wish to include provision relating to a pension or to PPF compensation in your consent order you should first seek legal advice as this area of law is complex. Court staff are unable to assist, as they are not trained to give legal advice.)

14. Has notice been served on every person responsible for any pension arrangement under Rules 9.33(1) or 9.34, and/or the PPF Board under 9.42 or 9.43 of the Family Procedure Rules 2010?

    ☐ Yes   ☐ No

15. Has any objection to an attachment order been made by the person responsible for the pension arrangements within 21 days from the date when the notice of the application was served?

    ☐ Yes   ☐ No

Pension or PPF compensation sharing on divorce, dissolution or nullity

These questions are to be answered by the Petitioner/Applicant where the terms of an order include provision for a pension or a PPF compensation sharing order.

(Please note that if you wish to include provision relating to a pension or a PPF compensation in your consent order you should first seek legal advice. Court staff are unable to assist, as they are not trained to give legal advice.)

16. (For pension sharing only) Has the Pension Arrangement furnished the information required by Regulation 4 of the Pensions on Divorce etc. (Provision of Information) Regulations 2000?

    ☐ Yes   ☐ No

    (For PPF compensation sharing only) Has the PPF Board provided the information required by Regulation 5 of The Pension Protection Fund (Pension Compensation Sharing and Attachment on Divorce etc) Regulations 2011?

    ☐ Yes   ☐ No

4

17. (For pension sharing only) Does it appear from that information that there is power to make an order including provision under section 24B of the Matrimonial Causes Act 1973 or under paragraph 15 of Schedule 5 to the Civil Partnership Act 2004 (Pension Sharing)?

☐ Yes   ☐ No

(For PPF compensation sharing only) Does it appear from that information that there is power to make an order for compensation sharing?

☐ Yes   ☐ No

Proposed consent order

Please ensure that you attach the proposed consent order with this completed form when lodging at court, and if appropriate, any pension sharing/attachment annex or compensation sharing/annex.

I

[(Petitioner/Applicant's full name)]

confirm that I have read a fully completed Statement of information for a consent order from the [Respondent].

Signed   Dated   D D / M M / Y Y Y Y

I

[(Respondent's full name)]

confirm that I have read a fully completed Statement of information for a consent order from the [Applicant/ Petitioner].

Signed   Dated   D D / M M / Y Y Y Y

continued over the page ⇨

Petitioner/Applicant's Statement of Truth   *delete as appropriate

*I [   ]   [(Petitioner/Applicant's
                                              full name)]

believe that the facts stated in this Statement of information for a consent order are true and I
have made full disclosure of all relevant facts.

*I am duly authorised by the Petitioner/Applicant to sign this statement

Print full name [   ]

Name of Petitioner/
Applicant's solicitor's firm [   ]

Signed [   ]   Dated [D D / M M / Y Y Y Y]

*Petitioner/Applicant('s solicitor)('s litigation friend)

Position or office held
(if signing on behalf of firm
or company) [   ]

**Proceedings for contempt of court may be brought against a person who makes or
causes to be made, a false statement in a document verified by a statement of truth.**

Respondent's Statement of Truth   *delete as appropriate

*I [   ]   [(Respondent's full name)]

believe that the facts stated in this Statement of information for a consent order are true and I
have made full disclosure of all relevant facts.

*I am duly authorised by the Respondent to sign this statement

Print full name [   ]

Name of Respondent's
solicitor's firm [   ]

Signed [   ]   Dated [D D / M M / Y Y Y Y]

*(Respondent('s solicitor)('s litigation friend)

Position or office held
(if signing on behalf of firm
or company) [   ]

**Proceedings for contempt of court may be brought against a person who makes or
causes to be made, a false statement in a document verified by a statement of truth.**

6

(E)   Parental responsibility agreement (1)

Parental Responsibility Agreement
Section 4(1)(b) Children Act 1989

Keep this form in a safe place
Date recorded at The Central Family Court:

Read the notes on the other side before you make this agreement.

This is a Parental Responsibility Agreement regarding

the Child	*Full Name* _____

	Gender	*Date of birth*	*Date of 18th birthday*

Between
the Mother   *Name*

Address

and   the Father   *Name*

Address

We declare that   we are the mother and father of the above child and we agree that the child's father shall have parental responsibility for the child (in addition to the mother having parental responsibility).

Signed **(Mother)**	Signed **(Father)**

Date	Date

Certificate of witness

The following evidence of identity was produced by the person signing above:	The following evidence of identity was produced by the person signing above:

Signed in the presence of: *Name of Witness*	Signed in the presence of: *Name of Witness*

Address	*Address*

Signature of Witness	*Signature of Witness*

[A Justice of the Peace] [Justices' Clerk] [An assistant to a justices' clerk] [An officer of the court authorised by the judge to administer oaths]	[A Justice of the Peace] [Justices' Clerk] [An assistant to a justices' clerk] [An Officer of the Court authorised by the judge to administer oaths]

Notes about the Parental Responsibility Agreement

Read these notes before you make the agreement.

About the Parental Responsibility Agreement

The making of this agreement will affect the legal position of the mother and the father. You should both seek legal advice before you make the Agreement. You can obtain the name and address of a solicitor from the Children Panel (020 7242 1222)

or from
- a local office of the family court
- a Citizens Advice Bureau
- a Law Centre
- a local library.

You may be eligible for legal aid.

When you fill in the Agreement

Please use black ink (the Agreement will be copied). Put the name of one child only. If the father is to have parental responsibility for more than one child, fill in a separate form for each child. **Do not sign the Agreement.**

When you have filled in the Agreement

Take it to a local office of the family court, or The Central Family Court (the address is below).

A justice of the peace, a justices' clerk, an assistant to a justices' clerk, or a court official who is authorised by the judge to administer oaths, will witness your signature and he or she will sign the certificate of the witness. **A solicitor cannot witness your signature.**

To the mother: When you make the declaration you will have to prove that you are the child's mother so take to the court the child's full birth certificate.

You will also need evidence of your identity showing a photograph and signature (for example, a photocard, official pass or passport). **Please note that the child's birth certificate cannot be accepted as sufficient proof of your identity.**

To the father: You will need evidence of your identity showing a photograph and signature (for example, a photocard, official pass or passport).

When the Certificate has been signed and witnessed

Make 2 copies of the Agreement form. You do not need to copy these notes.

Take, or send, this form and the copies to **The Central Family Court, First Avenue House, 42-49 High Holborn, London, WC1V 6NP.**

The Court will record the Agreement and keep this form. The copies will be stamped and sent back to each parent at the address on the Agreement. The Agreement will not take effect until it has been received and recorded at The Central Family Court.

Ending the Agreement

Once a parental responsibility agreement has been made it can only end
- by an order of the court made on the application of any person who has parental responsibility for the child
- by an order of the court made on the application of the child with permission of the court
- when the child reaches the age of 18.

C(PRA1) (Notes) (08.14)

Step-Parent Parental Responsibility Agreement

Section 4A(1)(a) Children Act 1989

Keep this form in a safe place
Date recorded at The Central Family Court:

Read the notes on the other side before you make this agreement.

This is a Step-Parent Parental Responsibility Agreement regarding

the Child	*Full Name* _____		

Gender	*Date of birth*	*Date of 18th birthday*

Between
Parent A   *Name*

                   Address

and
*the other parent   *Name*
(with parental
responsibility)   *Address*

and
the step-parent   *Name*

                   Address

We declare that	we are the parents and step-parent of the above child and we agree that the above mentioned step-parent shall have parental responsibility for the child (in addition to those already having parental responsibility).

	Signed (**Parent A**)	*Signed (**Other Parent**)	Signed (**Step-Parent**)
	Date	Date	Date
Certificate of witness	The following evidence of identity was produced by the person signing above:	The following evidence of identity was produced by the person signing above:	The following evidence of identity was produced by the person signing above:
	Signed in the presence of: *Name of Witness*	Signed in the presence of: *Name of Witness*	Signed in the presence of: *Name of Witness*
	Address	*Address*	*Address*
*If there is only one parent with parental responsibility, please delete this section.	*Signature of Witness*	*Signature of Witness*	*Signature of Witness*
	[A Justice of the Peace] [Justices' Clerk] [An assistant to a justices' clerk] [An Officer of the Court authorised by the judge to administer oaths]	[A Justice of the Peace] [Justices' Clerk] [An assistant to a justices' clerk] [An Officer of the Court authorised by the judge to administer oaths]	[A Justice of the Peace] [Justices' Clerk] [An assistant to a justices' clerk] [An Officer of the Court authorised by the judge to administer oaths]

C(PRA2) (08.14)   © Crown copyright 2014

Notes about the Step-Parent Parental Responsibility Form
Read these notes before you make the Agreement

About the Step-Parent Parental Responsibility Agreement

The making of this agreement will affect the legal position of the parent(s) and the step-parent. You should seek legal advice before you make the Agreement. You can obtain the name and address of a solicitor from the Children Panel (020 7242 1222) or from:

- a local office of the family court,
- a Citizens Advice Bureau,
- a Law Centre,
- a local library.

You may be eligible for legal aid.

When you fill in the Agreement

Please use black ink (the Agreement will be copied). Put the name of one child only. If the step-parent is to have parental responsibility for more than one child, fill in a separate form for each child. **Do not sign the Agreement.**

When you have filled in the Agreement

Take it to a local office of the family court, or The Central Family Court (the address is below).

A justice of the peace, a justices' clerk, an assistant to a justices' clerk, or a court official who is authorised by the judge to administer oaths, will witness your signature and he or she will sign the certificate of the witness. **A solicitor cannot witness your signature.**

To Parent A and the Other Parent with parental responsibility:

When you make the declaration you will have to prove that you have parental responsibility for the child. You should therefore take with you to the court one of the following documents:

- the child's full birth certificate and a marriage certificate or civil partnership certificate to show that the parents were married to each other or were in a civil partnership with each other at the time of birth or subsequently,
- a court order granting parental responsibility,
- a registered Parental Responsibility Agreement Form between the child's mother and father or other parent,
- if the birth was registered after the 1 December 2003, the child's full birth certificate showing that the parents jointly registered the child's birth.

You will also require evidence of your (both parents') identity showing a photograph and signature (for example, a photocard, official pass or passport) **(Please note that the child's birth certificate cannot be accepted as sufficient proof of your identity.)**

To the step-parent: When you make the declaration you will have to prove that you are married to, or the civil partner of, a parent of the child so take to the court your marriage certificate or certificate of civil partnership.

You will also need evidence of your identity showing a photograph and signature (for example, a photocard, official pass or passport).

When the Certificate has been signed and witnessed

Make sufficient copies of the Agreement Form for each person who has signed the form. You do not need to copy these notes.

Take, or send, the original form and the copies to: **The Central Family Court, First Avenue House, 42-49 High Holborn, London, WC1V 6NP.**

The Court will record the Agreement and retain the original form. The copies will be stamped with the seal of the court and sent back to every person with parental responsibility who has signed the Agreement Form and to the step-parent. The Agreement will not take effect until it has been received and recorded at The Central Family Court.

Ending the Agreement

Once a step-parent parental responsibility agreement has been made it can only end:

- by an order of the court made on the application of any person who has parental responsibility for the child,
- by an order of the court made on the application of the child with permission of the court,
- when the child reaches the age of 18.

(G)   Form C1 (Children Act application)

Application for an order   Form C1

Children Act 1989 except care and supervision orders, Section 8 orders and orders related to enforcement of a contact order.

If you are applying for a section 8 order or an order related to enforcement of a contact order you will need to use a different application form (Form C100 for Section 8 orders and Form C79 for enforcement). Booklet 'CB1 - Making an application - children and the family courts' gives more information. These leaflets are available from your local court or online at hmctsformfinder.justice.gov.uk.

If you are applying for one of the following private law Children Act 1989 orders you **must** file a separate completed FM1 form with this application:

- A parental responsibility order (sections 4(1)(c), 4ZA(1)(c) or 4A(1)(b) of the Children Act 1989) or an order terminating parental responsibility (sections 4(2A), 4ZA(5) or 4A(3) of that Act).

- An order appointing a child's guardian (section 5(1) of the Children Act 1989) or an order terminating the appointment (section 6(7) of that Act).

- An order giving permission to change a child's surname or remove a child from the United Kingdom (sections 13(1) or 14C of the Children Act 1989).

- A special guardianship order or an order varying or discharging such an order (section 14D of the Children Act 1989).

If you are applying for a care or supervision order, you will need to use Form C110A, which is available online at hmctsformfinder.justice.gov.uk.

Cafcass/CAFCASS CYMRU will carry out checks as it considers necessary.

Cafcass - Children and Family Court Advisory and Support Service (in England); CAFCASS CYMRU - Children and Family Court Advisory and Support Service Wales.

Help with Fees – Ref no. (if applicable)	H W F - ☐☐☐ - ☐☐☐

The family court sitting at	To be completed by the court
	Date issued
	Case number
The full name(s) of the child(ren)	Child(ren)'s number(s)

Important Note
You should only answer question 7 if you are applying for a **Parental Responsibility Order.**

---

1 About you (the person completing this form known as 'the applicant')

If you do not wish your address or telephone number to be made known to the respondent, leave the address details blank and complete Confidential contact details form C8. You can get a copy of this form from any family court office or from our website at hmctsformfinder.justice.gov.uk

Please ensure that any documents submitted with this form or at a later date, do not include the confidential contact details you wish to withhold.

State:
- *your title, full name, address, telephone number, date of birth and relationship to each child above*
- *your solicitor's name, address, reference, telephone, FAX and DX numbers.*

Solicitor's fee account no.	

C1

2 The child(ren) and the order(s) you are applying for

For each child state:
- *the full name, date of birth and sex*
- *the type of order(s) you are applying for (for example, Parental Responsibility Order).*

3 Other cases which concern the child(ren)

If there have ever been, or there are pending, any court cases which concern:
- *a child whose name you have put in paragraph 2*
- *a full, half or step brother or sister of a child whose name you have put in paragraph 2*
- *a person in this case who is or has been, involved in caring for a child whose name you have put in paragraph 2*

attach a copy of the relevant order and give:
- *the name of the court*
- *the name and contact address (if known) of the children's guardian, if appointed*
- *the name and contact address (if known) of the children and family reporter, if appointed*
- *the name and contact address (if known) of the welfare officer, if appointed*
- *the name and contact address (if known) of the solicitor appointed for the child(ren).*

C1

4 The respondent(s)

Family Procedure Rules 2010, SI 2010/2955, 12.3

For each respondent state:
- *the title, full name and address*
- *the date of birth (if known) or the age*
- *the relationship to each child.*

C1

4

5 Others to whom notice is to be given

Practice Direction 12C to the Family Procedure Rules 2010 - Service of application in certain proceedings relating to children

For each person state:
- *the title, full name and address*
- *the date of birth (if known) or the age*
- *the relationship to each child.*

6 The care of the child(ren)

For each child in paragraph 2 state:
- *the child's current address and how long the child has lived there*
- *whether it is the child's usual address and who cares for the child there*
- *the child's relationship to the other children (if any).*

7 Domestic abuse, violence or harm

Do you believe that the child(ren) named above have suffered or are at risk of suffering any harm from any of the following:
- *any form of domestic abuse*
- *violence within the household*
- *child abduction*
- *other conduct or behaviour*

by any person who is or has been involved in caring for the child(ren) or lives with, or has contact with, the child(ren)?

Yes   No

Please tick the box which applies ☐   ☐

If you tick the Yes box, you must also fill in Supplemental Information Form (form C1A). You can obtain a copy of this from a court office if one has not been enclosed with the papers served on you.

C1

5

8 Social Services

For each child in paragraph 2 state:
- *whether the child is known to the Social Services. If so, give the name of the social worker and the address of the Social Services department.*
- *whether the child is, or has been, on the Child Protection Register. If so, give details of registration.*

9 The education and health of the child(ren)

For each child state:
- *the name of the school, college or place of training which the child attends*
- *whether the child is in good health. Give details of any serious disabilities or ill health.*
- *whether the child has any special needs.*

10 The parents of the child(ren)

For each child state:
- *the full name of the child's parents*
- *whether the parents are, or have been, married to each other or civil partners of each other*
- *whether the parents live together. If so, where.*
- *whether, to your knowledge, either of the parents have been involved in a court case concerning a child. If so, give the date and the name of the court.*

C1

6

11 The family of the child(ren) (other children)

For any other child not already mentioned in the family (for example, a brother or half sister) state:
- *the full name and address*
- *the date of birth (if known) or age*
- *the relationship of the child to you.*

12 Other adults

State:
- *the full name of any other adults (for example, lodgers) who live at the same address as any child named in paragraph 2*
- *whether they live there all the time*
- *whether, to your knowledge, the adult has been involved in a court case concerning a child. If so, give the date and the name of the court.*

13 Your reason(s) for applying and any plans for the child(ren)

State briefly your reasons for applying and what you want the court to order.
- ***Do not** complete this section if this form is accompanied by a supplementary form.*

C1

14　Attending the court

State:
- *whether you will need an interpreter at court. If so, please indicate what language and dialect you will use. If you require an interpreter you must notify the court immediately so that one can be arranged.*
- *whether you have a disability for which you require special assistance or special facilities. If so, please say what your needs are. The court staff will get in touch with you about your requirements.*

15　Parenting Information – Arrangements after Separation

	Yes	No
Have you received a Parenting Plan booklet? *(If No, you may obtain a copy from a court office,* *a citizen's advice bureau or other family advice service.)*	☐	☐
Have you agreed to a Parenting Plan? *(If Yes, please include a copy of the Plan when you send* *your application to the court)*	☐	☐
If you did agree a Parenting Plan, has the Plan *broken down?*	☐	☐

If Yes, please explain briefly why the Plan broke down –

C1

Statement of truth

I understand that proceedings for contempt of court may be brought against anyone who makes, or causes to be made, a false statement in a document verified by a statement of truth without an honest belief in its truth.

☐ **I believe** that the facts stated in this form and any continuation sheets are true.

☐ **The applicant** believes that the facts stated in this form and any continuation sheets are true. **I am authorised** by the applicant to sign this statement.

Signature

☐ Applicant

☐ Applicant's legal representative (as defined by FPR 2.3(1))

Date

Day   Month   Year

Full name

Name of Applicant's legal representative's firm

If signing on behalf of firm or company give position or office held

C1

9

(H)   Form C100 (Application for a s 8 order)

Application under section 8 of the Children Act 1989 for a child arrangements, prohibited steps, specific issue order or to vary or discharge or ask permission to make a section 8 order

To be completed by the court	
The family court sitting at	
Case number	Date issued

Help with Fees – Ref no. (if applicable)	H W F – ☐☐☐ – ☐☐☐

Before completing this form please read the leaflet 'CB1 – Making an application – Children and the Family Courts' and the leaflet 'CB7 – Guide for separated parents: children and the family courts'. **These and other forms and leaflets are available from your local court or online at hmctsformfinder.justice.gov.uk**

First name(s) of applicant(s)	Last name of applicant(s)

First name(s) of respondent(s)	Last name of the respondent(s)

Nature of application

What order(s) are you applying for?

☐ Child Arrangements Order

☐ Prohibited Steps Order

☐ Specific Issue Order

Please specify the nature of the order you seek. *For example, an order about with whom a child is to live, or how often they spend time with the applicant and for how long.*

Concerns about risk of harm

Are you alleging that the child(ren) named in Section 1 of this form have experienced, or are at risk of experiencing, harm from any of the following by any person who has had contact with the child?

any form of domestic abuse	☐ Yes	☐ No
child abduction	☐ Yes	☐ No
child abuse	☐ Yes	☐ No
drugs, alcohol or substance abuse	☐ Yes	☐ No
other safety or welfare concerns	☐ Yes	☐ No

If you answered Yes to any of the above, **you must complete form C1A** (Supplemental information form) **and file it with this C100 form.**

Additional information required

Are you asking for permission to make this application, where that is required?	☐ Yes	☐ No	If Yes, complete section 5a
Is an urgent hearing or without notice hearing required?	☐ Yes	☐ No	If Yes, complete section 6a or 6b
Are there previous or ongoing proceedings for the child(ren)?	☐ Yes	☐ No	If Yes, complete section 7
Are you applying for an order to formalise an agreement (consent order)?	☐ Yes	☐ No	If Yes, **attach the draft order to this form**
Is this a case with an international element or factors affecting litigation capacity?	☐ Yes	☐ No	If Yes, complete section 8 or 9
Will the child or any of the people involved need to use spoken or written Welsh during the course of the proceedings?	☐ Yes	☐ No	If Yes, complete section 10

1. The Child(ren)

Please also read the information notes and complete the checklist at the end of the form.

- Failure to complete every question or state if it does not apply, could delay the case, as the court will have to ask you to provide the additional information required.
- If there is not enough space please attach separate sheets clearly showing the details of the children, parties, question and page number they refer to.
- Cafcass/CAFCASS CYMRU will carry out checks as it considers necessary. See Section J of leaflet CB1 for more information about Cafcass and CAFCASS CYMRU.

Summary of children's details

Please list the name(s) of the child(ren) and the type(s) of order you are applying for, starting with the oldest. To understand which order to apply for read the booklet CB1 Section D.

Child 1 - First name(s)	Last name	Date of birth	☐ Don't know

Gender	Orders applied for
☐ Female ☐ Male	

Applicant(s) relationship to the child	Respondent(s) relationship to the child

Child 2 - First name(s)	Last name	Date of birth	☐ Don't know

Gender	Orders applied for
☐ Female ☐ Male	

Applicant(s) relationship to the child	Respondent(s) relationship to the child

Child 3 - First name(s)	Last name	Date of birth	☐ Don't know

Gender	Orders applied for
☐ Female ☐ Male	

Applicant(s) relationship to the child	Respondent(s) relationship to the child

Child 4 - First name(s)	Last name	Date of birth	☐ Don't know

Gender	Orders applied for
☐ Female ☐ Male	

Applicant(s) relationship to the child	Respondent(s) relationship to the child

1a. Are any of the children known to the local authority children's services?

☐ Yes   ☐ No   ☐ Don't know

If Yes please state which child and the name of the Local Authority and Social worker (if known)

1b. Are any of the children the subject of a child protection plan?

☐ Yes   ☐ No   ☐ Don't know

1c. Do all the children have the same parents?

☐ Yes   ☐ No

If Yes, what are the names of the parents?

If No, please give details of each parent and their children involved in this application

Please state everyone who has parental responsibility for each child and how they have parental responsibility (e.g. 'child's mother', 'child's father and was married to the mother when the child was born' etc.)
(See Section E of leaflet CB1 for more information)

1d. Who do the children currently live with?

☐ Applicant(s)   ☐ Respondent(s)   ☐ Other

If other, please give the full address of the child, the names of any adults living with the children and their relationship to or involvement with the child.

If you do not wish this information to be made known to the Respondent, leave the details blank and complete Confidential contact details Form C8.

3

2. Requirement to attend a Mediation, Information and Assessment Meeting (MIAM)

Before making an application for a child arrangements order, prohibited steps order or specific issue order (a section 8 order) you must first attend a Mediation, Information and Assessment Meeting (MIAM). At the MIAM an authorised family mediator will consider with you (and the other party if present) whether family mediation, or another form of non-court dispute resolution, would be a more appropriate alternative to court. The mediator will also be able to sign post you to other help and support services.

You **must** have attended a MIAM before making this application **unless** the requirement to attend a MIAM does not apply because the section 8 order you are applying for:

- is for a consent order; **or**
- concerns a child who is the subject of separate ongoing emergency proceedings, care proceedings or supervision proceedings (or is already the subject of an emergency, care or supervision order); **or**
- you are exempt from the requirement to attend a MIAM. (Some exemptions you can claim yourself, others must be certified by an authorised family mediator).

All applicants must complete sections 1, 2 and 5 to 14 before signing this form.

In addition, you must tick one of the boxes below and ensure that you, your legal adviser or a family mediator completes (and where indicated signs) the relevant section(s) of this form as shown.

2a. If you ticked 'Yes' to the question on page 1 about current or previous court cases, are/were any of those cases about an emergency protection, care or supervision order?	☐ Yes	☐ No	**If Yes, complete section 7** to provide additional details. **Do not complete sections 3 and 4** **If No**, please **answer question 2b.**
2b. Are you claiming exemption from the requirement to attend a MIAM?	☐ Yes	☐ No	**If Yes, complete section 3.** **If No**, please **answer question 2c.**
2c. Has a family mediator informed you that a mediator's exemption applies, and you do not need to attend a MIAM?	☐ Yes	☐ No	**If Yes**, you must ensure that the **family mediator completes and signs section 4a.** **If No**, please **answer question 2d.**
2d. Have you attended a MIAM?	☐ Yes	☐ No	**If Yes**, you must ensure that **the family mediator completes and signs section 4b.** **If No, you cannot make this application.**

4

3. Applicant claims exemption(s) from attendance at a Mediation, Information and Assessment Meeting (MIAM)

(To be completed by the person intending to make a court application or their solicitor)

The applicant has not attended a MIAM because the following MIAM exemption(s) applies:

☐ Domestic violence (you must complete **section 3a**)

☐ Child protection concerns (you must complete **section 3b**)

☐ Urgency (you must complete **section 3c**)

☐ Previous MIAM attendance or previous MIAM exemption (you must complete **section 3d**)

☐ Other (you must complete **section 3e**)

Now complete the relevant section 3a, b, c, d or e by ticking the appropriate box(s)

Further details of MIAM exemption(s) claimed by the applicant

If you have claimed a MIAM exemption above you must also tick the relevant box(s), as shown below to confirm that you have the necessary evidence to support your ground(s) for exemption and should bring it to the first hearing. Where you are asked to provide additional details you must do so.

Section 3a - Domestic violence evidence

The applicant confirms that there is evidence of domestic violence, as specified below:

☐ evidence that a prospective party has been arrested for a relevant domestic violence offence;

☐ evidence of a relevant police caution for a domestic violence offence;

☐ evidence of relevant criminal proceedings for a domestic violence offence which have not concluded;

☐ evidence of a relevant conviction for a domestic violence offence;

☐ a court order binding a prospective party over in connection with a domestic violence offence;

☐ a domestic violence protection notice issued under section 24 of the Crime and Security Act 2010 against a prospective party;

☐ a relevant protective injunction;

☐ an undertaking given in England and Wales under section 46 or 63E of the Family Law Act 1996 (or given in Scotland or Northern Ireland in place of a protective injunction) by a prospective party, provided that a cross-undertaking relating to domestic violence was not given by another prospective party;

☐ a copy of a finding of fact, made in proceedings in the United Kingdom, that there has been domestic violence by a prospective party;

☐ an expert report produced as evidence in proceedings in the United Kingdom for the benefit of a court or tribunal confirming that a person with whom a prospective party is or was in a family relationship, was assessed as being, or at risk of being, a victim of domestic violence by that prospective party;

☐ a letter or report from an appropriate health professional confirming that-

(i) that professional, or another appropriate health professional, has examined a prospective party in person; and

5

(ii) in the reasonable professional judgment of the author or the examining appropriate health professional, that prospective party has, or has had, injuries or a condition consistent with being a victim of domestic violence;

☐ a letter or report from-

   (i) the appropriate health professional who made the referral described below;

   (ii) an appropriate health professional who has access to the medical records of the prospective party referred to below; or

   (iii) the person to whom the referral described below was made;

   confirming that there was a referral by an appropriate health professional of a prospective party to a person who provides specialist support or assistance for victims of, or those at risk of, domestic violence;

☐ a letter from any person who is a member of a multi-agency risk assessment conference (or other suitable local safeguarding forum) confirming that a prospective party, or a person with whom that prospective party is in a family relationship, is or has been at risk of harm from domestic violence by another prospective party;

☐ a letter from an independent domestic violence advisor confirming that they are providing support to a prospective party;

☐ a letter from an independent sexual violence advisor confirming that they are providing support to a prospective party relating to sexual violence by another prospective party;

☐ a letter from an officer employed by a local authority or housing association (or their equivalent in Scotland or Northern Ireland) for the purpose of supporting tenants containing-

   (i) a statement to the effect that, in their reasonable professional judgment, a person with whom a prospective party is or has been in a family relationship is, or is at risk of being, a victim of domestic violence by that prospective party;

   (ii) a description of the specific matters relied upon to support that judgment; and

   (iii) a description of the support they provided to the victim of domestic violence or the person at risk of domestic violence by that prospective party;

☐ a letter which-

   (i) is from an organisation providing domestic violence support services, or a registered charity, which letter confirms that it-

      (a) is situated in England and Wales,

      (b) has been operating for an uninterrupted period of six months or more; and

      (c) provided a prospective party with support in relation to that person's needs as a victim, or a person at risk, of domestic violence; and

   (ii) contains-

      (a) a statement to the effect that, in the reasonable professional judgment of the author of the letter, the prospective party is, or is at risk of being, a victim of domestic violence;

      (b) a description of the specific matters relied upon to support that judgment;

      (c) a description of the support provided to the prospective party; and

6

Section 3a - Domestic violence evidence - continued

(d) a statement of the reasons why the prospective party needed that support;

☐ a letter or report from an organisation providing domestic violence support services in the United Kingdom confirming-

(i) that a person with whom a prospective party is or was in a family relationship was refused admission to a refuge;

(ii) the date on which they were refused admission to the refuge; and

(iii) they sought admission to the refuge because of allegations of domestic violence by the prospective party referred to in paragraph (i);

☐ a letter from a public authority confirming that a person with whom a prospective party is or was in a family relationship, was assessed as being, or at risk of being, a victim of domestic violence by that prospective party (or a copy of that assessment);

☐ a letter from the Secretary of State for the Home Department confirming that a prospective party has been granted leave to remain in the United Kingdom under paragraph 289B of the Rules made by the Home Secretary under section 3(2) of the Immigration Act 1971, which can be found at https://www.gov.uk/guidance/immigration-rules/immigration-rules-index;

☐ evidence which demonstrates that a prospective party has been, or is at risk of being, the victim of domestic violence by another prospective party in the form of abuse which relates to financial matters.

Section 3b – Child protection concerns

The applicant confirms that a child would be the subject of the application and that child or another child of the family who is living with that child is currently—

☐ the subject of enquiries by a local authority under section 47 of the Children Act 1989 Act; or

☐ the subject of a child protection plan put in place by a local authority.

Section 3c – Urgency

The applicant confirms that the application must be made urgently because:

☐ there is risk to the life, liberty or physical safety of the prospective applicant or his or her family or his or her home; or

☐ any delay caused by attending a MIAM would cause—

☐ a risk of harm to a child; or

☐ a risk of unlawful removal of a child from the United Kingdom, or a risk of unlawful retention of a child who is currently outside England and Wales; or

☐ a significant risk of a miscarriage of justice; or

☐ unreasonable hardship to the prospective applicant; or

☐ irretrievable problems in dealing with the dispute (including the irretrievable loss of significant evidence); or

☐ there is a significant risk that in the period necessary to schedule and attend a MIAM, proceedings relating to the dispute will be brought in another state in which a valid claim to jurisdiction may exist, such that a court in that other State would be seized of the dispute before a court in England and Wales.

7

Section 3d – Previous MIAM attendance or MIAM exemption

The applicant confirms that one of the following applies:

☐ in the 4 months prior to making the application, the person attended a MIAM or participated in another form of non-court dispute resolution relating to the same or substantially the same dispute; or

☐ at the time of making the application, the person is participating in another form of non-court dispute resolution relating to the same or substantially the same dispute; or

☐ in the 4 months prior to making the application, the person filed a relevant family application confirming that a MIAM exemption applied and that application related to the same or substantially the same dispute; or

☐ the application would be made in existing proceedings which are continuing and the prospective applicant attended a MIAM before initiating those proceedings; or

☐ the application would be made in existing proceedings which are continuing and a MIAM exemption applied to the application for those proceedings.

Section 3e – Other exemptions

The applicant confirms that one of the following other grounds for exemption applies:

☐ the prospective applicant does not have sufficient contact details for any of the prospective respondents to enable a family mediator to contact any of the prospective respondents for the purpose of scheduling the MIAM.

☐ the application would be made without notice (Paragraph 5.1 of Practice Direction 18A sets out the circumstances in which applications may be made without notice.)

☐ (i) the prospective applicant is or all of the prospective respondents are subject to a disability or other inability that would prevent attendance at a MIAM unless appropriate facilities can be offered by an authorised mediator; (ii) the prospective applicant has contacted as many authorised family mediators as have an office within fifteen miles of his or her home (or three of them if there are three or more), and all have stated that they are unable to provide such facilities; and (iii) the names, postal addresses and telephone numbers or e-mail addresses for such authorised family mediators, and the dates of contact, can be provided to the court if requested.

☐ the prospective applicant or all of the prospective respondents cannot attend a MIAM because he or she is, or they are, as the case may be (i) in prison or any other institution in which he or she is or they are required to be detained; (ii) subject to conditions of bail that prevent contact with the other person; or (iii) subject to a licence with a prohibited contact requirement in relation to the other person.

☐ the prospective applicant or all of the prospective respondents are not habitually resident in England and Wales.

☐ a child is one of the prospective parties by virtue of Rule 12.3(1).

☐ (i) the prospective applicant has contacted as many authorised family mediators as have an office within fifteen miles of his or her home (or three of them if there are three or more), and all of them have stated that they are not available to conduct a MIAM within fifteen business days of the date of contact; and (ii) the names, postal addresses and telephone numbers or e-mail addresses for such authorised family mediators, and the dates of contact, can be provided to the court if requested.

☐ there is no authorised family mediator with an office within fifteen miles of the prospective applicant's home.

Now complete Section 5.

8

4. Mediator certifies that the prospective applicant is exempt from attendance at Mediation Information and Assessment Meeting (MIAM) or confirms MIAM attendance

(To be completed and signed by the authorised family mediator) (tick the boxes that apply)

4a.

The following MIAM exemption(s) applies:

☐ An authorised family mediator confirms that he or she is satisfied that -

  ☐ (a) mediation is not suitable as a means of resolving the dispute because none of the respondents is willing to attend a MIAM; or

  ☐ (b) mediation is not suitable as a means of resolving the dispute because all of the respondents failed without good reason to attend a MIAM appointment; or

  ☐ (c) mediation is otherwise not suitable as a means of resolving the dispute.

4b.

The prospective applicant attended a MIAM:

☐ The prospective applicant only attended a MIAM.

☐ The prospective applicant and respondent party(s) attended the MIAM together.

☐ The prospective applicant and respondent(s) have each attended a separate MIAM.

☐ The prospective respondent party(s) has/have made or is/are making arrangements to attend a separate MIAM.

Mediation or other form of Dispute Resolution is not proceeding because:

☐ The applicant has attended a MIAM alone and

- the applicant does not wish to start or continue mediation; or
- the mediator has determined that mediation is unsuitable; or
- the respondent did not wish to attend a MIAM

☐ Both the applicant and respondent have attended a MIAM (separately or together) and

- the applicant does not wish to start or continue mediation; or
- the respondent does not wish to start or continue mediation; or
- the mediator has determined that mediation is unsuitable

☐ Mediation has started, but has:

- broken down; or
- concluded with some or all issues unresolved

Signed	
	Authorised Family Mediator (a family mediator who is authorised to undertake MIAMs)
FMC Registration no.	
Family Mediation Service name	
Sole trader name	
Address	
Dated	☐☐/☐☐/☐☐☐☐

9

5. Why are you making this application?

Have you applied to the court for permission to make this application?

☐ Yes   ☐ No - permission not required   ☐ No - permission now sought

5a. Reasons for permission if permission is required.

5b. Please give brief details:

- any previous agreements (formal or informal) or parenting plans, and how they have broken down
- your reasons for bringing this application to the court
- what you want the court to do
- reasons given by the respondent(s) for their actions in relation to this application.

Do not give a full statement, please provide a summary of any relevant reasons. You may be asked to provide a full statement later.

5c. Have you previously prepared a Parenting Plan?

☐ Yes   ☐ No

If No, you can download a copy from the website www.cafcass.gov.uk/parentingplan

If Yes, please attach the plan to this application form

6. Urgent and without notice hearings

Complete this section if you have ticked the relevant box on the front of the form

6a. Urgent hearing

Set out the order(s)/directions sought

Set out the reasons for urgency

Proposed timetable

The application should be considered within [   ] hours/days

If consideration is sought within 48 hours, you must complete the section below

What efforts have you made to put each respondent on notice of the application?

11

Complete this section if you have ticked the relevant box on the front of the form

6b. Without notice hearing

Set out the reasons for the application to be considered without notice. (This information is a requirement, a without notice hearing will **not** be directed without reason)

Do you require a without notice hearing because it is not possible to give notice including abridged or informal notice?

☐ Yes   ☐ No

If Yes, please set out reasons below

Do you require a without notice hearing because notice to a respondent will frustrate the order that is being applied for?

☐ Yes   ☐ No

If Yes, please set out reasons below

12

7. Other court cases which concern the child(ren) listed in Section 1

Complete this section if you have ticked the relevant box on the front of this form.

Use this section to provide details of any other court cases now, or at any time in the past, which concern any of the child(ren) listed in section 1.

Additional details

Name of child(ren)

Name of the court where proceedings heard

Case no.

Date/year (if known)

Name and office (if known) of Cafcass/CAFCASS CYMRU officer

Type of proceedings if known - please tick all that apply

	Yes	No
Emergency Protection Order	☐ Yes	☐ No
Supervision Order	☐ Yes	☐ No
Care Order	☐ Yes	☐ No
Child abduction	☐ Yes	☐ No
Family Law Act 1996 Part 4 (proceedings for non-molestation order or occupation order)	☐ Yes	☐ No
A contact or residence order (Section 8 Children Act 1989) made within proceedings for a divorce or dissolution of a civil partnership	☐ Yes	☐ No
A contact or residence order (Section 8 Children Act 1989) made in connection with an Adoption Order	☐ Yes	☐ No
An order relating to child maintenance (Schedule 1 Children Act 1989)	☐ Yes	☐ No
A child arrangements order (Section 8 Children Act 1989)	☐ Yes	☐ No

Please tick if additional sheets are attached.   ☐

Please attach a copy of any relevant order.

13

8. Cases with an international element

Complete this section if you have ticked the relevant box on the front of this form.

Do you have any reason to believe that any child, parent or potentially significant adult in the child's life may be habitually resident in another state?

☐ Yes   ☐ No

If Yes, please give details

Do you have any reason to believe that there may be an issue as to jurisdiction in this case?

☐ Yes   ☐ No

If Yes, please give details

Has a request been made or should a request be made to a Central Authority or other competent authority in a foreign state or a consular authority in England and Wales?

☐ Yes   ☐ No

If Yes, please give details

9. Factors affecting ability to participate in proceedings

Complete this section if you have ticked the relevant box on the front of this form.

Please give details of any factors affecting litigation capacity

Provide details of any referral to or assessment by the Adult Learning Disability team, and/or any adult health service, where known, together with the outcome

Are you aware of any other factors which may affect the ability of the person concerned to take part in the proceedings?

14

10. Attending the court

Section N of the booklet **'CB1 - Making an application - Children and the Family Courts'** and the leaflet 'CB7 - Guide for separated parents: children and the family courts' provide information about attending court.

If you require an interpreter, you must tell the court now so that one can be arranged.

Please note that in any court proceedings in Wales you have the right to speak Welsh at any court hearing.

10a. Do you or any other party need to use spoken Welsh in the course of the proceedings or require written documentation in Welsh?

☐ Yes   ☐ No

If Yes, please give the names of the parties/witnesses/children involved who need to use written or spoken Welsh?

	Spoken	Written	Both
	☐ Spoken	☐ Written	☐ Both
	☐ Spoken	☐ Written	☐ Both
	☐ Spoken	☐ Written	☐ Both
	☐ Spoken	☐ Written	☐ Both
	☐ Spoken	☐ Written	☐ Both
	☐ Spoken	☐ Written	☐ Both
	☐ Spoken	☐ Written	☐ Both

10b. Do you or any of the parties require the court to appoint an interpreter or arrange any other assistance (e.g. sign language)?

☐ Yes   ☐ No

If Yes, who requires the interpreter

☐ applicant   ☐ respondent   ☐ Other party *(please specify)*

and please specify the language and dialect required:

10c. Are you aware of whether an intermediary will be required?

☐ Yes   ☐ No

If Yes, please give details

10d. If attending the court, do you or any of the parties involved have a disability for which you require special assistance or special facilities?

☐ Yes   ☐ No

If Yes, please say what the needs are

Please say whether there is a need for the court to make any special arrangements for you or any relevant children to attend court (e.g. providing you with a separate waiting room from the respondent or other security provisions).

Court staff may get in touch with you about the requirements

15

11. About you (the applicant(s))

	Applicant 1 (You)	Applicant 2 (if applicable)
First name(s)		
Last name(s)		
Previous names (if any)		
Gender	☐ Male ☐ Female	☐ Male ☐ Female
Date of birth (If under 18 read section Q of leaflet CB1)	☐☐/☐☐/☐☐☐☐	☐☐/☐☐/☐☐☐☐
Place of birth (town/county/country)		

If you do not wish your address to be made known to the respondent, leave the details below blank and complete Confidential contact details Form C8. Please ensure that any documents submitted with this form or at a later date, **do not** disclose the confidential contact details you wish to withhold

	Applicant 1 (You)	Applicant 2 (if applicable)
Address		
	Postcode ☐☐☐☐ ☐☐☐☐	Postcode ☐☐☐☐ ☐☐☐☐
Home telephone number		
Mobile telephone number		
Email address		
Have you lived at this address for more than 5 years?	☐ Yes ☐ No	☐ Yes ☐ No

If No, please provide details of all previous addresses you have lived at for the last 5 years.

Applicant 1 (You)	Applicant 2 (if applicable)

16

12. The respondent(s)

Sections G and H of the booklet **'CB1 - Making an application - Children and the Family Courts'** explain who a respondent is.

If there are more than 2 respondents please continue on a separate sheet.

	Respondent 1	**Respondent 2**
First name(s)		
Last name(s)		
Previous names (if known)		
Gender	☐ Male ☐ Female	☐ Male ☐ Female
Date of birth (If party under 18 read section Q of leaflet CB1)	D D / M M / Y Y Y Y ☐ Don't know	D D / M M / Y Y Y Y ☐ Don't know
Place of birth (town/county/country)		
Address (to which documents relating to this application should be sent)	Postcode ☐☐☐☐ ☐☐☐☐ ☐ Don't know	Postcode ☐☐☐☐ ☐☐☐☐ ☐ Don't know
Home telephone number		
Mobile telephone number	☐ Don't know	☐ Don't know
Email address	☐ Don't know	☐ Don't know
Have they lived at this address for more than 5 years?	☐ Yes ☐ No ☐ Don't know	☐ Yes ☐ No ☐ Don't know

If No, please provide details of all previous addresses for the last 5 years below (if known, including the dates and starting with the most recent)

17

13. Others who should be given notice

There may be other people who should be notified of your application, for example, someone who cares for the child but is not a parent. Sections G and I of the booklet **'CB1 - Making an application - Children and the Family Courts'** explain who others are.

	Person1	Person 2
First name(s)		
Last name(s)		
Previous names (if known)		
Gender	☐ Male ☐ Female	☐ Male ☐ Female
Date of birth	☐☐/☐☐/☐☐☐☐ ☐ Don't know	☐☐/☐☐/☐☐☐☐ ☐ Don't know
Address	Postcode ☐☐☐☐ ☐☐☐☐ ☐ Don't know	Postcode ☐☐☐☐ ☐☐☐☐ ☐ Don't know
Please state their relationship to the children listed on page 1. If their relationship is not the same to each child please state their relationship to each child.		

13a. Other children not part of the application.

Full name of child	Date of birth	Gender
	☐☐/☐☐/☐☐☐☐ ☐ Don't know	☐ Male ☐ Female
Relationship to applicant(s)	Relationship to respondent(s)	

Full name of child	Date of birth	Gender
	☐☐/☐☐/☐☐☐☐ ☐ Don't know	☐ Male ☐ Female
Relationship to applicant(s)	Relationship to respondent(s)	

18

14. Solicitor's details

Do you have a solicitor acting for you?

☐ Yes   ☐ No   If No, see section Q of leaflet CB1 for more information

If Yes, please give the following details

Your solicitor's name

Name of firm

Address

Postcode ☐☐☐☐ ☐☐☐☐

Telephone number

Fax number

DX number

Solicitor's Reference

Fee account no.

Email address

19

15. Checklist

1. Have you completed section 1 relating to the child(ren) in full? ☐ Yes ☐ No

2. Have you completed sections 2, 3 and 4 relating to Mediation in full? ☐ Yes ☐ No

3. Have you completed sections 5 and 6 relating to reasons for making the application in full? ☐ Yes ☐ No

4. Have you completed section 7 relating to Other Court cases in full? ☐ Yes ☐ No

5. Have you completed sections 8, 9 and 10 about the factors affecting the proceedings? ☐ Yes ☐ No

6. Have you completed section 11 relating to you the applicant in full? ☐ Yes ☐ No

7. Have you completed section 12, 13 and 14 relating to the Respondent and others who should be given notice ☐ Yes ☐ No

8. Have you completed section 16 relating to statement of truth in full? ☐ Yes ☐ No

You must send the court at least three copies of this form.

16. Statement of truth

*[I believe] [The applicant believes] that the facts stated in this application are true.

*delete as appropriate

*I am duly authorised by the applicant to sign this statement.

Print full name	
Name of applicant solicitors firm	
Signed	

(Applicant) (Applicant's solicitor)

Dated ☐☐/☐☐/☐☐☐☐

Position or office held (If signing on behalf of firm or company)

Proceedings for contempt of court may be brought against a person who makes or causes to be made, a false statement in a document verified by a statement of truth.

Court fee – Are you paying the court fee by credit or debit card?

☐ **Yes**, the court will contact you, using the details given in your application, within three working days to take payment

☐ **No**

What you do next
You should normally make your application to the Designated Family Centre for your area. You can find this, and a full list of courts and what type of work they do online at courttribunalfinder.service.gov.uk

Fees
You may need to pay a fee with your application. You should read leaflet **EX50 Civil and family court fees** to find out what fee, if any, you need to pay. This leaflet is available from your local court or online at hmctsformfinder.justice.gov.uk

20

Guidance note for completing form C100

Relevant sections of this application will be provided to Cafcass/CAFCASS CYMRU upon issue of proceedings. The information contained in this form enables Cafcass/CAFCASS CYMRU to conduct enquiries prior to the first court hearing. Without it they cannot conduct their initial safeguarding checks and enquiries.

Every question in this form should be completed, or stated that the information is not available. This essential information is required by Cafcass/CAFCASS CYMRU and failure to provide this information could lead to unnecessary delays to proceedings:

Page 1

Specify in the box the nature of the order you seek

You need to complete this form if you want to ask the court to make an (or change an existing) order about a child(ren) and your application is for:

- a child arrangements order (where a child should live, who a child should spend time with or both); or

- a specific issue order (for example, if you are asking the court to decide whether a child's surname should be changed); or

- a prohibited steps order (for example, if you are asking the court to prevent a person from removing a child from a school).

These orders are known as 'Section 8 orders' and are orders made by the court under section 8 of the Children Act 1989 to decide issues in relation to a child. You must tick the relevant box on page 1 to indicate which type of order(s) you are applying for. (If you wish to ask the court to enforce a previous Section 8 order you need to complete a different court form – Form 'C79 (Application related to enforcement of a child arrangements order)).

If you have any concerns about the risk of harm, tick the relevant box(s) and complete a separate Form C1A (Allegations of harm and domestic violence) and give this to the court with your completed Form C100.

Tick whether you are asking permission to make this application (and if so complete section 5a)

Tick whether the application is urgent (and if so complete section 6a) or whether the application is to be made without notice to another party (and if so complete section 6b)

Tick whether there are linked proceedings (and if so complete section 7). When providing information about linked proceedings, please provide as much detail as possible about previous or current court cases that you are aware of in relation to the child(ren).

Tick whether your application is for an order to formalise an agreement (consent order) and if so attach the draft order to this form.

Tick whether your case has an international element or whether there are any factors that affect the ability of any party to these proceedings to participate in proceedings.

Page 4

Answer questions 2a to 2d about whether there are parallel proceedings for an emergency protection, care or supervision order, whether a MIAM exemption applies or whether you have attended a MIAM.

Pages 5 to 9

If you answered question 2b on page 4 with 'Yes' you must tick one of the first five boxes box in section 3 to indicate the category of MIAM exemption that you are claiming. You must then complete section 3a, b, c, d or e as shown.

If a family mediator needs to certify that a mediator's exemption applies you must ask them to complete section 4 of this form and sign where shown.

If you have attended a MIAM you must ask the family mediator who conducted it to complete section 4 of the form and sign where shown.

Page 10

Tick whether you have or are applying for permission to make this application (and if seeking permission complete section 5a).

Complete section 5b to provide brief details about why you are making the application

Complete section 5c about any previously prepared Parenting Plan.

Page 15

Answer questions 10a to 10c by ticking the relevant boxes and provide details in the box of any special arrangements you need in order to be able to attend court.

Page 16

If you (the applicant) does not wish the address to be made known it should be included in an accompanying Form C8 (Confidential contact details). Please ensure that any documents submitted with this form or at a later date, **do not** include the confidential contact details you wish to withhold.

Page 17

The respondent's address, including the Postcode

The respondent's telephone number and if applicable, mobile telephone

Whether the respondent has lived at their address for more than 5 years

Page 18

Full details for other parties who should be given notice of the application

Page 20

Check that you (or your solicitor if relevant) have completed and signed the statement of truth.

General information for completing this form

Requirement to attend a Mediation, Information and Assessment Meeting

1. It is now a legal requirement that, unless an exemption applies, a person who wishes to apply to court for one or more of the orders listed at paragraph 1 of these notes must first attend a Mediation, Information and Assessment Meeting (a MIAM). At the stage before proceedings the other party (the respondent) is expected to attend either the same MIAM or a separate MIAM.

2. At the MIAM, a trained family mediator will give you (the applicant) and the other person if present (the respondent) information about family mediation and other types of non-court dispute resolution. They will consider with you whether non-court dispute resolution would be an appropriate way to resolve the dispute. It is then for the applicant and respondent to decide whether or not to do so.

3. The requirement for the applicant to attend a MIAM does not apply if a Section 8 order is being applied for and:

   • the other person is in agreement about what you are asking the court to order (the order is a 'consent order'); or

   • there is an ongoing case about the child(ren) who would be the subject of the Section 8 application and that case concerns an emergency protection order, a supervision order or a care order, or if one of those orders has previously been made.

4. You must tick the relevant box in Section 2 of this form so that the court knows whether the MIAM requirement applies, whether an exemption applies (and why) or whether you have attended a MIAM.

MIAM exemptions and MIAM attendance

5. As the applicant you are expected to have contacted an authorised family mediator in order to make arrangements to attend a MIAM unless :

   • the MIAM requirement does not apply for one of the reasons explained at paragraph 9 of these notes, or

   • you are claiming a MIAM exemption, or a family mediator certifies that a mediator's exemption applies.

6. You can find an authorised family mediator by using the 'Find your local mediator' search facility available at: www.familymediationcouncil.org.uk

7. You should give the mediator the contact details of the other person so that the family mediator can contact them to check their willingness to attend a MIAM. If the other persons (or none of the other persons if there is more than one respondent) is or are unwilling to attend a MIAM this is a ground for the family mediator to exempt you from attending a MIAM.

8. If you or your solicitor believe that you have grounds for claiming exemption from MIAM attendance you or your solicitor must tick the relevant box in Section 2 of this form and complete Section 13.

9. If a family mediator wishes to certify that a mediator's exemption applies, so that you do not need to attend a MIAM, you must ask the family mediator to complete Section 4 of this form and sign it where shown.

10. If you have attended a MIAM you must ask the family mediator who conducted the MIAM to complete Section 4 of this form and sign it where shown.

11. If you claim a MIAM exemption and make an application to the court, the court will inquire into the grounds for exemption. The court may ask you to produce written evidence (see Section 3 of this form for details against each exemption shown).

12. If the court determines that the exemption was not validly claimed it may direct you, or you and the other party, to attend a MIAM and, if the case has already progressed to the first hearing, may adjourn the case to enable you to make arrangements to attend a MIAM.

13. The detailed procedure relating to the MIAM requirement and MIAM exemptions and attendance is set out in Part 3 of the Family Procedure Rules and in supporting Practice Direction 3A (judicial guidance). These are available online at: www.justice.gov.uk/courts/procedure-rules/family/ practice_directions/pd_part_03a

Paying for MIAM attendance or for family mediation

14. Legal aid is available for MIAMs and for family mediation. If you are eligible for legal aid you could receive both the MIAM and mediation sessions free of charge, as well as some advice from a solicitor to support you in the mediation process.

15. If you, or the prospective respondent, is eligible for Legal Aid then the total cost of MIAM attendance can be met by the Legal Aid Agency, whether you and the prospective respondent attend the same MIAM or separate MIAMs.

16. If neither you nor the respective respondent is eligible for Legal Aid then the mediator will agree with you how the cost of MIAM attendance is to be met.

17. See paragraph 33 below on how to find out whether you are eligible for Legal Aid.

Safety and MIAM attendance

18. Please note: the family mediator will discuss with you and with the other person whether you wish to attend the MIAM separately or together. Family mediators have a responsibility to ensure the safety and security of all concerned and will always check with each of you that attending together is your individual choice and is safe.

Information about mediation

19. If suitable, mediation can be a better way of resolving issues about arrangements for children when you and your partner separate or divorce. Mediation can be less expensive than going to court and much less stressful for all the family. It can also help you as parents to focus on your child(ren)'s needs in making decisions about them.

20. Family Mediation is an impartial process that involves an independent third person who assists both parties involved in a family dispute to reach a resolution. Family mediation can be used to settle any or all of the following issues:

    • Arrangements for children

    • Financial arrangements and dividing up property

    • Any combination of these

    • Any other disputes to do with separation and divorce.

21. Family Mediation is not just for divorcing or separating couples – it is a means for resolving a range of family disputes, whether they arise from divorce or the separation of cohabiting parents. Family Mediation could also help resolve issues with wider family members such as grandparents.

22. The family mediator helps the process of negotiation between the parties to agree their own arrangements by way of a Memorandum of Understanding. You can ask a solicitor, if you have one, to check the Memorandum of Understanding.

23. If both parties agree, you can ask the court to endorse what you have agreed by issuing a consent order. The mediator will help you to decide whether your case is complicated and does in fact need the court to consider your situation and make an order. The mediator should also tell you about other local services and options for resolving your dispute.

24. A statutory Mediation Information and Assessment Meeting (MIAM) is reserved for "authorised mediators" under the Family Procedure Rules. "Authorised family mediator" means a person identified by the Family Mediation Council as qualified to conduct a MIAM. "Qualified to conduct a MIAM" is interpreted as holding current Family Mediation Council accreditation (FMCA). FMCA mediators are issued with a unique FMC registration number. Authorised mediators are requested to enter this number in the box provided.

Further information and sources of help

25. General information about family mediation is available from the Family Mediation Council website at: www.familymediationcouncil.org.uk

26. The family mediator who undertakes the MIAM for you must be a member of a national mediation organisation which adheres to the Family Mediation Council's Code of Conduct and the mediator must be authorised to conduct MIAMs. The service finder will help you find such a local mediator.

27. You can find out more about legal aid for family matters, including whether you may eligible for legal aid, on the Legal Aid Information Service on the Gov.UK site at: www.gov.uk/check-legal-aid or you can telephone the Civil Legal Advice direct helpline 0345 345 4345.

28. For general advice on separation services and options for resolving disputes: www.sortingoutseparation.org.uk

29. For general advice about sorting out arrangements for children, the use of post-separation mediation, and/or going to court: www.advicenow.org.uk; www.advicenow.org.uk/guides/survival-guide-sorting-out-arrangements-your-children

30. For general advice about sorting out arrangements for children: www.theparentconnection.org.uk/

31. For advice about Contact Centres, which are neutral places where children of separated families can enjoy contact with their non-resident parents and sometimes other family members, in a comfortable and safe environment; and information about where they are: www.naccc.org.uk

32. For help with taking a case to court without a solicitor, the Personal Support Unit: www.thepsu.org/

33. For guidance on representing yourself at court, including a list of commonly used terms that you may come across: http://www.barcouncil.org.uk/using-a-barrister/representing-yourself-in-court/

34. For advice about finding and using a family law solicitor see: Law Society www.lawsociety.org.uk, and Resolution (family law solicitors): www.resolution.org.uk

35. For advice about finding using a family law barrister: see http://www.barcouncil.org.uk/using-a-barrister/find-a-barrister/ and for arrangements for using a barrister directly see http://www.barcouncil.org.uk/using-a-barrister/how-to-instruct-a-barrister/

36. Judicial guidance that sets out the approach of the courts to deciding child arrangements is available online at: www.justice.gov.uk/courts/procedure-rules/family/practice_directions/pd_part_12b

Online videos

37. There are several videos explain more about the mediation process, making your application, what will happen in court and will help you prepare for the hearing. To watch the videos visit www.bit.ly/guides_for_separating_parents

(I)   Form C1A (Allegations of harm and domestic violence)

C1A **Allegations of harm and domestic violence** (Supplemental information form) This form cannot be used to make an application for a court order. It must be sent to the court **together with** the relevant application form.	**To be completed by the court**
	The Family Court sitting at
	Date issued
	Case number
	Order(s) applied for

Please read the notes at the end of this form before completing it.

If completing this form by hand, please use **black ink** and BLOCK CAPITAL LETTERS.

You are completing this form because there are allegations that the child(ren) listed in this form may have suffered or be at risk of suffering domestic abuse, violence/abuse.

"Domestic violence/abuse" means any incident of threatening behaviour, violence or abuse (psychological, physical, sexual, financial or emotional) between adults who are or have been intimate partners or family members regardless of gender or sexuality.

The Children Act 1989 defines the following terms as:

"Harm" means ill treatment or damage to health and development, including, for example, damage suffered from seeing or hearing the ill treatment of another.

"Development" means physical, intellectual, emotional, social or behavioural development.

"Health" means physical or mental health.

"Ill-treatment" includes sexual abuse and forms of ill-treatment which are not physical.

Section 1 - About you (the person completing this form)

Your full name

Gender ☐ Male ☐ Female

Are you the ☐ Applicant ☐ Respondent

Contact telephone number

Have you completed the form C8 (Confidential contact details)? ☐ Yes ☐ No ☐ Not applicable
See Section 1 of the guidance notes.

Name of child(ren)	Date of birth	Gender	Relationship to you
	☐☐/☐☐/☐☐☐☐	☐ Male ☐ Female	
	☐☐/☐☐/☐☐☐☐	☐ Male ☐ Female	
	☐☐/☐☐/☐☐☐☐	☐ Male ☐ Female	

	Do you have a solicitor acting for you?	☐ Yes ☐ No

If Yes, please give the following details

Your solicitor's details ——————————————

Your solicitor's name	
Name of firm	
Address	
	Postcode ☐☐☐☐ ☐☐☐
Telephone number	
Fax number	
DX number	
Email address	
Solicitor's Reference	

Section 2 - Details of domestic violence/abuse

In this section outline the nature and frequency of the abuse experienced by you or the child(ren) and if this has led to any involvement with the police, social services, children's services, your doctor (GP) or any other outside agency(ies). (Provide the details in the table on the page 3).

Tick any of the following kinds of abuse that you or the child(ren) have experienced:

	Physical	Emotional	Psychological	Sexual	Financial
You	☐	☐	☐	☐	☐
Child(ren)	☐	☐	☐	☐	☐

Have you had or do you currently have any of the following orders and are they current?

	Date issued	Length of order	Current Yes/No	Name of court
Non-molestation order				
Occupation order				
Forced marriage protection order				
Restraining order				
Other injunctive order				
Undertaking in place of order				

If you have any copies of the above orders please attached them to this form

2

Give a short description of what happened and any relevant information so the court can decide what needs to be done.
There will be further opportunities to make a detailed statement

When did the behaviour start and how long did it continue? (Does not need to be exact date and indicate if abuse is ongoing)	Nature of behaviour/what happened	If you have sought help, please say who from	Did they do anything? If Yes, what did they do?
1.			
2.			
3.			
4.			
5.			

Section 3 - Abduction

| Do you believe that the children are at risk of being abducted? | ☐ Yes   If Yes, please complete this Section |
| | ☐ No   If No, go to Section 4 |

Why do you believe the child(ren) may be abducted?

Have there been any previous threats, attempts to abduct or actual abduction of the child(ren)?

☐ Yes   ☐ No

If Yes, please give details

Where is/are the child(ren) now?

Has the passport office been notified?

☐ Yes   ☐ No

Do(es) the child(ren) have more than one passport?

☐ Yes   ☐ No

Who is in possession of the child(ren)'s passport(s)?

☐ Mother   ☐ Father

☐ Other (please give details below)

Were the police in this and/ or another country or any organisation or agency including any private investigators involved in any previous incident of attempted abduction or abduction.

☐ Yes   ☐ No

If Yes, please give details below

Section 4 - Other concerns about your child(ren)

Do you have any other concerns about your child(ren)'s safety and wellbeing?

☐ Yes   ☐ No

If Yes, please give details

(Do not give full statement, please provide a summary of your concerns. You may be asked to provide a full statement later.)

Section 5 - Steps or orders required to protect the safety and wellbeing

What steps or orders do you want the court to take or make to protect the safety of the child(ren) and/or yourself?

Non-molestation order: The court may decide to make a non-molestation order under Part IV of the Family Law Act 1996. A non-molestation order requires that the person against whom the order has been made may not be violent or threaten violence, harass, pester or annoy the person who applied for the order, by any means, including social media (text messages, Facebook etc.).

The different types of orders that can be applied for under section 8 of the Children Act 1989 are as follows:

Prohibited Steps: this prevents a parent from taking a particular action as set out in the order without the permission of the court. This also applies to actions by any other person named in the order.

Specific issue: this decides specific questions e.g. about education, medical treatment or a foreign holiday or visit where parents or those with parental responsibility cannot agree.

Do you agree to the child(ren) spending **unsupervised** time with the other person in receipt of this form?

☐ Yes   ☐ No

Do you agree to the child(ren) spending **supervised** time with the other person in receipt of this form?

☐ Yes   ☐ No

Do you agree to the child having other forms of contact with the other person in receipt of this form? (by telephone, text, email, social media)

☐ Yes   ☐ No

6

Section 6 - Statement of truth

*delete as appropriate

*[I believe] [The applicant/respondent believes] that the facts stated in this application are true.

*I am duly authorised by the applicant/respondent to sign this statement.

Print full name

Name of solicitors firm

Signed

Dated [ ] / [ ] / [   ]

(Applicant) (Respondent) ('s Solicitor)

Position or office held
(If signing on behalf of firm or company)

Proceedings for contempt of court may be brought against a person who makes or causes to be made, a false statement in a document verified by a statement of truth.

Section 7 - Attending court

Please indicate whether you intend to request any special arrangements to be made for you to attend court. The court will make every effort to meet these needs, subject to facilities available. Please telephone the court in advance of the hearing to clarify what arrangements can be made.

- [ ] Separate waiting rooms
- [ ] Separate e xits and entrances
- [ ] Screens
- [ ] Video links
- [ ] Separate toilets
- [ ] Advance viewing of the Court
- [ ] Interpreter
- [ ] a disability for which you require special assistance or special facilities
- [ ] a sign language signer
- [ ] Other _____

7

Checklist

Before sending your forms to the court, please complete this checklist to confirm that you have enclosed the following items:

- [ ] If you are the applicant - for a child arrangements or other section 8 order under the Children Act 1989 C100 or if you are the respondent – C7 (Response to an application under the Children Act 1989).

- [ ] If you are the applicant for a non-section 8 order under the Children Act 1989 - C1, or if you are the respondent - C7 (Response to an application under the Children Act 1989).

- [ ] C8 (Confidential contact details)
Note: Only attach this form if you want to withhold your contact details from the other party.

- [ ] Copies of any orders made by the court for your protection — see section 2.

- [ ] Any other written evidence which you are able to provide at this stage to support your allegations made in the table on page 3.

If you have any concerns about your safety and that of your children you can call the **National Domestic Violence Helpline** on **freephone 0808 2000 247** or you get more information from **www.nationaldomesticviolencehelpline.org.uk**

If you are a man and have concerns for your safety and that of your children you can call the **Men's Advice Line and Enquiry** on **freephone 0808 801 0327** or you get more information from **www.mensadviceline.org.uk**

Other organisations that may be able to provide advice for children or young people are:
Childline on freephone 0800 1111 and **NSPCC Child Protection Helpline on freephone 0808 800 5000**

Response to allegations of harm - To be completed by the person in receipt of this form

You do not have to complete this section unless you wish to comment on any of the information given in this form.

Please give brief comments on the information provided on the table on page 3 of this form. You will have an opportunity to make a more detailed statement later in the proceedings.

1.	
2.	
3.	
4.	
5.	

Any other comments you have on the information provided in this form

Statement of truth

*[I believe] [The applicant/respondent believes] that the facts stated in this
form are true.

*delete as
appropriate *I am duly authorised by the applicant/respondent to sign this statement.

Print full name

Name of solicitors firm

Signed   Dated [ ]/[ ]/[   ]

(Applicant) (Respondent) ('s Solicitor)

Position or office held
(If signing on behalf of firm or
company)

**Proceedings for contempt of court may be brought against a person who
makes, or causes to be made, a false statement in a document verified by
a statement of truth.**

9

Notes for Guidance and Checklist
For Supplemental Information Form C1A

About these notes:

- They explain some of the terms used in this form that may be unfamiliar to you and will help you to complete the form.

- You should read all these notes and the checklist before beginning to complete this form.

- These notes are only a guide to help you complete this form. If you need further help you could speak to a solicitor, Citizen's Advice Bureau, legal advice centre or law centre. Legal aid may be available. You can get further information at www.gov.uk/check-legal-aid or by phoning 0345 345 4345.

Please note that while court staff will help on procedural matters, they cannot offer any legal advice

Section 1

About You

If you do not wish your contact details to be made known to the respondent, leave the space on the form blank and complete Confidential contact details (form C8). You can get a copy of this form from any family court office or from our website at hmctsformfinder.justice.gov.uk It should be sent to the court at the same time as you submit this form.

Section 2 – Further Information

1. Incidents of domestic violence/abuse and their outcomes

The definitions of harm and domestic violence/abuse are set out on page one of the form

This section is to outline the nature and frequency of the abuse experienced by you or the child(ren) and any action that may have taken place as a consequence.

The first part asks what type of abuse that you or the child(ren) may have experienced.

The second part asks if you have any of the following court orders, when they were issued, how long they are for, and which court they were made in.

Non-molestation order – requires that the person against whom the order has been made may not be violent or threaten violence, harass, pester or annoy the person who applied for the order

Occupation order – sets out who can live in a property and can exclude a person totally from the property or prohibit a person from entering certain rooms within the property.

Forced Marriage Protection Order – can require that a person's passport is surrendered, prohibit intimidation and violence, order a person to reveal the whereabouts of a person and stop someone from being taken abroad for the purpose of being forced into marriage.

Restraining order – prohibits the convicted person from further conduct which causes harassment or will cause a fear of violence.

Other injunctive order – any other injunction you may have obtained against the person whom you are alleging harm.

If you have been granted any of the above orders please attach copies of the orders with the form.

2. Information about incidents

The table is intended to give a short description of what happened and relevant information. The following is a brief description of what is required in each column:

Approximate date/when/how long did the behaviour continue – this can be either specific/approximate dates of individual incidents, or a timeframe over which multiple incidents occurred.

Nature of behaviour/what happened – a brief description on the incidents, please note that you can describe the same type of behaviour that happened over a period of time in one entry.

Have you ever sought help? If so, from who? – This could be the police, social services, your doctor, a medical professional, a voluntary sector worker, the Citizen's Advice Bureau or any agency you may have approached for help. It could also be a friend or family member.

Did they do anything? – What help did they give you? Were you referred to anyone else? Is there any ongoing contact with them?

Section 3 – Abduction

This section asks about any concerns you may have about a child being abducted from your care.

'Child abduction' is the wrongful removal of a child from any person having, or entitled to, lawful control of that child.

'International child abduction' is the wrongful removal or wrongful retention away from the country where the child usually lives.

If the child has a passport it is important that you fill in the section about who is in possession of the child's passport.

Section 4

Are there any other concerns you would like to raise regarding your Child(ren)?

This section is for any concerns not already raised in the form regarding the childs safety and wellbeing.

Section 5

Attending the Court

This section asks if you require any special measures put in place when you attend court. The court will try to supply you and your witnesses with a separate waiting area and the other measures listed. However, this is not always possible and can depend on the court facilities as to whether these measures are available.

Response to allegations of harm (page 9)

This section should only be filled in if the other party (the applicant) has served a completed form C1A and has sent it to the respondent.

If no form C1A is sent in with the application for an order the respondent themselves will need to complete the form C1A to be returned with form C7 Response to an application under the Children Act 1989.

(J)   Form C110A (Application for a care or supervision order)

Application for a care or supervision order and other orders under Part 4 of the Children Act 1989 or an Emergency Protection Order under section 44 of the Children Act 1989

To be completed by the court	
The family court sitting at	
Case number	Date issued
Child(ren)'s name(s)	
Fee charged	

Name of applicant

Full name of respondent(s)

Nature of application

What order(s) are you applying for? *(tick all which apply)*

☐ **Care and supervision or other Part 4**

☐ Care

☐ Supervision

☐ Interim care order

☐ Interim supervision order

☐ Other *(please specify)*

Is the Local Authority considering adoption?

☐ Yes   ☐ No

If Yes, please complete Section 7b

☐ **Emergency Protection Order**

☐ information on the whereabouts of the child[ren] (Section 48(1) Children Act 1989).

☐ authorisation for entry of premises (Section 48(3) Children Act 1989).

☐ authorisation to search for another child on the premises (Section 48(4) Children Act 1989).

☐ Other *(please specify)*

Additional information required

Is an urgent hearing required?	☐ Yes	☐ No	If Yes, complete Section 1
Is a without notice hearing required?	☐ Yes	☐ No	If Yes, complete Section 2
Are there previous or ongoing proceedings for the child(ren)?	☐ Yes	☐ No	If Yes, complete Section 3
Are there factors affecting litigation capacity?	☐ Yes	☐ No	If Yes, complete Section 4
Is this a case with an international element?	☐ Yes	☐ No	If Yes, complete Section 5
Will the child or any of the people involved need to use spoken or written Welsh during the course of the proceedings?	☐ Yes	☐ No	If Yes, complete Section 9

Summary of children's details

Child 1 - Full name of child	Date of birth	Order(s) applied for (including interim orders)
	D D / M M / Y Y Y Y	
	Is the child accommodated? ☐ Yes ☐ No	
	If Yes, from what date? D D / M M / Y Y Y Y	

Name of mother	Name of father	Parental Responsibility
		☐ Yes ☐ No

Child 2 - Full name of child	Date of birth	Order(s) applied for (including interim orders)
	D D / M M / Y Y Y Y	
	Is the child accommodated? ☐ Yes ☐ No	
	If Yes, from what date? D D / M M / Y Y Y Y	

Name of mother	Name of father	Parental Responsibility
		☐ Yes ☐ No

Child 3 - Full name of child	Date of birth	Order(s) applied for (including interim orders)
	D D / M M / Y Y Y Y	
	Is the child accommodated? ☐ Yes ☐ No	
	If Yes, from what date? D D / M M / Y Y Y Y	

Name of mother	Name of father	Parental Responsibility
		☐ Yes ☐ No

Child 4 - Full name of child	Date of birth	Order(s) applied for (including interim orders)
	D D / M M / Y Y Y Y	
	Is the child accommodated? ☐ Yes ☐ No	
	If Yes, from what date? D D / M M / Y Y Y Y	

Name of mother	Name of father	Parental Responsibility
		☐ Yes ☐ No

2

1. Is the application for urgent consideration?

Complete this section if you have ticked the relevant box on the front of the form

Is the urgent hearing for:
(tick as required)

☐ Contested ICO

☐ EPO

☐ urgent preliminary Case Management Hearing

Part A - All applications

Set out the order(s)/directions sought

Set out the reasons for urgency

Proposed timetable

The application should be considered within [   ] hours/days

If consideration is sought within 48 hours, you must complete the section below

What efforts have been made to put each respondent on notice of the application?

3

If the application is for an Emergency Protection Order only, please complete B, C and D as appropriate

B – The grounds are

Any applicant

☐ that there is reasonable cause to believe that [this] [these] child[ren] [is] [are] likely to suffer significant harm if

or ☐ the child[ren] [is] [are] not removed to accommodation provided by or on behalf of this applicant

or ☐ the child[ren] [does] [do] not remain in the place where [the child] [they] [is] [are] currently being accommodated.

Local authority applicants

☐ that enquiries are being made about the welfare of the child[ren] under Section 47(1)(b) of Children Act 1989 **and** those enquiries are being frustrated by access to the child[ren] being unreasonably refused to someone who is authorised to seek access **and** there is reasonable cause to believe that access to the child[ren] is required as a matter of urgency.

Authorised person applicants

☐ that there is reasonable cause to suspect that the child[ren] [is] [are] suffering, or [is] [are] likely to suffer, significant harm **and** enquiries are being made with respect to the welfare of the child[ren] **and** those enquiries are being frustrated by access to the child[ren] being unreasonably refused to someone who is authorised to seek access **and** there is reasonable cause to believe that access to the child[ren] is required as a matter of urgency.

C – The additional order(s) applied for

☐ information on the whereabouts of the child[ren] (Section 48(1) Children Act 1989).

☐ authorisation for entry of premises (Section 48(3) Children Act 1989).

☐ authorisation to search for another child on the premises (Section 48(4) Children Act 1989).

D – The direction(s) sought

☐ contact with any named person (Section 44(6)(a) Children Act 1989).

☐ a medical or psychiatric examination or other assessment of the child[ren] (Section 44(6)(b) Children Act 1989).

☐ to be accompanied by a registered medical practitioner, registered nurse or registered midwife (Section 45(12) Children Act 1989).

☐ an exclusion requirement (Section 44A(1) Children Act 1989).

4

2. Is the application for a without notice hearing?

Complete this section if you have ticked the relevant box on the front of the form

Set out the order/directions sought

Set out the reasons for the application to be considered without notice. (This information is a requirement, a without notice hearing will **not** be directed without reason)

Do you require a without notice hearing because it is not possible to give notice including abridged or informal notice?

☐ Yes   ☐ No

If Yes, please set out reasons below

Do you require a without notice hearing because notice to a respondent will frustrate the order that is being applied for?

☐ Yes   ☐ No

If Yes, please set out reasons below

Other *(please specify)*

5

3. Previous or ongoing proceedings

Complete this section if you have ticked the relevant box on the front of this form.

Please give details (include name of child(ren), case no., date(s) of application, dates proceedings concluded, order made)

Please also provide the name of any children's guardian who has been involved in any previous or ongoing proceedings involving a child of one or both respondents

Is continuity of the children's guardian required?

☐ Yes   ☐ No

If No, why not?

4. Factors affecting ability to participate in proceedings

Complete this section if you have ticked the relevant box on the front of this form.

Please give details of any factors affecting litigation capacity

Provide details of any referral to or assessment by the Adult Learning Disability team, and/or any adult health service, where known, together with the outcome

Are you aware of any other factors which may affect the ability of the person concerned to take part in the proceedings?

7

5. Cases with an international element

Complete this section if you have ticked the relevant box on the front of this form.

Do you have any reason to believe that any child, parent or potentially significant adult in the child's life may be habitually resident in another state?

☐ Yes   ☐ No

If Yes, please give details

Do you have any reason to believe that there may be an issue as to jurisdiction in this case (for example under Brussels 2 revised)?

☐ Yes   ☐ No

If Yes, please give details

Has a request been made or should a request be made to a Central Authority or other competent authority in a foreign state or a consular authority in England and Wales?

☐ Yes   ☐ No

If Yes, please give details

6. Grounds for the application

The grounds for the application are that the child(ren) is suffering or is likely to suffer, significant harm and the harm or likelihood of harm is because the child is:

☐ not receiving care that would be reasonably expected from a parent

☐ beyond parental control

Set out in not more than the two following pages the threshold criteria relied upon

Continued from overleaf – Set out
the threshold criteria relied upon

10

7. Plans for the child(ren)

7a. Please give a brief summary of the plans for the child(ren).

The summary must include any contact arrangements that are in place or are proposed.

What is the local authority's proposal including placement and support services and are there any requirements which the local authority wish the court to impose under Part 1 of Schedule 3 Children Act 1989?

It is not sufficient just to refer to or repeat the Care Plan.

7b. Having regard to s. 22 Adoption and Children Act 2002 is the local authority considering adoption?

☐ Yes   ☐ No

Does the application for a placement order(s) accompany this application?

☐ Yes   ☐ No

If not, why not and when will it be submitted?

Have you notified the relevant Central Authority or the competent authority in the foreign state in cases to which section 5 of this form applies?

☐ Yes   ☐ No

11

8. Timetable for the child(ren)

The timetable for the child will be set by the court to take account of dates of the significant steps in the child's life that are likely to take place during the proceedings. Those steps include not only legal steps, but also social, care, health, education and developmental steps and any timetable for a case with an international element.

Please give any relevant dates/events in relation to the child(ren)
• it may be necessary to give different dates for each child.

Are you aware of any significant event in the timetable, before which the case should be concluded?

☐ Yes   ☐ No

If Yes, please give a date

[D D / M M / Y Y Y Y]

and give your reasons

By what date should the child(ren) be placed on a permanent basis?

Name of child

[D D / M M / Y Y Y Y]

Name of child

[D D / M M / Y Y Y Y]

Name of child

[D D / M M / Y Y Y Y]

Name of child

[D D / M M / Y Y Y Y]

Please give your reasons

12

9. Attending the court

If you require an interpreter, you must tell the court now so that one can be arranged.

9a. Do you or any other party need to use spoken or written Welsh in the course of the proceedings?

☐ Yes   ☐ No

If Yes, please give the names of the parties/witnesses/children involved who need to use written or spoken Welsh?

	Spoken	Written	Both
	☐ Spoken	☐ Written	☐ Both
	☐ Spoken	☐ Written	☐ Both
	☐ Spoken	☐ Written	☐ Both
	☐ Spoken	☐ Written	☐ Both
	☐ Spoken	☐ Written	☐ Both
	☐ Spoken	☐ Written	☐ Both
	☐ Spoken	☐ Written	☐ Both

9b. Do you or any of the parties require the court to appoint an interpreter or arrange any other assistance (e.g. sign language signer)?

☐ Yes   ☐ No

If Yes, who requires the interpreter

☐ applicant   ☐ respondent   ☐ Other party *(please specify)*

and please specify the language and dialect required:

9c. Are you aware of whether an intermediary will be required?

☐ Yes   ☐ No

If Yes, please give details

9d. If attending the court, do you or any of the parties involved have a disability for which you require special assistance or special facilities?

☐ Yes   ☐ No

If Yes, please say what the needs are

Please say whether there is a need for the court to make any special arrangements for you or any relevant children to attend court (e.g. providing you with a separate waiting room from the respondent or other security provisions).

Court staff may get in touch with you about the requirements

13

10. Allocation proposal

Part 1 (To be completed by the applicant Local Authority on issue)

Judicial continuity
Please give the following details of other proceedings:

Case number

Name of Judge

Date of last relevant order

Are proceedings finished or outstanding?

☐ Finished   ☐ Outstanding

Applicant's allocation proposal

☐ Lay justices

☐ District Judge level

☐ Circuit Judge level

☐ DFJ/Section 9 sitting as a Judge of the High Court

☐ High Court Judge level

Set out the applicable paragraphs of the schedule to the President's Guidance on the distribution of business

Part 2 (To be completed by the Court)

Allocation decision in accordance with the Allocation Rules and the President's Guidance on the distribution of business

☐ Lay justices

☐ District Judge level

☐ Circuit Judge level

☐ High Court Judge level

Listed for Case Management Hearing

Time ☐   Date ☐☐/☐☐/☐☐☐☐

14

Allocated by	Location of court	
	or	
	Name of Judge	
	District Judge	
	Legal Adviser	
	Date	[2 0 / M M / Y Y Y Y]

11. Signature

Print full name	
Your role/position held	

The facts in this application are true to the best of my knowledge and belief and the opinions set out are my own.

Signed	
	Applicant
Date	[D D / M M / Y Y Y Y]

15

Details of parties – please complete this section in full

The applicant

Name of applicant
(local authority or authorised person)

Name of contact

Job title

Address

Postcode

Contact telephone number

Mobile telephone number

Fax number

Email

DX number

Solicitor's details

Solicitor's name

Address

Postcode

Telephone number

Mobile telephone number

Fax number

Email

DX number

Solicitor's Reference

Fee account no.

16

If there are more than two respondents please continue on a separate sheet.

The respondents

Respondent 1

Respondent's full name

Date of birth [ ] / [ ] / [ ]   Gender ☐ Male ☐ Female

Place of birth
(town/county/country, if known)

Current address

Postcode [ ][ ][ ] [ ][ ][ ]

Telephone number

Relationship to the child(ren)

Name of child(ren)	Relationship	Parental Responsibility	
		☐ Yes	☐ No
		☐ Yes	☐ No
		☐ Yes	☐ No
		☐ Yes	☐ No

Respondent 2

Respondent's full name

Date of birth [ ] / [ ] / [ ]   Gender ☐ Male ☐ Female

Place of birth
(town/county/country, if known)

Current address

Postcode [ ][ ][ ] [ ][ ][ ]

Telephone number

Relationship to the child(ren)

Name of child(ren)	Relationship	Parental Responsibility	
		☐ Yes	☐ No
		☐ Yes	☐ No
		☐ Yes	☐ No
		☐ Yes	☐ No

17

The child(ren)

Please give details of the child(ren) and the order(s) you are applying for.
If there are more than four children please continue on a separate sheet.

Child 1

Child's full name

Date of birth ☐☐ / ☐☐ / ☐☐☐☐   Gender ☐ Male ☐ Female

Name of social worker and telephone number

If the child is not accommodated, who does the child live with?

At which address does the child live?

Postcode ☐☐☐☐ ☐☐☐☐

Child 2

Child's full name

Date of birth ☐☐ / ☐☐ / ☐☐☐☐   Gender ☐ Male ☐ Female

Name of social worker and telephone number

If the child is not accommodated, who does the child live with?

At which address does the child live?

Postcode ☐☐☐☐ ☐☐☐☐

18

Child 3

Child's full name

Date of birth [D D / M M / Y Y Y Y]   Gender ☐ Male   ☐ Female

Name of social worker and telephone number

If the child is not accommodated, who does the child live with?

At which address does the child live?

Postcode [   ] [   ]

Child 4

Child's full name

Date of birth [D D / M M / Y Y Y Y]   Gender ☐ Male   ☐ Female

Name of social worker and telephone number

If the child is not accommodated, who does the child live with?

At which address does the child live?

Postcode [   ] [   ]

If more than four children, continue on a separate sheet.

19

Others who should be given notice

Person 1

Person's full name	
Date of birth	☐ ☐ / ☐ ☐ / ☐ ☐ ☐ ☐ Gender ☐ Male ☐ Female
Address	
	Postcode ☐☐☐☐ ☐☐☐☐

Relationship to the child(ren)

Name of child	Relationship	Parental Responsibility
		☐ Yes ☐ No
		☐ Yes ☐ No
		☐ Yes ☐ No
		☐ Yes ☐ No

Relationship to the respondents

Name of respondent	Relationship

Person 2

Person's full name	
Date of birth	☐ ☐ / ☐ ☐ / ☐ ☐ ☐ ☐ Gender ☐ Male ☐ Female
Address	
	Postcode ☐☐☐☐ ☐☐☐☐

Relationship to the child(ren)

Name of child	Relationship	Parental Responsibility
		☐ Yes ☐ No
		☐ Yes ☐ No
		☐ Yes ☐ No
		☐ Yes ☐ No

Relationship to the respondents

Name of respondent	Relationship

20

Annex Documents

This annex must be completed by the applicant with any application for a care, supervision or other Part 4 order.

The documents specified in this annex must be filed with the application if available.

If any relevant document is not filed with the application, the reason and any expected date of filing must be stated.

All documents filed with the application must be clearly marked with their title and numbered consecutively.

1. Social Work Chronology
(A succinct summary)

☐ attached   ☐ to follow

If **to follow** please give reasons why not included and the date when the document will be sent to the court.

2. Social Work Statement and genogram

☐ attached   ☐ to follow

If **to follow** please give reasons why not included and the date when the document will be sent to the court.

3. The current assessment relating to the child and/or the family and friends of the child to which the Social Work Statement refers and on which the local authority relies

☐ attached   ☐ to follow

If **to follow** please give reasons why not included and the date when the document will be sent to the court.

4. Care plan

☐ attached   ☐ to follow

If **to follow** please give reasons why not included and the date when the document will be sent to the court.

5. Index of checklist documents

☐ attached   ☐ to follow

If **to follow** please give reasons why not included and the date when the document will be sent to the court.

What to do once you have completed this form

Ensure that you have:

☐ attached copies of any **annex** documents.

☐ **signed** the form at Section 11.

☐ provided a **copy** of the application and attached documents for each of the respondents, and for Cafcass or CAFCASS CYMRU.

☐ given details of the additional children if there are more than four.

☐ given details of the additional respondents if there are more than two.

☐ the correct fee.

It is good practice to inform Cafcass or CAFCASS CYMRU that you are making this application. The court will expect the local authority to have informed Cafcass or CAFCASS CYMRU that proceedings are being issued.

Have you notified Cafcass - Children and Family Court Advisory and Support Service (for England)
or
CAFCASS CYMRU - Children and Family Court Advisory and Support Service Wales.

☐ Yes   ☐ No

If Yes, please give the date of notification

☐ ☐ / ☐ ☐ / ☐ ☐ ☐ ☐

Now take or send your application with the correct fee and four copies to the court.

Please refer to the Family Proceedings Fees Order for the correct fee in respect of your application.

Apply for a non-molestation or occupation order

Family Law Act 1996 (Part 4)

You can use this form to apply for a:

- **Non-molestation order:** Protects you and any relevant child from abuse or harassment. This order can also prevent someone coming to or near your home.

- **Occupation order:** The court decides who should live in, or return to, the home or any part of it.

There are no court fees for applying. You can apply for either order or both, depending on your situation.

Support with applying for an order

CourtNav is an online tool (provided by RCJ Citizens Advice) that will help you in putting together your application. The tool will also put you in touch with legal advisors to discuss your options.

Visit https://injunction.courtnav.org.uk to register and apply. If you choose to use CourtNav, you will not need to complete this FL401 form or a supporting statement – CourtNav will complete both for you.

Support if you are experiencing domestic abuse

Visit www.gov.uk/report-domestic-abuse for a list of organisations that can provide help and advice about domestic abuse. Call 999 if it's an emergency or you're in immediate danger

Applications without the respondent being told

In exceptional circumstances, such as your safety is immediately threatened, the court may make an order without telling the 'respondent' (the person the order is against). This is called an 'ex parte' or 'without notice' order. It means the court can consider your application without the respondent present. A hearing will be held later and the respondent will be given notice to attend. You can request this in section 1 of this form. You must tell the court why you are applying for a without notice order and what you think might happen if the court does not grant it.

If you want to keep your information confidential

If you do not want your or your child's contact details to be shared with the respondent, do not put these in at any point on the form, even when asked. Instead complete a confidential contact details (C8) form and send it with this application. Visit GOV.UK and search form 'C8'.

Do not include your contact details on any other documents sent to the court, such as supporting evidence.

If you are living in a refuge, it is very important that you keep your address details confidential and only include the address details on a form C8.

Before you start

How old are you?

☐ **18 years old or older.** You can continue to apply using this form.

☐ **16 to 18 years old.** Someone over 18 must help you apply, such as a parent. They will also need to complete form '**FP9**' to include with your application.

☐ **Under 16 years old**. You will need permission from the court to apply. With the help of someone over 18, you must also complete form '**FP2**' and they will need to complete form '**FP9**' and include these with your application. Visit GOV.UK and search form '**FP2**' and form '**FP9**'.

1. Your situation

1.1   Which order(s) are you applying for?

☐ **Non-molestation order** – to stop abusive behaviour

☐ **Occupation order** – to decide who lives in or can return to a property

---

Without notice orders

The court may, in any case where it considers that it is just and convenient to do so, make an occupation order or a non-molestation order even though the respondent has not been given prior notice of the proceedings, as would otherwise be required by rules of court.

Please see the guidance on the right to help work out if this may be an option for you.

1.2   Do you want to apply for the order without giving notice to the respondent?

☐ Yes

☐ No. **Go to question 1.5**

Note 1.1: 'Molestation' is a word used in law and by the court to cover all kinds of unwanted, harassing and abusive behaviours.

Note 1.2 and 1.3: This is sometimes called 'ex parte' and means the order can be made without the respondent knowing in advance. This is only an option if:

- you think there's a risk that the respondent may try to harm you or your child **(a)**

- you feel like you may be prevented or put off from applying if an order is not made immediately **(b)**

- you think the respondent will try to avoid court proceedings, including being served with the order* – and any delay caused by this could affect your application or the health, safety or wellbeing of you or your child **(c)**

* Usually the respondent will be given the order by hand. In some cases, the court may decide that the order should be served in another way, such as by email or text message. This is called 'substituted' or 'alternative' service.

The court or police cannot act if the respondent does something the order says they aren't allowed to until they have been served with the order.

1.3 Why do you want to apply without giving notice to the respondent?
You can select more than one reason – see guidance note for help.

☐ **a)** there is risk of significant harm to me or a relevant child, attributable to conduct of the respondent, if the order is not made immediately

☐ **b)** it is likely that I will be deterred or prevented from pursuing the application if an order is not made immediately

☐ **c)** I believe that the respondent is aware of the proceedings but is deliberately evading service and that I or a relevant child will be seriously prejudiced by the delay in effecting substituted service

1.4 Why do you think one or more of the reasons you have chosen for question 1.3 may happen?

Note 1.4: Please describe as best as you can why these things may happen. This could include things the respondent has said or done in the past.

1.5 As far as you know, are there any bail conditions stopping the respondent from contacting or coming near you?

☐ Yes

☐ No. **Go to question 1.7**

1.6 When do the bail conditions end?

Day   Month   Year

1.7   Is there anything else about your situation that you would like the court to know about or consider?

Note 1.7: It is important for the court to know about any special characteristics relating to you, the respondent or a child of the family. This could include whether there are any illnesses or disabilities suffered by anybody, or if you are pregnant.

You can provide more details about your situation in your supporting witness statement.

2. Your details

2.1 Your full name

First name(s)

[   ]

Last name

[   ]

2.2 Any other names you have been known by

[   ]

2.3 Your date of birth

Day   Month   Year

[   ]   [   ]   [   ]

2.4 Can your contact details be shared with the respondent?

☐ Yes

☐ No. Complete the separate **C8** form with your details.

2.5 Your full current address

Building and street

[   ]

Second line of address

[   ]

Town or city

[   ]

County (optional)

[   ]

Postcode

[   ]

Note 2.4: If you do not wish to disclose your contact details you should leave those details blank and complete form C8 Confidential contact details.

Note 2.5: The address you provide will be where the court will send your documents.

If you think the respondent may open your post or hide it from you, give us a different address to send the documents. Write the request on a separate sheet and include it with this application.

If you do provide a different address, make sure that it is of someone you trust and they can contact you.

If you are keeping your contact details confidential you should include both your address and the different address on the C8 form.

2.6 Your phone number

2.7 Your email address

2.8 How do you prefer to be contacted?

☐ Phone

☐ Email

2.9 Contact instructions, including safe call times

2.10 Do you have a legal representative?

☐ Yes

☐ No. **Go to Section 3**

2.11 Your legal representative's name

2.12 Name of your legal representative's firm

Note 2.8: Do not select phone for contact preference if it is not safe for you to take calls. If there is a safe time to call, please let us know when that is by providing a contact instruction (question 2.9).

If you are worried that the respondent has access to your email account, please create a new email account and use that address here.

This will be the email address used on your application to the court.

Note 2.9: Your safe call times will be when you are not going to be with the respondent. Please provide hours between 9am and 5pm.

2.13 Address of your legal representative's firm

Building and street

Second line of address

Town or city

County (optional)

Postcode

DX number (if known)

2.14 Your legal representative's phone number

2.15 Your legal representative's address email address

2.16 Your legal representative's reference

3. Respondent's details

3.1 Their name

First name(s)

[   ]

Last name

[   ]

3.2 Any other names the respondent has been known by

[   ]

3.3 Their date of birth

Day   Month   Year

[   ]   [   ]   [   ]

3.4 Does the respondent live with you?

☐ Yes

☐ No

3.5 Their full current address

Building and street

[   ]

Second line of address

[   ]

Town or city

[   ]

County (optional)

[   ]

Postcode

[| | | | |]

Note 3: The 'respondent' is the person you are asking the court to make the order against. In any court papers or hearings this person will be called 'the respondent'. You will be called 'the applicant'.

Note 3.5: An address for the respondent is needed so any order can be 'personally served' on them. The order is usually handed directly to the respondent. See the first page of this form for more information and guidance.

If you don't know their address, include an alternative address, such as a family member of the respondent or workplace where you know they are likely to be.

It is very important to include an address for the respondent as the order cannot be enforced until it has been served on them or they are aware of it. This means the police or court may not be able to take any action if the respondent does something the order says they aren't allowed to.

3.6 Their phone number (if you know it)

3.7 Their email address (if you know it)

4. Your relationship with the respondent

4.1 If your relationship with the respondent is one of the following, select the one which best describes your relationship and go to question 4.2.

☐ Married or in a civil partnership

☐ Formerly married or in a civil partnership

☐ Engaged or proposed civil partnership

☐ Formerly engaged or proposed civil partnership

☐ Live together as a couple

☐ Formerly lived together as a couple

☐ Boyfriend, girlfriend or partner who does not live with me

☐ Former boyfriend, girlfriend or partner who did not live with me

☐ None of the above. **Go to question 4.4**

4.2 When did your relationship start and when did it end?

Start

Day	Month	Year

End (if applicable)

Day	Month	Year

4.3 If you are or were previously married or in a civil partnership with the respondent, what date was your wedding or civil ceremony?

Day	Month	Year

Note 4: To get an injunction against the respondent, you will need to show the court that you have a connection to them. The courts call this being an 'associated person'.

The questions in this section are used to decide if you are an associated person for this application

Note 4.2: If you don't know the exact date your relationship started or ended, give your best guess of the month and year.

4.4 What is the respondent's relationship to you (if not answered in question 4.1)?

My

☐ Father   ☐ Mother   ☐ Son   ☐ Daughter

☐ Brother   ☐ Sister   ☐ Grandfather   ☐ Grandmother

☐ Uncle   ☐ Aunt   ☐ Nephew   ☐ Niece

☐ Cousin

☐ Other – please specify

[   ]

4.5 Do you have any children, have parental responsibility for any children or need to protect other children with this application?

☐ Yes. **Go to Section 5 – Your family**

☐ No. **Go to Section 6 – Respondent's behaviour**

Note 4.4: If the respondent is your relative by birth, please check the appropriate box.

If the respondent is your relative by marriage or other association, please select other and specify. This includes in-laws and step relatives of you or your partner.

The respondent must be, or have been, someone listed in question 4.1, **or** a relative by birth, marriage or other association. If they are not, then you cannot apply for a non-molestation or occupation order and should seek legal advice.

5. Your family

5.1 Who is this application for?

☐ You only. **Go to Section 6 – Respondent's behaviour**

☐ You and your child/children

Note 5.2: Parental responsibility means all the responsibilities and rights that a parent has towards their child. A mother automatically has parental responsibility for her child from birth. A father usually has parental responsibility if he's either married to the child's mother or listed on the birth certificate.

For more information visit www.gov.uk/parental-rights-responsibilities

5.2 Details of the child or children to be protected by the order:

Child's full name	Child's date of birth	Your relationship to the child	Do you and the respondent both have parental responsibility for this child?	Respondent's relationship to the child

5.3 Are there any ongoing family court proceedings involving both of you?

☐ Yes

☐ No. **Go to Section 6 – Respondent's behaviour**

Note 5.3: Such as a case about child arrangements or one where the respondent has asked for an injunction against you. This could also include divorce proceedings.

5.4 Family court proceedings

Name of court	Case number	Type of case and any other details

6. Respondent's behaviour

Note 6: This section is to capture a summary of the type of behaviours from the respondent that you want to stop.

6.1 Are you applying for a non-molestation order?

☐ Yes

☐ No. **Go to Section 7 – The home**

6.2 What do you want to stop the respondent from doing?

☐ Being violent towards me or threatening me

☐ Harassing or intimidating me

☐ Posting or publishing about me either in print or digitally

☐ Contacting me directly

☐ Causing damage to my possessions

☐ Causing damage to my home

☐ Coming into my home

☐ Coming near my home

☐ Coming near my place of work

6.3 What do you want to stop the respondent from doing to your child or children (if applicable)?

☐ Being violent towards my children or threatening my children

☐ Harassing or intimidating my children

☐ Posting or publishing anything about my children in print, or digitally

☐ Contacting my children directly without my consent

☐ Going to or near my children's school or nursery

Note 6.2 and 6.3: You can choose more than one option for questions 6.2 and 6.3.

You will be asked to provide more detail in your supporting witness statement, including information about specific incidents.

6.4 Is there anything else you want the respondent to stop doing that is not mentioned in question 6.1 or 6.2?

Note 6.4: The kinds of abusive behaviour you might want to stop could for example be sexual, psychological, physical, emotional, financial.

7. The home

7.1   Are you applying for an occupation order?

☐ Yes

☐ No. **Go to Section 8 – Going to court**

Note 7: Please only complete this section if you are applying for an occupation order. This is where a court decides who lives or stays in a property, or who should be excluded from a property.

If you are not applying for an occupation order, please go the next section, 'Going to court' (section 8).

7.2   To what address do you want the occupation order to apply?

Building and street

[   ]

Second line of address

[   ]

Town or city

[   ]

County (optional)

[   ]

Postcode

[| | | | |]

7.3   Who currently lives at the address?

Please select all that apply.

☐ Me

☐ The respondent

☐ My child or children

☐ Someone else – please specify

[   ]

Note 7.3: If selecting 'someone else', please provide their name and why they live there. For example, they rent a room, they are a lodger, they are a relative, they are a dependent parent.

7.4   Have you or the respondent ever lived at the address but don't live there currently?

☐ Yes, both of us

☐ Yes, myself

☐ Yes, the respondent

☐ No

7.5 If you answered 'No' to question 7.4, did you or the respondent ever intend to live at the address?

☐ Yes, both of us

☐ Yes, myself

☐ Yes, the respondent

☐ No

7.6 If any children live at the address, please provide their name(s) and age(s).

a) Any children that both you and the respondent are parents of or responsible for:

Child's name	Child's age

b) Other children that you are the parent of or are responsible for that the respondent is not:

Do not complete this question if you want to keep your child or children's information confidential from the respondent. See notes on the first page for more information and instructions.

Child's name	Child's age

7.7 Is the property specially adapted in any way for you, your children or anyone else living there?

☐ Yes

☐ No. **Go to question 7.9**

Note 7.7: For example, changes made to a property to support someone with a physical or mental health disability.

7.8 Please provide details of how the property is specially adapted.

[blank box]

7.9 Is there a mortgage on the property?

[ ] Yes

[ ] No. **Go to question 7.13**

Note 7.9: Please do not select 'Yes' if thinking of a mortgage your landlord may have. See question 7.13 for landlord information.

7.10 Who is named on the mortgage? Please select all that apply

[ ] Me

[ ] The respondent

[ ] Someone else – please specify

[blank box]

Note 7.10: If selecting 'someone else', please provide their name and their relationship to you and/or the respondent.

7.11 Please provide your mortgage number, if you know it

[blank box]

7.12 What is the name and address of the mortgage lender?

Name

[blank box]

Building and street

[blank box]

Second line of address

[blank box]

Town or city

[blank box]

County (optional)

[blank box]

Postcode

[blank box]

Note 7.12: The mortgage lender is usually a bank, building society or savings and loans association.

You must serve your mortgage company or landlord with the application. They will be given the opportunity to provide information to the court about the mortgage or tenancy.

7.13 Is the property rented?

☐ Yes

☐ No. **Go to question 7.16**

7.14 Who is named on the rental agreement? Please select all that apply

☐ Me

☐ The respondent

☐ Someone else – please specify

[ ]

Note 7.14: If selecting someone else, please provide their name and their relationship to you and/or the respondent.

7.15 What is the name and address of the landlord?

Name

[ ]

Building and street

[ ]

Second line of address

[ ]

Town or city

[ ]

County (optional)

[ ]

Postcode

[ ]

7.16 Do you have any home rights?

☐ Yes

☐ No

Note 7.16: Home rights mean you have a right to live in the property whether or not your name is on a legal agreement. This could be, for example, where you are married to the respondent but your name is not on the mortgage or rental agreement. You may wish to seek legal advice.

7.17 What exactly do you want to happen with your living situation?

☐ I want to be able to stay in my home

☐ I want to be able to return to my home

☐ I don't want the respondent to be able to enter my home

☐ I want to keep the respondent away from the area surrounding my home

☐ I want to limit where in the home the respondent can go

7.18 Is there anything else you want to happen with the family home?

☐ I need the respondent to pay for or contribute to repairs or maintenance to the home

☐ I need the respondent to pay for or contribute to the rent or mortgage

☐ I need the use of the furniture or other household contents

7.19 Is there anything else you want to be considered by the court?

Note 7.17: There are several options available to you when you apply for an occupation order, for example removing the respondent from the property altogether or limiting areas of the property they can live in, for example that they cannot go into a specific room, such as a bedroom.

Note 7.19: This should include information about where you and your children will be able to live if unable to stay in your home or return to it.

Please also include details of any hardship you might face if you are not able to stay in your home or return to it. For example, you may not be able to attend your workplace or your child may not be able to attend their school or nursery.

If you can also demonstrate that the respondent is able to live elsewhere and is not entirely dependent upon the home, this may support your application.

8. Going to court

8.1 Do you need an interpreter at court?

☐ Yes

☐ No. **Go to question 8.3**

8.2 Please tell us what language and/or dialect.

Language

Dialect

Note 8: The court will try to provide you and any witnesses with the special assistance that you ask for. However, this is not always possible and can depend on the facilities available at your local court.

It is a good idea to contact the court before your court hearing to find out whether they can supply the special assistance that you have requested.

8.3 Do we need to provide something different in court or when we contact you, because of a disability?

☐ Yes

☐ No

8.4 Explain how your disability affects you, giving as much information as you can.

Note 8.3: We know that people with disabilities sometimes need our help and support to use our services. This can mean that we need to provide something different so you can access and use our services in the same way as a person without a disability.

Explaining how your disability affects you will help court staff or the judge to consider any help we can provide.

8.5 Special measures can be put in place to keep you separate from the respondent when you attend court. Please select any of the following measures you would like to request.

☐ a separate waiting room in the court building

☐ a separate entrance and exit from the court building

☐ to be shielded by a privacy screen in the courtroom

☐ to join the hearing by video link rather than in person

Note 8.5: A privacy screen would mean the respondent would not be able to see you while in the courtroom.

Statement of truth

I understand that proceedings for contempt of court may be brought against anyone who makes, or causes to be made, a false statement in a document verified by a statement of truth without an honest belief in its truth.

☐ **I believe** that the facts stated in this form and any continuation sheets are true.

☐ **The applicant** believes that the facts stated in this form and any continuation sheets are true. **I am authorised** by the applicant to sign this statement.

Signature

You can sign the application by hand or type your name in if completing electronically.

☐ Applicant

☐ Applicant's legal representative

This application is to be served on the respondent.

Date

Day   Month   Year

You must not serve the documents yourself on the person you are seeking the order against. See the first page of this form for more information and instructions about serving the documents.

Full name

Name of applicant's legal representative's firm

If signing on behalf of firm or company give position or office held

Index

access to justice
  bank loans 19
  court orders 18–19
  creative options 19
  litigation insurance 19
  public funding *see* **public funding**
  Sears Tooth agreement 18
acknowledgement of service
  divorce petition 43–4
  section 8 orders 214
adultery
  co-respondent 30–1
  cohabitation after 31
  confession of 30
  intolerability 29–30, 31
  meaning 30
  proof 30
agreements *see individual types eg* **cohabitation agreements**
alternative dispute resolution 20–4
  arbitration 23–4, 160
  collaborative law 22, 160
  mediation *see* **mediation**
ancillary relief *see* **financial provisions**
annulment *see* **nullity**
appeals
  arbitral awards 169
  financial orders 168–9
  maintenance assessments 169
  welfare benefits 169
arbitral awards
  appeals 169
arbitration 23–4, 160
  Certainty Project 24
arrest
  domestic abuse order enforcement 276
  power of 276
  warrant of 276
attachment of earnings 164–5

bank loans 19
bankruptcy
  financial provision 125–6
  matrimonial home 125
behaviour in divorce
  cohabitation and 32
  respondent's 31–2
'big money' cases
  capital tied up 106
  fairness 57–8
  lump sums 122–3
Brexit
  choice of divorce forum 28–9
budgeting advance 87

capital assets
  see also **matrimonial home**
  'big money' cases 122–3

capital assets – *continued*
  lump sums 121–3
  pensions 123–5
  protection of 118–19
    injunctions 120–1
    in joint names 119
    matrimonial home rights 119–20
    pending land action 120
    in sole name 119–21
capital gains tax
  disposal of assets 79–80
  marriage breakdown 78–80
  matrimonial home
    deferred charge 79, 112, 116, 144
    deferred trust of land 79, 112, 114, 144
    future sale 79
    private residence exemption 78
    sale to third party 78–9
    transfer between spouses 79
capital orders 54–6
  clean break 70
  homes *see* **matrimonial home**
  lump sums 52, 55, 70, 72, 73, 121–3, 143
  orders for sale 52, 55–6, 112–13, 145, 165
  pension sharing compensation orders 52, 56, 72
  pension sharing orders 52, 56
  property adjustment orders 52, 55, 73, 117–18, 144–5, 168, 291–2
care orders
  advocates' meeting 253
  application 236
  application form 251, 553–74
  availability to court 239
  care plans 240, 257–8
  Case Management Hearing
    attendance 254
    timetable for proceedings 253
  causation of harm 238
  children's guardian 252–3
  choice of order 244
  concurrent applications 239
  contact 241–3, 246
  discharge 243
  discharge of s.8 order by 241
  disclosure 255
  effect 224, 240–1
  evidence
    admissibility 254
    disclosure 255
    expert evidence 254–5
    witness statements 254
  exclusion requirement 246
  final hearing 255–6
  grounds 236
  human rights 241, 256–7
  independence of child 243
  interim 244–6

care orders – *continued*
'is likely to suffer' 237–8
'is suffering' 237
issue of application 251–2
issues resolution hearing 255
judgment 256
kinship assessments 250
letter before proceedings 250
meaning 236
meeting with parents 250
name change 241
once made 256
parental responsibility 240
parties to application 251
'pathway plan' 243
pre-proceedings action 250
procedure 249–56
  checklist 259
public funding 249–50
service of application 252
significant harm 236–7
solicitor appointment 253
stage 1 251–3
welfare principle 239, 257
care plans 240, 257–8
Case Management Hearing
care and supervision orders 253–5
change of name
care orders and 241
child arrangements orders 191–2
charging order 165
child abduction 220–1
Child Abduction Act 1984 221–2
criminal offences 221–2
Family Law Act 1986 221
international 223
passports
  preventing issue 222
  surrender 222–3
'port alert' procedure 222
practical advice 223
prohibited steps orders 201
recovery of child 223
section 8 orders 221
Child Abduction Act 1984
text 320–1
child arrangements orders 190–201
activities 199
activity conditions 198–9
activity directions 198–9
children of cohabitants 290
conditions 191, 194, 195
contact regulation 194–8
directions 191, 195
domestic violence 196–8
duration 219
enforcement 199–201
grandparents 196
interim 244–6
intractable cases 199–200
leaving UK 192–4
letters, email or telephone contact 194
monitoring contact 199

child arrangements orders – *continued*
name change 191–2
physical contact 194
Practice Direction 197–8
relocation within UK 194
step-parents 195
with whom child lives 190–1
Child Arrangements Programme 212–17
child assessment orders 224, 249
child benefit 84
Child Contact Centre 195
child of the family 67–8
Child Maintenance and Enforcement Commission 92
see also **Child Maintenance Service**
Child Maintenance Options 92, 94
Child Maintenance Service 224
apportionment 99
calculation of maintenance 97–101
  apportionment 99
  basic rate 98
  existing court orders 99
  flat rate 99
  formula 97
  nil rate 99
  reduced rate 98
  review 102
  shared care 99–100
  special cases 99–100
  special expenses 100–1
  variations 100–2
    downwards 101
  voluntary payments 102
child
  with disability 94
  meaning 92
clean break and 113–14
Collect & Pay scheme 92, 167
collection by 167–8
default maintenance decision 102
Direct Pay scheme 167
educational expenses 94
enforcement 167–8
fees 92
habitual residence 93
interim maintenance decision 102
jurisdiction of court 93–4
legislation 91–2
maintenance assessment *see* calculation of maintenance
non-resident parent 92, 93
parent 92–3
parentage determination 93
person with care 93
qualifying child 92, 93
reform 102
shared care 99–100
step-children 93
step-parents 93
supplementary maintenance 94
voluntary payments 102
child protection
abduction *see* **child abduction**
care orders *see* **care orders**
care plans 240, 257–8

child protection – *continued*
  child assessment orders 249
  conferences 235–6
  contact
    application to court 242
    initial considerations 241
    local authority duties 242
    refusal 242–3
  emergency protection orders 224, 246–8
  general 223–4
  investigation
    court-directed 235
    local authorities 204, 235
  local authorities *see* **children, public law**
  neglect or abuse 234
  police protection 248
  supervision orders *see* **supervision orders**
  wardship 224
child protection conferences 235–6
Child Support Act 1991
  text 380–9
Child Support Agency 92
  see also **Child Maintenance Service**
children
  abduction *see* **child abduction**
  child arrangements orders 190–201, 290
    change of surname 191–2
    conditions 191, 194, 195
    directions 191, 195
    domestic violence 196–8
    enforcement 199–201
    grandparents 196
    interim 244–6
    intractable cases 199–200
    leaving UK 192–4
    letters, email or telephone contact 194
    monitoring contact 199
    physical contact 194
    Practice Direction 197–8
    relocation within UK 194
    step-parents 195
    with whom child lives 190–1
  child of the family 67–8
  consent orders 95–6
  delay avoidance 209–10
  with disability 68, 94
  divorce and
    service of petition 43
    welfare of child 36
  family assistance order 202–3
  financial provision 67
    see also **Child Maintenance Service**
    child with disability 68
    child of the family 67–8
    Child Maintenance Service *see* **Child Maintenance Service**
    Children Act 1989 relief 225–6
    'Christmas' orders 96
    consent orders 95–6
    during marriage 225
    family-based arrangements 95
    flowchart 96–7
    jurisdiction 224

children – *continued*
    maintenance agreements 95, 180
    matrimonial breakdown and 67–8
    matrimonial proceedings 225
    property orders 291–2
    Segal orders 96, 102
    separation agreements 95
    step-children 68
    unmarried parents 224, 291–2
  guardianship 187
  human rights 205
  legislation 183–4
  local authority and *see* **children, public law**
  maintenance agreements 95
  matrimonial home and 112–13
  name change
    care orders 241
    child arrangements orders 191–2
  'no order' presumption 209
  nullity of marriage and 37
  parental involvement 205–6
  parental responsibility
    agreement 185
    artificial insemination/IVF 188
    child arrangements orders 187
    civil partners 187
    cohabitants 290–1
    delegation of 189
    exercise of 189
    guardianship 187
    human rights 291
    local authority 188
    loss of 188–9
    meaning 184
    order 185–7
      refusal 186
      termination 186
    persons with 184
    removal 291
    same-sex couples 291
    special guardianship orders 203
    step-parents 187–8
    supervision orders 243
    unmarried fathers 184–7, 290–1
      refusal of order 186
  as party to proceedings 213
  passports
    preventing issue 222
    surrender 222–3
  prohibited steps orders 201–2
  protection *see* **child protection; children, public law**
  section 8 orders *see* **section 8 orders** *and individual orders eg* **child arrangements orders**
  separation agreements and 180
  special guardianship orders 203
  special guardianship support services 203
  specific issues order 202
  step-children 68, 93
  of unmarried parents
    appointment of guardian 290
    child arrangements order 290
    financial provision orders 291–2
    guardianship 290

children – *continued*
    human rights 291
    occupation of home 289
    parental responsibility 290–1
        removal 291
    property orders 291–2
    s.8 orders 290
    same-sex couples 291
    welfare principle *see* **welfare principle**
Children Act 1989
    text 322–79
**Children and Family Court Advisory and Support Service
    (Cafcass) 184, 214**
children, public law 229–58
    accommodation provision 232–3
        duty 232
        limits 232–3
        preventing removal 233
    care orders
        advocates' meeting 253
        application 236
        application form 251, 553–74
        availability to court 239
        care plans 240, 257–8
        Case Management Hearing
            attendance 254
            timetable for proceedings 253
        causation of harm 238
        children's guardian 252–3
        choice of order 244
        concurrent applications 239
        contact 241–3, 246
        discharge 243
        discharge of s.8 order by 241
        disclosure 255
        effect 240–1
        evidence
            admissibility 254
            disclosure 255
            expert evidence 254–5
            witness statements 254
        exclusion requirement 246
        final hearing 255–6
        grounds 236, 260
        human rights 241, 256–7
        independence of child 243
        Independent Reviewing Officer 241
        interim 244–6
        'is likely to suffer' 237–8
        'is suffering' 237
        issue of application 251–2
        issues resolution hearing 255
        judgment 256
        kinship assessments 250
        letter before proceedings 250
        meeting with parents 250
        name change 241
        once made 256
        parental responsibility 240
        parties to application 251
        'pathway plan' 243
        pre-proceedings action 250
        procedure 249–56

children, public law – *continued*
        procedure checklist 260
        public funding 249–50
        service of application 252
        significant harm 236–7
        solicitor appointment 253
        stage 1 251–3
        welfare principle 239, 257
    care plans 240, 257–8
    challenging local authority 234
        complaints 234
        judicial review 234
    child assessment orders 224, 249
    child protection conferences 235–6
    child support 231–4
    Children Act applications 507–15
    children in need
        definition 231
        duty to 232
    children 'looked after' 233
    compensation for failures 258
    contact
        application to court 242
        emergency protection orders 248
        initial considerations 241
        interim care order 246
        local authorities and 242, 246, 248
        public funding 249–50
        refusal 242–3
    costs 256
    emergency protection orders 224, 246–8
    human rights 256–7
    increase in applications 230–1
    Independent Reviewing Officer 241
    investigation
        court-directed 235
        local authority 204, 235
    issue of application 251–2
    issues resolution hearing 255
    kinship assessments 250
    letter before proceedings 250
    meeting with parents 250
    neglect or abuse
        child protection conferences 235–6
        court-directed investigation 235
        local authority investigation 204, 235
    parties to application 251
    pre-proceedings action 250
    prevention of harm 231
    protection of child 224
    provision of services 233–4
    Public Law Outline 230, 249, 250
    settlement conference 230
    stage 1 251–3
    supervision orders
        advocates' meeting 253
        application 236
        application form 251, 553–74
        availability to court 239
        Case Management Hearing
            attendance 254
            timetable for proceedings 253
        causation of harm 238

children, public law – *continued*
children's guardian 252–3
choice of 244
concurrent applications 239
disclosure 255
duration 244
duties of supervisor 244
effect of 243–4
evidence
admissibility 254
disclosure 255
expert evidence 254–5
witness statements 254
final hearing 255–6
grounds 236, 260
human rights implications 256–7
interim 244–6
'is likely to suffer' 237–8
issue of application 251–2
issues resolution hearing 255
judgment 256
kinship assessments 250
letter before proceedings 250
meeting with parents 250
parental responsibility 243
parties to application 251
pre-proceedings action 250
procedure 249–56
public funding 249–50
service of application 252
significant harm 236–7
'is suffering' 237
solicitor appointment 253
stage 1 251–3
welfare principle 239, 257
welfare principle 239, 257
children's guardian 247
appointment 252–3
duties 252–3
'Christmas' orders 96
civil partnership 281–2
see also **matrimonial home**
dissolution 25–6, 27, 29
parental responsibility 187
clean break
capital orders 70
Child Maintenance Service and 113–14
deferred 70
drafting order 145–6
duty to consider 68–9
income orders 69–70
matrimonial home 112
principle 68–9
co-respondent 30–1
service of divorce petition on 43
coercive and controlling behaviour 278
cohabitation
after adultery 31
after desertion 33
after separation (2 years) 34
after separation (5 years) 36
agreements *see* **cohabitation agreements**
bankruptcy 292

cohabitation – *continued*
behaviour and 32
breaking up 285–90
occupation of home 288–9
ownership of home 285–8
sale of property 289–90
tenancies 290
children
appointment of guardian 290
child arrangements order 290
financial provision orders 291–2
guardianship 290
human rights 291
parental responsibility 290–1
removal 291
same-sex couples 291
property orders 291–2
s.8 orders 290
civil partnerships 281–2
death of cohabitant
family provision 292–3
intestacy 292
ownership rights 292
pensions 293
widowed parent's allowance 293
domestic abuse 263
life insurance 283
'Living Together' (Dept of Constitutional Affairs 2004) 281
occupation of home
breaking up 288–9
children and 289
contractual licence 288
Family Law Act 1996 289
licence by estoppel 288–9
ownership of home
acting to detriment 286
breaking up and 285–8
common intention 286, 287
conduct of parties 287
constructive trust 286–7
contribution 287
declaration of interests 282–3
detrimental reliance 287
duty of buyers' solicitor 282
jointly owned 282, 285–6
mortgages 283
proprietary estoppel 288
resulting trust 286
size of share 287–8
sole legal ownership 286–8
sale of property 289–90
same-sex couples 281–2
setting up home together 282–4
tenancies 290
wills 283
cohabitation agreements 177
certainty 284
consideration 284
enforcement 284
intention 284
matters to be covered 284
public policy 283

cohabitation agreements – *continued*
  undue influence 284
  validity 283–4
cold weather payments 87
collaborative law 22, 160
consent orders
  attendance at court 160
  financial provision 141
  online application 132
  procedures 159–60
  statement of information 497–502
contact, local authorities and
  application to court 242
  emergency protection orders 248
  initial considerations 241
  interim care order 246
  local authority duties 242
  public funding 249–50
  refusal 242–3
contact orders
  see also **child arrangements orders**
  replacement 190
costs
  children cases 256
  cost rules 139–40
  deferred payment of legal fees 18
  divorce 47
  drafting orders 146
  financial provision proceedings 139–40
    conduct of party 139–40
    offers to settle 140
  offers to settle 140
  public funding 15
  solicitor's 15
council tax support 87
counselling 6
county courts
  variation of orders 171–5
court forms 130, 132, 133, 135, 136, 137, 140, 212–13, 251, 437–594

death
  of cohabitant
    family provision 292–3
    intestacy 292
    ownership rights 292
    pensions 293
    widowed parent's allowance 293
  presumption of 38
  widowed parent's allowance 293
decree absolute
  petitioner's application 45–6
  religious marriages 46
  respondent's application 46
decree nisi 45
  application 44
defended divorce
  filing an answer 46
  notice of intent 46
  procedure 46–7
delay
  children and 209–10

desertion
  cohabitation after 33
  elements 33
directions for hearing
  divorce 44–5
disabilities, persons with *see* **person under disability**
disclosure
  care and supervision orders 255
  financial provision procedure 132–3
discretionary housing payments 87
Dispute Resolution Appointment 217
divorce
  acknowledgement of service 43–4
  adultery
    co-respondent 30–1
    cohabitation after 31
    confession of 30
    intolerability 29–30, 31
    meaning 30
    proof 30
  behaviour
    cohabitation and 32
    respondent's 31–2
  checklist 50
  child protection, welfare of child 36
  choice of nullity or 37
  co-respondent 30–1
  costs 47
  decree absolute
    petitioner's application 45–6
    religious marriages 46
    respondent's application 46
  decree nisi 45
  defended
    filing an answer 46
    notice of intent 46
    procedure 46–7
  desertion
    cohabitation and 33
    elements 33
  directions for hearing 44–5
  divorce centres 41
  exemption from fees 41
  fees 41
  filing of petition 41
  first interview 38–9
  five facts *see individual facts eg* adultery
  future law reform 47–8
  irretrievable breakdown ground 29
  jurisdiction of courts 26–7
    choice of forum 28–9
    domicile 27–8
    habitual residence 27
    recognition of foreign decrees 29
  legal help 38–9
  nullity *see* **nullity**
  one-year rule 26
  online process 38
  pensions and 70–3
  petition *see* **divorce petition**
  public funding 38–9
  reform 26

divorce – *continued*
  same-sex 25, 27
  separation (2 years) with consent
    calculation of period 33
    cohabitation after 34
    consent 34
    financial position 34–5
    mental element 34
    separation 33–4
  separation (5 years)
    cohabitation after 36
    financial hardship 35
    grave hardship 35
    meaning 35
  service of petition *see* **divorce petition**
  summary 49
Divorce, Dissolution and Separation Act 2020 47–8
divorce petition
  acknowledgement of service 43–4
  amendments 40
  exemption from fees 41
  fees 41
  filing 41
  form 437–52
  marriage certificate 40
  minor corrections 40
  prescribed form 39–40
  service 41
    alternative methods 42–3
    children 43
    co-respondent 43
    deemed service 42
    dispensing with 42–3
    finding respondent 43
    outside England and Wales 43
    personal service 42
    protected parties 43
    service copies 41
    usual method 41
  statement of reconciliation 41
  statement in support 44
  supporting documents 40–1
domestic abuse
  applicants 263
  child applicants 263
  coercive and controlling behaviour 278
  cohabitants 263
  definition 12, 261
  distressed client 262
  Domestic Abuse Act 2021 261–2
  Domestic Violence Protection Notice 262
  Domestic Violence Protection Order 262
  emergency applications 271
  emergency legal representation 272
  enforcement of orders
    penalty available 276–7
    power of arrest 276
    warrant of arrest 276
  Family Law Act 1996 protection 263–77
  human rights issues 277
  Integrated Domestic Abuse Courts 262
  legal aid 12, 272
  legal help 272

domestic abuse – *continued*
  legal representation 272
  legislation 262, 263
  local authority housing 88
  non-molestation orders *see* **non-molestation orders**
  occupation orders *see* **occupation orders**
  orders available 263
  procedure 272–4
    checklist 274–5
  protection from harassment 277–8
  public funding 272
  reform 262
  refuges 262
  undertakings 271–2
  with notice application 273–4
  without notice application 272–3
Domestic Abuse Commissioner 262
Domestic Proceedings and Magistrates' Courts Act 1978
  text 318–19
Domestic Violence Protection Notice 262
Domestic Violence Protection Order 262
domicile
  of choice 28
  of dependence 28
  divorce 27–8
  of origin 28
drafting financial provisions 141–2
  clean break orders 145–6
  form of order 142
  lump sums 143
  orders for sale 145
  pensions 145
  periodical payments 143
  property adjustment orders 144–5
  undertakings 142–3

early neutral evaluation 23
emergency applications
  domestic abuse 271
emergency legal representation
  domestic abuse 272
emergency protection orders 224
  application 247
  children's guardian 247
  contact during currency of 248
  duration 248
  effect of order 247
  examination or assessment 248
  grounds 246–7
  police protection 248
enforcement
  attachment of earnings 164–5
  charging order 165
  child arrangements orders 199–201
  Child Maintenance Service 167–8
  cohabitation agreements 284
  domestic abuse orders 275–7
  in family court 164–7
  judgment summons 165–6
  non-molestation orders 275
  occupation orders 276–7
  order for sale 165
  power of arrest 276

enforcement – *continued*
  preliminary steps 164
  property adjustment orders 168
  reform 166–7
  separation/maintenance agreements 181
  third party debt order 165
  warrant of arrest 276
  warrant of control 165
evidence
  care and supervision orders 254–5
  expert 215, 254–5
  financial provision procedure 133–4
  section 8 proceedings 215
expert evidence
  care and supervision procedure 254–5
  section 8 proceedings 215

family assistance order 202–3
family client 1–3
family court 7
  enforcement 164–7
  reforms 8
  section 8 orders 212
    checklist 220
  transparency of proceedings 7
family court orders
  enforcement 164–7
Family Drug and Alcohol Court (FDAC) 230
family help (higher) 128
  alternative sources 14
  availability 14
  care and supervision orders 249
  cost benefit test 14
  financial eligibility 14
family help (lower) 128
  availability 13
  care and supervision orders 249
  cost benefit test 14
  financial eligibility 14
family home (cohabitants)
  bankruptcy of cohabitant 292
  breaking up partnership 285–90
  death of cohabitant 292–3
  married couples *see* **matrimonial home**
  occupation
    breaking up 288–9
    children and 289
    contractual licence 288
    Family Law Act 1996 289
    licence by estoppel 288–9
  ownership
    acting to detriment 286
    breaking up and 285–8
    common intention 286, 287
    conduct of parties 287
    constructive trust 286–7
    contribution 287
    declaration of interests 282–3
    detrimental reliance 287
    duty of buyers' solicitor 282
    jointly owned 282, 285–6
    mortgages 283
    proprietary estoppel 288

family home (cohabitants) – *continued*
    resulting trust 286
    size of share 287–8
    sole legal ownership 286–8
  sale of property 289–90
  tenancies 290
Family Law Act 1986
  child abduction 221
Family Law Act 1996
  domestic abuse protection 263–77
  text 390–406
family practitioner
  advisory role 4
  changing role 8–9
  emotions of client 5–6
  interviewing skills 5
  long-term objectives 4–5
  negotiation skills 5
  professional conduct 3–4
  vulnerability of clients 4
Family Procedure Rules 2010 408–34
final hearing
  care and supervision orders 255–6
  financial provision 137–8
  section 8 orders 217
Financial Dispute Resolution (FDR) appointment 136–7
financial provisions
  accelerated first appointment 160
  appeals *see* **appeals**
  application 157–9
    at early stage 130
    dismissal 145
    filing 131–2
    Form A 130, 132, 453–67
    making application 130
    pre-application protocol 130
    remarriage trap 130
    service on respondent 132
  arbitration 160
  bankruptcy 125–6
  capital assets *see* **capital assets; matrimonial home**
  capital orders 52, 54–6
    clean break 70
  children 67
    child of the family 67–8
    Child Maintenance Service *see* **Child Maintenance Service**
    Children Act 1989 relief 225–6
    'Christmas' orders 96
    consent orders 95–6
    during marriage 225
    family-based arrangements 95
    flowchart 96–7
    jurisdictions 224
    maintenance agreements 95, 180
    matrimonial breakdown and 67–8
    matrimonial proceedings 225
    property orders 291–2
    Segal orders 96, 102
    separation agreements 95
    step-children 68
    unmarried parents 224, 291–2
    with disability 68

financial provisions – *continued*
   choice of order 56–68
   clean break *see* **clean break**
   collaborative law 160
   consent orders 141
   costs 139–40
      drafting orders 146
      offers to settle 140
   dismissal of application 145
   drafting 141–2
      clean break orders 145–6
      costs 146
      form of order 142
      'liberty to apply' 146
      lump sums 143
      orders for sale 145
      pensions 145
      periodical payments 143
      property adjustment orders 144–5
      side-letters 146
      specimen orders 146–56
      undertakings 142–3
   fast track procedure 127, 138–9
   final hearing 137–8
   Financial Remedies Unit 131
   first appointment 134–6
      accelerated 160
   Form A 130, 132, 160, 453–67
   Form E 133, 136, 469–95
   Form H 134, 136
   Form H1 137, 140
   Form P 135
   hearings
      FDR appointment 136–7
      final 137–8
      first appointment 134–6
   income orders 52–4
      clean break 69–70
   interim orders 138
   lump sum orders 52, 55, 70, 72, 73, 121–3, 143
   maintenance pending suit 52–3
   marriage 73–4
      agreed applications 74
      contested applications 74
      duration of periodic payments 74
      failure to make reasonable provision 73
      MCA 1973 73
   matrimonial breakdown 56–67
      age of parties 63–4
      'big money' cases 57–8, 106
      children 67–8
      conduct 65–6
      contributions to family 57, 64–5
      court guidance 105–6
      courts' approach 57–9
      disability 64
      duration of marriage 63–4
      earning capacity 57, 59
      equal sharing principle 57
      factors to be considered 57
      fairness 57
      future prospects 60–1
      high income families 106

financial provisions – *continued*
      human rights 67
      inherited assets 62
      lost assets 62
      low income families 108–9
      middle income families 106–8
      misconduct 65–6
      needs 62–3
      negative contribution 65
      non-matrimonial assets 61–2
      pension rights 66–7
      potential financial loss 66–7
      reasonable requirements 57
      resources 59–62
      second family 60, 62, 130, 135
      second spouse's income 60
      spouses 105–9
      standard of living 63
      welfare benefits 59–60
      yardstick of equality 58
   millionaire's defence 136
   negotiations 140–1
   new partners 60, 62, 135
   orders available *see individual orders eg* periodical payments
   orders for sale 52, 55–6, 145
   pensions 135–6, 145
      see also **pensions**
      information required 132, 135–6
      pension sharing compensation orders 52, 56, 72
      pension sharing orders 52
   periodical payments 52, 53–4, 69–70, 73–4, 143, 180
   powers of court 52
   procedure
      application *see* application
      consent orders 141, 159–60
      costs 139–40
      court hearings *see* hearings
      disclosure 132–3
      dismissal of application 145
      documentation required 133–4
      first appointment 134–6
      negotiations 140–1
      obtaining evidence 133–4
      overview 128–9
      public funding 128
      summary of procedure 157–60
   property adjustment orders 52, 55, 73, 117–18, 144–5, 168, 291–2
   reform 73, 160–1
   remarriage trap 130
   school fees 94
   second marriages 60, 62, 130, 135
   secured periodical payments 52, 54, 55
   setting aside orders 169–71
   term maintenance 70
   undertakings 142–3, 174–5
   universal credit 109
   valuation
      of business 135
      of home 135
   variation of orders, county court orders 171–5
   welfare benefits and 109
   when orders available 52

Financial Remedies Courts 131
Financial Remedies Unit 131
Financial Remedies Working Group 160–1
First Hearing Dispute Resolution Appointment (FHDRA)
    214–17
first interview
    divorce 38–9
forced marriage 278–9
funeral grants 87

grandparents
    child arrangements orders 196
    leave to apply for section 8 order 211
guardianship 187, 290
    children of cohabitants 290

habitual residence
    child support 93
    divorce 27
harassment *see* domestic abuse; protection from
    harassment
Harvey order 116
hearings
    care and supervision orders
        Case Management Hearing 253–5
        final 255–6
    financial provision
        directions 134–5
        FDR appointment 136–7
        final 137–8
        first appointment 134–6
help with family mediation 14
High Court 7
Hildebrand rules 133
homelessness
    domestic abuse 88
    intentional 88
    local authority housing 88–90
    meaning 88
homes
    married couples *see* matrimonial home
    unmarried partners *see* family home (cohabitants)
housing payments, discretionary 87
human rights
    care orders 241
    care and supervision orders 256–7
    children 205
    domestic abuse orders 277
    European Convention 8, 16–17
    financial provisions 67
    Human Rights Act 1998 8, 17
    marriage 26
    non-molestation orders 277
    occupation orders 277
    public funding 16–17
    unmarried fathers 291

income orders
    clean break 69–70
    maintenance pending suit 52–3
    periodical payments 52, 53–4, 69–70, 73–4
    secured periodical payments 52, 54, 55
    term maintenance 70

income tax
    marriage breakdown 77–8
Inheritance (Provision for Family and Dependants) Act
    1975
    text 315–17
inheritance tax 80
    dispositions
        family maintenance 80
        without donative intent 80
    spouse exemption 80
insurance
    life insurance 283
    litigation insurance 19
intentional homelessness 88
interim orders 138
    care orders 244–6
    child arrangements orders 244–6
    supervision orders 244–6
international issues
    jurisdiction *see* jurisdiction
    service of divorce petition 43
intimidation *see* domestic abuse
investigations, child protection
    court-directed 235
    local authorities 204, 235
issues resolution hearing 255

judgment
    care and supervision orders 256
    section 8 orders 217–18
judgment summons 165–6
judicial review
    local authority services 234
judicial separation 37
    effect of decree 37
    grounds 37
    reasons for seeking 38
jurisdiction
    dissolution of civil partnership 25–6, 27
    divorce
        choice of forum 28–9
        domicile 27–8
        habitual residence 27
        recognition of foreign decrees 29
    relocation within UK 194
    same-sex divorces 27
    section 8 orders 210
    taking child from UK 192–4

Legal Aid Agency 12
Legal Aid, Sentencing and Punishment of Offenders Act
    2012 11
legal help
    advice 13
    domestic abuse 272
    financial eligibility 13
    financial order 128
    sufficient benefit test 13
legal representation 14
    care and supervision orders 249
    domestic abuse 272
lenders
    property adjustment orders 117–18

lenders – *continued*
  'put on inquiry' 117
  undue influence 116–17
life insurance
  cohabitants 283
litigants in person 6
'Living Together' (Dept of Constitutional Affairs 2004) 281
local assistance schemes 87
local authorities, child protection
  accommodation provision
    duty 232
    limits 232–3
    preventing removal 233
  care orders
    advocates' meeting 253
    application 236
    application form 251, 553–74
    availability to court 239
    care plans 240, 257–8
    Case Management Hearing
      attendance 254
      timetable for proceedings 253
    causation of harm 238
    children's guardian 252–3
    choice of order 244
    concurrent applications 239
    contact 241–3, 246
    discharge 243
    discharge of s.8 order by 241
    disclosure 255
    effect 240–1
    evidence
      admissibility 254
      disclosure 255
      expert evidence 254–5
      witness statements 254
    exclusion requirement 246
    final hearing 255–6
    grounds 236, 260
    human rights 241, 256–7
    independence of child 243
    Independent Reviewing Officer 241
    interim 244–6
    'is likely to suffer' 237–8
    'is suffering' 237
    issue of application 251–2
    issues resolution hearings 255
    judgment 256
    kinship assessments 250
    letter before proceedings 250
    meeting with parents 250
    name change 241
    parental responsibility 240
    parties to application 251
    'pathway plan' 243
    pre-proceedings action 250
    procedure 249–56
    procedure checklist 260
    public funding 249–50
    service of application 252
    significant harm 236–7
    solicitor appointment 253
    stage 1 251–3

local authorities, child protection – *continued*
  welfare principle 239, 257
  care plans 240, 257–8
  challenging local authority
    complaints 234
    judicial review 234
  child assessment orders 224, 249
  child protection conferences 235–6
  child support 231–4
  children 'looked after' 233
  children in need
    definition 231
    duty to 232
  compensation for failures 258
  contact
    application to court 242
    emergency protection orders 248
    initial considerations 241
    interim care order 246
    local authorities and 246, 248
    local authority duties 242
    public funding 249–50
    refusal 242–3
  emergency protection orders 224, 246–8
  human rights, care and supervision orders 256–7
  investigation
    court-directed 235
    local authority 204, 235
  neglect or abuse
    child protection conferences 235–6
    court-directed investigation 235
    local authority investigation 204, 235
  parental responsibility 188
  prevention of harm 231
  protection of child 224
  provision of services 233–4
  special guardianship orders 204
  supervision orders
    advocates' meeting 253
    application 236
    application form 251, 553–74
    availability to court 239
    Case Management Hearing
      attendance 254
      timetable for proceedings 253
    causation of harm 238
    children's guardian 252–3
    choice of 244
    concurrent applications 239
    disclosure 255
    duration 244
    duties of supervisor 244
    effect of 243–4
    evidence
      admissibility 254
      disclosure 255
      expert evidence 254–5
      witness statements 254
    final hearing 255–6
    grounds 236, 260
    human rights 256–7
    interim 244–6
    'is likely to suffer' 237–8

local authorities, child protection – *continued*
    issue of application 251–2
    issues resolution hearings 255
    judgment 256
    kinship assessments 250
    letter before proceedings 250
    meeting with parents 250
    parental responsibility 243
    parties to application 251
    pre-proceedings action 250
    procedure 249–56
    public funding 249–50
    service of application 252
    significant harm 236–7
      'is suffering' 237
    solicitor appointment 253
    stage 1 251–3
    welfare principle 239, 257
  welfare principle 239, 257
local authority housing
  domestic abuse 88
  duties of local authority 89
  homelessness 88–90
  intentional homelessness 88
  local connection provision 89
  priority need 89
  tenancies 89–90
local connection 89
lump sums 52, 55, 70, 72, 73
  'big money' cases 122–3
  Child Maintenance Service 93
  drafting orders 143
  orders 93
  pensions 123–5
  welfare benefits 88

maintenance
  child support *see* **Child Maintenance Service**
  marriage breakdown *see* **financial provisions**
  term 70
maintenance agreements 179–82
  advantages 180
  agreement to separate 180
  children 180
  disadvantages 181
  enforceability 181
  finality 181
  flexibility 180
  periodical payments 180
  property 180
  speed 180
  variation 181, 182
    court jurisdiction 181
maintenance pending suit 52–3
marriage
  annulment *see* **nullity**
  divorce *see* **divorce**
  forced marriage 278–9
  judicial separation *see* **judicial separation**
  presumption of death 38
  religious 46
  void 36
  voidable 36–7

marriage breakdown
  see also **divorce; nullity**
  ancillary orders *see* **financial provisions**
  capital gains tax 78–80
  income tax 77–8
  inheritance tax 80
  stamp duty land tax 81
  taxation *see individual taxes*
***Martin* order 115–16**
maternity grants 87
Matrimonial Causes Act 1973
  text 297–314
matrimonial home 70
  bankruptcy 125
  'buy out' 113
  capital gains tax
    deferred charge 79, 112, 116, 144
    deferred trust of land 79, 112, 114, 144
    future sale 79
    private residence exemption 78
    sale to third party 78–9
    transfer between spouses 79
  clean break 112
  deferred charge 79, 112, 116, 144
  deferred trust of land 79, 112, 114, 144
  Harvey order 116
  injunctions
    avoiding enforcement 121
    preventing disposal 120–1
    setting aside disposition 121
  joint names 119
  lenders
    mortgages 116–17
    property adjustment orders 117–18
    undue influence 116–17
  Martin order 115–16
  Mesher order 114–15
  minor children and 112–13
  mortgages 112, 116–17
    redemption from sale 112
  order for sale 112–13, 145
  pending land action 120
  property adjustment orders 117–18
  registration of charge 119
  rented 118
  retention by one party 113
  rights of non-owning spouse 119–21
  separation agreements 180
  in sole name 119–21
  statutory tenancies 118
  third parties
    co-owners 116
    lenders 116–18
  transfer between spouses
    CMS payments and 113–14
    outright transfer 113–14, 144
  transfer of tenancy 118, 145
  unmarried partners *see* **family home (cohabitants)**
mediation 21–2
  help with family mediation 14
  hybrid 22
  Mediation Information and Assessment Meeting 129,
    184, 210, 215

Mesher order
triggering events 114–15
use 115
misconduct
financial provision and 65–6
relating to proceedings 65–6
mortgages 112
see also **lenders**
cohabitants 283
matrimonial home 116–17
occupation orders and payment 267
redemption from sale 112

name of child, changing
care orders 241
child arrangements orders 191–2
negotiation skills 5
negotiations 21
financial provision 140–1
'no order' presumption 209
non-molestation orders
applicants 263–4
application form 575–94
breach 275
duration 264
emergency applications 271
enforcement 275
factors to consider 264
human rights 277
pestering 263
power of arrest 277
procedure checklist 274–5
undertakings 271–2
with notice application 273–4
without notice application 272–3
nullity
children 37
choice of divorce or 37
consequences of decree 37
financial provisions 37
void marriage 36
voidable marriage 36–7
wills 37

occupation orders
additional provisions 269
applicants 263
cohabitant 267
with existing occupation right 264–6
flowchart 270
former cohabitant 267
former spouse 266
neither party with rights 268
with no existing right 266–8
application form 575–94
balance of harm test 265, 266, 267
breach 276–7
duration 266–8
emergency applications 271
enforcement 269, 276–7
examples 268
human rights 277
mortgage payments 267, 269

occupation orders – *continued*
penalties 276–7
power of arrest 276, 277
procedure checklist 274–5
undertakings 271–2
warrant of arrest 276
with notice application 273–4
without notice application 272–3
off-setting pensions 71
offers to settle
costs 140
one-year rule 26
orders for sale 52, 55–6, 112–13, 165
drafting 145
jointly owned property 56

parentage, determination 93
parental responsibility
acquisition 184–8
agreement 185, 503–4
artificial insemination/IVF 188
civil partners 187
cohabitants 290
delegation of 189
exercise of 189
guardianship 187
local authority 188
loss of 188–9
meaning 184
order 185–7
refusal 186
termination 186
paternity disputes 185
persons with 184
removal 291
s.8 orders 290
same-sex couples 291
special guardianship orders 203
step-parents 187–8, 505–6
supervision orders 243
unmarried fathers 184–7, 290–1
refusal of order 186
paternity disputes 185
'pathway plan' 243
pensions
cash equivalent transfer value 72
court powers 71
death of cohabitant 293
divorce and 70–3
external transfer 72
financial order applications 132, 135–6
future benefits 71
internal transfer 72
loss of rights on matrimonial breakdown 66–7
lump sums 123–5
payable on retirement 72
off-setting 71
'pension attachments' 71–2
pension credit 72
pension debit 72
pension sharing 72–3, 145
compensation order 52, 56, 72
order 52, 56, 72–3

pensions – *continued*
    types of pension 72
    traditional approach 71
    valuation 72, 124
periodical payments 52, 53–4
    Child Maintenance Service 93
    clean breaks 69–70
    drafting orders 143
    during marriage 73–4
    maintenance agreements 180
    secured 52, 54, 55
person under disability
    children 68, 94
    service of divorce petition 43
    spouse 64
pestering 263
police protection 248
'port alert' procedure 222
post-nuptial agreements *see* **maintenance agreements**
power of arrest 276, 277
pre-application protocol
    financial provisions 129
pre-marital agreements 177–9
    general contract principles 179
    law reform 182
private residence exemption 78
professional conduct 3–4, 6
prohibited steps orders 201–2
    duration 219
property adjustment orders 52, 55, 73, 112
    Child Maintenance Service 93
    children 291–2
    deferred charge 112, 116, 144
    deferred trusts of land 112, 114, 144
    drafting 144–5
    enforcement 168
    lenders and 117–18
    outright transfers 113–14, 144
    preliminary considerations 144
    transfer of tenancies 118, 145
    welfare benefits 88
protected parties *see* **person under disability**
protection from harassment 277–8
public funding
    care orders 249–50
    costs 14
    domestic abuse 12, 272
    emergency legal representation 272
    family help (higher) 128, 249
        alternative sources 14
        availability 14
        cost benefit test 14
        financial eligibility 14
    family help (lower) 128, 249
        availability 13
        cost benefit test 14
        financial eligibility 14
    financial provisions 128
    help with family mediation 14
    human rights 16–17
    legal help
        advice 13
        domestic abuse 272

public funding – *continued*
    financial eligibility 13
    financial order 128
    sufficient benefit test 13
    legal representation 14, 249, 272
    notification duty 14
    reform 11–12
    scope of legal aid 12–13
    section 8 orders 210
    solicitor-client relationship 14
    statutory charge 15–16
    supervision orders 249–50
    types 13–14
Public Law Outline 230, 249, 250

refuges 262
religious marriage 46
relocation within UK 194
residence orders
    see also **child arrangements orders**
    replacement 190
Resolution Code of Practice 4–5, 435

same-sex couples 281–2
    see also **cohabitation**
    parental responsibility 291
***Sears Tooth* agreement 18**
section 8 orders
    acknowledgement of service 214
    allegations of harm and domestic violence form 213, 541–51
    applicants
        child 211–12
        leave to apply 210–11
    application 212–13
        acknowledgement of service 214
        child as party 213
        forms 212–13, 517–40
        parties 213
        service 213
        without notice 213–14
    child abduction 221
    child applicant 211–12
        leave of court 212
        merits of case 212
        public funding 211
        solicitor to act 211
    child arrangements orders 190–201
        conditions 191, 194
        contact regulation 194–8
        directions 191, 194
        domestic violence 196–8
        duration 219
        enforcement 199–201
        grandparents 196
        interim 244–6
        intractable cases 199–200
        leaving UK 192–4
        letters, email or telephone contact 194
        monitoring contact 199
        name change 191–2
        physical contact 194
        Practice Direction 197–8

Section 8 orders – *continued*
    relocation within UK 194
    step-parents 195
  costs 218
  duration 219
  emergency protection 221
  family court 212
    checklist 220
  final hearing 217
  First Hearing Dispute Resolution Appointment (FHDRA) 214–17
    case management 216–17
    consent orders 215
    dispute resolution 215
    expert evidence 215
    Mediation Information and Assessment Meeting 215
    orders 217
    safeguarding 214–15
    timetable 217
    welfare reports 215
    wishes and feelings of child 216
    witness statements 216
  judgment 217–18
  jurisdiction 210
  leave to apply 210–11
  no further application without leave of court 218
  parental responsibility 290
  procedure 210–19
  prohibited steps orders 201–2, 219
  public funding 210, 211
  risk assessments 214
  safety checks 214
  service of application 213
    acknowledgement 214
  specific issues order 202
  witness statements 216
    filing 216
    hearsay evidence in 216
secured periodical payments 52, 54, 55
Segal **orders** 96, 102
separation (2 years) with consent
  calculation of period 33
  cohabitation after 34
  consent 34
  financial position 34–5
  mental element 34
  separation 33–4
separation (5 years)
  cohabitation after 36
  financial hardship 35
  grave hardship 35
  meaning 35
separation agreements 179–82
  advantages 180
  agreement to separate 180
  children 180
  disadvantages 181
  enforceability 181
  finality 181
  flexibility 180
  periodical payments 180
  property 180
  speed 180

separation agreements – *continued*
  variation 181, 182
    court jurisdiction 181
service
  care order application 252
  divorce petition 41
    alternative methods 42–3
    children 43
    co-respondent 43
    deemed service 42
    dispensing with 42–3
    finding respondent 43
    outside England and Wales 43
    personal service 42
    protected parties 43
    service copies 41
    usual method 41
  financial provision application 132
  section 8 order application 213
  supervision order application 252
setting aside orders
  grounds 169–71
settlement conference 230
side-letters
  drafting 146
solicitor's costs 15
special guardianship orders 203
  application 203–4
  effect 203
  procedure 204
special guardianship support services 204
specific issues order 202, 290
  duration 219
stamp duty land tax 81
statutory charge
  exemptions 16
  operation of 15
  postponement 16
step-children 68
  Child Maintenance Service 93
step-parents
  child arrangements orders 195
  child support 93
  parental responsibility 187–8
supervision orders
  advocates' meeting 253
  application 236
  application form 251, 553–74
  availability to court 239
  Case Management Hearing
    attendance 254
    timetable for proceedings 253
  causation of harm 238
  children's guardian 252–3
  choice of 244
  concurrent applications 239
  disclosure 255
  duration 244
  duties of supervisor 244
  effect of 224, 243–4
  evidence
    admissibility 254
    disclosure 255

supervision orders – *continued*
    expert evidence 254–5
    witness statements 254
  final hearing 255–6
  grounds 236, 260
  human rights implications 256–7
  interim 244–6
  'is likely to suffer' 237–8
  issue of application 251–2
  issue resolution hearings 255
  judgment 256
  kinship assessments 250
  letter before proceedings 250
  meaning 236
  meetings with parents 250
  parental responsibility 243
  parties to application 251
  pre-proceedings action 250
  procedure 249–56
  public funding 249–50
  service of application 252
  significant harm 236–7
    'is suffering' 237
  solicitor appointment 253
  stage 1 251–3
  welfare principle 239, 257

tax credits
  universal credit 84–6, 109
term maintenance 70
third party debt order 165
Trusts of Land and Appointment of Trustees Act 1996
  text 407

undertakings
  domestic abuse 271–2
  financial provision 142–3, 174–5
undue influence
  cohabitation agreements 284
  matrimonial home lenders 116–17
universal credit 84–6, 109
  amount 85
  claimant commitment 86
  eligibility 84–5
  income 85–6
  maintenance and 87–8
  passport benefits 86
unmarried families *see* **cohabitation**
unmarried fathers
  human rights 291
  parental responsibility 184–7, 290–1
    refusal of order 186

violence *see* **domestic abuse**

void marriage 36
  wills 37
voidable marriage 36–7
  wills 37

wardship 224
warrant of arrest 276
warrant of control 165
welfare benefits
  see also **local authority housing**
  appeals 169
  benefits cap 87
  child benefit 84
  discretionary housing payments 87
  financial provision 109
  Flexible Support Fund 87
  lump sums 88
  property adjustment 88
  universal credit 84–6, 109
welfare principle 204–5
  age of child 208
  background of child 208
  capability of parent or carer 208–9
  care orders 239
  care and supervision orders 257
  change of circumstances, effect of 207
  characteristics of child 208
  checklist 206–9
  delay 209–10
  educational needs 207
  emotional needs 207
  feelings of child 206–7
  harm, past or future 208
  human rights 205
  'no order' presumption 209
  parental involvement 205–6
  physical needs 207
  powers of court 209
  sex of child 208
  supervision orders 239
  wishes of child 206–7
welfare reports
  section 8 proceedings 215
widowed parent's allowance 293
wills
  cohabitants 283
  void marriage and 37
  voidable marriage and 37
winter fuel payments 87
witness statements
  care and supervision orders 254
  section 8 proceedings 216

yardstick of equality 58